Meet the *Southern Living* Foods Staff

On these pages we present the *Southern Living* Foods
Staff (left to right in each photograph).

*Susan Dosier, Assistant Foods Editor; Dana Adkins
Campbell, Assistant Foods Editor*

Jean Wickstrom Liles, Senior Foods Editor

*Patty Vann, Assistant Test Kitchens Director; Kaye Adams,
Test Kitchens Director*

*Charles Walton IV, Senior Foods Photographer; Beverly
Morrow Perrine, Senior Photo Stylist*

Susan Payne, Foods Editor; Leslie Byars, Photo Stylist

Peggy Smith, Marketing Manager; Jane Cairns, Test Kitchens Home Economist

Judy Feagin and Diane Hogan, Test Kitchens Home Economists

Cathy Dunklin and Karen Brechin, Editorial Assistants

Southern Living®

1991 ANNUAL RECIPES

Oxmoor House®

©1991 by Oxmoor House, Inc.
Book Division of Southern Progress Corporation
P.O. Box 2463, Birmingham, Alabama 35201

Southern Living®, Summer Suppers®, and *Holiday Dinners®*
are federally registered trademarks of Southern Living, Inc.

Library of Congress Catalog Number: 79-88364
ISBN: 0-8487-1072-X
ISSN: 0272-2003

Manufactured in the United States of America
First printing 1991

Southern Living®

Senior Foods Editor: Jean Wickstrom Liles
Foods Editor: Susan Payne
Assistant Foods Editors: Dana Adkins Campbell,
     Susan Dosier
Editorial Assistants: Karen Brechin, Cathy Dunklin
Test Kitchens Director: Kaye Adams
Assistant Test Kitchens Director: Patty Vann
Test Kitchens Staff: Jane Cairns, Judy Feagin,
     Diane Hogan, Peggy Smith
Senior Photo Stylist: Beverly Morrow Perrine
Photo Stylist: Leslie Byars
Senior Foods Photographer: Charles E. Walton IV
Additional photography by Howard L. Puckett, pages 152 and
     153; Sylvia Martin, page 304
Production Manager: Clay Nordan
Assistant Production Manager: Amy Roth
Production Traffic Manager: Vicki Weathers

Oxmoor House, Inc.
Executive Editor: Ann H. Harvey
Director of Manufacturing: Jerry R. Higdon
Art Director: James Boone

Southern Living® 1991 Annual Recipes

Senior Editor: Olivia Kindig Wells
Copy Chief: Mary Ann Laurens
Copy Editor: Donna Baldone
Editorial Assistant: Carole Cain

Production Manager: Rick Litton
Associate Production Manager: Theresa L. Beste
Production Assistant: Pam Beasley Bullock

Designer and Illustrator: Carol Middleton

Cover: *Apricot Mousse (page 297) makes an impressive presentation for
Christmas or any other time of the year.*

Back cover: *Spumoni and Berries (page 204) served with juicy, fresh
strawberries features a trio of delicate sherbet flavors.*

Page 1: *The refreshing flavors of the fruits highlight the pastries in (from
front) Berry Good Lemon Tarts, Peachy Keen Tarts, and Fancy Fruit
Tart. (Recipes begin on page 118.)*

Page 4: *Herbed Turkey-in-a-Bag (page 253) bakes to a golden brown in
an oven cooking bag. Fresh herbs make a fitting garnish.*

To find out how you can receive *Southern Living* magazine, write
to *Southern Living®,* P.O. Box 830119, Birmingham, AL 35283.

Table of Contents

Our Year At Southern Living.

Welcome to our *1991 Annual Recipes,* a collection of all the recipes we published this year. Many of you have been loyal *Southern Living* subscribers over 25 years and have collected our *Annual Recipes* since the cookbook series began in 1979. Whether you're new to our magazine or a seasoned subscriber, we hope you realize how highly we prize the recipes and food ideas in each issue.

This thirteenth volume of our collection recaptures every food story appearing in 1991. Because recipes come from readers all across the South, you'll find here an appetizing variety of dishes and menus. We like to think our recipes offer something for everyone—from the experienced to the novice cook.

The *1991 Annual Recipes* is organized into monthly chapters designed to spotlight foods and great entertaining ideas for each season. This winter you can take the chill away with traditional Brunswick stew or Southern gumbo or add variety to your menus with Natchitoches Meat Pies.

Get inspiration on food and decorations for wedding celebrations with our menus beginning on page 97. We've included easy make-ahead recipes for a bridal shower, bridesmaids' luncheon, rehearsal dinner, and a simple or elaborate wedding reception.

In April we offer fresh new ways to entertain family and friends in "Brunches & Lunches." Sample recipes from our host in Meridian, Mississippi, or pack our portable picnic and head outdoors.

Throughout the book you'll glean tips on reducing fat, sodium, and calories in our monthly "On The Light Side" features. The special light section in June is packed with nutritional information and healthful recipes for all ages.

Cool off in the July heat with our children's poolside bash. This clever menu, spotlighting Peanut Butter-and-Jelly "Fish" Sandwiches and Chocolate Seashells, is served in sand buckets. Or get a headstart on summer plans with a festive tropical buffet, an ice cream party, or a Southwestern fiesta in "Summer Suppers."

If you're planning a fall festival, you'll find valuable tips and ideas for old-fashioned fun in October. Both Halloween and Christmas offer opportunities for youngsters to express creativity in the kitchen. Our Great Pumpkin Cookies, Jolly Reindeer Cookies, and Quick-Fix Christmas Cottage are fun projects guaranteeing big smiles and happy faces.

Usher in the holiday season with "Holiday Dinners," where you'll find fabulous recipes along with years and years of holiday traditions shared by our readers. As you make plans for this glorious season, consider adopting some of these special traditions for your family. To help you celebrate the season with your entire neighborhood or a multitude of friends, we suggest the gala progressive dinner hosted in Columbia, South Carolina, as a guide to menus, recipes, and plans.

Variety abounds in the desserts we selected to wrap up the year. Choose quick-and-easy Chocolate Pizza, glamorous Apricot Mousse, or another of our dazzling desserts appropriate for any occasion.

This *1991 Annual Recipes* is more than a collection of special recipes. It brings back a year of fond memories as the foods staff handpicked, tested, and tasted each recipe for your enjoyment. We hope that you will be inspired by these new recipes and stirred by your own warm memories of serving favorite *Southern Living* recipes to your family and friends.

Jean Wickstrom Liles

JANUARY

When Southerners usher in the New Year, the dress ranges

from blue jeans to black tie, and the food offers just as much

variety. Choose your menu from this month's festive offering.

And to warm the chilly days or nights throughout the winter,

serve a piping-hot cobbler, an old-fashioned favorite now

made with modern ease and convenience.

New Year's Menus
To Match The Festive Mood

Whether you plan a rip-roaring party for friends or a quiet dinner for your family on New Year's Day, don't forget to put lucky foods on the menu to be true to Southern tradition. It's debatable whether eating the special foods revered on this day really has anything to do with your fortune during the year, but one thing is sure:

Few born-and-bred Southerners let the sun set on New Year's Day without sampling a bite of each dish.

When it comes to the peas that supposedly provide good luck, stick with the traditional black-eyed variety. They can be canned, fresh, frozen, or dried, but they must display the little black "eye"—any imposter won't do.

Southern Ham and Biscuits
Caviar Tomatoes
Black-Eyed Pea Pâté
Fresh peppers
Turnip Green Dip
Baguette slices
Lucky Almond Tassies

CAVIAR TOMATOES

48 cherry tomatoes
2 (8-ounce) packages cream cheese, softened
½ cup mayonnaise or salad dressing
⅓ cup minced onion
⅛ teaspoon hot sauce
1 (3½-ounce) jar black caviar, drained

Wash tomatoes thoroughly. Cut a thin slice from top of each tomato; carefully scoop out pulp, reserving pulp for other uses. Invert shells on paper towels to drain.

Combine cream cheese and mayonnaise in a small mixing bowl; beat at low speed of an electric mixer until smooth. Stir in onion and hot sauce. Spoon or pipe mixture into tomato shells. Cover and chill if preparing ahead of time. Let tomatoes stand at room temperature 20 minutes, and top each stuffed tomato with a small amount of caviar just before serving. Yield: 4 dozen.

SOUTHERN HAM AND BISCUITS

1 cup butter or margarine
4 cups self-rising flour
1½ cups buttermilk
Butter or margarine, melted
Chive-Mustard Spread
3 (8-ounce) packages cooked country or regular ham slices, cut into 1¼-inch squares

Cut 1 cup butter into flour with a pastry blender until mixture resembles coarse meal. Add buttermilk, stirring until dry ingredients are moistened. Turn dough out onto a lightly floured surface, and knead lightly 3 or 4 times.

Roll dough to ½-inch thickness; cut with a 1½-inch biscuit cutter. Place on lightly greased baking sheets. Bake at 425° for 12 to 14 minutes. Brush with melted butter. Serve with Chive-Mustard Spread and ham. Yield: 5 dozen.

Chive-Mustard Spread

⅓ cup sugar
¼ cup dry mustard
1½ tablespoons all-purpose flour
¼ teaspoon salt
¾ cup milk
⅓ cup white vinegar
1 egg yolk
3 tablespoons minced fresh or frozen chives

Combine first 4 ingredients in a small saucepan; stir well. Combine milk, vinegar, and egg yolk; beat well. Gradually stir milk mixture into mustard mixture; cook over low heat, stirring constantly, until thickened and bubbly. Stir in chives. Cool completely, and store in refrigerator. Yield: 1⅓ cups.

BLACK-EYED PEA PÂTÉ

2 (3-ounce) packages cream cheese, softened
2 (16-ounce) cans black-eyed peas, drained
1 medium onion, quartered
1 to 2 cloves garlic
½ cup medium picante sauce
3 tablespoons Worcestershire sauce
1 teaspoon hot sauce
2 envelopes unflavored gelatin
2 tablespoons cold water
¼ cup minced fresh parsley
Red, yellow, and green pepper pieces

Position knife blade in food processor bowl; add first 7 ingredients. Process 1 minute or until smooth.

Sprinkle gelatin over cold water in a small saucepan; let stand 1 minute. Cook over low heat, stirring until gelatin dissolves. Add gelatin mixture to pea mixture; process 30 seconds. Spoon into an oiled 9-inch round cakepan; cover and chill until firm. Unmold pâté, and sprinkle with minced parsley. Serve with pepper pieces. Yield: about 4½ cups.

TURNIP GREEN DIP

1 cup chopped onion
2 tablespoons butter or margarine, melted
¼ cup dry white wine
2 (10-ounce) packages frozen chopped turnip greens, thawed and drained
2 (8-ounce) packages cream cheese, softened
1 (8-ounce) carton sour cream
¾ cup milk
1 teaspoon hot sauce
¼ teaspoon salt

Sauté onion in butter until tender. Stir in wine, and simmer 2 minutes; stir in turnip greens and remaining ingredients, and cook over medium heat until thoroughly heated, stirring occasionally. Transfer to a chafing dish, and keep warm. Serve with toasted baguette slices. Yield: about 4 cups.

■ Serve Lucky Almond Tassies for a New Year's party or any festive gathering. A whole almond is hidden beneath the filling of one of the desserts, and the lucky recipient is guaranteed good fortune.

LUCKY ALMOND TASSIES

¾ cup firmly packed brown sugar
¾ cup sliced almonds, toasted
1 egg
1 tablespoon butter or margarine, melted
½ teaspoon vanilla extract
¼ teaspoon almond extract
Dash of salt
1 whole almond
Tart Shells

Combine first 7 ingredients in a medium mixing bowl. Place whole almond in one tart shell. Spoon almond mixture evenly into tart shells, filling three-fourths full. Bake at 350° for 20 to 25 minutes or until tassies are browned. Yield: 2 dozen.

Tart Shells

1 cup all-purpose flour
1 (3-ounce) package cream cheese, softened
¼ cup plus 3 tablespoons butter, softened

Combine all ingredients in a medium bowl; stir until blended. Shape dough into 24 balls; chill. Place balls in ungreased miniature (1¾-inch) muffin pans, shaping each ball into a shell. Yield: 2 dozen.

Glazed Ham Steak
Black-Eyed Peas With Rice
Spinach-Stuffed Squash
Corn sticks

GLAZED HAM STEAK

½ cup red currant jelly
¼ cup chopped onion
2 tablespoons prepared mustard
1 (1-inch-thick) smoked, fully cooked ham steak (about 2 pounds)

Combine first 3 ingredients; set aside. Cook ham in a nonstick skillet over medium heat 10 minutes, turning once; remove from skillet. Add jelly mixture to skillet; cook about 5 minutes or until jelly melts, stirring often. Return ham to skillet; cook 3 to 5 minutes, turning once. Transfer ham to a serving platter; spoon sauce over ham. Yield: 6 servings.

Microwave Directions: Combine first 3 ingredients in a 12- x 8- x 2-inch baking dish. Microwave at HIGH 5 to

7 minutes, stirring after 3 minutes. Add ham to sauce; turn to coat both sides. Cover tightly with heavy-duty plastic wrap; fold back a small corner of wrap to allow steam to escape. Microwave at MEDIUM (50% power) 6 minutes.
Joanne Neely
Duluth, Georgia

BLACK-EYED PEAS WITH RICE

3 slices bacon
1 small onion, chopped
1 (16-ounce) can black-eyed peas, drained
1 (14½-ounce) can stewed tomatoes, undrained and chopped
1½ cups cooked rice
¼ teaspoon hot sauce
⅛ teaspoon garlic powder
⅛ teaspoon pepper

Cook bacon in a large skillet until crisp; remove bacon, reserving drippings in skillet. Crumble bacon, and set aside.

Sauté onion in drippings until tender. Drain onion, and discard drippings; return onion to skillet.

Add peas and remaining ingredients; cover and cook over low heat 8 to 10 minutes. Spoon into a serving dish; sprinkle crumbled bacon over top. Yield: 6 servings.

Tip: *When grains, such as rice, are served together with dried beans or peas, the two dishes complement each other, providing a good source of high quality protein.*

SPINACH-STUFFED SQUASH

3 medium-size yellow squash
¼ cup butter or margarine
1 tablespoon all-purpose flour
½ cup whipping cream
½ teaspoon salt
⅛ teaspoon ground nutmeg
1 (10-ounce) package frozen
   chopped spinach, thawed

Steam squash 8 to 10 minutes or until tender. Cut squash in half lengthwise; scoop out pulp, leaving shells intact. Keep warm.

Melt butter in a heavy saucepan over low heat; add flour, stirring until smooth. Cook 1 minute, stirring constantly. Gradually add whipping cream; cook over medium heat, stirring constantly, until thickened and bubbly. Stir salt and nutmeg. Stir spinach into creamed mixture, and cook until thoroughly heated. Spoon mixture into squash shells. Serve immediately. Yield: 6 servings.

Brew A Little Brunswick Stew

There's an age-old, fun-loving feud still simmering in the South, and this War Between the States appears to have no end in sight. Since the turn of the century, Brunswick County, Virginia, and Brunswick, Georgia, have firmly stood their ground, spoons and forks drawn in battle. The meat of the matter is who lays rightful claim to the origin of Brunswick stew—a hearty dish traditionally cooked outdoors over an open fire in a huge cauldron or vat, stirred constantly with wooden paddles throughout a lengthy vigil.

Both Virginia and Georgia tell their palate-pleasing sides of the Brunswick stew story, so grab your bowl and get ready to choose.

■ While Brunswick stew was making it onto the books in Richmond, stewmaster Harold Blick was outside on the state capitol steps making a pot of the famous dish. He says the "Proclamation Stew" recipe he used is Van Doyle's, who has scaled it down to family size here.

VAN DOYLE'S FAMILY-SIZE BRUNSWICK STEW

1 (2½- to 3-pound) broiler-fryer
2 celery stalks
1 small onion
1 quart water
2 (28-ounce) cans whole tomatoes,
   undrained
1 (16-ounce) can whole tomatoes,
   undrained
1 cup chopped onion
3 medium potatoes, peeled
2 (10-ounce) packages frozen baby
   lima beans
2 (10-ounce) packages frozen whole
   kernel corn
¼ cup plus 1 tablespoon sugar
1 teaspoon salt
½ teaspoon red pepper
¼ teaspoon pepper

Combine first 4 ingredients in a large Dutch oven or stockpot; bring to a boil. Cover, reduce heat, and simmer 2 hours. Remove chicken from broth, reserving broth in Dutch oven; discard celery and onion. Skim and discard fat from surface of broth. Cool chicken; skin, bone, and coarsely chop meat. Set aside.

Add tomatoes, chopped onion, and whole potatoes to broth; bring mixture to a boil. Cover, reduce heat, and simmer 30 minutes or until potatoes are tender. Remove potatoes; mash and return to stew.

Add chopped chicken, baby lima beans, and remaining ingredients; bring to a boil. Cover, reduce heat, and simmer 3 hours, stirring often. Yield: 5½ quarts. *Van Doyle*
Lawrenceville, Virginia

■ Smoked chicken, smoked pork, and the secret ingredient of allspice give Breeden Liles's recipe its own twist and will have stew aficionados asking for more.

BREEDEN LILES'S BRUNSWICK STEW

1 (3-pound) broiler-fryer, smoked
   and skinned
4 bay leaves
6 celery tops with leaves
4½ quarts water
1½ teaspoons salt
1 teaspoon hot sauce
3 medium onions, chopped
1 (16-ounce) package frozen whole
   kernel corn
1 (16-ounce) package frozen lima
   beans
1 (16-ounce) package frozen
   English peas
1 (28-ounce) can crushed tomatoes,
   undrained
1 pound ground beef
1 pound smoked pork, chopped
½ cup Worcestershire sauce
2 teaspoons garlic salt
2 teaspoons ground allspice
1 to 2 teaspoons black pepper
½ to 1 teaspoon red pepper

Combine first 6 ingredients in a large Dutch oven or stockpot; bring to a boil. Cook, uncovered, 15 minutes. Reduce heat, and simmer, uncovered, 1 hour. Remove chicken from broth, reserving broth in Dutch oven; discard bay leaves and celery tops. Cool chicken; bone and coarsely chop meat. Set aside.

Add onion and next 4 ingredients to broth; bring to a boil. Cook 15 minutes. Reduce heat, and simmer 1 hour, stirring often.

Cook ground beef in a skillet over medium heat until browned, stirring to crumble. Drain well; add ground beef, chicken, pork, and remaining ingredients to stew. Simmer, uncovered, 2 hours, stirring occasionally. Yield: 4½ quarts. *Breeden Liles*
St. Simon's Island, Georgia

The Brunswick Stew
War Between The States

Since Georgia and Virginia threw their pots into the ring years ago, Brunswick County, North Carolina, occasionally added fuel to the fire, but no sincere interest has been sparked. For North Carolinians, Brunswick stew only serves as an accompaniment for—but, as a main dish, doesn't hold a candle to—their revered barbecue.

So what are the magical ingredients in those big pots? In either state, you're likely to find chicken, lima beans, corn, tomatoes, and often potatoes, but that's where the similarity ends—and the trouble begins. The additional ingredients and how they're put together lead to some serious but friendly bone picking.

Virginians tend to stick to just chicken, while many Georgians add pork and beef to their renditions. A couple of our recipe contributors from the Peach State use smoked meats or barbecue sauces for flavor. Some Georgians strive for a chunky stew on their spoons, while most Virginians know that when the stirring paddle stands upright in the pot unassisted, the stew is thick enough to eat with a fork, if you want.

The issue that's still astir is who was first with Brunswick stew. Well, Virginia documents theirs back to 1828 when, as legend has it, "Uncle Jimmy" Matthews, a black cook, prepared it for Dr. Creed Haskins and his buddies on a hunting expedition near the Nottoway River. The original version was hardly akin to today's; it was mainly squirrel, onion, butter, and bread. Due to changing tastes and the outlaw of wild game sales for profit, you'll find no squirrel in this dish so often used for fund raisers across the South.

According to Virginia, Georgia is just too little, too late. Georgia's evidence for inventing Brunswick Stew is a monument on St. Simon's Island—a black cauldron labeled as the first one to contain the sacred potion in the South—on July 2, 1898. Well, that's 70 years later than Virginia's claim.

Resorting to a "my House is better than your House" argument, both states have now passed tongue-in-cheek resolutions through their respective legislatures. But again, Virginia beat Georgia to the punch—by three days—in February 1988. In the last few years, the states have exchanged invitations as well as good-humored insults. Virginians have traveled south, and Georgians have trekked north, taking part in "stew-offs" and "stew bilees" to try to settle the matter once and for all.

Dale Lewis, organizer of one of the Virginia events, comments on the opposition, "I think it's only fitting Georgia should aspire to claim Brunswick stew." He pauses, and a sly smile steals across his face. "And when they learn how to cook it, maybe we'll give it to them!"

Georgia stewmaster Dan Dickerson reminisces about a recent venture to Virginia. "We had a pretty big time up there. Of course, we packed all our own Georgia ingredients, even our water. You know you can't trust even the water in Virginia!" he jests.

Of course, team spirit and state pride prevail throughout. Some stewmasters represent their homes on their own; others form groups and call themselves such names as "The Red Oak Stew Crew" or "Swine and Roses" (obviously supporters of adding pork to the pot).

They may appear to be pots apart, but both states have a mutual goal. It all boils down to upholding the tradition of Brunswick stew, and to that end they'll stick together through thick and thin, chunky and mushy.

Former Georgia state representative Virginia Ramsey (ironically named) who sponsored her home's bill says, "It's all a good, friendly promotion of both areas." And Georgia stewmistress Fran Kelly concluded after one contest, "I never knew Brunswick stew could be so much fun!"

It may never be known who was really *first* with Brunswick stew, but it'll be fun to find out who's *best*. A word of warning: Keep a lid on your choice!

■ A Georgia native and resident of Brunswick for more than 40 years, former state representative Virginia Ramsey gives her special version of Brunswick stew.

VIRGINIA RAMSEY'S FAVORITE BRUNSWICK STEW

1 (2½-pound) broiler-fryer
1 (1½- to 2-pound) boneless chuck roast
1 (2½- to 3-pound) boneless pork roast
2 quarts water
3 large onions, quartered
1 (46-ounce) can tomato juice
4 (17-ounce) cans cream-style corn
¼ cup cider vinegar
¼ cup Worcestershire sauce
1½ tablespoons poultry seasoning
1 tablespoon salt
1 teaspoon black pepper
½ teaspoon red pepper
½ teaspoon liquid smoke

Combine first 4 ingredients in a large Dutch oven or stockpot; bring to a boil. Cover, reduce heat, and simmer 2 hours or until meat is tender. Remove meat from broth, reserving broth. Cool meat; skin, bone, and coarsely chop meat.

Refrigerate chopped meat and broth in separate containers 8 hours. Remove fat layer from broth. Position knife blade in bowl of food processor. Add a small amount of meat and onion. Process 1 minute or until finely chopped. Repeat procedure with remaining meat and onion.

Combine broth, meat mixture, tomato juice, and remaining ingredients in large Dutch oven. Bring mixture to a boil; reduce heat, and simmer, uncovered, 2 hours, stirring often to prevent sticking. Yield: 6½ quarts.

Virginia Ramsey
Brunswick, Georgia

■ About his Georgia stew, Dan Dickerson confides, "This recipe will get you close to perfection, but the real secret is in the preparation method—cold beer, a smoker full of fresh pork, cooking all night, and telling a zillion lies with your buddies!"

DAN DICKERSON'S BRUNSWICK STEW
(pictured on page 40)

½ cup butter or margarine
3 cups chopped cooked chicken
3 cups chopped potatoes
2 cups chopped smoked pork (½ pound)
1 cup chopped onion
2 (14½-ounce) cans ready-to-serve chicken broth
2 (14½-ounce) cans stewed tomatoes
1 (16-ounce) can lima beans, drained
1 (17-ounce) can cream-style corn
1 (8½-ounce) can English peas, drained
¼ cup liquid smoke
Barbecue Sauce

Melt butter in a large Dutch oven. Stir in chicken, potatoes, smoked pork, onion, and chicken broth. Bring to a boil; reduce heat, and simmer, uncovered, 20 minutes. Add tomatoes and remaining ingredients; bring mixture to a boil. Reduce heat, and simmer, uncovered, 2 hours, stirring occasionally. Yield: 3 quarts.

Barbecue Sauce

¼ cup butter or margarine, melted
1¾ cups catsup
¼ cup firmly packed brown sugar
¼ cup prepared mustard
¼ cup white vinegar
2 tablespoons Worcestershire sauce
1 to 2 tablespoons hot sauce
1 tablespoon liquid smoke
1½ teaspoons lemon juice
1½ teaspoons minced garlic
1 teaspoon coarsely ground black pepper
½ teaspoon crushed red pepper

Combine all ingredients in a large heavy saucepan. Cook over low heat 25 to 30 minutes, stirring often. Yield: 1½ cups.

Dan Dickerson
Brunswick, Georgia

■ Jeff Daniel shares his secret to cooking Brunswick stew. He is adamant about the type poultry found in his stewpot. It must be a hen—not a broiler-fryer—for more fat, and thus a richer flavor. If you've got a good broth, then you've got a good stew, says this stewmaster.

JEFF DANIEL'S BRUNSWICK STEW

1 (5- to 5½-pound) hen, cut up and skinned
¼ pound fatback, snipped at ½-inch intervals around edges
3 medium onions, chopped
2 quarts water
1½ pounds potatoes, peeled and cubed
1 (28-ounce) can whole tomatoes, drained and chopped
1 (16-ounce) can whole tomatoes, drained and chopped
1 (17-ounce) can lima beans, drained and mashed
1 (8.5-ounce) can lima beans, drained and mashed
1 (17-ounce) can cream-style corn
1 (8¾-ounce) can cream-style corn
2 tablespoons butter or margarine
1 tablespoon sugar
1½ teaspoons salt
1 teaspoon black pepper
¼ teaspoon red pepper

Combine hen, fatback, onions, and 2 quarts water in a large Dutch oven; bring to a boil. Cover, reduce heat, and simmer 2½ to 3 hours or until hen is tender. Remove hen, reserving broth mixture in Dutch oven. Cool hen; bone and chop meat.

Add chopped meat, potatoes, and tomatoes to broth; bring to a boil. Reduce heat, and simmer, uncovered, 1

hour and 15 minutes, stirring occasionally. Add lima beans and remaining ingredients; simmer, uncovered, 30 minutes or until thickened. Remove and discard fatback before serving. Yield: 4½ quarts.   *Jeff Daniel*
Alberta, Virginia

■ Brunswick stew figures prominently into the annals of Southern history. A county historian, Gay Neale has published a book on her home, including the story behind Brunswick stew. She shares her Virginia rendition with us.

GAY NEALE'S BRUNSWICK STEW
(pictured on page 40)

1 (3-pound) broiler-fryer
2 stalks celery, cut into 1-inch pieces
1 small onion, quartered
7 cups water, divided
2 (10-ounce) packages frozen baby lima beans
2 (10-ounce) packages frozen whole kernel corn
1 cup chopped onion
2 (28-ounce) cans whole tomatoes, undrained and chopped
1 (8-ounce) can whole tomatoes, undrained and chopped
3 medium potatoes, peeled and diced
2 tablespoons butter or margarine
1 tablespoon salt
1 to 1½ teaspoons black pepper
½ to 1 teaspoon red pepper
10 saltine crackers, crumbled

Combine broiler-fryer, celery, quartered onion, and 5 cups water in a large Dutch oven or stockpot; bring to a boil. Cover, reduce heat, and simmer 1 hour. Remove chicken, celery, and onion from broth, reserving broth in Dutch oven; discard celery and onion. Cool chicken; skin, bone, and coarsely chop meat.
Add chopped cooked chicken, baby lima beans, and remaining ingredients

except saltines to broth in Dutch oven; bring mixture to a boil. Reduce heat, and simmer, uncovered, about 4½ hours or to desired consistency, stirring often.
Add remaining 2 cups water as needed. Add cracker crumbs to stew, and cook an additional 15 minutes. Yield: 3½ quarts.   *Gay Neale*
Brodnax, Virginia

ON THE LIGHT SIDE

Nibble Your Way To Better Nutrition

Remember when eating between meals was considered a bad habit? Nowadays nutritionists are recommending eating six or eight small meals each day instead of three large ones to help control weight and possibly lower cholesterol levels. Frequent eating tames hunger pangs so that you're not ravenous at meals. And it gives the body a chance to metabolize food better.
Just by adding chili powder and garlic powder to plain popcorn it becomes anything but plain in Chili Popcorn. Here are other healthy options for snack foods that you and your kids can prepare. Serve them with a glass of juice or skim milk.

CHILI POPCORN

1 tablespoon margarine, melted
½ teaspoon chili powder
⅛ teaspoon salt
⅛ teaspoon garlic powder
⅛ teaspoon paprika
6 cups popped corn (popped without salt or fat)

Combine first 5 ingredients, and drizzle over warm popcorn. Yield: 6 servings (41 calories per 1-cup serving).

□ *0.8 gram protein, 2.2 grams fat, 4.8 grams carbohydrate, 0 milligrams cholesterol, 70 milligrams sodium, and 2 milligrams calcium.*

VEGETABLE NACHOS

1 cup diced tomato
¼ cup diced green pepper
2 tablespoons sliced green onions
2 tablespoons chopped ripe olives
2 tablespoons chopped green chiles
2 teaspoons white vinegar
¼ teaspoon garlic powder
⅛ teaspoon freshly ground pepper
Corn Tortilla Chips
¼ cup (1 ounce) shredded 40%-less-fat sharp Cheddar cheese

Combine first 8 ingredients. Spoon 2 teaspoons vegetable mixture on each tortilla chip; divide cheese evenly among chips. Broil 6 inches from heat 1 minute or until cheese melts. Yield: 26 appetizers (18 calories each).

□ *0.8 gram protein, 0.5 gram fat, 2.8 grams carbohydrate, 1 milligram cholesterol, 25 milligrams sodium, and 18 milligrams calcium.*

Corn Tortilla Chips

9 (6-inch) corn tortillas
Cold water

Cut 3 circles from each tortilla, using a 2½-inch biscuit cutter. Dip rounds in water; drain on paper towels. Place rounds in a single layer on an ungreased baking sheet. Bake at 350° for 10 minutes or until chips are crisp and begin to brown. Remove from oven, and let cool. Yield: 26 chips (12 calories per chip).

□ *0.4 gram protein, 0.2 gram fat, 2.2 grams carbohydrate, 0 milligrams cholesterol, 9 milligrams sodium, and 7 milligrams calcium.*

POTATO SKIN SNACK

2 (6¾-ounce) baking potatoes
Vegetable cooking spray
2 tablespoons commercial oil-free
    Italian salad dressing
2 teaspoons salt-free
    herb-and-seasoning blend (regular
    or spicy)

Scrub potatoes, and coat with cooking spray; bake at 400° for 1 hour or until done. Allow potatoes to cool.

Cut potatoes in half lengthwise; carefully scoop out pulp, leaving a ¼-inch shell. (Pulp may be reserved for other uses.) Cut shells into 5 (½-inch-wide) strips. Place strips, skin side down, on a baking sheet. Brush with dressing; sprinkle with seasoning blend. Broil 6 inches from heat 5 minutes or until browned. Serve warm. Yield: 20 appetizers (11 calories each).

□ 0.2 gram protein, 0 grams fat, 2.6 grams carbohydrate, 0 milligrams cholesterol, 17 milligrams sodium, and 1 milligram calcium.   Eileen Wehling
Austin, Texas

APRICOT FRUIT FLIP

1 (12-ounce) can apricot nectar
1 medium-size ripe banana
¼ cup instant nonfat dry milk
    powder
2 tablespoons lemon juice
1 tablespoon honey
1 teaspoon grated lemon rind
Ice cubes

Combine all ingredients except ice cubes in container of an electric blender. Add enough ice cubes to measure 4 cups; blend until smooth. Serve immediately. Yield: 4 cups (108 calories per 1-cup serving).

□ 2.1 grams protein, 0.2 gram fat, 26.5 grams carbohydrate, 1 milligram cholesterol, 27 milligrams sodium, 62 milligrams calcium.   Cathy Williams
Vale, North Carolina

OAT BRAN-BANANA MUFFINS

a bit more liquid

1½ cups oat bran *less*
¾ cup all-purpose flour *more*
1 teaspoon baking powder
¼ teaspoon salt
¼ cup firmly packed brown sugar
1 cup mashed ripe banana
¾ cup skim milk
2 egg whites, slightly beaten
1 tablespoon vegetable oil
Vegetable cooking spray

Combine first 5 ingredients in a large bowl; make a well in center of mixture. Combine banana, milk, egg whites, and oil; add to dry ingredients, stirring just until moistened.

Spoon batter into muffin pans or muffin liners coated with cooking spray, filling three-fourths full. Bake at 425° for 18 to 20 minutes. Remove from pans immediately. Yield: 14 muffins (101 calories per muffin).

□ 3.6 grams protein, 2 grams fat, 17.5 grams carbohydrate, 0 milligrams cholesterol, 78 milligrams sodium, and 41 milligrams calcium.

LIGHT MENU

Savory Jambalaya Dinner

Along the coast of South Carolina they serve a version of jambalaya that's similar to those offered in Louisiana. Red Rice Jambalaya is a light version of this dish.

On cold winter nights, serve Red Rice Jambalaya and Cornmeal Muffins (page 19), along with a green salad with oil-free dressing and Spicy Grapefruit-Berry Compote.

RED RICE JAMBALAYA

Vegetable cooking spray
4 (6-ounce) skinned chicken breast
    halves
1 cup lean diced cooked ham
1 cup diced onion
4 large cloves garlic, sliced
1 cup diced sweet red pepper,
    divided
1 cup sliced green onions,
    divided
2 (10½-ounce) cans ready-to-serve,
    no-salt-added chicken broth
1 (8-ounce) can no-salt-added
    tomato sauce
½ teaspoon salt
¼ teaspoon red pepper
¾ teaspoon liquid smoke
1 bay leaf
1¾ cups long-grain rice,
    uncooked

Coat a Dutch oven with cooking spray; place over medium heat until hot. Add chicken, meat side down; cover and cook 15 minutes. Turn chicken, and add ham; cover and cook 15 minutes. Remove chicken from Dutch oven, and let cool.

Add 1 cup diced onion, garlic, and half each of sweet red pepper and green onions to Dutch oven; sauté until crisp-tender. Stir in chicken broth and remaining ingredients. Bring to a boil; cover, reduce heat, and simmer 20 minutes.

Remove chicken from bone; shred. Add chicken and remaining sweet red pepper and green onions to Dutch oven; toss gently, and cook until thoroughly heated. Remove bay leaf. Yield: 8 cups (395 calories per 1¼-cup serving).

□ 30.1 grams protein, 5.6 grams fat, 52.3 grams carbohydrate, 67 milligrams cholesterol, 650 milligrams sodium, and 51 milligrams calcium.

SPICY GRAPEFRUIT-BERRY COMPOTE

1 (10-ounce) package frozen
  raspberries, thawed
2 tablespoons sugar
½ teaspoon whole cloves
1 (3-inch) stick cinnamon
¼ cup water
2 large white grapefruit

Drain thawed raspberries, reserving juice. Combine reserved juice, sugar, and next 3 ingredients in a saucepan. Bring to a boil; reduce heat, and simmer, uncovered, 10 minutes.

Strain; discard cloves and cinnamon stick. Cover and chill.

Peel and section grapefruit; divide evenly into compotes. Spoon raspberries and syrup evenly over each compote. Yield: 6 servings (98 calories per serving).

□ *0.9 gram protein, 0.2 gram fat, 24.9 grams carbohydrate, 0 milligrams cholesterol, 1 milligram sodium, and 28 milligrams calcium. Alice McNamara Eucha, Oklahoma*

CORNMEAL MUFFINS
(pictured on page 40)

1 cup yellow cornmeal
1 cup all-purpose flour
2 teaspoons baking powder
1 teaspoon baking soda
½ teaspoon salt
1 teaspoon sugar
¼ cup egg substitute or 2 egg
  whites
1¼ cups plain nonfat yogurt
¼ cup vegetable oil
Vegetable cooking spray

Combine cornmeal, flour, baking powder, soda, salt, and sugar in a large bowl; make a well in center of mixture. Combine egg substitute, yogurt, and oil; add to dry ingredients, stirring just until moistened.

Spoon mixture into muffin pans coated with cooking spray, filling three-fourths full. Bake at 425° for 12 to 14 minutes or until golden brown. Remove muffins from pans immediately. Yield: 1½ dozen (96 calories per muffin).

□ *2.7 grams protein, 3.5 grams fat, 13.5 grams carbohydrate, 0 milligrams cholesterol, 161 milligrams sodium, and 65 milligrams calcium.*

QUICK!

Cold Days, Warm Cobblers

What's in a name? Why, the hint of things to come. Our readers identify these recipes with several titles — slump, crinkle, crisp, cobbler, and more. Regardless of what name sticks, these desserts rate as favorites with young and old alike.

Commercial refrigerated piecrust, cake mix, or butter and oats or graham cracker crumbs make each crust crumbly good. Keep such simple and convenient ingredients on hand for those chilly days and nights when a warm, toasty cobbler would be mighty inviting.

LIGHT FAVORITE

Southern Cornmeal Muffins

Cornmeal muffins sound healthy enough until you take a look at the ingredients. Bacon drippings or shortening, eggs, and even sour cream are basics in many recipes.

We took our favorite cornmeal muffin recipe from *The Southern Living Cookbook* and replaced an egg, sour cream, and shortening with egg substitute, nonfat yogurt, and vegetable oil. We think you'll like this new healthier recipe as much as the original version.

COMPARE THE NUTRIENTS
(per serving)

	Traditional	Light
Calories	134	96
Fat	7.1g	3.5g
Cholesterol	19mg	0mg

CREAMY DUTCH APPLE DESSERT

3 tablespoons butter or margarine,
  melted
1 cup graham cracker crumbs
1 (14-ounce) can sweetened
  condensed milk
¼ cup lemon juice
1 (8-ounce) carton sour cream
1 (21-ounce) can apple pie filling
¼ cup chopped walnuts
½ teaspoon ground cinnamon

Combine butter and cracker crumbs in an 8-inch square baking dish; firmly press mixture in bottom of dish, and set aside.

Combine condensed milk and lemon juice; stir in sour cream. Spread cream mixture over crust. Spoon pie filling over cream mixture. Bake at 400° for 18 minutes.

Combine walnuts and cinnamon; sprinkle on top. Serve warm. Yield: 8 servings.
          *Peggy H. Amos
          Martinsville, Virginia*

QUICK FRUIT COBBLER

1 (21-ounce) can cherry or
  blueberry pie filling
1 (8-ounce) can unsweetened
  crushed pineapple, drained
1 (9-ounce) package yellow cake
  mix
⅓ cup butter or margarine, melted

Spoon pie filling into a lightly greased
8-inch square baking dish. Spoon pineapple over pie filling. Sprinkle cake
mix evenly over pineapple. Drizzle
butter over cake mix. Bake at 425° for
20 to 22 minutes. Yield: 8 servings.
Brenda Teal
Austin, Texas

CHERRY CRISP

1 (21-ounce) can cherry pie filling
2 teaspoons lemon juice
2 tablespoons all-purpose flour
¼ cup firmly packed brown sugar
½ teaspoon ground cinnamon
2 tablespoons butter or margarine
½ cup regular oats, uncooked

Combine cherry pie filling and lemon
juice; spoon into a lightly greased
1-quart casserole. Combine flour,
brown sugar, and cinnamon; cut in
butter with a pastry blender until mixture is crumbly. Stir in oats. Sprinkle
mixture over pie filling.
  Bake at 425° for 20 to 24 minutes.
Serve with ice cream, if desired.
Yield: 4 to 6 servings.   *Gwen Louer*
Roswell, Georgia

QUICK BLUEBERRY SLUMP

½ cup all-purpose flour
¼ teaspoon salt
1½ cups sugar
5 cups fresh or frozen blueberries,
  thawed
2 tablespoons lemon juice
2 tablespoons butter or margarine
1 (9-inch) refrigerated piecrust

Combine flour, salt, and sugar in a
medium bowl. Add blueberries; toss
gently. Spoon into a lightly greased
8-inch square baking dish. Sprinkle
lemon juice over blueberry mixture,
and dot with butter.
  Cut pastry to fit top; place over
filling. Make several slits in pastry to
allow steam to escape. Bake at 450°
for 18 to 20 minutes or until crust is
golden. Yield: 8 servings.
Marilee P. Curry
Lovettsville, Virginia

PEACH CRINKLE

1 (29-ounce) can sliced peaches,
  drained
1 teaspoon grated lemon rind
1 (9-ounce) package piecrust mix
⅔ cup firmly packed light brown
  sugar
¼ cup butter or margarine
Vanilla ice cream

Place peaches in a lightly greased 12-
x 8- x 2-inch baking dish. Sprinkle
with lemon rind.
  Combine piecrust mix and brown
sugar; sprinkle over rind. Dot with
butter. Bake at 425° for 15 to 20 minutes. Serve with ice cream. Yield: 6 to
8 servings.   *Mrs. Rosco Preston*
Williamsport, Kentucky

Marvelous Mascarpone

Mascarpone, a soft, rich, buttery
cheese made from fresh cream, is the
base for a number of Italian desserts,
or it can be served alone as a spread
for bread or as a dip for strawberries
or biscotti. Once you learn about mascarpone, you have the key to many
Italian treats.

Tiramisù is just one of the tempting
desserts that starts with mascarpone.
Our reader's version, like many others, uses brandy, but some call for
Marsala instead. Most recipes list ladyfingers, while a few use sponge
cake. Either grated chocolate or
sprinkled cocoa can top the custard
filling.
  You can find mascarpone in gourmet
shops or upscale supermarkets, but if
you have no luck in your area, try our
substitute of cream cheese, sour
cream, and whipping cream—not
quite as good, but very close. After
you've made tiramisù with our alternative, you'll have enough leftover
cream cheese mixture to try Cannoli.
Instructions for homemade cannoli
shells are included, but feel free to
use commercial ones if you're in a
hurry. Cannoli forms for the made-
from-scratch version are available in
kitchen shops.

CANNOLI

2 cups all-purpose flour
⅛ teaspoon salt
1 tablespoon sugar
½ cup butter or margarine
1 egg, slightly beaten
¼ cup white wine
Vegetable oil
1 cup ricotta cheese
1 cup mascarpone cheese (see note)
¾ cup sifted powdered sugar
1 tablespoon amaretto (optional)
3 (1-ounce) squares semisweet
  chocolate, grated and divided
¼ cup sifted powdered sugar

Combine first 3 ingredients in a medium bowl. Cut in butter until mixture
resembles coarse meal; stir in beaten
egg. Gradually stir in wine, mixing
well. Shape dough into a ball; cover
and refrigerate 30 minutes.
  Turn dough out onto a lightly
floured surface; roll dough to 1/16-inch
thickness. Cut into 3½-inch circles;
roll circles into 5-inch ovals with a rolling pin. Place a cannoli form down the

lengthwise center of oval, and roll dough around form. Moisten seam with water to seal.

Pour oil to a depth of 3 inches into a Dutch oven; heat to 350°. Fry cannoli shells 1 minute or until golden brown. Drain on paper towels, and cool about 5 seconds. Carefully remove cannoli form. Cool shells completely.

Thoroughly drain ricotta cheese in a strainer, discarding liquid. Place ricotta cheese in container of an electric blender or food processor, and process until smooth.

Combine ricotta, mascarpone cheese, ¾ cup powdered sugar, and, if desired, amaretto in a medium mixing bowl; beat at medium speed of an electric mixer until light and fluffy. Fold in 2 grated squares of chocolate; chill 4 hours.

Pipe or spoon filling into shells. Sprinkle shells with ¼ cup powdered sugar and exposed filling with remaining grated chocolate. Serve immediately. Yield: 12 to 15 servings.

Note: As a substitute for mascarpone cheese, combine 2 (8-ounce) packages cream cheese, ⅓ cup sour cream, and ¼ cup whipping cream; beat well. Use 1 cup mixture for recipe, reserving remainder for other uses.

TIRAMISÙ

6 egg yolks
1¼ cups sugar
1¼ cups mascarpone cheese (see note)
1¾ cups whipping cream
¾ cup water
2 teaspoons instant coffee granules
1½ tablespoons brandy
2 (3-ounce) packages ladyfingers
Garnishes: piped whipped cream, grated unsweetened chocolate

Combine egg yolks and sugar in top of a double boiler; beat at medium speed of an electric mixer until thick and lemon colored. Bring water to a boil; reduce heat to low, and cook 8 to 10 minutes, stirring constantly. Remove

from heat. Add mascarpone, and beat until smooth.

Beat whipping cream in a medium bowl until soft peaks form; fold into cheese mixture.

Combine water, coffee granules, and brandy; brush on cut side of ladyfingers. Line sides and bottom of a trifle bowl or 3-quart soufflé dish with 36 ladyfingers; pour in half of filling. Layer remaining ladyfingers on top; cover with remaining filling. Garnish, if desired; cover and chill 8 hours. Yield: 10 to 12 servings.

Note: As a substitute for mascarpone cheese, combine 2 (8-ounce) packages cream cheese, ⅓ cup sour cream, and ¼ cup whipping cream; beat well. Use 1¼ cups mixture for recipe, reserving remainder for other uses.

Trenda Leigh
Richmond, Virginia

Breads Are A Rising Success

You'll have guests scratching their heads in wonder when you reveal that the luscious breads they're eating *weren't* made from scratch. Start with a loaf of frozen bread dough from your grocer, and you've got some tasty options ahead.

CHEESE-FILLED MONKEY BREAD

1 (16-ounce) loaf frozen bread dough, thawed
4 ounces Cheddar cheese, cut into 32 (½-inch) cubes
2 tablespoons butter or margarine, melted

Cut bread dough into 32 equal pieces. Place 1 cheese cube in center of each

dough piece, shaping dough into a ball around cheese. Pinch dough to seal. Dip dough balls in butter.

Layer dough balls, seam side up, in a greased Bundt pan. Cover and let rise in a warm place (85°), free from drafts, 30 to 40 minutes or until doubled in bulk. Bake at 375° for 30 minutes or until golden brown. Invert onto a platter, and serve warm. Yield: one 10-inch ring.

To reheat: Wrap bread in aluminum foil, and bake at 300° for 15 to 20 minutes or until thoroughly heated.

Laura Jane Richardson
Greenville, South Carolina

BROCCOLI-CHEDDAR ROLLS

1 (16-ounce) loaf frozen bread dough, thawed
1 (10-ounce) package frozen chopped broccoli, thawed and well drained
1 cup (4 ounces) shredded Cheddar cheese
1 egg, beaten
2 tablespoons instant minced onion
1 teaspoon onion salt
2 tablespoons butter or margarine, melted

Roll dough to a 12-inch square on a lightly floured surface. Combine broccoli and next 4 ingredients; stir well. Spread mixture evenly over dough, leaving a ½-inch border. Starting on one side, roll dough tightly, jellyroll fashion. Moisten seam of dough with water; press securely to seal, turning seam side down.

Cut roll into 8 slices. Cut each slice almost in half again, cutting to within ½ inch of bottom. Gently open out halves, invert, and place on a lightly greased baking sheet. Brush with melted butter. Cover and let rise in a warm place (85°), free from drafts, 45 minutes or until doubled in bulk. Bake at 375° for 18 to 20 minutes or until golden brown. Serve immediately. Yield: 8 servings. *Sandra Russell*
Gainesville, Florida

FETA CHEESE-SPINACH ROLL

1 (10-ounce) package frozen
   chopped spinach, thawed and well
   drained
1 (7-ounce) package feta cheese,
   crumbled
½ cup cottage cheese
1 egg
½ teaspoon pepper
¼ teaspoon garlic powder
1 (16-ounce) loaf frozen bread
   dough, thawed
1 (3-ounce) package cream cheese,
   softened
1 egg, beaten

Combine first 6 ingredients; set mixture aside.

Place bread dough on a lightly greased baking sheet; roll to a 14- x 10-inch rectangle. Spread cream cheese on dough, and spoon spinach mixture lengthwise down center. Moisten all edges of dough with water. Bring each long edge of dough to center; press edges together to seal. Seal ends, and invert roll. Let rise in a warm place (85°), free from drafts, 45 minutes or until doubled in bulk.

Brush dough with beaten egg. Bake at 375° for 25 to 30 minutes or until golden brown. Serve immediately. Yield: one 12-inch loaf.

Clarine Spetzler
Salem, Virginia

ALMOND COFFEE CAKE TWIST

⅓ cup butter or margarine
¼ cup sugar
¼ teaspoon almond extract
2 (16-ounce) loaves frozen bread
   dough, thawed
¼ cup sliced almonds
1½ cups sifted powdered sugar
3 tablespoons milk
¼ teaspoon almond extract

Combine first 3 ingredients in a small saucepan; cook over medium heat until butter melts. Remove from heat, and let cool.

Cut each bread loaf crosswise into 4 pieces; roll each piece to an 18-inch strip on a lightly floured surface. While twisting dough several times, coil 1 strip in center of a lightly greased 12-inch pizza pan. Attach second strip to end of first; twist and coil. Repeat procedure with remaining dough. Spoon butter mixture over top. Let rise in a warm place (85°), free from drafts, 30 minutes or until dough is doubled in bulk.

Bake at 350° for 15 minutes; sprinkle with almonds. Shield roll with aluminum foil to prevent overbrowning, and bake an additional 15 minutes.

Let coffee cake cool 10 minutes. Combine powdered sugar, milk, and almond extract; stir until smooth. Drizzle glaze over coffee cake. Yield: one 12-inch coffee cake.

From Our Kitchen To Yours

Before preparing extra food to serve guests or to freeze, consider your time, space, and equipment. If you double or triple recipes, allow time for pre-preparation, and adjust cooking or chilling times if two or more recipes are combined in larger containers. Don't expect the food processor, blender, and mixer to handle larger quantities, and be sure your mixing bowls and cookware will hold the increased amounts.

You'll need ample refrigeration or freezer space to store large containers or additional ones. Also check to be sure your oven will accommodate large containers or multiple ones.

It isn't always practical to double a recipe because you may not be able to achieve the desired texture or thoroughly blend flavors. The easiest recipes to double or triple are casseroles, sauces, cookies, muffins, appetizers, soups, vegetables, and beverages. However, don't automatically double or triple salt, pepper, herbs, and spices; taste and adjust carefully because it doesn't take much seasoning to permeate an entire dish.

Pastries, yeast breads, and reduction sauces are not practical recipes to increase. The additional time and flour needed to work the extra amount of dough will cause a tougher pastry or bread, and cooking down twice the amount of liquid for a reduction sauce takes too long. We recommend you make the same recipe twice.

When packaging foods for freezing, choose moisture- and vapor-proof materials, such as plastic wrap, aluminum foil, and freezer paper. Strong plastic

Can Size		Cup Measure	
6	ounce	¾	cup
8	ounce	1	cup
10½	ounce	1¼	cups
16	ounce	2	cups
20	ounce	2½	cups
29	ounce	3½	cups
46	ounce	5¾	cups

Ingredient Equivalents

Beans, dry: 1 pound = 6 cups cooked

Carrots: 1 pound = 2 cups sliced

Celery: 1 medium bunch = 4½ cups chopped

Corn: 2 medium ears = 1 cup kernels

Lettuce: 1 pound head = 6¼ cups torn

Noodles, medium egg: 4 ounces = 3 cups cooked

Peppers, sweet: 1 large = 1 cup chopped

Potatoes: 3 medium = 2 cups cubed cooked

Rice, long-grain: 1 cup = 3 to 4 cups cooked

Rice, quick-cooking: 1 cup = 2 cups cooked

Tomatoes: 1 medium = ½ cup cooked

containers, heat-sealed cooking pouches, and wax paper- or plastic-lined paperboard cartons also work.

You'll find calculating ingredient amounts easier by using these charts. For doubling or tripling recipes, keep this guide to can sizes handy. When marketing, eliminate the guesswork by using these ingredient equivalents.

Pizza In A Double Crust

Most Southerners think of double-crust pies filled with aromatic apples or Grandmother's creamy chicken and vegetables. But this recipe presents pizza in a thick double-crusted variation with layers of ricotta and mozzarella cheeses, mushrooms, and a rich tomato sauce.

PIZZA PIE

¼ cup chopped onion
2 cloves garlic, minced
2 tablespoons olive oil
1 (10-ounce) can tomato puree
¼ cup tomato paste
½ teaspoon marjoram leaves
1 teaspoon dried whole oregano
1 cup sliced ripe olives
2 eggs, beaten
1 pound ricotta cheese
2 tablespoons chopped onion
1 cup grated Parmesan cheese
1 tablespoon chopped fresh parsley
¼ teaspoon salt
¼ teaspoon pepper
Pastry
1 (6-ounce) package sliced
   mozzarella cheese
1½ cups sliced fresh mushrooms
Garnishes: fresh mushroom slices,
   fresh parsley sprigs

Sauté ¼ cup chopped onion and garlic in olive oil until tender. Add tomato puree, tomato paste, marjoram, oregano, and sliced olives, mixing well. Set aside.

Combine eggs and next 6 ingredients, mixing well. Set aside.

Roll half of pastry to ⅛-inch thickness on a lightly floured surface. Place in a 10-inch pieplate.

Spread 3 tablespoons tomato puree mixture in pastry shell. Layer with half of ricotta mixture and half of mozzarella slices. Cover with half of remaining tomato puree mixture and 1½ cups mushrooms. Repeat layers with remaining ricotta mixture, mozzarella, and tomato puree mixture.

Roll remaining pastry to ⅛-inch thickness, and place over pizza mixture. Trim off excess pastry along edges. Fold edges under, and flute. Cut slits in top for steam to escape.

Bake at 425° for 40 minutes or until done. Let stand 30 minutes before serving. Garnish, if desired. Yield: one 10-inch pie.

Pastry

2 cups unbleached flour
½ teaspoon salt
½ teaspoon sugar
¾ cup butter or margarine
¼ teaspoon lemon juice
¼ cup ice water

Combine flour, salt, and sugar; cut in butter with a pastry blender until mixture resembles coarse meal. Combine lemon juice and water; sprinkle over flour mixture until dry ingredients are moistened. Shape into a ball. Wrap in wax paper; chill at least 1 hour. Yield: pastry for one double-crust 10-inch pie.
Tasha Riggins
Nashville, Tennessee

Cash In On Canned Salmon

It's hard to top the nutrition and convenience offered by a can of salmon. This well-known fish is rich in several vitamins and minerals, especially when you don't remove the tiny calcium-rich bones commonly found in the processed fish.

Fully cooked and ready to eat from the can, you can stir salmon into salads to serve immediately, or you can blend it with other ingredients and bake popular patties, such as those offered here.

SIMPLE SALMON SALAD

1 (15½-ounce) can salmon, drained
1 (10-ounce) package frozen
   English peas, thawed
1 (10-ounce) package frozen long-grain white and wild rice, thawed
4 ounces Swiss cheese, cubed
¼ teaspoon dried whole dillweed
2 cups loosely packed spinach
   leaves
1 (8-ounce) bottle creamy cucumber
   salad dressing
½ cup shredded carrot

Remove skin and bones from salmon, if desired; flake salmon with a fork. Add peas and next 3 ingredients, tossing well. Cover and chill.

When ready to serve, arrange spinach leaves on individual plates; top with salmon mixture. Drizzle evenly with dressing, and sprinkle with carrot. Yield: 4 to 6 servings.
Sara A. McCullough
Zavalla, Texas

Tip: *Remember that the darker the orange color of carrots, the greater the content of vitamin A.*

SALMON PATTIES WITH LEMON-CHEESE SAUCE

1 (15½-ounce) can salmon
2 tablespoons butter or margarine
½ cup all-purpose flour
½ cup milk
¼ cup grated onion
1 tablespoon minced fresh parsley
1 teaspoon dry mustard
1 teaspoon lemon juice
¼ teaspoon salt
¼ teaspoon pepper
¼ teaspoon Beau Monde seasoning
¼ teaspoon hot sauce
1 egg, beaten
1 cup Italian-seasoned
  breadcrumbs, divided
Vegetable oil
Lemon-Cheese Sauce

Drain salmon, reserving ½ cup liquid; set liquid aside. Remove bones and skin from salmon, if desired; flake salmon with a fork, and set aside.

Melt butter in a saucepan over low heat; add flour, stirring constantly. Gradually add reserved liquid and milk; cook over medium heat, stirring constantly, until mixture is thickened and bubbly. Remove from heat. Add onion and next 7 ingredients, stirring well. Stir in salmon, egg, and ½ cup breadcrumbs.

Shape mixture into 6 patties; dredge patties in remaining breadcrumbs. Pour oil to a depth of ¼ inch into a skillet. Fry patties in hot oil over medium heat 5 minutes or until brown; drain. Serve with Lemon-Cheese Sauce. Yield: 6 servings.

Lemon-Cheese Sauce

2 tablespoons butter or margarine
2 tablespoons all-purpose flour
1 cup milk
¼ teaspoon salt
Dash of pepper
2 egg yolks
2 ounces process cheese spread,
  cubed
2 tablespoons lemon juice

Melt butter in a heavy saucepan over low heat; add flour, stirring constantly. Gradually add milk; cook over medium heat, stirring constantly, until thickened and bubbly. Stir in salt and pepper. Gradually stir about one-fourth of hot mixture into yolks; add to remaining hot mixture, stirring constantly. Add cheese and lemon juice; stir 2 minutes over low heat. Yield: 1¼ cups.
Mrs. Sam Rigsby
Daphne, Alabama

Sample Blue-Ribbon Crêpes

Special Steak Crêpes—what an elegant and tasty way to stretch a pound of sirloin steak. Hot sauce, cream sherry, and Pickapeppa sauce accent the steak, and horseradish seasons the sour cream topping.

Gloria Different of Austin, Texas, had a great idea when she created this combination. Several years ago it won a prize in a cooking contest sponsored by *The Times-Picayune,* the New Orleans newspaper.

SPECIAL STEAK CRÊPES

1 pound boneless sirloin steak
2 tablespoons butter or margarine,
  melted
½ cup chopped onion
¼ teaspoon salt
¼ teaspoon freshly ground pepper
⅛ teaspoon dry mustard
1 teaspoon Pickapeppa sauce
¼ teaspoon hot sauce
2 tablespoons cream sherry
Crêpes (recipe follows)
16 fresh mushroom slices
1 teaspoon vegetable oil
1 tablespoon prepared horseradish
½ cup sour cream

Partially freeze steak; slice diagonally across grain into 2- x ¼-inch strips, and sauté in butter until brown. Add onion and next 5 ingredients; stir well. Cover, reduce heat, and simmer 10 minutes. Stir in cream sherry; remove from heat.

Spoon beef mixture into center of 8 crêpes; roll up, and place crêpes, seam side up, in a lightly greased 12- x 8- x 2-inch baking dish. Cover and bake at 350° for 15 minutes or until crêpes are thoroughly heated.

Sauté mushroom slices in hot oil until tender; drain on paper towels, and set aside.

Combine horseradish and sour cream; stir well, and spoon over crêpes. Garnish with mushroom slices. Yield: 4 servings.

Crêpes

1 cup all-purpose flour
¼ teaspoon salt
1¼ cups milk
2 eggs
2 tablespoons butter or margarine,
  melted
Vegetable oil

Combine flour, salt, and milk, beating at medium speed of an electric mixer until smooth. Add eggs, and beat well; stir in butter. Refrigerate batter 1 hour. (This allows flour particles to swell and soften so that crêpes will be light in texture.)

Brush bottom of a 6-inch crêpe pan or heavy skillet lightly with oil; place over medium heat just until hot, not smoking.

Pour 2 tablespoons batter into pan; quickly tilt pan in all directions so that batter covers pan with a thin film. Cook about 1 minute or until lightly browned.

Lift edge of crêpe to test for doneness. Crêpe is ready for flipping when it can be shaken loose from pan. Flip crêpe, and cook about 30 seconds on other side. (This side of the crêpe is usually spotty brown and is the side on which the filling is placed.)

Place crêpes on a towel to cool. Stack crêpes between layers of wax paper to prevent sticking. Repeat until all batter is used. Yield: 16 to 18 (6-inch) crêpes.

Note: Crêpes may be frozen, if desired. Thaw at room temperature; fill as directed.

FEBRUARY

Perk up your menus with flavorful variations on old favorites.

For starters, prepare a sensational salad for main dish or

accompaniment. Or bring together unusual combinations of

beans and vegetables in soups and chilis. For celebration

menus, try one of the tempting selections in

"Easy, Elegant Chicken."

Easy, Elegant Chicken

A fine meal with friends begins with an appealing entrée. And celebration meals require special attention and an entrée that goes beyond the everyday. These chicken selections answer your needs beautifully.

There's no more tempting aroma than meat hot off the grill. That's why we chose to highlight Grilled Ginger-Orange Chicken. Wedges of orange add color and an extra splash of flavor to this basic yet showy dish. Serve it with simple vegetables, such as tender steamed asparagus.

Any of these selections may be paired with a salad and hot bread. It's fine to add the honoree's favorite side dish and dessert, too.

GRILLED CHICKEN WITH VEGETABLES VINAIGRETTE
(pictured on page 37)

4 chicken breast halves, skinned
  and boned
2 (8-ounce) bottles olive oil
  vinaigrette salad dressing, divided
2 sweet red peppers, seeded
2 small zucchini
2 carrots, scraped
2 small yellow squash

Combine chicken and 1 bottle salad dressing in a shallow dish; cover and marinate 4 hours in refrigerator.

Cut vegetables into ¼-inch strips; place in a shallow dish. Add remaining salad dressing, tossing to coat. Cover and marinate 4 hours in refrigerator.

Remove chicken from marinade, reserving marinade. Grill chicken, covered, over medium coals 5 to 6 minutes on each side, basting twice with marinade.

Remove vegetables from marinade; drain and discard marinade. Arrange vegetables in steaming rack, and place over boiling water. Cover and steam 3 to 4 minutes or until crisp-tender. Serve chicken on steamed vegetables. Yield: 4 servings.   *Valerie East*
Houston, Texas

GRILLED GINGER-ORANGE CHICKEN
(pictured on page 37)

¼ cup orange marmalade
¼ cup Dijon mustard
2 tablespoons orange juice
2 green onions, finely chopped
6 chicken breast halves, skinned
Ginger Butter
Garnishes: orange wedges, kale,
  and green onion and orange rind
  strips

Combine first 4 ingredients; brush on both sides of chicken breasts. Grill chicken, uncovered, over medium coals 9 to 10 minutes on each side or until done. Serve with Ginger Butter; garnish, if desired. Yield: 6 servings.

Ginger Butter

½ cup butter or margarine,
  softened
½ teaspoon grated orange rind
¼ teaspoon ground ginger

Combine all ingredients; chill. Shape butter into curls. Yield: ½ cup.

HERB-STUFFED CHICKEN WITH SAUTÉED PEPPERS AND MUSHROOMS

1 cup herb stuffing mix
½ cup boiling water
1 tablespoon butter or margarine,
  melted
4 chicken breast halves, skinned
  and boned
3 ounces Monterey Jack cheese
1 egg, slightly beaten
⅓ cup Italian-seasoned
  breadcrumbs
Butter-flavored vegetable cooking
  spray
3 green onions, sliced diagonally
1 small sweet red pepper, cut into
  julienne strips
2 tablespoons butter or margarine,
  melted
6 fresh mushrooms, sliced
¼ cup white wine Worcestershire
  sauce

Combine first 3 ingredients in a small bowl; set aside.

Place chicken breasts between two sheets of heavy-duty plastic wrap. Flatten to ¼-inch thickness, using a meat mallet; set aside.

Cut cheese into four 2½- x 1- x ¼-inch strips. Place a cheese strip in center of each chicken breast. Spoon stuffing mixture evenly over cheese; fold sides of chicken breast over stuffing. Roll up chicken breast, and secure with a wooden pick.

Dip chicken in egg; roll in breadcrumbs, and place in a lightly greased 8-inch square baking dish. Spray chicken breast with cooking spray. Bake at 375° for 35 minutes or until done. Remove from oven, and spray with cooking spray.

Sauté sliced green onions and red pepper strips in 2 tablespoons melted butter until vegetables are crisp-tender. Stir in sliced mushrooms and Worcestershire sauce; spoon vegetables over chicken. Serve immediately. Yield: 4 servings.   *April Rhodes*
Atlanta, Georgia

MEDITERRANEAN CHICKEN

3 tablespoons olive oil
4 chicken leg-thigh combinations, skinned
1 medium onion, sliced and separated into rings
2 large cloves garlic, crushed
1 cup dried tomatoes
1½ cups tomato juice
1 (2-ounce) can anchovies, drained and chopped
½ cup pitted ripe olives
⅓ cup capers
1 tablespoon dried Italian herbs
1 tablespoon balsamic vinegar
⅛ teaspoon red pepper flakes

Heat oil in a large skillet over medium-high heat; add chicken, and sauté 3 minutes on each side or until golden brown. Remove chicken from skillet; set aside.

Add onion rings and garlic to skillet; sauté over medium heat until onion is tender. Stir in dried tomatoes and remaining ingredients; add chicken, and bring mixture to a boil. Cover, reduce heat, and simmer 45 minutes or until chicken is tender; stir occasionally. Serve immediately. Yield: 4 servings.
Mike Singleton
Memphis, Tennessee

Salads With A Different Twist

Take a break from tossed greens and try one of these salads that offer something a little different. Most need to be made ahead of time, which makes them great for busy cooks.

Wild rice mix and shoe peg corn are combined with a variety of vegetables and spices in Pebble Salad. Sunflower kernels and almonds added just before serving give the salad an interesting taste and texture.

Prepare Greek-Style Salad in the morning for a special treat at supper. The flavors of marinated artichoke hearts, red wine vinegar, ripe olives, and feta cheese mingle with the other ingredients for a savory salad that's sure to be popular.

GREEK-STYLE SALAD

2 medium tomatoes, cut into wedges
1 medium zucchini, cut into julienne strips
1 medium cucumber, sliced
1 cup pitted ripe olives
1 medium-size purple onion, thinly sliced and separated into rings
¾ cup feta cheese, drained and crumbled
1 (6-ounce) jar marinated artichoke hearts, undrained
¼ cup red wine vinegar
¼ teaspoon freshly ground pepper
Lettuce leaves

Combine first 6 ingredients in a large bowl; toss gently. Drain artichoke hearts, reserving marinade. Add artichoke hearts to tomato mixture.

Combine reserved marinade, vinegar, and pepper; pour over tomato mixture. Toss. Cover and chill 8 hours. Drain; serve on lettuce. Yield: 4 to 6 servings.
Mrs. Randall L. Wilson
Louisville, Kentucky

CORN SALAD

1 (15.25-ounce) can whole kernel corn, drained
2 tablespoons chopped onion
1 tablespoon white vinegar
1 teaspoon sugar
⅛ to ¼ teaspoon dried whole oregano
⅛ teaspoon pepper
1 medium carrot, scraped and shredded

Combine first 6 ingredients in a small saucepan; cook over low heat 5 minutes. Stir in carrot, and chill. Yield: 4 servings.
Edith Askins
Greenville, Texas

PEBBLE SALAD

1 (6-ounce) package long-grain and wild rice mix
1 (12-ounce) can white shoe peg corn, drained
1 small cucumber, seeded and chopped
2 medium carrots, chopped
¼ cup sliced green onions
⅓ cup chopped fresh parsley
¼ cup olive oil
¼ cup lemon juice
1 clove garlic, minced
½ teaspoon dried whole dillweed
¼ teaspoon dry mustard
⅛ teaspoon pepper
½ cup dry-roasted sunflower kernels
Romaine lettuce leaves
⅓ cup slivered almonds, toasted

Prepare rice according to package directions; cool.

Combine rice, corn, cucumber, carrot, green onions, and parsley in a large bowl; set aside. Combine oil and next 5 ingredients; pour over rice mixture, and toss gently. Cover and chill 3 hours.

Just before serving, stir in sunflower kernels. Arrange lettuce leaves in a large serving dish; spoon salad on top, and sprinkle with almonds. Yield: 8 to 10 servings. *Diane Mikulecky*
Birmingham, Alabama

MEMPHIS SLAW

½ cup sugar
½ cup prepared mustard
¼ cup white vinegar
2 tablespoons sweet pickle juice
¼ teaspoon salt
1 small cabbage, grated (6 cups)
¼ cup chopped sweet pickles

Combine first 5 ingredients; stir with a wire whisk until sugar dissolves. Combine cabbage and pickles; add dressing, and toss gently. Chill 1 hour. Yield: 6 to 8 servings.

Chill-Chasing Soups And Chilis

While awaiting the frosty season's thaw into spring and the return of fresh produce at the market, you'll want to try these winter-warming soups that feature the convenience of dried, frozen, and canned beans. These key ingredients are richly enhanced by the hearty flavors of meats, other vegetables, and an array of spices. You'll never notice they weren't just picked from the garden.

LENTIL SOUP

1 pound dried lentils
1 pound smoked sausage, thinly sliced
1 stalk celery, chopped
4 cloves garlic, minced
½ to 1 teaspoon salt
½ teaspoon black peppercorns
½ teaspoon ground cumin

Sort and wash lentils; place in a large Dutch oven. Cover with water 2 inches above lentils; bring to a boil. Cover, reduce heat, and simmer 40 minutes or until tender.

Brown sausage in a heavy skillet; drain. Add sausage and remaining ingredients to lentils; simmer mixture 5 minutes. Remove peppercorns. Yield: 2½ quarts.
Emily Danho
Birmingham, Alabama

SPICY THREE-BEAN SOUP

2 chicken breast halves, skinned
3 cups water
1 (28-ounce) can whole tomatoes, undrained and chopped
1 (10-ounce) package frozen cut green beans
1 (10-ounce) package frozen baby lima beans
1 bay leaf
2 teaspoons Creole seasoning
1 teaspoon chili powder
1 teaspoon paprika
¼ teaspoon garlic powder
¼ teaspoon onion powder
¼ teaspoon red pepper
Dash of hot sauce
Dash of soy sauce
Dash of Worcestershire sauce
1 (15-ounce) can black beans, drained

Combine all ingredients except black beans in a Dutch oven. Bring to a boil over medium heat. Cover, reduce heat, and simmer 1 hour. Remove chicken from soup; let chicken cool to touch, remove meat from bone, and cut into bite-size pieces. Return chicken to Dutch oven; add black beans, and cook until thoroughly heated. Remove bay leaf before serving. Yield: 2½ quarts. *Janet Kauder*
Hampton, Virginia

Tip: *Store spices in a cool place and away from any direct source of heat, because the heat will destroy their flavor. Red spices will maintain flavor and retain color longer if stored in the refrigerator.*

HEARTY KIELBASA CHILI

1 pound ground beef
½ pound kielbasa, cut into ½-inch slices
2 medium onions, chopped
2 cloves garlic, minced
1 (29-ounce) can tomato sauce
2 (15-ounce) cans red kidney beans, undrained
½ cup water
2 teaspoons chili powder
¼ teaspoon seasoned pepper
¼ teaspoon freshly ground black pepper

Combine first 4 ingredients in a Dutch oven; cook until meat is browned, stirring to crumble. Drain.

Stir in tomato sauce and remaining ingredients. Bring to a boil; cover, reduce heat, and simmer 1 hour, stirring occasionally. Yield: 2 quarts.

To freeze: Prepare recipe as above. Place in airtight plastic containers or freezer bags. Freeze.

To defrost and reheat: For **conventional** method, thaw chili, and cook in Dutch oven until thoroughly heated. For **microwave** oven, cover and defrost at MEDIUM LOW (30% power) 30 minutes, stirring at 10-minute intervals. Microwave at HIGH 30 minutes, rotating dish and stirring chili at 10-minute intervals.
Brian Hamilton
Knoxville, Tennessee

VEGETABLE CHILI

1½ cups chopped onion
1¼ cups chopped green pepper
½ cup chopped celery
1 clove garlic, minced
2 tablespoons vegetable oil
2 (16-ounce) cans tomatoes, undrained and chopped
2 tablespoons chili powder
2 teaspoons ground cumin
½ teaspoon ground red pepper
2 (16-ounce) cans pinto beans, undrained and divided

Sauté first 4 ingredients in oil in a large Dutch oven until tender. Add tomatoes, chili powder, cumin, and red pepper.

Pour 1 can of beans into container of an electric blender; blend until smooth. Add to tomato mixture with remaining can of beans. Bring to a boil; reduce heat, and simmer, uncovered, 30 minutes or to desired consistency. Yield: about 2 quarts.

Kathleen Stone
Houston, Texas

An Order For Seafood

Ocean breezes blow through the kitchen when you cook these tasty seafood entrées. Each takes advantage of the seafood brought home from the coast or available at the nearest seafood counter or fish market. The recipes are quick, too, with most being ready in less than 45 minutes.

SHRIMP WITH RÉMOULADE SAUCE

6 cups water
2 pounds unpeeled medium-size fresh shrimp
7 green onions, cut into 1-inch pieces
1 stalk celery, sliced
1 clove garlic, minced
3 tablespoons chopped fresh parsley
¼ cup hot Creole mustard
2 tablespoons paprika
⅛ teaspoon salt
⅛ teaspoon pepper
⅓ cup white vinegar
⅓ cup vegetable oil
⅓ cup olive oil
Lettuce leaves

Bring water to a boil; add shrimp, and cook 3 to 5 minutes. Drain well; rinse with cold water. Chill. Peel and devein shrimp. Set aside.

Combine green onions, celery, garlic, and parsley in food processor bowl fitted with a steel blade. Process 30 seconds, scraping sides of processor bowl occasionally. Add mustard and next 4 ingredients; process 10 seconds or until ingredients are blended. Gradually add vegetable oil and olive oil through food chute with processor running; continue processing until oil is blended and mixture is thickened.

To serve, arrange shrimp on lettuce, and top with dressing. Yield: 4 to 6 servings.   *Beverly Adams Mantz*
Washington, D.C.

GULF COAST FRIED SHRIMP

2 pounds unpeeled medium-size fresh shrimp
4 eggs, beaten
⅔ cup commercial spicy French dressing
1½ tablespoons lemon juice
¾ teaspoon onion powder
1⅓ cups saltine cracker crumbs
⅓ cup white cornmeal
⅔ cup corn flake cereal crumbs
Vegetable oil
Commercial cocktail sauce

Peel and devein shrimp, leaving tails intact. Combine eggs and next 3 ingredients; pour over shrimp. Stir gently; cover and chill 3 hours.

Combine cracker crumbs, cornmeal, and corn flake crumbs. Remove shrimp from marinade; discard marinade. Dredge shrimp in crumb mixture. Pour oil to a depth of 2 to 3 inches in a Dutch oven; heat to 375°. Fry shrimp in hot oil until golden. Serve with cocktail sauce. Yield: 4 to 6 servings.   *Laurie McIntyre*
Lake Jackson, Texas

ORANGE ROUGHY FILLETS WITH HERB SAUCE

1 cup club cracker crumbs
¼ cup all-purpose flour
1 teaspoon salt-free lemon herb-and-spice blend
⅓ cup sour cream
¼ cup water
6 (4- to 6-ounce) orange roughy fillets
¼ cup butter or margarine, melted
Herb Sauce

Combine first 3 ingredients in a dish. Combine sour cream and water; dip fillets in sour cream mixture, and coat with cracker crumb mixture. Arrange fillets on a greased 15- x 10- x 1-inch jellyroll pan. Drizzle with butter. Bake at 350° for 20 minutes or until fish flakes easily when tested with a fork. Serve fillets with Herb Sauce. Yield: 6 servings.

Herb Sauce

1½ cups boiling water
1 chicken-flavored bouillon cube
2 tablespoons butter or margarine
2½ tablespoons all-purpose flour
1 teaspoon dried whole dillweed
1 teaspoon onion powder
1 teaspoon dried whole parsley
½ teaspoon dried whole tarragon
¼ cup sour cream

Combine boiling water and bouillon cube, stirring to dissolve; set aside.

Melt butter in a heavy saucepan over low heat; add flour, stirring until smooth. Cook 1 minute, stirring constantly. Gradually add bouillon, dillweed, and next 3 ingredients. Cook over medium heat, stirring constantly, until thickened and bubbly. Remove mixture from heat, and gradually stir in sour cream. Yield: 1⅓ cups.

Wanda Edwards
Fayetteville, North Carolina

Tip: *Use fish as an economical dish. It has very little waste. A pound of dressed fish will yield two full-size servings.*

Perk Up Menus With Pasta

Bring on the pasta! Its versatility allows it to fit into just about any kind of menu. Our readers have come up with a variety of recipes using some familiar types of pasta.

GARDEN SPIRAL PRIMAVERA

8 ounces vegetable-flavored corkscrew macaroni, uncooked
2 tablespoons olive oil
¼ cup butter or margarine
1 small onion, thinly sliced
1 clove garlic, minced
1½ cups broccoli flowerets
1 carrot, scraped and sliced
4 ounces fresh mushrooms, sliced
3 tablespoons white wine
½ teaspoon dried whole basil or 1½ teaspoons chopped fresh basil
½ teaspoon dried parsley flakes or 1½ teaspoons chopped fresh parsley
¼ teaspoon white pepper
½ cup grated Parmesan cheese

Cook macaroni according to package directions; drain.

Heat olive oil and butter in a large skillet; add onion and garlic. Cook over medium heat 2 minutes, stirring frequently. Add broccoli and carrot; cook 2 minutes. Add mushrooms, and cook 1 minute, stirring occasionally. Add wine, basil, parsley, and pepper; bring to a boil. Cover, reduce heat, and simmer 3 minutes or until vegetables are tender.

Add vegetables and Parmesan cheese to pasta, stirring well. Serve immediately. Yield: 4 servings.
Heather Riggins
Nashville, Tennessee

SZECHUAN NOODLE TOSS

1 (8-ounce) package thin spaghetti
¼ cup sesame oil, divided
2 large sweet red peppers, cut into julienne strips
4 green onions, cut into 1-inch pieces
1 clove garlic, crushed
1 (10-ounce) package fresh, trimmed spinach, torn into bite-size pieces
2 cups cubed cooked chicken
1 (8-ounce) can sliced water chestnuts, drained
¼ cup soy sauce
2 tablespoons rice vinegar
1½ teaspoons crushed red pepper
1 teaspoon minced fresh gingerroot

Cook spaghetti according to package directions; drain. Rinse with cold water; drain. Place spaghetti in a large salad bowl; set aside.

Heat 2 tablespoons sesame oil in a large skillet. Add red pepper strips, green onions, and garlic; sauté 2 minutes. Stir in spinach; cover and cook over medium heat 3 minutes or until spinach wilts. Remove from heat; cool. Spoon mixture over pasta. Add chicken and water chestnuts.

Combine remaining 2 tablespoons sesame oil, soy sauce, and remaining ingredients; stir well. Pour over pasta; toss gently to coat. Yield: 6 servings.
Kimberly J. Orr
Fort Worth, Texas

LINGUINE WITH SPINACH

1 (8-ounce) package linguine
1 cup sliced carrot
1 cup sliced celery
1 cup chopped onion
2 tablespoons butter or margarine, melted
2 cups water
1 chicken-flavored bouillon cube
1 onion-flavored bouillon cube
1 teaspoon garlic powder
1 (10-ounce) package frozen chopped spinach, thawed and drained

Break linguine into 1-inch lengths, and set aside.

Sauté carrot, celery, and onion in butter in a Dutch oven until crisp-tender; add linguine, and cook, stirring constantly, until pasta begins to brown. Add water, bouillon cubes, and garlic powder. Bring to a boil; cover, reduce heat, and simmer 15 minutes or until water is absorbed. Place spinach on top of pasta; cover and simmer 5 minutes. Toss mixture. Serve immediately. Yield: 4 to 6 servings.
Becky Pinckney
Atlanta, Georgia

VEGETABLE NOODLE CASSEROLE

4 ounces egg noodles, uncooked
1 stalk celery, sliced
1 small onion, chopped
1 small green pepper, chopped
1 cup coarsely chopped fresh broccoli
2 tablespoons vegetable oil
½ cup milk
¼ teaspoon salt
¼ teaspoon pepper
1½ cups (6 ounces) shredded Monterey Jack cheese
3 tablespoons fine, dry breadcrumbs
1 tablespoon butter or margarine, melted

Cook noodles according to package directions; drain and set aside.

Sauté celery, onion, green pepper, and broccoli in oil until tender. Stir in milk and next 3 ingredients. Add noodles, and spoon into a lightly greased 1½-quart baking dish. Cover and bake at 350° for 15 minutes. Sprinkle with breadcrumbs, and drizzle with butter; bake, uncovered, 10 minutes. Yield: 4 to 6 servings.
Joy Garcia
Bartlett, Tennessee

QUICK!

Frozen Vegetables

If you're craving vegetables and don't have much time to cook, take heart. These frozen vegetable recipes are ready in 30 minutes or less. Preparation is easy, too—just pull the frozen food straight from the freezer, and cook conventionally or in the microwave oven.

QUICK VEGGIE SOUP

1 (16-ounce) package frozen mixed vegetables
1 (1-ounce) envelope onion soup mix
1 (46-ounce) can cocktail vegetable juice
1 pound lean ground beef

Combine first 3 ingredients in a Dutch oven; bring to a boil.

Cook ground beef in a nonstick skillet until meat is browned, stirring to crumble; drain. Stir meat into vegetable mixture; reduce heat, and simmer 20 minutes. Yield: 2 quarts.

Note: To microwave 1 pound ground beef, crumble into a microwave-safe colander; place colander in a 9-inch pieplate. Cover with wax paper, and microwave at HIGH 5 to 6 minutes, stirring once.
Marie Prevost
Greenville, South Carolina

LEMON-SESAME ASPARAGUS

1 (10-ounce) package frozen asparagus spears
1 tablespoon butter or margarine
2 teaspoons sesame seeds
2 teaspoons lemon juice

Cook asparagus according to package directions; drain. Combine butter and sesame seeds in a small skillet; cook over medium heat 2 to 3 minutes or until sesame seeds are lightly browned. Stir in lemon juice; pour over asparagus. Yield: 3 servings.

Microwave Directions: Microwave asparagus according to package directions; drain. Combine butter and sesame seeds in a 6-ounce custard cup. Cover with wax paper; microwave at HIGH 1½ minutes. Stir in lemon juice; pour over asparagus.
Leona Holland
Wynnewood, Oklahoma

COMPANY GREEN PEAS

1 (10-ounce) package frozen English peas
1 (4-ounce) can sliced mushrooms, drained
1 tablespoon butter or margarine, melted
½ tablespoon dried onion flakes
¼ teaspoon salt
¼ teaspoon pepper

Cook peas according to package directions; drain. Add remaining ingredients; cover and let stand 5 minutes. Yield: 3 to 4 servings.

Microwave Directions: Defrost peas in package at MEDIUM (50% power) 2½ minutes. Place peas in a 1-quart casserole; cover with heavy-duty plastic wrap; fold back a small corner of wrap to allow steam to escape. Microwave at HIGH 2 to 3½ minutes. Stir in mushrooms and remaining ingredients; cover and microwave at HIGH 2 to 3 minutes. Cover and let stand 5 minutes.
Sabrina McFarling
Hawesville, Kentucky

SPINACH CASSEROLE

2 (10-ounce) packages frozen chopped spinach
2 (3-ounce) packages cream cheese, softened
2 tablespoons butter or margarine, melted
2 tablespoons grated Parmesan cheese

Cook spinach according to package directions; drain well, and set aside.

Combine cream cheese and butter; beat at medium speed of an electric mixer until smooth. Stir in spinach. Spoon into a lightly greased 1-quart casserole; sprinkle with Parmesan cheese. Cover and bake at 350° for 20 minutes. Yield: 6 servings.

Microwave Directions: Cook spinach according to package directions; drain well, and set aside.

Combine cream cheese and butter; beat at medium speed of an electric mixer until smooth. Stir in spinach. Spoon into a greased 1-quart casserole; sprinkle with Parmesan cheese. Cover and microwave at HIGH 5 to 6 minutes, giving dish a half-turn after 3 minutes.
Jane C. Moore
Lawrenceville, Georgia

Freezer Tips

■ If power to your freezer is interrupted, do not open the door unnecessarily. Food in a full freezer will stay frozen 2 days, and food in a half-filled freezer about one day. If power is not resumed within this time, use dry ice to prevent spoilage, or move your frozen food to a locker plant nearby.

■ For the quickest freezing, leave a little space between containers so that air can circulate freely. Place containers closer together after they are frozen.

Steam For Healthy Cuisine

Steaming is simple, quick, economical, and nutritious and produces bright-colored, crisp vegetables as well as tender fish, poultry, and meat. Food prepared this way retains nearly all its natural vitamin content, and no extra fat is added.

This process can be done in specially designed cookware or in a saucepan or Dutch oven with a simple rack that prevents food from touching the boiling water. A good steamer should be both deep and wide so that the mist can circulate around the food.

Steamers or vessels that hold steamers need tight-fitting lids, but they shouldn't be so tight that they don't allow some steam to escape when pressure builds up. Remember, steam can inflict severe burns, so be sure to lift lids so that the steam escapes away from you.

Cooking a whole meal by steaming makes for easy preparation and cleanup. Foods that require the longest cooking time should be placed in the vessel first so that they will be ready with the rest of the meal.

STEAMED FISH AND VEGETABLES

4 small new potatoes
2 (4-ounce) grouper fillets or other lean white fish
2 small squash
8 medium okra
½ pound fresh or frozen green beans
1 cup sweet red pepper slices
½ cup sliced onion
1 tablespoon reduced-calorie margarine
½ teaspoon salt-free herb-and-spice blend

Place potatoes in a vegetable steamer over boiling water; cover and steam 10 minutes. Add fish and next 3 ingredients; cover and steam 10 minutes. Add red pepper slices and onion. Dot with margarine, and sprinkle with herb-and-spice blend; cover and steam 5 minutes. Yield: 2 servings (298 calories per 4 ounces cooked fish, 2 potatoes, 1 squash, 4 okra, and 1 cup vegetable mixture).

☐ *28.6 grams protein, 5.5 grams fat, 36.5 grams carbohydrate, 42 milligrams cholesterol, 136 milligrams sodium, and 128 milligrams calcium.*
Lucile Morgan Blevins
Rising Fawn, Georgia

MEATBALLS AND VEGETABLES WITH HORSERADISH DRESSING

6 ounces ground chuck
1½ tablespoons seasoned, dry breadcrumbs
⅛ teaspoon salt
⅛ teaspoon pepper
¼ teaspoon browning-and-seasoning sauce
Vegetable cooking spray
½ cup cauliflower flowerets
⅓ cup julienne-cut carrots
¼ cup coarsely chopped onion
1 cup ½-inch sliced zucchini
¾ cup snow pea pods, trimmed (about 24)
4 cherry tomatoes
Horseradish Dressing

Combine ground chuck, breadcrumbs, salt, pepper, and browning-and-seasoning sauce; shape meat mixture into 6 meatballs.

Coat a vegetable steamer with cooking spray, and place over boiling water. Add meatballs; cover and steam 5 to 7 minutes.

Add cauliflower, carrot, and onion; cover and steam 10 minutes. Add zucchini, snow peas, and tomatoes; cover and steam 2 to 3 minutes. Serve with Horseradish Dressing. Yield: 2 servings (287 calories per 3 meatballs, 1½ cups vegetables, and 2½ tablespoons dressing).

☐ *18.2 grams protein, 15.8 grams fat, 18.5 grams carbohydrate, 53 milligrams cholesterol, 329 milligrams sodium, and 119 milligrams calcium.*

Horseradish Dressing

¼ cup plain low-fat yogurt
1½ tablespoons reduced-calorie mayonnaise
1 teaspoon prepared horseradish
½ teaspoon lemon juice

Combine yogurt (at room temperature) and remaining ingredients in a saucepan. Place over low heat; cook, stirring constantly, until heated (do not boil). Yield: 6 tablespoons (16 calories per tablespoon).

☐ *0.5 gram protein, 1.1 grams fat, 1 gram carbohydrate, 2 milligrams cholesterol, 29 milligrams sodium, and 18 milligrams calcium.*

CHICKEN AND VEGETABLES WITH GINGER-SOY SAUCE

2 (4-ounce) skinned, boned chicken breast halves
¾ cup onion wedges
1 cup whole fresh mushrooms
¼ teaspoon onion powder
¼ teaspoon garlic powder
2 cups broccoli flowerets
1½ cups hot cooked long-grain rice (cooked without salt or fat)
Ginger-Soy Sauce

Layer chicken, onion, and mushrooms in a vegetable steamer over boiling water. Sprinkle with onion powder and garlic powder. Cover and steam 10 minutes. Add broccoli; cover and steam an additional 10 minutes or until chicken is done.

Serve chicken and vegetables over rice; top with Ginger-Soy Sauce. Yield: 2 servings (379 calories per 1 chicken breast half, 1½ cups vegetables, and ½ cup sauce).

□ *32.7 grams protein, 4.9 grams fat, 50.3 grams carbohydrate, 70 milligrams cholesterol, 802 milligrams sodium, and 80 milligrams calcium.*

Ginger-Soy Sauce

1 teaspoon sugar
1 tablespoon cornstarch
1 teaspoon chicken bouillon
    granules
¼ teaspoon ground ginger
1 cup water
1 tablespoon reduced-sodium soy
    sauce
1 tablespoon dry sherry

Combine all ingredients in a heavy saucepan. Place over medium heat, and bring to a boil; boil 1 minute, stirring constantly. Yield: 1 cup (4 calories per tablespoon).

□ *0.1 gram protein, 0.1 gram fat, 0.9 gram carbohydrate, 0 milligrams cholesterol, 90 milligrams sodium, and 0 milligrams calcium.*

Lynda L. Medaugh
Sassafras, Kentucky

LIGHT MENU

A "Not-So-Traditional" Pork Chop Dinner

Ease and simplicity are key factors in this health-minded menu that's full of flavor and color. Whether you serve it to family and friends on St. Valentine's Day or for a cozy supper, it's sure to be requested often.

Barley-Vegetable Pilaf, which is similar to rice pilaf, is a new way to serve barley. Its considerable complex carbohydrate and soluble fiber content (the kind that may lower cholesterol levels) makes it a sure bet for healthy eating.

Slide slices of tomato into fanned zucchini for an attractive presentation. Spraying the fans with vegetable cooking spray before sprinkling with basil and pepper helps the seasonings adhere to the vegetables.

Complete this pork chop dinner menu with a 2-ounce slice of commercial angel food cake. Top each slice with ½ cup sliced fresh strawberries for a meal that is less than 575 calories and only 20% fat per serving.

Honey-Lime Pork Chops
Barley-Vegetable Pilaf
Zucchini Fans
Angel food cake
with sliced strawberries

HONEY-LIME PORK CHOPS

6 (4-ounce) lean, boneless center-
    cut loin pork chops (¾-inch thick)
½ cup lime juice
½ cup reduced-sodium soy sauce
2 tablespoons honey
3 cloves garlic, crushed
Vegetable cooking spray

Trim fat from pork chops; place chops in a shallow 2-quart baking dish. Combine lime juice and next 3 ingredients; pour over pork chops. Cover and refrigerate about 4 hours, turning pork chops occasionally.

Coat a large, nonstick skillet with cooking spray. Place over medium-high heat until hot. Add pork chops, reserving marinade. Brown meat 2 to 3 minutes on each side. Add marinade; cover and cook 5 minutes or to desired degree of doneness, turning once. Yield: 6 servings (234 calories per pork chop).

□ *23.5 grams protein, 10.8 grams fat, 8.2 grams carbohydrate, 74 milligrams cholesterol, 576 milligrams sodium, and 10 milligrams calcium.*

Nancy Collis
Washington, North Carolina

BARLEY-VEGETABLE PILAF

2 (10½-ounce) cans ready-to-serve,
    no-salt-added chicken broth
1 cup barley
1 cup chopped onion
½ cup sliced green onions
½ cup grated carrot
¼ teaspoon garlic powder
¼ teaspoon salt
1 tablespoon chopped fresh parsley

Bring chicken broth to a boil in a medium saucepan; add barley. Cover, reduce heat, and simmer 15 minutes. Stir in chopped onion and next 4 ingredients; cover and cook 10 minutes or until barley is tender and broth is absorbed. Stir in parsley. Yield: 4 cups (134 calories per ⅔-cup serving).

□ *4.6 grams protein, 0.8 gram fat, 26.9 grams carbohydrate, 0 milligrams cholesterol, 108 milligrams sodium, and 26 milligrams calcium.*

Sue Corbett
Fairfax, Virginia

ZUCCHINI FANS

6 small zucchini (1¼ pounds)
18 small tomato slices, ¼-inch
    thick
Olive oil-flavored vegetable cooking
    spray
½ teaspoon dried whole basil
¼ teaspoon freshly ground pepper

Cut each zucchini into 4 lengthwise slices, leaving slices attached at stem end. Fan slices out; place a tomato slice in a staggered pattern between each slice. Place in a 13- x 9- x 2-inch baking dish coated with cooking spray. Coat each fan with cooking spray, and sprinkle with basil and pepper. Cover and bake at 350° for 20 minutes. Yield: 6 servings (27 calories each).

□ *1.6 grams protein, 0.6 gram fat, 5.3 grams carbohydrate, 0 milligrams cholesterol, 7 milligrams sodium, and 20 milligrams calcium.*

Charlotte Stirling
Beaumont, Texas

Muffins: Savory, Not Sweet

Muffins aren't always sweet and served for breakfast; some can be hearty and incorporated into your lunch or dinner menus. Here are some good reasons to include muffins with your next midday or evening meal.

—Muffins are easy on the cook. You will probably have most of these ingredients on hand.

—They mix up quickly and bake in 15 to 20 minutes, allowing time to prepare a second dish while they bake.

—Muffins are versatile. You can mix and match them with other types of food for quick, easy meals.

For the best muffins, be sure to mix dry ingredients separately. When the liquid and dry ingredients are combined, limit stirring to avoid peaked tops or tunnels inside the muffin. The perfect muffin batter should be lumpy, not smooth.

■ Here's a savory idea. Pair a homemade pasta salad or one from the deli with **Chive Muffins**. It's a lunch to take to the office or pack for a spring picnic. What an easy way to plan an outing for friends.

CHIVE MUFFINS

2 cups all-purpose flour
1 tablespoon baking powder
¼ cup dried chives
1 tablespoon sugar
1 tablespoon brown sugar
1 egg, lightly beaten
1 cup milk
¼ cup butter or margarine, melted

Combine first 5 ingredients in a large bowl; make a well in center of mixture. Combine egg, milk, and butter; add to dry ingredients, stirring just until moistened.

Spoon batter into greased muffin pans, filling about two-thirds full. Bake at 400° for 18 to 20 minutes or until

muffins are lightly browned. Remove muffins from pans immediately. Yield: 1 dozen.
Heather Riggins
Nashville, Tennessee

■ Make a cheese omelet for Sunday night supper and serve **Southwestern Muffins** on the side. Hashbrowns complete the menu, which may become a family favorite.

SOUTHWESTERN MUFFINS

½ cup finely chopped sweet red pepper
½ cup finely chopped sweet yellow pepper
¼ cup finely chopped onion
2 tablespoons vegetable oil
¾ cup diced cooked ham
1½ cups blue cornmeal or yellow cornmeal
1 cup all-purpose flour
1 tablespoon baking powder
1 teaspoon salt
¼ cup sugar
2 eggs, beaten
1 cup milk
½ cup whipping cream
¼ cup vegetable oil
¼ cup butter or margarine, melted

Sauté peppers and onion in 2 tablespoons oil until tender; stir in ham.

Combine cornmeal, flour, baking powder, salt, and sugar in a large bowl; make a well in center of mixture. Combine eggs and remaining ingredients; add to dry ingredients with pepper mixture, stirring just until moistened. Spoon into greased muffin pans, filling two-thirds full. Bake at 425° for 15 to 20 minutes or until golden. Remove from pans immediately. Yield: about 2 dozen.

Note: Blue cornmeal, available at specialty food stores, is ground from speckled Indian blue corn. It's nuttier tasting than white or yellow cornmeal and is traditionally used in Southwestern breads, tortillas, and tamales.
Helen H. Maurer
Christmas, Florida

■ Serve **Poppy Seed Muffins** with a tangy fruit salad and baked ham slices. This winning combination makes a delicious lunch or brunch.

POPPY SEED MUFFINS

½ cup butter or margarine, softened
¾ cup sugar
2 eggs
¾ cup sour cream
1½ teaspoons vanilla extract
2 cups all-purpose flour
¼ teaspoon baking soda
½ teaspoon salt
¼ cup poppy seeds

Cream butter; gradually add sugar, beating well at medium speed of an electric mixer. Add eggs, one at a time, beating after each. Add sour cream and vanilla.

Combine flour, soda, salt, and poppy seeds; add to creamed mixture. Spoon into greased muffin pans, filling two-thirds full. Bake at 400° for 20 minutes or until golden. Remove from pans immediately. Yield: 16 muffins.
Ann C. McConnel
Kensington, Maryland

Candy Full Of Flavor

The shapes of these candies are identical, but the color of the icing or the type nut on top identifies the flavor inside. That makes it easy to package an assortment of candies that leaves no question about the filling.

For cream-filled varieties, spoon chocolate into molds, and brush it onto the sides to create cavities of chocolate for the filling. Spoon additional chocolate over the filling to entirely seal it in chocolate. Invert the hardened candy from the molds, and drizzle it with a similar color icing. Use green icing for Crème de Menthe Chocolates, white for White Chocolate

Surprises, pink for Raspberry Cream Chocolates, and a golden color for Chocolate Caramels.

Make Chocolate Nut Teasers from pecans, peanuts, almonds, or pistachios. These candies use the same molds as the others, but the technique is a little different. In this case, place a small amount of nuts in the mold before adding the chocolate.

You can prepare these chocolates using ordinary melted semisweet chocolate, but to give the candy a shiny, professional-looking surface you'll need to temper the chocolate.

Tempering monitors the temperature to which the chocolate is exposed so that it never gets high enough to make the chocolate sticky after it hardens. Each candy recipe calls for a certain amount of tempered chocolate, and a separate recipe gives directions for the tempering process.

TEMPERED CHOCOLATE

Semisweet chocolate squares

Grate or finely chop the amount of chocolate called for in recipe. Place two-thirds of grated chocolate in top of a double boiler, and heat, stirring constantly, over hot, not boiling, water until chocolate melts and temperature registers 115°. (Make sure water is below, not touching, top of boiler.)

Remove top of double boiler, and place on a dry towel. Add remaining one-third of grated chocolate to chocolate in double boiler, stirring constantly until melted.

Pour melted chocolate onto a marble or laminate surface. Using a spatula or pastry scraper, scrape and stir chocolate to smooth and cool it. When chocolate cools to between 80° and 82°, return it to top of double boiler.

Place top of double boiler over hot, not boiling, water, and heat again, stirring constantly, until mixture reaches 87° to 91°. Remove top part of double boiler, and use chocolate as directed.

DRIZZLING ICING

3¼ cups sifted powdered
    sugar
3 tablespoons water
1 tablespoon lemon juice
⅛ teaspoon vanilla extract

Combine all ingredients in a small bowl; mix well (mixture will be thick). Yield: ⅔ cup.

CHOCOLATE CARAMELS

2 cups sugar
1½ cups half-and-half
½ cup light corn syrup
¼ cup butter or margarine
1 teaspoon vanilla extract
14 ounces Tempered Chocolate (see
    separate recipe)
Brown paste food coloring
Drizzling Icing (see separate recipe)

Combine first 4 ingredients in a large, heavy saucepan; cook over low heat, stirring gently, until sugar dissolves. Cover and cook over medium heat 2 to 3 minutes to wash down sugar crystals from sides of pan. Uncover and cook to firm ball stage (246°). Stir in vanilla; remove from heat. Pour into a buttered 9-inch square pan, without stirring; let cool. Remove from pan; shape mixture into ¾-inch balls.

Spoon about ½ teaspoon Tempered Chocolate into each 1-inch plastic candy mold (molds should be clean and dry). Spread chocolate to cover bottom and sides of molds, using an art brush or the back of a small spoon. Freeze 10 minutes or until firm.

Carefully place 1 caramel ball into each chocolate-filled candy mold, pressing caramel gently to flatten. Spoon about ½ teaspoon Tempered Chocolate over filling.

Tap molds on counter to remove air bubbles. Freeze 10 minutes or until firm. Invert molds; remove candies.

Stir a small amount of food coloring into Drizzling Icing to color icing like caramel. Spoon icing into a decorating bag fitted with small round tip No. 2.

Drizzle icing over top of each piece of candy. Store at cool room temperature. Let stand 24 hours before serving to soften. Yield: 5½ dozen.

CHOCOLATE NUT TEASERS

¾ cup pecan pieces, peanut halves,
    slivered almonds, or pistachio
    pieces, toasted
14 ounces Tempered Chocolate
    (see separate recipe)
Nut Filling

Spoon about ½ teaspoon nuts into each 1-inch plastic candy mold (molds should be clean and dry). Spoon ¾ teaspoon Tempered Chocolate over nuts in candy molds; spread to cover sides, using an art brush or the back of a small spoon. Freeze 10 minutes or until firm.

Carefully spoon about ¾ teaspoon Nut Filling into each chocolate-filled candy mold. Spoon about ½ teaspoon Tempered Chocolate over filling.

Gently tap molds on counter to remove air bubbles. Freeze 10 minutes or until firm. Invert molds, and remove candies. Store at cool room temperature. Yield: 4½ dozen.

Nut Filling

1 cup butter or margarine
1 cup sugar
2 tablespoons water
1 tablespoon light corn syrup
⅔ cup finely chopped pecans,
    peanuts, almonds, or pistachios,
    toasted
½ teaspoon vanilla extract

Melt butter in a heavy saucepan. Gradually add sugar, water, and corn syrup, stirring once. Cook over low heat until sugar dissolves, stirring once. Bring mixture to a boil. Cover, reduce heat to medium, and cook 2 to 3 minutes to wash down sugar crystals from sides of pan. Uncover and cook to soft ball stage (235°). Remove from heat, and stir in nuts and vanilla. Pour mixture into a greased pan, and cool. Yield: 1¼ cups.

CRÈME DE MENTHE CHOCOLATES

1 (14-ounce) can sweetened
  condensed milk
2 tablespoons butter or margarine
¼ cup green crème de menthe
⅛ teaspoon peppermint extract
8 ounces Tempered Chocolate (see
  recipe, page 35)
Green paste food coloring
Drizzling Icing (see recipe, page 35)

Combine condensed milk and butter in a small saucepan; cook over medium heat, stirring constantly, until mixture comes to a boil. Reduce heat, and simmer 5 minutes or until thickened, stirring constantly. Remove from heat, and stir in crème de menthe and peppermint extract. Set aside to cool.

Spoon about ½ teaspoon Tempered Chocolate into each 1-inch plastic candy mold (molds should be clean and dry). Spread chocolate to cover bottom and sides of molds, using an art brush or the back of a small spoon. Freeze 10 minutes or until firm.

Carefully spoon about ¾ teaspoon crème de menthe filling into each chocolate-filled mold. Spoon about ½ teaspoon Tempered Chocolate over filling.

Gently tap molds on counter to remove air bubbles. Freeze 10 minutes or until firm. Invert molds, and remove candies.

Stir a small amount of food coloring into Drizzling Icing. Spoon icing into a decorating bag fitted with small round tip No. 2. Drizzle icing over top of each piece of candy. Store at cool room temperature. Yield: 3 dozen.

Raspberry Cream Chocolates: Prepare recipe for Crème de Menthe Chocolates, omitting peppermint extract, substituting crème de framboises for crème de menthe, and substituting red food coloring for green in Drizzling Icing. Add red food coloring to filling mixture, if desired.

WHITE CHOCOLATE SURPRISES

⅓ cup whipping cream
1½ tablespoons sour cream
8 ounces grated white chocolate or
  vanilla-flavored baking bars
About ½ cup sifted powdered sugar
12 ounces Tempered Chocolate (see
  recipe, page 35)
2 ounces grated white chocolate or
  vanilla-flavored baking bars,
  melted

Bring whipping cream to a simmer in a heavy saucepan. Reduce heat to low, and stir in sour cream. Add 8 ounces grated white chocolate, and stir until chocolate melts; remove from heat. Pour white chocolate mixture into a buttered 9-inch square pan, and freeze 20 minutes or until mixture is firm enough to hold its shape.

Place a large piece of wax paper on a baking sheet, and sprinkle with powdered sugar. Spoon white chocolate mixture into mounds (about ¾ teaspoon) on wax paper, and freeze 10 minutes or until almost firm.

Roll each mound of candy in powdered sugar to make a ball; set aside.

Spoon about ½ teaspoon Tempered Chocolate into each 1-inch plastic candy mold (molds should be clean and dry). Spread chocolate to cover bottom and sides of molds, using an art brush or the back of a spoon. Freeze 10 minutes or until firm.

Carefully place 1 ball of white chocolate filling into each chocolate-filled candy mold, pressing gently to flatten. Spoon about ½ teaspoon Tempered Chocolate over filling.

Tap molds on counter to remove air bubbles. Freeze 10 minutes or until firm. Invert molds; remove candies.

Spoon 2 ounces melted white chocolate into a decorating bag fitted with small round tip No. 2. Drizzle white chocolate over top of each piece of candy. Store at cool room temperature. Yield: 3½ dozen.

Note: We tested this recipe using white chocolate sold in bulk at candy counters of large department stores, as well as with vanilla-flavored baking bars sold in grocery stores.

Winter Stirrings

Winter's chill is far away in the presence of good conversation and a treasured friend. These beverages are tailored for afternoons spent chatting by the fire.

MOLASSES RUM TODDY

3 (6-ounce) cans pineapple juice
Juice of 1 lime or lemon
¼ cup molasses
½ cup rum
Cinnamon sticks (optional)

Combine pineapple juice, lime juice, and molasses in a saucepan; cook over low heat, stirring until molasses dissolves. Remove from heat; stir in rum. Serve with cinnamon stick stirrers, if desired. Yield: 3 cups.
Alice Lewis
Knoxville, Tennessee

HOT SPICED BREW

3 cups milk
2 tablespoons instant coffee
  granules
2 tablespoons brown sugar
⅛ teaspoon ground cinnamon
Cinnamon sticks (optional)

Combine first 4 ingredients in a saucepan; bring to a boil. Reduce heat, and simmer, stirring constantly, until sugar dissolves. Serve immediately with cinnamon stick stirrers, if desired. Yield: 3 cups. *Linda H. Sutton*
Winston-Salem, North Carolina

Right: *Grilled Ginger-Orange Chicken (top) and Grilled Chicken With Vegetables Vinaigrette appeal to the eye and palate. (Recipes, page 26.)*

Tangy, sweet, and refreshing, the light flavors of citrus pies capture the bright spirit of spring: (from left) Florida Orange Pie (page 43), Key Lime Pie (page 42).

The down-home goodness of Cornmeal Muffins (page 19) will convince longtime cornbread lovers that eating healthy doesn't mean giving up flavor.

Gay Neale's Brunswick Stew (page 17) and Dan Dickerson's Brunswick Stew (page 16) are 20th-century renditions of a dish that's been a Southern staple since the 1800s. Other recipes as well as a history of Brunswick stew begin on page 14.

MARCH

Looking for light, nutritious recipes and ideas? "On the Light Side" spotlights pork, served in a variety of delicious ways— all developed to cut fat, cholesterol, and calories. In addition, there is another healthy choice in an Oriental menu. Salads, the traditional favorite of light eaters, show a burst of vivid color and unusual texture in "A Fresh Approach to Salads."

Sunny Citrus Pies

Peel a sun-soaked orange or cut open a vibrant lemon, and a spray of spring fragrance tickles your nose. Pies filled with these succulent citrus fruits, bursting with flavor and ablaze with color, become the upper crust of desserts. Just a slice of any of our tart treats is the pièce de résistance.

In particular, a Key lime pie—an authentic one—is especially good and comes as a surprise to folks who've been eating lime gelatin concoctions tagged as the real thing. Floridians deem that only pastries (not graham cracker crusts) filled with sweetened condensed milk, egg yolks, and freshly squeezed juice from Key limes

make the cut. These golf ball-size, yellow fruits are shipped from the Florida Keys, thus the name. The familiar green Persian limes come close, but they are less acidic and have a milder flavor.

Why sweetened condensed milk? Anyone who loves to dip a sampling finger into the can while cooking may ask why not, but there is a reason. In the mid-1800s, before refrigeration, tropical weather in the Keys ruined any hopes of storing fresh milk. Canned milk's long shelf life beat the heat, and paired with abundant Key limes, spawned this classic, meringue-topped dessert.

Tradition and flavor have kept these sweets popular for generations, but suddenly time-honored cooking methods for them have changed. With increasing salmonella cases linked to raw or undercooked egg yolks (a key ingredient in many citrus pies) we'd already changed cooking procedures with yolks. The USDA has recently found that egg whites can be a problem, too, and can cause temporary flu-like symptoms or, in rare cases, can even be fatal. But don't worry; we've changed some techniques and substituted ingredients in our recipes so that you can still have your pie and eat it, too—safely.

KEY LIME PIE
(pictured on pages 38 and 39)

4 eggs, separated
1 (14-ounce) can sweetened
   condensed milk
⅓ cup Key lime juice
½ teaspoon cream of tartar
⅓ cup sugar
1 baked 9-inch pastry shell

Combine egg yolks, condensed milk, and Key lime juice in a heavy saucepan. Cook over low heat, stirring constantly, until mixture reaches 160° (about 10 minutes).

Beat egg whites and cream of tartar at high speed of an electric mixer just until foamy. Gradually add sugar, 1 tablespoon at a time, beating until stiff peaks form and sugar dissolves (2 to 4 minutes).

Pour hot filling into shell. Immediately spread meringue over filling, sealing to edge. Bake at 325° for 25 to 28 minutes. Yield: one 9-inch pie.

LEMONADE PIE

4 egg yolks
½ cup sugar
⅛ teaspoon salt
1 envelope unflavored gelatin
½ cup cold water
1 (6-ounce) can frozen lemonade
   concentrate, thawed and
   undiluted
1½ cups whipping cream, whipped
   and divided
1 baked 9-inch pastry shell

Combine egg yolks, sugar, and salt in top of a double boiler; bring water to a boil. Reduce heat to low; cook, stirring constantly, until temperature reaches 160° (about 20 minutes). Remove egg yolk mixture from heat, and set aside.

Sprinkle unflavored gelatin over cold water in a small saucepan; stir and let stand 1 minute. Cook over low heat, stirring constantly, until gelatin dissolves. Stir gelatin mixture and

lemonade concentrate into yolk mixture. Chill until consistency of unbeaten egg white.

Fold two-thirds of whipped cream into chilled mixture; spoon into pastry shell. Chill at least 4 hours. Garnish with remaining whipped cream. Yield: one 9-inch pie. *Valerie Stutsman*
Norfolk, Virginia

Tip: *For an easy and attractive garnish, slice a lemon or lime into ¼-inch-thick slices; make a cut from the center of the slice to the outside edge, and gently twist the cut slice in opposite directions to form an "S" shaped twist.*

FLORIDA ORANGE PIE
(pictured on pages 38 and 39)

3 egg yolks
½ cup sugar
1 cup orange juice, divided
1 envelope unflavored gelatin
2 tablespoons grated orange rind
1 teaspoon grated lemon rind
2 cups whipping cream, divided
⅔ cup powdered sugar
⅛ teaspoon salt
½ cup flaked coconut
1 cup diced orange sections,
    drained
1 baked 9-inch pastry shell
3 tablespoons powdered sugar
Garnishes: toasted flaked coconut,
    orange sections, and fresh mint
    sprigs

Beat egg yolks slightly. Combine yolks, ½ cup sugar, and ½ cup orange juice in a heavy saucepan. Cook over low heat, stirring constantly, 10 to 12 minutes or until mixture reaches 160°. Remove from heat.

Sprinkle gelatin over remaining ½ cup orange juice; stir and let stand 1 minute. Add gelatin mixture and grated rinds to yolk mixture. Chill until consistency of unbeaten egg white.

Beat ½ cup whipping cream, ⅔ cup powdered sugar, and salt at high speed of an electric mixer until stiff peaks form. Fold in gelatin mixture; fold in coconut and diced orange sections. Spoon mixture into pastry shell; chill until firm.

Beat remaining 1½ cups whipping cream until foamy; gradually add 3 tablespoons powdered sugar, beating until soft peaks form. Spread about half of whipped cream over pie. Dollop or pipe remaining whipped cream around outer edge of pie. Garnish, if desired. Yield: one 9-inch pie.
Mrs. Harland J. Stone
Ocala, Florida

A Fresh Approach To Salads

Lots of options are available when it's time to make a salad. Flowers nest as rightfully as carrots in produce markets, while pasta displays a rainbow of colors and flavors on supermarket shelves. And gourmet greens are at hand almost year-round. Flashy ingredients like these team up to offer new ideas in each of these salads.

When preparing cold pasta salads like Tuna-Pasta Salad, always rinse the pasta under cold water after cooking to help keep it from becoming gummy after it chills.

There's no real trick to serving pretty flowers in a salad other than knowing what kinds are safe to eat. The two most common edible flowers are nasturtiums and pansies. Just be sure the flowers haven't been sprayed with an insecticide. Either select flowers labeled edible in the produce section of supermarkets or use those grown in your own garden.

ORIENTAL CHICKEN SALAD

⅔ cup vegetable oil
¼ cup soy sauce
¼ cup lemon juice
3 tablespoons rice salad vinegar
1 clove garlic, minced
¼ teaspoon ground ginger
½ teaspoon salt
¼ teaspoon pepper
1½ pounds skinned, boned chicken
    breasts
1 tablespoon vegetable oil
⅔ cup fresh bean sprouts
1 sweet red pepper, cut into 1-inch
    strips
4 green onions, cut into 1-inch
    pieces
1 (10-ounce) package frozen snow
    pea pods, thawed and drained
2 cups torn fresh spinach
2 (5-ounce) cans chow mein noodles

Combine first 8 ingredients in a jar; cover tightly, and shake vigorously.

Pour half of mixture into a shallow dish. Set aside remaining mixture.

Cut chicken into bite-size pieces, using kitchen shears, and place in marinade in dish, tossing gently. Cover and chill 1 hour. Drain chicken, discarding marinade.

Heat 1 tablespoon oil in a large skillet; sauté chicken until done. Drain. Combine chicken, bean sprouts, red pepper strips, green onions, snow peas, and reserved marinade mixture. Cover and chill 2 hours. Toss spinach with chicken mixture just before serving. Serve over chow mein noodles. Yield: 6 servings.

TUNA-PASTA SALAD

6 ounces spinach or tri-colored
    corkscrew noodles
½ cup sliced green onions
½ cup sweet yellow or green
    pepper strips
½ cup sliced ripe olives
1 cup halved cherry tomatoes
1 carrot, scraped and shredded
2 (6½-ounce) cans chunk light
    tuna, drained and flaked
½ cup vegetable oil
3 tablespoons white wine vinegar
2 tablespoons lemon juice
3 tablespoons minced fresh parsley
½ teaspoon salt
¼ teaspoon pepper
1 green onion, cut into 1-inch
    pieces
1 large clove garlic, halved
Lettuce leaves

Cook pasta according to package directions; drain. Rinse with cold water; drain. Combine pasta, sliced green onions, pepper strips, ripe olives, cherry tomatoes, carrot, and tuna. Set aside.

Combine oil and remaining ingredients except lettuce leaves in an electric blender, and process until mixture is smooth.

Pour dressing over salad, and toss gently. Cover and chill at least 8 hours, stirring occasionally. Spoon salad over lettuce leaves, using a slotted spoon. Yield: 6 to 8 servings.

GARDEN TORTELLINI SALAD

1 (9-ounce) package cheese-filled tortellini
1 (7-ounce) package cheese-filled spinach tortellini
3 cups fresh broccoli flowerets
½ pound carrots, scraped and sliced
2 small green onions, sliced
1 small sweet red pepper, cut into strips
¼ cup finely chopped fresh basil
2 tablespoons egg substitute
1 tablespoon lemon juice
1½ teaspoons Dijon mustard
1½ teaspoons balsamic vinegar
½ cup vegetable oil
¼ cup olive oil
1½ teaspoons grated orange rind
½ teaspoon dried whole thyme
½ teaspoon salt
⅛ teaspoon white pepper

Cook tortellini according to package directions; drain. Rinse with cold water; drain.

Cook broccoli and carrot in a small amount of boiling water 5 minutes or just until crisp-tender; drain.

Combine tortellini, broccoli, carrot, green onions, red pepper strips, and basil in a large bowl.

Position knife blade in food processor bowl; add egg substitute, lemon juice, mustard, and vinegar. Process 30 seconds. Remove food pusher. Slowly pour oils through food chute with processor running, blending just until smooth. Add orange rind and remaining ingredients; process 30 seconds. Spoon dressing over pasta mixture; toss well. Chill salad at least 2 hours. Yield: 10 to 12 servings.

Rublelene Singleton
Scotts Hill, Tennessee

BEANS-AND-RICE SALAD

1 (15-ounce) can black beans, drained
¼ cup commercial Italian salad dressing
¼ teaspoon pepper
¾ cup long-grain rice, uncooked
¼ cup commercial Italian salad dressing
Lettuce leaves
¾ cup (3 ounces) shredded Cheddar cheese
3 green onions, thinly sliced
1 medium tomato, chopped
Sour cream (optional)

Combine first 3 ingredients; cover and chill at least 8 hours.

Cook rice according to package directions, omitting salt, if desired. Rinse with cold water; drain. Combine rice and ¼ cup salad dressing, stirring well. Chill at least 8 hours.

Spoon rice onto individual lettuce-lined plates. Spoon bean mixture over rice. Top with cheese, green onions, tomato, and, if desired, sour cream. Yield: 4 servings.

A SALAD BOUQUET

1 head Romaine lettuce, torn
1 head Bibb lettuce, torn
1 carrot, scraped and shredded
Garlic-Chive Vinaigrette
1 cup loosely packed edible nasturtiums or pansies

Combine first 3 ingredients in a salad bowl. Just before serving, toss salad with Garlic-Chive Vinaigrette; add flowers, and toss gently. Serve immediately. Yield: 6 to 8 servings.

Garlic-Chive Vinaigrette

⅓ cup olive oil
3 tablespoons balsamic vinegar
1 clove garlic, pressed
2 tablespoons minced fresh or frozen chives
¼ teaspoon salt
⅛ teaspoon white pepper

Combine olive oil, vinegar, garlic, chives, salt, and white pepper in a jar. Cover tightly; shake vigorously before tossing with greens. Yield: ½ cup.

CURRIED COUSCOUS SALAD

1½ cups canned chicken broth
½ cup currants
1 teaspoon curry powder
1 cup couscous, uncooked
⅓ cup vegetable oil
2 tablespoons lemon juice
½ cup whole natural almonds, toasted
Lettuce leaves
1 (20-ounce) can pineapple slices, drained
1 (8-ounce) can pineapple slices, drained
⅓ cup sliced green onions

Combine first 3 ingredients in a saucepan; bring to a boil. Remove from heat, and stir in couscous. Cover and let stand 5 minutes. Fluff with a fork; let cool, uncovered. Combine oil and lemon juice; toss couscous with juice mixture and almonds.

Line salad plates with lettuce; arrange 2 pineapple slices on each. Spoon salad over pineapple; sprinkle with green onions. Yield: 6 servings.

AVOCADO-ORANGE SALAD

2 tablespoons chopped fresh parsley
1 tablespoon chopped green onions
2 tablespoons lime juice
1 tablespoon vegetable oil
¼ teaspoon salt
¼ teaspoon sugar
⅛ teaspoon freshly ground pepper
2 oranges, peeled and sectioned
1 avocado, peeled and sliced
2 cups torn fresh watercress

Combine first 7 ingredients in container of an electric blender; blend well. Set aside.

Arrange orange sections and avocado slices on a bed of watercress on individual salad plates; drizzle dressing over top. Yield: 4 servings.

Sara A. McCullough
Zavalla, Texas

Vegetables Bring Spring To The Table

As spring approaches and daylight lingers, team broiled or grilled chicken breasts or fish fillets with a pasta or rice side dish and spring vegetables. New potatoes fresh from the earth, straight-as-an-arrow stalks of asparagus, and brilliantly hued carrots and squash await at the market. These natural treasures become even more special in the easy recipes found here, so don't be surprised if they outshine the entrée.

ASPARAGUS-CARROT-SQUASH TOSS

½ pound asparagus, cut diagonally
  into 1-inch pieces
½ pound carrots, cut into julienne
  strips
1 yellow squash, sliced
3 tablespoons butter or margarine,
  melted
3 tablespoons lemon juice
1 tablespoon chopped fresh dillweed
  or 1 teaspoon dried whole
  dillweed
¼ teaspoon salt

Combine vegetables, and place in a steamer rack over boiling water in a Dutch oven. Steam 8 to 10 minutes or just until vegetables are crisp-tender. Transfer to a serving dish.
  Combine butter, lemon juice, dillweed, and salt; add to vegetables,

tossing gently. Serve immediately. Yield: 4 to 6 servings.

Microwave Directions: Place butter in a microwave-safe 2-quart shallow casserole; microwave at HIGH 50 seconds or until melted. Stir in lemon juice, dillweed, and salt; add vegetables, stirring well. Cover tightly with heavy-duty plastic wrap; fold back a small corner of wrap to allow steam to escape. Microwave at HIGH 6 to 8 minutes, stirring after 3 minutes.

GARDEN VEGETABLE MEDLEY

2 small yellow squash, sliced
1 medium zucchini, sliced
1 small onion, sliced and separated
  into rings
¼ cup water
1 tomato, sliced
½ teaspoon seasoned salt
½ teaspoon dried whole basil
½ teaspoon dried whole thyme
2 tablespoons grated Parmesan
  cheese

Combine first 4 ingredients in a skillet; bring to a boil. Cover, reduce heat, and simmer 3 to 4 minutes. Add tomato, salt, basil, and thyme, and toss gently. Cover and simmer 2 minutes. Sprinkle with Parmesan cheese. Serve immediately. Yield: 3 to 4 servings.

Microwave Directions: Combine first 4 ingredients in a shallow 1-quart casserole. Cover tightly with heavy-duty plastic wrap; fold back a small corner of wrap to allow steam to escape. Microwave at HIGH 6 minutes, giving dish a half-turn after 3 minutes. Add tomato, salt, basil, and thyme; toss gently. Cover and microwave at HIGH 1½ to 2 minutes. Sprinkle with cheese. Serve immediately.

Nancy Walter
Myrtle Beach, South Carolina

Vegetable Tips

■ Use a stiff vegetable brush to scrub vegetables rather than peel them. Peeling causes a loss of vitamins found in and just under the skin. For many vegetables, such as squash, peeling is not necessary.

■ Sand and dirt can be removed from fresh vegetables by soaking in warm salted water 5 minutes.

■ When selecting yellow squash, be sure to look at the stem; it can indicate the quality of the squash. If the stem is hard, dry, shriveled, or darkened, the squash is not fresh.

■ Onions offer outstanding nutritive value. They are a good source of calcium and vitamins A and C. They contain iron, riboflavin, thiamine, and niacin; have a high percentage of water; and supply essential bulk. They are low in calories and have only a trace of fat.

■ To make use of thick asparagus stalks, peel the lower part up to the tender part with a vegetable peeler.

■ Steaming fresh vegetables over boiling water preserves more vitamins than cooking in boiling water.

■ Remove the tops of carrots before refrigerating. The tops drain the carrots of moisture, making them limp and dry.

■ Remember that leftover vegetables go nicely in a salad. Or make a chef's salad with leftover meats, cheeses, and cold cuts cut in strips and tossed with leftover vegetables, greens, and salad dressing.

NEW POTATOES WITH BASIL CREAM SAUCE

2 pounds new potatoes, unpeeled
  and sliced
2 tablespoons dry white wine
2 tablespoons finely chopped shallot
1½ cups whipping cream
¼ cup chopped fresh basil
¼ teaspoon salt
⅛ teaspoon white pepper

Cook potatoes in boiling salted water to cover 10 to 15 minutes. Drain carefully, leaving skins intact. Keep potatoes warm.

Combine wine and shallot in a large saucepan. Bring to a boil, and cook 1 minute. Add whipping cream; return to a boil. Reduce heat, and simmer 20 minutes, stirring occasionally. Stir in basil, salt, and pepper.

Arrange potatoes on a serving plate; spoon sauce over potatoes. Serve immediately. Yield: about 8 servings.

MARINATED VEGGIES

1 (12-ounce) bag fresh baby carrots,
  scraped
½ pound fresh mushrooms,
  quartered
1 cup pitted ripe olives
1 cup sliced celery
1 (14-ounce) can artichoke hearts,
  drained and halved
1 (2-ounce) jar diced pimiento,
  drained
⅔ cup olive oil
⅓ cup red wine vinegar
¼ cup diced onion
2 cloves garlic, minced
1 teaspoon dried whole basil
1 teaspoon dried whole oregano
1 teaspoon sugar
1 teaspoon salt
½ teaspoon pepper
Lettuce leaves (optional)

Cook carrots in boiling water to cover 5 minutes or until carrots are crisp-tender. Drain and let cool. Combine carrots and next 5 ingredients in a shallow dish; set aside.

Combine olive oil and remaining ingredients except lettuce in a jar; cover tightly, and shake vigorously. Pour marinade over vegetables; toss gently. Cover and chill. Drain and serve in a lettuce-lined bowl, if desired. Yield: 10 to 12 servings.
Gwen Louer
Roswell, Georgia

Beef Up Your Menu

Beef fits a variety of lifestyles— whether you're looking for lighter, leaner choices or selections that are practical and inexpensive. If you take advantage of leaner, "skinnier" cuts with "loin" or "round" in their name, beef can be a healthy choice. It is also a good source of iron and other nutrients, such as zinc, vitamins B-12, thiamin, and niacin.

From a practical standpoint, beef supplies protein, and some of the less-expensive cuts, such as chuck roast, offer ideal meal options for families watching their finances. In addition, beef still tastes great.

■ Because **Beef-and-Broccoli Stir-Fry** requires only a small amount of oil, it's a healthy way to utilize sirloin steak, one of the "skinniest six" lean cuts of beef.

BEEF-AND-BROCCOLI STIR-FRY

1 pound fresh broccoli
1 pound boneless sirloin steak
3 tablespoons vegetable oil,
  divided
2 tablespoons soy sauce
2 teaspoons cornstarch
⅔ cup chicken broth
2 tablespoons sherry (optional)
½ teaspoon sugar
Hot cooked rice

Trim off large leaves of broccoli, and remove tough ends of lower stalks. Wash broccoli thoroughly. Cut into flowerets; set aside.

Slice steak diagonally across grain into 2- x ¼-inch strips. Pour 1 tablespoon oil around top of preheated wok or skillet, coating sides. Add meat, and stir-fry 2 minutes; remove meat from wok.

Pour remaining 2 tablespoons oil around top of wok. Add broccoli, and stir-fry 2 to 3 minutes; remove broccoli from wok.

Combine soy sauce and cornstarch; add chicken broth, sherry, if desired, and sugar. Add to wok, and cook over medium heat until thickened and bubbly. Add meat and broccoli to wok, and stir-fry 2 minutes. Serve over rice. Yield: 4 servings.
Elizabeth McCall
Columbia, South Carolina

■ **Beef With Red Wine Marinade** is made from top round steak— sometimes called London broil. It's known as one of the "skinniest six" cuts of lean beef. The other "skinny" cuts include round tip, eye of round, top loin, tenderloin, and sirloin. You may substitute flank steak for top round in this recipe.

BEEF WITH RED WINE MARINADE

1 (1½-pound) top round steak or
  flank steak
1 cup red wine
¼ cup soy sauce
¼ cup vegetable oil
1 teaspoon seasoned salt
1 teaspoon pepper
1 teaspoon dried whole oregano
1 teaspoon garlic juice

Place steak in a shallow dish or zip-top heavy-duty plastic bag. Combine remaining ingredients in a small bowl; stir well. Pour marinade over steak. Cover or seal, and chill 8 hours, turning occasionally.

Remove steak from marinade; grill over medium (300° to 400°) coals 7 to 9 minutes on each side or to desired degree of doneness.

To serve, slice grilled steak across grain into thin slices. Yield: about 6 servings.
Maggie Cates
Greenville, Texas

■ Here's a meal that's easy to prepare. It takes only 10 minutes to get **Chuck Roast in Sauce** ready to marinate and cook.

CHUCK ROAST IN SAUCE

1 (8-ounce) can tomato sauce
½ cup beef broth
1 medium onion, chopped
1 (3- to 4-pound) boneless chuck roast
2 tablespoons vegetable oil
½ cup cider vinegar
¼ cup catsup
2 teaspoons Worcestershire sauce
1 teaspoon prepared mustard
1 teaspoon paprika
⅛ teaspoon garlic powder

Combine first 3 ingredients in a shallow dish; add roast. Cover and marinate in refrigerator 8 hours.

Remove roast from marinade, reserving marinade. Place roast in a Dutch oven. Combine marinade and remaining ingredients; pour over roast. Cover and bake at 350° for 2½ to 3 hours or until roast is tender. Skim fat from sauce. Serve sauce with roast. Yield: 6 servings.
Mrs. A. Mayer
Richmond, Virginia

Tip: *When cooking on the grill, never allow the coals to flame during cooking, because the flames may either burn the food or cause it to dry out. Just remember to keep a container of water nearby so that you can douse flames as they appear.*

QUICK!

Pasta On The Side

Fettuccine, linguine, tortellini, macaroni, mostaccioli—there's a pasta to please almost every palate. The seemingly endless variety of shapes, sizes, and flavors will complement most entrées.

Pasta cooks quickly; use plenty of water when cooking it. When the water begins to boil, drop the pasta in gradually. Let the water return to a boil; then cook until the pasta is limp but slightly resistant to chewing.

MOSTACCIOLI ALFREDO

1 (16-ounce) package mostaccioli
1 cup whipping cream
½ cup butter or margarine
½ cup grated Parmesan cheese
¼ cup chopped fresh parsley
1 teaspoon salt
¼ teaspoon freshly ground pepper
⅛ teaspoon garlic powder

Cook mostaccioli according to package directions; drain. Combine whipping cream and butter in a Dutch oven; heat until butter melts, stirring occasionally (do not boil). Add cheese and remaining ingredients; stir well. Add mostaccioli, and toss well. Serve immediately. Yield: 8 servings.
Mrs. William Murphy
Pinehurst, North Carolina

SPAGHETTI WITH TOMATOES AND GARLIC

3 large ripe tomatoes
8 ounces thin spaghetti, uncooked
1 teaspoon salt
4 cloves garlic, minced
5 ripe olives, sliced
1 Anaheim chile, seeded and chopped or ¼ cup canned chopped green chiles
1 tablespoon olive oil
1½ tablespoons lime juice
1 tablespoon chopped fresh cilantro or parsley
⅛ teaspoon salt
⅛ teaspoon pepper

Chop tomatoes; drain. Cook spaghetti according to package directions, using 1 teaspoon salt; drain.

Combine garlic, olives, chile, olive oil, lime juice, cilantro, salt, and pepper; add tomatoes to mixture. Toss tomato mixture with spaghetti; serve immediately. Yield: 4 servings.
Mary B. Quesenberry
Dugspur, Virginia

TORTELLINI CARBONARA

1 (9-ounce) package cheese-filled tortellini
1 small clove garlic, minced
1½ teaspoons olive oil
½ teaspoon white vinegar
3 slices bacon, cooked and crumbled
⅓ cup grated Parmesan cheese
¼ cup whipping cream
1 tablespoon minced fresh parsley
¼ teaspoon pepper

Cook tortellini according to package directions; drain. Sauté garlic in olive oil; stir in vinegar. Toss mixture with tortellini.

Combine bacon, Parmesan cheese, whipping cream, parsley, and pepper in a small bowl; toss mixture with tortellini. Serve tortellini immediately. Yield: 3 to 4 servings. *Christine Orth*
Signal Mountain, Tennessee

FETTUCCINE WITH POPPY SEEDS

6 ounces fettuccine, uncooked
⅓ cup butter or margarine, melted
¾ teaspoon garlic salt
¾ teaspoon dried parsley flakes
½ teaspoon poppy seeds
⅛ teaspoon pepper
½ cup sour cream
½ cup grated Parmesan cheese

Cook fettuccine according to package directions; drain. Combine butter and next 4 ingredients; stir in sour cream. Combine fettuccine and sour cream mixture; add cheese, and toss until fettuccine is coated. Serve immediately. Yield: 6 servings.

Lynne Teal Weeks
Columbus, Georgia

Vintage Entertaining

For the entertaining events on your calendar, earmark these recipes for spirited appetizers, desserts, and of course, main dishes. To be sure the results meet your high standards, keep these tips in mind when cooking with wine:

—**More is not always better.** If you use more wine than the recipe calls for, you'll probably end up with too much of a good thing.

—**Cut it down to size.** Most wine-laced dishes use only a cup or two of the alcohol—about what you might have left over from an open bottle. Transfer the wine to a smaller container with a tight lid so that there will be less contact with the air.

—**Go for the real thing.** Cooking wine from your grocer's shelf won't give you the spectacular taste table wine will. Cooking wine is of poorer quality and has salt added, which may require altering the recipe.

SCALLOPS IN WINE

1 pound fresh bay scallops
¼ cup butter or margarine, melted
½ cup sliced fresh mushrooms
¼ cup chopped onion
1 clove garlic, minced
½ cup dry white wine
3 tablespoons lemon juice
3 tablespoons lime juice
½ teaspoon dried whole oregano
½ teaspoon celery salt
¼ teaspoon pepper
Hot cooked vermicelli
Garnish: chopped fresh parsley

Sauté scallops in butter in a large skillet 3 minutes or until tender. Remove scallops from skillet, reserving drippings. Sauté mushrooms, onion, and garlic 3 to 5 minutes; remove vegetables, reserving drippings. Add wine, juices, and seasonings to skillet. Bring to a boil, and cook 8 minutes. Stir in scallops and vegetables; cook until thoroughly heated. Serve over hot vermicelli. Garnish, if desired. Yield: 3 to 4 servings.

Skip Weeks
Columbus, Georgia

SWISS CHEESE FONDUE

6 cups (1½ pounds) shredded Swiss cheese
2 cups (8 ounces) shredded Gruyère cheese
2 tablespoons cornstarch
2 cloves garlic, halved
2 cups dry white wine
2 tablespoons lemon juice
⅓ cup dry sherry or kirsch
1 teaspoon salt
¼ teaspoon white pepper
French bread, cut into cubes

Combine first 3 ingredients, stirring well; set aside.

Rub inside of a large heavy saucepan with garlic; discard garlic. Add wine; cook over medium heat until hot, but not boiling. Add lemon juice. Gradually add cheese mixture; cook, stirring constantly, until cheese melts. Stir in sherry, salt, and pepper. Pour mixture into a fondue pot, keeping warm. Serve with bread cubes. Yield: about 4 cups.

Connie Palmer
Macon, Georgia

BAKED PEARS ELEGANT

4 pears, peeled, cored, and halved lengthwise
1 cup Burgundy or other dry red wine
1 cup sugar
3 (3-inch) sticks cinnamon
6 whole cloves
⅛ teaspoon salt
1 lemon, thinly sliced
Sweetened whipped cream (optional)

Arrange pear halves, cut side down, in a 12- x 8- x 2-inch baking dish. Set dish aside.

Combine Burgundy and next 5 ingredients in a small saucepan; bring to a boil. Pour mixture over pears; cover and bake at 350° for 30 minutes or until pears are tender, basting occasionally with wine mixture.

Remove from oven, and cool. Chill at least 2 hours. Serve cut side up with whipped cream, if desired. Yield: 4 servings.

Margaret Cotton
Franklin, Virginia

ON THE LIGHT SIDE

Pig Out! It's Healthy

Today the "little piggies that go to market" are leaner than ever—about 50% leaner than they were in the 1960s. A 3-ounce serving of roasted pork tenderloin, for example, has fewer than 150 calories and only 4.1 grams of fat—about the same amount as 3 ounces of roasted, skinless chicken breast.

One of the major concerns of eating any type of meat is its saturated fat content. Saturated fat has the potential to raise blood cholesterol levels. However, the fat in meat is not all saturated, and lean cuts of pork are only about one-third saturated fat.

Nutritionists consider lean pork a nutrient-dense food. That is, it has lots of nutrients for its calorie content. Protein, iron, thiamin, riboflavin, vitamins B6 and B12, and zinc can all be found in pork. As more research is done, the benefits of eating foods that contain zinc are becoming more evident. Zinc plays a vital role in wound healing, bone and tissue growth, and our senses of smell and taste.

Time-conscious cooks will find that fresh, lean pork cooks quickly. The National Pork Producers Council recently revised their cooking recommendations for pork to an internal temperature of 160° for medium doneness. At this temperature pork will be tender, juicy, and slightly pink in the middle. Regular cut top loin chops (¾-inch thick) will broil in 7 to 9 minutes and thick ones (1½ inches thick) in 16 to 18 minutes. It will take only about 20 minutes per pound for a top loin roast to cook to 160°. Overcooked pork will be tough and dry.

PORK TENDERLOIN WITH ORANGE MARMALADE

1½ tablespoons coarse-grained mustard
1 clove garlic, minced
¼ teaspoon dried whole rosemary
¼ teaspoon pepper
1 (1-pound) pork tenderloin
¼ cup low-sugar orange marmalade, divided
Vegetable cooking spray
½ cup water
¼ cup ready-to-serve, no-salt-added chicken broth

Combine first 4 ingredients; set aside. Trim fat from tenderloin. Slice tenderloin lengthwise, cutting almost to, but not through, outer edge. Spread mustard mixture in pocket; press gently to close. Tie tenderloin securely with heavy string at 2-inch intervals. Spread 2 tablespoons orange marmalade over tenderloin.

Place tenderloin on rack coated with cooking spray. Place rack in broiler pan; add water to pan. Bake at 325° for 40 to 45 minutes or until meat thermometer inserted into thickest portion of tenderloin registers 160°.

Combine remaining 2 tablespoons orange marmalade and chicken broth in a saucepan; cook 2 to 3 minutes or until thickened. Slice tenderloin; spoon sauce over slices, and serve. Yield: 4 servings (161 calories per 3-ounce serving).

□ *26.3 grams protein, 4.7 grams fat, 1.6 grams carbohydrate, 83 milligrams cholesterol, 117 milligrams sodium, and 17 milligrams calcium.*

Jackie Broome
Greenville, South Carolina

CREOLE-STYLE PORK CHOPS

4 (4-ounce) lean, boneless top loin pork chops (¾-inch thick)
Vegetable cooking spray
½ cup chopped onion
½ cup chopped celery
½ cup chopped green pepper
½ cup chopped sweet red pepper
3 large cloves garlic, crushed
1 (8½-ounce) can whole tomatoes, undrained and chopped
½ teaspoon hot sauce
¼ teaspoon pepper
2 cups hot cooked rice (cooked without salt or fat)
1 teaspoon cornstarch
¼ cup ready-to-serve, no-salt-added chicken broth

Trim fat from chops. Coat a nonstick skillet with cooking spray; place over medium-high heat until hot. Add pork chops, and brown on all sides. Remove from skillet.

Coat a nonstick skillet with cooking spray; place over medium-high heat until hot. Add onion and next 4 ingredients; sauté until tender. Remove ½ cup vegetable mixture from skillet; set aside. Add tomatoes, hot sauce, and pepper to skillet. Return pork chops to skillet; cover and cook 15 minutes, turning chops once.

Stir reserved ½ cup vegetable mixture into rice; spoon onto a serving plate. Arrange pork chops on top of rice. Combine cornstarch and chicken broth; add to vegetable mixture in skillet. Cook over medium heat, stirring constantly, until mixture begins to boil; boil 1 minute, stirring constantly, until mixture is thickened. Spoon over chops. Yield: 4 servings (368 calories per chop with ⅔ cup rice mixture).

□ *27.4 grams protein, 11.4 grams fat, 37 grams carbohydrate, 74 milligrams cholesterol, 299 milligrams sodium, and 54 milligrams calcium.*

Mrs. Joe Mann
Pearsall, Texas

Three Lean Cuts of Pork
(Nutrition analysis based on a 3-ounce cooked serving)

Pork Tenderloin	
Calories	133
Fat	4.1g
Saturated fat	1.4g
Cholesterol	67mg

Boneless Top Loin Chops	
Calories	165
Fat	6.6g
Saturated fat	2.3g
Cholesterol	68mg

Boneless Top Loin Roast	
Calories	160
Fat	6.4g
Saturated fat	2.4g
Cholesterol	66mg

OVEN-BARBECUED PORK ROAST

1 (3-pound) boneless rolled top loin
  pork roast
3 large cloves garlic, sliced
1 teaspoon coarsely ground pepper
½ teaspoon dried whole sage
½ teaspoon dried whole thyme
Vegetable cooking spray
1 cup sliced onion
½ cup ready-to-serve, no-salt-added
  chicken broth
1 (8-ounce) can tomato sauce
¼ cup chili sauce
¼ cup reduced-calorie catsup
¼ cup cider vinegar
¼ cup lemon juice
3 tablespoons low-sodium
  Worcestershire sauce
2 tablespoons brown sugar
2 teaspoons Dijon mustard
½ teaspoon paprika
⅛ teaspoon red pepper

Remove strings from pork roast; trim fat, and retie roast securely with heavy string at 2-inch intervals. Cut deep slits in roast, and insert garlic. Combine pepper, sage, and thyme; rub over surface of roast.

Coat a nonstick skillet with cooking spray; place over medium-high heat until hot. Add pork roast, and brown on all sides. Add onion; sauté until tender. Add chicken broth; bring to a boil. Transfer to a 9-inch square pan. Bake roast, uncovered, at 350° for 30 minutes.

Combine tomato sauce and remaining ingredients in a medium saucepan. Bring to a boil over medium heat; pour sauce over pork roast. Bake an additional 35 minutes or until meat thermometer inserted in center of roast registers 160°. Slice roast; serve with sauce. Yield: 12 servings (228 calories per 3 ounces meat and 2 tablespoons sauce).

□ *24 grams protein, 10.9 grams fat, 7.3 grams carbohydrate, 74 milligrams cholesterol, 288 milligrams sodium, and 17 milligrams calcium.*
Barbara Sherrer
Bay City, Texas

Stay In For Oriental

Whether you're eating in a restaurant or cooking at home, Oriental food is a good bet for healthy eating. Oriental cooking's reliance on stir-frying and steaming keeps food low in fat and high in nutrients. And its recipes take advantage of a variety of vegetables, lean meats, rice, and noodles.

This menu is a filling combination that derives 50% of calories from complex carbohydrates and less than 30% from fat.

HOT-AND-SOUR SOUP

3 (10½-ounce) cans ready-to-serve,
  no-salt-added chicken broth
½ cup sliced fresh mushrooms
1 teaspoon minced fresh gingerroot
1 (4-ounce) skinned, boned chicken
  breast half, cut into thin strips
⅓ cup canned bamboo shoots, cut
  into thin strips
3 tablespoons rice vinegar
3 tablespoons reduced-sodium soy
  sauce
¼ teaspoon hot sauce
⅛ teaspoon pepper
1 egg white, slightly beaten
¼ cup sliced green onions
¼ cup fresh snow pea pods
1 tablespoon cornstarch
¼ cup water

Combine chicken broth, fresh mushrooms, and gingerroot in a 2-quart saucepan; bring to a boil. Add chicken, and simmer 10 minutes. Add bamboo shoots; simmer 5 minutes. Add vinegar, soy sauce, hot sauce, and pepper; return to a boil. Slowly pour egg white into soup, stirring constantly. (The egg white forms lacy strands as it cooks.) Stir in green onions and snow peas.

Combine cornstarch and water in a small bowl. Add to soup, and return to a boil; boil 1 minute, stirring gently. Yield: 1 quart (79 calories per 1-cup serving).

□ *8.5 grams protein, 0.5 gram fat, 6.3 grams carbohydrate, 16 milligrams cholesterol, 332 milligrams sodium, and 14 milligrams calcium.*

ORANGE ROUGHY-AND-VEGETABLE STIR-FRY

Vegetable cooking spray
2 teaspoons vegetable oil
1 tablespoon peeled, minced fresh
  gingerroot
1 clove garlic, sliced
1 pound orange roughy, cut into 1-
  inch cubes
1 medium onion, cut into thin
  wedges
2 cups sliced fresh broccoli
1 cup sliced fresh mushrooms
1 large sweet red pepper, cut into
  strips
1 teaspoon cornstarch
2 tablespoons water
2 tablespoons Chablis or other dry
  white wine
2 tablespoons reduced-sodium soy
  sauce
¼ teaspoon hot sauce
4 cups hot cooked rice (cooked
  without salt or fat)

Coat a wok or heavy skillet with cooking spray; add oil, and heat to medium high (325°) for 2 minutes. Add gingerroot and garlic; stir-fry 2 to 3 minutes. Add orange roughy, and stir-fry just until fish is cooked. Remove fish from wok; let wok cool.

Coat wok or heavy skillet with cooking spray; add onion, and stir-fry 1 minute. Add broccoli, mushrooms, and red pepper; stir-fry 3 minutes or until broccoli is crisp-tender. Stir fish into vegetables.

Combine cornstarch and water; stir in wine, soy sauce, and hot sauce. Pour over fish, and stir-fry until thickened and bubbly. Serve over rice.

Yield: 4 servings (471 calories per 1¼ cups stir-fry and 1 cup rice).

□ *24.5 grams protein, 11.4 grams fat, 65.3 grams carbohydrate, 23 milligrams cholesterol, 287 milligrams sodium, and 57 milligrams calcium.*
Pat Watt
Smiths Grove, Kentucky

ALMOND COOKIES

½ cup margarine, softened
¼ cup sugar
1 egg yolk
1 tablespoon water
½ teaspoon almond extract
1¼ cups all-purpose flour

Beat margarine and sugar at medium speed of an electric mixer until light and fluffy. Add egg yolk, water, and almond extract to mixture; beat well. Stir in flour.

Use a cookie press or decorator pastry bag fitted with a bar disk to shape dough into long strips; cut strips into 2-inch pieces. Place on ungreased cookie sheets; bake at 400° for 6 minutes or until lightly browned. Remove from cookie sheets, and cool completely on wire racks. Store in an airtight container. Yield: 4 dozen (34 calories per cookie).

□ *0.4 gram protein, 2 grams fat, 3.5 grams carbohydrate, 6 milligrams cholesterol, 19 milligrams sodium, and 1 milligram calcium.* *Lynn Aigner*
Woodsboro, Texas

Tip: *If separating eggs seems like a difficult task, break the eggs into a small funnel. The whites will slip through; the yolks won't.*

Turn Sloppy Joes Into Sloppy Toms

Mrs. Roy Turner of St. Petersburg, Florida, developed her recipe for Sloppy Toms while trying to lose weight. "I added extra vegetables to my Sloppy Joes and substituted turkey for beef."

SLOPPY TOMS

Vegetable cooking spray
1 pound raw ground turkey
¾ cup chopped onion
⅔ cup chopped green pepper
2 cloves garlic, minced
1 (8-ounce) can no-salt-added tomato sauce
¼ cup reduced-calorie catsup
1 teaspoon chili powder
½ teaspoon dried whole basil
½ teaspoon dried whole oregano
¼ teaspoon salt
¼ teaspoon pepper
1¼ cups shredded zucchini
⅔ cup shredded carrot
6 whole wheat hamburger buns

Coat a large, nonstick skillet with cooking spray; place skillet over medium-high heat. Add ground turkey, onion, green pepper, and garlic; cook until browned, stirring well to crumble turkey. Drain well on paper towels.

Return turkey mixture to skillet; add tomato sauce and remaining ingredients except buns. Cook over medium heat 10 minutes, stirring occasionally. Divide mixture evenly among hamburger buns; cover with top half of bun. Yield: 6 servings (318 calories per serving).

□ *21.5 grams protein, 11.5 grams fat, 33.4 grams carbohydrate, 68 milligrams cholesterol, 485 milligrams sodium, and 70 milligrams calcium.*

COMPARE THE NUTRIENTS (per serving)		
	Traditional	Light
Calories	422	318
Fat	30.6g	11.5g
Cholesterol	96mg	68mg

Cheese Breads Take A Bow

Dinner bread plays a passive role on the menu when you serve the same plain muffins or yeast breads night after night. But try one of these recipes flavored with cheese, and the bread will take center stage.

CHEDDAR-RAISIN MUFFINS

2 cups all-purpose flour
3½ teaspoons baking powder
½ teaspoon salt
1 teaspoon paprika
¼ cup butter or margarine
1 cup (4 ounces) shredded Cheddar cheese
⅔ cup raisins
1 egg, beaten
1 cup milk

Combine first 4 ingredients in a large bowl; cut in butter with a pastry blender until mixture resembles coarse meal. Stir in cheese and raisins. Make a well in center of mixture.

Combine egg and milk; add to dry ingredients, stirring just until moistened. Spoon batter into greased and floured muffin pans. Bake at 425° for 20 to 25 minutes. Remove from pans. Yield: 14 muffins. *Joyce Maurer*
Christmas, Florida

BUTTERMILK-CHEESE LOAF

2 cups all-purpose flour
1½ teaspoons baking powder
½ teaspoon baking soda
¼ teaspoon salt
1 cup (4 ounces) shredded Cheddar
  cheese
2 eggs, beaten
1 cup buttermilk
¼ cup vegetable oil

Combine first 4 ingredients in a large bowl; stir in cheese. Make a well in center of mixture. Combine eggs, buttermilk, and oil; add to flour mixture, stirring just until moistened.

Spoon batter into a greased and floured 8½- x 4½- x 3-inch loafpan. Bake at 375° for 30 to 35 minutes or until a wooden pick inserted in center comes out clean. Cool in pan 10 minutes; remove from pan. Yield: 1 loaf.
Shelby Brennan
Richmond, Virginia

GOUDA BREAD

5¼ cups all-purpose flour, divided
2 teaspoons salt
2 tablespoons sugar
½ cup instant nonfat dry milk
  powder
2 packages dry yeast
2 cups warm water (120° to 130°)
2 tablespoons vegetable oil
1¾ cups (7 ounces) shredded Gouda
  cheese

Combine 2 cups flour and next 4 ingredients in a large mixing bowl; stir well. Combine water and oil; gradually add to flour mixture, beating 2 minutes at medium speed of an electric mixer. Gradually add 1 cup flour, beating 1 minute at medium speed.

Combine ¼ cup flour and cheese in a small bowl; add to dough, and beat 1 minute at medium speed. Gradually stir in remaining 2 cups flour. Cover and let rise in a warm place (85°), free from drafts, 45 minutes or until doubled in bulk.

Punch dough down, and stir with a wooden spoon 20 strokes. Place

dough in a well-greased round 2½-quart baking dish. Bake at 350° for 30 minutes. Shield bread with aluminum foil, and bake an additional 30 minutes. Remove from baking dish immediately. Yield: 1 round loaf.
Marie A. Davis
Charlotte, North Carolina

POPPY SEED-SWISS CHEESE BREAD

3½ cups all-purpose flour
1½ tablespoons baking powder
½ teaspoon salt
1 tablespoon sugar
⅓ cup butter or margarine
2 cups (8 ounces) shredded Swiss
  cheese
1 tablespoon poppy seeds
2 eggs, slightly beaten
1½ cups milk
2 teaspoons prepared mustard

Combine first 4 ingredients in a large bowl; cut in butter with a pastry blender until mixture resembles coarse meal. Stir in shredded cheese and poppy seeds. Make a well in center of mixture.

Combine eggs, milk, and mustard; add to dry ingredients, stirring just until moistened. Spoon batter into a greased and floured 9- x 5- x 3-inch loafpan. Bake at 350° for 1 hour and 10 minutes or until a wooden pick inserted in center comes out clean, tenting with aluminum foil after 50 minutes, if necessary. Cool bread in pan 10 minutes; remove from pan. Yield: 1 loaf.
Eleanor K. Brandt
Arlington, Texas

A Head Start On Yeast Rolls

Some folks call the bakery for dinner rolls when they entertain because they feel as though they don't have time to mix, rise, shape, and bake

fresh yeast dough in addition to preparing the rest of the menu. These recipes, however, offer you an option. They let you do part of the preparation ahead of time—up to a month in advance—and still pull fresh homemade rolls hot from the oven in time for dinner.

The recipes for both Whole Wheat Dinner Rolls and Brown-and-Serve Pan Rolls let you mix and shape the dough ahead of time and freeze it up to a month. Just thaw the dough according to directions, and bake it just before dinner.

For Refrigerator Rolls, you can mix the dough and chill it up to three days ahead of time. Then you'll need to shape the rolls and let them rise just before baking them.

BROWN-AND-SERVE PAN ROLLS

1 package dry yeast
1 cup warm water (105° to 115°)
2 tablespoons shortening
3 tablespoons sugar
2 teaspoons salt
1 teaspoon cider vinegar
1 egg
3¼ to 3¾ cups all-purpose flour,
  divided

Dissolve yeast in warm water in a large mixing bowl; let stand 5 minutes. Add shortening, sugar, salt, vinegar, egg, and half of flour; beat at medium speed of an electric mixer until well blended. Gradually stir in enough remaining flour to make a moderately stiff dough.

Turn dough out onto a lightly floured surface, and knead 4 or 5 times. Place in a well-greased bowl, turning to grease top. Cover and let rise in a warm place (85°), free from drafts, 1 hour or until doubled in bulk.

Punch dough down. Turn out onto a lightly floured surface. Knead 4 or 5 times, and roll to ½-inch thickness. Cut with a 2½-inch biscuit cutter, and place rounds in a lightly greased 13- x 9- x 2-inch pan.

Cover and let rise in a warm place, free from drafts, 30 minutes or until doubled in bulk. Bake at 300° for 15 minutes; cool. Remove from pan, and wrap in aluminum foil, folding edges to seal securely. Place foil package in a zip-top heavy-duty plastic bag, and freeze up to 1 month.

To serve, remove foil package from bag, and let rolls thaw to room temperature. Remove foil wrapping, and return rolls to pan. Bake at 350° for 15 to 17 minutes or until golden brown. Yield: 15 rolls.

Roxie Adair
Victoria, Texas

WHOLE WHEAT DINNER ROLLS

2 cups water
2 tablespoons molasses
¾ cup shortening
3¾ to 4¼ cups all-purpose flour, divided
3 cups whole wheat flour, divided
2 teaspoons salt
2 eggs, beaten
½ cup sugar
2 packages dry yeast

Combine water, molasses, and shortening in a small saucepan; heat until shortening melts, stirring occasionally. Cool to 120° to 130°.

Combine 2 cups all-purpose flour, 1 cup whole wheat flour, and remaining ingredients in a large mixing bowl, and stir well.

Gradually add liquid mixture to flour mixture, beating 4 minutes at medium speed of an electric mixer. Stir in remaining 2 cups whole wheat flour and enough remaining all-purpose flour to make a stiff dough.

Turn dough out onto a heavily floured surface, and knead until smooth and elastic (about 5 minutes). Place in a lightly greased bowl, turning to grease top. Let rest 20 minutes. Punch dough down; divide dough into 36 balls. Place balls on a lightly greased baking sheet. Cover with plastic wrap; freeze until firm. Transfer frozen balls to zip-top heavy-duty plastic bags. Freeze up to 1 month.

Remove from freezer; place 2 inches apart on greased baking sheets. Cover and let rise in a warm place (85°), free from drafts, 1½ hours or until doubled in bulk. Bake at 375° for 15 minutes or until golden brown. Yield: 3 dozen.

Nell H. Amador
Guntersville, Alabama

REFRIGERATOR ROLLS

2 cups water
⅔ cup butter or margarine
½ cup sugar
6 cups all-purpose flour, divided
2 teaspoons salt
2 packages dry yeast
2 eggs

Combine water, butter, and sugar in a saucepan; heat until butter melts, stirring occasionally. Cool to 120° to 130°.

Combine 2 cups flour, salt, and yeast in a large mixing bowl; stir well. Gradually add liquid mixture to flour mixture, beating well at high speed of an electric mixer. Add eggs, and beat an additional 2 minutes at medium speed. Gradually stir in remaining 4 cups flour, making a soft dough. Cover and refrigerate up to 3 days; punch dough down and cover if it begins rising out of bowl.

When ready to use, punch dough down; turn out onto a floured surface, and knead lightly 4 or 5 times. Divide dough into thirds. Divide each third into 12 pieces; shape each into a ball. Place each ball in cup of lightly greased muffin pans. Repeat procedure with remaining dough.

Cover and let rise in a warm place (85°), free from drafts, 1 hour or until doubled in bulk. Bake at 400° for 12 minutes or until golden brown. Yield: 3 dozen.

Note: For **cloverleaf rolls,** punch dough down; divide and shape into 108 balls; place 3 balls in each cup of lightly greased muffin pans. Cover and let rise until doubled in bulk; bake as directed.

Edith McClure
Bethany, Missouri

Dessert For Passover

Although Jewish dietary restrictions during Passover may leave some cooks wondering what to serve their family or friends for dessert, Sally Wolfish of Dallas, Texas, wisely offers Passover Cheesecake.

To make this creamy dessert, crushed matzos are used in place of graham cracker crumbs for the crust. The cream cheese must be manufactured under rabbinic supervision to be kosher. Ask the local rabbi what brands may be used, or look for the kosher symbol located on the package (either a K or a U inside a circle).

Matzos and other kosher foods are available at large supermarkets, usually in a special section designated for such foods.

PASSOVER CHEESECAKE

1 cup crushed matzos
¼ cup sugar
¼ cup butter, melted
3 (8-ounce) packages cream cheese, softened
1 cup sugar
3 eggs
½ teaspoon grated lemon rind
1 tablespoon lemon juice
Garnish: lemon slices

Combine first 3 ingredients in a bowl; blend well. Press in bottom of an ungreased 9-inch springform pan. Set pan aside.

Combine cream cheese and 1 cup sugar; beat at medium speed of an electric mixer until fluffy. Add eggs, one at a time, beating after each addition. Add lemon rind and lemon juice; mix well. Spoon cream cheese mixture over crust. Bake at 375° for 45 minutes or until cheesecake is set. Remove from oven, and cool on wire rack; chill 8 hours. Garnish, if desired. Yield: 8 to 10 servings.

Braided Bread For Easter

"We wouldn't celebrate Easter without Easter bread!" Faye Hicks says emphatically. A resident of Charleston, West Virginia, Faye has made Easter bread for her family many times. "We like it for breakfast or brunch—and with lots of butter, applesauce, or orange marmalade.

"My mother's great-great-grandmother had the recipe and passed it down through her family," she says. She remembers watching her grandmother make the bread when she was a little girl. Today Faye and her family carry on the tradition and bake the bread each spring.

GOLDEN EASTER BREAD

1 package dry yeast
¾ cup warm water (105° to 115°)
¼ cup sugar
¼ cup vegetable oil
2 teaspoons salt
3 eggs, slightly beaten
1 teaspoon grated lemon rind
4 to 5 cups all-purpose flour, divided
⅓ cup raisins
Butter or margarine, melted

Dissolve yeast in warm water in a large mixing bowl; let stand 5 minutes. Stir sugar, oil, and salt into yeast mixture. Add eggs, lemon rind, and 2 cups flour. Beat at low speed of an electric mixer until mixture is smooth. Stir in enough remaining flour to make a soft dough.

Turn dough out onto a floured surface; add raisins, and knead until smooth and elastic (about 8 to 10 minutes). Place in a well-greased bowl, turning to grease top. Cover and let rise in a warm place (85°), free from drafts, 1 hour or until doubled in bulk.

Punch dough down, and divide into thirds. Shape each third into a 16-inch rope. Place ropes on a greased baking sheet (do not stretch); pinch ropes together at one end to seal. Braid ropes; pinch ends to seal. Tuck ends under; with fingers, gently lift and loosen braids in center to form an oval-shaped loaf. Brush braid with melted butter. Let rise in a warm place (85°), free from drafts, 40 minutes or until doubled in bulk.

Bake at 350° for 25 to 30 minutes or until golden, shielding with aluminum foil, if necessary. Brush bread with melted butter. Yield: 1 loaf.

Note: Before second rising, loaf may be sprayed with vegetable cooking spray rather than brushed with melted butter.

Some Tasty Reasons To Drink Coffee

Coffee cake boasts the brew in its name—not because coffee is an ingredient but because someone discovered how well the two pair up. We think the recipes here are fine mates for coffee, too. Just step into the kitchen—a blend of tantalizing flavor and aroma awaits you.

ST. TIMOTHY'S COFFEE CAKE

1 cup butter or margarine, softened
2 cups sugar
2 eggs
½ teaspoon vanilla extract
2 cups all-purpose flour
1 teaspoon baking powder
¼ teaspoon salt
1 teaspoon ground cinnamon
1 cup chopped pecans
½ cup golden raisins
1 cup sour cream
1 tablespoon sugar
¼ teaspoon ground cinnamon

Beat butter at medium speed of an electric mixer until fluffy; gradually add 2 cups sugar, beating well. Add eggs, one at a time, beating after each addition. Stir in vanilla.

Combine flour and next 5 ingredients; add to creamed mixture alternately with sour cream, beginning and ending with flour mixture. Mix just until blended after each addition.

Spoon batter into a greased and floured 12-cup Bundt pan. Combine 1 tablespoon sugar and ¼ teaspoon cinnamon; sprinkle half of mixture on top of cake.

Bake at 350° for 55 minutes or until a wooden pick inserted in center comes out clean. Cool in pan 10 minutes; remove from pan, and sprinkle top with remaining cinnamon mixture. Cool completely on a wire rack. Yield: one 10-inch coffee cake. *Kim Shelton Snow Camp, North Carolina*

Something's Brewing

■ Keep your coffee fresh—don't heat it for more than 10 minutes after it's brewed. Exposure to air saps the aroma from the coffee; continued heat adds a bitter, acidic taste. The solution lies in pouring freshly made coffee into a sealed, insulated thermal container—a carafe, coffee butler, or thermos—as soon as the coffee brews. It should stay fresh and aromatic up to four hours.

■ For the freshest taste, store ground coffee or beans in an airtight container in the refrigerator or freezer. They may become rancid at room temperature.

■ "Grind" describes the size of ground coffee bean particles. Some manufacturers label the package according to what coffee maker is best suited for a particular grind.

■ One, two, or three level tablespoons of ground coffee should be used per 6-ounce cup of water to produce mild, average, or strong coffee, respectively.

PRUNE-NUT BREAD

¾ cup prune juice
¼ cup water
½ cup coarsely chopped pitted
   prunes
3 tablespoons butter or margarine
1 egg, slightly beaten
¾ teaspoon vanilla extract
1½ cups all-purpose flour
1 teaspoon baking soda
⅛ teaspoon salt
½ cup sugar
½ cup chopped pecans

Combine prune juice and water in a small saucepan; bring to a boil. Remove from heat, and stir in prunes and butter. Cool mixture to lukewarm. Stir in egg and vanilla.

Combine flour and remaining ingredients in a large bowl; add prune mixture, stirring just until dry ingredients are moistened.

Spoon batter into a greased and floured 8½- x 4½- x 3-inch loafpan. Bake at 325° for 50 to 55 minutes or until a wooden pick inserted in center comes out clean. Cool in pan 10 minutes; remove from pan, and let cool on a wire rack. Yield: 1 loaf.

Light-As-A-Cloud Cakes

Often grouped together in cookbooks under the classification of "foam" cakes, angel food, sponge, and chiffon cakes contain a common element that's responsible for their similarity and characteristic lightness—beaten egg whites. But key differences distinguish these three cakes.

Angel food cakes are the purest of the foam cakes. They contain no leavening, no egg yolks, and no shortening. In contrast, sponge cakes contain yolks and sometimes leavening, but never shortening. Chiffon cakes get their lightness from beaten egg whites, but they always contain yolks, leavening, and shortening or oil.

Foam cakes are commonly baked in ungreased tube pans. This allows the batter to cling to the sides of the pan and rise higher. Cool foam cakes upside-down to prevent shrinking and falling.

COFFEE SPONGE CAKE

1 tablespoon instant coffee granules
1 cup boiling water
6 eggs, separated
2 cups sugar, divided
1 teaspoon vanilla extract
2 cups all-purpose flour
1 tablespoon baking powder
1 teaspoon salt
¼ teaspoon cream of tartar
1½ teaspoons instant coffee
   granules
2 tablespoons hot milk
3 tablespoons butter or margarine,
   softened
3 cups sifted powdered sugar
1 cup chopped pecans

Dissolve 1 tablespoon coffee granules in boiling water; set aside to cool.

Beat egg yolks, 1½ cups sugar, and vanilla in a large mixing bowl at high speed of an electric mixer 4 minutes or until thick and lemon colored.

Combine flour, baking powder, and salt; add to egg mixture alternately with coffee mixture, beginning and ending with flour mixture. Set aside.

Beat egg whites and cream of tartar in a large mixing bowl at high speed of an electric mixer until soft peaks form. Add remaining ½ cup sugar, 2 tablespoons at a time, and beat until stiff peaks form; fold into batter.

Pour batter into an ungreased 10-inch tube pan, spreading evenly. Bake at 350° for 1 hour or until cake springs back when lightly touched. Invert pan; cool 40 minutes. Loosen cake from sides of pan, using a narrow metal spatula; remove from pan.

Dissolve 1½ teaspoons coffee granules in 2 tablespoons hot milk; set mixture aside.

Beat butter at medium speed of an electric mixer; add powdered sugar and coffee mixture. Add additional milk, if necessary, to make frosting of spreading consistency. Frost top and sides of cake. Pat chopped pecans around sides of cake. Yield: one 10-inch cake.
Ruth Chellis
Easley, South Carolina

CHOCOLATE ANGEL FOOD CAKE

11 egg whites
1 teaspoon cream of tartar
⅛ teaspoon salt
1⅓ cups sugar
1 cup sifted cake flour
¼ cup cocoa
1 teaspoon vanilla extract
Garnishes: whipped cream,
   strawberries

Beat egg whites in a large mixing bowl at high speed of an electric mixer until foamy. Add cream of tartar and salt; beat until soft peaks form. Add sugar, 2 tablespoons at a time, beating until stiff peaks form. Combine flour and cocoa. Sprinkle flour mixture over egg white mixture, ¼ cup at a time; fold in carefully. Fold in vanilla.

Pour batter into an ungreased 10-inch tube pan, spreading evenly. Bake at 350° for 15 minutes. Reduce temperature to 300°; bake 35 to 40 minutes or until cake springs back when lightly touched. Invert pan; cool 40 minutes. Loosen cake from sides of pan, using a narrow metal spatula; remove from pan. Garnish each serving, if desired. Yield: one 10-inch cake.
Marie A. Davis
Charlotte, North Carolina

ORANGE CHIFFON CAKE

2¼ cups sifted cake flour
1 tablespoon baking powder
½ teaspoon salt
1½ cups sugar
½ cup vegetable oil
5 egg yolks
2 teaspoons grated orange rind
¾ cup orange juice
1 teaspoon vanilla extract
8 egg whites
½ teaspoon cream of tartar

Combine first 4 ingredients in a mixing bowl. Make a well in center; add oil, egg yolks, orange rind, orange juice, and vanilla. Beat at medium speed of an electric mixer until smooth.

Beat egg whites and cream of tartar in a large mixing bowl at high speed of electric mixer until soft peaks form. Pour egg yolk mixture in a thin, steady stream over egg whites; gently fold yolks into whites.

Pour batter into an ungreased 10-inch tube pan, spreading evenly. Bake at 325° for 1 hour or until cake springs back when lightly touched. Invert pan; cool 40 minutes. Loosen cake from sides of pan, using a narrow metal spatula; remove from pan. Yield: one 10-inch cake.

Here's The Scoop

It's no secret that ice cream ranks high on any dessert list. Hardly anything will satisfy more than a scoop of the frosty concoction on a warm, sunny day, but sometimes a fancier dessert might be in order when company is coming. In that case, take ice cream one step further.

Layer your favorite flavor into a pie, or top it with other ingredients to rival fancy ice cream parlor concoctions. No matter how you decide to serve the ice cream, you'll find it a little easier if you first let it soften.

BANANA-GRAHAM ICE CREAM

18 graham cracker squares
4 bananas, sliced
1 quart vanilla ice cream, softened
6 to 8 maraschino cherries

Break graham crackers into 1-inch pieces. Fold crackers and banana slices into ice cream. Freeze until firm. Top each serving with a cherry. Yield: 6 to 8 servings.   *Wanda Ford*
Denton, Texas

CHOCOLATE ICE CREAM PIE

18 cream-filled chocolate sandwich cookies, crushed
⅓ cup butter or margarine, melted
1 quart vanilla ice cream, softened
Chocolate Sauce
1 (8-ounce) container frozen whipped topping, thawed
2 tablespoons chopped pecans, toasted

Combine cookie crumbs and butter; mix well, and press into a buttered 9-inch pieplate. Spoon ice cream evenly over crust; cover and freeze.

Spoon Chocolate Sauce over ice cream; freeze until firm. Pipe or spread whipped topping on pie; sprinkle with pecans. Yield: one 9-inch pie.

Chocolate Sauce

½ cup sugar
3 tablespoons cocoa
⅔ cup cvaporated milk
½ teaspoon vanilla extract
1 tablespoon butter or margarine

Combine sugar, cocoa, and evaporated milk in a heavy saucepan; cook over medium heat until boiling, stirring occasionally.

Reduce heat to low, and cook 5 minutes or until thickened, stirring occasionally. Stir in vanilla and butter. Let cool completely. Yield: ⅔ cup.
Mrs. Charles L. Poteet
Little Rock, Arkansas

DECADENT ICE CREAM DESSERT

1¼ cups cream-filled chocolate sandwich cookie crumbs
3 tablespoons butter or margarine, melted
Caramel Sauce
1 quart chocolate ice cream, softened
1 quart vanilla ice cream, softened
6 (1.4-ounce) English toffee-flavored candy bars, crushed
Chocolate Sauce
1 quart coffee ice cream, softened

Combine cookie crumbs and butter, mixing well. Press crumb mixture firmly over bottom of a 10-inch springform pan. Bake at 350° for 6 minutes. Cool on a wire rack.

Spread ½ cup Caramel Sauce over crust, leaving a 1-inch border; freeze until set. Spread chocolate ice cream over Caramel Sauce; freeze until firm.

Combine vanilla ice cream and crushed candy bars. Spread mixture over chocolate ice cream; freeze until firm. Spread 1 cup Chocolate Sauce over vanilla ice cream; freeze until set. Spread coffee ice cream over Chocolate Sauce. Cover tightly, and freeze at least 8 hours. Remove dessert from freezer 10 minutes before serving; remove sides of springform pan, and slice dessert into wedges. Serve with remaining sauces. Yield: 12 to 14 servings.

Caramel Sauce

⅓ cup butter or margarine
2 cups firmly packed brown sugar
⅛ teaspoon salt
1 cup half-and-half, divided
2 teaspoons cornstarch
2 teaspoons vanilla extract

Combine butter, brown sugar, salt, and ¾ cup half-and-half in a heavy saucepan. Cook over low heat, stirring constantly, until sugar dissolves. Do not boil. Combine cornstarch and remaining ¼ cup half-and-half; gradually stir into brown sugar mixture.

Cook over low heat, stirring constantly, until mixture thickens. Stir in vanilla. Yield: 2 cups.

Chocolate Sauce

1 (6-ounce) package semisweet chocolate morsels
1 (12-ounce) can evaporated milk
2 cups sifted powdered sugar

Combine chocolate morsels and evaporated milk in a small heavy saucepan. Cook over medium heat, stirring constantly, until chocolate morsels melt. Stir in powdered sugar. Cook over medium heat, stirring frequently, 5 minutes or until sauce thickens. Yield: 2 cups.
Mary Andrew
Winston-Salem, North Carolina

APRICOT ICE CREAM SAUCE

1 (12-ounce) jar apricot preserves
⅓ cup firmly packed light brown sugar
⅓ cup unsweetened pineapple juice
1½ tablespoons grated lemon or orange rind

Combine all ingredients; stir until sugar dissolves. Serve over vanilla ice cream. Yield: 1½ cups.
Mrs. Thomas Byrd
Nashville, Tennessee

Tip: *When an ice cream pie recipe calls for a graham cracker crust, freeze the crust before adding the ice cream to prevent crumbs from getting mixed into the filling.*

A Torte Of Many Flavors

"Spring Torte is a wonderful dessert when strawberries are fresh and plentiful," says Mrs. Richard L. Brownell of Salisbury, North Carolina. "You may also serve it during other seasons by substituting canned pineapple or sliced bananas."

For a rainbow of colors, we've used all three of Mrs. Brownell's suggestions. Feel free to use your imagination by mixing your favorite fruits. Peaches alone or combined with strawberries would be delicious, or you may prefer fresh blueberries.

SPRING TORTE

½ cup butter or margarine
½ cup sugar
4 eggs, separated
1⅓ cups all-purpose flour
1½ teaspoons baking powder
¼ cup plus 1 tablespoon milk
1 teaspoon vanilla extract
½ teaspoon cream of tartar
1 cup sugar
2 cups whipping cream
½ cup sifted powdered sugar
2 bananas
Lemon juice
2 cups fresh strawberries, sliced
1 (8-ounce) can pineapple tidbits, well drained
¼ cup chopped pecans, toasted
Garnish: whole strawberries

Cream butter; gradually add ½ cup sugar, beating well at medium speed of an electric mixer. Add yolks, one at a time, beating after each addition.

Combine flour and baking powder; add to creamed mixture alternately with milk, beginning and ending with flour mixture. Mix well after each addition. Stir in vanilla. Pour batter into 2 greased and floured, wax paper-lined 9-inch round cakepans.

Beat egg whites and cream of tartar at high speed of an electric mixer 1 minute. Gradually add 1 cup sugar, 1 tablespoon at a time, beating until stiff peaks form and sugar dissolves (2 to 4 minutes). Spread half of meringue over batter in each pan; bake at 250° for 25 minutes. Increase heat to 350°; bake 20 minutes. Cool cake layers in pans on wire racks 10 minutes. Carefully remove cake layers from pans; cool completely on wire racks.

Combine whipping cream and powdered sugar; beat until soft peaks form. Set aside. Slice bananas, and coat with lemon juice.

Place one torte layer on a cake plate; spread with half of whipped cream. Arrange half of banana slices, sliced strawberries, and pineapple over whipped cream; sprinkle with half of pecans. Repeat with second torte layer, remaining whipped cream, fruit, and pecans. Garnish, if desired. Yield: 8 servings.

Cake Tips

■ When a recipe calls for a "greased pan," be sure to grease the pan with solid shortening or an oil unless specified.

■ To keep cake layers from sticking in the pan, grease the bottom and sides of the pan and line bottom with wax paper. (Trace outline of pan on wax paper and cut out.) Pour batter in pan and bake. Invert cake layer on rack to cool; gently peel off wax paper while the cake is still warm.

■ To keep the plate neat while frosting a cake, place three or four strips of wax paper over the edges of the plate. Position the cake on the plate, and fill and frost it; then carefully pull out the wax paper strips.

QUICK!

Toss A Fruit Salad

Certainly the *quickest* way to eat fruit is out of your hand, but making these salads ranks close behind. Some offer the convenience of spooning cut fruit from a can, while others suggest fresh fruit that's a snap to cut and toss into a salad. From start to finish, they take 10 to 20 minutes to prepare.

COLORFUL FRUIT BOWL

1 (8-ounce) carton plain yogurt
1 tablespoon sugar
1 teaspoon lemon juice
Dash of salt
2 medium oranges, chilled
1 medium-size pink grapefruit, chilled
1 medium banana, sliced
1 cup sliced strawberries
½ cup cubed honeydew

Combine first 4 ingredients; chill. Peel and section oranges and grapefruit, placing sections and any juice that accumulates in a bowl. Add remaining fruit, tossing gently.

To serve fruit, use a slotted spoon, and drizzle dressing over each serving. Serve immediately. Yield: 4 servings.
Marie A. Davis
Charlotte, North Carolina

YOGURT-GRANOLA FRUIT MEDLEY

2 bananas, sliced
1 (8-ounce) carton vanilla yogurt
1 cup granola
1¼ cups seedless grapes

Layer half of banana slices in a 1-quart bowl; lightly spread one-fourth of yogurt on top, and sprinkle with one-fourth of granola. Arrange half of grapes over granola; spread with one-fourth of yogurt, and sprinkle with one-fourth of granola. Repeat procedure with remaining ingredients. Cover and chill up to 3 hours. Yield: 4 servings.
Leslie Hamilton
Montgomery, Alabama

SUNNY FRUIT SALAD

½ cup plain yogurt
2 teaspoons honey
1 teaspoon lemon juice
Pinch of grated nutmeg
2 oranges, peeled, seeded, and sectioned
2 large bananas, peeled and cut into ½-inch slices
3 kiwifruit, peeled and cut into ½-inch slices
Lettuce leaves

Combine first 4 ingredients in a medium bowl. Add fruit, and toss gently. Serve on lettuce leaves. Yield: 4 servings.
Wylene B. Gillespie
Gallatin, Tennessee

LAYERED FRUIT SALAD

½ cup sliced strawberries
¼ cup sliced banana
¼ cup sour cream
½ cup pineapple chunks

Layer half each of strawberries and banana in a small serving dish; lightly spread with one-fourth of sour cream. Top with half of pineapple and one-fourth of sour cream. Repeat procedure with remaining ingredients. Yield: 2 servings.
Suzan L. Wiener
Spring Hill, Florida

BANANA SPLIT SALAD

1 (15¼-ounce) can unsweetened pineapple chunks, drained
1 (11-ounce) can mandarin oranges, drained
2 cups miniature marshmallows
½ cup sour cream
Lettuce leaves
6 small bananas, cut in half lengthwise
¼ cup flaked coconut, toasted
6 maraschino cherries

Combine pineapple, mandarin oranges, marshmallows, and sour cream in a large bowl, tossing gently. Line salad plates with lettuce leaves; spoon fruit mixture on lettuce. Place a banana half on each side of fruit mixture; sprinkle with coconut, and top with a cherry. Serve immediately. Yield: 6 servings.
Janice S. Brett
Bowling Green, Kentucky

GOLDEN PEAR SALAD

3 tablespoons shredded carrot
3 tablespoons shredded Cheddar cheese
1 tablespoon commercial French salad dressing
1 (8½-ounce) can pear halves, drained
Lettuce leaves

Combine carrot, cheese, and dressing in a small bowl; spoon into pear halves. Arrange on lettuce-lined salad plates. Yield: 2 servings.
Emma Prillhart
Kingsport, Tennessee

APRIL

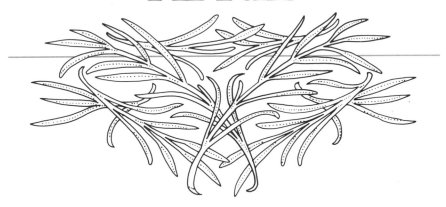

Warm spring days present perfect opportunities to entertain. For fresh ideas, turn to our "Brunches & Lunches" section. Morning to midday, these meals range from relaxing breakfast ideas to light lunches and even heartier fare. In addition to these morning meals, the menu featured in "You're Invited" also makes a tempting presentation, especially served outdoors. In fact, nothing says relaxing elegance quite as well as a linen-covered table set up for alfresco dining.

Let's Talk Turkey

Now you can prepare turkey all year long in a fraction of the time it takes to roast the big holiday bird. When health-conscious consumers found out that turkey is naturally low in fat and calories, they created a big demand for this versatile meat. That led the industry to slice, chop, and grind the bird down to family-size, quick-cooking portions.

In the poultry section of many grocery stores you'll find several cuts of tray-packed turkey that can be sautéed, stir-fried, and quickly roasted. It's a fitting substitute in many of the recipes where you may have previously used beef and pork.

The labeling of these turkey parts may vary by store and region, but as turkey becomes more available, labeling should become more consistent. (Refer to the boxed material on the facing page for the most common terms and cuts.)

You can refrigerate fresh turkey up to two days before cooking it and up to two additional days after cooking it. For longer storage, freeze ground turkey up to two months and turkey parts up to three months.

The low-fat and high-protein content of turkey makes it especially sensitive to high heat and overcooking, so cook it just until done—usually when the thickest part of the meat is no longer pink.

TURKEY SLICES WITH CURRIED CREAM SAUCE

1½ **pounds turkey tenderloins**
2 **tablespoons butter or margarine**
3 **tablespoons all-purpose flour**
1 **cup chicken broth**
¼ **cup milk**
½ **teaspoon curry powder**
½ **teaspoon grated lemon rind**
Hot cooked rice
¼ **cup chopped pitted dates**
¼ **cup chopped cashews**
¼ **cup chopped green onions**

Place tenderloins in a 13- x 9- x 2-inch pan; bake at 400° for 25 to 30 minutes or until meat thermometer registers 170°. Cut tenderloins into ½-inch slices, and keep warm.

Melt butter in a heavy saucepan over low heat; add flour, stirring until smooth. Cook 1 minute, stirring constantly. Gradually add broth and milk; cook over medium heat, stirring constantly, until mixture is thickened and bubbly. Stir in curry powder and lemon rind.

Place turkey slices on top of rice; pour sauce over turkey, and sprinkle with dates, cashews, and green onions. Yield: 6 servings.

Hilda Marshall
Front Royal, Virginia

TURKEY WITH TARRAGON CREAM

1 **pound cooked turkey breast**
2 **tablespoons butter or margarine,**
  divided
1 **tablespoon all-purpose flour**
¾ **cup milk**
2 **tablespoons chopped fresh parsley**
½ **teaspoon dried whole tarragon**
½ **cup sour cream**
1 **tablespoon Dijon mustard**
Hot cooked rice or noodles
  (optional)

Cut turkey into ¼-inch slices. Melt 1 tablespoon butter in a large skillet; add turkey slices, and cook 2 minutes on each side. Arrange turkey slices on a platter; keep warm.

Melt remaining tablespoon butter in skillet over low heat; add flour, stirring until smooth. Cook 1 minute, stirring constantly. Gradually add milk; cook over medium heat, stirring constantly, until thickened and bubbly. Remove from heat; stir in parsley and next 3 ingredients. Pour sauce over turkey slices. Serve with rice or noodles, if desired. Yield:4 servings. *Mrs. Riley Christopher*
Iron Station, North Carolina

TURKEY STROGANOFF

½ pound fresh mushrooms, sliced
½ cup chopped onion
1 small clove garlic, minced
2 tablespoons butter or margarine
1 pound ground turkey
1 (10¾-ounce) can cream of celery
  soup, undiluted
1 tablespoon dry sherry
½ teaspoon salt
½ teaspoon dried whole dillweed
½ teaspoon paprika
Dash of red pepper
1 (8-ounce) carton sour cream
Hot cooked noodles

Sauté mushrooms, onion, and garlic in butter in a large skillet 5 minutes. Drain mixture, and set aside, reserving drippings in skillet. Add turkey to skillet; cook over medium heat until browned, stirring to crumble. Drain. Stir in soup and next 5 ingredients. Stir in reserved vegetable mixture. Cook over low heat 5 minutes, stirring often. Add sour cream; cook until thoroughly heated, stirring often (do not boil). Serve over noodles. Yield: 4 to 6 servings.
Edith Askins
Greenville, Texas

GRILLED TURKEY BURGERS

1 pound ground turkey
¼ cup finely chopped onion
1 clove garlic, minced
½ teaspoon salt
⅛ teaspoon pepper
¼ teaspoon dried whole basil
⅛ teaspoon dried whole thyme
⅛ teaspoon rubbed sage
Vegetable cooking spray
Hamburger buns

Combine first 8 ingredients; shape into four 4-inch patties. Coat grill rack with cooking spray; place on grill over medium-hot coals. Place patties on rack, and cook 8 minutes on each side or until done. Serve on buns. Yield: 4 servings.
JaLayne Eddy
Jacksonville, Texas

Turkey Talk

You'll find turkey in new forms in most supermarkets around the South. When shopping, look for these labels: tenderloins, cutlets, ground, and link sausages.

Tenderloins are fillets of turkey cut from the breast, which are especially good for baking, broiling, or grilling.

Cutlets are ⅛- to ⅜-inch-thick slices of turkey also cut from the breast. They take only about three minutes to cook on each side because they are so thin. Some supermarkets mistakenly label turkey cutlets as **steaks,** although the term "steak" refers to slices of turkey that are ½- to 1-inch thick.

Ground turkey, a blend of white and dark turkey meat, substitutes well for ground beef in many recipes. The fat content of ground turkey can vary, depending on how much dark meat (higher in fat) is used.

Turkey **sausage** is available in the form of links and patties in many areas of the South. And just like other types of sausage, turkey sausage can be pan-fried or broiled.

You'll find other forms of turkey on the market. Some supermarkets may also have boneless **turkey roasts** available, in addition to the more familiar **drumsticks, wings,** and **breasts.**

SKILLET TURKEY DINNER

1 (14-ounce) package link turkey
  sausage
Vegetable cooking spray
1 clove garlic, minced
1 medium onion, sliced
6 cups coarsely shredded cabbage
2 carrots, scraped and sliced
¼ cup water
¼ teaspoon salt
¼ teaspoon pepper

Cook sausage in a large skillet coated with cooking spray until browned; drain. Add garlic and remaining ingredients, tossing gently. Cover and cook over medium heat 10 minutes, stirring occasionally. Yield: 4 servings.
Martha Leder
Ulm, Arkansas

TURKEY CUTLETS
WITH TOMATO-CAPER SAUCE

¼ cup all-purpose flour
½ teaspoon dried whole rosemary
¼ teaspoon salt
¼ teaspoon pepper
1 pound turkey cutlets
¼ cup olive oil
3 medium tomatoes, peeled and
  diced
1 small onion, thinly sliced
2 tablespoons capers, drained

Combine flour, rosemary, salt, and pepper; dredge turkey cutlets in flour mixture, and set aside.

Heat olive oil in a large skillet until hot. Add turkey cutlets; cook 3 to 4 minutes on each side. Remove cutlets to a serving platter, and keep warm; reserve drippings in skillet. Add tomatoes and onion to drippings; cover and cook 8 to 10 minutes, stirring occasionally. Spoon sauce over turkey cutlets; sprinkle with capers. Yield: 4 servings.
Carol Y. Chastain
San Antonio, Texas

TURKEY-BROCCOLI STIR-FRY

1 (14½-ounce) can ready-to-serve
  chicken broth
3 tablespoons soy sauce
2 tablespoons cornstarch
½ teaspoon grated fresh gingerroot
1 tablespoon vegetable oil
½ teaspoon salt
¼ teaspoon white pepper
1 pound turkey cutlets, cut into
  ½-inch strips
1 clove garlic, crushed
4 green onions, sliced
1 pound fresh broccoli, cut into
  flowerets
1 sweet red pepper, cut into strips
Hot cooked rice
2 tablespoons sesame seeds, lightly
  toasted

Combine broth, soy sauce, cornstarch, and gingerroot in a small bowl;
set aside.

Pour oil around top of preheated
wok or skillet, coating sides; heat at
medium high (325°) for 1 minute.
Sprinkle salt and pepper over turkey.
Add turkey and garlic to wok; stir-fry
3 to 4 minutes. Add green onions,
broccoli, red pepper, and broth mixture; cover and cook 3 to 4 minutes or
until vegetables are crisp-tender.
Serve over rice. Sprinkle with sesame
seeds. Yield: 6 servings.

TURKEY ITALIANO

1 pound turkey cutlets
1 tablespoon butter or margarine
½ cup chicken broth, divided
¾ cup chopped onion
½ cup chopped green pepper
¼ cup sliced celery
1 (2.5-ounce) jar sliced mushrooms,
  drained
1 (8-ounce) can tomato sauce
1 teaspoon dried Italian seasoning
½ teaspoon salt
⅔ cup (2.6 ounces) shredded
  mozzarella cheese

Cook cutlets in butter in a skillet over
medium heat until browned. Remove

from heat, and place in a greased 12- x
8- x 2-inch baking dish.

Combine ¼ cup broth, onion, green
pepper, and celery in a small saucepan; bring to a boil. Cover, reduce
heat, and simmer 10 minutes or until
vegetables are tender. Stir in remaining ¼ cup broth, mushrooms, tomato
sauce, and seasonings; bring to a boil.
Reduce heat, and simmer 10 minutes.

Pour broth mixture over cutlets;
cover with aluminum foil, and bake at
325° for 40 minutes. Sprinkle with
cheese, and bake an additional 5 minutes. Yield: 4 servings.

Joanne A. Mackintosh
Kingsport, Tennessee

Cheesecake With A New Taste

Next time you find yourself searching
for a special luncheon entrée, try Layered Vegetable Cheesecake. Not only
is it tasty, but it can also be made the
day before it is to be served.

LAYERED VEGETABLE CHEESECAKE

1⅓ cups dry breadcrumbs
⅓ cup butter or margarine, melted
2 (8-ounce) packages Neufchâtel
  cheese, softened
2 eggs
⅓ cup all-purpose flour
1 (8-ounce) carton sour cream
¼ cup minced onion
¼ teaspoon salt
¼ teaspoon white pepper
¾ cup shredded carrots
¾ cup diced green pepper
¾ cup diced sweet red pepper
Cucumber-Dill Sauce
Garnishes: cucumber slices, fresh
  dillweed

Combine breadcrumbs and butter;
press on bottom and 1 inch up sides of
a 9-inch springform pan. Set aside.

Beat cheese at high speed of an
electric mixer until fluffy. Add eggs,
one at a time, beating well after each
addition. Add flour and next 4 ingredients; beat until blended.

Pour about one-fourth of sour
cream mixture into prepared pan;
sprinkle with carrots. Top with one-
third of remaining sour cream mixture; sprinkle with green pepper. Top
with half of remaining sour cream mixture; top with red pepper. Top with
remaining sour cream mixture. Bake
at 300° for 1 hour or until set. Turn
oven off, and partially open oven door;
leave cheesecake in oven 1 hour. Remove from oven, and let cool completely. Cover and chill. Serve with
Cucumber-Dill Sauce. Garnish, if desired. Yield: 6 to 8 servings.

Cucumber-Dill Sauce

1 (8-ounce) carton plain yogurt
⅓ cup mayonnaise or salad
  dressing
½ cup unpeeled, chopped cucumber
¼ teaspoon salt
¼ teaspoon dried whole dillweed

Combine all ingredients, stirring well;
cover and chill. Yield: 1½ cups.

Tip: *Most cheeses should be wrapped
in moisture-proof airtight wrappers.
One exception is "moldy" cheeses,
such as blue cheese, which need to
breathe and should be kept in covered containers with the tops loosened. Remember, too, that cheeses
should be stored in the refrigerator.*

Brunches & Lunches

For daytime entertaining, this special section offers a bounty of menu ideas, from picnics and parties to brunch buffets and sit-down luncheons.

This Architect Builds A Great Party

Here's a tip. If you are ever a luncheon guest at B. B. Archer's party, eat lots of the savory seafood appetizers. It may be an hour or more before you are served the entrée and the rest of the menu! Yet it's worth the wait to sample the offerings of this Meridian, Mississippi, architect.

Why wait so long for lunch? Well, when B. B. entertains, everybody gets into the act, either cheering on the cooks or cooking alongside the host. College fraternity brother Bobby Landry helps B. B. chop parsley, stir a sauce, mix drinks, and man the oven, while B. B.'s wife, Sally, makes everyone feel at home.

Today B. B. moves back and forth, frying fish and passing them to Bobby, who keeps them warm in the oven. Soon every dish is ready, and the guests line up and take their plates to the sunny porch.

Folks take a seat, finding it pleasant in the early afternoon sunlight. They begin to eat, savoring each bite. The tables are set simply, with wildflowers in vases. A light blush wine makes the perfect accompaniment to the spicy fish, and a keg on the porch satisfies heartier thirsts. Worth the wait? You bet it is.

Brunch for 6
Clam Diggers
Crabmeat Topping
Melba rounds
Smoked Oyster Spread
Pecan Roughy
With Brown Butter Sauce
Green Salad With B. B.'s Dressing
New potatoes
Fresh asparagus
Toasted French bread
Lemon Ice Cream

■ A Clam Digger is like a bloody Mary except it's made with clam-and-tomato juice. This version has a little kick to it.

CLAM DIGGERS

1½ quarts clam-and-tomato juice
½ cup vodka
¼ cup Worcestershire sauce
2 tablespoons lemon juice
3 dashes of hot sauce
½ teaspoon salt
½ to 1 teaspoon Greek seasoning
Freshly ground pepper
Garnish: celery stalks

Combine first 7 ingredients. Serve over ice; sprinkle each serving with pepper, and garnish, if desired. Yield: about 7 cups.

Tip: *When cooking for a crowd, make the most of your kitchen appliances. Plan your menu so that you can utilize several cooking appliances rather than just your oven. Don't forget to use the cooktop, microwave oven, electric skillet, and toaster oven, as well as smaller bread warmers.*

Brunches & Lunches

■ Our host says fresh crabmeat is the key to success with Crabmeat Topping. It's served in a chafing dish to keep it warm.

CRABMEAT TOPPING

1 cup chopped green onions and tops
¼ cup chopped fresh parsley
1 tablespoon minced garlic
¼ cup butter or margarine, melted
¼ cup dry white wine
1 pound fresh lump crabmeat, drained
2 tablespoons mayonnaise or salad dressing
⅛ teaspoon paprika
⅛ teaspoon red pepper
Garnishes: chopped green onions, paprika

Sauté 1 cup chopped green onions, parsley, and garlic in butter in a large skillet; stir in wine, and cook 1 minute. Stir in crabmeat.

Remove crabmeat mixture from heat, and stir in mayonnaise, ⅛ teaspoon paprika, and red pepper. Garnish, if desired. Serve in a chafing dish with melba rounds. Yield: 3¾ cups.

■ Smoked Oyster Spread is a good recipe to make ahead of time. Just retrieve the rolled cream cheese log from the refrigerator, and garnish when guests arrive.

SMOKED OYSTER SPREAD

2 (8-ounce) packages cream cheese, softened
2 tablespoons mayonnaise or salad dressing
2 teaspoons Worcestershire sauce
¾ teaspoon garlic powder
Vegetable cooking spray
2 (3.66-ounce) cans smoked oysters, drained and chopped
Garnishes: fresh parsley sprigs, paprika, lemon slices

Combine first 4 ingredients. Coat a 15-inch-long piece of wax paper with cooking spray. Spread cream cheese mixture on paper in a 10- x 6-inch rectangle.

Place oysters evenly over cheese; roll up jellyroll fashion, starting with long side. Cover and chill. Garnish, if desired. Serve with bagel chips and melba rounds. Yield: 16 appetizer servings.

■ B. B. says many folks like to make a simpler version of Pecan Roughy With Brown Butter Sauce—they just coat fish with the Seasoning Mix, batter, and fry.

PECAN ROUGHY WITH BROWN BUTTER SAUCE

6 (6-ounce) orange roughy fillets
Seasoning Mix, divided
½ cup milk
1 egg yolk
1 cup all-purpose flour
Vegetable oil
Brown Butter Sauce
Pecan-Butter Sauce
½ cup chopped pecans

Sprinkle fish with 1½ tablespoons Seasoning Mix; set aside.

Combine milk and egg yolk in a shallow dish. Combine flour and remaining 1½ tablespoons Seasoning Mix. Dredge fish in flour mixture; dip in milk mixture. Dredge again in flour mixture. Pour oil to a depth of 1 inch in an electric skillet; heat oil to 350°. Fry fish 2 to 3 minutes on each side. Drain well on paper towels, and keep warm in oven.

Spoon Brown Butter Sauce onto a serving platter. Place fish on sauce, and spread each fillet with 3 tablespoons Pecan-Butter Sauce. Sprinkle with ½ cup pecans. Serve immediately. Yield: 6 servings.

Seasoning Mix

2 tablespoons Greek seasoning
1 teaspoon onion powder
1 teaspoon paprika
1 teaspoon Creole seasoning
½ teaspoon red pepper
½ teaspoon black pepper
½ teaspoon white pepper

Combine all ingredients in a small bowl, stirring well to combine. Yield: about 3 tablespoons.

Party Tips

■ Make ice cubes for a party ahead of time and store in plastic bags in the freezer. Count on 350 cubes for 50 people or 7 cubes per person.

■ To keep appetizers appealingly hot—and you out of the kitchen—use your chafing dish and warming trays for serving.

■ The key to the best tasting coffee is buying fresh coffee beans and grinding them just before brewing.

■ It's easy to determine the amount of coffee needed. When making it for your next party, allow 1 pound of coffee and 2 gallons of water for 40 servings.

Brunches & Lunches

Brown Butter Sauce

1 cup chicken broth
1 teaspoon minced garlic
½ cup butter, divided
2 tablespoons all-purpose flour
¼ cup Worcestershire sauce
½ teaspoon hot sauce

Combine broth and garlic in a small saucepan; bring to a boil. Reduce heat, and simmer 2 to 3 minutes.

Melt ¼ cup butter in a heavy saucepan over low heat; add flour, stirring until smooth. Cook 1 minute, stirring constantly. Gradually add broth mixture, stirring constantly. Add remaining ¼ cup butter, Worcestershire sauce, and hot sauce; cook over medium heat, stirring constantly, until mixture is thickened and bubbly. Yield: 1½ cups.

Pecan-Butter Sauce

½ cup butter, melted
1 cup chopped pecans
2 tablespoons chopped onion
½ teaspoon minced garlic
1 tablespoon lemon juice
1 teaspoon hot sauce

Position knife blade in food processor bowl. Combine butter and remaining ingredients in processor bowl. Top with cover, and process until sauce is smooth. Yield: 1¼ cups.

Serving Tips From B. B. Archer

When frying orange roughy or other fish for a crowd, use an electric skillet. Pat the fish dry with a paper towel after cooking, and keep the cooked fish warm in the oven until ready to serve.

To present Pecan Roughy, spoon a pool of Brown Butter Sauce onto each plate and top it with the roughy. Then spread Pecan-Butter Sauce over it just like a mayonnaise.

Prepare the plates one at a time so that guests get their food when it's hot.

Serve on white plates so that you really see the food.

■ Sally lines a dough bowl with plastic wrap, which allows her to mix the salad and B. B.'s Salad Dressing and serve it. Whole green onions garnish the sides of the salad bowl.

GREEN SALAD WITH B. B.'s DRESSING

6 cups torn iceberg lettuce
6 cups torn leaf lettuce
3 cups torn escarole
1 small purple onion, sliced and separated into rings
1 large tomato, cut into wedges
1 cucumber, sliced
2 tablespoons chopped fresh mint
B. B.'s Salad Dressing
2 to 3 bunches green onions

Combine first 7 ingredients in a large bowl. Drizzle B. B.'s Salad Dressing over salad; toss gently. Place green onions around edge of bowl; serve immediately. Yield: 6 to 8 servings.

B. B.'s Salad Dressing

½ cup olive oil
¼ cup lemon juice
3 tablespoons water
¼ to ½ teaspoon white pepper
¼ to ½ teaspoon red pepper
¼ to ½ teaspoon black pepper
2 tablespoons Greek seasoning
2 tablespoons chopped fresh mint
1½ teaspoons minced garlic

Combine all ingredients in a jar. Cover tightly; shake vigorously. Yield: 1 cup.

■ Sally recommends the following recipe for Lemon Ice Cream. "This recipe is great to serve for dessert after having seafood or fish as an entrée," she says.

LEMON ICE CREAM

2 cups sugar
2 cups milk
2 cups half-and-half
2 teaspoons grated lemon rind
1 cup fresh lemon juice
6 to 8 drops of yellow food color
Garnishes: fresh strawberries, fresh mint sprigs

Combine first 6 ingredients in a large bowl. Pour mixture into a 13- x 9- x 2-inch pan; cover and freeze until almost firm. Spoon half of mixture into a food processor or blender; process until smooth. Set aside. Repeat procedure with remaining mixture.

Return all of mixture to pan. Cover and freeze until mixture is firm. Garnish, if desired. Yield: 1½ quarts.

Spring Sippers

A beverage, it seems, is the quickest tool of hospitality. Think about it. No sooner have you let a guest into your home than you say, "Can I get you something to drink?" Be it a large party that includes new acquaintances or an intimate visit with a longtime friend, a glass offering a welcome drink makes everyone comfortable.

FUNSHINE FIZZ

2 cups orange juice
2 cups pineapple juice
1 pint orange sherbet
1 cup club soda

Combine first 3 ingredients in container of an electric blender; blend until smooth. Stir in club soda. Serve immediately. Yield: 7 cups.
Brenda Russell
Signal Mountain, Tennessee

HAWAIIAN CRUSH

2 cups milk
1 cup unsweetened pineapple juice, chilled
⅓ cup crushed ice
3 tablespoons sugar
2 tablespoons orange juice
1 teaspoon lemon juice

Combine all ingredients in container of an electric blender; process 2 minutes. Serve immediately. Yield: about 1 quart.
Louise F. Joseph
Elizabethtown, North Carolina

FROSTY PINEAPPLE PUNCH

1 (46-ounce) can pineapple juice, chilled
1 (12-ounce) can frozen pineapple-orange juice concentrate, thawed and undiluted
1 (6-ounce) can frozen lemonade concentrate, thawed and undiluted
½ gallon pineapple or lemon sherbet, softened

Combine first 3 ingredients in a punch bowl. Just before serving, spoon sherbet into punch bowl by heaping tablespoonfuls; stir gently. Serve immediately. Yield: 3 quarts.
Beth Scoggins
Gainesville, Texas

BANANA FROSTEE

1 ripe banana, unpeeled and frozen
⅓ cup instant nonfat dry milk powder
⅓ cup water
¼ teaspoon chocolate extract
Ice cubes

Peel banana; place in container of an electric blender. Add milk powder, water, and chocolate extract; process until smooth. Add ice to make 2 cups; process until smooth. Yield: 2 cups.
Virginia H. Scheffelin
Texarkana, Texas

Tip: *Slushes are refreshing beverages that can be made ahead and kept in the freezer. Immediately before serving slush, add carbonated beverage to the frozen base and stir.*

CRANBERRY SPRITZER

2 cups cranberry juice cocktail, chilled
1½ cups Sauterne, chilled
½ cup Triple Sec or other orange-flavored liqueur
2 cups club soda, chilled

Combine chilled cranberry juice, Sauterne, and Triple Sec in a pitcher. Just before serving, add club soda. Serve over crushed ice. Yield: 1½ quarts.
Velma P. Kestner
Berwind, West Virginia

CREAMY STRAWBERRY DAIQUIRIS

1 cup crushed ice
1 cup sliced fresh strawberries
½ cup light rum
⅓ cup frozen pink lemonade concentrate, thawed
1 pint vanilla ice cream

Combine all ingredients in container of an electric blender; process until mixture is smooth. Serve immediately. Yield: 1 quart.
Mrs. J. David Stearns
Mobile, Alabama

Brunches & Lunches

Wake Up To Breakfast In Bed

Breakfast in bed hasn't gone out of vogue. But it may just be harder to find time for it. If you can manage a morning free from the bustle of everyday life, take a relaxing repast.

Cinnamon Buns can be made ahead of time and warmed in the oven for those who aren't quite their best at an early hour. Serve them with Marinated Fruit for an easy menu.

MARINATED FRUIT

1 (20-ounce) can unsweetened
  pineapple chunks, undrained
1 pear, cut into chunks
1 apple, cut into chunks
1 nectarine, cut into chunks
2 tablespoons orange juice
  concentrate, undiluted
1 tablespoon honey
1 teaspoon chopped fresh mint

Drain pineapple; reserve juice, and set aside. Combine pineapple, pear, apple, and nectarine in a medium bowl; set aside.

Combine reserved pineapple juice, orange juice concentrate, honey, and mint; pour over fruit, and toss gently. Cover and chill, stirring occasionally. Yield: 8 servings.

Note: Substitute frozen peach slices for nectarines if they are unavailable.
Romanza O. Johnson
Bowling Green, Kentucky

CHERRY CRÊPES

1 cup all-purpose flour
1 cup milk
1 teaspoon vanilla extract
1 egg
1 tablespoon vegetable oil
1 (8-ounce) carton plain low-fat
  yogurt
¼ cup sugar
¼ teaspoon ground cinnamon
Cherry Sauce

Combine first 3 ingredients; beat at medium speed of an electric mixer until smooth. Add egg, and beat well. Refrigerate batter at least 2 hours. (This allows flour particles to swell and soften so that crêpes are light in texture.)

Brush bottom of a 6-inch crêpe pan or heavy skillet with oil; place pan over medium heat just until hot, not smoking.

Pour 2 tablespoons batter into pan; quickly tilt pan in all directions so that batter covers pan in a thin film. Cook 1 minute or until lightly browned.

Lift edge of crêpe to test for doneness. Crêpe is ready for flipping when it can be shaken loose from pan. Flip crêpe and cook about 30 seconds on other side. (This side is usually spotty brown and is the side on which filling is placed.)

Place crêpes on a towel to cool. Stack between layers of wax paper to prevent sticking. Repeat until all batter is used.

Combine yogurt, sugar, and cinnamon; spread about 2 tablespoons on each crêpe. Roll up crêpes, and place seam side down in a lightly greased 12- x 8- x 2-inch baking dish. Pour Cherry Sauce over crêpes. Bake at 350° for 20 to 25 minutes or until thoroughly heated. Yield: 8 servings.

Cherry Sauce

¼ cup sugar
1 tablespoon cornstarch
1 cup cranberry juice cocktail
1 (16-ounce) can red sour pitted
  cherries, drained
1 teaspoon grated orange rind

Combine sugar and cornstarch in a medium saucepan; stir in cranberry juice, cherries, and orange rind. Cook over medium heat, stirring constantly, until thickened and bubbly. Yield: about 2½ cups.

Note: To make a day ahead, prepare crêpes as directed, and place in baking dish; refrigerate. Remove from refrigerator 30 minutes before serving; make Cherry Sauce, and pour over crêpes. Bake as directed.
Yetta J. Burrell
Valdosta, Georgia

Brunches & Lunches

ORANGE SLICES WITH HONEY YOGURT

½ cup plain low-fat yogurt
1 tablespoon honey
⅛ teaspoon ground cinnamon
3 oranges, peeled and sectioned

Combine low-fat yogurt, honey, and cinnamon. Place orange sections in individual bowls; spoon yogurt sauce over oranges. Serve immediately. Yield: 2 to 3 servings.

Charlotte Pierce
Greensburg, Kentucky

CINNAMON BUNS

1¼ cups milk
¼ cup butter or margarine
4 cups all-purpose flour, divided
¼ cup sugar
1 teaspoon salt
¾ teaspoon ground cinnamon
1 package dry yeast
1 egg
¾ cup sugar
2 teaspoons ground cinnamon
¼ cup butter or margarine, melted
2 cups sifted powdered sugar
3 tablespoons milk
1 teaspoon vanilla extract

Combine 1¼ cups milk and ¼ cup butter in a saucepan; heat until butter melts, stirring occasionally. Cool to 120° to 130°.

Combine 2 cups flour and next 4 ingredients in a large bowl; stir well.

Gradually add milk mixture to flour mixture, beating at medium speed of an electric mixer 1 minute. Add egg, and beat 2 minutes. Gradually add remaining 2 cups flour to make a soft dough. Place in a well-greased bowl, turning to grease top. Cover and let rise in a warm place (85°), free from drafts, 1 hour or until doubled in bulk.

Punch dough down; turn out onto a lightly floured surface. Knead lightly 3 or 4 times. Roll dough to an 18- x 12-inch rectangle. Combine ¾ cup sugar, 2 teaspoons cinnamon, and ¼ cup melted butter; spread evenly over dough, leaving a ½-inch border. Roll up jellyroll fashion, starting at long side. Pinch seam to seal. Cut roll into 18 slices; place rolls, cut side down, in 2 greased 9-inch square pans.

Cover and let rise in a warm place, free from drafts, 45 minutes or until rolls are doubled in bulk. Bake at 375° for 20 minutes or until done. Cool on wire racks.

Combine powdered sugar, 3 tablespoons milk, and vanilla; drizzle over warm rolls. Yield: 1½ dozen.

Marcia Luzier
Dublin, Virginia

GINGERBREAD WAFFLES

1½ cups all-purpose flour
1 teaspoon baking powder
1 teaspoon baking soda
½ teaspoon salt
1 teaspoon ground ginger
¼ cup sugar
3 eggs, beaten
1 cup buttermilk
½ cup molasses
⅓ cup shortening, melted

Combine first 6 ingredients; set aside. Combine eggs, buttermilk, molasses, and melted shortening, stirring well; add to flour mixture, stirring until blended.

Bake in preheated, oiled waffle iron. Serve with butter and syrup. Yield: 14 (4-inch) waffles.

Note: Waffles may be frozen and reheated in the microwave or conventional oven.

Erma Jackson
Huntsville, Alabama

HONEY-BANANA BREAD

½ cup butter or margarine, softened
¾ cup honey
2 eggs
1 cup mashed ripe banana
2 cups all-purpose flour
1 teaspoon baking soda
¼ teaspoon salt
1 cup chopped pecans, toasted

Beat butter at medium speed of an electric mixer in a large mixing bowl; add honey, beating well. Add eggs, one at a time, beating after each addition. Add banana, and mix well.

Combine flour, soda, and salt; stir in pecans. Add to creamed mixture, stirring until dry ingredients are moistened.

Spoon batter into a greased and floured 9- x 5- x 3-inch loafpan. Bake at 350° for 50 to 55 minutes or until a wooden pick inserted in center comes out clean. Shield corners with aluminum foil, if necessary. Cool 10 minutes; remove from pan, and cool on a wire rack. Yield: 1 loaf.

Lynne Teal Weeks
Columbus, Georgia

BREAKFAST POTATOES

4 large potatoes (10 ounces each)
1½ quarts water
2 teaspoons salt
1 small green pepper, chopped
1 small sweet red pepper, chopped
1 small sweet yellow pepper, chopped
1 large clove garlic, crushed
¾ cup chopped onion
2 tablespoons butter or margarine, melted
¼ teaspoon pepper
1 teaspoon chopped fresh rosemary
1 teaspoon chopped fresh parsley

Peel potatoes, and cut into 2- x ¼-inch strips. Combine potatoes, water, and salt in a large saucepan or Dutch oven. Bring to a boil; reduce heat, and simmer, uncovered, 4 to 6 minutes or until crisp-tender. Drain well, and keep warm.

Sauté chopped peppers, garlic, and onion in butter until tender. Add onion mixture, pepper, rosemary, and parsley to potatoes; toss gently. Yield: 8 servings.
Chip Schwab
Valle Crucis, North Carolina

Rethinking The Vegetable Plate

We think you'll like this break from tradition. It's the vegetable plate gone upscale, including soup and muffins with a surprise on the inside.

This balanced combination of vegetable dishes provides the necessary dietary protein even without a meat, so it's just right when you have a craving for fresh vegetables.

CREAM OF CARROT SOUP

2 pounds carrots, thinly sliced
1¼ cups chopped onion
1 cup sliced celery
¼ cup butter or margarine, melted
3⅓ cups chicken broth
⅔ cup half-and-half

Sauté carrots, onion, and celery in butter in a Dutch oven 10 minutes. Add broth; bring to a boil. Cover, reduce heat, and simmer 20 minutes. Remove from heat; cool 10 minutes.

Place half of mixture in container of an electric blender; blend until smooth. Repeat with remaining mixture. Return to Dutch oven. Stir in half-and-half, and cook just until soup is thoroughly heated (do not boil). Yield: 7 cups.
Gwen Louer
Roswell, Georgia

PASTA WITH PEPPERS AND BROCCOLI

1 (7.5-ounce) jar roasted peppers, drained and cut into strips
⅔ cup pine nuts
½ cup olive oil
½ cup chopped fresh parsley
1 bunch fresh broccoli
1 (12-ounce) package small shell pasta
1 cup freshly grated Parmesan cheese
⅛ teaspoon pepper
⅛ teaspoon ground red pepper

Combine first 4 ingredients in a skillet; cook over medium heat until nuts are golden brown, stirring often.

Trim off large leaves of broccoli, and remove tough ends of lower stalks. Wash broccoli thoroughly, and cut into flowerets. Set aside.

Cook pasta according to package directions, adding broccoli the last 2 minutes; drain. Add roasted pepper mixture, cheese, and remaining ingredients. Toss and serve immediately. Yield: 6 servings.
La Juan Coward
Jasper, Texas

CHEESE-STUFFED TOMATOES

3 large tomatoes
2 cups small-curd cottage cheese
3 tablespoons commercial blue cheese salad dressing
3 tablespoons chopped green onions
3 tablespoons finely chopped celery
Sliced green onions

Cut each tomato in half; scoop out tomato pulp, reserving for other uses. Combine cottage cheese and next 3 ingredients; spoon into each tomato. Sprinkle with sliced green onions. Yield: 6 servings.
Margaret Eder
Baltimore, Maryland

SQUASH MUFFINS

2 cups all-purpose flour
1 tablespoon baking powder
¼ teaspoon salt
2 tablespoons sugar
⅔ cup grated yellow squash
1 egg, beaten
¾ cup milk
2 tablespoons vegetable oil

Combine flour, baking powder, salt, sugar, and squash in large bowl; make a well in center of mixture. Combine egg, milk, and oil; add to dry ingredients, stirring just until moistened.

Spoon batter into lightly greased muffin pans, filling two-thirds full. Bake at 350° for 20 to 25 minutes. Remove muffins from pans immediately. Yield: 1 dozen.
Betty Norwood
Gainesville, Texas

Brunches & Lunches

ON THE LIGHT SIDE

Slimming Lunch Ideas

Planning to have a few friends over for lunch? Chances are they're just as concerned about getting into shape for summer as you are. So make the menu light and healthy. Choose from these three easy entrées.

BEEF FAJITA SALAD

1 pound top round steak
⅓ cup lime juice
3 cloves garlic, minced
½ teaspoon ground cumin
½ teaspoon pepper
6 cups mixed salad greens
2 medium tomatoes, cut into wedges
½ cup sliced red onion, separated into rings
1 cup picante sauce
¼ cup plain low-fat yogurt

Trim fat from steak. Place steak in a zip-top heavy-duty plastic bag; add lime juice and next 3 ingredients to bag, and seal securely. Marinate in refrigerator 6 to 8 hours.

Remove steak from bag, and discard marinade. Grill steak over medium coals 2 to 3 minutes on each side or to desired degree of doneness. Cut steak diagonally across grain into thin slices.

Arrange equal amounts of salad greens, steak, tomato, and onion on serving plates. Serve each salad with

¼ cup picante sauce and 1 tablespoon yogurt. Yield: 4 servings (223 calories per salad).

□ 31 grams protein, 6.1 grams fat, 11.2 grams carbohydrate, 74 milligrams cholesterol, 77 milligrams sodium, and 67 milligrams calcium.

GRILLED CHICKEN WITH TABBOULEH SALAD

6 (4-ounce) skinned, boned chicken breast halves
¼ cup commercial oil-free Italian salad dressing
Tabbouleh Salad

Place chicken in a shallow dish. Pour salad dressing over chicken; cover and chill at least 4 hours. Grill chicken, covered, over medium coals 8 to 10 minutes on each side. Serve with Tabbouleh Salad. Yield: 6 servings (296 calories per chicken breast with ¾-cup Tabbouleh Salad).

□ 30.5 grams protein, 5.5 grams fat, 28.8 grams carbohydrate, 70 milligrams cholesterol, 180 milligrams sodium, and 40 milligrams calcium.

Tabbouleh Salad

1 cup ready-to-serve, no-salt-added chicken broth
¼ cup water
1 cup couscous, uncooked
1¼ cups chopped tomato
½ cup sliced green onions
½ cup chopped fresh parsley
¼ cup chopped fresh mint
3 tablespoons lemon juice
1 tablespoon vegetable oil
6 romaine lettuce leaves

Combine chicken broth and water in a medium saucepan; bring to a boil. Add

couscous; cover and remove from heat. Let stand 5 minutes. Uncover and cool.

Combine couscous, tomato, and next 5 ingredients. Cover and chill several hours. Serve on romaine leaves. Yield: 4½ cups (154 calories per ¾-cup serving).

□ 4.8 grams protein, 2.6 grams fat, 27.6 grams carbohydrate, 0 milligrams cholesterol, 11 milligrams sodium, and 26 milligrams calcium.

Lisa Grable Wallace
Raleigh, North Carolina

SCALLOPS IN VEGETABLE NESTS

2 cups sliced zucchini
1½ cups mushrooms, halved
1 pound sea scallops, halved
¼ cup reduced-calorie margarine, melted
1 tablespoon minced fresh parsley
¼ teaspoon salt
¼ teaspoon dried whole dillweed
Dash of pepper
3 tablespoons lemon juice

Cover zucchini with boiling water; let stand 5 minutes. Drain. Place zucchini in 4 individual ovenproof baking dishes; add mushrooms, and top with scallops.

Combine margarine and remaining ingredients; spoon equal amounts over each dish. Cover with aluminum foil. Bake at 350° for 30 minutes or until done. Yield: 4 servings (179 calories per serving).

□ 20.4 grams protein, 8.3 grams fat, 6.9 grams carbohydrate, 37 milligrams cholesterol, 443 milligrams sodium, and 43 milligrams calcium.

Micki Bowman
Martinez, Georgia

A Christening Brunch

Like a wedding, a baby's christening is usually an event long dreamed about by the parents and one that should be remembered as one of life's most special days. You can make a fond memory for family and close friends by hosting a brunch after the baptism.

This menu for eight from Barbara Carson of Hollywood, Florida, will serve as an intimate meal for parents and godparents, or it can be doubled or tripled to handle other friends and relatives. Add a special touch to the table by borrowing silver baby accessories or christening photographs from past generations. You might want to give the child a keepsake gift along the same lines and think of the day years from now when it, too, will be part of a future generation's christening day.

Champagne With Orange Juice
Artichoke Quiche
Swiss-and-Cheddar Baked Grits
Commercial croissants
Strawberry Butter
Fresh fruit platter
Coffee   Tea

CHAMPAGNE WITH ORANGE JUICE

5 cups champagne, chilled
5 cups orange juice, chilled
Fresh strawberries

Combine champagne and orange juice. Place a strawberry on rim of each glass; pour in champagne mixture. Yield: 2½ quarts.

ARTICHOKE QUICHE

1½ tablespoons olive oil
1 tablespoon butter or margarine
½ cup chopped onion
1 tablespoon diced celery
2 cloves garlic, minced
2 teaspoons chopped fresh parsley
2 (14-ounce) cans artichoke hearts, drained and chopped
1 (4-ounce) can sliced mushrooms, drained
⅓ cup (1.3 ounces) shredded Swiss cheese
1¼ cups milk
4 eggs
⅔ cup biscuit mix
¼ cup grated Parmesan cheese
¼ teaspoon garlic powder
¼ teaspoon pepper
Garnishes: sweet red pepper rings, celery leaves

Heat olive oil and butter in a skillet. Add onion and next 3 ingredients; sauté until tender. Remove from heat; stir in artichokes. Spoon into a greased 10-inch quiche dish. Top with mushrooms; sprinkle with shredded Swiss cheese.

Combine milk, eggs, biscuit mix, Parmesan cheese, garlic powder, and pepper in container of an electric blender; blend 10 seconds or until smooth, stopping to scrape sides, if necessary. Pour over artichoke mixture. Bake at 350° for 30 to 35 minutes or until set. Garnish, if desired. Yield: one 10-inch quiche.

SWISS-AND-CHEDDAR BAKED GRITS

4⅓ cups water
½ teaspoon salt
1¼ cups quick-cooking grits, uncooked
¼ cup butter or margarine
1½ cups (6 ounces) shredded Cheddar cheese, divided
¼ teaspoon salt
¼ teaspoon pepper
3 eggs, beaten
1¼ cups (5 ounces) shredded Swiss cheese

Bring water and ½ teaspoon salt to a boil in a heavy saucepan. Gradually stir in grits; return to a boil. Cover, reduce heat, and simmer, stirring occasionally, 5 minutes or until done.

Remove saucepan from heat; stir in ¼ cup butter, 1¼ cups Cheddar cheese, ¼ teaspoon salt, and pepper. Set mixture aside, and let cool 15 minutes. Stir in beaten eggs.

Pour half of grits into a lightly greased 12- x 8- x 2-inch baking dish; sprinkle Swiss cheese over top. Spoon remaining grits over cheese. Cover and bake at 350° for 1 hour or until set. Uncover and sprinkle remaining ¼ cup Cheddar cheese over top. Bake, uncovered, 5 minutes or until cheese melts. Yield: 8 to 10 servings.

STRAWBERRY BUTTER

½ cup unsalted butter, softened
⅔ cup strawberry preserves

Combine butter and preserves; beat at low speed of an electric mixer 1 minute or until well mixed. Cover and chill. Remove from refrigerator 30 minutes before serving. Serve with croissants. Yield: about 1¼ cups.

Pack A Meal To Go

If you routinely think of fried chicken when you plan a picnic, think again. This menu provides a flavor diversion for picnickers as well as a new look for transporting and setup. And you can even make everything the day before.

We filled containers—some with cork tops and others with hinged ones—with soup, pasta, and peaches, and nestled them into the ice for our short trip.

As a word of caution, galvanized tubs with ice are not intended to substitute as an insulated cooler when you need to keep food cold for an extended time, but it's a great alternative when your picnic is nearby.

Chicken-Pasta Primavera
Watercress-Zucchini Soup
Spiced Peaches
Commercial baguettes
Old-Fashioned Tea Cakes

CHICKEN-PASTA PRIMAVERA

8 ounces vermicelli, uncooked
1½ cups commercial Italian salad
    dressing, divided
3 cups cubed cooked chicken
1 (10-ounce) package frozen snow
    pea pods, thawed
15 fresh mushrooms, sliced
¾ cup pine nuts
⅓ cup chopped fresh basil
¼ cup chopped fresh parsley
¼ teaspoon pepper
12 cherry tomatoes, halved

Cook pasta according to package directions; drain. Rinse with cold water; drain. Combine pasta and ½ cup salad dressing, tossing to coat; cover and chill 3 hours.

Combine chicken, remaining 1 cup salad dressing, snow peas, and remaining ingredients except tomatoes, tossing well; cover and chill 3 hours.

When ready to serve, combine pasta mixture, chicken mixture, and cherry tomatoes, tossing well. Yield: 6 servings.
Linda Tompkins
Birmingham, Alabama

WATERCRESS-ZUCCHINI SOUP

3 leeks, sliced (about 2 pounds)
1 tablespoon butter or margarine
1½ pounds zucchini, peeled and
    sliced
4 cups ready-to-serve chicken broth
1 bunch fresh watercress
⅛ teaspoon pepper
⅓ cup whipping cream

Sauté leeks in butter in a Dutch oven 3 minutes. Stir in zucchini, and sauté 2 minutes. Add broth; bring to a boil, reduce heat, and simmer 4 minutes. Add watercress and pepper; simmer 1 minute.

Spoon one-third of soup mixture into container of an electric blender, and puree; repeat process twice until all mixture is pureed. Stir in whipping cream; chill. Yield: 7⅓ cups.
Valerie Stutsman
Norfolk, Virginia

SPICED PEACHES

2 (29-ounce) cans peach halves,
    undrained
1 teaspoon cornstarch
½ teaspoon ground cinnamon
½ teaspoon whole cloves
¼ teaspoon grated orange rind
⅛ teaspoon ground nutmeg
⅛ teaspoon ground allspice

Drain peaches, reserving syrup. Set peaches aside.

Combine syrup, cornstarch, and remaining ingredients in a small Dutch oven; bring to a boil, stirring constantly. Reduce heat; add peaches, and simmer 1 minute. Let cool 30 minutes; chill. Yield: 6 servings.
Lynette Maginnis
Pearl River, Louisiana

OLD-FASHIONED TEA CAKES

½ cup butter, softened
1 cup sugar
2 eggs
2½ cups all-purpose flour
2 teaspoons baking powder
½ teaspoon ground nutmeg
1 tablespoon milk

Beat butter at medium speed of an electric mixer; gradually add sugar, beating well. Add eggs; beat well. Combine flour, baking powder, and nutmeg. Add to creamed mixture alternately with milk; mix well. Cover and chill 1 hour.

Work with half of dough at a time, and store remainder in refrigerator. Place stockinette cover on rolling pin; flour well. Roll dough to ¼-inch thickness on a lightly floured pastry cloth. Cut with a 2¼-inch round cutter, and carefully place dough rounds on greased cookie sheets.

Bake at 350° for 8 minutes. (Cookies will be pale.) Cool on wire racks. Yield: 3½ dozen. *Imogene Narmore*
Russellville, Alabama

Welcome the season with a spring menu featuring Grilled Flank Steak, Lemon-Carrot Bundles, Refrigerator Yeast Rolls, Garden New Potatoes, and Fruited Mint Tea. (Recipes begin on page 80.) Served alfresco, the meal will be a grand occasion for hostess and guests alike.

For a nutritious one-dish meal, try Black Beans and Rice topped with tomato, green onions, and yogurt; one serving has 12 grams of fiber. (Recipe, page 82.)

Yogurt Crescent Rolls (page 123), which smell wonderful as they bake, go well with just about any menu. And best of all, this "Light Favorite" recipe cuts calories, fat, and cholesterol.

Lump crab is combined with a spicy breadcrumb mixture to make this light version of Crab Cakes (page 122). The perfect accompaniment is Roasted Red Pepper Corn (page 122).

(Clockwise from front) Gazpacho, Dill-Oat Bread, and Date-Filled Cookies provide ready-to-eat treats for a friend in need of home-cooked food. (Recipes begin on page 94.)

Brunches & Lunches

A Taste Of Tex-Mex

Whether you live in Texas or hundreds of miles away, plan your next brunch around the spicy flavors of the Tex-Mex tradition. Chiles and tortillas take to eggs as naturally as a spoonful of grits, and they offer fun as well as a flavorful, colorful variation of the typical morning meal.

TEX-MEX BRUNCH
Huevos Rancheros
or
Brunch Burritos
Breakfast Chorizo
Mexican-Style Potatoes
Fresh fruit
Sopaipillas
Mexican Coffee

HUEVOS RANCHEROS

6 (6-inch) corn tortillas
2 tablespoons vegetable oil
½ cup chopped onion
1 clove garlic, minced
3 large tomatoes, peeled and chopped
1 (4-ounce) can chopped green chiles, undrained
¼ teaspoon salt
6 eggs
½ cup (2 ounces) shredded Cheddar or Monterey Jack cheese

Fry tortillas, one at a time, in hot oil 5 seconds on each side or just until softened. Drain tortillas on paper towels; reserve oil in skillet. Line a 12- x 8- x 2-inch baking dish with tortillas, letting tortillas extend ½ inch up sides of dish. Set baking dish aside.

Sauté onion and garlic in oil in skillet until crisp-tender. Add tomato, chiles, and salt; simmer, uncovered, 10 minutes, stirring occasionally. Pour mixture over tortillas. Make 6 indentations in tomato mixture, and break an egg into each. Cover and bake at 350° for 25 minutes.

Sprinkle with cheese, and bake an additional 2 minutes. Serve immediately. Yield: 6 servings.

Martha T. Leoni
New Bern, North Carolina

BRUNCH BURRITOS

1 green pepper, chopped
⅔ cup chopped onion
2 tablespoons butter or margarine, melted
8 eggs, beaten
1 cup (4 ounces) shredded Monterey Jack or Cheddar cheese
1 (16-ounce) jar picante sauce
6 (8-inch) flour tortillas
Sour cream (optional)

Sauté green pepper and onion in butter in a large nonstick skillet until tender. Combine eggs and cheese; add to skillet. Cook over low heat, stirring gently, until eggs are set.

Heat picante sauce in a small skillet until warm. Dip each tortilla in picante sauce. Spoon about ½ cup egg mixture into center of each tortilla. Roll tortilla up, and place seam side down in a lightly greased 13- x 9- x 2-inch baking dish. Top with remaining picante sauce. Cover and bake at 350° for 10 minutes or until burritos are hot. Serve with sour cream, if desired. Yield: 6 servings.

Mary Jane Wilson
Bovina, Texas

BREAKFAST CHORIZO

1 pound mild bulk pork sausage
1½ tablespoons chili powder
1 clove garlic, minced
Dash of ground cumin
Dash of ground oregano
Garnish: fresh parsley sprigs

Combine first 5 ingredients, mixing well. Shape sausage mixture into patties. Cook in a skillet over medium heat until browned, turning once. Drain well. Garnish, if desired. Yield: 6 to 8 patties.

Note: To prepare chorizo ahead of time, cook patties until browned; drain. Cover and refrigerate up to two days. Place sausage patties on a baking sheet, and bake at 300° for 10 minutes or until hot.

MEXICAN-STYLE POTATOES

6 medium unpeeled potatoes, boiled
  and chilled
4 slices bacon
¾ teaspoon salt
1½ teaspoons chili powder
2 tablespoons chopped fresh parsley
  or 2 teaspoons parsley flakes

Cut potatoes into ¼-inch slices, and
set aside.

Cook bacon in skillet until crisp; remove bacon, reserving 2 tablespoons
drippings in skillet. Crumble bacon,
and set aside. Add salt and chili powder to skillet, stirring well. Add potatoes to skillet; gently stir to coat with
seasoning.

Spoon potatoes into a lightly
greased 9-inch square baking dish.
Sprinkle with bacon and parsley;
cover and bake at 350° for 25 minutes
or until thoroughly heated. Yield: 6
servings.
Evelyn Appelbee
Henderson, Texas

SOPAIPILLAS

1 package dry yeast
1½ cups warm water (105° to 115°)
1 tablespoon shortening, melted
1 tablespoon sugar
4 cups all-purpose flour
1 teaspoon salt
Vegetable oil
Sifted powdered sugar
Honey (optional)

Dissolve yeast in warm water in a
large mixing bowl; let stand 5 minutes. Stir in 1 tablespoon shortening
and sugar. Combine flour and salt; add
to yeast mixture, stirring well.

Turn dough out onto a lightly
floured surface, and knead until
smooth and elastic (about 2 minutes).

Place in a well-greased bowl, turning
to grease top. Cover and let rise in a
warm place (85°), free from drafts, 1
hour or until doubled in bulk. Punch
dough down; roll dough to ¼-inch
thickness. Cut into 2½-inch squares.

Pour oil to a depth of 3 inches into a
Dutch oven; heat to 375°. Fry a few
sopaipillas at a time in hot oil, lightly
pressing down with the back of a fork
until dough starts to puff. Release
pressure, and continue frying until
golden brown, turning once; drain.

Sprinkle with powdered sugar, and,
if desired, serve with honey. Yield:
2 dozen.
Judy Newton
Allen, Texas

MEXICAN COFFEE

1 quart milk
1 teaspoon ground cinnamon
1 teaspoon vanilla extract
⅔ cup instant cocoa mix
8 cups boiling water
⅓ cup instant coffee granules
Whipped cream
Garnish: cinnamon sticks

Combine first 3 ingredients in a Dutch
oven; cook over medium heat until
thoroughly heated. Stir in instant cocoa mix.

Combine boiling water and coffee
granules; stir into milk mixture. Serve
with a dollop of whipped cream; garnish, if desired. Yield: 3 quarts.
Dorothy D. Warner
Whispering Pines, North Carolina

Planning a Brunch

Most hostesses enjoy giving
brunches because a brunch is more
relaxed than a formal dinner, and
guests find morning a good time
to attend a party. Brunch usually takes place between 10 a.m.
and 1 p.m., so there's time to
tend to last-minute details before
guests arrive.

The secret to a successful
brunch is planning ahead. By doing as much in advance as possible, you will have more time to
have fun with your guests. Here
are some tips to make it run
smoothly.

■ Brunch menus allow for lots of
flexibility. This is the ideal time
to be creative and add a surprise
or two to the menu. You might
consider serving anything from
eggs to seafood.

■ Decide what type of brunch
you are going to have. Consider
the occasion and your resources,
such as space, time, budget, and
talents.

■ Select a theme; this helps
when you're planning the menu
and decorations.

■ Plan the menu well in advance,
and carefully select the wine,
champagne, or other beverages.

■ Use recipes you have prepared
before that can be assembled
ahead of time.

■ Make a list of all jobs and
errands that need to be done—
clean house, polish silver, set
table, shop, and cook—and
delegate what you can.

It's Time For Sweet Onions

As spring approaches, many of the South's cooks start eyeing roadside markets and produce counters for sweet onions. Their mild, sweet flavor makes them a great choice for baking, grilling, or eating raw.

Georgia and Texas produce the largest amount of sweet onions in the South. Vidalia Sweets are grown in a select area of southeast Georgia and are available fresh only from approximately May to July. The Rio Grande is home to Texas SpringSweets. One of the best known SpringSweet types is the 1015, which actually gets its name from the planting date of the original strain of onion, the 15th of October. The 1015s are harvested during the months of April and May.

To store sweet onions for year-round enjoyment, arrange them in a single layer on a wire rack or screen. Then place in a cool, dry place with good air circulation. Onions may also be stored in legs of pantyhose by tying a knot between each onion.

ONION RELISH

2 pounds large sweet onions, chopped
2 stalks celery, sliced
1 sweet red pepper, chopped
1 tablespoon butter or margarine, melted
¾ cup cider vinegar
¼ cup water
2 tablespoons brown sugar
1 teaspoon celery seeds
¼ teaspoon salt

Sauté onion, celery, and red pepper in butter in a small Dutch oven 15 minutes or until tender. Add vinegar and remaining ingredients. Bring to a boil; reduce heat, and simmer, uncovered, 20 minutes. Store in refrigerator. Serve chilled or at room temperature. Yield: 1 quart. *Betty Sue Adams*
Fort Payne, Alabama

STUFFED SWEET ONIONS

4 (½-pound) sweet onions
1 cup frozen English peas, thawed
⅔ cup sliced fresh mushrooms
⅛ teaspoon dried whole thyme, crushed
Dash of pepper
2 tablespoons butter or margarine
¼ cup boiling water
½ teaspoon chicken-flavored bouillon granules

Cut a slice from top of each onion, and scoop out centers, leaving ¼-inch-thick shells. Reserve centers for other uses. Place shells in a lightly greased 8-inch square baking dish.

Combine peas, mushrooms, thyme, and pepper; spoon evenly into onions, and dot with butter. Combine water and bouillon granules; pour over stuffed onions. Cover tightly with heavy-duty plastic wrap; fold back a small corner of wrap to allow steam to escape. Microwave at HIGH 7 to 9 minutes, giving dish a half-turn after 4 minutes. Let stand 3 minutes. Yield: 4 servings. *Mrs. Harland J. Stone*
Ocala, Florida

BAKED SWEET ONIONS

4 pounds large sweet onions
¼ cup butter or margarine, melted
1 (10¾-ounce) can cream of mushroom soup, undiluted
1 cup half-and-half
¼ teaspoon salt
¼ teaspoon pepper
1 cup (4 ounces) shredded sharp Cheddar cheese
8 (¾-inch-thick) slices French bread
3 tablespoons butter or margarine, melted

Slice onions; cut each slice in half. Sauté onion in ¼ cup butter in a Dutch oven until crisp-tender; spoon into a lightly greased 13- x 9- x 2-inch baking dish. Set aside.

Combine soup, half-and-half, salt, and pepper; pour mixture over onion. Sprinkle cheese evenly over sauce; arrange bread slices on top, and brush with 3 tablespoons melted butter. Bake at 350° for 35 minutes or until golden brown. Yield: 8 servings. *Gwen Louer*
Roswell, Georgia

Tip: *Wash or chop vegetables and open cans before you begin preparing any recipe. It is also a good idea to have most ingredients measured before beginning to cook.*

You're Invited

Step outside and enjoy spring with a menu that's fresh and tempting—and not too hard.

This simple menu serves six and is a perfect choice to allow you time to enjoy your guests. If you prefer, you may even grill the steak ahead of time and serve it cold. The side dishes of carrots and new potatoes can be prepared quickly and easily.

Grilled Flank Steak
Lemon-Carrot Bundles
Garden New Potatoes
Refrigerator Yeast Rolls
Fruited Mint Tea
Fresh strawberries

GRILLED FLANK STEAK
(pictured on page 73)

1 (1½-pound) flank steak
1 cup vegetable oil
½ cup firmly packed brown
   sugar
½ cup soy sauce
¼ cup red wine
1 tablespoon minced garlic
1 tablespoon minced gingerroot or
   1 teaspoon ground ginger

Trim excess fat from steak; score steak on both sides in 1½-inch squares. Place steak in a large shallow dish or zip-top heavy-duty plastic bag.

Combine oil and remaining ingredients, stirring well. Pour over steak. Cover or seal; marinate in refrigerator 8 hours, turning occasionally.

Drain steak, reserving marinade. Grill, covered, over medium (300° to 400°) coals 6 to 8 minutes on each side or to desired degree of doneness, basting twice with marinade. Discard remaining marinade. To serve, slice steak across the grain into thin slices. Yield: 6 servings.

Note: Steak may be grilled ahead of time and served cold.   *Des Keller*
Homewood, Alabama

LEMON-CARROT BUNDLES
(pictured on page 73)

1½ pounds carrots, scraped
6 leek strips
⅓ cup lemon juice
3 tablespoons butter or margarine,
   melted
2 tablespoons sugar
¼ teaspoon salt

Cut carrots into 3-inch julienne sticks. Arrange carrots on a steaming rack, and place over boiling water; cover and steam 8 to 10 minutes. Remove carrots, and plunge into ice water to stop the cooking process; drain. Separate carrots into 6 bundles.

Place leek strips in boiling water for 1 minute; drain. Carefully tie a leek strip around each carrot bundle, and set aside.

Combine lemon juice and remaining ingredients in a small Dutch oven; bring to a boil. Reduce heat, and simmer 1 minute or until sugar dissolves. Carefully add carrot bundles, and cook over medium heat 3 minutes or until thoroughly heated, spooning lemon mixture over carrots frequently. Yield: 6 servings.

Mrs. Gordon P. Bobbitt
Burleson, Texas

GARDEN NEW POTATOES
(pictured on page 73)

6 slices bacon, cut into ½-inch
   pieces
1½ pounds new potatoes, peeled
   (about 24 potatoes)
12 pearl onions, peeled
¾ cup chicken broth
½ pound fresh mushrooms, sliced
¼ teaspoon salt
¼ teaspoon freshly ground pepper
¼ cup minced fresh parsley

Cook bacon in a large skillet until crisp; remove bacon, reserving 2 tablespoons drippings in skillet. Add potatoes and onions to bacon drippings; cook over high heat until lightly browned. Drain excess bacon drippings. Add chicken broth. Bring to a boil; cover, reduce heat, and simmer 10 minutes or until potatoes are tender. Add mushrooms, and cook, uncovered, over high heat, stirring constantly, until liquid evaporates. Stir in bacon, salt, pepper, and parsley. Yield: 6 servings.

Note: Rather than peeling the entire potato, a small ring may be peeled around the center of the potato.

Caroline W. Kennedy
Newborn, Georgia

REFRIGERATOR YEAST ROLLS
(pictured on page 73)

2 cups milk
½ cup shortening
½ cup sugar
1 package dry yeast
5 cups all-purpose flour,
   divided
½ teaspoon baking powder
½ teaspoon baking soda
1 teaspoon salt

Combine first 3 ingredients in a saucepan; heat until shortening melts. Cool to 105° to 115°. Place yeast in a large bowl; add milk mixture, and let stand 5 minutes. Stir in 3 cups flour. Cover and let stand at room temperature 1½ hours. Add remaining 2 cups flour, baking powder, soda, and salt, stirring well. Cover tightly, and refrigerate 8 hours or up to 5 days.

Punch dough down; shape into 36 (1½-inch) balls. Place dough balls 2 inches apart on lightly greased baking sheets.

Cover and let rise in a warm place (85°), free from drafts, 25 minutes or until dough is doubled in bulk. Bake at 375° for 10 to 12 minutes or until golden. Yield: 3 dozen.

Loretta Vinson
Jonesboro, Arkansas

FRUITED MINT TEA

(pictured on page 73)

3 cups boiling water
4 regular-size tea bags
12 fresh mint sprigs
1 cup sugar
¼ cup lemon juice
1 cup orange juice
5 cups water
Garnishes: fresh mint sprigs,
    orange slices

Pour boiling water over tea bags and 12 mint sprigs; cover and steep 5 minutes. Remove tea bags and mint, squeezing gently. Stir in sugar and next 3 ingredients. Serve over ice. Garnish, if desired. Yield: 2½ quarts.

Alice Byars
Mayfield, Kentucky

Fiber Joins The Cancer Fight

Go ahead. Take that extra helping of vegetables, fresh fruit, or whole-grain bread or cereal; these fiber-rich foods may actually decrease your chances of getting cancer.

Exactly how fiber protects us from cancer is not known, but many cancer researchers believe eating fiber-rich foods may reduce the risk of developing colon and rectal cancers. Some of the scientists suspect that because it is bulky, fiber pushes cancer-causing agents through the digestive tract and out of the body. Still another possibility under consideration these days is that fiber binds or dilutes cancer-producing agents.

The National Cancer Institute recommends boosting your dietary fiber intake to 25 to 35 grams a day—or about twice as much as most of us eat. As with many things, more *isn't* always better. Very large amounts of fiber, 45 grams or more, can interfere with the absorption of important minerals, such as iron and calcium.

There is an added benefit to increasing the amount of fiber in the diet—it can help you lose weight. Fiber takes up room in the stomach and makes you feel full faster. Many high-fiber foods also take longer to chew and force you to eat more slowly, and therefore eat less.

BARLEY AND VEGETABLES

2 (10½-ounce) cans ready-to-serve,
    no-salt-added chicken broth
1 cup quick-cooking barley,
    uncooked
1 cup chopped onion
1 cup chopped green pepper
2½ cups chopped tomato
1 teaspoon dried whole oregano,
    crushed
½ teaspoon salt
¼ teaspoon freshly ground pepper

Bring broth to a boil in a saucepan. Stir in barley, onion, and green pepper; cover, reduce heat, and simmer 10 minutes or until barley is tender, stirring occasionally. Drain. Stir in tomato and remaining ingredients; cook until heated. Yield: 9 servings (99 calories per ½-cup serving).

□ *3.5 grams protein, 0.7 gram fat, 20.1 grams carbohydrate, 4.8 grams fiber, 0 milligrams cholesterol, 139 milligrams sodium, and 20 milligrams calcium.*

Heather Check
Oxford, Alabama

Tip: *Revive the flavor of long-dried herbs by soaking them for 10 minutes in lemon juice.*

How Much Fiber Is In Your Food?

	Serving Size	Fiber (g)		Serving Size	Fiber (g)
Breads and Cereals			**Vegetables**		
Barley, uncooked	⅓ cup	5.0	Artichoke	1 each	1.1
Bulgur wheat, cooked	½ cup	1.5	Beans, green, cooked	½ cup	1.2
Grits, corn, quick	½ cup	0.3	Broccoli, cooked	½ cup	2.0
Hominy, canned	½ cup	2.0	Brussels sprouts, cooked	½ cup	3.4
Oatmeal, cooked	½ cup	1.1	Cabbage, cooked	½ cup	0.8
Oat bran, uncooked	⅓ cup	4.1	Carrots, cooked	½ cup	1.5
Rice, brown, cooked	½ cup	1.7	Okra, cooked	½ cup	0.6
Rice, white, cooked	½ cup	0.5	Potato, with skin, baked	1 medium	3.6
Whole wheat bread	1 slice	2.1	Spinach, cooked	½ cup	2.4
Fruits			Squash, cooked	½ cup	1.4
Apple, raw	1 medium	4.3	Sweet potato, cooked	1 medium	3.4
Applesauce, canned, unsweetened	½ cup	1.8	Tomato, raw	1 medium	1.6
Apricots, dried	½ cup	5.1	**Legumes**		
Banana, raw	1 medium	1.9	Black beans, cooked	½ cup	3.6
Blackberries, raw	½ cup	5.3	Black-eyed peas, cooked	½ cup	1.5
Blueberries, raw	½ cup	2.2	Kidney beans, cooked	½ cup	3.2
Dates, dried	½ cup	7.8	Lentils, cooked	½ cup	4.0
Kiwifruit, raw	1 each	2.4	Navy beans, cooked	½ cup	3.3
Nectarine, raw	1 medium	2.2	Split peas, cooked	½ cup	2.3
Orange, raw	1 medium	3.1	**Nuts and Seeds**		
Peach, raw	1 medium	1.4	Almonds, blanched	¼ cup	2.9
Pear, raw	1 medium	4.3	Cashews, dry roasted	¼ cup	2.1
Prunes, dried	½ cup	5.8	Peanuts, dry roasted	¼ cup	2.9
Raisins, dried	½ cup	3.8	Peanut butter, chunky	¼ cup	4.3
Strawberries, raw	½ cup	1.9	Pecans, raw	¼ cup	1.8

Based on analysis for total dietary fiber by Computrition, Inc.

BROWN RICE PILAF

2 cups ready-to-serve, no-salt-added chicken broth
1 cup brown rice, uncooked
½ cup grated carrot
½ cup finely chopped celery
¼ cup finely sliced green onions
1 clove garlic, minced
½ teaspoon salt
¼ teaspoon red pepper
3 tablespoons slivered almonds, toasted

Bring broth to a boil in a heavy saucepan; stir in rice and remaining ingredients except almonds. Cover, reduce heat, and simmer 25 to 30 minutes or until liquid is absorbed. Stir in almonds. Yield: 8 servings (111 calories per ½-cup serving).

□ *2.7 grams protein, 2 grams fat, 20.1 grams carbohydrate, 1.5 grams fiber, 0 milligrams cholesterol, 159 milligrams sodium, and 20 milligrams calcium.*
Pat Rush Benigno
Gulfport, Mississippi

BLACK BEANS AND RICE
(pictured on page 74)

1¼ cups dried black beans
Vegetable cooking spray
1 cup chopped onion
1 cup chopped green pepper
5 cloves garlic, minced
½ teaspoon salt
½ teaspoon pepper
¼ teaspoon crushed red pepper
1 tablespoon red wine vinegar
3 cups water
1 (6-ounce) can tomato paste
3 cups hot cooked rice (cooked without salt or fat)
½ cup chopped tomato
¼ cup sliced green onions
4 teaspoons plain nonfat yogurt

Sort and wash beans; place in a Dutch oven. Cover with water 2 inches above beans; let soak 8 hours. Drain.

Coat a Dutch oven with cooking spray; place over medium-high heat until hot. Add chopped onion, green pepper, and garlic; sauté until tender. Add beans, salt, and next 4 ingredients, and bring mixture to a boil. Cover, reduce heat, and simmer 1½ hours or until beans are tender, stirring occasionally. Add tomato paste; cook an additional 15 minutes.

Serve over rice. Top each serving with tomato, green onions, and yogurt. Yield: 4 servings (468 calories per 1 cup beans, ¾ cup rice, 2 tablespoons tomato, 1 tablespoon green onions, and 1 teaspoon yogurt).

☐ *19.6 grams protein, 2.1 grams fat, 95.1 grams carbohydrate, 12 grams fiber, 0 milligrams cholesterol, 336 milligrams sodium, and 139 milligrams calcium.*

WILD RICE BULGUR

Olive oil-flavored vegetable cooking
　spray
¾ cup chopped onion
¾ cup chopped celery
2 cloves garlic, minced
3 cups ready-to-serve, no-salt-added
　chicken broth
1 cup bulgur wheat
⅓ cup instant wild rice
½ teaspoon salt

Coat a Dutch oven with cooking spray; place over medium-high heat until hot. Add onion, celery, and garlic; sauté until crisp-tender. Add broth, and bring to a boil. Stir in bulgur wheat, wild rice, and salt; cover, reduce heat, and simmer 25 to 30 minutes. Yield: 8 servings (101 calories per ½-cup serving).

☐ *3.6 grams protein, 0.4 gram fat, 20.8 grams carbohydrate, 4 grams fiber, 0 milligrams cholesterol, 162 milligrams sodium, and 18 milligrams calcium.*
Lynette Walther
East Palatka, Florida

OATMEAL-BRAN MUFFINS

¾ cup morsels of wheat bran cereal
¾ cup regular oats, uncooked
1¼ cups skim milk
1 egg or ¼ cup egg substitute
¼ cup vegetable oil
½ cup raisins
1¼ cups all-purpose flour
1 tablespoon baking powder
½ teaspoon salt
½ cup sugar
Vegetable cooking spray

Combine first 3 ingredients in a bowl; let stand 5 minutes. Stir in egg, oil, and raisins. Combine flour, baking powder, salt, and sugar; make a well in center of mixture. Add bran mixture, stirring just until moistened.

Spoon batter into muffin pans coated with cooking spray, filling three-fourths full. Bake at 400° for 20 to 25 minutes. Yield: 1½ dozen (126 calories per muffin).

☐ *3 grams protein, 4 grams fat, 21.2 grams carbohydrate, 1.8 grams fiber, 12 milligrams cholesterol, 150 milligrams sodium, and 62 milligrams calcium.*
Mary R. Schuessler
North Fort Myers, Florida

CARROT-PINEAPPLE SALAD

1 envelope unflavored gelatin
1 cup water
½ teaspoon grated orange rind
1 (6-ounce) can frozen unsweetened
　orange juice concentrate, thawed
　and undiluted
1 (8-ounce) can unsweetened
　crushed pineapple, undrained
½ cup raisins
1 cup finely grated carrot
Vegetable cooking spray
Lettuce leaves

Sprinkle gelatin over water in a small saucepan; let stand 1 minute. Cook over medium heat until gelatin dissolves, stirring constantly; remove

from heat. Stir in orange rind and orange juice concentrate. Chill until the consistency of unbeaten egg white. Fold in pineapple, raisins, and carrot. Spoon into six ½-cup molds coated with cooking spray. Cover and chill until firm. Unmold onto lettuce-lined plates. Yield: 6 servings (139 calories per ½-cup serving).

☐ *3.1 grams protein, 0.7 gram fat, 32.2 grams carbohydrate, 1.8 grams fiber, 0 milligrams cholesterol, 13 milligrams sodium, and 35 milligrams calcium.*
Mrs. C. E. Atwell
Rotan, Texas

All about Rice

■ Reheat cooked rice in a metal strainer or colander over a pan of steaming water. Cover the strainer with aluminum foil, and steam the rice for 15 minutes.

■ Cooked rice freezes well by itself or combined with other foods that are suitable for freezing. It may be frozen for up to four months. Store cooked rice in the refrigerator for up to 1 week.

■ For a tasty variation, cook rice in a flavorful liquid, such as chicken broth, beef broth, or fruit juice, instead of water.

■ Herbs and spices, such as thyme, parsley, basil, and curry, add extra flavor to rice.

■ Be sure to keep rice and other staples, as well as all dry foods, in their original containers or airtight ones. White rice can be stored in a container almost indefinitely.

Preserves Flavor The Pork

Preserves do more than make a biscuit irresistible. They make particularly good glazes and sauces, especially for pork, which is naturally complemented by the flavor of fruit. Here, our readers use preserves as the base of several glazes and sauces.

Today's pork is much leaner than in previous years, and you'll find an extensive variety of cuts to choose from at the meat counter, some labeled pork and some labeled ham. The leg of pork becomes ham after being cured and seasoned or smoked. The label will specify how the ham has been cured and whether it's cooked or uncooked. Hams labeled "fully cooked" do not require further heating and may be eaten cold. You may cook and glaze these hams, however, for more flavor. Strawberry-Glazed Ham is an example.

It's best to cook fresh roasts and hams that require further cooking to an internal temperature of 160°. For optimal flavor, heat fully cooked hams to 140°. Be careful to check the temperature by inserting a meat thermometer into the meat, being sure not to touch fat or bone.

STRAWBERRY-GLAZED HAM

1 (5- to 7-pound) fully cooked
   ham half
Whole cloves
½ cup strawberry preserves
1 tablespoon lemon juice
⅛ teaspoon ground cinnamon
⅛ teaspoon ground cloves

Remove and discard skin from ham; score fat in a diamond design, and stud with whole cloves.

Combine preserves and remaining ingredients; stir well. Set aside.

Place ham, fat side up, on a rack in a shallow roasting pan. Insert meat thermometer, making sure it does not touch fat or bone. Bake, uncovered, at 325° for 1 hour. Spread strawberry mixture over ham, and continue baking, uncovered, 30 minutes to 1 hour or until thermometer registers 140° (18 to 24 minutes per pound). Yield: 10 to 14 servings.

Note: If fat on ham is trimmed to less than ¼-inch thick, cover ham with aluminum foil for first hour of baking.

Kay Castleman Cooper
Burke, Virginia

ORANGE-GLAZED PORK CHOPS

¼ teaspoon salt
¼ teaspoon pepper
¼ teaspoon paprika
4 (¾-inch-thick) boneless butterfly
   pork chops
1 tablespoon vegetable oil
1 cup orange juice
¼ cup maple-flavored syrup
2 tablespoons orange marmalade

Combine first 3 ingredients; sprinkle on both sides of each pork chop.

Heat oil in a large skillet over medium heat; add chops, and brown on both sides. Add orange juice; cover, reduce heat, and simmer 8 to 10 minutes. Turn chops over; cover and cook an additional 8 to 10 minutes. Drizzle syrup over chops; spread each with orange marmalade. Yield: 4 servings.

Beth Pryor
Salisbury, Maryland

CHERRY-GLAZED PORK ROAST

1 (14-ounce) jar cherry preserves
¼ cup red wine vinegar
3 tablespoons light corn syrup
¼ teaspoon salt
¼ teaspoon ground cinnamon
¼ teaspoon ground nutmeg
¼ teaspoon ground cloves
3 tablespoons slivered almonds,
   toasted
1 (3-pound) boneless pork loin roast
½ teaspoon salt
¼ teaspoon pepper
Garnishes: celery leaves, whole
   almonds

Combine first 7 ingredients in a small saucepan. Bring mixture to a boil; reduce heat, and simmer 2 minutes. Add slivered almonds.

Sprinkle roast with salt and pepper. Place roast, fat side up, on rack in a shallow roasting pan. Bake, uncovered, at 325° for 45 minutes or until browned. Brush with cherry mixture;

turn roast, and brush with cherry mixture. Insert meat thermometer, making sure it does not touch fat. Bake, uncovered, an additional 20 minutes or until thermometer registers 160°, basting frequently with cherry mixture. Let stand 10 to 15 minutes before slicing. Garnish, if desired. Yield: 10 servings.   *Sharron Kay Johnston*
                                          Fort Worth, Texas

Entrées With Sauces

Vegetable sauces add flavor and color to poultry, fish, and cheese dishes. Made from a few simple ingredients, they provide a special touch to a meal.

Take advantage of the abundance of peppers available this time of year with Red or Green Pepper Sauce. Red peppers yield a sauce that's a little sweeter and milder than one that's made with green peppers.

Add zest to plain entrées with creamy Watercress Sauce. When preparing it, loosely pack the watercress leaves in a measuring cup to ensure getting an accurate amount.

WATERCRESS SAUCE

1 cup chicken broth
1½ cups watercress leaves
½ cup sour cream
⅛ teaspoon freshly ground pepper

Bring chicken broth to a boil in a small saucepan; boil until broth is reduced to ½ cup (about 5 minutes). Add watercress, and boil 1 minute. Cool. Spoon mixture into container of an electric blender or food processor. Process until smooth; strain. Return strained mixture to saucepan; stir in sour cream and pepper. Cook, stirring constantly, until thoroughly heated. (Do not boil.) Serve with chicken or fish. Yield: ¾ cup.

BROCCOLI SAUCE

3 cups chopped fresh broccoli
½ cup boiling water
1 chicken-flavored bouillon cube
¼ cup chopped onion
2 tablespoons butter or margarine, melted
2 tablespoons all-purpose flour
¾ cup milk
½ teaspoon dried whole dillweed
½ teaspoon freshly ground pepper

Cook broccoli, covered, in a small amount of boiling water 10 minutes or until tender. Drain. Place broccoli in container of an electric blender or food processor. Combine ½ cup water and bouillon cube; add to broccoli. Process until smooth.

Sauté onion in butter in a saucepan; add flour, stirring until smooth. Cook 1 minute, stirring constantly. Gradually add milk; cook over medium heat, stirring constantly, until thickened and bubbly. Stir in broccoli, dillweed, and pepper; cook until thoroughly heated. Yield: 2 cups.

RED OR GREEN PEPPER SAUCE

2 tablespoons finely chopped onion
1 clove garlic, minced
1 tablespoon olive oil
2 medium-size sweet red or green peppers, chopped
1 cup chicken broth
1 tablespoon minced fresh parsley
½ teaspoon sugar
¼ teaspoon freshly ground pepper

Sauté onion and garlic in oil in a large skillet until tender. Stir in remaining ingredients. Bring to a boil; reduce heat, and simmer, uncovered, 20 minutes. Spoon mixture into container of an electric blender; process until smooth. Return mixture to skillet, and heat thoroughly. Serve with chicken or fish. Yield: 1 cup.

TOMATO BASIL SAUCE

1 clove garlic, minced
1 medium onion, chopped
3 stalks celery, diced
2 tablespoons olive oil
6 large ripe tomatoes, peeled, seeded, and chopped
½ cup minced fresh basil
¾ teaspoon sugar
⅛ teaspoon white pepper
1 teaspoon dried whole oregano
1 tablespoon chopped fresh parsley

Sauté garlic, onion, and celery in oil in a saucepan until crisp-tender. Add tomato, and bring to a boil; cover, reduce heat, and simmer 1 hour.

Spoon mixture into container of an electric blender or food processor; process 30 seconds or until smooth. Return mixture to saucepan; add basil and remaining ingredients. Cover and simmer 30 minutes or until mixture is thickened. Yield: 2¾ cups.

Vegetables Set The Stage

Need a recipe that goes beyond the everyday? These just might fit the bill. Each takes a familiar vegetable—cabbage, carrot, broccoli, or a plump eggplant—and makes it into something special.

FRESH BROCCOLI SOUP

1¾ pounds fresh broccoli
1 large onion, chopped
1 large carrot, scraped and diced
1 stalk celery, chopped
1 cup water
3 tablespoons butter or margarine
3 tablespoons all-purpose flour
2½ cups milk
1½ cups chicken broth
1¼ cups (5 ounces) shredded sharp American cheese
¼ teaspoon salt
½ teaspoon pepper
½ teaspoon Worcestershire sauce
Garnish: carrot curls

Trim off large leaves of broccoli, and remove tough ends of lower stalks. Wash broccoli thoroughly, and chop. Place broccoli in a Dutch oven; add water to a depth of 1 inch. Bring to a boil; cover, reduce heat, and simmer 10 to 12 minutes or until tender. Drain and set aside.

Combine onion, diced carrot, celery, and 1 cup water in a saucepan. Bring to a boil; reduce heat, and simmer 15 minutes or until vegetables are tender. Cool; do not drain. Spoon vegetables and water into container of an electric blender. Process until mixture is smooth.

Melt butter in Dutch oven over low heat; add flour, stirring until smooth. Cook 1 minute, stirring constantly. Gradually add milk; cook over medium heat, stirring constantly, until mixture is thickened and bubbly. Add broccoli, pureed vegetables, broth, and next 4

ingredients. Cook over low heat, stirring occasionally, until cheese melts. Garnish, if desired. Yield: 2 quarts.
Glyna Meredith Gallrein
Anchorage, Kentucky

VEGETARIAN CABBAGE ROLLS

16 cabbage leaves
1 small zucchini, chopped
½ cup chopped onion
1 clove garlic, chopped
1 tablespoon butter or margarine, melted
1 teaspoon dried whole oregano
1 tablespoon parsley flakes
2 tablespoons soy sauce
2 cups cooked brown rice
2 cups (8 ounces) shredded Cheddar cheese
1 (12-ounce) carton low-fat cottage cheese
¼ cup sunflower kernels, toasted
2 (8-ounce) cans tomato sauce
Garnish: toasted sunflower kernels

Cook leaves in boiling salted water 5 to 8 minutes or just until tender; drain and set aside.

Sauté zucchini, onion, and garlic in butter in a large skillet. Add oregano and next 6 ingredients, mixing well. Place equal portions of vegetable mixture in center of each cabbage leaf. Fold 2 opposite ends over, and place rolls, seam side down, in a lightly greased 13- x 9- x 2-inch baking dish. Pour tomato sauce over cabbage rolls.

Cover and bake at 350° for 30 minutes. Uncover and bake an additional 30 minutes. Garnish, if desired. Yield: 8 servings.
Pam Thelen
Georgetown, Kentucky

Tip: *When buying garlic, select firm, plump bulbs that have dry, unbroken skins. Store in a cool, dry place that is well ventilated. The flavor will remain sharp up to four months.*

EGGPLANT CHILES RELLENOS

5 cups water
1 eggplant (about 1 pound), peeled and chopped
1 medium onion, chopped
2 eggs, slightly beaten
2½ tablespoons chopped canned green chiles
Dash of hot sauce
¾ cup (3 ounces) shredded extra-sharp Cheddar cheese
¾ cup (3 ounces) shredded Monterey Jack cheese
⅓ cup cracker crumbs
1 tablespoon butter or margarine, melted
Commercial picante sauce (optional)

Bring water to a boil in a Dutch oven; add eggplant and onion, and cook 10 minutes or until vegetables are tender. Drain well.

Combine eggs, green chiles, hot sauce, Cheddar cheese, and Monterey Jack cheese in a mixing bowl; stir well. Add eggplant mixture; beat at medium speed of an electric mixer until mixture is smooth.

Spoon eggplant mixture into a greased 1-quart casserole. Combine cracker crumbs and butter; sprinkle evenly over casserole. Bake at 375° for 45 minutes or until a knife inserted in center comes out clean. Serve casserole with picante sauce, if desired. Yield: 4 servings.
Merle R. Downs
Tryon, North Carolina

Taste Of The Southwest

The roots of Southwestern cooking reach from the heart of Texas to the desert plain of New Mexico. In the 1980s several young chefs began promoting a cuisine symbolic of the region—one that used ingredients indigenous to their Texas homeland. Our readers experiment with the same enthusiasm as those Southwestern chefs. Now sample their recipes and enjoy the distinctive taste of the Southwestern cuisine.

MEXICAN STUFFED SHELLS

21 jumbo pasta shells, uncooked
1 (16-ounce) jar picante sauce
1 (8-ounce) can tomato sauce
½ cup water
1 pound ground beef
1 (4-ounce) can chopped green chiles, drained
1 cup (4 ounces) shredded Monterey Jack cheese, divided
1 (2.8-ounce) can French fried onions, divided

Cook pasta shells according to package directions; drain.

Combine picante sauce, tomato sauce, and water. Set aside.

Cook ground beef over medium heat until meat is browned, stirring to crumble; drain. Add ½ cup picante mixture, green chiles, ½ cup cheese, and ½ can French fried onions. Fill each shell with about 2 tablespoons ground beef mixture.

Spoon about half of remaining picante mixture into a 13- x 9- x 2-inch dish. Place filled shells on sauce; top with remaining picante mixture. Cover and bake at 350° for 30 minutes. Uncover; sprinkle with remaining cheese and French fried onions. Bake an additional 5 minutes or until cheese melts. Yield: 4 servings. *Mary Baker Meeker, Oklahoma*

PICADILLO (SPANISH HASH)

2 pounds ground beef
2 medium onions, chopped
1 clove garlic, minced
2 apples, peeled, cored, and chopped
3 tomatoes, peeled, seeded, and chopped
3 canned jalapeños, seeded and sliced
½ cup raisins
¼ cup pimiento-stuffed olives, halved
¼ teaspoon salt
¼ teaspoon pepper
⅛ teaspoon ground cloves
⅛ teaspoon ground cinnamon
¼ cup slivered almonds, toasted

Combine first 3 ingredients in a Dutch oven; cook until browned, stirring to crumble. Drain. Add apple and next 8 ingredients. Bring to a boil; reduce heat, and simmer, uncovered, about 20 minutes, stirring occasionally.

Spoon mixture into a serving dish, and sprinkle with almonds. Serve on tortillas or in taco shells; top with salsa and shredded Cheddar cheese. Yield: 8 servings. *Betty L. Beske Arlington, Virginia*

GRILLED LIME-JALAPEÑO CHICKEN

4 chicken breast halves, skinned and boned
¼ cup vegetable oil
½ cup lime or lemon juice
1½ teaspoons garlic powder
1 tablespoon minced jalapeño pepper
¼ teaspoon salt
⅛ teaspoon pepper
Garnishes: lime wedges, jalapeño peppers, cherry tomatoes, fresh parsley sprigs

Place each chicken breast half between 2 sheets of wax paper; flatten to ¼-inch thickness, using a meat mallet or rolling pin.

Combine oil and next 3 ingredients in a zip-top heavy-duty plastic bag. Add chicken and marinate 1 hour; remove chicken from marinade, reserving marinade. Sprinkle chicken with salt and pepper. Grill chicken, covered, over medium-hot (300° to 400°) coals 7 minutes on each side, basting twice with marinade. Garnish, if desired. Yield: 4 servings.
Sharon Giordano, McLean, Virginia

Fancy The Flavor Of Tacos

Everywhere you turn these days, you see familiar taco flavorings and ingredients teamed with many foods other than the popular crisp shells. And our readers have jumped on the bandwagon, conjuring up all sorts of options in their kitchens. Here's a sample of their creations.

Instead of calling for traditional shells, the recipe for Soft Beef Tacos uses fresh flour tortillas. This makes them a little easier to eat and better for you than tacos served in fried shells. This one is folded in on one end to help enclose the filling.

There are other taco variations. In Greenville, Texas, Cindy Quebe turns tacos into a casserole called Deep-Dish Taco Squares, while Sandra Kondora of Harrison, Arkansas, stirs taco sauce into bread dough to make Taco Biscuit Bites.

SOFT BEEF TACOS

1 pound ground beef
1 small onion, minced
2 cloves garlic, minced
½ green pepper, chopped
1 jalapeño pepper, seeded and minced
1 cup water
1 teaspoon ground cumin
1 teaspoon chili powder
½ teaspoon dried whole oregano
¼ teaspoon salt
⅛ teaspoon pepper
8 (7-inch) flour tortillas
2 cups shredded lettuce
2 tomatoes, chopped
1 cup (4 ounces) shredded Cheddar cheese
1 (8-ounce) carton commercial guacamole
Commercial taco or picante sauce

Cook first 5 ingredients in a large skillet until meat is browned, stirring to crumble; drain well. Stir in water, cumin, chili powder, oregano, salt, and pepper; cover and simmer over low heat 30 minutes, stirring occasionally. Uncover and cook 8 to 10 minutes.

Wrap tortillas securely in aluminum foil; bake at 350° for 10 minutes or until thoroughly heated. Spoon about one-eighth of meat mixture lengthwise down center of a tortilla. Top with about one-eighth each of lettuce, tomato, cheese, guacamole, and desired amount of taco sauce. Fold bottom third of tortilla over filling. Fold sides of tortilla in toward center, leaving top open. Secure with wooden picks, if necessary. Repeat with remaining tortillas and fillings. Serve with additional taco sauce, if desired. Yield: 8 tacos.

Sally Murphy
Grapevine, Texas

DEEP-DISH TACO SQUARES

2 cups biscuit mix
½ cup cold water
1 pound ground beef
1 green pepper, chopped
2 tablespoons chopped onion
1 (8-ounce) can tomato sauce
1 (8-ounce) carton sour cream
1 cup (4 ounces) shredded sharp Cheddar cheese
⅓ cup mayonnaise or salad dressing
Paprika

Combine biscuit mix and water, stirring with a fork until blended. Press mixture in bottom of a lightly greased 12- x 8- x 2-inch baking dish. Bake at 375° for 9 minutes.

Cook ground beef, green pepper, and onion in a large skillet until meat is browned, stirring to crumble meat; drain well. Stir in tomato sauce; spoon over crust.

Combine sour cream, cheese, and mayonnaise in a medium bowl; spoon over meat mixture. Sprinkle top evenly with paprika. Bake at 375°, uncovered, for 25 minutes or until casserole is lightly browned. Cut into squares to serve. Yield: 6 servings.

Cindy Quebe
Greenville, Texas

TACO BISCUIT BITES

¼ cup commercial taco sauce
¼ cup milk
½ teaspoon dried onion flakes
2 cups biscuit mix
2 teaspoons butter or margarine, melted
2 tablespoons grated Parmesan cheese

Combine first 3 ingredients in a large bowl; let stand 5 minutes. Add biscuit mix, stirring just until dry ingredients are moistened. Turn dough out onto a lightly floured surface, and knead 4 or 5 times.

Roll dough to ½-inch thickness; cut with a 1½-inch biscuit cutter. Place on a lightly greased baking sheet. Brush tops with butter, and sprinkle with Parmesan cheese. Bake at 450° for 8 to 10 minutes or until biscuits are lightly browned. Serve immediately. Yield: about 1½ dozen.

Note: Dough may be chilled 2 hours before baking, if desired.

Sandra Kondora
Harrison, Arkansas

Crawfish: Beyond The Bayou

Sample these tasty gems of the bayou country in your favorite recipes from other lands. Here, our readers try them in lasagna and stroganoff, traditional favorites from Italian and German cuisines.

If you've never eaten crawfish before, you may not be exactly sure what you're about to consume. Crawfish tails are extracted from the tail of a red crustacean that looks like a miniature lobster. In coastal Mississippi and Louisiana, crawfish are plentiful and available fresh during the spring months. About 4 pounds of crawfish are peeled to get 1 pound of tails; that's why the frozen version is so handy, especially for landlocked folks. If you can't get crawfish, shrimp is a fairly close substitute.

Frozen, packaged crawfish tails come peeled, their plump meat ready to be used immediately. Their prices vary depending on the time of year, but you can expect to pay $8 to $12 per pound.

You can use either fresh or frozen crawfish tails in these recipes; let frozen tails thaw before using them. Most frozen crawfish have been cooked for a short period of time to extend the freezer life.

CRAWFISH LASAGNA

1 cup chopped onion
¾ cup chopped celery
¾ cup chopped green pepper
⅓ cup butter or margarine, melted
3 cloves garlic, minced
1 teaspoon dried whole basil
1 teaspoon dried whole oregano
¼ teaspoon salt
¼ teaspoon pepper
Dash of hot sauce
½ teaspoon liquid crab boil
⅓ cup all-purpose flour
3 cups milk
1 cup sour cream
4 cups (16 ounces) shredded Monterey Jack cheese, divided
2 pounds fresh or frozen peeled crawfish tails
⅔ cup chopped green onions
⅓ cup chopped fresh parsley
1 teaspoon dried whole oregano
1 teaspoon dried whole basil
½ teaspoon salt
½ teaspoon pepper
Dash of hot sauce
9 lasagna noodles
½ teaspoon liquid crab boil
1 tablespoon vegetable oil

Sauté first 3 ingredients in butter in a Dutch oven until tender. Add garlic and next 6 ingredients. Add flour, stirring until smooth. Cook 1 minute, stirring constantly. Gradually add milk; cook over medium heat, stirring constantly, until mixture is thickened and bubbly. Whisk in sour cream and 3 cups cheese, stirring until smooth.

Combine crawfish tails and green onions in a skillet, and cook until thoroughly heated; drain. Stir into white sauce; add parsley and next 5 ingredients. Simmer over low heat 5 to 6 minutes.

Cook lasagna noodles according to package directions, adding ½ teaspoon crab boil and oil to water; drain.

Place half of noodles in a lightly greased 13- x 9- x 2-inch baking dish. Layer half of sauce over noodles; repeat layers.

Bake at 350° for 40 minutes. Sprinkle with remaining 1 cup cheese, and bake an additional 5 minutes. Let lasagna stand 10 minutes before serving. Yield: 10 to 12 servings. *Fran Ginn*
Columbia, Mississippi

CRAWFISH STROGANOFF

1 medium onion, chopped
1 medium-size green pepper, chopped
1 tablespoon vegetable oil
¼ cup butter or margarine
⅓ cup all-purpose flour
⅔ cup water
1 pound fresh or frozen peeled crawfish tails
½ teaspoon salt
½ teaspoon pepper
1 (8-ounce) carton sour cream
Hot cooked noodles

Sauté onion and green pepper in hot oil in a large skillet. Remove from skillet, and set aside.

Melt butter in skillet over low heat; add flour, stirring until smooth. Cook 1 minute, stirring constantly. Gradually add water, stirring constantly. Add sautéed vegetables, crawfish, salt, and pepper; cover and simmer 30 minutes. Remove from heat, and stir in sour cream. Cook over medium heat until thoroughly heated. (Do not boil.) Serve over hot cooked noodles. Yield: 4 servings. *Anne Trapp*
Bay City, Texas

Down-Home Dinner Duo

Like salt and pepper, cream and sugar, and bacon and eggs, these two recipes seem to go together naturally. This rich rendition of creamed chicken, with the convenience of frozen vegetables, proved to be a perfect partner to the waffles.

CREAMED CHICKEN AND VEGETABLES

1 (10-ounce) package frozen mixed vegetables or frozen peas and carrots
¼ cup chopped celery
2 teaspoons finely chopped onion
3 tablespoons butter or margarine, melted
3 tablespoons all-purpose flour
1½ cups milk
1½ cups whipping cream
⅓ cup (1.3 ounces) shredded Cheddar cheese
1 teaspoon salt
½ teaspoon white pepper
¼ teaspoon red pepper
3 cups chopped cooked chicken
1 (2-ounce) jar diced pimiento, drained
Garnishes: shredded Cheddar cheese, paprika

Cook mixed vegetables according to package directions, omitting salt; drain and set aside.

Sauté celery and onion in butter until tender. Add flour, stirring until smooth. Cook 1 minute, stirring constantly. Gradually add milk and whipping cream; cook over medium heat, stirring constantly, until mixture is thickened and bubbly. Add ⅓ cup cheese, salt, and peppers; stir until cheese melts. Stir in chicken, diced pimiento, and cooked vegetables; cook until thoroughly heated. Serve over Cornbread Waffles, and garnish, if desired. Yield: 6 servings.

Gayle Wallace
Kingwood, Texas

CORNBREAD WAFFLES

1½ cups cornmeal
1½ cups all-purpose flour
2 tablespoons baking powder
1½ teaspoons salt
¼ cup sugar
3 eggs, beaten
1½ cups milk
¼ cup butter or margarine, melted

Combine first 5 ingredients in a medium bowl. Combine eggs, milk, and butter; add to flour mixture, stirring briskly until blended. Bake in preheated, oiled waffle iron. Cut waffles to make twelve 4-inch squares. Yield: three 8-inch waffles.

Beryl Wyatt
Columbia, Missouri

Onion Flavors This Bread

If in the past you haven't been confident enough in your bread-baking skills to make French bread yourself, maybe it's time to give this technique a try.

Making French Onion Bread is as easy as baking any basic yeast bread—just sprinkle a packet of dry onion soup mix into the yeast mixture, and follow the recipe instructions.

This recipe follows the rapid-mix method for making bread where the yeast is mixed with some of the dry ingredients before adding the liquid. This method eliminates the need to dissolve the yeast. When using this method, heat the liquid ingredient to 120° to 130°—a little hotter than for recipes that dissolve the yeast.

The ideal rising temperature for yeast bread is 85°. A gas oven with a pilot light or an electric oven with either the light on or with a large pan of hot water should provide this temperature and a draft-free spot.

FRENCH ONION BREAD

5 to 5½ cups all-purpose flour, divided
¼ cup dry onion soup mix
3 tablespoons sugar
2 teaspoons salt
2 packages dry yeast
2 tablespoons shortening
2 cups warm water (120° to 130°)
1 egg white
1 tablespoon water

Combine 2 cups flour, soup mix, sugar, salt, and yeast in a large mixing bowl; stir well. Add shortening and 2 cups warm water. Beat at medium speed of an electric mixer 3 minutes. Gradually stir in enough remaining flour to make a stiff dough.

Turn dough out onto a floured surface, and knead until smooth and elastic (about 3 minutes). Place in a well-greased bowl, turning to grease top. Cover and let rise in a warm place (85°), free from drafts, 1 hour or until doubled in bulk.

Punch dough down; turn out onto a lightly floured surface, and knead lightly 4 or 5 times. Divide dough in half. Roll each portion of dough to a 14- x 5-inch rectangle. Roll up dough, starting at long side, pressing firmly to eliminate air pockets; pinch seam and ends to seal. Place dough, seam side down, on a greased baking sheet.

Cover and let rise in a warm place, free from drafts, 45 minutes or until doubled in bulk. Make 3 or 4 diagonal slits about ½-inch deep diagonally across loaves, using a sharp knife. Combine egg white and 1 tablespoon water, beating until blended; brush gently over loaves. Bake at 375° for 30 to 35 minutes or until loaves sound hollow when tapped. Yield: 2 loaves.

Sandy Pichon
Slidell, Louisiana

Tip: *To know when yeast is doubled in bulk, press dough flat in a bowl, mark level on outside of bowl, and mark a measure on outside of bowl that is double the first.*

Spirits Enhance The Fruit

To truly enjoy the essence of sweet, juicy fruits, adorn them simply. These recipes do so by adding a splash of liquor, which accents their natural goodness.

Jan Wier adds cognac to Elegant Fruit for a refreshing dessert. A delicious mixture of honey, lemon juice, and kirsch sweetens Melon Balls and Cherries in Kirsch. Sauterne seasons Marinated Peaches.

If you like Bananas Foster, you'll love Nancy Monroe's version. Orange-Glazed Bananas Foster is baked—not cooked on top of the range. Orange juice, Grand Marnier, and a topping of brown sugar and walnuts lend rich flavor to bananas that are served over ice cream.

ORANGE-GLAZED BANANAS FOSTER

4 bananas, split and quartered
¾ cup orange juice
¼ cup Grand Marnier or other orange-flavored liqueur
2 tablespoons butter or margarine
⅓ cup chopped walnuts
⅓ cup firmly packed brown sugar
Vanilla ice cream

Arrange bananas in an 8-inch square baking dish. Combine orange juice and liqueur; pour over bananas, and dot with butter. Bake at 400° for 10 minutes, basting occasionally. Combine walnuts and brown sugar; sprinkle over bananas and bake an additional 5 minutes. Serve immediately over ice cream. Yield: 8 servings.
Nancy Monroe
Salisbury, North Carolina

ELEGANT FRUIT

1 fresh pineapple, peeled, cored, and cubed
3 cups sliced fresh peaches
3 cups seedless red grapes (about 1¼ pounds)
⅓ cup cognac
2 cups fresh or frozen blueberries
Marshmallow Sauce

Combine first 4 ingredients in a salad bowl; stir gently. Layer blueberries on top. Chill. Serve with Marshmallow Sauce. Yield: 10 servings.

Marshmallow Sauce

1 (8-ounce) package cream cheese, softened
1 (7-ounce) jar marshmallow cream

Combine ingredients; beat on low speed of an electric mixer until smooth. Yield: 1¼ cups.

Note: 1 (16-ounce) bag frozen sliced peaches, thawed, may be substituted for fresh peaches. *Jan Wier*
Dallas, Texas

MELON BALLS AND CHERRIES IN KIRSCH

4 cups honeydew melon balls (1 large honeydew)
3½ cups cantaloupe balls (1 large cantaloupe)
2 cups fresh cherries, pitted (¾ pound)
½ cup honey
1½ teaspoons lemon juice
¼ cup kirsch, divided
¾ cup sour cream

Combine first 3 ingredients in a large bowl. Combine honey, lemon juice, and 1½ teaspoons kirsch; pour over melon ball mixture, stirring well. Chill 2 hours, stirring occasionally.

Combine sour cream and remaining kirsch. Serve fruit with a slotted spoon and sour cream dressing. Yield: 8 to 10 servings. *Patricia Boschen*
Ashland, Virginia

HONEYDEW MELON WITH GRAPES

¼ cup sugar
2 teaspoons cornstarch
Pinch of salt
¾ cup dry white wine
¼ cup mint jelly
1 teaspoon lemon juice
3 tablespoons kirsch
3 cups honeydew melon balls (1 medium honeydew)
2 cups seedless red grapes (¾ pound)

Combine sugar, cornstarch, and salt in a small saucepan; stir in white wine. Bring to a boil; cook 1 minute. Add mint jelly and lemon juice, stirring until jelly melts. Stir in kirsch; pour over melon balls and grapes. Chill. Yield: 8 servings. *Mrs. J. H. Nichols*
Franklin, North Carolina

MARINATED PEACHES

¼ cup water
¼ cup sugar
1 tablespoon lemon juice
¾ cup Sauterne or sweet white wine
6 peaches, peeled and sliced

Combine first 3 ingredients in a small saucepan; bring to a boil and cook until sugar dissolves. Remove from heat; add wine. Pour marinade over peaches in a glass bowl; cover and chill several hours. Serve with a slotted spoon. Yield: 6 servings. *Betsy Rose*
Greensboro, North Carolina

Tip: *It is best to store most fruit in the refrigerator. Allow melons, avocados, and pears to ripen at room temperature; then refrigerate. Berries should be sorted to remove imperfect fruit before refrigerating; then wash and hull just before serving.*

From Our Kitchen To Yours

Children love to feel that they're being helpful. When children are 5 or 6, they may begin helping in the kitchen—stirring ingredients together, shaping cookie dough, counting vanilla wafers for banana pudding, and punching the buttons on the microwave oven. Cooking with them can be a special way of spending time together.

With an easy recipe, a child can learn measuring basics and the proper way to use the microwave oven—skills that he can apply later when making other foods on his own. You and your child might enjoy making this easy recipe.

MICROWAVE FUDGE

1 (16-ounce) package powdered
  sugar, sifted
½ cup cocoa
¼ teaspoon salt
½ cup butter or margarine
¼ cup milk
1 tablespoon vanilla extract

Combine first 3 ingredients in a 2-quart glass bowl; add butter. Microwave at HIGH, uncovered, 2 to 3 minutes; add milk, stirring until blended. Microwave at HIGH 1 minute. Stir in vanilla; pour into a lightly greased 8-inch square pan. Refrigerate until fudge is firm; cut into squares. Yield: 1½ pounds.

Using the Microwave Safely

Preparing Microwave Fudge can give a child a feeling of independence and achievement. Parents must help children learn to use the microwave oven with care. Supervising simple tasks, such as pushing the buttons, and then letting them help with putting the food in and taking it out of the microwave are good ways to begin. Knowing what your children are individually capable of doing helps establish rules when they use kitchen equipment, including the microwave.

To avoid injuries caused by spills and steam that scald fingers and faces, sometimes with second-degree burns, all children should have suitable supervision and instruction—especially those under age 7. Be sure the microwave oven is located where it can be reached easily and where the control panel is in full view. Discuss with your young assistants how foods react differently when heated in the microwave oven. Read with them and explain, if necessary, the directions on a food package or in a recipe. You'll also want to emphasize these safety guidelines:

■ When heating a liquid remember that the container may feel warm, but the liquid can be scalding. Let containers stand for several minutes before removing them from the microwave and before adding hot chocolate or other mixes.

■ Use potholders to remove containers; although the microwave oven doesn't get hot, foods and their containers do.

■ Heat foods in microwave-safe containers; some plastic containers, such as margarine tubs and plastic storage bags, are not intended for use in the microwave oven. Use an indelible marker to mark the cookware you want your children to use. Be sure to choose lightweight and unbreakable containers equipped with handles and covers.

■ When covering a container before cooking, turn back a small corner of the plastic wrap to let excess steam escape; never puncture plastic wrap after cooking because the wrap can split open, releasing hot steam.

■ Before cooking foods that have thick skins or membrane coverings (whole potatoes, hot dogs, or egg yolks), pierce or prick the skins or coverings to prevent bursting during cooking.

■ During the cooking process, stir or rotate the container a quarter- or half-turn to distribute heat, prevent dangerous hot spots, and ensure even cooking.

■ Follow the standing time instructions on convenience food packaging and in recipes; this time is necessary to complete the cooking process.

■ Uncover hot containers away from your face.

■ Do not heat eggs in the shell; when they are cracked, the pressure built up inside causes the egg to explode.

■ Unevenly heated foods burn mouths. Avoid overheating snacks; fillings such as jelly, fruit, pizza sauce, and cheese in pastry can be scalding while the outside is only warm. Break the pastry open before taking a bite.

■ Microwave packages that are designed to heat and crisp foods—pizza, French fries, waffles, popcorn—may get extremely hot. Handle with care.

MAY

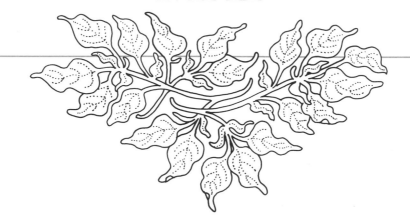

Southern hospitality—those words are synonymous with food, good food served in Southern homes. In another way, this famous hospitality can be expressed through gifts of food, such as a basket of cookies to welcome new neighbors or a casserole to help out friends. Recipes for these dishes and others make up "A Taste of Southern Hospitality." For hospitality on a grander scale, we offer a bonus section entitled "Our Wedding Celebration," which is filled with ideas, recipes, and menus for the wedding reception, bridal tea, bridesmaids' luncheon, and rehearsal dinner.

A Taste Of Southern Hospitality

The Southern philosophy is right; the gift of home-cooked meals—and the support behind them—do make things easier for others. When a friend or relative needs a helping hand, prepare one of these dishes, and head on over for a visit.

Your gift and concern will do more for them than you know. And don't be surprised if your serving dishes are returned filled with treats for you to enjoy. See "From Our Kitchen to Yours" on the facing page for packaging suggestions.

GAZPACHO
(pictured on page 76)

1 (46-ounce) can tomato juice
1 medium onion, finely chopped
2 large tomatoes, peeled and chopped
1 green pepper, finely chopped
1 cucumber, peeled, seeded, and diced
2 scallions, minced
1 clove garlic, crushed
¼ cup chopped fresh parsley
2 tablespoons olive oil
2 tablespoons lime juice
2 tablespoons red wine vinegar
1½ tablespoons lemon juice
1 teaspoon dried whole tarragon
1 teaspoon dried whole basil
1 teaspoon honey
½ teaspoon salt
¼ teaspoon pepper
¼ teaspoon ground cumin
Dash of hot sauce

Combine all ingredients; stir well. Chill at least 2 hours. Yield: 9 cups.
Joanne Shaughnessy
Birmingham, Alabama

PESTO SAUCE

2½ cups firmly packed fresh basil
½ cup freshly grated Parmesan cheese
½ cup pine nuts
2 large cloves garlic, crushed
¾ teaspoon salt
½ cup olive oil
Hot cooked linguine

Position knife blade in food processor bowl; add first 5 ingredients. Top with cover, and process until smooth. With processor running, pour oil through food chute in a slow, steady stream until blended. Toss with hot linguine. Yield: 1¼ cups.
Joe Rada
Birmingham, Alabama

CREAMY LASAGNA FLORENTINE

9 lasagna noodles, uncooked
1 pound bulk pork sausage
½ cup chopped onion
2 cups cubed cooked chicken
2 (10-ounce) packages frozen chopped spinach, thawed and well drained
Béchamel Sauce
¾ cup (3 ounces) shredded Swiss cheese, divided
½ cup grated Parmesan cheese
¼ teaspoon garlic powder
¼ cup soft breadcrumbs

Cook lasagna noodles according to package directions; drain well, and set noodles aside.

Combine sausage and onion in a large skillet; cook over medium heat until sausage is browned, stirring to crumble. Drain well on paper towels. Add chicken, spinach, and half each of Béchamel Sauce and shredded Swiss cheese. Stir in Parmesan cheese and garlic powder.

Spread ¼ cup of remaining Béchamel Sauce in a lightly greased 13- x 9- x 2-inch baking dish. Place 3 lasagna noodles over sauce; top with one-third of meat mixture. Repeat noodle and meat layers twice. Spread remaining Béchamel Sauce on top; sprinkle evenly with breadcrumbs. Cover and refrigerate 8 hours.

To bake, remove lasagna from refrigerator, and let stand at room temperature 30 minutes. Bake, uncovered, at 350° for 35 minutes. Cover and bake an additional 10 minutes. Uncover and sprinkle evenly with remaining Swiss cheese; bake lasagna an additional 5 minutes or until cheese melts. Yield: 8 servings.

Béchamel Sauce

3½ cups milk
½ cup finely chopped onion
2 bay leaves
¼ teaspoon ground thyme
3 tablespoons butter or margarine
⅓ cup all-purpose flour
½ teaspoon salt
¼ teaspoon cracked pepper
Pinch of ground nutmeg

Combine milk, onion, bay leaves, and thyme in a medium saucepan; bring to a boil over medium heat. Remove from heat, and cool.

Melt butter in a heavy saucepan over low heat; add flour, stirring until smooth. Cook 1 minute, stirring constantly. Gradually add milk mixture; cook over medium heat, stirring constantly, until mixture is thickened and bubbly. Stir in salt, pepper, and nutmeg; remove bay leaves and discard. Yield: 3½ cups.

Note: Unbaked casserole may be frozen. To bake, thaw in refrigerator 24 hours. Remove from refrigerator, and let stand at room temperature 30 minutes. Bake, covered, at 350° for 1 hour and 25 minutes. Sprinkle with ¼ cup plus 2 tablespoons shredded Swiss cheese; bake an additional 5 minutes or until cheese melts.

Michelle Bernhart
Stone Mountain, Georgia

DILL-OAT BREAD
(pictured on page 76)

1⅔ cups bread flour
1½ cups regular oats, uncooked
2 teaspoons salt
3 packages dry yeast
1¾ cups water
½ cup vegetable oil
2 eggs
½ cup sour cream
2½ cups whole wheat flour
1¾ cups bread flour, divided
2 tablespoons dried whole dillweed

Combine first 4 ingredients in a large mixing bowl. Combine water and oil in a saucepan; heat to 120° to 130°. Gradually add liquid mixture to flour mixture, beating at low speed of an electric mixer until blended. Add eggs, and beat at low speed until blended. Add sour cream, and beat 3 minutes at medium speed. Gradually stir in wheat flour, ¼ cup bread flour, and dillweed to make a soft dough.

Turn dough out onto a lightly floured surface. Knead until smooth and elastic (about 10 minutes). Add enough remaining 1½ cups bread flour while kneading to keep dough from sticking to hands. Place dough in a large greased bowl, turning to grease top. Cover and let rise in a warm place (85°), free from drafts, 1 hour or until doubled in bulk.

Punch dough down; let rest 15 minutes. Divide dough in half. Shape each half into a loaf, and place in 2 well-greased 9- x 5- x 3-inch loafpans. Let rise in a warm place, free from drafts, 40 minutes or until doubled in bulk. Bake at 375° for 35 minutes or until loaves sound hollow when tapped. Remove from pans, and cool completely on wire racks. Yield: 2 loaves.

DATE-FILLED COOKIES
(pictured on page 76)

1 (8-ounce) package chopped dates
½ cup water
½ cup finely chopped pecans
½ cup butter or margarine, softened
½ cup sugar
½ cup firmly packed brown sugar
1 egg, beaten
1 teaspoon vanilla extract
2 cups all-purpose flour
½ teaspoon baking soda
½ teaspoon salt

Combine dates and water in a small saucepan; cook over medium heat 3 minutes or until thickened, stirring constantly. Remove from heat; stir in pecans. Set aside to cool.

Cream butter; gradually add sugars, beating well at medium speed of an electric mixer. Add egg and vanilla.

Combine flour, soda, and salt; gradually add to creamed mixture, mixing well. Divide dough in half, and shape into two balls. Roll half of dough to an 8-inch square on a lightly floured surface. Spread half of filling over dough, leaving a ¼-inch margin on all sides. Carefully roll dough, jellyroll fashion; pinch seam to seal. Repeat procedure with remaining half of dough and filling. Wrap dough in wax paper, and chill 8 hours or overnight.

Unwrap rolls, and cut into ¼-inch slices. Place 1 inch apart on greased cookie sheets. Bake at 400° for 8 to 10 minutes. Cool on wire racks. Yield: 5 dozen. *Wanda Edwards*
Fayetteville, North Carolina

From Our Kitchen To Yours

Regardless of what your message is—get well, congratulations, sympathy, or welcome—the recipes we suggest as gifts from the heart (left and on facing page) will be well received. Here we share packaging ideas to help you add a personal touch, and we've included storing and freezing tips.

If **Gazpacho** is a favorite at your house, you'll probably have many ingredients on hand, needing only to run out to the garden or the store for fresh vegetables. Deliver this chilled soup on a napkin-lined tray with bowls and a basket of breadsticks. Or fill a jar with this mixture, and adorn it with ribbon and a fresh herb sprig to cheer most anyone.

For emergencies, make loaves of **Dill-Oat Bread** when you have extra time, and freeze them for up to three months. To freeze, wrap the cooled bread in aluminum foil, and seal it tightly in a heavy-duty plastic bag; then label and date the package. Thaw foil-wrapped bread at room temperature for two to three hours. It's fun to give a loaf tied to a cutting board or tray, with the ribbon wrapped around both bread and board; tuck a fresh sprig of dillweed or a fresh flower into the ribbon.

Browse in antique or junk stores and at garage sales, and buy some unusual containers and linens. Pile **Date-Filled Cookies** in a decorative box lined with an antique linen or paper doily, and take along a flavored coffee or tea.

When your herb pots are overflowing with basil, make batches of **Pesto**

Sauce, and freeze separately in airtight containers for up to six months. Give this gift in a jar or crock nestled in a cloth-lined basket with commercial pasta.

Often it's comforting to have dinner in the freezer. Give wrapped and frozen unbaked **Creamy Lasagna Florentine** in a decorated shirt box tied with yarn, lace, or paper ribbon (ribbon in a snakelike coil that you carefully untwist); include baking instructions and a zip-top plastic bag with the shredded Swiss cheese for the top. Double the recipe, and bake one for supper, and freeze the other to give. To freeze, line the dish with aluminum foil, leaving a 1½-inch foil collar. Fill with food, cover with foil, and fold the edges together, sealing tightly and pressing out air; then freeze. When it's frozen, lift the foil package from the dish, and return it to freezer. When reheating, remove foil, and return lasagna to baking dish.

A Little Mousse Magic

To some cooks, making a mousse is about as easy as pulling a rabbit out of a hat. But once you learn a few tricks of the trade, there's nothing to it. To solve the first mystery, mousse is simply a French term for "froth." Its consistency is light because of the air incorporated into it.

Traditionally, beaten egg whites were a common ingredient that gave mousses their volume, but to keep up with new safety standards of avoiding raw eggs in recipes, we've used another familiar option—whipped cream. It works just as well as beaten egg whites to fluff these sweets, but adds richer flavor and more calories than the whites. Unflavored gelatin helps versions chilled in a mold hold their shape once removed from their containers. Whichever version you choose, these treats are sure to make dessert a magical finale.

PUMPKIN MOUSSE

1 envelope unflavored gelatin
¼ cup light rum
4 egg yolks
⅔ cup sugar
1 cup cooked, mashed pumpkin
½ teaspoon ground cinnamon
½ teaspoon ground ginger
¼ teaspoon ground mace
¼ teaspoon ground cloves
1½ cups whipping cream, whipped
Garnishes: whipped cream, walnut halves

Sprinkle gelatin over rum in a small saucepan; stir and let stand 1 minute. Cook over low heat, stirring until gelatin dissolves; remove from heat.

Combine egg yolks and sugar in top of a double boiler; gradually stir in gelatin mixture. Bring water to a boil. Cook yolk mixture, stirring constantly, until mixture reaches 160° (about 20 minutes).

Gradually stir in pumpkin and spices. Fold whipped cream into pumpkin mixture. Spoon into a 1-quart soufflé dish, and chill until firm. Garnish, if desired. Yield: 6 to 8 servings.
Margaret Cotton
Franklin, Virginia

LEMON MOUSSE WITH RASPBERRY SAUCE

1 envelope unflavored gelatin
2 tablespoons Chablis or other dry white wine
1½ tablespoons grated lemon rind
⅓ cup lemon juice
3 egg yolks
½ cup sugar, divided
1⅓ cups whipping cream
Raspberry Sauce

Sprinkle gelatin over wine in a heavy-duty 1-quart saucepan; stir and let stand 1 minute. Stir in lemon rind and juice. Cook over low heat, stirring until gelatin dissolves.

Combine egg yolks and 3 tablespoons sugar; add to gelatin mixture, and cook, stirring constantly, until mixture reaches 160°. Cool 5 to 10

minutes, stirring often with a wire whisk. (Do not let mixture congeal.)

Beat whipping cream until foamy; gradually add remaining 5 tablespoons sugar, beating until soft peaks form. Fold into lemon mixture. Spoon into individual serving dishes; chill until set. Serve with Raspberry Sauce. Yield: 6 servings.

Raspberry Sauce

1 (10-ounce) package frozen raspberries, thawed and drained
2 tablespoons sugar
1 tablespoon lemon juice
1 tablespoon Grand Marnier or other orange-flavored liqueur

Combine raspberries, sugar, and lemon juice in container of an electric blender; process until smooth. Strain raspberry mixture, and discard seeds. Stir in Grand Marnier. Yield: ½ cup.
Betty Watts
Panama City, Florida

FROZEN WATERMELON MOUSSE

2½ cups seeded, diced watermelon
1 envelope unflavored gelatin
1 cup sugar
1 tablespoon lemon juice
1 cup whipping cream, whipped

Place watermelon in container of an electric blender, and process until smooth. Reserve 2¼ cups puree, discarding any remaining puree.

Combine gelatin and ¼ cup watermelon puree. Bring remaining 2 cups puree to a boil in a small saucepan. Remove from heat; add gelatin mixture, and stir until gelatin dissolves. Stir in sugar and lemon juice, and chill mixture until consistency of unbeaten egg white.

Fold whipped cream into chilled watermelon mixture. Spoon into a lightly oiled 6-cup mold. Cover and freeze 8 hours or until firm; unmold onto serving plate. Yield: 8 to 10 servings.
Mrs. E. W. Hanley
Palm Harbor, Florida

OUR *Wedding* CELEBRATION

To help you celebrate your wedding, we've designed special menus and recipes,

complete with serving suggestions, for the festivities—a wedding reception,

bridal tea, bridesmaids' luncheon, and rehearsal dinner.

Here's To A Grand Feast

The mere "popping of the question" stirs other inevitable questions in the minds of many near and dear to the bride and groom . . . friendly debates about the wedding cake, reception, rehearsal dinner, bridesmaids' luncheon, and of course, wedding showers and parties. We know you have questions about wedding festivities because many of you have directed your inquiries to us.

Now we can't supply *all* the answers within these pages, but we do have lots of menus, recipes, and ideas to guide you, whether you opt for professional catering services or you handle the food preparation yourself. Our wedding section begins with the wedding reception because it's usually the largest and most difficult event to mastermind. The next part focuses on menus for a rehearsal dinner and a bridesmaids' luncheon, with the third part offering recipes and tips for bridal parties and showers.

What's on the Menu?

The trend today is to personalize the wedding food and festivities to match the personalities of the bride and groom. Consequently, about the

only food guests can be sure to see at a reception is wedding cake, but even this tradition is witnessing changes. The traditional white bridal cake is sometimes replaced with spice cake, fruitcake, or carrot cake, frequently with cream cheese frosting. The groom's cake, originating as a smaller chocolate cake served to accompany the bride's cake, may boast similar flavor variations or may be replaced altogether with another culinary sensation, such as an elaborate tiered display of fine chocolate candies or a cheesecake bar, complete with choice of fruit, nut, and chocolate toppings.

Our Double Chocolate Wedding Cake combines the bride's and groom's cake into one stately creation; with a single slice a guest can sample the bride's white chocolate cake along with the groom's milk chocolate cake. White chocolate curls and swags of greenery offer wonderful decorations that are easier to make than elaborate piped or hand-shaped icing flowers. See "From Our Kitchen to Yours" on page 99 for the recipe plus details about flowers and foliage that are safe to use with food, as well as other tips for making the cake.

A wedding-day reminder: Save the top of the cake for your first anniversary. It may be necessary to remove this layer before the cake is cut. Wrap it well before freezing.

Around the Clock

The time of day scheduled for the wedding in large part determines what type foods should be served at the reception. Our menu was planned to guide your choice of party foods, from a simple wedding spread to an elaborate feast. Make-ahead suggestions are incorporated into each recipe as appropriate, and the menu was put together to let you take advantage of deli foods and convenience products. Feel free to substitute your own favorite recipes when commercially prepared products, such as commercial date-nut bread and orange marmalade, are suggested.

For **an early-afternoon wedding** guests expect a very simple menu. All that is really necessary is wedding cake and punch, and perhaps mints and nuts. A simple appetizer or two may be added to the menu, if desired.

In addition to the wedding cake, the menu for **a morning wedding** calls

for light appetizers along a brunch theme. We suggest the Savory Cheese Bar and Prosciutto-Wrapped Asparagus for a reception at this time of day.

The menu should be a little heavier for **a late-afternoon wedding.** Adding Curried Chicken Balls and Fresh Berry Tartlets to the cheese bar and asparagus makes a substantial appetizer feast for late afternoon.

Guests will almost expect a meal if a **noon wedding,** or one at **dinnertime,** is planned, so expand the same menu to include little sandwiches guests can assemble from sliced smoked turkey and party rolls. Offer mayonnaise and horseradish on the side as condiments.

All of these recipes were planned to serve 25 guests, except the cake, which serves 75. Double or triple the recipes for an expanded guest list.

CURRIED CHICKEN BALLS
(pictured on pages 114 and 115)

2 (3-ounce) packages cream cheese, softened
2 tablespoons orange marmalade
2 teaspoons curry powder
¾ teaspoon salt
¼ teaspoon white pepper
3 cups finely chopped cooked chicken
3 tablespoons minced green onions
3 tablespoons minced celery
1 cup finely chopped macadamia nuts or almonds, toasted

Combine first 5 ingredients in a mixing bowl; beat at medium speed of an electric mixer until smooth. Stir in chicken, green onions, and celery. Shape into 1-inch balls, and roll in nuts. Chill up to 2 days, or freeze up to 1 month. Yield: 3½ dozen.

PROSCIUTTO-WRAPPED ASPARAGUS
(pictured on pages 114 and 115)

50 fresh asparagus spears (about 3 pounds)
About 2 tablespoons Dijon mustard
50 thin slices prosciutto or fully cooked ham (about 1 pound)

Snap off tough ends of asparagus. Remove scales from stalks with a knife or vegetable peeler, if desired. Cook asparagus in a small amount of boiling water 3 to 4 minutes. Drain; plunge asparagus into ice water. Drain.

Spread about ⅛ teaspoon mustard on one side of each slice of prosciutto. Wrap prosciutto, mustard side in, around asparagus. Cover tightly, and chill up to 2 days. Yield: 25 appetizer servings.
Missy Wilson
Birmingham, Alabama

SAVORY CHEESE BAR
(pictured on page 114)

Set up a cheese bar with spreadable cheeses, assorted breads and crackers, and toppings. It makes an elaborate presentation with little effort.

For cheeses, offer Brie and cream cheese that have been glazed and garnished. Offer commercial water wafers, sliced date-nut bread, and gingersnaps, and 1½ cups each of commercial chopped chutney, orange marmalade, and green pepper jelly. Or you can substitute other commercial jellies or sauces of your choice.

Garnished Cheese

1 (5-inch) round Brie or 1 recipe Shapely Cream Cheese
Chive leaves or flat-leaf parsley
1 envelope unflavored gelatin
1 cup water
Garnish: edible violets

Cut a piece of thin white cardboard ¼ inch smaller than round of Brie. Cover cardboard with plastic wrap. Place Brie on cardboard base on a wire rack. Garnish cheese with desired herb leaves, placing them to one side of cheese. (Guests can first cut cheese from the opposite side and leave garnish untouched.)

Soften gelatin in water in a small saucepan. Cook over low heat until gelatin dissolves. Remove from heat; let stand until cooled slightly but not set. Drizzle 2 or 3 thin coats of gelatin mixture over cheese, chilling 20 minutes between each coat. Cover loosely, and chill up to 5 days. Garnish, if desired, just before serving. Yield: 25 appetizer servings.

Shapely Cream Cheese

Cut a piece of thin white cardboard ¼ inch smaller than an 8-inch heart-shaped pan. Cover cardboard with plastic wrap. Line pan with plastic wrap, extending it 4 inches from pan on 2 sides. Place cardboard liner in heart-shaped pan.

Spread 3 (8-ounce) packages softened cream cheese into prepared pan. Cover and chill at least 8 hours. Remove cream cheese heart on cardboard base from pan. Place on wire rack. Glaze and garnish cream cheese as described above.

FRESH BERRY TARTLETS
(pictured on pages 114 and 115)

2 (3-ounce) packages cream cheese, softened
⅔ cup butter or margarine, softened
2½ cups all-purpose flour
½ cup ground almonds
Crème Fraîche
Fresh raspberries, blueberries, and sliced strawberries

Position knife blade in food processor bowl. Add first 4 ingredients; process until mixture leaves sides of bowl and forms a ball. Remove dough from bowl. Shape into 50 balls; chill 15 minutes. Place in ungreased miniature (1¾-inch) muffin pans, shaping dough to make shells. Prick bottom of shells several times with a fork; bake at 450° for 8 to 10 minutes or until browned. Remove from pans; cool on wire racks. Just before serving spoon Crème Fraîche into pastry shells; top with choice of fruit. Yield: 50 tartlets.

Crème Fraîche

1 (3-ounce) package cream cheese, softened
1½ cups whipping cream
½ cup sour cream
⅔ cup sifted powdered sugar
2 tablespoons amaretto

Beat cream cheese at medium speed of an electric mixer until light and fluffy. Add remaining ingredients; beat until thickened. Cover and chill 8 hours or up to 4 days. (Mixture may thin upon agitation, but will thicken upon standing.) Yield: 2¾ cups.

Note: Pastry shells may be made ahead and frozen in airtight containers up to 1 month. Let thaw at room temperature before filling.

From Our Kitchen To Yours

When the foods staff planned the wedding reception beginning on page 97, we wanted an unforgettable cake in flavor and design. The Double Chocolate Wedding Cake was tested nine times before our expectations were met. If you need to practice assembling and decorating the cake, substitute plastic foam rounds for the cake layers, and make an extra batch of frosting for a trial run.

The cake created for you is simple to make, yet white chocolate curls and greenery make it sensational to see. Everyone assumes that making a wedding cake is difficult, but the following tips and techniques based on our experiences will help.

What about White Chocolate?

For the white layers of Double Chocolate Wedding Cake, we used white chocolate available by the pound at candy counters of many department stores. You may substitute an equal amount of vanilla-flavored candy coating or vanilla-flavored morsels, if desired. But do not use white baking bars, as these make the cake too tender to stack as a wedding cake. Don't be alarmed if the candy coating doesn't blend with the water when melted. The texture of the cake was good with each substitution; however, the flavor was more like that of a plain white cake.

When making white chocolate curls, we found it better to substitute vanilla-flavored candy coating for real white chocolate. Candy coating is easier to work with and makes smoother, prettier curls. Do not use white baking bars for making curls.

Baking the Layers

Bake the smaller layers on the same rack in a preheated oven; stagger the 6-inch and 8-inch pans so that they do not touch each other or the oven sides. Bake the large 12-inch layer separately. After cooling in the pans 10 minutes, loosen edges of layers with a spatula, and invert the pans onto towel-covered wire racks. Quickly turn each layer upright on another rack to cool thoroughly before storing; covering a warm cake makes it sticky. For cooling the 12-inch layers, use your extra oven racks. When the layers are completely cool, wrap each in plastic wrap and then in aluminum foil; refrigerate up to two days or freeze up to two months. To decorate, thaw wrapped frozen layers at room temperature about four hours; it is easier to work with a cold cake.

Adding the Frosting

White Chocolate Frosting has a rich, creamy flavor and spreads easily. The three frosting recipes can be made two days ahead, covered, and refrigerated. Let them stand at room temperature until softened to a spreading consistency. Frost the layers the day before the wedding, and pipe the grapevine design on the sides of the cake, if desired. Refrigerate leftover frosting to use on the day of the wedding for piping the shell border and, if desired, the columns.

Follow the recipe directions carefully when spreading frosting between layers; too much frosting and failure to leave a ½-inch border will cause frosting to ooze out the sides, making a ring of frosting on the sides of the cake. Frost the sides of the cake first, working from the bottom toward the top with long, even strokes. Then heap the frosting on center top and spread it toward edges. To completely cover the cake and get a smooth surface, apply the frosting thicker than you would normally.

To smooth the frosting, place the cake on a turntable. Dip a spatula in hot water; place the wet spatula halfway across the top of the cake, and press down lightly, holding the spatula still; turn the turntable, smoothing frosting as you go. (Excess water on frosting will evaporate.) Smooth the sides by holding the spatula vertically and repeating the same technique several times, discarding excess frosting as the sides become smooth. If crumbs show, apply more frosting and smooth with wet spatula.

The Final Touches

Adding the decorative touches to the cake is simple using a large decorating bag fitted with a small coupler, five standard metal tips, white chocolate curls and shavings, silk ivy, and fresh fern leaves.

To pipe the **grapevine design** (see sketch, shown actual size) on the cake, first trace the pattern on wax paper; then flip the wax paper over to continue tracing the design. Practice piping frosting on the wax paper, and then piping the design on the sides of cake pans or plastic foam. It is easier to work at eye level. Using plain round metal tip No. 3, pipe the long curved vine, applying even pressure and maintaining a steady flow as you move the tip across the surface. The bunches of grapes are placed inside the curves. Holding the tip at a 45° angle, make an outline of the bunch using small dots; apply pressure, and lift the tip as you release to form the outline of each grape. Then fill in the center with additional dots. Draw curved lines to simulate stems for grapes and leaves. Make small curled twigs using the same tip and a series of slight oval movements. Change to metal tip No. 66 (a small leaf tube). Apply a small amount of pressure at a 45° angle; at the halfway point, discontinue pressure, and lift away from the surface to draw the leaf out to a point. Pipe this design on the sides of the tiers the day before the wedding.

Greenery is a natural to use as decoration on a cake, but be sure that any fresh greenery you use is nonpoisonous and has not been sprayed with insecticides. We teamed fresh climbing fern leaves with silk ivy leaves (real ivy is poisonous, but we liked the look of ivy on the cake). Smilax and baby's breath are also safe to use fresh.

DOUBLE CHOCOLATE WEDDING CAKE
(pictured on page 116)

3 recipes White Chocolate Frosting
Milk Chocolate Pound Cake
3 ounces white chocolate, grated
White Chocolate Pound Cake
White Chocolate Curls and
  Shavings

Cover 8- and 12-inch sturdy cardboard circles with aluminum foil. Spread a small amount of White Chocolate Frosting on the 12-inch circle, and place 12-inch milk chocolate cake layer on top. Measure 2 cups frosting; stir in 3 ounces grated white chocolate. Spread about 1 cup frosting with grated chocolate on top of cake layer, spreading to within ½ inch of edges. (Set remaining frosting with grated chocolate aside to spread between other layers.) Top with 12-inch white chocolate cake layer. Vertically insert 4 wooden sticks cut the depth of 12-inch tier into 12-inch layers about 3 inches from sides, spacing evenly to support weight of other layers. Spread sides and top of 12-inch cake thinly with frosting; let stand 5 minutes. Then spread a regular amount of frosting. Smooth top and sides with a wet metal spatula.

Assemble 8-inch tier on its cardboard base, filling layers with about ¾ cup frosting with grated chocolate. Frost 8-inch layers as described

Double Chocolate Wedding Cake

above. Position 8-inch tier in center of 12-inch tier. Center a 7-inch plastic divider plate (available as a set of 2 divider plates and 4 columns in department stores or kitchen supply stores) on 8-inch tier; spread plate with frosting, leaving a small mound in center to support decorations (white chocolate curls and ivy). Spread a small amount of frosting on top of other 7-inch divider plate; assemble 6-inch layers on divider plate, filling layers with remaining frosting containing grated chocolate. Frost 6-inch layers, and place a small mound of frosting in center of top of tier as described above. If desired, pipe grapevine design on sides of tiers using tips No. 3 and 66.

Spread a small amount of frosting in center of cake stand. Place two stacked tiers carefully in center of cake stand. (Frosting on cake stand will help hold finished cake steady as you transfer cake to desired location.) Transport cake at this stage.

When you're ready to complete the decorating, prepare a large decorating bag with a coupler and metal tip No. 30. Spoon frosting into bag; fold corners of bag over, and crease until all air is pressed out. Starting with bottom tier, pipe a top and bottom shell border around sides of cake. Repeat piping procedure for remaining tiers, piping top tier carefully because of its smaller base.

Arrange greenery and chocolate curls on mound of frosting on top of plastic divider plate. (We used fresh fern leaves and silk ivy.)

If desired, pipe strips of frosting on 3-inch columns using metal tip No. 48, and pipe small dots of frosting to fill in between strips using metal tip No. 3. Attach columns onto bottom divider plate, and carefully attach top tier onto columns. Pipe drop flowers on exposed top and bottom portions of columns using metal tip No. 16. Sprinkle white chocolate shavings on tops of 12-inch and 8-inch tiers. Arrange greenery as desired on top and sides. (When inserting greenery into cake, first wrap stems with plastic wrap.) Place chocolate curls on top. Yield: about 75 servings.

White Chocolate Pound Cake

¾ pound white chocolate
¾ cup boiling water
1 cup butter or margarine, softened
3 cups sugar
7 eggs
1 tablespoon vanilla extract
5 cups all-purpose flour
1 teaspoon baking soda
⅛ teaspoon salt
2 cups buttermilk

Grease and flour one 6-inch, 8-inch, and 12-inch round cakepan, and set aside. Combine white chocolate and water, stirring until chocolate melts; set mixture aside to cool.

Cream butter; gradually add sugar, beating at medium speed of an electric mixer until well blended. Add eggs, one at a time, beating after each addition. Stir in white chocolate mixture and vanilla.

Combine flour, soda, and salt; add to chocolate mixture alternately with buttermilk, beginning and ending with flour mixture. Mix after each addition.

Spoon 1¾ cups batter into 6-inch pan, 3½ cups batter into 8-inch pan, and remaining batter into 12-inch pan. Bake at 300° for 45 to 50 minutes for 6-inch layer, 50 to 55 minutes for 8-inch layer, and 1 hour for 12-inch layer or until a wooden pick inserted in center comes out clean. Cool in pans 10 minutes; remove from pans, and let cool on wire racks. Brush excess crumbs from cake. Yield: one 6-, 8-, and 12-inch layer.

Milk Chocolate Pound Cake: For Milk Chocolate Pound Cake, prepare recipe for White Chocolate Pound Cake, substituting 1 cup milk chocolate morsels for white chocolate, and adding ¼ cup cocoa to flour mixture. Spoon batter into pans, and bake as directed above.

White Chocolate Frosting

¾ cup butter, softened
¾ cup shortening
3 ounces white chocolate, melted
3 (16-ounce) packages powdered sugar, sifted
½ teaspoon salt
2 teaspoons vanilla extract
½ teaspoon almond extract
1½ tablespoons lemon juice
⅔ to ¾ cup whipping cream

Cream butter and shortening in a large mixing bowl at medium speed of an electric mixer; add melted chocolate. Gradually add 4 cups powdered sugar; beat well. Add salt, flavorings, and lemon juice. Gradually add remaining powdered sugar and whipping cream alternately, beginning and ending with sugar. Mix well after each addition. Yield: 7 cups.

White Chocolate Curls and Shavings

To make white chocolate curls, place squares or wafers of vanilla-flavored candy coating in top of a double boiler (about 24 ounces). Bring water to a boil; reduce heat to low. Cook until coating melts; stir often.

Pour coating out in several streams onto a wax paper-lined baking sheet, and spread coating with a spatula into 2-inch-wide strips. Smooth top of strips with spatula.

Let stand at room temperature about 30 minutes or until coating hardens. Do not refrigerate. If coating is too hard, curls will break; if too soft, coating won't curl.

Gently pull a cheese plane or vegetable peeler across length of coating until curl forms, letting coating curl up on top of cheese plane. Reserve broken pieces to use as shavings.

Perfect Preludes To The Wedding

Here comes the bride—and her guests and the wedding party! The best weddings are those where friends and family enjoy time together and celebrate the union of two special people. Our menus for a rehearsal dinner and bridesmaids' luncheon keep the focus on easy yet elegant entertaining—a style that allows the host family and friends to have as much fun as the new couple. Each menu is designed to allow the host or hostess to entertain at home or offer ideas to a caterer. Because oven space and time are at a premium in most homes, microwave instructions are included for some recipes, too. Suggestions for menus, decorations and flowers, and even garnishes (see sidebar on facing page) are included. Add your own special touches, and enjoy.

Rehearsal Dinner at Home
(Serves 10 or 20)
Shrimp-and-Chicken Casserole
Tomatoes With
Walnut-Rice Stuffing
Marinated Carrots
Commercial rolls
Chocolate-Mint Cheesecake
Coffee   Tea

Pulling It All Together: Tips That Help

■ Decorate the sideboard with candles, a silver ice bucket filled with flowers, and champagne goblets tied with ribbon.
■ Prepare the main-dish casserole, carrots, stuffed tomatoes, and cheesecake ahead of time, and refrigerate. Bake the casserole and stuffed tomatoes when you return from the rehearsal.
■ Ice down two or three bottles of champagne in a punch bowl placed on a tray in the living room. Greet guests at the door with a glass of champagne.

SHRIMP-AND-CHICKEN CASSEROLE
(pictured on pages 112 and 113)

1 (2½- to 3-pound) broiler-fryer
1 teaspoon salt
4 cups water
1 pound unpeeled medium-size fresh shrimp
2 (16-ounce) packages frozen broccoli cuts, thawed and well drained
1 cup mayonnaise or salad dressing
1 (10¾-ounce) can cream of chicken soup, undiluted
1 (10¾-ounce) can cream of celery soup, undiluted
3 tablespoons lemon juice
¼ teaspoon white pepper
1 cup (4 ounces) shredded Cheddar cheese
½ cup soft breadcrumbs
1 tablespoon butter or margarine, melted
Paprika
Garnishes: shrimp and fresh parsley sprigs

Combine chicken and salt in a Dutch oven; add enough water to cover, and bring to a boil. Cook 45 minutes or until tender. Bone chicken; cut into bite-size pieces, and set aside.

Bring 4 cups water to a boil; add shrimp, and cook 3 to 5 minutes. Drain well; rinse with cold water. Peel and devein shrimp. Set 3 shrimp aside for garnish, if desired.

Spread broccoli evenly in a lightly greased 13- x 9- x 2-inch baking dish; set aside. Combine mayonnaise and next 4 ingredients; spread about one-third over broccoli. Set aside remaining sauce. Combine chicken and shrimp; spread evenly over casserole, and top with remaining sauce. Cover and chill up to 8 hours.

Remove casserole from refrigerator, and let stand at room temperature 30 minutes. Cover and bake at 350° for 30 minutes. Uncover; sprinkle with cheese. Combine breadcrumbs and butter; sprinkle over cheese. Bake an additional 15 minutes or until casserole is hot and bubbly. Sprinkle with paprika. Garnish, if desired. Yield: 10 servings.

Note: Casserole may be assembled and baked immediately.

Marianne Absher
Raleigh, North Carolina

TOMATOES WITH WALNUT-RICE STUFFING
(pictured on pages 112 and 113)

10 small tomatoes
Salt
2¼ cups quick-cooking brown rice, uncooked
1 cup chopped onion
2 tablespoons olive oil
½ cup chopped walnuts, toasted
3 tablespoons chopped fresh parsley
½ teaspoon salt
¼ teaspoon pepper
2 tablespoons olive oil
¼ cup Chablis or other dry white wine
Garnish: fresh parsley sprigs

Slice top off each tomato; set tops aside. Scoop out pulp, reserving pulp for other uses. Sprinkle inside of each tomato shell with a pinch of salt, and invert on paper towels to drain.

Cook rice according to package directions, omitting salt and fat.

Sauté onion in 2 tablespoons oil until tender. Combine rice, sautéed onion, walnuts, chopped parsley, ½ teaspoon salt, and pepper.

Spoon rice mixture into tomato shells; place in a lightly greased 12- x 8- x 2-inch baking dish. Combine 2 tablespoons olive oil and wine; spoon over tomatoes. Cover and bake at 350° for 25 minutes. Place tomato tops on each stuffed tomato, and bake an additional 5 minutes. Garnish, if desired. Yield: 10 servings.

Microwave Directions: Slice top off each tomato; set tops aside. Scoop out pulp, reserving pulp for other uses. Sprinkle inside of each tomato shell with a pinch of salt, and invert on paper towels to drain.

Cook rice according to package directions, omitting salt and fat.

Combine onion and 2 tablespoons olive oil in a 9-inch pieplate. Microwave at HIGH 3 minutes or until onion is slightly transparent. Combine rice, onion, walnuts, and next 3 ingredients. Spoon rice mixture into tomato shells; place in a lightly greased 12- x 8- x 2-inch baking dish. Combine 2 tablespoons olive oil and wine; spoon over tomatoes. Cover tightly with heavy-duty plastic wrap; fold back a small corner of wrap to allow steam to escape. Microwave at HIGH 4 minutes. Remove plastic wrap; place tomato tops on each stuffed tomato, and microwave at HIGH, uncovered, 2 minutes. Garnish, if desired.

Tony Jones
Atlanta, Georgia

Tip: *For an unusual appetizer, wrap melon wedges or fresh figs with prosciutto (thinly sliced Italian ham).*

Make the Food Look Special

Adding garnishes isn't complicated, as illustrated in the photographs of our wedding rehearsal dinner and bridesmaids' luncheon beginning on page 109. Many people feel that a plate isn't complete unless tastefully arranged or garnished. You'll find these garnishing tips helpful.

■ A garnish should enhance food. Fresh raspberries and a sprig of fresh mint add an appealing touch to Sherbet-Cantaloupe Surprise.

■ Here's a quick garnish: Use a vegetable peeler to make chocolate curls. Just pull the peeler firmly down the flat surface of a chocolate bar.

■ Artfully arrange food on the plate rather than make a garnish. (See photograph of luncheon menu, page 109.)

■ Fresh fruits and vegetables are simple to use as garnishes. For example, lettuce leaves and radicchio line the bowl of Marinated Carrots.

■ Garnishes should be edible and complementary. To garnish Tomatoes With Walnut-Rice Stuffing, cut a slit in the tops of the tomatoes from the outer edge to the center; insert sprigs of fresh parsley, and replace the tops on the stuffed tomatoes.

■ To spruce up a punch bowl, add whole fruit and a fruit-filled ice ring of the same ingredients used in the punch.

■ Sometimes ingredients in the recipe lend themselves to being used as a garnish. Reserve a few whole shrimp, and pair them with fresh parsley sprigs to garnish the Shrimp-and-Chicken Casserole.

MARINATED CARROTS
(pictured on pages 112 and 113)

2½ pounds carrots, scraped and diagonally sliced
1 small purple onion, sliced and separated into rings
1 cup white wine vinegar
1 cup water
2 tablespoons olive oil
¾ cup sugar
2 cloves garlic, crushed
1½ teaspoons seasoned salt
½ teaspoon dry mustard
Radicchio
Leaf lettuce

Combine carrots and onion in a bowl; set aside.

Combine vinegar, water, olive oil, sugar, garlic, seasoned salt, and dry mustard; stir until sugar dissolves. Pour over carrots; toss gently. Cover and chill 8 hours. Drain well. Spoon carrots onto a serving platter lined with radicchio and leaf lettuce. Yield: 10 servings.
Eileen Wehling
Austin, Texas

CHOCOLATE-MINT CHEESECAKE
(pictured on page 113)

2 cups chocolate wafer crumbs
¼ cup sugar
¼ cup butter or margarine, melted
4 (8-ounce) packages cream cheese, softened
1 (3-ounce) package cream cheese, softened
1⅔ cups sugar
5 eggs
⅓ cup green crème de menthe
1 tablespoon vanilla extract
½ cup butter or margarine
¾ cup cocoa
2¾ cups sifted powdered sugar
½ cup milk
1½ teaspoons vanilla extract
Garnish: chocolate marble leaves (directions, sidebar at right)

Combine first 3 ingredients; firmly press mixture evenly over bottom and 2 inches up sides of a 10-inch springform pan. Bake at 325° for 7 minutes, and cool.

Beat cream cheese at high speed of an electric mixer until light and fluffy; gradually add 1⅔ cups sugar, beating well. Add eggs, beating just until combined. Stir in crème de menthe and 1 tablespoon vanilla. Pour into prepared pan. Bake at 325° for 1 hour and 15 minutes (center may be soft but will firm when chilled). Let cool to room temperature on a wire rack.

Melt ½ cup butter in a small saucepan; add cocoa, and stir until smooth. Remove from heat, and cool. Pour chocolate mixture into a small mixing bowl; gradually add powdered sugar alternately with milk, beating at medium speed of an electric mixer until smooth. Stir in 1½ teaspoons vanilla. Spread mixture over top of cheesecake. Garnish, if desired. Yield: 10 to 12 servings. *Ann Ferguson Ward Morgantown, West Virginia*

Swirling the Leaves

To garnish Chocolate-Mint Cheesecake, paint and swirl candy coating on lemon balm mint leaves. The leaves curl gracefully because they are placed on a rounded object to cool.

For the chocolate marbled leaves, select **12 to 14 nonpoisonous leaves,** such as mint or rose. Wash leaves, and pat dry with paper towels. Place 1 ounce **vanilla-flavored candy coating** in a 6-ounce custard cup; microwave at MEDIUM (50% power) 1 to 2 minutes or until coating melts, stirring after 1 minute. Stir a small amount of **green-paste food coloring** into coating. Place custard cup in a shallow pan; pour hot water to a depth of ½ inch into pan, if desired, to prevent coating from hardening quickly. Set aside. Place **1 ounce chocolate-flavored candy coating** in a 6-ounce custard cup. Microwave at MEDIUM 1 to 2 minutes or until coating melts, stirring after 1 minute; place cup in pan of water, if desired.

Using an artist's brush, coat tops of leaves with green coating. Place three small dots of chocolate-flavored coating on leaves; using the tip of a wooden pick, draw lines through dots to create a marbled effect. Place leaves over a banana or other rounded object; let coated leaves stand at room temperature until coating cools and is firm. Reverse colors on remaining mint leaves.

Grasp leaf at stem end, and carefully peel leaf away from coating. Cover and store marbled leaves in a cool, dry place until ready to use.

Luncheon for Bridesmaids
(Serves 8)
Chicken Breasts in Phyllo Pastry
Marinated Asparagus Medley
Sherbet-Cantaloupe Surprise
Mint tea

Pulling It All Together: Tips That Help

■ The day before the luncheon, prepare raspberry sauce and asparagus. Scoop pineapple sherbet into balls, and freeze on wax paper to make assembling the dessert easier.

■ The morning of the luncheon, prepare chicken; bake 45 minutes before serving.

■ The centerpiece can be fancy or simple. Be sure arrangements don't block the view of guests when they are seated. Fresh flowers in vases, violets or miniature ferns in bright baskets, a single orchid floating in water in a brandy snifter, or tussie mussie bouquets (also known as nosegays) are a few examples.

■ For a gift from the bride, frame a photograph of each attendant or guest to mark her place setting. (See luncheon photo, page 109.)

CHICKEN BREASTS
IN PHYLLO PASTRY
(pictured on page 109)

1 cup mayonnaise or salad dressing
⅔ cup chopped green onions
3½ tablespoons fresh lemon juice
1 small clove garlic, minced
¾ teaspoon dried whole tarragon
8 chicken breast halves, skinned
   and boned
¼ teaspoon salt
⅛ teaspoon pepper
16 sheets commercial frozen phyllo
   pastry, thawed
Butter-flavored vegetable cooking
   spray
3½ tablespoons grated Parmesan
   cheese

Combine mayonnaise, green onions, lemon juice, garlic, and tarragon in a small mixing bowl. Set mayonnaise mixture aside.

Sprinkle chicken breasts with salt and pepper. Place one sheet of phyllo pastry on a sheet of plastic wrap; spray evenly with cooking spray. Place another sheet of phyllo on top; spray with cooking spray. Spread about 3 tablespoons mayonnaise mixture on both sides of 1 chicken breast; place breast diagonally in one corner of stacked pastry sheets. Fold corner over breast; fold sides over, and carefully roll up in pastry. Place seam side down in an ungreased 15- x 10- x 1-inch jellyroll pan. Repeat procedure with remaining phyllo, cooking spray, mayonnaise mixture, and chicken breasts. Spray tops of pastry bundles with cooking spray; sprinkle with Parmesan cheese. Bake at 350° for 40 to 45 minutes or until chicken breasts are done. Serve immediately. Yield: 8 servings.

Note: Melted butter or margarine may be substituted for butter-flavored cooking spray, if you perfer.

Judith Hafner
Murray, Kentucky

MARINATED ASPARAGUS
MEDLEY
(pictured on page 109)

2 pounds fresh asparagus
⅓ cup chopped fresh parsley
⅓ cup sliced black olives
⅓ cup sliced stuffed green olives
1 (2-ounce) jar diced pimiento,
   drained
2 tablespoons sliced green onions
1½ cups vegetable oil
½ cup red wine vinegar
2 teaspoons lemon juice
1 teaspoon Worcestershire sauce
1 tablespoon dried whole basil
2 teaspoons coarsely ground pepper
1 teaspoon dried whole oregano
½ teaspoon garlic powder
½ teaspoon salt
¼ teaspoon sugar
Bibb lettuce
12 to 16 large cherry tomatoes,
   sliced

Snap off tough ends of asparagus. Remove scales with a vegetable peeler or knife, if desired. Cook asparagus, covered, in boiling water 6 to 8 minutes or until crisp-tender. Drain. Place asparagus in a shallow dish. Arrange parsley, olives, pimiento, and green onions over asparagus; set dish aside.

Combine oil and next 9 ingredients in a jar. Cover tightly, and shake vigorously; pour marinade over asparagus. Cover and chill 8 hours.

Line plates with lettuce leaves. Remove asparagus-olive mixture from marinade; arrange on lettuce. Place sliced tomatoes on lettuce. Yield: 8 servings.

Kaki Hockersmith
Little Rock, Arkansas

SHERBET-CANTALOUPE
SURPRISE

1 (10-ounce) package frozen
   raspberries, thawed
½ cup red currant jelly
1 tablespoon cornstarch
1 tablespoon water
1 cantaloupe
1 quart pineapple sherbet
Garnishes: fresh raspberries, fresh
   mint sprigs

Place raspberries in a strainer. Press raspberries with back of spoon against the sides of the strainer to squeeze out juice (about ½ to ¾ cup). Discard pulp and seeds remaining in strainer. Combine raspberry juice and jelly in a small saucepan; bring mixture to a boil over medium heat. Combine cornstarch and water; stir into raspberry juice mixture. Boil 1 minute, stirring constantly. Cool.

Peel cantaloupe; cut into 8 wedges. Scoop sherbet into 8 balls. To serve, place scoop of sherbet in cantaloupe wedge; secure with short wooden picks. Top with raspberry sauce. Garnish, if desired. Yield: 8 servings.

Millie Givens
Savannah, Georgia

Tip: *For an interesting change, use fresh pineapple, cantaloupe, or other shells as containers for dips and spreads. Pineapple halves scooped out are beautiful for serving cheese dips or salads. Other fruit shells, such as melon, are nice containers for salads or appetizers.*

Showers & Parties

Here's To The New Life Ahead

As the wedding date nears, the bride and groom are hardly alone in their excitement over the upcoming event. They are usually surrounded by friends eager to express their sentiments, and one of the most special ways is to give the couple a party.

You might want to consider some of the new trends toward evening parties that include the husband-to-be and his father and friends or even ones for men only, with casual menus. But no matter how much fun these may be, the favorite bridal parties continue to be traditional teas or showers.

Our menu serves 25 and can easily be doubled or tripled for larger gatherings. One person can prepare all the food, but it's easier if the work and the cost are divided among several hostesses. Check with the bride to schedule the event within the last two months before the wedding—not the week of the wedding.

Party Punch
Calla Lily Sandwiches
Cocktail Puffs
Sweet Ravioli
Savory Rosettes
Spritz Hearts
Almond Biscotti and fresh
strawberries with
Chocolate-Almond Cream
Chocolate Truffles

PARTY PUNCH
(pictured on pages 110 and 111)

1 (46-ounce) can unsweetened pineapple juice, chilled
2 (33.8-ounce) bottles ginger ale, chilled
3 quarts raspberry sherbet, softened

Combine all ingredients in a punch bowl. Yield: 5½ quarts.
Millie Givens
Savannah, Georgia

CALLA LILY SANDWICHES
(pictured on page 111)

1 (2-ounce) package slivered almonds
2 to 3 drops of yellow food coloring
54 slices white sandwich bread
1 (8-ounce) package cream cheese, softened
2 tablespoons orange marmalade

Combine almonds and food coloring in a jar; cover with lid, and shake vigorously until almonds are evenly coated.

Roll each slice of bread to ⅛-inch thickness with a rolling pin; cut with a 2½-inch biscuit cutter. Combine

cream cheese and marmalade; spread about 1 teaspoon on each bread round. Pinch the edges of one portion of the circle together to form a calla lily. Press a tinted slivered almond into the pinched portion to represent the flower's stamen. Yield: 4½ dozen.
Rublelene Singleton
Scotts Hill, Tennessee

COCKTAIL PUFFS
(pictured on page 111)

1 cup water
½ cup butter or margarine
1 cup all-purpose flour
¼ teaspoon salt
4 eggs
1½ cups fresh lump crabmeat
2 cups (8 ounces) shredded sharp Cheddar cheese
1 cup mayonnaise
½ cup finely chopped celery
1½ teaspoons minced onion
1 tablespoon Worcestershire sauce
1 teaspoon hot sauce
Garnish: fresh parsley sprigs

Combine water and butter in a medium saucepan; bring to a boil. Add flour and salt all at once, stirring vigorously with a wooden spoon until mixture leaves sides of pan and forms a smooth ball. Remove from heat, and cool 5 minutes.

Add eggs, one at a time, beating with a wooden spoon after each addition; beat until batter is smooth. Drop batter by teaspoonfuls 2 inches apart onto lightly greased baking sheets.

Bake at 400° for 20 minutes. Turn oven off; remove puffs. Make a horizontal slit about one-third of the way down in top of puffs (do not cut completely through). Return puffs to oven for 10 minutes to dry out. Remove from oven; cool on wire racks. Complete slit to slice top from each puff.

Combine crabmeat and remaining ingredients, stirring well. Spoon about

2 teaspoons crab mixture into each cream puff; replace tops. Cover and chill until ready to serve. Garnish, if desired. Yield: 4½ dozen.

Note: One pound fresh medium shrimp, boiled and peeled, can be substituted for crabmeat.

Eleanor K. Brandt
Arlington, Texas

SWEET RAVIOLI
(pictured on page 110)

1 cup butter or margarine, softened
⅔ cup sugar
1 egg, beaten
1 teaspoon grated lemon rind
1½ teaspoons vanilla extract
¼ teaspoon almond extract
2½ cups all-purpose flour
¼ teaspoon baking soda
⅛ teaspoon salt
About ½ cup raspberry preserves
Sifted powdered sugar

Beat butter at medium speed of an electric mixer; gradually add ⅔ cup sugar, beating well. Add egg, lemon rind, and extracts; mix well.

Combine flour, soda, and salt; add to creamed mixture. Divide dough in half. Roll each portion of dough between 2 sheets of wax paper to a 12-inch square. Chill at least 1 hour.

Remove one portion of dough from refrigerator; remove top piece of wax paper, and cut dough into 1½-inch squares. Place ¼ teaspoon raspberry preserves in center of half of squares; brush edges of filled squares with water. Place unfilled squares over filled squares; press edges to seal. Cut an X on top of each. Repeat with remaining dough and preserves.

Place cookies on greased cookie sheets, and bake at 350° for 9 to 11 minutes or until edges are lightly

browned. Remove from oven, and cool on baking sheets 4 to 5 minutes. Transfer cookies to wire racks, and cool competely. Sprinkle with powdered sugar. Yield: 4 dozen.

Elizabeth S. Evins
Atlanta, Georgia

SAVORY ROSETTES
(pictured on page 110)

3 eggs, beaten
1½ teaspoons sugar
¼ teaspoon salt
1½ cups all-purpose flour
1 cup milk
2 tablespoons butter or margarine, melted
1 tablespoon lemon juice
Vegetable oil
½ cup grated Parmesan cheese
½ teaspoon garlic salt

Combine first 3 ingredients, beating well at low speed of an electric mixer. Add flour, milk, butter, and lemon juice, beating until smooth. Chill at least 1 hour.

Pour oil to a depth of 3 inches into a Dutch oven; heat to 375°. Heat rosette iron by dipping into hot oil 1 minute. Drain excess oil from iron, and dip iron into batter, being careful not to coat top of iron with batter. Immediately dip iron into hot oil; fry rosette 30 seconds or until golden brown.

Remove iron from hot oil; carefully remove rosette from iron with a fork. (Some rosettes will float off the iron while cooking.) Drain upside down on paper towels.

Combine Parmesan cheese and garlic salt in a large zip-top plastic bag. Place several rosettes in bag; shake gently. Let cool completely before storing in an airtight container. Yield: 4½ dozen.
Abreena Tompkins
Ennice, North Carolina

SPRITZ HEARTS
(pictured on page 110)

2 cups butter, softened
1 cup sugar
4 egg yolks
4 cups all-purpose flour
1 to 2 teaspoons vanilla extract
3 to 4 drops of red food coloring
24 ounces vanilla-flavored candy coating

Beat butter at medium speed of an electric mixer; gradually add sugar, beating well. Add egg yolks, mixing well. Add flour; stir in vanilla and food coloring.

Use a cookie gun, following manufacturer's instructions, to shape cookies into hearts or as desired. Place cookies on ungreased cookie sheets. Bake at 375° for 8 to 10 minutes or until cookies are lightly browned. Let cool on wire racks.

Melt candy coating in a heavy saucepan over low heat. Dip half of each heart into coating; place on wax paper to cool. Store in airtight containers, placing wax paper between each layer. Yield: 12 dozen.
Mrs. Curtis H. Ward
Auburn, Alabama

Tip: *When preparing finger sandwiches in advance, keep them from drying out by placing them in a shallow container lined with a damp towel and wax paper. Separate sandwich layers with wax paper, and cover with another layer of wax paper and a damp towel; refrigerate.*

ALMOND BISCOTTI
(pictured on page 110)

2 eggs
½ cup sugar
1 teaspoon vanilla extract
½ teaspoon almond extract
1½ cups all-purpose flour
1 teaspoon baking powder
¼ teaspoon salt
½ cup whole almonds, finely chopped

Line a cookie sheet with heavy-duty aluminum foil; set aside. Beat eggs and sugar at medium speed of an electric mixer until well blended; add flavorings. Combine flour and remaining ingredients; add to creamed mixture. Using lightly floured hands, shape dough into an 8- x 4-inch rectangle, and place on prepared pan. Bake at 375° for 20 minutes; cool.

Cut into ¼-inch slices. Cut each slice in half crosswise, and place on cookie sheets. Bake at 350° for 10 minutes or until crisp and golden brown. Cool on wire racks. Yield: about 5 dozen.

Mrs. Harland J. Stone
Ocala, Florida

CHOCOLATE-ALMOND CREAM
(pictured on page 110)

1 cup whipping cream
2 tablespoons powdered sugar
½ teaspoon chocolate almondine or almond extract
Garnish: grated chocolate

Beat whipping cream until foamy; gradually add powdered sugar, beating until soft peaks form. Stir in flavoring. Garnish, if desired. Serve with biscotti and strawberries. Yield: 2 cups.

Pulling It All Together			
One month before party:	**One week before party:**	**Three days ahead:**	**Day before party:**
Bake and freeze Spritz Hearts.	Prepare Sweet Ravioli and Almond Biscotti; store in airtight containers.	Prepare Chocolate Truffles; refrigerate in an airtight container. Prepare Savory Rosettes and cream puffs for Cocktail Puffs; store in airtight containers.	Prepare cream cheese filling and tinted almonds for Calla Lily Sandwiches and chill. Prepare filling for Cocktail Puffs; chill.
Morning of party:	**Two hours before party:**	**30 minutes before party:**	**Just before guests arrive:**
Assemble Calla Lily Sandwiches and chill. Wash and arrange strawberries for Almond Biscotti; chill.	Fill cream puffs for Cocktail Puffs; chill. Make Chocolate-Almond Cream.	Arrange refrigerated items on table for serving.	Prepare Party Punch in bowl.

CHOCOLATE TRUFFLES
(pictured on pages 110 and 111)

1 (6-ounce) package semisweet chocolate morsels
1 (9-ounce) package chocolate wafers, crushed
2 cups sifted powdered sugar
1 cup finely chopped walnuts, toasted
½ cup orange juice
½ teaspoon rum extract
Chocolate decorator sprinkles

Place chocolate morsels in top of a double boiler; bring water to a boil. Reduce heat to low; cook until chocolate melts. Remove from heat. Add wafer crumbs and next 4 ingredients; mix well. Cover; chill 30 minutes.

Shape mixture into 1-inch balls; roll lightly in chocolate sprinkles. Chill until firm. Store in an airtight container in refrigerator. Yield: about 7 dozen.

M. K. Quesenberry
Dugspur, Virginia

Right: *Framed photographs of guests serve as place cards at the bridesmaids' luncheon. The menu, featuring Chicken Breasts in Phyllo Pastry and Marinated Asparagus Medley, begins on page 104.*

(Front table, clockwise from top) Party Punch, Spritz Hearts, Almond Biscotti and strawberries with Chocolate-Almond Cream, Sweet Ravioli, Chocolate Truffles, and (in center of table) Savory Rosettes grace the table at this tradtional bridal tea. (Recipes and menu plan begin on page 106.)

A cornhusk angel bride is perfect for a sideboard arrangement including (from top) Chocolate Truffles, Calla Lily Sandwiches, and Cocktail Puffs. (Recipes begin on page 106.)

Cool, refreshing Party Punch (page 106) will be a hit at any bridal tea or shower. In making your preparations for this recipe, keep in mind that people tend to drink more of any beverage in warm weather. Therefore, you may want to have enough ingredients on hand for an extra batch.

Chocolate-Mint Cheesecake (page 104) is the perfect finale to a memorable evening.

Serve the rehearsal dinner from a decorated sideboard. The menu includes Tomatoes With Walnut-Rice Stuffing, commercial rolls, Marinated Carrots, and Shrimp-and-Chicken Casserole. (Recipes begin on page 102.)

A simple centerpiece of potted ivy and violets showcases the wedding reception food—Fresh Berry Tartlets, Curried Chicken Balls, and Prosciutto-Wrapped Asparagus— without overpowering it. These appetizers, along with others from the Savory Cheese Bar, grace the plate shown left. (Recipes, page 98.)

Savory Cheese Bar makes a special presentation of ordinary crackers and cheese. Serve commercial sauces on the side as toppings. Embed sprigs of fresh herbs in a clear gelatin mixture drizzled over the top of cheeses. Edible violets dress the cheese nicely. (Recipes and suggestions, page 98.)

Greenery and white chocolate curls decorate Double Chocolate Wedding Cake (page 100). Slicing the cake (see inset) reveals layers of both white and milk chocolate pound cake.

Artichokes And Asparagus Aplenty

April showers have brought May flowers and a welcome deluge of fresh spring vegetables. Two seasonal favorites—artichokes and asparagus—are a great start to lots of delicious dishes. A couple offered here taste equally good prepared conventionally or in the microwave.

STUFFED ARTICHOKES

4 artichokes
Lemon wedge
2 cups sliced green onions
4 cloves garlic, minced
½ cup butter or margarine, melted
1 cup Italian-seasoned breadcrumbs
1 cup grated Parmesan cheese
1 cup chopped fresh parsley
¼ cup water

Wash artichokes by plunging them up and down in cold water. Cut off stem end, and trim about ½ inch from top of each artichoke. Remove any loose bottom leaves. With scissors, trim away about a fourth of each outer leaf. Rub top and edges of leaves with a lemon wedge to prevent discoloration.

Place artichokes in a large Dutch oven; cover with water, and bring to a boil. Cover, reduce heat, and simmer 30 minutes or until lower leaves pull out easily; drain. Spread leaves apart; scrape out each fuzzy thistle center (choke) with a spoon, and set artichokes aside.

Sauté green onions and garlic in butter in a large skillet until tender; remove from heat. Stir in breadcrumbs, cheese, and parsley. Spoon vegetable mixture into artichoke cavities. Arrange artichokes in an 8-inch square baking dish; add ¼ cup water to dish. Cover and bake at 350° for 25 to 30 minutes. Yield: 4 servings.

Microwave Directions: Wash and trim artichokes following instructions above, and place in an 8-inch square baking dish; add ¼ cup water. Cover with heavy-duty plastic wrap; fold back a small corner of wrap to allow steam to escape. Microwave at HIGH 10 to 15 minutes or until lower leaves pull out easily, giving dish a half-turn after 7 minutes. Spread leaves apart; scrape out each fuzzy thistle center (choke) with a spoon. Set the artichokes aside.

Combine green onions, garlic, and butter in a 1-quart glass measure; microwave at HIGH 2 to 4 minutes or until onions are tender. Stir in breadcrumbs, cheese, and parsley. Spoon vegetable mixture into artichoke cavities. Arrange artichokes in an 8-inch square baking dish; add ¼ cup water to dish. Cover with heavy-duty plastic wrap; fold back a small corner of wrap to allow steam to escape. Microwave at HIGH 8 minutes, giving dish a half-turn after 4 minutes. *Dottie Placke Katy, Texas*

ASPARAGUS WITH ALMOND SAUCE

1 pound fresh asparagus spears
¼ cup slivered almonds
1 tablespoon butter or margarine
⅓ cup water
1 teaspoon cornstarch
½ teaspoon chicken-flavored bouillon granules
2 teaspoons lemon juice
Dash of pepper

Snap off tough ends of asparagus. Remove scales from stalks with a knife or vegetable peeler, if desired. Cook asparagus, covered, in a small amount of boiling water 6 to 8 minutes or until crisp-tender. Drain. Arrange on a serving platter; keep warm.

Sauté almonds in butter in a small saucepan 3 to 5 minutes or until golden brown. Combine water and remaining ingredients, stirring until blended, and add to sautéed almonds. Cook over medium heat, stirring constantly, until mixture comes to a boil. Boil 1 minute. Pour sauce over asparagus. Yield: 4 servings.

Microwave Directions: Snap off tough ends of asparagus. Remove scales from stalks, if desired. Combine asparagus and ¼ cup water in a shallow 2-quart baking dish. Cover tightly with heavy-duty plastic wrap; fold back a small corner of wrap to allow steam to escape. Microwave at HIGH 5 to 6 minutes; drain. Set aside, and keep warm.

Combine almonds and butter in a 1-quart glass measure; microwave at HIGH 1½ minutes, stirring after 1 minute. Combine ⅓ cup water and remaining ingredients, stirring until blended; add to almonds. Microwave at HIGH 2 to 3 minutes, stirring at 1-minute intervals. Pour sauce over asparagus. *Sandra Russell Gainesville, Florida*

ASPARAGUS HAM ROLLS

12 fresh asparagus spears
2 tablespoons butter or margarine
2 tablespoons all-purpose flour
½ teaspoon dry mustard
1 cup milk
4 (1-ounce) slices cooked ham
½ cup (2 ounces) shredded Cheddar cheese

Snap off tough ends of asparagus. Remove scales from stalks with a knife or vegetable peeler, if desired. Cook asparagus, covered, in a small amount of boiling water 6 to 8 minutes. Drain.

Melt butter in a heavy saucepan over low heat; add flour and mustard, stirring until smooth. Cook 1 minute, stirring constantly. Gradually add milk; cook over medium heat, stirring constantly, until mixture is thickened and bubbly.

Place 3 asparagus spears on each slice of ham; roll and secure with a wooden pick. Arrange rolls in a 1-quart casserole; pour sauce over rolls. Bake, uncovered, at 350° for 20 minutes or until thoroughly heated. Sprinkle with cheese, and bake an additional 3 to 5 minutes or until cheese melts. Yield: 2 to 3 servings. *Nancy Monroe Salisbury, North Carolina*

Fabulous Fruit Tarts

It's hard to top a fruit pie in terms of a luscious dessert, except if it's with one of these fruit tarts. The fillings are equally colorful and refreshing, but their shapely and freestanding pastry shells dress them for the fanciest of occasions.

Most large tarts are made in two-piece tart pans that have a bottom plate and a removable ring that shapes the sides of the crust. Leave the sides in place until serving time to protect the crust. To remove the sides, place your hand under the bottom center of the pan, and let the outer ring slip down over your wrist. You can also remove the bottom plate from firm tarts, but you may want to leave it intact as support for larger and more fragile tarts.

Miniature tart pans, such as those used for Berry Good Lemon Tarts, are usually one piece but can be slipped easily from the tiny pastries after cooling.

Most large department stores and kitchen specialty shops sell miniature tart pans, as well as the large ones.

PEACHY KEEN TARTS
(pictured on page 1)

Tart Pastry
1 (3-ounce) package cream cheese, softened
2 tablespoons powdered sugar
½ teaspoon grated orange rind
2 teaspoons orange juice
3 large fresh peaches
¾ cup apricot preserves
2 tablespoons Cointreau

Roll each portion of pastry to ⅛-inch thickness on a floured surface. Fit pastry into six 4-inch shallow tart pans or quiche pans. Roll over top of tart pans with a rolling pin to trim excess pastry. Prick bottom of pastry with a fork. Bake at 450° for 10 minutes or until lightly browned. Cool.

Combine cream cheese and next 3 ingredients in a mixing bowl; beat at medium speed of an electric mixer until blended. Spoon mixture evenly into 6 tart pans, spreading to edges.

Place peaches in a large saucepan of boiling water 10 seconds; drain and cool slightly. Carefully peel peaches, and cut in half lengthwise; remove pits. Cut peaches into ⅛-inch-thick lengthwise slices, keeping slices in order as they are cut. Arrange slices over cream cheese mixture in the shape of peach halves, letting slices fan out slightly.

Heat preserves over low heat until melted. Press preserves through a sieve to remove lumps. Stir Cointreau into preserves, and brush liberally over peaches. Yield: 6 servings.

Tart Pastry

1½ cups all-purpose flour
½ teaspoon baking powder
½ teaspoon salt
¼ cup butter or margarine
¼ cup shortening
4 to 6 tablespoons milk

Combine first 3 ingredients; cut in butter and shortening with a pastry blender until mixture resembles coarse meal. Sprinkle milk evenly over surface of mixture; stir with a fork until dry ingredients are moistened. Divide into 6 equal portions. Wrap in plastic wrap; chill. Yield: pastry for six 4-inch tarts.

PICK-A-BERRY TART
(pictured on page 149)

¾ cup sugar
1 tablespoon cornstarch
⅛ teaspoon salt
4 cups fresh blueberries, blackberries, or raspberries
1 tablespoon butter or margarine
1 tablespoon lemon juice
Tart Pastry

Combine sugar, cornstarch, and salt in a medium saucepan, stirring well to remove lumps. Add berries; stir well. Cook over low heat, stirring constantly, until mixture comes to a boil. Boil 1 minute. Add butter and lemon juice, stirring until butter melts. Remove from heat, and set aside to cool.

Roll one-third of Tart Pastry to ⅛-inch thickness on a lightly floured surface; fit into a 10-inch round tart pan with removable bottom. Pour cooled mixture into unbaked shell.

Roll another one-third of pastry to ⅛-inch thickness. Cut into ½-inch strips, using a fluted pastry wheel. Carefully weave strips together on wax paper, weaving strips as close together as possible. Roll last one-third of pastry to ⅛-inch thickness, cutting and weaving enough of it to make lattice measure 10½ inches square. Fold pastry in half with wax paper on the inside. Carefully unfold pastry over filling. Gently remove wax paper. Roll over top of tart pan with rolling pin to trim excess pastry.

Bake at 400° for 20 minutes. Reduce heat to 350°; bake 30 to 35 minutes or until crust is browned. Cool. Yield: one 10-inch tart.

Tart Pastry

3½ cups all-purpose flour
1¼ teaspoons baking powder
1⅛ teaspoons salt
⅔ cup shortening
½ cup butter or margarine
¾ to 1 cup milk

Combine first 3 ingredients; cut in shortening and butter with a pastry blender until mixture resembles coarse meal. Sprinkle milk evenly over surface of mixture; stir with a fork until dry ingredients are moistened. Divide into 3 portions. Wrap in plastic wrap; chill. Yield: pastry for one double-crust 10-inch tart.

FANCY FRUIT TART
(pictured on page 1)

Sugar Cookie Pastry
Lemon Cream
½ cup fresh blueberries
½ cup fresh blackberries
½ cup grape halves
⅔ cup fresh raspberries
1 cup halved strawberries
1 peach, peeled and sliced
1 cup peach preserves

Roll Sugar Cookie Pastry to a rectangle of ⅛-inch thickness between two sheets of wax paper; chill. Remove one sheet of paper, and invert pastry into an 11- x 7½- x 1-inch tart pan, paper side up. Carefully peel away paper, and press pastry into pan. Roll over top of tart pan with a rolling pin to trim excess pastry. (Sugar Cookie Pastry is fragile; patch with pastry trimmings, if necessary.)

Carefully line pastry with aluminum foil, and fill foil with pastry weights or dried beans. Bake at 375° for 15 minutes. Carefully remove foil and weights, and bake an additional 7 minutes or until pastry is browned. Cool on wire rack.

Spoon Lemon Cream into baked pastry. Arrange fruit over Lemon Cream. Heat preserves over low heat until melted. Press preserves through a sieve to remove lumps. Brush strained preserves lightly over fruit. Yield: one 11- x 7½-inch tart.

Sugar Cookie Pastry

1¼ cups all-purpose flour
1½ tablespoons sugar
½ cup butter or margarine
3 to 4 tablespoons ice water
1 egg yolk, lightly beaten

Combine flour and sugar; cut in butter until mixture resembles coarse meal. Combine water and egg yolk; sprinkle yolk mixture (1 tablespoon at a time)

evenly over surface; stir with a fork until dry ingredients are moistened.

Shape into a ball; cover and chill at least 1 hour. Yield: pastry for one 11- x 7½-inch tart.

Lemon Cream

4 egg yolks
⅔ cup sugar
¼ cup lemon juice
⅓ cup butter or margarine
3 tablespoons half-and-half

Combine all ingredients in a heavy saucepan, beating well. Cook over medium-low heat 10 minutes or until mixture thickens, stirring constantly. Remove from heat; let mixture cool. Yield: 1¼ cups.

BERRY GOOD LEMON TARTS
(pictured on page 1)

Basic Pastry
3 egg yolks
⅔ cup sugar
¼ cup lemon juice
⅓ cup butter or margarine
2 teaspoons grated lemon rind
Garnish: blueberries, blackberries, raspberries, or strawberries

Divide Basic Pastry into 18 equal portions; gently press each portion into 2-inch tart pans. Prick bottom of pastry generously with a fork. Bake at 375° for 12 to 15 minutes or until lightly browned.

Combine egg yolks, sugar, and lemon juice in a small heavy saucepan, stirring until blended. Cook over low heat, stirring constantly, 5 minutes or until thickened. Remove from heat, and stir in butter and lemon rind. Cool and spoon into tart shells. Cover and chill thoroughly. Garnish, if desired. Yield: 1½ dozen.

Basic Pastry

1¼ cups all-purpose flour
½ teaspoon salt
⅓ cup plus 2 tablespoons shortening
3 to 4 tablespoons cold water

Combine flour and salt; cut in shortening with a pastry blender until mixture resembles coarse meal. Sprinkle water evenly over surface of mixture; stir with a fork until dry ingredients are moistened. Shape into a ball; chill. Yield: pastry for 18 (2-inch) tarts.

Peas For The Picking

There are so many kinds of peas to keep straight—English, snow, Sugar Snap—and the list goes on. But no matter what the type, the delicate aroma and succulent flavor are unmistakable when fresh. The only problem may be picking a favorite from these garden treasures. Out of the list of hundreds, we've chosen dishes for the three most popular spring peas.

MINTED PEA SALAD

2 cups fresh or frozen English peas
¼ cup mayonnaise or salad dressing
¼ cup sour cream
¼ cup thinly sliced green onions
1 tablespoon minced fresh mint
½ teaspoon Dijon mustard
⅛ teaspoon salt
⅛ teaspoon white pepper
Radicchio leaves
Garnish: fresh mint sprigs

Cover peas with water in a saucepan, and bring to a boil. Cover, reduce heat, and simmer 12 to 15 minutes or until peas are tender. Drain; plunge in ice water. Drain.

Combine mayonnaise and next 6 ingredients; stir well. Add peas, and toss lightly to coat; chill. Serve on radicchio leaves. Garnish, if desired. Yield: 4 servings.
Gwen Louer
Roswell, Georgia

Spring Peas

Before you head to the garden or market, recipes in hand, we'll arm you with basic information about the peas you'll likely find this time of year.

- **English**—Also called garden or green peas, English peas are available fresh, frozen, and canned. The pods are discarded, and only the familiar bright-green, round peas inside are eaten.

- **Snow**—Because they're so often used in Oriental cuisine, these wafer-thin pods are also known as Chinese pea pods. After washing and trimming both ends, eat the pod and all, raw or cooked. You can also find them in the frozen foods section.

- **Sugar Snap**—A cross between English and snow peas, these are darker green and have a fatter pod and thicker skin than snow peas. Wash, remove ends and strings, and cook only a few minutes before serving. Sugar Snaps, available both fresh and frozen, are relatively new, so they may be harder to find.

POTATO SALAD WITH SUGAR SNAP PEAS

½ pound Sugar Snap peas
¾ pound new potatoes
3 tablespoons chopped shallots
2 tablespoons peanut or
  vegetable oil
2 tablespoons white wine vinegar
¼ cup minced fresh parsley
½ teaspoon minced garlic
¼ teaspoon freshly ground pepper

Wash pea pods, and remove strings and ends. Cook peas in boiling, salted water 3 to 5 minutes or until crisp-tender; drain.

Cook potatoes in boiling, salted water to cover 15 minutes or until tender. Drain and let potatoes cool to touch. Cut potatoes into ¼-inch slices, leaving skins intact, if desired. Combine potatoes and peas.

Combine shallots and remaining ingredients; pour over potatoes and peas. Toss. Serve warm or cold. Yield: 4 servings. *Joyce M. Maurer Christmas, Florida*

COLD CURRIED PEA SOUP

1 cup fresh or frozen English peas
1 medium onion, sliced
1 carrot, scraped and sliced
1 small potato, peeled and sliced
1 stalk celery with leaves, sliced
1 clove garlic, minced
1 teaspoon curry powder
½ teaspoon salt
1 (10¾-ounce) can condensed
  chicken broth, undiluted and
  divided
1 cup milk
¾ cup whipping cream

Combine first 8 ingredients in a saucepan. Add 1 cup chicken broth; bring to a boil. Cover, reduce heat, and simmer 15 minutes or until vegetables are tender. Cool slightly, and spoon mixture into container of an electric blender; add remaining broth, and process until smooth.

Return vegetable mixture to saucepan; stir in milk and cream. Chill. Yield: 4½ cups. *Marie H. Webb Roanoke, Virginia*

SNOW PEAS AND PINEAPPLE

1 (15¼-ounce) can unsweetened
  pineappple tidbits, undrained
2 teaspoons sugar
1½ teaspoons cornstarch
1 tablespoon soy sauce
1½ cups fresh snow pea pods,
  trimmed, or 1 (6-ounce) package
  frozen snow pea pods

Drain pineapple, reserving ½ cup juice; set pineapple aside. Combine juice, sugar, cornstarch, and soy sauce in a large skillet. Cook over medium heat, stirring constantly, until thickened and bubbly. Add snow peas and pineapple; bring to a boil. Boil 1 to 2 minutes, stirring constantly. Serve immediately. Yield: 4 to 6 servings. *Mrs. Earl Faulkenberry Lancaster, South Carolina*

ON THE LIGHT SIDE

You'll Be Surprised, It's Oven Fried

We searched through hundreds of oven-fried recipes to find the ones offered here that are comparable to pan-fried and deep-fried. Our test kitchens staff tested several different recipes of each food to make sure we selected the best.

NO-FRY-PAN CHICKEN FINGERS

1 (8½-ounce) can chow mein
  noodles
½ cup nonfat buttermilk
1 teaspoon reduced-sodium soy
  sauce
½ teaspoon salt-free herb-and-spice
  blend
¼ teaspoon garlic powder
¼ teaspoon pepper
6 (4-ounce) skinned, boned chicken
  breast halves, cut into 18 strips
Vegetable cooking spray

Place noodles in container of an electric blender or food processor; process until crumbs form. Place in a shallow dish, and set aside.

Combine buttermilk and next 4 ingredients. Dip each chicken strip into buttermilk mixture; coat with crumbs. Place on a baking sheet coated with cooking spray. Bake at 350° for 18 minutes; turn and bake an additional 15 minutes or until golden. Yield: 6 servings (357 calories per 3 strips).

□ *29.7 grams protein, 15.4 grams fat, 24.4 grams carbohydrate, 71 milligrams cholesterol, 269 milligrams sodium, and 43 milligrams calcium.*

Judi Grigoraci
Charleston, West Virginia

BREADED HERBED FISH FILLETS

½ cup fine, dry breadcrumbs
¼ cup all-purpose flour
2 teaspoons chicken-flavored bouillon granules
1 teaspoon dried onion flakes
1 teaspoon paprika
1 teaspoon dried parsley flakes
½ teaspoon dried whole dillweed
½ teaspoon dried whole thyme
¼ teaspoon garlic powder
4 (4-ounce) farm-raised catfish fillets
Butter-flavored vegetable cooking spray

Combine first 9 ingredients in a shallow dish. Coat fillets with cooking spray; dredge in breadcrumb mixture. Place fillets on a broiler pan coated with cooking spray; bake, uncovered, at 400° for 20 minutes or until fish flakes easily when tested with a fork. Serve immediately. Yield: 4 servings (225 calories per fillet).

□ *23.7 grams protein, 6.2 grams fat, 17.2 grams carbohydrate, 66 milligrams cholesterol, 630 milligrams sodium, and 70 milligrams calcium.*

Elizabeth Benbenek
Ballwin, Missouri

OVEN-FRIED TURKEY CUTLETS

1 egg
2 teaspoons vegetable oil
½ cup Italian-seasoned breadcrumbs
2 tablespoons grated Parmesan cheese
1 pound turkey breast cutlets
Vegetable cooking spray
½ cup commercial marinara sauce

Combine egg and oil in a shallow dish; beat well, and set aside. Combine breadcrumbs and Parmesan cheese in a shallow dish. Dip turkey in egg mixture; dredge in breadcrumb mixture.
Place turkey on a baking sheet coated with cooking spray. Spray each cutlet lightly with cooking spray. Bake at 350° for 8 to 10 minutes or until done. Serve turkey with commercial marinara sauce. Yield: 4 servings (271 calories per cutlet with 2 tablespoons marinara sauce).

□ *38.2 grams protein, 7.1 grams fat, 14.1 grams carbohydrate, 122 milligrams cholesterol, 725 milligrams sodium, and 62 milligrams calcium.*

Barbara Ek
Kansas City, Missouri

OVEN-FRIED OKRA

1 pound fresh okra
¼ cup egg substitute
¼ cup nonfat buttermilk
⅔ cup cornmeal
⅓ cup all-purpose flour
1 teaspoon baking powder
½ teaspoon salt
1 tablespoon vegetable oil
Vegetable cooking spray

Wash okra, and drain. Remove tips and stem ends; cut okra crosswise into ½-inch slices.
Combine egg substitute and buttermilk; add okra, stirring to coat well. Let stand 10 minutes.
Combine cornmeal and next 3 ingredients in a zip-top plastic bag.

Drain okra, small portions at a time, using a slotted spoon; place okra in bag with cornmeal mixture, shaking gently to coat. Brush oil on a 15- x 10- x 1-inch jellyroll pan; add okra in a single layer.
Coat okra with cooking spray, and bake at 450° for 8 minutes. Stir well, and spray with cooking spray again; bake an additional 7 to 8 minutes. After last baking, broil 4 inches from heat 4 to 5 minutes or until browned, stirring occasionally. Yield: 7 servings (114 calories per ½-cup serving).

□ *3.7 grams protein, 2.8 grams fat, 19.2 grams carbohydrate, 0 milligrams cholesterol, 233 milligrams sodium, and 84 milligrams calcium.*

OVEN-FRIED ZUCCHINI SPEARS

3 tablespoons herb-seasoned breadcrumbs
1 tablespoon grated Parmesan cheese
⅛ teaspoon garlic powder
⅛ teaspoon paprika
⅛ teaspoon pepper
2 medium zucchini (about 12 ounces)
2 teaspoons vegetable oil
2 tablespoons water
Vegetable cooking spray

Combine breadcrumbs, Parmesan cheese, garlic powder, paprika, and pepper in a shallow dish; set aside.
Cut each zucchini lengthwise into 4 pieces; cut each piece in half crosswise. Place zucchini in a zip-top plastic bag; add oil and water. Shake.
Dredge zucchini in breadcrumb mixture, and place on a baking sheet coated with cooking spray. Bake at 475° for 10 minutes or until brown and tender. Yield: 4 servings (60 calories per 4 wedges).

□ *2.3 grams protein, 3.1 grams fat, 6.6 grams carbohydrate, 1 milligram cholesterol, 175 milligrams sodium, and 36 milligrams calcium.*

Donna Jelley
Stillwater, Oklahoma

OVEN FRENCH FRIES

½ cup grated Parmesan cheese
2 teaspoons dried whole oregano
2 (8-ounce) baking potatoes, unpeeled
1 egg white, beaten
Vegetable cooking spray

Combine Parmesan cheese and oregano; set aside.

Cut each potato lengthwise into 8 wedges; dip into egg white, and dredge in Parmesan cheese mixture. Place fries on a baking sheet coated with vegetable cooking spray. Bake at 425° for 25 minutes. Yield: 4 servings (137 calories per 4 wedges).

☐ *7.5 grams protein, 3.4 grams fat, 19.8 grams carbohydrate, 8 milligrams cholesterol, 206 milligrams sodium, and 165 milligrams calcium.*
Mrs. Gordon P. Bobbitt
Burleson, Texas

OVEN-FRIED GREEN TOMATOES

⅓ cup cornmeal
⅓ cup all-purpose flour
½ teaspoon salt
½ teaspoon pepper
4 medium-size green tomatoes, cut into ½-inch slices
Vegetable cooking spray
1 tablespoon grated Parmesan cheese

Combine first 4 ingredients in a shallow dish; set aside. Dip tomato slices in water; dredge in cornmeal mixture. Place tomato slices on a baking sheet coated with cooking spray. Coat each slice with cooking spray. Bake at 400° for 15 minutes; sprinkle with Parmesan cheese, and bake an additional 5 minutes or until golden. Serve immediately. Yield: 8 servings (64 calories per 2 slices).

☐ *2.1 grams protein, 1.1 grams fat, 12.1 grams carbohydrate, 0 milligrams cholesterol, 168 milligrams sodium, and 20 milligrams calcium.*
Lynne Teal Weeks
Columbus, Georgia

Put Crab Cakes In The Spotlight

If you ask residents of Maryland's Eastern shore how they serve crab, they're likely to reply "crab cakes." Keeping that in mind, we created a healthy menu featuring crab cakes. We've minimized the fat and calories by replacing the eggs with egg whites, using reduced-calorie mayonnaise, and frying the cakes in a nonstick skillet coated with vegetable cooking spray. The cakes are moist inside with a crusty outside.

Roasted Red Pepper Corn makes a colorful complement for Crab Cakes. At fewer than 550 calories and less than 20% fat, the menu is a delicious way to eat light and healthy.

Crab Cakes
Roasted Red Pepper Corn
Green salad with
oil-free dressing
Yogurt Crescent Rolls
Grapefruit Ice

CRAB CAKES
(pictured on page 75)

2 egg whites, slightly beaten
2 tablespoons reduced-calorie mayonnaise
2 teaspoons chopped fresh parsley
1¼ teaspoons Old Bay seasoning
1 teaspoon reduced-sodium Worcestershire sauce
1 teaspoon dry mustard
¼ teaspoon pepper
½ cup soft breadcrumbs
1 pound fresh, lump crabmeat, drained
Olive oil-flavored vegetable cooking spray

Combine first 7 ingredients. Stir in breadcrumbs and crabmeat, and shape into 8 (2½-inch) patties. Place on a baking sheet lined with wax paper; chill 30 minutes.

Coat a large nonstick skillet with cooking spray; place over medium-high heat until hot. Add crab cakes, and cook 3 minutes on each side or until browned. Yield: 4 servings (206 calories per 2 crab cakes).

☐ *26.5 grams protein, 5.1 grams fat, 11.5 grams carbohydrate, 117 milligrams cholesterol, 664 milligrams sodium, and 145 milligrams calcium.*
Audrey Mulcare
Lehigh Acres, Florida

ROASTED RED PEPPER CORN
(pictured on page 75)

4 medium-size ears fresh corn
Butter-flavored vegetable cooking spray
¼ cup diced sweet red pepper

Remove husks and silks from corn. Place each ear on a piece of heavy-duty aluminum foil, and coat with cooking spray. Sprinkle 1 tablespoon sweet red pepper on each ear of corn. Roll foil lengthwise around corn, and twist foil at each end. Bake at 500° for 20 minutes. Yield: 4 servings (89 calories each).

☐ *2.5 grams protein, 1.6 grams fat, 19.3 grams carbohydrate, 0 milligrams cholesterol, 13 milligrams sodium, and 2 milligrams calcium.*

GRAPEFRUIT ICE

⅔ cup sugar
2⅓ cups grapefruit juice
½ teaspoon grated grapefruit rind
2 cups champagne, chilled

Combine sugar and grapefruit juice in a saucepan; bring to a boil, stirring constantly. Cover, reduce heat, and simmer 5 minutes. Let cool.

Combine grapefruit mixture, grape-fruit rind, and champagne; pour into a 13- x 9- x 2-inch pan. Freeze until almost firm. Spoon mixture into a bowl, and beat at medium speed of an electric mixer until slushy.

Return to pan. Freeze mixture 8 hours. Spoon into sherbet glasses, and serve immediately. Yield: 8 servings (136 calories per 1-cup serving).

□ *0.5 gram protein, 0.1 gram fat, 23.8 grams carbohydrate, 0 milligrams cholesterol, 3 milligrams sodium, and 7 milligrams calcium.*

LIGHT FAVORITE

Crescent Rolls With Half The Fat

Most breads are a healthy addition to a meal; however, the fat in them can turn bread into a not-so-healthy food. Sour Cream Crescent Rolls is a good example of a bread that is high in fat. To make them healthier we substituted yogurt for sour cream and vegetable oil for butter. Then we decreased the amount of oil. The result is tender Yogurt Crescent Rolls with 1.9 grams of fat each.

YOGURT CRESCENT ROLLS
(pictured on page 74)

⅓ cup vegetable oil
1 (8-ounce) carton plain low-fat
  yogurt
½ cup sugar
2 packages dry yeast
½ cup warm water (105° to 115°)
1 egg
1 egg white
4 cups all-purpose flour
1 teaspoon salt
Butter-flavored vegetable cooking
  spray

Combine first 3 ingredients; set aside. Dissolve yeast in warm water in a large mixing bowl; let stand 5 minutes. Stir in yogurt mixture, egg, and egg white.

Combine flour and salt. Stir 2 cups flour mixture into yogurt mixture; beat at medium speed of an electric mixer until smooth. Gradually stir in remaining flour mixture. Cover and refrigerate 8 hours.

Punch dough down, and divide into 4 equal portions. Roll each portion to a 10-inch circle on a floured surface; coat with cooking spray. Cut each circle into 12 wedges; roll up each wedge, beginning at wide end. Place on baking sheets coated with cooking spray, point side down.

Cover and let rise in a warm place (85°), free from drafts, 45 minutes or until doubled in bulk. Bake at 375° for 10 to 12 minutes or until rolls are golden brown. Yield: 4 dozen (66 calories per roll).

□ *1.7 grams protein, 1.9 grams fat, 10.5 grams carbohydrate, 5 milligrams cholesterol, 56 milligrams sodium, and 11 milligrams calcium.*

COMPARE THE NUTRIENTS		
(per serving)		
	Traditional	Light
Calories	89	66
Fat	4.6g	1.9g
Cholesterol	19mg	5mg

QUICK!

Speedy Stir-Fry

These recipes combine meat and vegetables over rice, making an easy, complete meal. When shopping for stir-fry ingredients, check out the rice section, too. You'll find a diversity of rices and flavored rice mixes to add variety and convenience. For the best use of your time, begin cooking the rice before you start the stir-fry. Remember, regular rice takes 20 minutes; instant, 4 to 7 minutes; boil in bags, 10 minutes; and flavored mixes vary according to package directions.

QUICK BEEF AND BROCCOLI

1 pound flank steak
¼ cup soy sauce
1 tablespoon dry sherry
1 tablespoon cornstarch
1 teaspoon sugar
2 stalks broccoli
3 tablespoons vegetable oil, divided
1 small onion, cut into strips
½ cup sliced fresh mushrooms
Hot cooked rice

Slice steak diagonally across grain into thin strips, and place in a shallow dish. Combine soy sauce, sherry, cornstarch, and sugar in a small bowl; pour over steak, and set aside.

Cut flowerets from broccoli; cut stalks into thin slices.

Pour 2 tablespoons oil into a wok or large skillet, coating bottom and sides; heat to medium high (325°) for 1 minute. Add broccoli and onion; stir-fry 2 minutes. Remove from wok.

Pour remaining 1 tablespoon oil into wok, coating sides. Add steak; stir-fry 2 minutes. Add mushrooms; stir-fry 1 to 2 minutes. Stir in broccoli mixture. Serve over rice. Yield: 4 servings.
Terri Cohen
North Potomac, Maryland

STIR-FRY BEEF AND ASPARAGUS

1 pound boneless sirloin steak
1 tablespoon cornstarch, divided
3 tablespoons dry sherry, divided
3 tablespoons soy sauce, divided
1½ tablespoons vegetable oil
1 pound fresh asparagus, cut diagonally into 1-inch lengths
3 tablespoons beef broth
Hot cooked rice

Slice steak diagonally across grain into thin strips; place in a shallow dish. Combine 2 teaspoons cornstarch, 2 tablespoons sherry, and 2 tablespoons soy sauce; pour over steak, and marinate 10 minutes. Remove steak from marinade.

Pour oil into a wok or large skillet, coating bottom and sides; heat to medium high (325°) for 2 minutes. Add steak, and stir-fry 4 minutes or until browned. Remove steak from wok. Add asparagus and beef broth. Bring to a boil; cover, reduce heat, and simmer 3 minutes.

Combine remaining 1 teaspoon cornstarch, 1 tablespoon sherry, and 1 tablespoon soy sauce. Add cornstarch mixture and steak to wok; bring to a boil. Cook, stirring constantly, 1 minute. Serve over rice. Yield: 3 or 4 servings.

Marge Killmon
Annandale, Virginia

HURRY-UP CHICKEN STIR-FRY

2 tablespoons vegetable oil, divided
1 cup broccoli flowerets
1 cup cauliflower flowerets
1 large carrot, cut into 2-inch strips
3 green onions, sliced
1 clove garlic, minced
3 chicken breast halves, skinned, boned, and cut into 1-inch pieces
½ cup commercial Italian salad dressing
1 tablespoon soy sauce
½ teaspoon ground ginger
Hot cooked rice

Pour 1 tablespoon oil into a wok or large skillet, coating bottom and sides; heat to medium high (325°) for 2 minutes. Add broccoli and next 4 ingredients; stir-fry 4 minutes. Remove vegetables from skillet. Pour remaining 1 tablespoon oil into wok. Add chicken; stir-fry 4 minutes or until tender. Return vegetables to wok; stir in salad dressing, soy sauce, and ginger. Serve over rice. Yield: 3 servings.

Louise Osborne
Lexington, Kentucky

EASY CHICKEN STIR-FRY

2 tablespoons vegetable oil
4 chicken breast halves, skinned, boned, and cut into strips
1 (2.25-ounce) package sliced almonds
1 (16-ounce) package frozen broccoli, baby carrots, and water chestnuts
¼ cup soy sauce
3 tablespoons pineapple juice
1½ teaspoons cornstarch
Hot cooked rice

Pour oil into a wok or skillet, coating bottom and sides; heat to medium high (325°) for 2 minutes. Add chicken and almonds; stir-fry 2 minutes. Add vegetables; cover and cook 4 minutes, stirring occasionally. Combine soy sauce, pineapple juice, and cornstarch; add to vegetables, and cook 2 minutes or until thickened. Serve over rice. Yield: 4 servings.

Serve A Fancy Spread

Do you ever need a quick appetizer that's also special? If you do, you'll want to keep this recipe for Herb-Cheese Spread close at hand. "You can make it when you get home from work and serve it as guests arrive for dinner," explains Libby Idom of Houston, Texas.

HERB-CHEESE SPREAD

1 teaspoon Dijon mustard
1 (12-ounce) package Havarti cheese
1 teaspoon dried parsley flakes
½ teaspoon freeze-dried chives
¼ teaspoon dried whole dillweed
¼ teaspoon dried whole basil
¼ teaspoon fennel seeds
½ (17¼-ounce) package frozen puff pastry, thawed
1 egg, beaten

Spread mustard over top of cheese; sprinkle with parsley flakes and next 4 ingredients. Place cheese, mustard side down, in center of pastry. Wrap package style, trimming excess pastry. Seal seam. Place seam side down on a lightly greased baking sheet. Brush with egg; chill 30 minutes. Bake at 375° for 20 minutes; brush with egg, and bake an additional 10 minutes or until golden brown. Serve warm with assorted crackers or sliced apples or pears. Yield: 8 to 10 appetizer servings.

Tip: *Use finely chopped fresh herbs whenever possible. Dried whole herbs are usually the next best choice since they maintain their strength longer than the commercially ground form. Remember to use 3 times more fresh herbs in a recipe if it calls for the more potent dried form.*

JUNE

It's time to enjoy the sweet harvest of summer. And what better way than with our new recipes that give a little twist to the natural goodness of fresh corn, peppers, melons, and strawberries? Fresh *and* light *are the key words to good food these days, and you'll find plenty of information, recipes, and menus on the subject in the special section called "On the Light Side."*

Summer's Sweet Harvest

The summer harvest will bring an abundance of berries, peppers, corn, and melons, so get out in the garden or a pick-your-own patch—and taste nature's precious treasures. Then fill a basket with a colorful assortment, and try our recipes that highlight summer's freshness.

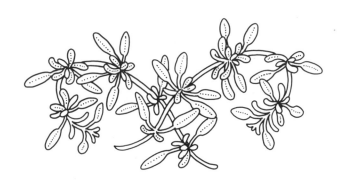

RAINBOW PEPPER MEDLEY
(pictured on page 151)

2 green peppers
2 sweet red peppers
1 sweet yellow pepper
1 purple onion (optional)
⅓ cup vegetable oil
2 tablespoons tarragon vinegar
1 tablespoon Dijon mustard
2 teaspoons sugar
1 teaspoon salt
¼ teaspoon freshly ground pepper
¼ teaspoon hot sauce
1 jalapeño pepper, minced
2 teaspoons caraway seeds
1 teaspoon grated lime rind

Cut peppers and, if desired, onion into julienne strips; set aside.

Combine oil and next 6 ingredients in a large bowl; beat with a wire whisk until thickened. Add reserved vegetables, jalapeño pepper, caraway seeds, and lime rind, tossing gently.

Cover and refrigerate 3 hours. Yield: 8 to 10 servings.

Peggy H. Amos
Martinsville, Virginia

FRESH CORN SALAD
(pictured on page 151)

3 cups corn cut from cob
  (about 6 ears)
1 large onion, chopped
2 medium zucchini, unpeeled
  and cubed
1 bunch green onions, sliced
1 sweet red pepper, chopped
1 green pepper, chopped
¼ cup minced fresh parsley
1 clove garlic, minced
¼ teaspoon salt
⅛ teaspoon pepper
2 teaspoons sugar
1 teaspoon ground cumin
2 teaspoons Dijon mustard
½ teaspoon hot sauce
⅔ cup vegetable oil
⅓ cup white vinegar

Cook corn, covered, in boiling water to cover 8 to 10 minutes; drain and cool. Combine corn and next 6 ingredients. Set aside.

Combine garlic and remaining ingredients, stirring well. Toss gently with vegetables. Chill 8 hours. Serve salad with a slotted spoon. Yield: 12 to 14 servings.

Eileen Wehling
Austin, Texas

CANTALOUPE GREEN SALAD
(pictured on page 151)

4 cups cantaloupe balls
1 head Bibb lettuce
1 small onion, sliced and separated
  into rings
4 slices bacon, cooked and
  crumbled
Sweet-and-Sour Dressing

Arrange cantaloupe balls on lettuce leaves on individual salad plates. Top cantaloupe with onion rings and bacon. Drizzle Sweet-and-Sour Dressing over salad. Yield: 4 servings.

Sweet-and-Sour Dressing

¼ cup vegetable oil
1½ tablespoons honey
1½ tablespoons white wine vinegar
½ teaspoon dried whole basil
½ teaspoon minced onion
¼ teaspoon dry mustard
Pinch of salt

Combine all ingredients, stirring with a wire whisk; cover dressing and chill. Yield: ⅓ cup.

STRAWBERRIES ROMANOFF
(pictured on page 151)

2 pints fresh strawberries
⅓ cup sugar
⅓ cup Grand Marnier or other
  orange-flavored liqueur
Zest or grated rind of 1 orange
Sweetened whipped cream
  (optional)

Wash and hull strawberries, and pat dry. Combine sugar, Grand Marnier, and orange zest in a large bowl; stir until sugar dissolves. Add strawberries; stir gently to coat.

Cover and chill 2 to 3 hours, stirring occasionally. Spoon into individual dishes; top with whipped cream, if desired. Yield: 4 to 6 servings.

Note: Kitchen shops carry citrus zesters for cutting orange rind into short, fine shreds or "zest."

Barbara W. Davis
Lilburn, Georgia

QUICK!
Weeknight Solutions

Even a gourmet cook relies on short-cuts for busy days. Besides, commercial soups, sauces, and convenience products make easy work of these meal-in-one casseroles. They're just right for hectic times.

BEEF-STUFFED PEPPERS

4 medium-size green peppers
1 egg, lightly beaten
1 (14-ounce) jar spaghetti sauce, divided
1 cup seasoned croutons, crushed
1 teaspoon dried onion flakes
¼ teaspoon pepper
¾ pound ground chuck
Grated Parmesan cheese

Cut off tops of green peppers, and remove seeds. Wash peppers.

Combine egg, ¾ cup spaghetti sauce, and next 4 ingredients, stirring well. Stuff peppers with meat mixture, and place peppers in a lightly greased 8-inch square baking dish. Cover loosely with wax paper. Microwave at HIGH 12 to 14 minutes, giving dish a half-turn after 6 minutes. Spoon a small amount of remaining spaghetti sauce over tops of peppers; sprinkle with Parmesan cheese. Heat remaining spaghetti sauce, and serve with peppers. Yield: 4 servings.

Tip: *When you are selecting peppers, size is not an indication of quality. Look for peppers with smooth, slick skin that has not shriveled.*

HAM ROLL CASSEROLE

2 (10-ounce) packages frozen broccoli spears
8 (1-ounce) slices Swiss cheese
8 (6- x 4-inch) slices cooked ham
1 (10¾-ounce) can cream of mushroom soup, undiluted
½ cup sour cream
2 teaspoons Dijon mustard
2 tablespoons sliced almonds

Place broccoli in a 12- x 8- x 2-inch baking dish. Cover tightly with heavy-duty plastic wrap; fold back a small corner of wrap to allow steam to escape. Microwave at HIGH 2 to 3 minutes. Rearrange spears. Cover and microwave at HIGH an additional 3 to 4 minutes. Drain broccoli; set aside.

Place 1 slice of cheese on each ham slice. Divide broccoli into 8 portions; arrange a portion on each ham slice, placing stems in the center and flowerets to the outside. Roll up securely, and place seam side down in greased 12- x 8- x 2-inch baking dish.

Combine soup, sour cream, and mustard; pour over ham rolls. Sprinkle with almonds. Cover with heavy-duty plastic wrap; fold back a small corner of wrap to allow steam to escape. Microwave at HIGH 8 to 10 minutes or until casserole is thoroughly heated, giving dish a half-turn after 5 minutes. Yield: 4 to 6 servings.

Conventional Directions: Cook broccoli according to package directions. Assemble casserole; cover and bake at 350° for 20 minutes or until bubbly.
Carol Y. Chastain
San Antonio, Texas

CHICKEN MEXICANA

4 chicken breast halves, skinned and boned
1 (10¾-ounce) can cream of chicken soup, undiluted
1 (11-ounce) can Cheddar cheese soup, undiluted
1 (10-ounce) can diced tomatoes and green chiles
2½ cups crushed corn chips

Cut chicken into bite-size pieces; arrange in an 8-inch square baking dish. Cover with wax paper, and microwave at HIGH 6 to 8 minutes or until chicken is done. Cool; cut chicken into smaller pieces, if desired.

Combine chicken soup, cheese soup, and tomatoes and green chiles. Layer half of chips and all of chicken in a lightly greased 12- x 8- x 2-inch baking dish; pour soup mixture over chicken. Microwave at HIGH 10 to 12 minutes, turning dish after 5 minutes. Sprinkle remaining chips on top, and microwave at HIGH 1 to 1½ additional minutes. Yield: 6 servings.
Doris B. Williams
Tulsa, Oklahoma

LOTS OF NOODLES LASAGNA

4 ounces medium egg noodles
1 (8-ounce) package cream cheese
1 cup cream-style cottage cheese
½ cup sour cream
1 pound ground chuck
1 (14-ounce) jar spaghetti sauce
½ cup grated Parmesan cheese

Cook noodles according to package directions; drain. Spoon into a lightly greased 12- x 8- x 2-inch baking dish.

Place cream cheese in a 1-quart microwave-safe bowl; microwave at HIGH 30 to 50 seconds. Add cottage cheese and sour cream; stir well. Spread mixture over noodles.

Crumble beef into a microwave-safe colander; place in a 9-inch pieplate. Cover beef with wax paper; microwave at HIGH 5 to 7 minutes or until meat is no longer pink, stirring after 3 minutes.

Combine beef and spaghetti sauce; spoon over cream cheese mixture. Sprinkle with Parmesan cheese. Cover tightly with heavy-duty plastic wrap; fold back a small corner of wrap to allow steam to escape. Microwave at HIGH 8 to 10 minutes, giving dish a half-turn after 4 minutes. Yield: 6 servings.
Pat Graham
Wallace, North Carolina

Snip Chives, And Add Onion Flavor

One bite of Cheesy Chive-Stuffed Potatoes and you might think they're flavored with onion, but guess again. This familiar flavor actually comes from chives, an herb akin to the onion that's skillfully used to season vegetables and delicately flavored egg and seafood dishes.

Chives grow in bunches of long, slender green leaves that come back just like grass when snipped. In fact, the more you clip chives, the more their growth is encouraged.

Chives are easily grown in the garden or in a pot. You can begin by planting seeds, but the easiest method is to buy a small pot of seedlings from a garden center or your grocer. Space them 8 inches apart in a sunny spot. They'll look lonesome, but they will fill in. If you plan to grow them in a pot, set seedlings about an inch apart in a 4- or 6-inch diameter container.

Chives go dormant in winter, but you can freeze cut chives during the summer. Use kitchen shears to snip a handful of foliage. Then hold it over a freezer container, cut the foliage into short segments, and freeze.

If you don't have chives growing in your garden, you can purchase the herb in dried form as well as in frozen chopped form in most supermarkets. Fresh, frozen, or dried chives can be used interchangeably in most recipes.

COUNTRY OMELETS

¾ pound new potatoes
3 tablespoons butter or margarine, divided
6 eggs
3 tablespoons water
2 tablespoons chopped chives
¼ teaspoon salt
⅛ teaspoon pepper

Cook potatoes in boiling salted water to cover 15 minutes or until tender.

Drain and cool slightly. Peel and cube potatoes.

Melt 2 tablespoons butter in an 8-inch omelet pan or heavy skillet; add potatoes, and cook over medium heat until potatoes are browned. Remove potatoes with a slotted spoon.

Combine eggs, water, chives, salt, and pepper; stir briskly with a fork until blended. Heat omelet pan; pour one-third of egg mixture into pan. As mixture starts to cook, gently lift edges of omelet with a spatula, and tilt pan so uncooked portion flows underneath. Spoon one-third of potatoes over half of omelet. Loosen omelet with spatula; fold omelet in half, and transfer to serving plate. Repeat procedure twice with remaining egg mixture and potatoes, using remaining butter, if needed. Yield: 3 servings.

Dean Knight
Forest, Mississippi

CHEESY CHIVE-STUFFED POTATOES

3 (8-ounce) baking potatoes
Vegetable oil
½ cup commercial buttermilk salad dressing
⅓ cup (1.3 ounces) shredded Cheddar cheese
⅓ cup chopped chives
2 tablespoons butter or margarine, melted
⅛ teaspoon salt

Wash potatoes, and rub skins with vegetable oil. Bake at 400° for 1 hour or until done. Allow potatoes to cool to touch. Cut in half lengthwise; carefully scoop out pulp, leaving shells intact. Coarsely chop pulp.

Combine potato pulp, salad dressing, and remaining ingredients; stir until blended. Stuff shells with potato mixture. Bake at 300° for 10 minutes or until thoroughly heated. Yield: 6 servings.

Mary Carden
Hartford, Kentucky

ROYAL FLOUNDER FILLETS

1 pound flounder fillets
¼ teaspoon salt
¼ teaspoon pepper
¼ cup mayonnaise or salad dressing
2 tablespoons chopped chives
1 tablespoon lemon juice
Pinch of salt
1 egg white
¼ cup saltine cracker crumbs
¼ teaspoon paprika

Sprinkle fillets evenly with ¼ teaspoon salt and pepper, and arrange in a lightly greased 13- x 9- x 2-inch pan. Bake at 350° for 10 minutes. Remove fillets with a slotted spatula; place on a heated ovenproof platter, and keep warm.

Combine mayonnaise and next 3 ingredients. Beat egg white until stiff but not dry; fold into mayonnaise mixture, and spread over fillets.

Combine cracker crumbs and paprika; sprinkle over mayonnaise mixture. Bake at 350° for 10 minutes or until fish is opaque and flakes easily when tested with a fork. Yield: 4 servings.

Violet Moore
Montezuma, Georgia

Tip: *You should not thaw fish at room temperature or in warm water; it will lose moisture and flavor. Instead, place the fish in the refrigerator to thaw. Keep in mind that you should allow 18 to 24 hours for thawing a 1-pound package. Of course, you should never refreeze thawed fish.*

ON THE
Light Side

Paint A Picture
For Eating Right Through Life

Like most Southerners, you've probably realized that healthy eating and regular exercise are the framework of healthy living. And chances are you've already taken steps to improve the way you eat. While it's best to start healthy habits early in life, making positive lifestyle changes at any age can have real rewards.

Nutritional needs vary during each stage of life. The food you choose today can make a difference tomorrow, so let's take a look at eating right throughout life.

A Healthy Start

When it comes to feeding babies, there are no rules carved in stone. The first few months require a simple liquid diet of infant formula or breast milk, which has the unique ability to protect infants from disease and allergic reactions. The benefits of breast-feeding are so great that the American Academy of Pediatrics suggests that every mother who can nurse do so, even if it's just for a short while. Infant formulas will also meet the nutritional needs of babies.

At about 4 to 6 months, infants are ready to begin eating semisolid foods. It's best to introduce one food at a time and wait three or four days before adding another new food. This way a problem food can be identified more easily.

With all the concern about fat and cholesterol in the diet, it's important

to note that children under 2 years old *need* fat and cholesterol to grow and develop properly. Fat provides essential fatty acids, aids in the absorption and storage of fat-soluble vitamins (vitamins A, D, E, and K), and is a concentrated source of calories needed by small appetites.

Building a Strong Kid

From 2 to 12 years old, children learn lifelong eating habits. It stands to reason that children adopt their parents' eating habits, so if you eat a variety of healthy foods, chances are your children will learn to also. You can encourage healthy eating by involving your children in meal preparation. Let them tear lettuce for a salad, stir muffin batter, or help with making sandwiches.

As children grow, their appetites may be unpredictable. One day it may be hard to fill them up, and the next they will hardly eat. However, their calorie and nutrient intake usually averages out over several days.

During the school-age years, girls and boys have similar nutrient needs. Use the basic four food groups as a guide to make sure your children are getting the variety of foods they need daily. Children under 12 should get three servings from the milk group, two from the meat group, four servings from the grain group, as well as four servings from the fruit-and-vegetable group.

Recent studies show that heart disease can begin early in life. And children over 2 years old, like their parents, will benefit from light-and-healthy eating. Children learn by example, and there is no time that you're going to have more control over what they eat than during these early years.

Food for Growing

Teenagers, especially boys, can eat you out of house and home. Physically active boys may need over 4,000 calories a day just to maintain their weight. Teenage girls also need more calories but not as many as boys.

Calcium and iron are the most important micronutrients during the teen years. Calcium is important because these are peak bone-building years. (See "Calcium: Milk Is Just a Start" on page 130.) And iron is needed for the growth spurts that occur during puberty. It can be found in lean red meats, poultry, and fish and in smaller amounts in legumes, dried fruits, whole-grain breads and cereals, green leafy vegetables, and nuts.

Anyone who has teenagers knows that there's no way to control what they eat. But encouraging good eating habits at home and keeping healthy snack foods on hand is a step in the right direction. Fresh and dried fruits, fruit juices, skim milk, raw vegetables (washed and cut up), yogurt, popcorn, healthy oatmeal cookies, peanut butter, and nuts are just a few examples

of healthy snacks. Chips generally have a lot more calories and fat than nutrients, but when made the light way (see "Crispy Chips Without All the Fat" on page 137) they easily fit into healthy snacking.

Probably the greatest nutrition concern facing adolescents is weight control. And evidence substantiates that fat children and fat teenagers are most likely to become fat adults.

Undue concern with weight control can lead to eating disorders, especially in girls. Bulimia and anorexia have become household words because of the prevalence of the disorders among teenagers.

Maintaining Nutrition Through Middle Life

Adulthood is generally a busy, high-pressured time of life when careers and family responsibilities are most demanding. Rushed or missed meals, snacks, and restaurant eating can sabotage the best laid plans for eating healthy. (It's important not to get sidetracked from following simple plans such as eating 5 servings of fruits and vegetables a day.)

Pregnancy and nursing place special nutrition requirements on women. Higher amounts of calories, vitamins, and minerals, particularly calcium and folacin, are needed. And nursing demands even more vitamins A and C than pregnancy.

Young and middle-aged adults may be short on dietary calcium and iron because they don't eat enough dairy products and red meat. Though it's best to get these nutrients from food, a supplement, especially for those constantly dieting, shouldn't be out of the question.

From age 40 to 60 the body's metabolism begins to slow down; this means the body burns fewer calories. Weight tends to creep up during this stage of life, which makes it a good time to increase efforts to eat healthy and exercise regularly.

Living Better In the Later Years

A healthy diet can help to limit the impact of disease and allow older folks to enjoy maximum energy, while poor nutrition can clearly shorten life.

Although people need fewer calories as they grow older, the need for vital nutrients remains the same. In order to pack the same amount of nutrients into fewer calories, foods must be chosen primarily for their nutrient density. (See "Eating in the Later Years" on page 134.)

Nutrition research on older folks has just begun, but already it suggests that the sooner healthy eating habits are begun, the greater the benefits for vitality and longevity.

Calcium: Milk Is Just A Start

Male or female, young or old, we all need calcium to help form bones and make them stronger and denser. And a diet rich in calcium, along with a regular exercise program, may help head off osteoporosis, the brittle-bone disease that leads to hip, spine, and wrist fractures in later years.

Weight-bearing exercises—walking, bicycling, aerobic dance, jogging, jumping rope, and weight training—pull and stress the longer bones of the body, making them stronger and thicker. This type of exercise appears to be a vital factor in preventing osteoporosis. A balanced diet adequate in calcium and containing moderate amounts of protein is also a key factor in preventing this disease.

In 1989 the Recommended Dietary Allowance (RDA) for calcium increased to 1,200 milligrams a day for folks age 11 to 24. This increase provides adequate calcium during adolescent growth spurts so teenagers and young adults can build stronger bones. The RDA for adults remains 800 milligrams, even though many authorities believe that women at certain stages of their lives need more calcium than the RDA.

To increase calcium in your diet, choose at least three servings of calcium-rich foods each day (see chart on facing page) or choose recipes that use calcium-rich foods, such as the ones below. A serving of Corn Chowder (page 132) containing 425 milligrams of calcium beats most foods on our chart, yet only about 19% of its calories come from fat. And Turkey Lasagna takes advantage of part-skim mozzarella cheese and 1% low-fat cottage cheese, which add calcium without excess fat.

TURKEY LASAGNA

Vegetable cooking spray
1½ pounds raw ground turkey
1¼ cups chopped onion
1 cup chopped green pepper
2 cloves garlic, chopped
½ teaspoon dried Italian seasoning
¼ cup chopped fresh parsley
2 (6-ounce) cans tomato paste
1 (10-ounce) can tomatoes and chiles, undrained
1½ cups water
2 egg whites, lightly beaten
2 cups 1% low-fat cottage cheese
2 tablespoons chopped fresh parsley
10 lasagna noodles (cooked without salt or fat)
½ cup grated Parmesan cheese
1 cup (4 ounces) shredded part-skim mozzarella cheese

Coat a large, nonstick skillet with cooking spray; place over medium-high heat until hot. Add ground turkey

and next 3 ingredients; cook until meat is browned and vegetables are tender, stirring to crumble meat. Drain and pat dry with paper towels. Wipe drippings from skillet.

Return turkey mixture to skillet; add Italian seasoning, parsley, tomato paste, tomatoes and chiles, and water; cover and cook over medium heat 30 minutes, stirring often.

Combine egg whites, cottage cheese, and parsley; set aside.

Coat a 13- x 9- x 2-inch baking dish with cooking spray. Place 5 noodles in bottom of dish. Top with half each of turkey mixture and cheese mixture. Repeat layers. Cover and bake at 350° for 25 minutes. Uncover and sprinkle with Parmesan and mozzarella cheeses; bake, uncovered, 5 minutes or until cheese melts. Let stand 10 minutes. Yield: 8 servings (407 calories per serving).

□ *35.9 grams protein, 11.6 grams fat, 40.1 grams carbohydrate, 14 milligrams cholesterol, 591 milligrams sodium, and 286 milligrams calcium.*
Alzina Toups
Galliano, Louisiana

MEXICAN-STUFFED POTATOES
(pictured on page 152)

4 medium-size baking potatoes
  (1½ pounds)
1 (8-ounce) carton plain low-fat
  yogurt
¼ cup skim milk
⅛ teaspoon pepper
1 (4-ounce) can chopped green
  chiles, drained
1 (2-ounce) jar diced pimiento,
  drained
4 large, pitted ripe olives, chopped
½ cup (2 ounces) shredded
  40%-less-fat sharp Cheddar
  cheese, divided

Wash potatoes; prick several times with a fork. Bake at 400° for 1 hour or until done. Let cool to touch. Cut potatoes in half lengthwise; carefully scoop out pulp, leaving shells intact. Set aside. Combine potato pulp, yogurt, milk, and pepper; mash until light and fluffy.

Stir chiles, pimiento, olives, and half of Cheddar cheese into potato mixture. Stuff shells with potato mixture; place on an ungreased baking sheet. Bake at 375° for 10 minutes. Sprinkle evenly with remaining cheese, and bake an additional 2 minutes. Yield: 8 servings (113 calories per stuffed potato half).

□ *5.8 grams protein, 2.2 grams fat, 17.9 grams carbohydrate, 7 milligrams cholesterol, 124 milligrams sodium, and 138 milligrams calcium.*
Louise Ellis
Talbott, Tennessee

Calcium-Rich Foods		
	Serving size	Calcium (mgs)
Sardines with bones	4 ounces	433
Yogurt, plain, low-fat	1 cup	415
Spinach, cooked	1 cup	299
Milk, skim	1 cup	279
Milk, whole	1 cup	270
Salmon with bones, canned	4 ounces	242
Turnip greens, cooked	1 cup	198
Mozzarella cheese, part-skim	1 ounce	183
Okra, cooked	1 cup	178
Ricotta cheese, part-skim	¼ cup	168
Frozen yogurt, soft	4 ounces	149
Cottage cheese, 1% low-fat	1 cup	138
Collard greens, cooked	1 cup	133
Mustard greens, cooked	1 cup	104
Almonds, dry roasted	¼ cup	97
Broccoli, cooked	1 cup	94
Ice milk or ice cream	½ cup	88
Orange	1 medium	52

CORN CHOWDER

½ cup chopped onion
½ cup chopped celery
2 tablespoons reduced-calorie
   margarine, melted
1 tablespoon all-purpose flour
4 cups skim milk
1 (17-ounce) can no-salt-added
   yellow cream-style corn
¼ teaspoon salt
¼ teaspoon white pepper
¼ teaspoon dried whole thyme
⅛ teaspoon paprika

Sauté onion and celery in margarine in a Dutch oven until tender. Add flour, and cook 1 minute, stirring constantly. Gradually add milk, stirring until mixture boils.

Stir in corn and next 3 ingredients. Reduce heat; simmer 20 minutes, stirring occasionally. Spoon into bowls; sprinkle evenly with paprika. Yield: 3 servings (294 calories per 1⅔-cup serving).

□ *14.7 grams protein, 6.2 grams fat, 49.9 grams carbohydrate, 7 milligrams cholesterol, 462 milligrams sodium, and 425 milligrams calcium.*
Elizabeth Thompson
Connelly Springs, North Carolina

PINEAPPLE-YOGURT WHIRL

¾ cup frozen unsweetened
   pineapple juice concentrate,
   thawed
1 (8-ounce) carton vanilla low-fat
   yogurt
½ cup skim milk
½ cup water
2 tablespoons sugar
1½ teaspoons vanilla extract
Ice cubes

Combine first 6 ingredients in container of an electric blender; process

until smooth. Add enough ice cubes to bring mixture to 5-cup level; process until frothy. Yield: 5 servings (148 calories per 1-cup serving).

□ *3.6 grams protein, 0.7 gram fat, 32 grams carbohydrate, 3 milligrams cholesterol, 44 milligrams sodium, and 125 milligrams calcium.*   *Linda Keith*
Carrollton, Texas

Focus On Fiber

Dietary fiber, soluble fiber, insoluble fiber, cellulose, hemicellulose, pectin, lignin, guar—with so many kinds of fiber out there, how's a person to know what kind to eat? The answer: all of them. Let's take a closer look at their differences and see why they're an important part of healthful eating.

Dietary fiber includes all the different kinds. Soluble and insoluble fiber are two categories of dietary fiber. Soluble fibers mesh with water and form gels. Pectin, lignin, guar, and the fiber in oats, oat bran, legumes, grits, and barley are all soluble fiber. They're best known for their ability to lower blood cholesterol.

Insoluble fiber absorbs lots of water—up to 15 times its weight—and moves quickly through the digestive tract. This is why it's thought to protect the body against cancer and other digestive problems. The most common source of insoluble fiber is cellulose; whole-grain products, wheat bran, vegetables, fruits, and nuts are all high in insoluble fiber.

Both soluble and insoluble fibers are important for overall health. The National Cancer Institute recommends 25 to 35 grams of dietary fiber a day with 10 grams of that as soluble fiber. To make sure there's enough fiber in your diet, each day eat six servings of

whole grains and/or legumes, five servings of fruits and vegetables, and 100% whole wheat bread (read labels to make sure).

It's hard to get enough fiber if you don't start with a fiber-rich breakfast. Give your diet a jumpstart with All-Bran Oat Bran Muffins (page 134); with nearly 4 grams of fiber and less than 100 calories, they're a nutritious way to begin your day.

CHICKEN-FRIED WILD RICE
(pictured on pages 152 and 153)

1 pound skinned, boned chicken
   breasts
¼ cup low-sodium teriyaki sauce
¼ cup low-sodium soy sauce
¼ cup Chablis or other dry white
   wine
2 cloves garlic, minced
½ teaspoon peeled, grated
   gingerroot
¼ teaspoon Chinese five-spice
   powder
1 (4-ounce) package uncooked wild
   rice
1 teaspoon vegetable oil
1 cup sliced green pepper
⅔ cup sliced carrot
⅔ cup chopped onion
⅔ cup sliced fresh mushrooms
½ cup frozen English peas, thawed
Vegetable cooking spray
2 tablespoons slivered almonds,
   toasted

Cut chicken into 1-inch pieces; place in a small bowl. Add teriyaki sauce and next 5 ingredients; stir well. Cover and marinate chicken in refrigerator at least 1 hour.

Cook rice according to package directions, omitting salt; keep warm.

Add oil to wok or heavy skillet, and heat to medium high (325°) for 1 minute. Add green pepper, carrot, and onion; stir-fry 3 minutes. Add mushrooms and peas; stir-fry 2 minutes. Stir into rice; set aside.

Coat wok with cooking spray; place over medium-high heat until hot. Add chicken and marinade to wok; stir-fry 4 minutes or until done. Add rice and vegetables; stir-fry 1 to 2 minutes or until heated. Sprinkle with almonds. Yield: 4 servings (322 calories per 1½-cup serving).

□ *33.5 grams protein, 4.9 grams fat, 33.7 grams carbohydrate, 66 milligrams cholesterol, 3.7 grams fiber, 754 milligrams sodium, and 49.3 milligrams calcium.* Marise Meier
Kennesaw, Georgia

THREE-BEAN ENCHILADAS

½ cup dried kidney beans
½ cup dried navy beans
½ cup dried pinto beans
6 cups water
½ teaspoon salt
½ cup chopped onion
2 cloves garlic
1 teaspoon chili powder
1 teaspoon ground cumin
¼ teaspoon salt
1 (4-ounce) can chopped green chiles, undrained
12 (6-inch) corn tortillas
Vegetable cooking spray
1 (10-ounce) can commercial enchilada sauce
½ cup (2 ounces) shredded 40%-less-fat Monterey Jack cheese

Sort and wash beans; place in a Dutch oven. Cover with water 2 inches above beans, and bring to a boil; cover and cook 2 minutes. Remove from heat, and let stand 1 hour. Drain beans; return to Dutch oven.

Add 6 cups water and ½ teaspoon salt. Bring to a boil; cover, reduce heat, and simmer 1 hour or until beans are tender. Drain, reserving ¼ cup liquid (add water, if necessary, to make ¼ cup).

Place beans in container of an electric blender or food processor; add reserved ¼ cup liquid, onion, and next 5 ingredients. Process 5 seconds or until mixture is chunky.

Brush tortillas with water. Divide bean mixture among tortillas. Roll up; place seam side down in a 12- x 8- x 2-inch baking dish coated with cooking spray. Pour enchilada sauce over tortillas; cover and bake at 350° for 20 minutes. Top with cheese, and bake, uncovered, 5 minutes. Yield: 12 servings (177 calories per enchilada).

□ *9.8 grams protein, 2.1 grams fat, 31.5 grams carbohydrate, 4.5 grams fiber, 2 milligrams cholesterol, 233 milligrams sodium, and 136 milligrams calcium.*

BAKED BARLEY

1 cup barley
2 cups ready-to-serve, salt-free chicken broth
Vegetable cooking spray
1 cup chopped onion
3 cups mushrooms, sliced
½ cup diced green pepper
½ teaspoon salt
¼ teaspoon pepper
3 tablespoons slivered almonds, toasted

Spread barley on a baking sheet; bake at 350° for 8 minutes or until lightly browned. Combine barley and chicken broth in a medium saucepan; bring to a boil. Cover, reduce heat, and simmer 30 minutes or until barley is tender and broth is absorbed.

Coat a nonstick skillet with cooking spray; place over medium-high heat until hot. Add onion, mushrooms, and green pepper; sauté until tender. Combine barley, vegetables, salt, and pepper in a 1½-quart baking dish coated with cooking spray. Cover and

bake at 350° for 30 minutes. Sprinkle with almonds; bake, uncovered, 5 minutes. Yield: 5 servings (196 calories per ½-cup serving).

□ *7.2 grams protein, 3.9 grams fat, 34.1 grams carbohydrate, 8.3 grams fiber, 0 milligrams cholesterol, 244 milligrams sodium, and 39 milligrams calcium.* Gwen Louer
Roswell, Georgia

MEXICAN HOMINY

Vegetable cooking spray
½ cup chopped onion
1 clove garlic, minced
1 (15-ounce) can yellow hominy, drained
1 cup chopped tomato
2 tablespoons canned chopped green chiles
½ teaspoon chili powder
⅛ teaspoon salt
¼ teaspoon pepper
¼ cup (1 ounce) shredded 40%-less-fat sharp Cheddar cheese

Coat a nonstick skillet with cooking spray; place over medium-high heat until hot. Add onion and garlic; sauté until tender. Stir in hominy and remaining ingredients except cheese. Spoon mixture into a 1-quart baking dish coated with cooking spray. Bake, uncovered, at 350° for 25 minutes. Sprinkle with cheese, and bake 5 minutes. Yield: 4 servings (94 calories per ¾-cup serving).

□ *3.9 grams protein, 2.3 grams fat, 14.7 grams carbohydrate, 2.8 grams fiber, 5 milligrams cholesterol, 289 milligrams sodium, and 82 milligrams calcium.*

BRAN-AND-FRUIT MUESLI

2 cups bran flakes
1½ cups corn-bran cereal
½ cup toasted wheat germ
⅓ cup chopped pitted dates
⅓ cup chopped dried apples
¼ cup chopped walnuts, toasted
¼ cup unsalted sunflower kernels, toasted
¼ cup dried banana chips, crushed

Combine all ingredients; store in an airtight container in a cool, dry place. Serve with milk. Yield: 10 servings (139 calories per ½-cup serving).

□ *4.8 grams protein, 4.6 grams fat, 23.2 grams carbohydrate, 4.0 grams fiber, 0 milligrams cholesterol, 124 milligrams sodium, and 22 milligrams calcium.* Thelma Holt
Mooresville, North Carolina

ALL-BRAN OAT BRAN MUFFINS

1¼ cups oat bran
½ cup firmly packed brown sugar
1 tablespoon baking powder
1½ teaspoons ground cinnamon
½ teaspoon salt
1½ cups shreds of wheat bran cereal
1¼ cups skim milk
¼ cup egg substitute or 1 egg
2 tablespoons vegetable oil
1 teaspoon vanilla extract
½ cup raisins
Vegetable cooking spray

Combine first 5 ingredients in a large bowl; make a well in center of mixture, and set aside.

Combine wheat bran cereal and milk, and let stand 2 minutes; stir in egg substitute and next 3 ingredients. Add to dry ingredients, stirring just until moistened.

Spoon batter into muffin pans coated with cooking spray, filling two-thirds full. Bake at 375° for 22 minutes. Remove from pans. Yield: 1½ dozen (93 calories per muffin).

□ *3.2 grams protein, 2.5 grams fat, 20.1 grams carbohydrate, 3.8 grams fiber, 0 milligrams cholesterol, 196 milligrams sodium, and 72 milligrams calcium.* Beverly S. Rose
Memphis, Tennessee

Eating In The Later Years

Kudos for older folks—they're setting trends in healthy eating, physical fitness, and overall lifestyle. Never before have so many over 50 been as health conscious.

Limiting fat to 30% or less of calories, and cholesterol to 300 milligrams or less each day may help prevent heart disease. And a high-fiber diet has been shown to decrease the incidence of certain kinds of cancer and to lower cholesterol levels (see "Focus on Fiber," page 132).

CHICKEN IN FOIL

2 (6-ounce) skinned chicken breast halves
¼ cup sliced onion
½ tomato, sliced
1 medium-size baking potato, sliced
1 small carrot, sliced
1 stalk celery, sliced
¼ teaspoon pepper
⅛ teaspoon dried whole tarragon
1 teaspoon lemon juice

Cut two 15- x 12-inch pieces of heavy-duty aluminum foil; place a chicken breast in center of each. Top with onion and remaining ingredients. Wrap well; place on baking sheet. Bake at 350° for 1 hour. Yield: 2 servings (221 calories per serving).

□ *29.5 grams protein, 1.8 grams fat, 21.5 grams carbohydrate, 66 milligrams cholesterol, 111 milligrams sodium, and 72 milligrams calcium.* Susan Kamer-Shinaberry
Charleston, West Virginia

BEEF STROGANOFF

1 pound lean, boneless top sirloin steak
Vegetable cooking spray
3 cups sliced fresh mushrooms
¾ cup chopped onion
2 cloves garlic, crushed
1 teaspoon beef-flavored bouillon granules
1 cup hot water
1 tablespoon reduced-calorie margarine
2 tablespoons all-purpose flour
⅛ teaspoon salt
¼ teaspoon freshly ground pepper
1 tablespoon cornstarch
¾ cup plain low-fat yogurt
3 cups hot cooked noodles (cooked without salt or fat)
2 tablespoons chopped fresh parsley

Trim fat from steak; partially freeze steak. Slice steak diagonally across grain into thin strips, and set aside.

Coat a nonstick skillet with cooking spray; place over medium-high heat until hot. Add steak, mushrooms, onion, and garlic; sauté until steak and vegetables are tender. Drain; wipe drippings from pan.

Combine bouillon granules and hot water; set aside. Melt margarine in skillet over low heat; add flour, stirring until smooth. Cook about 1

minute; stir constantly. Gradually add bouillon mixture; cook over medium heat, stirring constantly with a wire whisk until thickened. Stir in salt, pepper, and steak mixture. Cook until heated. Remove from heat.

Combine cornstarch and yogurt (at room temperature); stir into meat mixture (do not reheat). Serve meat mixture over noodles; sprinkle evenly with parsley. Yield: 6 servings (424 calories per ¾ cup meat mixture plus ¾ cup noodles).

□ *35.1 grams protein, 11.6 grams fat, 43.3 grams carbohydrate, 71 milligrams cholesterol, 447 milligrams sodium, and 221 milligrams calcium.*

TWICE BAKED COTTAGE-STYLE POTATOES

2 medium-size baking potatoes
½ cup 1% low-fat cottage cheese
2 tablespoons skim milk
2 teaspoons sliced green onions
⅛ teaspoon salt
⅛ teaspoon pepper
⅛ teaspoon paprika
Garnish: fresh parsley sprigs

Wash potatoes; prick several times with a fork. Bake at 400° for 1 hour or until done. Let cool to touch. Slice skin away from top of each potato. Carefully scoop out pulp, leaving shells intact. Set aside. Mash pulp.

Combine cottage cheese and milk in container of an electric blender or food processor; process until smooth. Add cottage cheese mixture, green onions, salt, and pepper to potato pulp; stir well. Stuff shells with potato mixture; sprinkle with paprika. Bake at 400° for 10 minutes or until thoroughly heated. Garnish, if desired. Yield: 2 servings (155 calories each).

□ *10.7 grams protein, 1.1 grams fat, 26.1 grams carbohydrate, 3 milligrams cholesterol, 394 milligrams sodium, and 75 milligrams calcium.*

Mrs. Hugh McCarley
McKinney, Texas

A Summer Menu

As the days grow longer, you'll want to be outside. So why not try this healthy menu that includes a grilled entrée, rice, and vegetables?

For Poblano Salsa, you'll need tomatillos, poblano chiles, and serrano chiles, which can be found in specialty markets, or use the canned.

Grilled Tuna With Poblano Salsa
Yellow Rice
Summer Vegetables
Four-Flavor Pound Cake

GRILLED TUNA WITH POBLANO SALSA

2 tablespoons lime juice
1 teaspoon olive oil
4 (4-ounce) tuna steaks
Vegetable cooking spray
Poblano Salsa

Combine lime juice and olive oil; brush on tuna. Coat grill rack with cooking spray; place on grill over medium-hot coals. Place tuna on rack, and cook, covered, 5 minutes on each side or until done. Serve with Poblano Salsa. Yield: 4 servings (232 calories per tuna steak with 2 tablespoons salsa).

□ *34.5 grams protein, 8.4 grams fat, 3.3 grams carbohydrate, 56 milligrams cholesterol, 133 milligrams sodium, and 8 milligrams calcium.*

Poblano Salsa

4 medium-size poblano chiles or 2 (4-ounce) cans chopped green chiles
⅓ cup fresh or canned tomatillos
1 small serrano or jalapeño chile, seeded and diced
½ cup chopped tomato
¼ cup diced onion
2 tablespoons chopped fresh parsley or cilantro
2 tablespoons lime juice
½ teaspoon ground cumin
½ teaspoon salt

Place poblano chiles on a baking sheet; broil 6 inches from heat, turning often with tongs until peppers are blistered on all sides. Immediately place in a plastic storage bag; fasten securely, and let steam 10 to 15 minutes. Remove peel of each chile; seed and dice chiles. Combine chiles, tomatillos, and remaining ingredients. Cover and chill thoroughly. Yield: 2 cups (6 calories per tablespoon).

□ *0.3 gram protein, 0 grams fat, 1.3 grams carbohydrate, 0 milligrams cholesterol, 38 milligrams sodium, and 3 milligrams calcium.*

YELLOW RICE

Olive oil-flavored vegetable cooking
  spray
¼ cup diced onion
2 cups ready-to-serve, no-salt-added
  chicken broth
1 cup long-grain rice, uncooked
¼ teaspoon salt
⅛ teaspoon ground turmeric
1 bay leaf

Coat a nonstick skillet with cooking
spray; place over medium-high heat
until hot. Add onion, and sauté until
tender. Add broth and remaining ingredients. Bring to a boil; cover, reduce heat, and simmer 20 minutes or
until rice is tender and liquid is absorbed. Remove and discard bay leaf.
Yield: 4 servings (186 calories per
½-cup serving).

☐ *3.7 grams protein, 0.5 gram fat,
38.9 grams carbohydrate, 0 milligrams
cholesterol, 151 milligrams sodium,
and 19 milligrams calcium.*
Carol S. Noble
Burgaw, North Carolina

SUMMER VEGETABLES

Vegetable cooking spray
4 cloves garlic, minced
2 cups sliced zucchini
2 cups sliced yellow squash
1 cup chopped tomato
½ cup julienne-sliced green pepper
½ cup ready-to-serve, no-salt-added
  chicken broth
1 tablespoon chopped fresh basil or
  1 teaspoon dried whole basil

Coat a large nonstick skillet with cooking spray; place over medium-high
heat until hot. Add garlic, and cook 1
minute. Add zucchini and next 4 ingredients. Cook 3 minutes or until vegetables are crisp-tender, stirring

constantly. Stir in basil. Yield: 4 servings (41 calories per ¾-cup serving).

☐ *2.2 grams protein, 0.5 gram fat, 8.3
grams carbohydrate, 0 milligrams cholesterol, 8 milligrams sodium, and 31
milligrams calcium.* Frances Wiltshire
Richmond, Virginia

FOUR-FLAVOR POUND CAKE

Vegetable cooking spray
1¾ cups sifted cake flour
2 teaspoons baking powder
¼ teaspoon salt
¾ cup sugar
½ cup vegetable oil
½ cup skim milk
½ teaspoon grated lemon rind
¼ teaspoon almond extract
¼ teaspoon rum extract
¼ teaspoon lemon extract
¼ teaspoon vanilla extract
4 egg whites, stiffly beaten
Fresh strawberries

Coat the bottom of an 8½- x 4½- x
3-inch loafpan with cooking spray;
dust with flour, and set aside.
  Combine 1¾ cups flour and next 3
ingredients in a large bowl. Add oil and
milk; beat at medium speed of an electric mixer until batter is smooth (batter will be thick). Add lemon rind and
next 4 ingredients; fold in about one-
third of egg whites. Gently fold in remaining egg whites.
  Pour batter into pan. Bake at 350°
for 40 minutes or until a wooden pick
inserted in center comes out clean.
  Cool in pan 10 minutes; remove
from pan, and cool on a wire rack.
Serve ¾ cup fresh strawberries with
each slice. Yield: 16 servings (183 calories per ½-inch slice and ¾ cup
strawberries).

☐ *2.7 grams protein, 7.4 grams fat,
27.2 grams carbohydrate, 0 milligrams
cholesterol, 91 milligrams sodium, and
52 milligrams calcium.*

Cooking For A Twosome?

Tea for two is easy to fix, but what
about an entrée for two? Most recipes
serve four, six, or eight, leaving folks
cooking for two performing major sur-
gery on favorite recipes.
  Our readers have come up with
some tasty recipes for two. Donice
Rogers of Columbia, Mississippi, cut
down her recipe for Pork Chops in
Gravy and made it light and healthy.
  For a fancier entrée, why not try
Linda Keith's Shrimp Cancun en Papillote (poppy-YOTE). "Shrimp and
salsa are regular items on most Tex-
ans' grocery list," Linda explains. "I
decided to try them together and
found they make a nice combination. If
they're baked in parchment bundles,
they give a special effect."

SHRIMP CANCUN
EN PAPILLOTE
(pictured on page 155)

10 ounces unpeeled medium-size
  fresh shrimp
Vegetable cooking spray
¾ cup chunky salsa, divided
½ cup (2 ounces) shredded part-
  skim mozzarella cheese
3 whole ripe olives, sliced

Peel and devein shrimp. Cut two 15- x
12-inch pieces of parchment paper or
aluminum foil; fold in half lengthwise.
Trim each into a heart shape. Place
hearts on a baking sheet. Coat one
side of each with cooking spray. Divide shrimp equally and place on side
of each heart coated with cooking
spray. Top each with ¼ cup salsa.
  Fold over remaining half of paper or
foil. Pleat and crimp edges together to
seal. Twist end slightly to seal.

On THE
Light Side

Bake at 400° for 10 to 12 minutes or until parchment is puffed and lightly browned. Cut an X in top of paper, and top each with cheese and olives. Bake 1 minute or until cheese melts. Serve with ¼ cup salsa. Yield: 2 servings (223 calories each).

□ *30.9 grams protein, 7.5 grams fat, 7.1 grams carbohydrate, 189 milligrams cholesterol, 356 milligrams sodium, and 259 milligrams calcium.*
Linda Keith
Carrollton, Texas

PORK CHOPS IN GRAVY

2 (4-ounce) lean boneless center-cut loin pork chops
1½ tablespoons all-purpose flour
1 teaspoon paprika
¼ teaspoon salt
¼ teaspoon pepper
Vegetable cooking spray
½ cup sliced fresh mushrooms
⅓ cup diced onion
⅓ cup diced green pepper
1 cup skim milk
2 tablespoons lemon juice
1 cup hot cooked rice (cooked without salt or fat)

Trim excess fat from pork; set aside. Combine flour and next 3 ingredients; dredge pork chops in flour mixture, reserving remaining flour mixture.

Coat a nonstick skillet with cooking spray; place over medium-high heat until hot. Add pork chops, and brown on each side; remove to a 1-quart casserole coated with cooking spray. Add mushrooms, onion, and green pepper to skillet; sauté until tender. Stir in reserved flour mixture; cook 1 minute, stirring constantly. Gradually stir in milk; cook until thickened, stirring constantly. Stir in lemon juice. Pour gravy over pork chops. Cover and bake at 350° for 30 minutes; uncover

and bake an additional 10 minutes. Serve over rice. Yield: 2 servings (408 calories per pork chop, ¾ cup gravy, and ½ cup rice).

□ *33.6 grams protein, 9.3 grams fat, 45.3 grams carbohydrate, 74 milligrams cholesterol, 436 milligrams sodium, and 184 milligrams calcium.*
Donice Rogers
Columbia, Mississippi

TURKEY PICATTA

1 tablespoon lemon juice
2 (4-ounce) turkey breast cutlets
1½ tablespoons all-purpose flour
½ teaspoon paprika
¼ teaspoon white pepper
½ teaspoon olive oil
¼ cup Chablis or other dry white wine
1 tablespoon lemon juice
1 tablespoon capers
½ tablespoon chopped fresh parsley

Drizzle 1 tablespoon lemon juice over cutlets; set aside. Combine flour, paprika, and pepper; dredge cutlets in flour mixture.

Heat oil in a large, nonstick skillet over medium-high heat until hot. Add turkey, and cook 2 to 3 minutes on each side or until browned. Transfer to a serving platter; keep warm.

Combine wine and 1 tablespoon lemon juice in skillet; bring to a boil over medium heat, stirring constantly. Add capers, and cook 1 minute. Pour over cutlets; sprinkle with parsley. Yield: 2 servings (207 calories per serving).

□ *35.1 grams protein, 2.1 grams fat, 10.2 grams carbohydrate, 94 milligrams cholesterol, 398 milligrams sodium, and 21 milligrams calcium.*
Jennifer Cairns
Jacksonville, Alabama

Crispy Chips Without All The Fat

Hurrah! No longer do chip lovers have to suffer the consequences of a snack that gets 60% or more of its calories from fat. Now there's a wide variety of crunchy chips that are light and healthy.

Lime juice and a sprinkling of seasonings give our light Tortilla Chips an authentic Mexican flavor. They have less than one-fourth the fat and calories of most commercial tortilla chips.

TORTILLA CHIPS

12 (6-inch) corn tortillas
½ cup lime juice
¼ cup water
¼ teaspoon salt
½ teaspoon garlic powder
⅛ teaspoon ground cumin
⅛ teaspoon red pepper

Using a cookie cutter or kitchen shears, cut 3 (2-inch) rounds from each tortilla. Combine lime juice and water in a small bowl; set aside. Combine salt and remaining ingredients.

Dip tortillas in lime juice mixture; drain on paper towels. Arrange tortillas in a single layer on an ungreased baking sheet; sprinkle evenly with salt mixture. Bake at 350° for 10 to 12 minutes or until chips are crisp. Cool; store in airtight containers. Yield: 3 dozen (23 calories per chip).

□ *0.7 gram protein, 0.4 gram fat, 4.6 grams carbohydrate, 0 milligrams cholesterol, 34 milligrams sodium, and 15 milligrams calcium.*

PITA CHIPS

3 (6-inch) whole-wheat pita bread
   rounds
Butter-flavored vegetable cooking
   spray
1½ teaspoons lemon juice
1 clove garlic, crushed
¼ teaspoon salt
⅛ teaspoon pepper
1 tablespoon minced fresh parsley
1½ teaspoons minced fresh chives

Separate each pita bread into 2 rounds; cut each into 8 wedges to make 48 triangles. Arrange in a single layer on an ungreased baking sheet, cut side up. Coat with cooking spray. Combine lemon juice and garlic; lightly brush over each triangle. Combine salt and remaining ingredients; sprinkle evenly over triangles. Bake at 350° for 15 minutes or until crisp and lightly browned. Let cool. Yield: 4 dozen (8 calories per chip).

□ *0.2 gram protein, 0.1 gram fat, 1.5 grams carbohydrate, 0 milligrams cholesterol, 12 milligrams sodium, and 3 milligrams calcium.*

Wilmina R. Smith
St. Petersburg, Florida

BAKED WONTON CHIPS

56 (2-inch-square) wonton skins
Water.

Cut wonton skins in half diagonally. Arrange in a single layer on ungreased baking sheets. Spray lightly with water. Bake at 375° for 8 minutes or until light brown. Serve warm or cold. Yield: 9⅓ dozen (3 calories per chip).

□ *0.1 gram protein, 0.1 gram fat, 0.6 gram carbohydrate, 3 milligrams cholesterol, 8 milligrams sodium, and 0 milligrams calcium.*

Parmesan Cheese Wonton Chips: Sprinkle 2 teaspoons grated Parmesan cheese evenly over wonton chips sprayed with water (4 calories per chip).

□ *0.2 gram protein, 0.1 gram fat, 0.6 gram carbohydrate, 3 milligrams cholesterol, 8 milligrams sodium, and 1 milligram calcium.*

Lemon-and-Herb Wonton Chips: Sprinkle 2 teaspoons salt-free lemon-and-herb spice blend evenly over chips sprayed with water (4 calories per chip).

□ *0.1 gram protein, 0.1 gram fat, 0.6 gram carbohydrate, 3 milligrams cholesterol, 8 milligrams sodium, and 0 milligrams calcium.*

Garlic Wonton Chips: Sprinkle 1½ teaspoons garlic powder evenly over wonton chips sprayed with water (4 calories per chip).

□ *0.1 gram protein, 0.1 gram fat, 0.6 gram carbohydrate, 3 milligrams cholesterol, 8 milligrams sodium, and 1 milligram calcium.*

Cinnamon-and-Sugar Wonton Chips: Combine ¼ teaspoon ground cinnamon and 1½ teaspoons sugar. Sprinkle mixture evenly over wonton chips sprayed with water (4 calories per chip).

□ *0.1 gram protein, 0.1 gram fat, 0.6 gram carbohydrate, 3 milligrams cholesterol, 8 milligrams sodium, and 1 milligram calcium.*

Delana W. Pearce
Lakeland, Florida

SWEET POTATO CHIPS

1 (½-pound) sweet potato, peeled
Vegetable cooking spray
¼ teaspoon salt

Using a very sharp knife or vegetable cutter, slice sweet potato crosswise into ⅛-inch slices; arrange in a single layer on baking sheets coated with cooking spray. Spray slices with cooking spray. Bake at 325° for 14 minutes or until crisp. Remove chips from baking sheet as they begin to brown, and cool. Sprinkle with salt. Store in an airtight container. Yield: 3 dozen (7 calories per chip).

□ *0.1 gram protein, 0.1 gram fat, 1.5 grams carbohydrate, 0 milligrams cholesterol, 17 milligrams sodium, and 1 milligram calcium.*

BAGEL CHIPS

6 plain bagels
Butter-flavored vegetable cooking
   spray

Using an electric slicer or serrated knife, horizontally cut each bagel into 6 (¼-inch) slices. Arrange slices in a single layer on wire racks; place racks on baking sheets. Coat slices with cooking spray. Bake at 325° for 12 to 15 minutes or until crisp and lightly browned. Remove from oven; let cool. Store in an airtight container. Yield: 3 dozen (28 calories per chip).

□ *1 gram protein, 0.4 gram fat, 5.1 grams carbohydrate, 0 milligrams cholesterol, 54 milligrams sodium, and 3 milligrams calcium.*

Parmesan Cheese Bagel Chips: Sprinkle 2 teaspoons of grated Parmesan cheese evenly over bagel chips

coated with cooking spray (28 calories per chip).

□ *1 gram protein, 0.4 gram fat, 5.1 grams carbohydrate, 0 milligrams cholesterol, 55 milligrams sodium, and 4 milligrams calcium.*

Lemon-and-Herb Bagel Chips: Sprinkle 2 teaspoons salt-free lemon-and-herb spice blend evenly over bagel chips coated with cooking spray (29 calories per chip).

□ *1 gram protein, 0.4 gram fat, 5.3 grams carbohydrate, 0 milligrams cholesterol, 54 milligrams sodium, and 3 milligrams calcium.*

Garlic Bagel Chips: Sprinkle 1 teaspoon garlic powder evenly over bagel chips coated with cooking spray (28 calories per chip).

□ *1 gram protein, 0.4 gram fat, 5.1 grams carbohydrate, 0 milligrams cholesterol, 54 milligrams sodium, and 3 milligrams calcium.*

Cinnamon-and-Sugar Bagel Chips: Combine ¼ teaspoon ground cinnamon and 1½ teaspoons sugar; sprinkle mixture evenly over bagel chips coated with cooking spray (29 calories per chip).

□ *1 gram protein, 0.4 gram fat, 5.2 grams carbohydrate, 0 milligrams cholesterol, 54 milligrams sodium, and 3 milligrams calcium.* Tracy Rogers
Hattiesburg, Mississippi

Healthy Breakfasts To Make And Freeze

Commercial frozen breakfast entrées are "selling like hot cakes." These entrées have encouraged more folks to eat breakfast. Unfortunately, many of these commercial products are too high in fat, calories, and sodium to be a part of healthful eating.

With a small investment of time, healthy muffins, pancakes, and waffles can be made ahead and frozen to use later. Most can be popped into the microwave and are ready to eat in 1 to 2 minutes.

Store breakfast items in an airtight container in the freezer, and heat them in the microwave as needed. With the addition of a glass of skim milk and fresh fruit or juice, you have a balanced breakfast in minutes.

HONEY PANCAKES

3 cups all-purpose flour
2 tablespoons baking powder
½ teaspoon salt
3 cups skim milk
½ cup egg substitute
¼ cup honey
¼ cup vegetable oil

Combine first 3 ingredients in a large bowl. Combine milk and remaining ingredients; add to flour mixture, stirring until smooth.

For each pancake, pour about ¼ cup batter onto a hot, lightly greased griddle. Turn pancakes when tops are covered with bubbles and edges look cooked. Yield: 28 (4-inch) pancakes (92 calories each).

□ *2.9 grams protein, 2.1 grams fat, 15.1 grams carbohydrate, 1 milligram cholesterol, 127 milligrams sodium, and 77 milligrams calcium.*

To freeze: Place pancakes on a wax paper-lined baking sheet; freeze. Place frozen pancakes in an airtight container; return to freezer. To reheat frozen pancakes, microwave 1 pancake at HIGH 30 to 45 seconds; 2 pancakes at HIGH 1 minute to 1 minute and 10 seconds; 3 pancakes at HIGH 1 minute and 15 seconds to 1 minute and 30 seconds or until thoroughly heated.

LIGHT WAFFLES

4 cups self-rising flour
2 tablespoons sugar
¼ teaspoon baking soda
4 cups nonfat buttermilk
½ cup vegetable oil
8 egg whites
Vegetable cooking spray

Combine flour, sugar, and soda in a large bowl. Combine buttermilk and oil; stir well. Add to dry ingredients, stirring just until moistened.

Beat egg whites until stiff peaks form; carefully fold into batter. Coat a waffle iron with cooking spray, and allow waffle iron to preheat. Pour batter onto hot waffle iron and bake. Yield: 32 (4-inch) waffles (105 calories per waffle).

□ *3.4 grams protein, 3.8 grams fat, 14 grams carbohydrate, 1 milligram cholesterol, 249 milligrams sodium, and 93 milligrams calcium.*

To freeze: Place waffles on a wax paper-lined baking sheet; freeze. Place frozen waffles in an airtight container; return to freezer. To reheat frozen waffles, broil 6 inches from heat 4 to 5 minutes or until thoroughly heated, turning after 2 minutes.
Betty Haygood
Liberty, Mississippi

Margarine Still Comes Out On Top

Margarine has taken a hit. For years nutritionists have told folks they could cut down on saturated fat and cholesterol by switching from butter to margarine. Now a Dutch study suggests that the trans fatty acids in margarine *raise* LDL-cholesterol (the "bad" cholesterol that clogs arteries) and *lower* HDL-cholesterol (the "good" cholesterol that helps unclog arteries). The big question to consider is whether this study makes margarine as bad a choice as butter when it comes to raising blood cholesterol levels.

Here's what happens. To make margarine from vegetable oil, the oil must undergo a process called hydrogenation. During hydrogenation some of the unsaturated fats in oil are converted from their naturally occurring cis form to a trans form. It's these trans fatty acids that are accused of raising blood cholesterol levels.

Margarines vary in the amount of trans fatty acids they contain. Stick margarines in the U.S. usually have 25% to 35% trans fatty acids; tub margarines have about 13% to 20%; and squeeze bottle margarines and spreads probably contain even less.

The average American diet contains only about 2% to 4% of its daily calories as trans fatty acids. This is about one-fourth the amount fed to participants in the Dutch study. So it stands to reason that the Dutch study did not depict the typical American diet. In fact, the National Academy of Sciences, along with the Surgeon General and other authorities in this country, has concluded that the levels of trans fatty acids found in a balanced diet are safe.

As you can see, currently there's not enough evidence to justify switching from margarine to butter. At over 60% saturated fat (the kind known to clog arteries) and about 33 grams of cholesterol per tablespoon, butter is a spread you'll live better without.

When choosing margarine, read the label and pick one that lists liquid vegetable oil rather than partially hydrogenated vegetable oil as the first ingredient. And make sure the amount of cholesterol-raising saturated fat is no more than 2 grams per tablespoon. The remaining 9 grams of fat per tablespoon is a combination of the more "heart healthy" monounsaturated and polyunsaturated fats. The healthiest are "diet," squeeze bottle, and tub margarines; they have the least saturated fat.

Remember that all margarine and margarine-like spreads are cholesterol free as long as they're made with only vegetable oil. So it's best to ignore the "no cholesterol" label, and look at the type of fat they contain.

BLUEBERRY MUFFINS

1 cup all-purpose flour
¾ cup whole wheat flour
2 teaspoons baking powder
¼ teaspoon salt
½ teaspoon ground cinnamon
1 cup fresh or frozen blueberries, thawed and drained
¾ cup skim milk
⅓ cup sugar
¼ cup vegetable oil
2 egg whites, lightly beaten
1 teaspoon grated orange rind
1 teaspoon vanilla extract
Vegetable cooking spray

Combine first 5 ingredients in a large bowl; add blueberries, and toss gently to coat. Make a well in center of mixture, and set aside.

Combine milk and next 5 ingredients; add to dry ingredients, stirring just until moistened. Spoon into muffin pans coated with cooking spray, filling two-thirds full. Bake at 350° for 15 to 20 minutes or until done. Yield: 1 dozen (146 calories each).

□ *3.3 grams protein, 5.1 grams fat, 21.9 grams carbohydrate, 0 milligrams cholesterol, 116 milligrams sodium, and 57 milligrams calcium.*

To freeze: Place muffins in an airtight container; freeze. To reheat frozen muffins, microwave 1 muffin at HIGH 40 to 50 seconds; 2 muffins at HIGH 1 minute to 1 minute and 30 seconds or until thoroughly heated.

Melissa Shores
Kansas City, Missouri

Tip: *To protect the natural flavor of whole wheat flour and ensure a long shelf life, store in a moisture-proof bag in the refrigerator or freezer.*

FREEZER BRAN MUFFINS

3 cups shreds of wheat bran cereal
1 cup raisins
½ cup vegetable oil
1 cup boiling water
½ cup egg substitute
2 cups buttermilk
¼ cup molasses
2¼ cups whole wheat flour
2½ teaspoons baking soda
1½ tablespoons sugar
Vegetable cooking spray

Combine first 4 ingredients in a large bowl; stir well, and let stand 10 minutes until cereal is moistened. Combine egg substitute, buttermilk, and molasses; add to cereal mixture, stirring well.

Combine flour, soda, and sugar; add to cereal mixture, stirring just until dry ingredients are moistened. Cover batter, and let stand at room temperature 15 minutes. Spoon batter into muffin pans coated with vegetable cooking spray, filling two-thirds full. Bake at 400° for 18 to 20 minutes or until done. Yield: 2 dozen (142 calories each).

□ *4.4 grams protein, 5.3 grams fat, 24.1 grams carbohydrate, 0 milligrams cholesterol, 202 milligrams sodium, and 63 milligrams calcium.*

To freeze: Place muffins in an airtight container, and freeze. To reheat frozen muffins, microwave 1 muffin at HIGH 35 to 45 seconds; 2 muffins at HIGH 1 minute and 10 seconds to 1 minute and 30 seconds or until thoroughly heated.

Note: For larger muffins, spoon batter into 8 (6-ounce) custard cups coated with cooking spray. To reheat frozen muffins, microwave 1 muffin at HIGH 1 minute and 10 seconds to 1 minute and 30 seconds or until thoroughly heated.
Vi Yount
Baldwin, Maryland

APPLESAUCE MUFFINS

1 cup all-purpose flour
1 cup regular oats, uncooked
¼ cup unprocessed oat bran
¼ cup sugar
1½ teaspoons baking soda
1 teaspoon baking powder
⅔ cup raisins or chopped dates
⅓ cup chopped pecans
2 egg whites, lightly beaten
¾ cup nonfat buttermilk
¾ cup unsweetened applesauce
¼ cup vegetable oil
1 teaspoon vanilla extract
Vegetable cooking spray
1 tablespoon sugar
½ teaspoon ground cinnamon

Combine first 8 ingredients in a large bowl; make a well in center of mixture. Combine egg whites and next 4 ingredients; add to dry ingredients, stirring just until moistened.

Spoon ¼ cup batter into muffin pans coated with cooking spray. Combine 1 tablespoon sugar and cinnamon; sprinkle on top of muffin batter. Bake at 400° for 20 minutes. Yield: 16 muffins (147 calories each).

□ *3.1 grams protein, 5.8 grams fat, 21.4 grams carbohydrate, 0 milligrams cholesterol, 115 milligrams sodium, and 53 milligrams calcium.*

To freeze: Place muffins in an airtight container; freeze. To reheat frozen muffins, microwave 1 muffin at HIGH 35 to 40 seconds; 2 muffins at HIGH 1 minute to 1 minute and 10 seconds or until thoroughly heated.
Doris Phillips
Fayetteville, Arkansas

Wholesome Muffins

■ If you grease more muffin cups than you need, fill the empty cups with water to keep grease from baking on the cups.

■ The secret of good muffins is in the mixing. Combine all the dry ingredients in a bowl, and form a well in the center of the mixture. Add the liquid all at once and stir only enough to moisten the dry ingredients. The mixture will be lumpy, but further mixing will make the muffins tough.

■ When preparing a whole wheat flour recipe, be sure not to sift the flour. Instead, stir flour lightly before measuring.

■ For easy chopping of dried fruit, place fruit in freezer 2 hours before chopping. Cut with knife or kitchen shears dipped frequently in hot water to prevent sticking.

■ Unless otherwise specified, always preheat the oven at least 20 minutes before baking.

■ If muffins are done ahead of serving time, loosen them from their cups, tilt slightly, and slide the pan back into the oven to stay warm. This keeps the muffins from steaming on bottom.

Chocolate Without Guilt

What's the most craved food in the South? If you guessed chocolate, you're right! Chocolate has long been considered a sinful, high-fat food because of the cocoa butter in it. However, various chocolate products have different amounts of fat.

Over 90% of the calories in unsweetened baking chocolate come from fat. Milk chocolate, semisweet, and sweet chocolate have 50% fat. But unsweetened cocoa, with 28% fat, and chocolate syrup, with only ¼% fat, easily fit healthy eating.

A good example of guilt-free chocolate is the recipe for Chocolate Fondue. It uses unsweetened cocoa and only ¼ cup sugar.

CHOCOLATE-CHEESE CUPS

½ cup sugar
2 tablespoons unsweetened cocoa
¼ teaspoon ground cinnamon
1 cup (8 ounces) part-skim ricotta cheese
¼ cup evaporated skimmed milk
¼ cup egg substitute
2 teaspoons vanilla extract
3 egg whites
⅛ teaspoon salt
Vegetable cooking spray
2 tablespoons graham cracker crumbs
1 tablespoon chopped almonds, toasted

Combine first 7 ingredients in container of an electric blender; blend on high until smooth. Pour into a large bowl; set aside.

Combine egg whites and salt in a medium bowl; beat at medium speed of an electric mixer until stiff peaks form. Fold into chocolate mixture. Coat paper muffin pan liners with cooking spray; sprinkle evenly with graham cracker crumbs. Spoon batter into liners, filling three-fourths full. Bake at 225° for 30 minutes. Turn oven off, and leave in oven 30 minutes. Remove to wire racks to cool completely. Cover and chill. Before serving, sprinkle with almonds. Yield: 16 servings (63 calories each).

□ *3.1 grams protein, 1.8 grams fat, 8.5 grams carbohydrate, 5 milligrams cholesterol, 60 milligrams sodium, and 56 milligrams calcium.*

CHOCOLATE FONDUE

2 teaspoons cornstarch
1 cup water
¼ cup unsweetened cocoa
¼ cup sugar
1 teaspoon vanilla extract

Combine cornstarch and water in a small saucepan. Add remaining ingredients; stir until smooth. Cook over medium heat until mixture boils, stirring constantly. Boil 1 minute, stirring constantly. Serve warm as a dip with fresh fruit. Yield: 1 cup (18 calories per 1 tablespoon).

□ *0.1 gram protein, 0.2 gram fat, 3.9 grams carbohydrate, 0 milligrams cholesterol, 0 milligrams sodium, and 4 milligrams calcium.*

Bettina Hambrick
Muskogee, Oklahoma

CHOCOLATE-BRAN RAISIN JUMBOS

½ cup reduced-calorie margarine, softened
½ cup firmly packed brown sugar
½ cup instant hot cocoa mix
¼ cup egg substitute
½ teaspoon vanilla extract
1 cup whole wheat flour
½ teaspoon baking soda
⅛ teaspoon salt
1½ cups wheat bran flakes cereal with raisins
Vegetable cooking spray

Beat margarine; gradually add sugar, beating well at medium speed of an electric mixer. Add cocoa mix, egg substitute, and vanilla, beating until well blended. Combine flour, soda, and salt; add to creamed mixture, mixing well. Stir in cereal.

Drop dough by rounded tablespoonfuls onto cookie sheet coated with cooking spray. Bake at 375° for 10 minutes or until lightly browned. Remove to wire racks; cool. Yield: 1¼ dozen (96 calories per cookie).

□ *2.1 grams protein, 4 grams fat, 14.7 grams carbohydrate, 0 milligrams cholesterol, 149 milligrams sodium, and 21 milligrams calcium.*

School's Out For Summer

School days give way to summer craze, and that's a good reason for kids to celebrate! Help them usher in vacation with an end-of-the-year party that's easy on you and fun for a class of 25 young scholars embarking on summer adventure. Fix-it-yourself sandwich and ice-cream sundae bars are the bulk of this easy menu, and they require simply buying and arranging deli and convenience products from your grocer. You can use our quick recipes for a beverage, dip with chips, and pasta salad, or you can substitute store-bought versions to save even more time.

You may want to divide the food list and cost of about $115 (a bargain for such a spread) among four or five parents, or let the parents prepare the recipes and ask each guest to bring an item for the sandwich or sundae bar. This can be written on each invitation. Collect food items from arriving guests, and while they enjoy Cola Punch and Chili Dip as an appetizer, you can set out the sandwich fixings. After they've polished off the main course, start the party activity, a scavenger hunt (see box, far right). While they're out collecting treasures, do a little cleanup and bring out the sundae bar. An easy test of your entertaining skills, this party will earn you a top grade.

VEGETABLE PASTA SALAD

1 (16-ounce) package rotini, uncooked
4 cups broccoli flowerets
2 cups sliced carrots
1 large sweet red pepper, cut into julienne strips
¾ cup sliced celery
1½ cups commercial Italian salad dressing

Cook rotini according to package directions, omitting salt. Drain. Rinse in cold water, and drain. Add broccoli and remaining ingredients, tossing well. Cover and chill at least 4 hours. Yield: 25 servings.

SUPER SUMMER SANDWICH BAR

1½ pounds thinly sliced deli roast turkey
1½ pounds thinly sliced deli ham
1½ pounds thinly sliced deli roast beef
1½ pounds bacon slices, cooked
1 (16-ounce) package American cheese slices
1 (16-ounce) package Swiss cheese slices
1 (16-ounce) package mozzarella cheese slices
2 to 3 heads leaf lettuce
5 large tomatoes, sliced
1 medium-size purple onion, sliced and separated into rings
1 (32-ounce) jar sliced dill pickles
1 (16-ounce) jar mayonnaise or salad dressing
1 (9-ounce) jar prepared mustard
1 (8-ounce) jar Dijon mustard
1 (16-ounce) loaf rye bread slices
1 (16-ounce) package onion buns
1 (12-ounce) package wheat sub rolls
1 (12-ounce) package white sub rolls

Set up the sandwich bar with meats and cheeses arranged with lettuce, tomatoes, onion rings, pickles, and other condiments. Serve with breads. Yield: 25 servings.

CHILI DIP

2 (10¾-ounce) cans chili-beef soup, undiluted
2 (11-ounce) cans Cheddar cheese soup, undiluted
1 (2½-ounce) can chopped black olives
1 (2-ounce) jar diced pimiento
3 (10-ounce) bags tortilla chips

Combine first 4 ingredients in a saucepan; cook over low heat until thoroughly heated, stirring often. Serve warm with tortilla chips. Yield: 6 cups.
Gwen Louer
Roswell, Georgia

Scavenger Hunt

Before the party, compose a list of ordinary household items and a courteous letter of explanation to neighbors who will be called on by partygoers. Divide the kids into teams of five, and give each team a list, a letter, a few ribbons, and a colorful, decorative bag for collecting treasures. Then explain to the group the objectives and rules of the game.

In a 30-minute time limit, they will collect as many items on the list as possible by knocking on neighbors' doors within a set boundary. Kids should give the neighbors the letter that tells them this is a party game, kindly requests their participation, and asks them to give only one item to each group. When they leave, the group should tie a ribbon on the doorknob to let other teams know that neighbor has contributed. When there are three ribbons on a doorknob, no more teams can knock there so that each neighbor has only a total of three visits.

After 30 minutes, teams return to the party and show their collections. The team that comes back with the most items wins a fun, inexpensive prize.

ICE CREAM GALORE AND MORE

1 ½-gallon carton each of chocolate, strawberry, and vanilla ice cream
1 pint fresh strawberries, sliced
1 (12-ounce) jar chocolate sauce
1 (12-ounce) jar butterscotch sauce
1 (12.25-ounce) jar caramel sauce
1 (16-ounce) bag candy-coated chocolate pieces
1 (8-ounce) bag chopped pecans
2 (8-ounce) cans whipped dessert topping

Tip: Scoop ice cream into balls a day before the party, and freeze on jelly-roll pans overnight. To serve, place scoops of each flavor into separate large bowls with toppings on the side.

COLA PUNCH

Grated rind of 6 lemons (optional)
2¼ cups fresh lemon juice
9 cups water
4½ cups sugar
1 (3-liter) bottle cola-flavored beverage

Combine lemon rind (if desired), juice, water, and sugar, stirring until sugar dissolves. Chill at least 4 hours or overnight. Stir in cola just before serving. Serve over crushed ice. Yield: 6½ quarts.   *Anna Robinson*
Oak Ridge, Tennessee

Tip: *When squeezing fresh lemons, limes, or oranges for juice, first grate the rind by rubbing the washed fruit against surface of grater, taking care to remove only the outer colored portion of the rind. Wrap the rind in plastic in teaspoon portions, and freeze for future use.*

From Our Kitchen To Yours

When it's time to cut a three-layer cake, do you hesitate before picking up a knife? Should you choose the long heavy knife with the smooth-edged blade or the long slender one with the serrated edge? Selecting the latter one will keep the cake from tearing and falling apart.

When shopping for knives, you'll find there just isn't an all-purpose knife. Knives come in a variety of shapes and sizes; each is made for specific tasks. Using a sharp knife and choosing the right blade make each cutting job easier.

The **chef's knife** blade is shaped like an elongated triangle and ranges from 8 to 10 inches in length. It is heavy and wide, gradually tapering to a point. Despite its size, this large knife can be used for many chores, such as chopping, mincing, and slicing most fruits and vegetables. Its shape lets the blade rock back and forth while the weight does the work. Mincing and chopping is simple—grasp the handle with one hand, and hold the back of the blade near the tip between the thumb and forefinger of the other hand. Lift handle up and down in a rapid rocking motion, moving blade in an arc and pulling the food you're chopping back into a pile to make sure it is evenly chopped.

Slicing knife blades are narrower than the blades on a chef's knife, and they vary in length. The tips can be pointed or rounded, and the blades can have either a smooth or serrated edge.

The long smooth-edged blade cuts thin, even slices of meats and large vegetables, as well as blocks of cheese. The long serrated-edged slicing knife (also called a **bread knife**) slices bread and layer cakes with ease. As you exert gentle downward pressure, drawing the knife toward you, its toothed or notched edge cuts through foods with a firm or crisp crust without tearing or crushing the soft insides. The smaller version of a slicing knife zips through tomatoes and smaller cuts of meat and poultry.

A small, lightweight 3- to 4-inch **paring knife** is easy to grasp and control. It is handy for garnishing and trimming foods, peeling and slicing small fruits and vegetables, and performing other small jobs.

The **utility** or **boning knife** is often used more than any of the others. This versatile knife's blade, which is 5 to 7 inches long is excellent for many chores. It peels, slices, chops, and carves. It also separates cooked or uncooked meat from the bone.

A **sharpening steel** is included in many knife sets. This tool acts like a file on the knife's edge and realigns the edge, keeping the blade sharp. A sharp knife will provide maximum safety. Sharpening your knife is easy to do; hold the blade at a 20-degree angle against the steel, and draw the blade gently across the steel's surface in a slight arc using moderate pressure. Repeat on the other side of the blade. Repeat these steps five to ten times, always alternating the right and left side of the blade.

After many years of use, the steel may no longer restore the cutting edge; that will be the time for you to have your knives professionally sharpened. Look in the Yellow Pages under the heading "Sharpening Service," and check local hardware stores that sharpen knives.

Sharpen Your Knife-Buying Skills

Knife prices vary greatly. What's the difference? Quality. Knives are an investment, but you'll get your money's worth with years of use. For the best value, comparison shop and watch for sales. If a good set of knives isn't in your budget, plan to buy the knives one at a time.

To know what you're paying for, look for the telltale signs of a quality knife. As a general rule, the more expensive knives have nicer finishes; however, the best knives are not necessarily the most expensive. Keeping your price range in mind, look at the knife's construction.

The handles that are hardwood or wood-impregnated plastic will give you a good nonslip grip even when your hands are wet or greasy. You'll make a wiser purchase if you choose a knife with a full tang, which means that the blade extends throughout the length of the handle. Be careful that there aren't any gaps between the handle and the tang where food particles or dirt may collect.

Most stainless steel blades have serrated edges because the metal is harder to keep sharpened. High-carbon stainless steel is the best value; these blades, often called "no stain," remain sharp and are not affected by air or moisture.

Before making your final decision, be sure the knife fits comfortably in your hand and is well balanced. Test the knife by supporting it with two fingers at the point where the handle joins the blade; it should stay in a horizontal position.

By following these tips and referring to the sketches below, you should be able to find the perfect knife for any food-preparation task.

chef's knife

slicing knife

bread knife

sharpening steel

paring knife

utility or boning knife

It's Rhubarb Time!

Wake up your taste buds with the invigorating flavor of rhubarb. It's no longer limited to recipes for pies and preserves. Our readers have found new ways to enjoy it, including a congealed salad and a quick dessert.

TART RHUBARB SALAD

4 cups sliced rhubarb (about 1 pound)
1 cup water
¾ cup sugar
¼ teaspoon salt
1 (6-ounce) package strawberry-flavored gelatin
1¾ cups cold water
¼ cup lemon juice
2 (11-ounce) cans mandarin oranges, drained
1 cup diced celery
Lettuce leaves
Sour cream

Combine first 4 ingredients in a large saucepan. Bring to a boil; reduce heat, and simmer 3 to 5 minutes or until rhubarb is tender. Remove from heat. Add gelatin, and stir until dissolved. Stir in cold water and lemon juice; chill until consistency of unbeaten egg white. Fold in oranges and celery; pour into a 12- x 8- x 2-inch dish. Chill until firm. Cut into squares. Serve on lettuce leaves; dollop with sour cream. Yield: 12 servings.
Barbara Sherrer
Bay City, Texas

RHUBARB SALAD

2 cups chopped rhubarb (about ½ pound)
¾ cup sugar
1 envelope unflavored gelatin
½ cup cold water
2 tablespoons lemon juice
2 drops of red food coloring (optional)
1 cup chopped celery
½ cup chopped pecans
Lettuce leaves

Combine rhubarb and sugar in a saucepan; let stand 30 minutes, stirring often. Sprinkle gelatin over cold water; let stand 5 minutes.

Cook rhubarb over low heat 5 to 10 minutes or until tender. Add gelatin mixture, lemon juice, and, if desired, food coloring; stir well. Chill until consistency of unbeaten egg white. Fold in celery and pecans. Spoon into five ½-cup oiled molds; chill until firm. Unmold onto lettuce leaves. Yield: 5 servings.
Mary P. Richmond
Paintsville, Kentucky

RHUBARB SQUARES

1 cup all-purpose flour
½ cup sifted powdered sugar
½ cup butter or margarine, softened
1 cup sugar
¼ cup all-purpose flour
¾ teaspoon baking powder
2 eggs, beaten
3 cups diced rhubarb (about ¾ pound)

Combine 1 cup flour and powdered sugar; cut in butter with a pastry blender until mixture resembles coarse meal. Press mixture evenly into a lightly greased 13- x 9- x 2-inch pan. Bake at 350° for 12 minutes.

Combine sugar, ¼ cup flour, and baking powder; add eggs, and mix well. Stir in rhubarb, and pour over prepared crust. Bake at 325° for 45 to 50 minutes. Cool and cut into squares. Yield: 12 servings.
Mrs. Clayton J. Turner
DeFuniak Springs, Florida

RHUBARB CRISP

1 cup regular oats, uncooked
⅔ cup sugar
⅓ cup all-purpose flour
⅓ cup butter or margarine, melted
½ teaspoon ground cinnamon
6 cups chopped rhubarb (about 1½ pounds)
1 cup sugar

Combine first 5 ingredients; set aside. Combine rhubarb and 1 cup sugar; toss gently, and place in a greased 8-inch square baking dish. Top with oat mixture. Bake at 350° for 45 minutes or until lightly browned. Yield: 8 servings.
Georgia S. Hagan
Bristol, Tennessee

Curious about Rhubarb?

From April to June, tangy tart rhubarb is at its peak. Botanically a vegetable, it is usually enjoyed as a fruit. The leggy stalks, resembling celery, are most often sweetened for use in pies, preserves, and sauces. A favorite flavor combination in England is rhubarb and ginger, whereas Americans have traditionally combined rhubarb with strawberries.

In selecting and preparing rhubarb, keep these tips in mind:

■ When you select rhubarb at the produce counter, be sure to look for stalks that are crisp and of medium thickness. If you puncture the stalk with your thumbnail and juice runs out, you know the rhubarb is fresh.

■ Be sure to remove and discard any leaves that may be left on the stalks. The leaves can be toxic if consumed.

Sauce Up The Seafood

It's hard to imagine summertime without at least one trip to the beach and a seafood feast. But you can also enjoy seafood at home with oysters on the half shell or boiled shrimp and crab or possibly your catch of the day. The special occasion and seafood warrant homemade cocktail sauces.

Everyone has his favorite concoction of the essentials—catsup, chili sauce, or mayonnaise, seasoned with lemon juice, horseradish, garlic, and Worcestershire sauce. You're sure to find your favorite combination in one of these recipes.

TARTAR SAUCE

1 cup mayonnaise or salad dressing
¼ cup chopped dill pickle
1 tablespoon minced fresh parsley
2 teaspoons capers
2 teaspoons grated onion
1 teaspoon prepared mustard
1 teaspoon lemon juice
1 teaspoon sugar
¼ teaspoon garlic powder

Combine all ingredients. Cover and chill before serving. Serve with fish or shellfish. Yield: 1¼ cups.

Louise Denmon
Silsbee, Texas

RÉMOULADE SAUCE

1½ cups mayonnaise or salad dressing
2 hard-cooked egg yolks, sieved
2 tablespoons minced fresh parsley
2 cloves garlic, minced
1 tablespoon dried whole chervil
1 tablespoon paprika
1½ tablespoons Creole mustard
2 tablespoons white vinegar
1 tablespoon Worcestershire sauce
Dash of hot sauce
Garnishes: egg slices and parsley

Combine first 10 ingredients. Cover and chill before serving. Garnish, if desired. Serve with fish or shellfish. Yield: 1½ cups.

Linda E. Whitt
Missouri City, Texas

DELTA COCKTAIL SAUCE

1 cup mayonnaise or salad dressing
2 small cloves garlic, minced
Juice of 1 lemon
1 small onion, grated
½ cup vegetable oil
¼ cup catsup
¼ cup chili sauce
1 teaspoon paprika
1 teaspoon pepper
1 teaspoon prepared mustard
1 teaspoon Worcestershire sauce
Dash of hot sauce

Combine all ingredients. Cover and chill before serving. Serve with fish or shellfish. Yield: 2¼ cups.

Mary Brown
Yazoo City, Mississippi

ZIPPY RED SAUCE

1 cup chili sauce
1 cup catsup
2 tablespoons prepared horseradish
2 tablespoons picante sauce
3 tablespoons lemon juice
2 tablespoons Worcestershire sauce
1 teaspoon onion powder
1 teaspoon garlic powder

Combine all ingredients, stirring well. Cover and chill at least 2 hours. Serve with fish or shellfish. Yield: 2½ cups.

Laurie McIntyre
Lake Jackson, Texas

Cook Out This Weekend

If the party is at your house, plan on serving one of these grilled or smoked favorites. Cookouts are easy on the host and fun for guests.

Curt Treloar, of Largo, Florida, recommends his Smoked Pork Loin Mahogany. Curt advises, "It's easy to prepare the meat in the smoker. The key to success is to allow the Mahogany Sauce to simmer slowly."

No-fuss side dishes such as wild rice, tossed green salads with slices of tangy grapefruit or oranges, vegetable trays with dip, or toasted French bread make outdoor entertaining easy. Provide plenty of drinks, use colorful plates and napkins, and light a few torches or candles as the evening sun wanes.

SWORDFISH STEAK WITH CHERVIL BUTTER

½ cup olive oil
¼ cup lemon juice
¼ teaspoon salt
2 pounds (1-inch-thick) swordfish steaks
Mesquite chips
½ cup butter or margarine, softened
½ cup finely chopped fresh chervil or 2½ teaspoons dried whole chervil
½ teaspoon pepper

Combine first 3 ingredients; brush on swordfish. Cover and refrigerate 30 minutes. Soak mesquite chips in water 30 minutes. Combine butter, chervil, and pepper; set aside.

Prepare charcoal fire; let burn 15 to 20 minutes or until flames disappear and coals are white. Place mesquite chips over hot coals. Grill swordfish over hot (400° to 500°) coals 12 to 15 minutes or until done, turning once. Remove fish from grill; generously brush with butter mixture. Yield: 4 to 6 servings.

Terry Inman
West Monroe, Louisiana

BEEF-AND-VEGETABLE KABOBS

½ cup butter or margarine
¼ cup lemon juice
3 tablespoons chopped fresh chives
1 tablespoon Worcestershire sauce
1 teaspoon prepared mustard
½ teaspoon salt
Dash of pepper
2 medium-size green peppers
12 mushrooms (about ½ pound)
12 cherry tomatoes
6 small onions
2 pounds (1-inch-thick) sirloin
  steak, cut into 1-inch cubes

Combine butter, lemon juice, chives, Worcestershire sauce, mustard, salt, and pepper in a small saucepan. Bring to a boil; reduce heat, and simmer 5 minutes. Set aside ½ cup sauce. Use remaining sauce for basting.

Cut green peppers into 16 (1½-inch) squares. Place each vegetable on a separate (14-inch) skewer. Place beef cubes on 3 (14-inch) skewers. Cook only beef and onion kabobs over hot coals for the first 10 minutes, basting with sauce and turning often. Add green pepper kabob to grill alongside beef and onions; brush with sauce, and cook all 10 minutes. Place mushrooms and tomato kabobs on grill with other kabobs; brush with sauce, and cook 5 minutes. Remove all kabobs from grill. Serve with reserved sauce. Yield: 6 servings.

Note: Because some vegetables take less time to grill than others, cooking each vegetable on separate skewers allows each to be grilled to the correct degree of doneness. *Bill Tate*
Birmingham, Alabama

SHERRY-MARINATED CORNISH HENS

½ cup soy sauce
¼ cup dry sherry
¼ cup water
2 tablespoons sugar
1 tablespoon minced fresh
  gingerroot
1 clove garlic, minced
2 (1½-pound) Cornish hens, split
Garnishes: onion fans, cherry
  tomato halves

Combine soy sauce, sherry, water, sugar, gingerroot, and garlic in a small mixing bowl. Place hens in a shallow dish; pour marinade evenly over hens, and cover. Chill 3 hours, turning hens occasionally.

Prepare charcoal fire in one end of grill; let burn 15 to 20 minutes or until flames disappear and coals are white. Place a pan of water opposite the coals; arrange hens on rack placed over pan of water. Cover with grill hood. Open air vents halfway. Cook 2 hours or until meat thermometer registers 185° when inserted in breast. Turn and baste hens with marinade after 1 hour. Add more charcoal as needed. Garnish, if desired. Yield: 4 servings. *R. A. Colosimo*
Copperas Cove, Texas

SMOKED PORK LOIN MAHOGANY

1 (3- to 4-pound) rolled boneless
  pork loin roast
½ teaspoon freshly ground black
  pepper
½ teaspoon garlic salt
Mesquite or hickory chips
2 (12-ounce) cans beer
2⅔ cups Burgundy wine
Mahogany Sauce
Spiced Peaches
Garnishes: leaf lettuce, cinnamon
  sticks

Sprinkle pork roast with pepper and garlic salt; set aside.

Soak mesquite chips in water 30 minutes. Prepare charcoal fire in smoker; let burn 20 minutes. Place mesquite on coals. Place water pan in smoker; add beer and wine to pan.

Place roast on food rack. Cover with smoker lid; cook 2 to 3 hours or until meat thermometer registers 155° to 160° when inserted in center. Serve with Mahogany Sauce and Spiced Peaches. Garnish, if desired. Yield: 10 to 12 servings.

Mahogany Sauce

3 strips bacon, diced
½ cup chopped onion
1 cup grape jam
1 cup catsup
2 tablespoons cider vinegar

Sauté bacon and onion in a medium saucepan until onion is tender; drain. Add jam, catsup, and vinegar to saucepan; simmer 10 to 15 minutes, stirring occasionally. Yield: 2⅓ cups.

Spiced Peaches

2 (16-ounce) cans peach halves,
  undrained
½ cup brandy
¼ teaspoon ground cinnamon

Combine all ingredients in a saucepan; cook over medium heat until mixture is thoroughly heated. Yield: 10 to 12 servings.

Note: A rolled boneless pork loin roast is two pieces of loin packaged together and usually tied with string or netting. *Curt Treloar*
Largo, Florida

Right: It's your choice of blueberries, blackberries, or raspberries for Pick-a-Berry Tart (recipe, page 118). After the tart is baked, the filling peeks through the woven lattice.

Oregano and feta cheese provide substantial flavor for Tomato-Feta Salad (page 168).

Summer's harvest goes straight from the garden into the kitchen with fresh, new recipes: (from front) Cantaloupe Green Salad, Strawberries Romanoff, Fresh Corn Salad, and Rainbow Pepper Medley. (Recipes, page 126.)

Make the most of the season with pick-of-the-crop recipes, Green Beans Provençal and Green Beans Oriental. (Recipes, page 158.)

Mexican-Stuffed Potatoes, as colorful as they are tasty, will raise the calcium content of your next meal without adding lots of fat. (Recipe, page 131.)

Chicken-Fried Wild Rice blends Oriental flavors and wild rice for a tempting dish that's high in fiber. (This and other fiber-rich recipes begin on page 132.)

Grilled orange roughy is topped with Corn and Pepper Relish. At right, Southwestern Snapper is nestled in a bed of mixed greens and drizzled with a tangy dressing. (Recipes, page 195.)

For an elegant entrée, serve Shrimp Cancun en Papillote (page 136) in the packet in which it cooks.

Crabmeat Salad (page 169) boasts fresh lump crabmeat piled on a bed of shredded lettuce and served with artichokes, hard-cooked eggs, asparagus, and a zesty sauce.

Toasted coconut sprinkled over each serving of Piña Colada Ice Cream (page 181) adds a little crunch.

JULY

Summertime sets the stage for picnics and ice cream parties,

cookouts and luaus. Spotlighting these outdoor parties, our

"Summer Suppers" special section stars a tropical buffet and

a Southwestern fiesta, complete with menus, recipes, and

decorating ideas. Sharing the scene are features on fresh

seafood entrées, grilled meats, crisp salads,

and refreshing beverages.

Green Beans—Plain To Fancy

Peggy Amos of Martinsville, Virginia, a farm girl who grew up gardening, looks forward to this year's crop of green beans. "I like the little White Half Runner—that's my favorite bean. I look for freshness; that's number one," she says.

Peggy's recipe for Green Beans Provençal also takes advantage of ripe summer tomatoes. The tomatoes are chopped and simmered in wine to make an Italian-style sauce that's topped with sliced ripe olives.

Rebekah McKay of Glyndon, Maryland, values the versatility of her recipe for Garlic Green Beans. "It's good with baked ham, and great with grilled salmon or any seafood," she says.

The types of green beans don't make as much difference in cooking time as the maturity or size of the bean. A mature bean has been on the vine longer and is well formed in the pod. It takes about 10 to 12 minutes to cook. Younger, more slender beans take about 8 to 10 minutes. And remember, the standard for crisp-tender varies, depending on who stirs the pot. Just don't be tempted to overcook your fresh green beans.

GREEN BEANS PROVENÇAL
(pictured on pages 150 and 151)

1 pound fresh green beans
1 onion, coarsely chopped
4 cloves garlic, minced
2 tablespoons olive oil
4 large tomatoes, peeled, seeded, and coarsely chopped
½ cup dry white wine
1 (2¼-ounce) can sliced ripe olives, drained
1 tablespoon lemon juice
¼ teaspoon coarsely ground pepper

Wash green beans; trim ends, and remove strings. Bring ½ cup water to a boil in a large saucepan; add beans. Cover, reduce heat to medium, and cook 10 minutes or until tender. Drain beans. Set aside; keep warm.

Sauté onion and garlic in olive oil in a skillet over high heat 5 minutes or until crisp-tender. Stir in tomatoes and wine; bring to a boil. Reduce heat, and simmer, uncovered, 20 minutes, stirring occasionally. Stir in olives.

Spoon sauce over green beans. Pour lemon juice over sauce; sprinkle with pepper. Yield: 6 servings.

Peggy H. Amos
Martinsville, Virginia

GREEN BEANS ORIENTAL
(pictured on pages 150 and 151)

2 tablespoons sliced almonds
2 teaspoons butter or margarine, melted
1¼ pounds green beans
2 tablespoons butter or margarine
½ cup chicken broth
¼ teaspoon salt
¼ teaspoon pepper
1 teaspoon cornstarch
1 tablespoon water
1½ teaspoons lemon juice

Sauté almonds in 2 teaspoons butter in a small skillet until lightly browned; set almonds aside.

Wash green beans; trim ends, and remove strings. Cut beans into French-style strips. Melt 2 tablespoons butter in a large skillet; add green beans, and cook over high heat, stirring constantly, 5 minutes.

Add chicken broth, salt, and pepper; bring to a boil. Reduce heat; cover and simmer 8 to 10 minutes. Combine cornstarch and water; stir into beans. Cook 1 minute, stirring constantly. Stir in lemon juice. Sprinkle sautéed almonds over green beans. Yield: 5 servings.

Microwave Directions: Spread 2 tablespoons almonds on a glass pieplate; stir in 2 tablespoons butter. Microwave at HIGH 3 minutes, stirring once.

Wash green beans; trim ends, and remove strings. Cut beans into French-style strips. Place 2 tablespoons butter in a 2-quart baking dish; cover and microwave at HIGH 1 minute. Add beans; cover and microwave at HIGH 3 to 4 minutes. Add broth, salt, and pepper; stir. Cover; microwave at HIGH 6 to 8 minutes.

Combine cornstarch and water; stir into beans. Microwave at HIGH 1 minute. Stir and let stand 5 minutes. Stir in lemon juice, and sprinkle almonds over green beans.

Sally Murphy
Grapevine, Texas

GARLIC GREEN BEANS

1 pound fresh green beans
3 to 4 cloves garlic, crushed
3 tablespoons butter or margarine,
  melted
⅛ teaspoon salt
⅛ teaspoon pepper
⅓ cup chopped fresh parsley

Wash green beans; trim ends, and remove strings. Bring ½ cup water to a boil in a Dutch oven or saucepan. Add beans. Cover, reduce heat to medium, and cook 10 minutes, stirring occasionally. Drain and set aside.

Sauté garlic in butter in a large skillet; add beans, salt, and pepper. Cook over medium heat 3 minutes or until thoroughly heated, stirring occasionally. Stir in parsley. Yield: 4 servings.

Microwave Directions: Wash beans; trim ends, and remove strings. Place beans in a 2-quart baking dish; add ¼ cup water. Cover beans, and microwave at HIGH 10 to 12 minutes, stirring twice. Drain beans; cover and set aside.

Combine garlic, butter, salt, and pepper in a 2-cup measure. Microwave at HIGH 1 minute; pour over beans, tossing well. Stir in parsley.
Rebekah McKay
Glyndon, Maryland

FRESH GREEN BEANS WITH MARJORAM

1½ pounds fresh green beans
3 tablespoons butter or margarine
½ teaspoon salt
¼ teaspoon pepper
⅛ teaspoon dried whole marjoram

Wash green beans. Trim ends, and remove strings; cut into 1½-inch pieces. Bring ¾ cup water to a boil in a Dutch oven; add green beans. Cover, reduce heat to medium, and cook 8 minutes, stirring frequently. Drain, returning beans to pan. Add butter and remaining ingredients. Cook over medium heat 5 minutes or until crisp-tender, stirring often. Yield: 6 servings.

Microwave Directions: Wash green beans. Trim ends, and remove strings; cut into 1½-inch pieces. Combine beans and ½ cup water in a 2-quart baking dish. Cover and microwave at HIGH 10 to 12 minutes, giving dish a quarter turn and stirring after 5 minutes. Drain beans; cover and set aside.

Combine butter and remaining ingredients in a 2-cup measure. Microwave at HIGH 30 to 45 seconds or until butter melts. Pour over green beans; stir well.
Edith Askins
Greenville, Texas

GREEN BEANS-AND-CHEESE SALAD

1 pound fresh green beans
1 cup white wine vinegar
¾ cup vegetable oil
½ cup diced red onion
2 teaspoons grated lemon rind
Lettuce
1 cup crumbled blue cheese
½ cup chopped walnuts, toasted

Wash green beans; trim ends, and remove strings.

Bring ½ cup water to a boil in a large saucepan; add beans. Cover, reduce heat to low, and cook 5 minutes, stirring occasionally. Drain immediately, and place in ice water. Let stand 5 minutes; drain well.

Combine vinegar, oil, onion, and lemon rind in a jar; cover tightly, and shake vigorously. Pour mixture over beans; cover and chill at least 3 hours.

Remove beans with a slotted spoon onto a lettuce-lined plate; top with blue cheese and walnuts. Yield: 6 servings.

Microwave Directions: Wash beans; trim ends, and remove strings. Place beans in a 2-quart baking dish; add ¼ cup water. Cover with heavy-duty plastic wrap; microwave at HIGH 8 to 9 minutes or until crisp-tender, stirring once. Drain immediately, and place in ice water. Let stand 5 minutes; drain well.

Combine vinegar, oil, onion, and lemon rind in a jar; cover tightly, and shake vigorously. Pour mixture over beans; cover and chill at least 3 hours.

Remove beans with a slotted spoon onto a lettuce-lined plate; top with blue cheese and walnuts.

BAKED GREEN BEANS

1 pound fresh green beans
1 tablespoon instant minced onion
½ teaspoon dried whole tarragon
¼ teaspoon salt
¼ teaspoon pepper
½ cup low-fat cottage cheese
1 egg, beaten
3 tablespoons chopped fresh parsley
3 tablespoons sliced green onions
3 tablespoons shredded Cheddar
  cheese
⅛ teaspoon red pepper

Wash green beans. Trim ends, and remove strings; set aside.

Combine ½ cup water, minced onion, and next 3 ingredients in a small Dutch oven; bring to a boil. Add beans; cover, reduce heat, and cook 10 minutes, stirring occasionally. Drain and place beans in a lightly greased 1-quart baking dish.

Combine cottage cheese and remaining ingredients; spread over beans. Cover and bake at 325° for 15 to 20 minutes or until thoroughly heated. Yield: 4 servings.

Microwave Directions: Wash green beans; trim ends, and remove strings. Place beans in a lightly greased 1-quart baking dish. Add ¼ cup water, minced onion, and next 3 ingredients. Cover and microwave at HIGH 10 to 12 minutes, stirring twice.

Combine cottage cheese and remaining ingredients; spread over beans. Cover and microwave at HIGH 3 minutes or until thoroughly heated.
Mrs. Charles DeHaven
Owensboro, Kentucky

Start The Day With A Sandwich

Lunch and supper menus may have made the sandwich famous, but as sure as the sun comes up every morning, breakfast continually offers new options for sandwich savvy. Bagels, English muffins, croissants, and even plain sandwich bread slices make sturdy bases for layering breakfast or brunch.

On hectic weekday mornings, you will appreciate a breakfast that you can take with you as you leave your house. Just grab a Saucy Egg Sandwich on the way out the door.

When there's a little more time to appreciate a morning meal, try Strawberry-French Toast Sandwiches. The cream cheese-and-jam filling may ooze a little, so you'll need to eat these sandwiches with a fork, but they're quick to fix and taste great, too.

SAUCY EGG SANDWICHES

½ cup cream cheese with chives, softened
2 hard-cooked eggs, finely chopped
1½ tablespoons mayonnaise or salad dressing
½ teaspoon prepared mustard
¼ teaspoon Worcestershire sauce
Dash of salt and pepper
8 English muffins, split and toasted

Combine all ingredients except muffins; spread 2 tablespoons mixture on bottom half of muffins, and cover with top half. Yield: 8 servings.

Note: Eight slices rye bread may be substituted for English muffins, if desired. If using rye bread, spread ¼ cup mixture for each of 4 sandwiches.
Charlotte Pierce
Greensburg, Kentucky

STRAWBERRY-FRENCH TOAST SANDWICHES

¼ cup plus 2 tablespoons whipped cream cheese
12 slices sandwich bread
3 tablespoons strawberry jam
3 eggs
3 tablespoons milk
⅛ teaspoon salt
2 to 3 tablespoons butter or margarine, divided
Powdered sugar
Garnish: strawberry fans

Spread 1 tablespoon cream cheese on each of six bread slices; spread 1½ teaspoons jam over cream cheese. Top with remaining slices of bread.

Combine eggs, milk, and salt in a shallow dish, beating well. Dip each sandwich into egg mixture, turning to coat both sides.

Melt 2 tablespoons butter in a large skillet; cook 3 sandwiches in butter until browned, turning to brown both sides. Repeat procedure with remaining sandwiches, adding more butter if necessary. Sprinkle sandwiches with powdered sugar; serve immediately. Garnish, if desired. Yield: 6 servings.
Nancy Bass Pizey
Clinton, North Carolina

CROISSANT EGGWICHES

3 eggs, beaten
3 tablespoons milk
¼ teaspoon salt
Dash of pepper
¼ cup diced cooked ham
1 to 2 tablespoons minced green onions
1 tablespoon butter or margarine
4 croissants, sliced horizontally
2 (1-ounce) slices process American cheese, cut in half diagonally

Combine first 6 ingredients, mixing well. Melt butter in a large nonstick skillet over medium heat, tilting pan to coat bottom; add egg mixture. Cook without stirring until mixture begins to set on bottom. Draw a spatula across bottom of pan to form large curds. Continue until eggs are thickened, but still moist; do not stir constantly.

Spoon egg mixture evenly onto cut sides of croissant bottoms. Top with a slice of cheese and croissant tops. Place sandwiches on a baking sheet; bake at 350° for 8 minutes or until cheese melts and croissants are heated. Yield: 4 servings.

From Our Kitchen To Yours

When you're ready to prepare chicken for stir-frying, don't reach for a knife—instead, get out your kitchen shears. Besides making an easy job of cutting chicken into bite-size pieces, this versatile utensil can be used for other tasks:
—Trimming excess fat from cooked or uncooked meats
—Cutting ham or cooked chicken into strips for salads
—Cutting cooked or uncooked bacon into pieces
—Cutting fins off fish
—Chopping canned whole tomatoes in the can
—Trimming away the top of each outer leaf of an artichoke
—Cutting dates, dried fruit, and candied fruit
—Chopping parsley, chives, and other fresh herbs
—Cutting phyllo into desired size
—Cutting orange rind into strips
—Cutting up pizza
—Snipping tortillas into chips
—Splitting pita bread in half
—Snipping dough for Swedish tea rings or rolls
—Cutting slits in bread dough before baking
—Dividing canned biscuits into pieces for monkey bread
—Snipping a tiny hole in the end of a zip-top heavy-duty plastic bag to drizzle melted chocolate or glazes
—Cutting coffee cakes

Summer Suppers.

There's no better place to experience summer than in the South, and you'll

find some tasty ways to enjoy the season with the recipes and suggestions in

our Summer Suppers bonus section.

A Buffet Of Southwestern Flavor

Mexican, Tex-Mex, New Mexican, or Southwestern—whatever word you choose to describe the foods of the Southwest, it's sure to evoke images of bright colors, unique flavors, and a fiesta atmosphere. And now is a great time to host a sizzling summer fiesta. With the help of our readers, we've put together a menu that will thrill your family or friends.

Greet guests with a cool glass of punch or your favorite margarita. Then offer them Chiles-Rellenos Squares and Guacamole with commercial tortilla chips for an appetizer.

Spicy Chicken Fingers, served with Creamy Green Salsa, and Carne Adovada help set the mood for this buffet menu. Both are flavored with lots of authentic Southwestern spices, such as cumin, oregano, and chili powder. Serve Carne Adovada on a bed of shredded lettuce; have hot flour tortillas and sour cream nearby so guests can roll Carne Adovada into a tortilla.

Three-Pepper Salad and Mexican Hominy aren't quite as spicy as the entrées, yet both are bursting with color and flavor. Mexican Hominy is similar to the traditional Mexican dish posole, but it's quicker and easier to make. And Three-Pepper Salad has strips of jicama tossed in for extra flavor and crunch.

What better way to cool down taste buds and temperatures than with Mexican Chocolate Ice Cream? A hint of cinnamon and almond give this treat an enjoyable, interesting flavor.

Margaritas or punch
Chiles-Rellenos Squares
Guacamole with tortilla chips
Spicy Chicken Fingers
Carne Adovada
Three-Pepper Salad
Mexican Hominy
Mexican Chocolate Ice Cream

CHILES-RELLENOS SQUARES

4 cups (16 ounces) shredded
  Monterey Jack cheese
1 (4-ounce) can chopped green
  chiles
5 eggs, beaten

Layer cheese and chiles in a lightly greased 12- x 8- x 2-inch baking dish. Pour eggs over mixture. Bake at 300° for 45 minutes or until center is firm. Cut into 2-inch squares. Yield: 2 dozen appetizers.

To make ahead: Bake as directed; cool. Cover with foil and refrigerate. To reheat, bake, covered, at 300° for 20 minutes or until thoroughly heated.
Mrs. William Huffert
Maxwell Air Force Base, Alabama

GUACAMOLE

2 ripe avocados, peeled and mashed
1 (10-ounce) can tomatoes and
  green chiles, drained
3 tablespoons lemon juice
1 teaspoon seasoned salt
½ teaspoon dried onion flakes
⅛ to ¼ teaspoon garlic powder
⅛ teaspoon salt
⅛ teaspoon pepper
Dash of hot sauce

Combine all ingredients. Serve with tortilla chips. Yield: 2½ cups.
Sharon McClatchey
Muskogee, Oklahoma

SPICY CHICKEN FINGERS

2 pounds boned and skinned
   chicken breasts, cut into strips
¾ cup milk
⅔ cup masa harina or cornmeal
3 tablespoons chili powder
2 teaspoons ground cumin
2 teaspoons dried parsley flakes
1 teaspoon dried whole oregano
½ teaspoon garlic powder
½ teaspoon salt
¼ to ½ teaspoon red pepper
¾ cup all-purpose flour
½ teaspoon black pepper
Creamy Green Salsa

Combine chicken and milk; set aside. Combine masa harina and next 7 ingredients. Combine flour and black pepper in a separate bowl. To coat chicken, dip milk-soaked pieces first in flour, back in milk, and then in masa harina mixture. Place on wax paper; freeze at least 4 hours. Place frozen chicken fingers on a lightly greased baking sheet; bake at 400° for 30 minutes or until crisp. Serve chicken fingers with Creamy Green Salsa. Yield: 8 servings.

Creamy Green Salsa

½ cup sour cream
⅓ cup mayonnaise or salad
   dressing
⅓ to ½ cup commercial green salsa
1 tablespoon lemon juice
⅛ teaspoon chili powder

Combine all ingredients; chill. Yield: 1¼ cups.
Sheral Cade
Dallas, Texas

CARNE ADOVADA

3 pounds lean boneless center-cut
   loin pork chops, thinly sliced
⅓ cup chili powder
1 to 2 tablespoons crushed red
   pepper flakes
2 cloves garlic, crushed
1½ tablespoons ground cumin
1½ tablespoons dried whole
   oregano
1 teaspoon salt
3 cups water
Shredded lettuce
Sour cream or yogurt
Hot flour tortillas

Trim fat from chops; place in a 13- x 9- x 2-inch baking dish. Combine chili powder and next 6 ingredients; pour over pork chops, turning chops to coat. Cover and refrigerate at least 8 hours, turning chops occasionally.

Bake, covered, at 325° for 1 hour. Uncover and bake 1 to 1½ hours, spooning marinade over chops occasionally. Cool to room temperature; shred meat with fingers, and return to baking dish. Bake at 350° for 30 minutes or until most of water is absorbed and meat is saucy.

Serve with shredded lettuce, sour cream or yogurt, and hot flour tortillas. Yield: 5 cups.
Libby Idom
Houston, Texas

THREE-PEPPER SALAD

2 green peppers
2 sweet red peppers
2 sweet yellow peppers
2 tablespoons olive oil
½ teaspoon dried whole thyme
¼ teaspoon salt
¼ teaspoon freshly ground pepper
2 cups jicama strips

Seed peppers, and cut into ¼-inch strips. Sauté peppers in oil 5 minutes or until crisp-tender. Stir in seasonings. Chill. Stir in jicama just before serving. Yield: 8 servings.
Jean A. Stephens
La Grange, Georgia

MEXICAN HOMINY

8 slices bacon
1 cup chopped onion
2 (15½-ounce) cans hominy
1 tablespoon all-purpose flour
2 large tomatoes, peeled and
   chopped (about 2 cups)
1 cup (4 ounces) shredded Cheddar
   cheese, divided
1 teaspoon chili powder
¼ teaspoon salt
¼ teaspoon pepper

Cook bacon in a large skillet until crisp; remove bacon, reserving 2 tablespoons drippings in skillet. Crumble bacon, and set aside. Add onion and hominy to drippings in skillet; cook until onion is tender.

Combine bacon, flour, and tomatoes in a large bowl; add hominy mixture, ¾ cup cheese, and remaining ingredients. Spoon into a lightly greased 2-quart casserole; bake at 350° for 25 minutes. Add remaining ¼ cup cheese, and bake an additional 5 minutes or until cheese melts. Yield: 6 to 8 servings.
Joanne Everett
Vinita, Oklahoma

MEXICAN CHOCOLATE
ICE CREAM

3 eggs
1 cup sugar
2 quarts half-and-half
1 (16-ounce) can chocolate syrup
½ teaspoon ground cinnamon
1 tablespoon vanilla extract
¼ teaspoon almond extract

Beat eggs at medium speed of an electric mixer until frothy. Gradually add sugar, beating until thickened.

Heat half-and-half in a 3-quart saucepan over low heat until hot. Gradually stir about one-fourth of hot mixture into eggs; add to remaining hot mixture, stirring constantly. Cook over low heat until mixture is slightly thickened and reaches 165°, stirring constantly. Remove from heat, and stir in chocolate syrup and remaining ingredients. Cool in refrigerator. Pour into freezer can of a 1-gallon freezer. Freeze according to manufacturer's instructions. Let ripen at least 1 hour. Yield: about 1 gallon.

Put A Little Sizzle Into Supper

How many good reasons can you think of for having a cookout? A few favorites might include keeping the kitchen cool, easy preparation, and minimal cleanup. The very best reason, though, is the tantalizing flavor and aroma of grilled meat.

GRILLED LAMB CHOPS

½ cup white wine vinegar
½ cup vegetable oil
½ cup soy sauce
4 cloves garlic, sliced
⅛ teaspoon pepper
4 lamb chops (about 1 pound)

Combine first 5 ingredients; place mixture in a shallow container or zip-top heavy-duty plastic bag. Add chops; cover or seal, and chill 8 hours, turning chops occasionally.

Remove chops from container, reserving marinade for basting. Grill, covered, over medium coals (300° to 400°) for 5 to 6 minutes on each side or to desired degree of doneness, basting chops once with marinade. Yield: 2 servings.   *Alice Pahl*
Raleigh, North Carolina

GRILLED PORK TENDERLOIN

½ cup peanut oil
⅓ cup soy sauce
¼ cup red wine vinegar
3 tablespoons lemon juice
2 tablespoons Worcestershire sauce
1 clove garlic, crushed
1 tablespoon chopped fresh parsley
1 tablespoon dry mustard
1½ teaspoons pepper
2 (¾- to 1-pound) pork tenderloins

Combine first 9 ingredients; place in a shallow container or zip-top heavy-duty plastic bag. Add tenderloins, turning to coat. Cover or seal, and chill 4 hours, turning occasionally. Remove tenderloins from marinade. Grill, covered, 6 inches from medium coals (300° to 400°) for 12 to 14 minutes or until done, turning once. Yield: 6 servings.   *Laurie McIntyre*
Lake Jackson, Texas

BEEF-AND-BACON TWIRLS

10 slices bacon
2 (¾-pound) top round steaks
½ teaspoon garlic powder
Dash of freshly ground pepper
2 tablespoons chopped fresh parsley

Place bacon on a rack in a 12- x 8- x 2-inch baking dish; cover with paper towels. Microwave at HIGH 4 to 5 minutes or until bacon is partially cooked. Drain bacon; set aside.

Place steaks between two sheets of heavy-duty plastic wrap; pound to ½-inch thickness, using a meat mallet or rolling pin. Sprinkle ¼ teaspoon garlic powder, dash of pepper, and 1 tablespoon parsley over each steak. Arrange 5 slices bacon lengthwise over each steak. Starting at narrow end, roll up steaks; secure with wooden picks at 1-inch intervals. Cut into 1-inch slices.

Grill, covered, over hot coals (400° to 500°) for 4 to 5 minutes on each side or to desired degree of doneness. Yield: 6 servings.   *Pearl Lakey*
Seymour, Missouri

TERIYAKI CHICKEN

1 (8-ounce) can crushed pineapple, undrained
¼ cup teriyaki sauce
2 tablespoons lemon juice
2 tablespoons red wine vinegar
2 cloves garlic, minced
1 tablespoon olive oil
¼ teaspoon mesquite liquid smoke
6 chicken breast halves, skinned and boned

Combine first 7 ingredients; place in a shallow container or a zip-top heavy-duty plastic bag. Add chicken; cover or seal, and chill 1 to 2 hours, turning occasionally. Remove chicken from marinade. Grill chicken, covered, over medium coals (300° to 400°) for 4 to 5 minutes on each side. Yield: 6 servings.

Note: Chicken may be served in a sandwich or as an entrée.
Anthony Patterson
Birmingham, Alabama

Come Aboard For A Tropical Buffet

When Kaki Mehlburger puts together one of her great parties, there's no stopping the creativity. Just ask her friends. When they find one of Kaki's fun invitations in their mailbox, they know the gears of a well-oiled machine are already in motion and a good time is on the way.

This Little Rock, Arkansas, interior designer seems more like a playwright than a party planner. She loves carrying a theme through every detail to give her guests a trip into an imaginary world. And for each production, Kaki steps into all roles—creator, director, stagehand, and lead player—along with her husband, Max.

"Our concept is to make each occasion very personal, and the way we do that is to do all the work ourselves," Kaki explains. "We try to create an atmosphere that makes people feel special when they walk in the door. The personal touches are as important as good food."

From a handmade invitation that arrived a few weeks ago in a cool, ocean-blue envelope, two dozen friends know that this time—through Kaki's magic—they'll set sail on a tropical cruise to beat the Arkansas summer heat. Signal flags borrowed from the Mehlburgers' sailboat flank the sidewalk, ushering guests toward the adventure that awaits beyond the front door.

Kaki has set the stage for tonight's opening scene in her courtyard. By the exotic flowers she has arranged, the generous spread of fruit and seafood appetizers, and carefree calypso playing in the background, her friends are sure they've landed on a lush, undiscovered island. After a while, the setting sun drops the curtain on the first act, and the couple's friends move indoors where the dining room provides a backdrop for heavier appetizers which provide the main course of this cocktail buffet.

Whether it's creating the recipes or designing "the set" for a party, Kaki's success lies in her resourcefulness. Her theory is to gather familiar ingredients or items, take them out of their normal context, and think of them in new ways. For instance, she combines elements of the traditional guacamole and margarita to make Tequila Dip. She adds lime juice and tequila to the usual guacamole formula, dips the bowl's rim in salt, and adds a lime garnish for a new twist.

In keeping with the party theme, Kaki places simple flower arrangements in hollowed pineapples and coconuts instead of crystal vases. And Max's prize trays from regattas double as serving pieces for this occasion.

We invite you to peruse the Mehlburgers' shipshape buffet and pick out the things that will work for your special occasion this summer.

**Tropical Fruit
With Curried Rum Sauce
Sausage-Stuffed Mushrooms
Coconut Curried Chicken Balls
Scalloped Zucchini Bites
Spicy Crab Bites
Tequila Dip
Grilled Tenderloin
Marinated Shrimp and
Cucumber**

TROPICAL FRUIT WITH CURRIED RUM SAUCE

1 large fresh pineapple
3 cups watermelon balls
3 cups cantaloupe balls
3 cups honeydew balls
3 cups strawberries, hulled
Curried Rum Sauce

To make pineapple into an oblong "bowl," lay it on its side. Cut an oval shape down to, but not through, the other side; leave stem intact. Remove cut-out section; cut into cubes, discarding skin. Set pineapple bowl aside. Combine cubed pineapple, watermelon, and next 3 ingredients. Cover and chill until ready to use.

To serve, drizzle Curried Rum Sauce over fruit, and toss gently. Spoon a portion of mixture into pineapple bowl. Refill as necessary. Yield: 16 cups.

Curried Rum Sauce

⅓ cup raisins
1 cup hot water
3 tablespoons butter or margarine
1¼ cups firmly packed brown sugar
½ teaspoon grated orange rind
¼ cup orange juice
¼ cup dark rum
¼ teaspoon grated lemon rind
1 tablespoon lemon juice
½ teaspoon curry powder
¼ teaspoon ground ginger

Soak raisins in water 15 minutes; drain and set aside.

Melt butter in a skillet; add brown sugar and remaining ingredients. Cook over medium heat 10 minutes, stirring often. Remove from heat; cool. Yield: 1½ cups.

SAUSAGE-STUFFED MUSHROOMS

24 large fresh mushrooms
2 tablespoons butter or margarine, melted
½ pound bulk pork sausage
¼ cup chopped onion
½ teaspoon garlic powder
2½ tablespoons hot picante sauce
1 (8-ounce) loaf process cheese spread

Clean mushrooms with damp paper towels. Remove stems, and reserve for other uses. Brush caps with melted butter, and place, stem side up, in a lightly greased 13- x 9- x 2-inch baking dish. Set aside.

Cook sausage, onion, and garlic powder in a skillet until sausage browns, stirring to crumble. Drain and return sausage mixture to skillet. Stir in picante sauce; simmer 2 minutes, stirring occasionally.

Spoon sausage mixture evenly into mushroom caps. Thinly slice cheese, and cut each slice into four squares. Top each mushroom with a square of cheese. Bake at 400° for 8 minutes. Yield: 2 dozen appetizers.

COCONUT CURRIED CHICKEN BALLS

⅔ cup raisins
2 tablespoons dark rum
4 chicken breast halves
1⅓ cups pineapple cream cheese
3 tablespoons mango chutney
3 tablespoons mayonnaise or salad dressing
1 tablespoon teriyaki sauce
2 teaspoons curry powder
½ teaspoon ground ginger
½ teaspoon salt
¼ teaspoon red pepper
1 cup sliced almonds, toasted
1½ cups flaked coconut
Garnishes: apricots, orange slices, kiwifruit slices

Combine raisins and rum; set aside.

Place chicken in a large saucepan; cover with water. Bring to a boil; cover, reduce heat, and simmer 25 minutes or until tender. Remove chicken; let cool slightly, and bone. Position knife blade in food processor bowl; add half of chicken. Pulse 2 or 3 times until coarsely chopped. Repeat with remaining chicken.

Combine cream cheese and next 7 ingredients. Drain raisins. Add raisins, chicken, and almonds to cream cheese mixture, stirring until blended. Shape mixture into 1-inch balls; roll in coconut. Chill before serving. Arrange on a platter, and garnish, if desired. Yield: 44 appetizers.

Note: These appetizers may be frozen up to 1 week.

SCALLOPED ZUCCHINI BITES

5 medium zucchini
40 bay scallops
¼ cup fine, dry breadcrumbs
2 tablespoons butter or margarine, melted
1 tablespoon butter or margarine, melted
2 tablespoons vermouth
½ cup fresh corn cut from cob
1 cup chopped sweet red pepper
1 tablespoon chopped onion
¼ teaspoon garlic powder
¼ teaspoon hot sauce
½ cup half-and-half
Grated Parmesan cheese

Cut zucchini in half lengthwise. Scoop a small amount of pulp from center of each half, and scallop edges. Cut each half into 4 (1½-inch) pieces. Blanch zucchini shells 3 minutes in boiling water to cover; drain. Rinse in cold water; drain and set aside.

Coat scallops with breadcrumbs; cook in 2 tablespoons butter 1 minute on each side or until lightly browned. Drain on paper towels; set aside.

Combine 1 tablespoon butter, vermouth, and next 5 ingredients in a skillet; cook, stirring often, until vegetables are tender. Stir in half-and-half; remove from heat. Spoon mixture into zucchini shells; place on lightly greased 15- x 10- x 1-inch jellyroll pans. Top each with 1 scallop,

and sprinkle lightly with Parmesan cheese. Broil 6 inches from heat 1 to 2 minutes or until lightly browned. Yield: 40 appetizers.

SPICY CRAB BITES

1 pound fresh crabmeat, drained and flaked
1 egg, beaten
1 cup fine, dry breadcrumbs
½ cup finely chopped sweet red pepper
⅓ cup finely chopped fresh parsley
3 tablespoons mayonnaise or salad dressing
1 tablespoon finely chopped green onions
1 teaspoon coarsely ground pepper
½ teaspoon salt
1½ teaspoons Old Bay seasoning
1 teaspoon Worcestershire sauce
¼ teaspoon dry mustard
1⅛ teaspoons red pepper
½ cup fine, dry breadcrumbs
2 tablespoons vegetable oil
2 tablespoons butter or margarine
Garnishes: red and green grapes, fresh parsley, citrus fruit slices

Combine first 13 ingredients in a bowl; mix well. Shape into patties, using 1 tablespoon mixture for each; dredge in ½ cup breadcrumbs.

Combine oil and butter in a large skillet over medium-high heat. Cook crabmeat patties in hot oil mixture until golden brown on both sides. Drain well on paper towels. Arrange on a tray, and garnish, if desired. Yield: about 3 dozen appetizers.

Note: May be prepared and fried 30 minutes ahead and reheated at 350° for 5 to 10 minutes.

TEQUILA DIP

2 medium-size ripe avocados,
  peeled and seeded
2 tablespoons lime juice
2 (3-ounce) packages cream cheese,
  softened
3 tablespoons tequila
½ teaspoon hot sauce
½ teaspoon salt
¼ teaspoon pepper
Lime wedge
Salt
Garnish: lime slices

Mash avocados; stir in lime juice, and
set aside. Beat cream cheese at medium speed of an electric mixer until
smooth; stir in tequila, hot sauce, salt,
and pepper. Stir in avocado; set aside.
Rub rim of serving bowl with lime
wedge. Put salt on plate; dip rim of
bowl in salt, coating well. Spoon dip
into bowl; garnish, if desired. Serve
with nacho chips. Yield: 3 cups.

GRILLED TENDERLOIN

1 (4- to 6-pound) beef tenderloin,
  trimmed
1 cup teriyaki marinade
1 tablespoon cracked pepper
Party rolls (optional)
Horseradish sauce (optional)
Garnishes: purple kale, fresh
  parsley, orange slices, cherry
  tomatoes

Place meat in a zip-top heavy-duty
plastic bag. Pour marinade into bag,
and seal. Place plastic bag in a shallow
pan, and refrigerate 8 hours, turning
occasionally.
  Drain meat, discarding marinade;
sprinkle with pepper. Place meat on a
gas grill on high heat with lid closed 3
minutes; turn tenderloin, and cook 3
additional minutes. Reduce heat to
low, and cook 12 minutes or until meat

thermometer registers 140° (rare).
Chill several hours or overnight before slicing.
  If desired, serve sliced tenderloin
with party rolls and horseradish
sauce, and garnish. Yield: 20 to 25 appetizer servings.

MARINATED SHRIMP AND CUCUMBER

1 tablespoon chopped fresh basil or
  1 teaspoon dried whole basil
1 tablespoon chopped fresh oregano
  or 1 teaspoon dried whole
  oregano
1 tablespoon olive oil
2½ quarts water
3 pounds unpeeled, large fresh
  shrimp
2 cucumbers, sliced
1 purple onion, sliced
2 cups vegetable oil
1 cup red wine vinegar
1 teaspoon ground coriander
1 teaspoon salt
1 teaspoon coarsely ground black
  pepper
1 teaspoon crushed red pepper
  flakes
1 teaspoon sugar
2 or 3 cloves garlic, crushed
1 (3-ounce) jar capers, drained
1 tablespoon Worcestershire sauce
1 tablespoon lemon juice

Combine first 3 ingredients in a small
bowl, and set aside.
  Bring water to a boil; add shrimp,
and cook 3 to 5 minutes. Drain well;
rinse with cold water. Peel and devein
shrimp. Combine shrimp, cucumber,
and onion in a large bowl.
  Combine vegetable oil and next 7
ingredients in a large saucepan. Bring
to a boil; reduce heat, and simmer 3
minutes. Let cool. Stir in reserved

herb mixture, capers, Worcestershire
sauce, and lemon juice. Pour over
shrimp mixture; toss. Cover and chill
8 hours. Yield: 15 appetizer servings.

Sandwiches That Satisfy

The Earl of Sandwich was a fellow after our own hearts (and perhaps our
hectic schedules, as well). The sandwich supposedly took its name from
this gambling nobleman who was too
busy to stop for lunch. The story goes
that he had his lunch brought to him
between two slices of bread so he
could hold it with one hand while con-
tinuing to throw dice with the other.
  Now you might not have a servant
at your side to fetch a meal, but perhaps you can find a few moments to
layer your lunch in similar fashion.

TUNA SANDWICH BOATS

6 sourdough French rolls
1 (7-ounce) can tuna, drained
½ cup (2 ounces) shredded Cheddar
  cheese
¼ cup chopped water chestnuts
¼ cup chopped celery
¼ cup chopped green pepper
¼ cup slivered almonds, toasted
2 tablespoons grated onion
2 tablespoons pimiento-stuffed
  olives, sliced
Dash of Worcestershire sauce
Dash of hot sauce
⅓ cup mayonnaise or salad
  dressing
Garnish: pimiento strips

Cut a ½-inch slice from top of each roll; scoop out center, leaving a ½-inch shell.

Combine tuna and next 9 ingredients. Add mayonnaise; toss gently to coat. Spoon tuna mixture into shells; place on a baking sheet. Bake at 400° for 15 minutes. Garnish, if desired. Yield: 6 servings.   *Linda Myers*
Muskogee, Oklahoma

BEEF-AND-KRAUT SANDWICH

⅓ cup mayonnaise or salad
  dressing
¼ cup pickle relish
2 tablespoons Dijon mustard
1 teaspoon Worcestershire sauce
1 cup thin strips cooked roast beef
  or corned beef
1 cup (4 ounces) shredded Swiss
  cheese
1 (16-ounce) can sauerkraut,
  drained
12 slices rye bread

Combine first 4 ingredients; mix well. Stir in roast beef, cheese, and sauerkraut; cover and chill. Spread beef mixture evenly on 6 slices of bread; top with remaining bread. Yield: 6 servings.   *Laurie Thomas*
Lake Jackson, Texas

ROAST BEEF HERO SANDWICH

1 (16-ounce) loaf Italian bread
2 tablespoons mayonnaise or salad
  dressing
1 teaspoon Creole mustard
¼ cup chopped ripe olives
¼ cup finely chopped purple onion
1 pound sliced cooked roast beef
1 (8-ounce) package sliced Swiss
  cheese

Heat bread according to package directions. Slice bread in half horizontally. Combine mayonnaise, mustard, olives, and onion, stirring well; spread on cut surfaces of bread.

Layer half each of beef and cheese on bottom half of bread; repeat layers with remaining beef and cheese. Cover with bread top. Cut sandwich into 4 slices, and wrap each in aluminum foil. Bake at 400° for 20 minutes or until thoroughly heated. Yield: 4 servings.   *Carolene Martinez*
Natchez, Mississippi

TACO JOES

1 pound ground chuck
1 small onion, chopped
¾ cup commercial taco sauce
1 tablespoon chili powder
2 teaspoons Worcestershire sauce
½ teaspoon salt
¼ teaspoon garlic powder
8 hamburger buns
1 (6-ounce) package sliced
  American cheese

Cook ground chuck and onion in a skillet until meat is browned, stirring to crumble meat. Drain off pan drippings. Stir in taco sauce and next 4 ingredients; simmer 5 minutes or until thoroughly heated.

Place opened hamburger buns on a baking sheet. Spoon about ¼ cup meat mixture onto bottom half of each bun. Top meat mixture with a slice of cheese. Bake at 350° for 4 minutes or until cheese melts and buns are warmed. Place top of bun over cheese. Yield: 8 servings.

Note: To make sandwiches ahead, cool filling before spooning onto buns. Top with cheese and top of bun. Wrap each sandwich in foil, and chill up to 2 days. Bake sandwiches in foil at 350° for 25 minutes or until heated.

PINEAPPLE-HAM SANDWICH LOAF

1 (8-inch) round loaf white bread
Pineapple-Cheese Spread
Horseradish-Ham Spread

Cut bread horizontally into 6 equal slices, using an electric knife or bread knife. Spread about one-third of Pineapple-Cheese Spread on cut surface of bottom slice of bread, and top with second bread layer. Spread about half of Horseradish-Ham Spread on second bread layer. Repeat layering bread and spreads to use remaining ingredients, ending with top of loaf. Cut into wedges. Yield: 8 servings.

Pineapple-Cheese Spread

1 (8-ounce) package cream cheese,
  softened
1 (8-ounce) can crushed pineapple,
  drained
1½ tablespoons finely chopped
  green pepper
1½ teaspoons minced onion
Dash of seasoned salt

Combine all ingredients, and mix well. Yield: 1⅔ cups.

Horseradish-Ham Spread

3 cups coarsely ground cooked ham
⅓ cup sweet pickle relish
⅓ cup mayonnaise or salad
  dressing
1½ tablespoons prepared
  horseradish
1 teaspoon prepared mustard

Combine all ingredients, and mix well. Yield: 2 cups.

RAISIN COUNTRY SANDWICH

½ cup shredded apple
½ cup shredded carrot
½ cup (2 ounces) shredded Cheddar
   cheese
¼ cup diced celery
¼ cup raisins
2 tablespoons sliced green onions
2 tablespoons mayonnaise or salad
   dressing
2 tablespoons butter or margarine
8 slices raisin bread

Combine first 7 ingredients in a medium bowl, tossing gently until blended; set aside.

Spread butter on one side of each slice of bread. Spread apple mixture on buttered side of 4 slices of bread, and top with remaining bread, buttered side down. Yield: 4 servings.
Aimee Goodman
Corryton, Tennessee

Fresh And Flashy Salads

Throughout the months that gardens flourish with produce, salads reign as a menu mainstay in homes and restaurants alike. And judging from these recipes, Southerners sport a particular knack for blending and seasoning the bounty into salads as crisp as their garden-fresh flavor.

Though light on seasonings compared to many tomato concoctions, Tomato-Feta Salad is definitely not shy on flavor. A simple blend of feta cheese, onion, and oregano flavors tomato wedges. Lemon slices and juice in Cukes and Scallions offer a new look and taste for cucumbers.

TOMATO-FETA SALAD
(pictured on page 151)

1½ cups crumbled feta cheese
   (7 ounces)
¼ to ½ cup chopped onion
1½ teaspoons vegetable oil
1 teaspoon dried whole oregano
6 medium tomatoes (about 2½
   pounds), cut into wedges
Boston lettuce leaves

Combine first 5 ingredients; toss gently. Cover and refrigerate at least 2 hours. Spoon onto Boston lettuce leaves to serve. Yield: 6 to 8 servings.
Karen Mantzouris
Fayetteville, North Carolina

FIESTA ZUCCHINI COLESLAW

2 cups coarsely shredded zucchini
2 cups shredded cabbage
1 medium carrot, shredded
2 green onions, sliced
½ cup thinly sliced radishes
⅓ cup mayonnaise or salad
   dressing
⅓ cup mild picante sauce
½ teaspoon ground cumin

Drain shredded zucchini by gently pressing between layers of paper towels. Combine zucchini and next 4 ingredients; set aside. Combine mayonnaise and remaining ingredients; add to zucchini mixture, and toss gently. Cover and chill at least 1 hour. Yield: 6 servings.
Carrie Treichel
Johnson City, Tennessee

CUKES AND SCALLIONS

4 large cucumbers, thinly sliced
1 teaspoon salt
3 scallions, sliced
1 tablespoon chopped fresh dillweed
1 tablespoon chopped fresh parsley
1 lemon, thinly sliced
⅓ cup cider vinegar
1 tablespoon sugar
1 tablespoon lemon juice
1 tablespoon vegetable oil
¼ teaspoon pepper
Red-tipped lettuce leaves

Layer cucumber in a large bowl, sprinkling salt between layers. Cover and chill 2 hours. Drain and rinse with cold water; drain well. Add sliced scallions, dillweed, parsley, and lemon slices; toss gently.

Combine vinegar and next 4 ingredients in a jar; cover tightly, and shake vigorously. Pour over cucumber mixture, tossing gently. Cover and chill at least 1 hour. Spoon into a lettuce-lined bowl, using a slotted spoon. Yield: 8 to 10 servings.
Clairiece Gilbert Humphrey
Charlottesville, Virginia

FRESH FRUIT SALAD WITH POPPY SEED DRESSING

3 bananas, sliced
1½ teaspoons lemon juice
1 small head romaine lettuce
2 cups pineapple chunks
2 cups strawberries, halved
2 cups cantaloupe balls
2 cups honeydew balls
2 kiwifruit, peeled and sliced
Poppy Seed Dressing

Sprinkle banana slices with lemon juice. Line a serving platter with romaine; arrange fruit on lettuce. Serve with Poppy Seed Dressing. Yield: 6 servings.

Poppy Seed Dressing

1 cup vegetable oil
¾ cup sugar
⅓ cup white vinegar
2 tablespoons minced onion
1 teaspoon salt
½ teaspoon dry mustard
1½ teaspoons poppy seeds

Combine first 6 ingredients in container of an electric blender; process on low speed 30 seconds. Stir in poppy seeds. Cover and chill; stir before using. Yield: 1½ cups.

Sherry Marr
Burke, Virginia

Catch On
To Seafood

The Southern coastline offers a cornucopia of fresh seafood, most of which can be found in fish markets year-round. That's great news for folks who want an entrée that's satisfying but not too filling. From snapper fillets to shrimp to crabmeat, there is a recipe here that will suit your taste for seafood.

Shrimp-and-Vegetable Spaghetti features fresh shrimp cooked in a vegetable sauce and served over hot pasta. Add a green salad and a loaf of French bread to round out a meal.

Crabmeat Salad makes an attractive main dish that can be prepared an hour or two before serving and held in the refrigerator.

STRAWBERRY-SPINACH SALAD

¼ cup sugar
3 tablespoons lemon juice
¼ cup egg substitute
⅓ cup vegetable oil
1 (10-ounce) package fresh, trimmed spinach, torn
2 cups strawberries, sliced

Combine sugar and lemon juice in a small bowl; beat with a wire whisk until sugar dissolves. Add egg substitute; beat well. Add oil, 1 tablespoon at a time, beating until dressing is thick and creamy. Cover and chill.

Combine spinach and strawberries in a bowl; add dressing, and toss. Yield: 6 servings. *Carol Y. Chastain*
San Antonio, Texas

Tip: *Remember that salad greens should never be cut with a knife because it may discolor and bruise the leaves. Gently tearing the leaves is better and makes a prettier salad.*

CRABMEAT SALAD
(pictured on page 155)

1 dozen fresh asparagus spears
⅓ cup sour cream
⅓ cup mayonnaise or salad dressing
2 teaspoons Dijon mustard
2 teaspoons white wine vinegar
½ teaspoon dried whole tarragon
¼ teaspoon dried whole basil
1 tablespoon chopped green onions
½ teaspoon prepared horseradish
4 cups shredded lettuce
1 pound fresh lump crabmeat
4 marinated canned artichoke hearts, halved
2 hard-cooked eggs, quartered
Garnish: pimiento strips

Snap off tough ends of asparagus. Remove scales from stalks with a knife or vegetable peeler, if desired. Arrange asparagus in a steaming rack, and place over boiling water. Cover and steam 6 to 8 minutes or until crisp-tender. Drain. Chill 1 hour.

Combine sour cream and next 7 ingredients in a small bowl. Line each of 4 individual salad plates with 1 cup lettuce. Divide crabmeat among plates. Divide artichokes, asparagus, and hard-cooked eggs among plates, and arrange around crabmeat. Serve with dressing. Garnish, if desired. Yield: 4 servings. *Grace Bravos*
Timonium, Maryland

summer Suppers.

Seafood Tips

■ When purchasing scallops, count on 40 to a pound. Because they are highly perishable, cook scallops within two days of purchase. Before cooking, always wash scallops well to remove sand and grit.

■ When frozen, crabmeat becomes tough and watery, losing flavor. It's best to use crabmeat in a recipe and then freeze it. To serve, thaw crabmeat in the refrigerator and then follow recipe cooking instructions.

■ When buying whole fish, don't discard the head and tail; when cooked with the fish or by themselves, they make good fish stock for sauces, aspics, and chowders or other soups.

■ Fish that is fresh has practically no "fish" odor. The fish odor becomes more pronounced with the passage of time, but the odor should not be strong when fish is bought.

■ As a rule, thawed fish should not be kept longer than one day before cooking; the flavor is better if it is cooked immediately after thawing.

■ Count on 2 servings per ½ to 1 pound of shucked or shelled crab, lobsters, scallops, oysters, and shrimp.

SNAPPER PROVENÇAL

1 (7½-ounce) can whole tomatoes, undrained and chopped
¼ cup chopped green pepper
¼ cup chopped onion
¼ cup chopped fresh parsley
1 small clove garlic, crushed
¼ teaspoon dried whole oregano
6 (4-ounce) red snapper fillets
⅛ teaspoon freshly ground pepper

Combine first 6 ingredients in a 12- x 8- x 2-inch baking dish; stir to distribute vegetables evenly in dish. Cover tightly with heavy-duty plastic wrap; fold back a small corner of wrap to allow steam to escape. Microwave at HIGH 4 minutes, giving dish a half-turn after 2 minutes. Push vegetables to one side of dish, and arrange fish in dish with thickest portions to outside. Spoon vegetable mixture evenly over fish, and sprinkle with pepper. Cover and microwave at HIGH 5 to 6 minutes, giving dish a half-turn after 3 minutes. Cook until fish turns opaque. Let stand, covered, 3 to 5 minutes. Yield: 6 servings.

BROILED SCALLOPS

1 clove garlic, crushed
¼ teaspoon salt
2 tablespoons minced fresh parsley
1 tablespoon vegetable oil
¼ cup dry vermouth
1 pound fresh bay scallops
1 tablespoon butter or margarine
½ cup soft breadcrumbs
Paprika

Combine first 5 ingredients in a bowl. Add scallops; cover and chill 1 hour.
Spoon scallop mixture into 4 individual baking shells. Place shells on a baking sheet. Broil 2 inches from heat 3 minutes; stir and broil 2 minutes.

Combine butter and breadcrumbs; sprinkle over scallops, and broil 1 minute or until browned. Sprinkle with paprika. Yield: 4 servings.

Note: If desired, sea scallops, quartered, may be substituted for the bay scallops. *Rita W. Cook*
Corpus Christi, Texas

SHRIMP-AND-VEGETABLE SPAGHETTI

1 pound unpeeled medium-size fresh shrimp
4 slices bacon
1 cup chopped onion
1 medium-size green pepper, chopped
4 carrots, scraped and sliced diagonally
¼ teaspoon garlic powder
2 (14.5-ounce) cans whole tomatoes, undrained and chopped
1 (2.25-ounce) can sliced ripe olives, drained
1 teaspoon dried whole basil
1 teaspoon dried whole oregano
¼ teaspoon pepper
¼ teaspoon garlic salt
8 ounces fresh mushrooms, sliced
Hot cooked vermicelli
Grated Parmesan cheese

Peel and devein shrimp; set aside. Cook bacon in a large skillet until crisp; remove bacon, reserving 1 tablespoon drippings in skillet. Crumble bacon, and set aside. Sauté onion, green pepper, carrots, and garlic powder in drippings until carrots are crisp-tender. Add tomatoes and next 5 ingredients; bring to a boil. Cover, reduce heat, and simmer 3 to 5 minutes. Add shrimp and mushrooms; cook 10 minutes. Serve over vermicelli; sprinkle with bacon and cheese. Yield: 6 servings. *Terry C. Paulson*
Little Rock, Arkansas

Vacation Munchies

So you found the best souvenir, sent all the wildest postcards, and had more fun than anybody. When you invite your friends to view the vacation video recounting every detail, persuade them to sit trough the show by offering tempting refreshments. A good choice is Veggie Bites, which consists of chopped vegetables and cheese atop a crescent roll crust.

A few of these snacks even travel well if you're looking for some goodies to take with you on your next vacation. Pack Creole Snack Mix in an airtight container or zip-top plastic bag, and nibble on it in transit or after you arrive at your destination. If you're headed to Memphis, consider stopping at the Germantown Commissary Company. Walker Taylor, Jr., invites folks to sample his version of nachos seasoned with spicy barbecue pork. He also shares the recipe so that you can enjoy it at home—perhaps during the video.

VEGGIE BITES

2 (8-ounce) packages refrigerated crescent rolls
1 egg, beaten
2 (8-ounce) packages cream cheese
1 cup mayonnaise or salad dressing
1 (1-ounce) envelope ranch-style salad dressing mix
¾ cup (3 ounces) shredded Cheddar cheese
½ cup finely chopped broccoli
½ cup finely chopped cauliflower
½ cup finely chopped mushrooms
½ cup finely chopped green pepper
½ cup finely chopped tomato

Unroll crescent rolls, and place in bottom of an ungreased 15- x 10- x 1-inch jellyroll pan, pinching edges together to seal. Brush dough with beaten egg. Bake at 375° for 11 to 13 minutes, and cool completely.

Combine cream cheese, mayonnaise, and salad dressing mix; beat until well blended. Spread mixture over crust; sprinkle with cheese and vegetables. Chill 2 hours; cut into 1- x 1½-inch bites. Yield: 8 dozen.

Rita Frye
Marietta, Georgia

CREOLE SNACK MIX

3 cups corn-and-rice cereal
3 cups crispy wheat cereal squares
3 cups toasted oat O-shaped cereal
3 cups pretzel sticks
2 cups pecan halves
⅓ cup butter or margarine, melted
¼ cup grated Parmesan cheese
1 tablespoon Creole seasoning
¼ teaspoon garlic powder

Combine first 5 ingredients in a large roasting pan; set aside.

Drizzle half of butter over cereal mixture. Combine cheese and seasonings; sprinkle half over cereal. Stir; repeat procedure with remaining butter and seasonings. Bake at 250° for 1 hour, stirring every 15 minutes. Yield: 12 cups.

Tammy Dosier
Lenoir, North Carolina

COMMISSARY BARBECUE NACHOS

½ pound chopped barbecued pork shoulder
1 (10-ounce) package tortilla chips
1 cup Hot Cheese Dip
½ cup commercial barbecue sauce
¼ cup chopped fresh jalapeño peppers

Wrap chopped meat in aluminum foil; heat at 300° for 20 minutes or until thoroughly heated.

Place tortilla chips on a platter. Pour Hot Cheese Dip over chips; add meat and barbecue sauce over top. Sprinkle with jalapeño peppers. Serve immediately. Yield: 6 to 8 servings.

Hot Cheese Dip

1 (16-ounce) loaf process cheese spread
1 (10-ounce) can tomatoes with chiles, undrained

Combine ingredients in a heavy saucepan. Cook over low heat, stirring constantly, until cheese melts. Serve warm over tortilla chips, vegetables, or baked potatoes. Yield: 2⅔ cups.

Walker Taylor, Jr.
Germantown, Tennessee

Munchie Tips

■ For a wonderfully seasoned popcorn, add ½ to ¾ teaspoon curry powder to 4 cups buttered, salted popcorn. Serve with an ice-cold beverage.

■ To freshen stale pretzels or chips, bake at 325° for 5 to 10 minutes. Let cool.

QUICK!

All-American Favorites

Declare your independence from the kitchen this Fourth of July. These speedy dishes salute time-honored American fare. Gone are lengthy vigils over a pot of hot grease to get crisp, golden fried chicken or fish; our oven-fried versions cook in less than 20 minutes. And you never even have to turn on your oven for the traditional baked beans and banana pudding.

Jiffy Beans and Franks cooks in the microwave in a hurry, and all you need for No-Bake Banana Pudding is a refrigerator. Commercial whipped topping replaces the usual baked meringue *and* a cooking step.

CORN FLAKE CHICKEN

1 cup crushed corn flakes cereal
1 (0.6-ounce) envelope zesty Italian salad dressing mix
2 tablespoons grated Parmesan cheese
1 teaspoon dried parsley flakes
6 chicken breast halves, skinned and boned
¼ cup milk

Combine first 4 ingredients in a shallow dish. Dip each chicken breast in milk; roll in crumb mixture. Place chicken in a lightly greased 12- x 8- x 2-inch baking dish; bake at 375° for 18 minutes or until done. Yield: 6 servings.   *Sharon Faulkner*
Springfield, Missouri

JIFFY BEANS AND FRANKS

2 (16-ounce) cans pork and beans
½ cup chopped onion
½ cup catsup
¼ cup firmly packed brown sugar
½ teaspoon dry mustard
4 frankfurters, cut in ⅜-inch slices

Combine first 5 ingredients; spoon into a lightly greased, shallow 2-quart casserole. Cover with heavy-duty plastic wrap; fold back a small edge of wrap to allow steam to escape. Microwave at HIGH 8 to 9 minutes, stirring once. Add frankfurters. Microwave at HIGH 8 to 9 minutes, stirring once. Yield: 6 servings.   *Lila J. Hughes*
Richardson, Texas

OVEN-FRIED FISH

2 pounds catfish or snapper fillets
1 egg, beaten
½ cup Italian-seasoned breadcrumbs
¼ cup butter or margarine, melted
2 tablespoons lemon juice

Dip fillets in egg; lightly coat with breadcrumbs. Arrange fish in a single layer on a well-greased, shallow baking pan. Combine butter and lemon juice; drizzle over fish. Bake at 450° for 15 to 18 minutes or until fish flakes easily when tested with a fork. Yield: 6 to 8 servings.   *Melanie Keaton*
Richmond, Kentucky

Tip: *Fish and onion odors can be removed from the hands by rubbing them with a little vinegar, followed by washing in soapy water.*

SLOPPY JOES

1½ pounds ground beef
1 small onion, chopped
1 small green pepper, chopped
1 (10¾-ounce) can tomato soup, undiluted
1 (8-ounce) can tomato sauce
2 tablespoons brown sugar (optional)
1 tablespoon Worcestershire sauce
1 teaspoon prepared mustard
Pinch of garlic powder
6 hamburger buns, split and toasted

Cook ground beef, onion, and green pepper in a large skillet until beef is browned, stirring to crumble; drain. Stir in tomato soup and next 5 ingredients; simmer 10 to 15 minutes, stirring mixture often. Serve on toasted buns. Yield: 6 servings.

Cindy Quebe
Greenville, Texas

NO-BAKE BANANA PUDDING

2 (3.4-ounce) packages vanilla instant pudding mix
1 (8-ounce) carton sour cream
3½ cups milk
Vanilla wafers
3 large bananas
1 (8-ounce) carton frozen whipped topping, thawed

Combine first 3 ingredients in a large bowl; beat at low speed of an electric mixer 2 minutes or until thickened. Line bottom and sides of a 3-quart bowl with vanilla wafers. Slice one banana, and layer over wafers. Spoon one-third of pudding mixture over bananas. Repeat layers of vanilla wafers, bananas, and pudding twice; chill. Spread whipped topping over pudding. Yield: 10 to 12 servings.

Charlotte Hunt
Medon, Tennessee

ON THE LIGHT SIDE

Frosty, Fruity, And Light Treats

As summer heats up in the South you'll be looking for a way to cool off. And a frozen fruit dessert or snack is just the ticket—especially if it's light.

Refresh yourself with Frozen Strawberry Cups after a game of tennis or an afternoon swim. You'll enjoy these tasty snacks without feeling the guilt of eating richer treats.

Kids will love Pineapple-Yogurt Pops for an afternoon snack. Make up a batch, and keep them in the freezer. At less than 1 gram of fat each, you'll want to offer them often.

PINEAPPLE-YOGURT POPS

1 (20-ounce) can crushed pineapple
1 (8-ounce) carton low-fat pineapple yogurt
1 (6-ounce) can unsweetened pineapple juice
1 teaspoon grated lemon rind

Combine all ingredients; pour mixture into frozen pop molds or 12 (3-ounce) paper cups, inserting wooden sticks. Freeze until firm. Yield: 12 servings (59 calories per serving).

□ *1.3 grams protein, 0.3 gram fat, 13.5 grams carbohydrate, 1 milligram cholesterol, 15 milligrams sodium, and 43 milligrams calcium.*
Louise Jones
Lithia Springs, Georgia

WATERMELON ICE

8 cups cubed watermelon, seeded
½ cup sugar

Place watermelon in container of an electric blender or food processor. Top with cover, and process until smooth (should have 4 cups watermelon puree). Spoon into a medium-size mixing bowl; add sugar, and stir until sugar dissolves.

Pour mixture into an 8-inch square pan, and freeze just until firm. Break frozen mixture into chunks, and place in a chilled large mixing bowl. Beat at low speed of an electric mixer until smooth. Return mixture to pan, and freeze until firm. Let stand at room temperature 10 minutes before serving. Yield: 4½ cups (88 calories per ½-cup serving).

□ *0.9 gram protein, 0.6 gram fat, 21.2 grams carbohydrate, 0 milligrams cholesterol, 3 milligrams sodium, and 11.3 milligrams calcium.*

FROZEN STRAWBERRY CUPS

1 (16-ounce) package frozen whole unsweetened strawberries, thawed
1 (8-ounce) can unsweetened crushed pineapple, drained
1 (8-ounce) carton low-fat strawberry-flavored yogurt
1 large banana, diced
¼ cup finely chopped pecans
2 tablespoons sifted powdered sugar

Place thawed strawberries in container of a food processor or electric blender; process until smooth. Spoon strawberry puree into a large bowl;

add remaining ingredients, and stir mixture well.

Spoon ⅓ cup strawberry mixture into each of 12 paper-lined muffin pans. Freeze until firm. Remove from freezer 10 minutes before serving. Yield: 12 servings (75 calories per serving).

□ *1.4 grams protein, 2 grams fat, 14 grams carbohydrate, 2 milligrams cholesterol, 22 milligrams sodium, and 38.8 milligrams calcium.*
Mrs. John R. Boone
Spartanburg, South Carolina

APPLESAUCE FLUFF

1 envelope unflavored gelatin
½ cup water
¼ cup sugar
2 cups unsweetened applesauce
2 tablespoons lemon juice
½ cup water

Sprinkle gelatin over ½ cup water in a medium saucepan; let stand 1 minute. Add sugar, and cook over medium heat, stirring until mixture dissolves. Remove from heat; stir in remaining ingredients. Chill until consistency of unbeaten egg white.

Spoon mixture into a large mixing bowl; beat at high speed of an electric mixer until fluffy. Spoon into an 8-inch square pan; freeze until firm. Let stand at room temperature 10 minutes before serving. Yield: 6 servings (72 calories per ⅔-cup serving).

□ *1.2 grams protein, 0 grams fat, 17.9 grams carbohydrate, 0 milligrams cholesterol, 3 milligrams sodium, and 3 milligrams calcium.*
Mrs. Blair Cunnyngham
Cleveland, Tennessee

Throw An Ice Cream Party

Whether it's a family reunion, a birthday, or a get-together with friends, an ice cream party always lends itself to some simple yet flashy ideas.

This menu makes the party easy because you can do almost everything ahead of time. First, make homemade ice cream and give it a new look by freezing it into balls the day prior to the party.

Vanilla Ice Cream relies on instant pudding to provide a creamy, firm product that handles and freezes well. One freezer yields 30 to 35 scoops— enough to feed about 15 guests. For larger parties, make two or more freezers.

Include Fudge Sauce and Butter Pecan Sauce at a Build Your Own Sundae party. Also offer fresh fruit, sweetened whipped cream, and nuts. Chewy Chocolate Chip Squares and Butter Spritz Cookies complete the party menu.

**Vanilla Ice Cream
Fudge Sauce
Butter Pecan Sauce
Chewy Chocolate Chip Squares
Butter Spritz Cookies**

VANILLA ICE CREAM

6 cups milk
2 cups sugar
1 (12-ounce) can evaporated milk
1 (8-ounce) container frozen
 whipped topping, thawed
1 (5¼-ounce) package vanilla
 instant pudding mix

Combine all ingredients in a large bowl; beat at medium speed of an electric mixer until well blended. Pour mixture into freezer can of a 5-quart hand-turned or electric freezer. Freeze according to manufacturer's instructions. Let ripen at least 1 hour. Yield: 5 quarts.

Note: To make ice cream balls, spoon frozen ice cream into a 13- x 9- x 2-inch pan. Freeze 8 hours, and scoop ice cream into balls. Serve immediately, or place frozen balls on a wax paper-lined tray and return to freezer.
*Betty A. Bates
Elkton, Tennessee*

Creative Invitations

A party becomes more personal when the host or hostess makes the invitations. Think about why you're having the party, and a variety of themes will probably come to mind.

Keep the invitations in the same color scheme as the party; you might want to hand-deliver them if the guest list isn't too long. Attach your colorful invitations to helium balloons in order to "heighten" their impression.

To make clever party invitations, purchase brightly colored 4¼-inch x 6¼-inch note cards and envelopes. Cut triangles of **brown or white paper** to make cones. Crinkle colored **tissue paper** to make scoops of ice cream, and use **rubber cement** to adhere tissue and cones to the note cards.

Vinyl lettering (available at art stores) completes the message ("HOW ABOUT A SCOOP?") on the front. Include information, such as time and place, on the back with a **felt-tip pen.**

FUDGE SAUCE

⅓ cup cocoa
¼ cup water
1½ cups light corn syrup
Pinch of salt
1 tablespoon butter or margarine
1 teaspoon vanilla extract

Combine first 4 ingredients in a small saucepan. Cook over medium heat, stirring until mixture boils; reduce heat, and simmer 5 minutes.

Remove mixture from heat; add butter and vanilla, and stir until blended. Serve at room temperature. Yield: 1⅔ cups.
*Sandra Russell
Gainesville, Florida*

BUTTER PECAN SAUCE

½ cup coarsely chopped pecans
2 tablespoons butter or margarine, melted
1 (14-ounce) can sweetened condensed milk
½ cup water
1 teaspoon rum extract (optional)

Sauté pecans in butter in a saucepan until lightly browned. Add condensed milk and water, stirring until blended. Cook over medium heat 10 minutes or until thickened, stirring occasionally. Remove from heat; stir in rum extract. Let cool. Yield: 1¾ cups.
*Connie Burgess
Knoxville, Tennessee*

CHEWY CHOCOLATE CHIP SQUARES

1 cup butter or margarine, softened
½ cup sugar
½ cup firmly packed brown sugar
2 eggs
1 teaspoon vanilla extract
1¼ cups all-purpose flour
1 teaspoon baking soda
1½ cups quick-cooking oats, uncooked
1 (12-ounce) package semisweet chocolate morsels
1 cup chopped pecans

Cream butter; gradually add sugars, beating well at medium speed of an electric mixer. Add eggs and vanilla; beat well.
Combine flour and soda; add to creamed mixture, and mix well. Stir in oats, chocolate morsels, and pecans. Spread mixture into a greased 13- x 9- x 2-inch pan. Bake at 375° for 25 minutes. Cool and cut into squares. Yield: 4 dozen.
Eileen Wehling
Austin, Texas

BUTTER SPRITZ COOKIES

1½ cups butter or margarine, softened
1 cup sugar
1 egg
1 teaspoon vanilla extract
½ teaspoon almond extract
4 cups all-purpose flour
1 teaspoon baking powder

Cream butter; gradually add sugar, beating well at medium speed of an electric mixer. Add egg and flavorings; mix well. Combine flour and baking powder; gradually add to creamed mixture, mixing until smooth.
Use a cookie gun to shape dough as desired, following manufacturer's instructions. Place cookies on ungreased cookie sheets. Bake at 375° for 8 minutes. Cool on wire racks. Store cookies in airtight containers, placing wax paper between each layer. Yield: about 12 dozen.
Ashley Adams
Birmingham, Alabama

Cool Down With Beverages

Southerners know that a tall glass of a frosty beverage is a sure way to beat the heat. Most of these recipes take advantage of refreshing fruit juice, and each makes enough to keep a pitcher handy in the refrigerator in case guests drop by.

FRUIT JUICY RUM PUNCH

2 cups orange juice
2 cups lemonade drink
1 (6-ounce) can frozen orange juice concentrate, thawed and undiluted
1 (6-ounce) can frozen lemonade concentrate, thawed and undiluted
½ cup sugar
1½ cups light rum
7 cups ginger ale, chilled

Combine first 6 ingredients; freeze 8 hours. Before serving, let stand at room temperature 20 minutes; stir in ginger ale. Yield: 3½ quarts.
Patty Nealeans
Lewisville, North Carolina

WHISKEY PUNCH

1 (12-ounce) can frozen orange juice concentrate, thawed and undiluted
1 (12-ounce) can frozen lemonade concentrate, thawed and undiluted
1 cup lemon juice
1 quart bourbon
1 (2-liter) bottle lemon-lime carbonated beverage, chilled

Combine all ingredients except lemon-lime beverage. Chill. Stir in lemon-lime beverage, and serve over crushed ice. Yield: 1 gallon.
Mrs. J. David Stearns
Mobile, Alabama

STRAWBERRY-LEMONADE PUNCH

1 (6-ounce) can frozen lemonade concentrate, thawed and undiluted
1 (6-ounce) can frozen limeade concentrate, thawed and undiluted
1 (6-ounce) can frozen orange juice concentrate, thawed and undiluted
2 (10-ounce) packages frozen sliced strawberries, thawed
3 cups cold water
1 (2-liter) bottle ginger ale, chilled

Combine first 5 ingredients, and stir well. Add ginger ale, and stir gently. Yield: 1 gallon.
Judy K. Sivadon
Mounds, Oklahoma

Tip: *Create a tempting nonalcoholic bubbly beverage by adding sparkling mineral water to nutritious fruit juice concentrates.*

KAHLÚA HUMMER

⅓ to ½ cup light rum
⅓ to ½ cup Kahlúa
1 quart vanilla ice cream

Combine all ingredients in container of an electric blender or food processor; process until smooth. Serve immediately. Yield: 1 quart.

Mary B. Quesenberry
Dugspur, Virginia

CRANBERRY-CHERRY PUNCH

1 (3-ounce) package cherry-flavored gelatin
1 cup boiling water
1 (6-ounce) can frozen lemonade concentrate, thawed and undiluted
3 cups cold water
1 (32-ounce) bottle cranberry juice cocktail, chilled
1 (1-liter) bottle ginger ale, chilled

Dissolve gelatin in boiling water in a large bowl. Add lemonade concentrate; stir until dissolved. Stir in 3 cups water and remaining ingredients. Serve over ice. Yield: 3 quarts.

Marie Davis
Charlotte, North Carolina

PINEAPPLE SANGRÍA

1 (20-ounce) can pineapple chunks, undrained
1 apple, unpeeled, cored, and cut into chunks
1 lemon, sliced and quartered
1 orange, sliced and quartered
1 (750-milliliter) bottle Burgundy
1 (46-ounce) can pineapple juice
¼ cup brandy
¼ cup sugar

Drain pineapple, reserving juice. Skewer pineapple chunks, apple chunks, and lemon and orange slices onto wooden picks.

Combine reserved pineapple juice, Burgundy, and remaining ingredients in a container; add fruit kabobs. Refrigerate at least 1 hour; serve beverage over ice with fruit kabobs. Yield: 2½ quarts.

Mrs. J. Russell Buchanan
Dunwoody, Georgia

Pack A Special Picnic

Whether your favorite outdoor spot is in the country or the nearest urban park, the only things you will need to update the traditional summer picnic are some helpful packing and entertainment ideas.

First, you might want to take a couple of picnic baskets or totes. In one package, pack china and glasses among cloth napkins and a brightly colored tablecloth or sheet to spread on the ground. Also include knives, forks, and a corkscrew in this basket. You might want to visit a "gadget" store to purchase a compact utensil set that includes, among other things, drink stirrers and bottle openers. To get a headstart, pack this basket the day before you go.

All the food items should fit into a second basket. Using an insulated tote for keeping drinks cold (or warm) might be a convenient way to carry the food. Fresh fruit can also be packed in this package and provides a healthy dessert after eating. The fruit can also be used to make a quick arrangement. Be sure to pack heavy fruits in the bottom of your basket and berries at the top; otherwise they may get bruised.

Splurging at a local specialty shop for fresh bread, gourmet cheeses, ready-cut veggies, and prepackaged chilled pasta salad means less planning and makes your picnic special. Or stop by the local delicatessen for ready-made sandwiches and chips. A bottle of chilled wine or sparkling cider completes your menu and should stay cool until you reach the picnic site. Don't bring a lot of perishable items, however. You may not eat right away, and an ice chest is just extra baggage.

Freezer ice packs, found at drugstores and discount stores, should keep the beverages cold in the basket and should prevent the other items from perishing. The ice packs can be refrozen and then used again for your next summer outing.

For entertainment, plan an occasion, such as a birthday or anniversary, and celebrate by inviting a few surprise guests to meet you at your picnic destination. Or plan the picnic around a public performance of a concert or theatrical play. For several weeks in the summer, many cities offer free performances that take place in public areas, such as parks. And if the sounds of nature aren't enough and there is not a public concert to attend, bring a radio or cassette player and supply some background music of your own.

Kids Will Love This Pool Party

Imagine the excitement as a 5-year-old receives your invitation to a Back-to-the-Beach Bash, including a colorful menu describing the meal. Sand buckets filled with Peanut Butter-and-Jelly "Fish" Sandwiches, Fruity Mermaid Kabobs, Ants on a Float, and Chocolate Seashells will make the children all smiles.

Invite the moms, too. If they're not as fond of mermaids and fish-shaped sandwiches as the kids, a few simple revisions of the menu will satisfy adults. Arrange a platter of cut fruit for them, and serve some of the Orange Cream Cheese from the Ants on a Float recipe on the side to accompany the fruit. Assemble hoagie-type sandwiches to substitute for fish-shaped ones, or set out a tray of deli meat, cheese, and buns. The desserts and beverage please all ages.

Start a Day Ahead

The most important aspect of the party is that all the food can be made ahead of time, arranged in the buckets or on platters, and covered and chilled. Much of the food can actually be made the day before, with some details left for the morning of the party. Follow these suggestions for easy preparation.
—On the day before the party, stir up sandwich spread and cream cheese mixture for the celery; cover and chill them both. Then bake the cookies.
—The morning of the party, cut and spread the fish-shaped sandwiches, wrap them in plastic wrap, and chill. Cut and assemble the fruit kabobs, and stuff the celery.
—Line a sand pail for each child with colored plastic wrap. If there's room in the refrigerator, put the food in the buckets, and chill until time to eat. Otherwise, chill the food separately, and fill the buckets as you serve the meal. Combine the two ingredients for Beach Brew just before serving.

BEACH BREW

2 (12-ounce) cans frozen cranberry juice concentrate, thawed and undiluted
2 (33.8-ounce) bottles ginger ale, chilled

Combine ingredients just before serving. Serve beverage over crushed ice. Yield: 2¾ quarts.

PEANUT BUTTER-AND-JELLY "FISH" SANDWICHES

¼ cup peanut butter
2 tablespoons apple jelly
Dash of ground nutmeg
16 slices light wheat bread
16 currants

Combine first 3 ingredients.
Cut each slice of bread with a fish-shaped cookie cutter (or use kitchen shears to cut fish shapes). Spread peanut butter mixture on half of fish-shaped pieces of bread; top with remaining bread. Make tiny slits on each piece of bread, and insert currants for eyes. Yield: 8 servings.

FRUITY MERMAID KABOBS

8 small wedges of watermelon
8 large pitted prunes
8 cantaloupe balls
Alfalfa sprouts

For each kabob, thread a watermelon wedge, large end at the bottom, onto a 6-inch narrow cocktail straw to make the tail of a mermaid. Next, thread a prune onto straw, gently squeezing prune at the end next to the watermelon to tighten it to look like a waist. Next, thread a cantaloupe ball for the face. Pull a mound of alfalfa sprouts from the container of sprouts, and stretch the mound just enough to keep the sprouts bunched together, and shape them like hair. Insert mound of hair onto straw, letting hair drape around face. Yield: 8 servings.

ANTS ON A FLOAT

Orange Cream Cheese
8 (2½-inch) slices celery
24 raisins

Spread about 1 tablespoon Orange Cream Cheese on grooved side of celery slices. Place 3 raisins on cream cheese on each celery slice. Cover and chill. Yield: 8 servings.

Orange Cream Cheese

1 (3-ounce) package cream cheese
1 tablespoon frozen orange juice concentrate
1 teaspoon honey
¼ teaspoon grated orange rind

Combine all ingredients in a small mixing bowl; beat at medium speed of an electric mixer until blended. Cover and chill. Yield: ½ cup.

Add a Splash of Color

To protect the guests from splinters or rough concrete surfaces, lay out large sheets of colorful vinyl, overlapping the edges slightly to cover a large area. Scatter several sand-filled buckets where the pieces of vinyl overlap to hold them in place. Insert whirligigs and strips of festive bendable foam into the sand.

When the party's over, just wipe the vinyl with a damp cloth, and let it air-dry. Stack the pieces on top of each other, roll the vinyl up, and store it until the next party. (When you buy this vinyl, ask the salesperson for an extra cardboard tube on which the vinyl is rolled for shipping.) The vinyl is available by the yard in 54- to 56-inch widths at large fabric or variety stores.

When it's time to eat, just pass out the sand pails, set out the platters, and enjoy. Let the children take the pails and whirligigs home as favors.

CINNAMON SAND BARS

1 cup butter, softened
½ cup sifted powdered sugar
2 cups all-purpose flour
½ teaspoon ground cinnamon
1½ tablespoons sugar
½ teaspoon ground cinnamon

Cream butter; gradually add powdered sugar, beating until light and fluffy. Stir in flour and ½ teaspoon cinnamon (mixture will be stiff). Press into a lightly greased 15- x 10- x 1-inch jellyroll pan; prick all over with a fork.

Combine 1½ tablespoons sugar and ½ teaspoon ground cinnamon; sprinkle over dough. Bake at 375° for 5 minutes; reduce heat to 300°, and bake 20 minutes or until golden brown. Cut into 2- x 1-inch bars while warm. Yield: 6¼ dozen.

CHOCOLATE SEASHELLS

2 eggs
⅛ teaspoon salt
⅔ cup sugar
¾ teaspoon vanilla extract
½ cup all-purpose flour
2 tablespoons cocoa
½ cup butter or margarine, melted
Powdered sugar

Beat eggs and salt in a mixing bowl at high speed of an electric mixer until foamy. Gradually add sugar and vanilla; beat at high speed 15 minutes. Combine flour and cocoa; fold into egg mixture 2 tablespoons at a time. Fold butter into egg mixture 1 tablespoon at a time.

Spoon 1 tablespoon batter into each greased and floured madeleine mold; bake at 400° for 8 to 10 minutes. Cool in molds 3 minutes. Remove from molds, and cool on a wire rack, flat side down. Sprinkle with powdered sugar before serving. Yield: 2 dozen.

Summer Fruit Sampler

What's your favorite summer fruit? If you can't decide on just one, then you'll love tasting your way through this recipe assortment. And no matter what time of day the mood strikes to enjoy the season's sweet fruit, we've got an indulgence for you.

You can start the morning with a slice of toast slathered with Golden Peach Butter, while Fresh Pineapple Pie tops off an evening meal with old-fashioned flavor.

And when you find yourself loading your grocery basket with as many different fruits as you can find, bring them all home and toss a Summer Fruit Fantasy. A subtle touch of orange-flavored liqueur adds elegance to this dish.

FRESH PINEAPPLE PIE

Pastry for double-crust 9-inch pie
3 cups fresh pineapple chunks
2 eggs, beaten
1 tablespoon grated lemon rind
1 tablespoon lemon juice
1½ cups sugar
2 tablespoons all-purpose flour

Roll half of pastry to ⅛-inch thickness on a lightly floured surface. Place in a 9-inch pieplate; trim off excess pastry along edges. Set aside.

Combine pineapple and next 3 ingredients in a large bowl; stir well. Combine sugar and flour; sprinkle over pineapple mixture, tossing gently. Spoon into pastry shell.

Roll remaining pastry to ⅛-inch thickness; transfer to top of pie. Trim off excess pastry along edges. Fold edges under, and flute. Cut slits in top crust for steam to escape. Bake at 425° for 40 minutes, covering edges of pastry with strips of aluminum foil the last 10 minutes to prevent excessive browning, if necessary. Cool completely before serving. Yield: one 9-inch pie.   *Susan Wiener*
Spring Hill, Florida

SUMMER FRUIT FANTASY

3 grapefruits, peeled and sectioned
3 oranges, peeled and sectioned
2 fresh peaches, peeled, seeded, and cubed
2 cups diced fresh pineapple
2 cups fresh strawberries, sliced in half
1 cup seedless grapes
1 cup fresh or frozen blueberries, thawed
1 teaspoon grated orange rind
¼ cup orange juice
3 tablespoons orange-flavored liqueur
3 tablespoons sugar

Combine first 7 ingredients in a large bowl. Combine orange rind, juice, liqueur, and sugar, stirring until sugar dissolves. Pour over fruit mixture, tossing lightly. Cover and chill at least 30 minutes. To serve, use a slotted spoon. Yield: 10 to 12 servings.
Laura Morris
Bunnell, Florida

GOLDEN PEACH BUTTER

1 pound peaches, peeled, pitted, and chopped
1 cup orange juice
1 cup sugar
2 tablespoons white vinegar
1 teaspoon grated orange rind
⅛ teaspoon ground allspice

Combine peaches and orange juice in a large saucepan. Bring to a boil; reduce heat, and cook, uncovered, 10 minutes or until peaches are soft, stirring occasionally. Remove from heat.

Position knife blade in food processor bowl; add peach mixture. Process until smooth. Return mixture to saucepan; stir in sugar and remaining ingredients. Bring to a boil; reduce heat, and cook, uncovered, 15 minutes or until thickened, stirring often. Remove from heat; cool. Chill 3 hours before serving. Store in refrigerator. Yield: about 1⅔ cups. *Estelle Gilbert*
Stanardsville, Virginia

AUGUST

*Now is the time to make the most of the season. It's easy to
turn summer produce and seasonings into Mexican salsas
that add robust flavors to favorite foods. As for the season's
sweeter harvest, turn for inspiration to our fruit sampler and
the "Light Favorite" recipe, Angel Food Trifle, made with
fresh berries and kiwifruit. Other features in this
chapter offer additional recipes for vegetables and fruit
from the garden. Enjoy!*

Cool Summer Desserts

When temperatures soar and sipping an icy beverage or waving a makeshift fan doesn't cool you off, maybe these desserts will. They provide a boost of energy and a burst of cooling.

You may anticipate an occasion that's ripe for spooning into a bowl of Piña Colada Ice Cream or dipping into Bavarian Cream With Raspberry Sauce. These creamy desserts can be ready when you are if you'll plan a little in advance. Chill some a day or two ahead; the frozen treats can be made up to a month ahead.

SHERRY-BERRY DESSERT SOUP

2 cups fresh strawberries or
  raspberries
1 (8-ounce) carton sour cream
1 cup half-and-half
¼ cup sugar
2 tablespoons dry sherry
½ teaspoon vanilla extract
Garnish: fresh mint

Combine first 6 ingredients in container of an electric blender; process until smooth, stopping and scraping sides as necessary. Pour into individual bowls or wine glasses; garnish, if desired. Yield: 3½ cups.

Joel A. Allard
San Antonio, Texas

Tip: *Make all types of cold soups more appealing by serving them in stemmed glasses or crystal bowls nestled in crushed ice.*

BAVARIAN CREAM WITH RASPBERRY SAUCE

1½ cups sugar
2 envelopes unflavored gelatin
1 cup cold water
2 cups whipping cream
3 (8-ounce) cartons sour cream
2 teaspoons vanilla extract
Raspberry Sauce

Combine sugar and gelatin in a saucepan; add water, and stir well. Let stand 1 minute. Cook over medium heat, stirring constantly, until gelatin dissolves. Stir in whipping cream, and set aside.

Combine sour cream and vanilla in a large bowl. Gradually whisk in whipping cream mixture until blended. Pour into a lightly oiled 7-cup mold; cover and chill at least 8 hours. Unmold dessert onto a serving dish, and spoon Raspberry Sauce over top just before serving. Yield: 12 servings.

Raspberry Sauce

1 (10-ounce) package frozen
  raspberries, thawed
2 tablespoons sugar
1 tablespoon raspberry-flavored
  liqueur (optional)

Combine all ingredients in container of an electric blender; process until smooth. Strain mixture through 2 layers of cheesecloth; discard seeds. Yield: ¾ cup.

Kathy Hunt
Dallas, Texas

NUTTY ICE CREAM PIE

2 egg whites
¼ teaspoon salt
¼ cup sugar
1½ cups chopped pecans
1 pint vanilla ice cream, softened
1 pint butter brickle ice cream,
  softened
Caramel Sauce

Beat egg whites and salt at high speed of an electric mixer until foamy. Gradually add sugar, 1 tablespoon at a time, beating until stiff peaks form and sugar dissolves. Fold in pecans; spoon into a buttered 9-inch pieplate. Using back of spoon, shape meringue into a pie shell. Bake at 350° for 15 to 20 minutes. Cool.

Spoon vanilla ice cream into cool crust, spreading evenly; freeze until almost firm. Spread butter brickle ice cream over vanilla layer, and freeze until firm. When ready to serve, spoon warm Caramel Sauce over each slice. Yield: one 9-inch pie.

Caramel Sauce

1 cup firmly packed brown sugar
½ cup half-and-half
3 tablespoons butter or margarine,
  melted
1 tablespoon vanilla extract

Combine first 3 ingredients in a small saucepan; cook over medium heat 5 minutes, stirring constantly. Remove from heat; add vanilla. Cool slightly. Yield: 1 cup.

Eleanor K. Brandt
Arlington, Texas

PIÑA COLADA ICE CREAM
(pictured on page 156)

6 eggs, beaten
1½ cups sugar
5 cups milk
1 (10-ounce) can frozen piña colada
   tropical fruit mixer, thawed and
   undiluted
2 cups half-and-half
1 cup whipping cream
½ cup light rum
Garnish: toasted coconut

Combine eggs and sugar in a large heavy saucepan; gradually add milk, beating well. Cook over medium heat, stirring constantly, until thermometer reaches 160°. Remove from heat; let cool. Stir in thawed fruit mixer and next 3 ingredients.

Pour mixture into container of a 1-gallon hand-turned or electric freezer. Freeze according to manufacturer's instructions. Pack freezer with additional ice and salt; let stand 1 hour before serving (ice cream will be soft). Garnish each serving, if desired. Yield: about 1 gallon.

Note: To scoop ice cream into balls, spoon ice cream into an airtight container after standing time. Cover and freeze at least 8 hours.

Geneva Hammons
Harriman, Tennessee

For The Love Of Iced Tea

It's no wonder Southerners like iced tea so much. The tea plant is an evergreen that actually belongs to the camellia family. And camellias, so fragile and fragrant, are a long-time favorite in this region.

Soothing and classic, tea is cradled in the hands of countless memories. Think of all the times it has satisfied more than thirst—big, swaggering gulps after a sweltering day hoeing the garden; a patient, tentative drink after listening to a friend's tale that's just a little too long; or a deep, slow sip taken as the late afternoon sun sinks from the sky.

Americans really didn't drink *iced* tea until 1904. It was invented during a heat wave at the St. Louis World's Fair. Hot tea was being served in a Far East Pavilion. They poured it over ice to ward off the heat, and it was a hit. Today, iced tea is the second most popular drink, after water, in this country. Only the British import more tea than we do.

Down South, we're sweet on tea made with real sugar and fresh lemon. A few will skip the lemon or add additional flavors, but most agree that tea without sugar is like New Orleans without jazz.

The subject of tea is covered in the cookbook *Dishes and Beverages of the Old South,* written just after the turn of the century by Martha McCulloch-Williams. She tantalizes readers with her idea of what's *best* to add to iced tea. Here's a little sample:

My teamaking is unorthodox, but people like to drink the brew. Bring fresh water to a bubbling boil in a clean, wide kettle, throw in the tea—a tablespoonful to the gallon of water, let boil just one minute, then strain from the leaves into a pot that has stood five minutes full of freshly boiled water, and that is instantly wrapped about with a thick napkin, so it shall not cool. Serve in tall glasses with rum and lemon, or with a sherry syrup, flavored with lemon, add a Maraschino cherry or so, or a tiny bit of ginger-flavored citron.

To make our version, combine 2 quarts of just-brewed tea, sugar, about 10 mint sprigs, and a little lemon juice in your favorite pitcher. Then, fill a tall glass with ice, and perch fresh-cut lemon slices and mint on the rim. Add tea. You know what comes next. All that's left is to find a friend, a place in the shade, and conversation for the coming hour.

Salsas For A Snappy Touch

The technique is really quite simple, although the term may sound a little intimidating. *Salsa,* the Mexican word for sauce, refers to uncooked sauces intended to make food look and taste better. Innovative chefs have expanded the original definition—sauces made from tomatoes and chiles—to include all types of fruits, vegetables, and seasonings.

These spunky little sauces are guaranteed to tickle your taste buds—literally. Sometimes the sensation comes from the combination of sweet fruit and fiery jalapeño peppers offered in Mango Salsa. Or maybe it's the coolness of avocado and the tanginess of wine vinegar in Avocado Salsa. Perhaps it's simply the play of the cold salsa with hot food when you spoon any of these sauces over vegetables or meat.

That's the beauty of salsas. Freshness. Simplicity. Versatility. Try one of these recipes when you want to add new appeal to your favorite foods.

MIXED PEPPER SALSA
(pictured on page 191)

¼ cup white vinegar
2 tablespoons vegetable oil
2 teaspoons sugar
¼ teaspoon salt
¼ teaspoon pepper
1 medium-size sweet red
   pepper, diced
1 medium-size sweet yellow
   pepper, diced
1 medium-size green pepper, diced
2 tablespoons chopped fresh parsley

Combine first 5 ingredients in a small saucepan; bring to a boil, stirring until sugar dissolves. Remove from heat.

Combine peppers and parsley in a glass bowl; add hot vinegar mixture, and stir gently. Cool. Cover and chill. Serve salsa with pork or ham. Yield: 1⅔ cups.

AVOCADO SALSA
(pictured on page 190)

⅓ cup white wine vinegar
1 tablespoon honey
¾ teaspoon salt
½ teaspoon ground cumin
¼ teaspoon pepper
1 small onion, chopped
1 (4-ounce) can chopped green
  chiles, undrained
1 large clove garlic, minced
2 avocados, peeled and diced

Combine all ingredients except avocado, stirring well; cover and chill. Just before serving, add avocado, and toss gently. Serve with chips, chicken, or seafood. Yield: 1½ cups.

SALSA VERDE

10 tomatillos, diced
½ cup chopped Spanish onion
¼ cup minced fresh cilantro or
  parsley
2 jalapeño peppers, seeded and
  minced
2 teaspoons lime juice
½ teaspoon salt

Combine all ingredients; cover and chill. Serve with chips, seafood, or chicken. Yield: 2 cups.

GARDEN SALSA

¼ pound fresh green beans
2 ears fresh corn
3 medium tomatoes, diced
¼ cup olive oil
¼ cup diced green pepper
¼ cup diced purple onion
2 tablespoons minced fresh basil or
  2 teaspoons dried whole basil
1 tablespoon lime juice
1 teaspoon salt
¼ teaspoon freshly ground
  pepper
2 cloves garlic, minced

Wash beans, and remove strings. Remove husks and silks from corn. Place beans and corn in boiling water to cover. Return water to a boil; cook 4 minutes. Drain and immediately cover vegetables with ice water. Let stand until cool; drain. Cut corn from cob, and cut beans into ¼-inch pieces.

Combine beans, corn, tomatoes, and remaining ingredients, stirring gently; cover and chill. Serve with chips, fish, chicken, or over toasted French bread. Yield: 4 cups.

FRESH TOMATO SALSA
(pictured on pages 190 and 191)

5 medium tomatoes, diced
⅓ cup tomato sauce
¼ cup finely chopped purple onion
3 cloves garlic, minced
1 to 2 small jalapeño peppers,
  seeded and minced
2 tablespoons minced fresh cilantro
  or parsley
1 tablespoon minced fresh oregano
  or 1 teaspoon dried whole
  oregano
2 tablespoons lime juice
1 teaspoon salt

Combine all ingredients, stirring gently; cover and chill. Serve over toasted French bread or with chips, fish, or chicken. Yield: 3⅓ cups.

DOUBLE CHILE SALSA

2 cups chopped tomatoes (about
  1 pound)
½ cup finely chopped onion
⅓ cup chopped green pepper
1 (4-ounce) can chopped green
  chiles, drained
1 tablespoon seeded, chopped
  jalapeño pepper
½ to 1 teaspoon hot sauce
⅛ teaspoon garlic powder
⅛ teaspoon seasoning salt

Combine all ingredients, stirring gently; cover and chill at least 2 hours.

Serve with chips, fish, or chicken. Yield: 2 cups.
Rebecca Koster
Chantilly, Virginia

MEXI-CORN SALSA
(pictured on pages 190 and 191)

5 ears fresh yellow corn
1 medium tomato, diced
1 small jalapeño pepper, seeded and
  minced
1 clove garlic, crushed
1 (4-ounce) can chopped green
  chiles, undrained
¼ cup sliced green onions
2 tablespoons olive oil
2 tablespoons white vinegar
½ teaspoon salt

Remove husks and silks from corn. Place ears in boiling water to cover. Return water to a boil; cook 4 minutes. Drain and immediately cover ears with ice water. Drain corn, and cut from cob.

Combine corn and remaining ingredients, stirring gently; cover and chill. Serve salsa with chicken or pork. Yield: 3 cups.

MANGO SALSA

1½ cups chopped mango
1 small clove garlic, crushed
½ small jalapeño pepper, seeded
  and minced
1½ teaspoons chopped fresh
  parsley or cilantro
¼ cup sugar
¼ cup sliced green onions
¼ cup white vinegar
2 tablespoons lime juice

Combine first 4 ingredients in a medium bowl; set aside.

Combine sugar and remaining ingredients in a saucepan; bring to a boil, stirring until sugar dissolves. Pour hot mixture over mango mixture, stirring gently; cover and chill. Serve with cooked ham or pork. Yield: 1¾ cups.

PEACH SALSA

½ teaspoon minced fresh
   gingerroot
5 peaches, peeled, chopped, and
   divided
¼ cup minced green onions
1½ tablespoons sugar
½ teaspoon dry mustard
1½ tablespoons lime juice
⅛ teaspoon salt
⅛ teaspoon white pepper

Combine gingerroot and one-fourth of peaches in container of an electric blender; process until smooth.

Combine remaining peaches, pureed peach mixture, green onions, and remaining ingredients, stirring gently; cover and chill up to 4 hours. Serve with ham, pork, chicken, or seafood. Yield: 2½ cups.

ON THE LIGHT SIDE

Poach For Flavor, Not Fat

Hardly any cooking method offers more than poaching. It takes less time than most methods; it enhances natural flavors; it's as easy as boiling water; and it requires no special equipment. But most of all, poaching gives food flavor without adding fat or calories.

A saucepan or skillet (except cast iron) works just fine for poaching. Submerge the food into the simmering poaching liquid; then reheat the liquid to barely simmering for cooking. Boneless chicken breasts are done when they are opaque and feel resilient when touched with a spoon. Fish is done when it flakes easily when tested with a fork. And fruit is cooked when a knife pierces it as it would room-temperature margarine.

Poaching can also be done in the microwave. Simply heat the poaching liquid to boiling; arrange food in the liquid with the thickest portion to the outside of the dish, and microwave on high for the specified time or until the food is done.

POACHED SALMON WITH HORSERADISH SAUCE

4 cups water
1 lemon, sliced
1 carrot, sliced
1 stalk celery, sliced
1 teaspoon peppercorns
4 (4-ounce) salmon steaks
Horseradish Sauce

Combine first 5 ingredients in a large skillet; bring to a boil over medium-high heat. Cover, reduce heat, and simmer 10 minutes. Add salmon steaks; cover and simmer 10 minutes. Remove skillet from heat; let stand 8 minutes. Remove salmon steaks to a serving plate; serve with Horseradish Sauce. Yield: 4 servings (186 calories per 4-ounce salmon steak with 2 tablespoons Horseradish Sauce).

□ *23.6 grams protein, 7.1 grams fat, 14 grams carbohydrate, 89 milligrams cholesterol, 155 milligrams sodium, and 27 milligrams calcium.*

Horseradish Sauce

¼ cup reduced-calorie mayonnaise
¼ cup plain nonfat yogurt
2 teaspoons prepared horseradish
1½ teaspoons lemon juice
1½ teaspoons chopped fresh chives

Combine all ingredients in a small bowl; cover and chill. Yield: ½ cup (25 calories per tablespoon).

□ *0.4 gram protein, 1.9 grams fat, 1.2 grams carbohydrate, 2 milligrams cholesterol, 49 milligrams sodium, and 15 milligrams calcium.*

Charlotte Moret
St. Louis, Missouri

POACHED FISH WITH GREEK SAUCE

2 tablespoons chopped onion
2 sprigs fresh parsley
½ bay leaf
⅛ teaspoon salt
4 whole peppercorns
½ cup Chablis or other dry white
   wine
½ cup water
4 (4-ounce) skinned flounder fillets
   or other lean white fish
Greek Sauce

Combine first 7 ingredients in a 12- x 8- x 2-inch baking dish. Cover with heavy-duty plastic wrap; fold back a small corner of wrap for steam to escape. Microwave at HIGH 5 minutes or until boiling. Uncover; arrange fillets in liquid with thickest portion to outside of dish. Cover and microwave at HIGH 4 minutes, giving dish a half-turn after 2 minutes. Cook until fish turns opaque. Let stand, covered, 3 to 5 minutes. Fish is done if it flakes easily when tested with a fork.

Remove fish to a serving dish; reserve liquid for use in Greek Sauce. Serve fish with Greek Sauce. Yield: 4 servings (141 calories per serving of fish with 3 tablespoons sauce).

□ *19.8 grams protein, 5.1 grams fat, 3 grams carbohydrate, 6 milligrams cholesterol, 211 milligrams sodium, and 47 milligrams calcium.*

Greek Sauce

¼ cup reduced-calorie mayonnaise
¼ cup plain low-fat yogurt
¼ cup minced fresh parsley
2 tablespoons lemon juice
⅛ teaspoon freshly ground pepper
⅛ teaspoon garlic powder
2 tablespoons reserved poaching
   liquid

Combine all ingredients in a small bowl; stir well. Yield: ¾ cup (17 calories per tablespoon).

□ *0.3 gram protein, 1.4 grams fat, 1 gram carbohydrate, 2 milligrams cholesterol, 32 milligrams sodium, and 11 milligrams calcium.*

POACHED CHICKEN BREAST IN WINE

4 (4-ounce) skinned, boned chicken
  breast halves
¾ cup Chablis or other dry white
  wine
2½ cups sliced fresh mushrooms
2 tablespoons chopped fresh parsley
½ teaspoon dried whole tarragon
½ teaspoon salt
¼ teaspoon pepper
1 tablespoon cornstarch
2 teaspoons water

Place chicken between two sheets of heavy-duty plastic wrap; flatten to ¼-inch thickness, using a meat mallet or rolling pin; set aside.

Combine Chablis and next 5 ingredients in a large skillet; bring to a boil over high heat. Arrange chicken in a single layer in skillet; cover, reduce heat, and simmer 15 minutes or until chicken is tender. Remove chicken to a serving plate; keep warm. Combine cornstarch and water; stir into skillet. Bring mixture to a boil; boil 1 minute, stirring constantly. Pour sauce over chicken. Yield: 4 servings (169 calories per serving).

□ *27.5 grams protein, 1.7 grams fat, 10 grams carbohydrate, 66 milligrams cholesterol, 374 milligrams sodium, and 26 milligrams calcium.*

Thayer Wilson
Augusta, Georgia

LIGHT FAVORITE

A Dessert With Only A Trifle Of Fat

English Trifle has long been a favorite dessert in the South. It's traditionally made with buttery pound cake or macaroons, a rich custard, and whipped cream—all of which are high in fat, calories, and cholesterol.

But our Angel Food Trifle is a light version of this old favorite. It uses angel food cake and a creamy "custard" made with skim milk and vanilla low-fat yogurt to keep it light and healthy. Luscious strawberries and kiwifruit are sliced and layered in the bowl or trifle dish with the cake and sauce. And instead of whipped cream, elegant strawberry fans decorate the top of the dessert.

ANGEL FOOD TRIFLE

1 (16-ounce) package angel food
  cake mix
⅓ cup sugar
¼ cup cornstarch
¼ teaspoon salt
2 cups skim milk
¼ cup egg substitute
1 teaspoon grated lemon rind
¼ cup lemon juice
2 (8-ounce) cartons vanilla low-fat
  yogurt
2 cups sliced strawberries
3 kiwifruit, sliced
3 strawberry fans

Prepare cake mix according to package directions. Cut into bite-size cubes; set aside.

Combine sugar, cornstarch, and salt in a saucepan; gradually add milk, stirring well. Cook over medium heat until mixture begins to thicken, stirring constantly. Remove from heat; gradually add egg substitute, stirring constantly with a wire whisk. Cook over medium-low heat 2 minutes, stirring constantly. Remove from heat; cool slightly. Stir in lemon rind and lemon juice; chill. Fold yogurt into cream mixture; set aside.

Place one-third of cake in bottom of a 16-cup trifle bowl. Spoon one-third of custard over cake; arrange half each of strawberry slices and kiwi slices around lower edge of bowl and over custard. Repeat procedure with remaining ingredients, ending with strawberry fans on top. Cover and chill 3 to 4 hours. Yield: 15 servings (198 calories per ⅔-cup serving).

□ *5.9 grams protein, 0.7 gram fat, 42.9 grams carbohydrate, 2 milligrams cholesterol, 140 milligrams sodium, and 134 milligrams calcium.*

COMPARE THE NUTRIENTS
(per serving)

	Traditional	Light
Calories	715	198
Fat	35.5g	0.7g
Cholesterol	207mg	2mg

Teach The Kids To Cook

Very young children love to tear lettuce for salads and arrange canned biscuits on a baking sheet. Once they have "experience" like this, it's time to tackle more difficult tasks.

According to Susan Bellows, the mother of at least 2 creative cooks, the best age for children to start cooking seriously is between the ages of 7 and 11. "Before that they can't read a recipe for themselves; and if they haven't developed an interest in cooking before after-school activities set in—it's too late!" she chuckles.

Susan finds her daughters are more interested in cooking when it's *their* idea. So instead of pushing the activity on them, she waits for them to volunteer, which they do often. Once they're ready to cook, Susan is ready to help. She finds that her young cooks do best concentrating on one recipe at a time.

As your children express an interest in cooking, share these recipes, the checklist, and the measuring hints to teach the basics about cooking.

■ **Keri** (age 16) and **Katie** (age 13) **Bellows** of Vestavia Hills, Alabama, often prepare Twice-Baked Potatoes for a simple dinner. To keep peace in the family, each likes to mix her own potato—that ensures that the cheese and other ingredients prepared by each girl go into the *right* potato.

TWICE-BAKED POTATOES

2 (10-ounce) baking potatoes
Vegetable oil
¼ cup sour cream
2 tablespoons butter or margarine
2 tablespoons milk
1 tablespoon chopped green onions
¼ teaspoon salt
Dash of pepper
2 slices bacon, cooked and
  crumbled
¼ cup (1 ounce) shredded Cheddar
  cheese

Wash potatoes, and rub skins with vegetable oil. Bake at 400° for 1 hour or until done. Allow potatoes to cool to touch. Cut a 1-inch strip lengthwise from top of each potato; carefully scoop out pulp, leaving shells intact.

Combine potato pulp, sour cream, and remaining ingredients except cheese in a small mixing bowl. Beat at medium speed of an electric mixer just until potato lumps disappear (do not overbeat). Stuff shells with potato mixture. Bake at 350° for 15 minutes; top with cheese, and bake an additional 5 minutes. Yield: 2 servings.

Note: To prepare in the microwave, prick potatoes several times with a fork. Omit vegetable oil. Arrange potatoes on paper towels in microwave. Microwave at HIGH 7 to 9 minutes, turning and rearranging potatoes once. Let stand 5 minutes. Microwave again briefly if not done. After stuffing the potatoes, arrange them on a microwave-safe platter, and microwave at HIGH 2 to 3 minutes or until hot. Top with cheese, and microwave at MEDIUM (50% power) 2 minutes.

■ Sixteen-year old **Lisa Felts** of Valdosta, Georgia, got her recipe for Upside-Down Pizza from an aunt. She likes to try recipes recommended by friends and family. "I'd hate to cook something for the first time and have it flop," she explains.

UPSIDE-DOWN PIZZA

2 pounds ground chuck
1 cup chopped onion
2 (8-ounce) cans tomato sauce
1 (1¼-ounce) package spaghetti
  sauce mix
1 (8-ounce) carton sour cream
2 cups (8 ounces) shredded
  mozzarella cheese
1 (8-ounce) package refrigerated
  crescent rolls

Cook beef and onion in a large skillet until meat is browned, stirring to crumble meat; drain well. Stir in tomato sauce and spaghetti sauce mix; cook over low heat 10 minutes, stirring frequently.

Spoon mixture into a lightly greased 13- x 9- x 2-inch baking dish; top with

Beginner's Checklist

■ Always check with an adult before you start to cook.

■ Read the recipe all the way through before you begin.

■ Wash your hands before you begin. Wear an apron or old shirt.

■ Collect all the ingredients listed in the recipe. Measure the exact amount of each item.

■ Clean up as you go. When finished, wash and dry all equipment, and put it away. Wash counters and other surfaces.

■ If you turned appliances on, make sure you turned them off.

sour cream, and sprinkle evenly with cheese. Unroll crescent rolls, and place on top of cheese. Bake, uncovered, at 350° for 18 to 20 minutes. Yield: 8 servings.

■ In Columbus, Georgia, 9-year old **Jennifer Hammock** says it's easy to make Homemade Pretzels. (Her mother, Carol, steps in to help her get the right water temperature to dissolve the yeast; they both knead the dough a little, but it doesn't have to rise.) Instead of the regular pretzel shape, Jennifer likes to fashion letters and numbers out of the strips of dough. And sometimes the project turns into an activity for Jennifer's Sunday school class—her mother is the teacher.

HOMEMADE PRETZELS

1 teaspoon dry yeast
¾ cup warm water (105° to 115°)
1¼ teaspoons sugar
½ teaspoon salt
1¾ cups all-purpose flour
1 egg, slightly beaten
1 teaspoon kosher salt

Dissolve yeast in warm water in a large bowl; let stand 5 minutes. Add sugar, ½ teaspoon salt, and flour; stir until smooth.

Turn dough out onto a lightly floured surface, and knead until smooth (about 3 minutes). Cut dough into 18 pieces; roll each piece on a lightly floured surface into a 9-inch rope. Shape each rope as desired; place on greased baking sheets.

Brush pretzels with egg; sprinkle with kosher salt. Bake at 425° for 10 to 12 minutes or until golden brown. Yield: 1½ dozen.

Note: Rock or table salt may be substituted for kosher salt.

■ **Sarah Weiser** of Durham, North Carolina, has never met Cora (her grandmother's housekeeper more than 50 years ago), but she has her to thank for this first recipe she ever prepared. "It's been passed on for two generations, and it gives me wonderful memories of my mother teaching me to cook," Sarah reminisces.

CORA'S COFFEE CAKE

¾ cup firmly packed brown sugar
1 teaspoon ground cinnamon
2 tablespoons butter or margarine
¼ cup butter or margarine, softened
½ cup sugar
1 egg
2 cups all-purpose flour
1 tablespoon plus 1 teaspoon baking powder
¼ teaspoon salt
1 cup milk

Combine brown sugar and cinnamon; cut in 2 tablespoons butter with a pastry blender until well blended.

Beat ¼ cup butter; gradually add ½ cup sugar, beating well at medium speed of an electric mixer. Add egg; beat well. Combine flour, baking powder, and salt; add to creamed mixture alternately with milk, beginning and ending with flour mixture. Mix just until blended after each addition.

Pour batter into a greased 12- x 8- x 2-inch baking dish. Sprinkle brown sugar mixture over batter. Bake at 350° for 25 minutes or until a wooden pick inserted in center comes out clean. Yield: 12 servings.

QUICK!

Lunch Is Served

Wait a minute. The words "easy" and "luncheon" are a contradiction in terms, aren't they? Not anymore. Even our foods staff was surprised at how easily this fresh menu for six is prepared. This is a good choice for a first-time hostess, and a breeze for the accomplished cook. And we offer a plan so you can make the most effective use of your preparation time.

For a simple yet effective centerpiece, place a few fresh flowers and herbs in a crystal vase. Or fill a white wicker basket with ivy, an airy fern, or violets.

From start to finish in less than an hour: Peel and halve peaches for Peachy Sherbet Cooler; place in pineapple juice. Boil water for Easy Mint Tea, and steep tea bags. Combine salad ingredients; chill. Prepare Lemon-Dill Chicken Sauté. Toast French bread, if desired. Add juice and ginger ale to tea. Greet guests with a glass of tea and cheese straws. Arrange food on plates, and serve. A few minutes before the end of the meal, set sherbet out to soften. Assemble the dessert, and serve it to your guests.

■ "Sauté" means to fry lightly with a little oil or fat. With chicken breast halves and a light breading, **Lemon-Dill Chicken Sauté** takes only 15 minutes to cook.

LEMON-DILL CHICKEN SAUTÉ

½ cup dry breadcrumbs
1½ teaspoons lemon-pepper seasoning
½ teaspoon dried whole dillweed
6 chicken breast halves, skinned and boned
1 egg, beaten
2 tablespoons vegetable oil

Combine first 3 ingredients in a shallow dish. Dip chicken in egg; dredge in breadcrumb mixture.

Heat oil in a large skillet over medium heat. Add chicken, and cook 5 minutes on each side or until golden brown. Cover and cook 5 minutes. Yield: 6 servings.   *Irene S. Cawthon*
Norcross, Georgia

■ If you serve **Marinated Salad** from a buffet, layer the ingredients in a glass bowl or trifle dish for a showy presentation. To make ahead, combine the ingredients, and chill 8 hours.

MARINATED SALAD

1 (15-ounce) can white asparagus spears, drained
1 (14-ounce) can artichoke hearts, drained and cut in half
1 (14-ounce) can hearts of palm, drained and cut into ½-inch slices
1 (4-ounce) can sliced mushrooms, drained
½ cup ripe olives, sliced
½ cup pimiento-stuffed olives, sliced
12 cherry tomatoes, halved
½ purple onion, sliced and separated into rings
1 (8-ounce) bottle Italian salad dressing
Romaine lettuce

Combine all ingredients except romaine lettuce in a bowl, stirring gently. Refrigerate at least 30 minutes. Drain salad, and serve on lettuce. Yield: 6 servings.

Pour boiling water over tea bags; cover and steep 5 minutes. Remove tea bags, squeezing gently. Add sugar and lemon juice, stirring until sugar dissolves. Stir in 3 quarts water, pineapple juice, and ginger ale. Serve over ice. Yield: about 1½ gallons.

Renee Alexander
Savannah, Tennessee

slices with mayonnaise; dredge in breadcrumb mixture. Place on a lightly greased baking sheet. Bake at 400°, uncovered, for 10 to 12 minutes or until eggplant is browned. Garnish, if desired. Yield: 4 to 6 servings.

Josephine Jones
Charleston, South Carolina

■ If children are present at the luncheon, simply offer them **Peachy Sherbet Cooler** without the schnapps.

PEACHY SHERBET COOLER

3 peaches, peeled and halved
1 pint lime sherbet
1½ cups fresh raspberries
2 tablespoons peach
  schnapps

Place peach halves in individual serving dishes; top with a scoop of sherbet. Sprinkle with raspberries. Spoon 1 teaspoon peach schnapps over sherbet. Serve dessert immediately. Yield: 6 servings.

Note: To prepare ahead, peel and halve peaches. Place in a bowl, and cover with pineapple juice to prevent discoloration; drain peaches well before serving. *Pauline J. Thompson*
Lenoir, North Carolina

Fry Without The Spatter

If you are trying to cut back on the amount of fat in your diet (as many folks are), it's nice to know you don't have to give up some of your favorite fried vegetables. Try frying them in the oven.

Dredged in naturally crisp and golden coatings, such as breadcrumbs, cornmeal, and grated Parmesan cheese, these recipes take on an added crunch after baking in the oven. A light coating of butter, margarine, or vegetable cooking spray moistens the ingredients prior to baking, but the end product contains less fat than recipes that call for traditional frying—and without all the spattering!

CHEESY OVEN FRIES

3 medium potatoes
⅓ cup grated Parmesan cheese
¾ teaspoon salt
¾ teaspoon garlic powder
¾ teaspoon paprika
3 tablespoons butter or margarine,
  melted

Wash potatoes well, and cut each into 8 wedges; set aside.

Combine Parmesan cheese and next 3 ingredients, stirring well.

Dip potato wedges in melted butter; arrange in a single layer in a lightly greased 15- x 10- x 1-inch jellyroll pan. Sprinkle cheese mixture evenly over potatoes. Bake, uncovered, at 375° for 40 minutes or until potatoes are tender and browned. Yield: 4 to 6 servings. *Nell Hamm*
Louisville, Mississippi

■ You won't have to crush fresh mint and strain the tea for **Easy Mint Tea.** It uses mint-flavored tea bags.

EASY MINT TEA

1 quart boiling water
10 regular-size, mint-flavored tea
  bags
2 cups sugar
1½ cups lemon juice
3 quarts water
2 cups pineapple juice
1 (33.8-ounce) bottle ginger ale

OVEN-FRIED EGGPLANT

⅓ cup fine, dry breadcrumbs
2 tablespoons grated Parmesan
  cheese
¼ teaspoon salt
¼ teaspoon pepper
1 (¾-pound) eggplant
¼ cup mayonnaise or salad
  dressing
Garnish: fresh basil

Combine first 4 ingredients in a shallow dish.

Peel eggplant, and cut into ¼-inch slices. Spread both sides of eggplant

From Our Kitchen To Yours

Stretching food dollars while looking for value and convenience is a challenge. For that reason, we have come up with these guidelines to help you shop quickly and save money.
—Shop at one or two supermarkets near you, choosing the ones that offer the best value on items you usually need. When you're familiar with a

store's layout, it's easy to spot the un-advertised specials.

—Save itemized receipts from different stores to compare costs of items that aren't marked with prices. This will help you decide which store has the best values.

—Clip "cents off" coupons for products you usually buy, and compare costs on these name-brand items with the store's brand or generic products.

—Don't go shopping without a list. It eliminates extra trips to the store and keeps you from buying items you don't need. Before making your list, you may want to plan meals around advertised specials.

—Compare size and price to find the best buys. Buy quality bulk foods only in amounts you can use. The large economy size usually costs less per serving; however, this size isn't a bargain if you throw out leftovers or if you can't store it.

—Stock up on store specials in reasonable amounts; the "one to a customer" limited-purchase promotion is usually a good buy.

—If practical, shop at large supermarkets; you'll have a better opportunity to compare prices and find bargains. Take along a calculator to figure the cost per serving, or look carefully at the price-per-unit tags. Also look for alternates in other areas of the store. For example, compare canned fruits and vegetables with fresh and frozen ones to see which are the most economical in cost per serving.

—Make sure convenience foods (package mixes, canned and frozen foods) are worthwhile buys. They can be timesavers on busy days, but read the labels to see what you'll be eating, and remember that preparation costs and the packaging often add to the price. If you cook for only one or two, convenience products may be the least expensive choice for you.

—Be conscious of the environment; select foods in biodegradable or recyclable containers with a minimum amount of bulk packaging.

What's the Best Value?

Although prices vary in different seasons, areas, and stores, these comparisons show the benefit of smart shopping.*

Food Item	Size/Price	Cost Per Serving
Pancake mix	16 ounces/89 cents	4 cents
Shake-and-pour pancake mix	7.25 ounces/ 87 cents	9 cents
Frozen pancakes	15.2 ounces/$1.67	14 cents
Blueberry muffin mix	14 ounces/$1.65	21 cents
Frozen blueberry muffins	10 ounces/$1.69	42 cents
Bakery blueberry muffins	4 /$2.79	70 cents
Ready-sweetened cereal	20 ounces/$2.99	15 cents
Ready-sweetened cereal (individual packs)	6 ounces/$2.27	38 cents
Regular or quick oats	18 ounces/$1.55	9 cents
Instant oatmeal (individual packs)	12 ounces/$2.17	18 cents
Cheddar cheese	8 ounces/$1.67	21 cents
Shredded Cheddar cheese	8 ounces/$1.87	23 cents
Uncooked linguine	16 ounces/$1.00	13 cents
Fresh linguine	9 ounces/$1.69	38 cents
Pizza mix	16⅝ ounces/$1.97	49 cents
Frozen pizza	21 ounces/$3.97	99 cents
Apple juice	64 ounces/$1.49	9 cents
Frozen apple juice concentrate	12 ounces/$1.27	11 cents
Apple juice (4-oz. bottles)	24 ounces/$1.49	25 cents
Potatoes (bag)	5 pounds/$1.99	10 cents
Potatoes (loose)	1 pound/69 cents	17 cents
Fresh broccoli	1¼ pounds/$1.29	26 cents
Frozen broccoli spears	10 ounces/83 cents	21 cents
Frozen broccoli spears (store brand)	10 ounces/53 cents	13 cents
Fresh green beans	1 pound/99 cents	25 cents
Canned whole green beans	16 ounces/69 cents	17 cents
Frozen whole green beans	10 ounces/$1.15	29 cents
Canned cut green beans (store brand)	16 ounces/39 cents	10 cents
Frozen cut green beans (store brand)	10 ounces/49 cents	12 cents
Fresh strawberries	1 pint/99 cents	25 cents
Frozen strawberries	16 ounces/$1.89	47 cents
Frozen strawberries in syrup	10 ounces/$1.37	69 cents

*Based on August 1991 prices.

Set the table for an Italian dinner of Veal Marsala served over a bed of fettuccine and Hearts of Romaine With Caper Vinaigrette. (Recipes, page 310.)

These salsas become lively additions to simple menus; (from top) Fresh Tomato Salsa, Avocado Salsa, and Mexi-Corn Salsa. (Recipes, page 182.)

Above: *Serve Mixed Pepper Salsa (page 181) to accompany medaillons of pork.*

Inset above: *Fresh Tomato Salsa (page 182) and toasted baguette slices team in an appetizer.*

Left: *Spoon Mexi-Corn Salsa (page 182) over a chicken breast hot off the grill.*

Six tender layers of pastry stack up to make Chocolate Pastry Cake (page 196); chocolate curls adorn the top. You can whip out chocolate curls by pulling a vegetable peeler down the side of a 7-ounce milk chocolate bar.

SEPTEMBER

Summer may be over, but you can still have a taste of the season. Enjoy the flavors of the Gulf Coast and other waters with recipes featured in "Gumbo from the Gulf" and "Get Hooked on Fresh Fish." And for your sweet tooth, sample "For the Love of Chocolate," with three spectacular desserts.

Get Hooked On Fresh Fish

If you have ever wondered what to do with fresh fish, we have some answers for you. Try fish grilled and topped with a colorful pepper relish. Or broil snapper, and nestle it in a bed of fresh salad greens; then drizzle it with a warm, spicy dressing. Even the beginning cook will succeed with the recipes and tips offered here. We'll start with the basics on how to select fish, and then tell you how to cook and serve it like a pro.

Where to Start

Simply begin at one end of the supermarket seafood counter or the local fish market and work your way down, asking questions as you go.

As you shop you may discover a wide variety in both quality and price, even among the same kinds of fish. Therefore, get to know the person behind the counter. Ask questions about when fish is coming in, and what is a good buy. If the fish you want to cook isn't there, ask for a substitute. The availability of fish depends on where you live, and sometimes the day of the week is also a factor.

Is It Fresh?

Most of us have grown up thinking that fresh fish is the best to eat. The truth is that the fresh fish you see in your supermarket may be from 1 to 21 days old. An alternative is to look for **fresh-frozen** fish. These are frozen on the boat the day they're caught. The immediate freezing eliminates any chance of spoilage from the water to the market, so fresh-frozen fish is often of better quality than fresh. It's usually thawed right before it's sold at the retail counter. Ask your merchant which fish are fresh and which are fresh-frozen. In a quality market, they'll usually be marked.

The best test for freshness is the sniff test—if a fish smells "fishy" or like ammonia, don't buy it. It should smell more like an ocean breeze. The skin should be shiny, not slimy, and if you press the fish with your finger, it should spring back rather than show an indentation. If the smell is overpowering in a market, the fish probably isn't fresh.

Prepare fish within 24 hours after you buy it. If you have other errands,

bring an ice chest for packing the fish so that it doesn't end up sitting in a hot car. If you won't be cooking it for a few days, ask for fresh-frozen fish that hasn't been thawed; then defrost it in your refrigerator.

Cook It with Style

Fish can be prepared in many different ways; in fact, it is as versatile as chicken, but many of us are afraid of ruining it because it can be expensive. For your money, however, you get a healthful protein-rich, low-cholesterol food that dances on your taste buds—if it's prepared right. Buy ⅓ to ½ pound per serving.

Great Taste from the Grill

Lemon-Soy Marinade bathes fish with flavor. It's processed in the blender to disperse oil and flavors throughout the mixture; you will have fewer flare-ups when you use marinades made this way. Because highly acidic marinades can make fish mushy, marinate for only an hour. A fish grilling basket keeps fish from falling apart and makes turning easier.

EASY GRILLED FISH

1 to 1½ pounds fish fillets or steaks
Lemon-Soy Marinade
Vegetable cooking spray

Combine fish and Lemon-Soy Marinade in a shallow dish; cover and marinate fish 1 hour in refrigerator. Remove fish from marinade, reserving marinade. Place fish in a fish basket coated with cooking spray. Place on grill, and close cover of grill. (Because of the shape of the fish basket, the grill will not close completely.) Using

specific times listed in box on facing page, grill fish over medium coals (300° to 400°), turning once and brushing with Lemon-Soy Marinade. Yield: 2 to 4 servings.

Tip: *Successful grilling starts with a good fire. If you're using a charcoal fire, spread the briquets in a single layer with tongs, making sure the edges of the coals touch.*

LEMON-SOY MARINADE

¼ cup freshly squeezed lemon juice
2 tablespoons soy sauce
¼ teaspoon garlic powder
¼ teaspoon pepper
¼ teaspoon hot sauce
¼ cup olive oil

Combine first 5 ingredients in container of an electric blender; process 10 seconds. With motor running, gradually add olive oil in a slow, steady stream. Use as a marinade for fish. Yield: about ⅔ cup.

■ Grill the fish of your choice in Lemon-Soy Marinade, and top it with **Confetti Pepper Relish.**

CONFETTI PEPPER RELISH
(pictured on page 154)

2 sweet red peppers, seeded and chopped
2 green peppers, seeded and chopped
1 large onion, chopped
1 jalapeño pepper, chopped
½ cup white vinegar
½ cup sugar
¼ teaspoon salt

Combine red and green peppers, onion, and jalapeño pepper in a Dutch oven; add boiling water to cover pepper mixture. Let stand 5 minutes; drain well.

Combine vinegar, sugar, and salt, stirring well; pour over pepper mixture. Bring mixture to a boil over medium heat; boil 5 minutes, stirring occasionally. Chill. Serve with fish. Yield: 1 quart. *Myrtie Mincey Knoxville, Tennessee*

■ If you would prefer, orange roughy, red snapper, and grouper may be substituted for the amberjack in **Grilled Amberjack Sandwiches.** Cut large fillets in half to fit the buns.

GRILLED AMBERJACK SANDWICHES

4 (¾-inch-thick) amberjack fillets (about 1½ pounds)
Lemon-Soy Marinade
Vegetable cooking spray
¼ cup commercial tartar sauce
1 tablespoon capers
4 toasted whole wheat buns
Lettuce
4 tomato slices

Place fish fillets in Lemon-Soy Marinade; cover and chill 1 hour.

Remove fish fillets from marinade, and arrange in a fish basket coated with vegetable cooking spray. Cover and grill fillets over medium coals (300° to 400°) 9 minutes on each side, turning once and brushing with Lemon-Soy Marinade.

Combine tartar sauce and capers in a small bowl, stirring well. Spread tartar sauce mixture evenly on cut side of bun halves. Place lettuce on bottom halves of buns; top with grilled amberjack, tomato slices, and top bun halves. Serve immediately. Yield: 4 sandwiches.

■ Any fish fillet boasting a firm texture and mild to moderate flavor may be substituted in **Southwestern Snapper.** A few choices include grouper, halibut, sea bass, amberjack, mahi mahi, pompano, and shark.

SOUTHWESTERN SNAPPER
(pictured on page 154)

6 cups torn, mixed salad greens
½ cup fresh cilantro (see note)
1 small sweet red pepper, sliced into strips
1 small yellow pepper, sliced into strips
4 (6-ounce) red snapper fillets
2 tablespoons olive oil
¼ teaspoon freshly ground pepper
¼ cup pine nuts, toasted
Southwestern Dressing

Combine first 4 ingredients; chill. Arrange fillets in a shallow pan, skin side down. Combine olive oil and pepper; brush over fish. Broil 6 inches from heat 8 to 10 minutes or until fish flakes easily when tested with a fork.

Arrange salad green mixture on 4 individual plates. Place fillets on greens; sprinkle with pine nuts, and drizzle with Southwestern Dressing. Serve immediately. Yield: 4 servings.

Note: Cilantro, a leafy green herb, has a distinct lemon flavor. Substitute fresh parsley if cilantro is unavailable.

Southwestern Dressing

½ teaspoon dried whole oregano
½ teaspoon chili powder
¼ teaspoon salt
¼ teaspoon pepper
2 cloves garlic, minced
¼ cup lime juice
¼ cup olive oil

Combine all ingredients in a saucepan; cook over medium heat until thoroughly heated, stirring constantly. Serve warm. Yield: ½ cup.

Fish Grilling Times

Amberjack: 1½ pounds—4 (¾-inch fillets); grill 9 minutes on each side. Yield: 4 servings.
Grouper: 1 pound—may be fillets or one piece; grill 9 minutes on each side. Yield: 2 servings.
Halibut: 1 pound—1 (1-inch-thick) steak; grill 10 minutes on each side. Yield: 2 servings.
Orange roughy: 1½ pounds—4 (½-inch-thick) fillets; grill 7 minutes on each side. Yield: 4 servings.
Red snapper: 1 pound—2 (¾-inch-thick) fillets; grill fillets 9 minutes on each side. Yield: 2 servings.
Salmon: 1 pound—2 (1-inch-thick) steaks; grill 10 minutes on each side. Yield: 2 servings.
Swordfish: 1 pound—1 (1-inch-thick) steak; grill 8 to 10 minutes on each side. Yield: 2 servings.
Tuna: 1 pound—2 (1-inch-thick) steaks; grill 10 minutes on each side. Yield: 2 servings.

Note: The thickness of fillets or steaks will vary according to the way they are cut. Allow a few extra minutes of cooking time for thicker fillets or steaks and less for thinner ones.

■ **Fish-and-Vegetable Dinner** cooks in 25 minutes or less. Serve with hush puppies or garlic bread and a green salad toppped with a vinaigrette dressing.

FISH-AND-VEGETABLE DINNER

4 orange roughy fillets (about 1½ pounds)
½ teaspoon salt
¼ teaspoon pepper
½ cup commercial buttermilk salad dressing
2 cups broccoli flowerets
1 medium-size sweet red pepper, cut into strips
1 small onion, cut into strips

Place orange roughy fillets on a 12-inch square of heavy-duty aluminum foil; sprinkle with salt and pepper. Spread 2 tablespoons buttermilk salad dressing on each fillet; arrange vegetables over fish. Fold foil over, sealing edges securely.

Bake at 450° for 20 to 25 minutes or until fish flakes easily when tested with a fork. Remove to a serving platter. Yield: 4 servings.

Microwave Directions: Place orange roughy fillets in a 12- x 8- x 2-inch baking dish; sprinkle with salt and pepper. Spread 2 tablespoons salad dressing on each fillet; arrange vegetables over fish. Cover with heavy-duty plastic wrap; fold back a small corner of wrap to allow steam to escape. Microwave at HIGH 13 to 15 minutes or until fish flakes easily when tested with a fork, giving dish a half-turn after 7 minutes. *Louise Osborne Lexington, Kentucky*

■ For a crunchy topping, combine 1 tablespoon butter and ⅓ cup chopped pecans in skillet; stir over heat 3 to 5 minutes or until browned. Serve over **Pan-Fried Fish Fillets.**

PAN-FRIED FISH FILLETS

¼ cup all-purpose flour
¼ teaspoon salt
¼ teaspoon white pepper
2 grouper or orange roughy fillets (about ¾ pound)
1 egg, slightly beaten
1 tablespoon milk
¼ cup Italian-seasoned breadcrumbs
3 tablespoons butter or margarine

Combine first 3 ingredients; dredge fillets in mixture. Combine egg and milk; dip fillets in milk mixture, and dredge in breadcrumbs.

Melt butter in a nonstick skillet; add fillets, and cook 5 minutes on each side until golden brown or until fish flakes easily when tested with a fork. Yield: 2 servings. *Helen H. Maurer Christmas, Florida*

■ For **Curry-Baked Fish**, fillets with a delicate texture, such as flounder, sole, and cod, work as well as firm fish, such as orange roughy and snapper.

CURRY-BAKED FISH

⅓ cup mayonnaise
¾ teaspoon Creole mustard
¾ teaspoon lemon juice
¾ teaspoon hot sauce
¾ teaspoon Worcestershire sauce
½ teaspoon garlic powder
⅛ teaspoon curry powder
4 orange roughy fillets (about 1½ pounds)
2½ dozen round buttery crackers, crushed

Combine first 7 ingredients; brush over top of fillets. Dredge both sides of fillets in cracker crumbs. Place fillets, mayonnaise side up, in a lightly greased 13- x 9- x 2-inch baking dish.

Bake at 400° for 20 minutes or until fish flakes easily when tested with a fork. Serve immediately. Yield: 4 servings. *Geneva B. Costello Plaquemine, Louisiana*

For The Love Of Chocolate

To find these spectacular chocolate desserts, we flipped through the hundreds of dessert options in our reader recipe files: tortes, meringues, cheesecakes.

Many taste-testings and 14 desserts later, we selected 3. We *certainly* hope you enjoy them. We did.

CHOCOLATE PASTRY CAKE
(pictured on page 192)

2 (4-ounce) packages sweet baking chocolate
½ cup sugar
½ cup water
1½ teaspoons instant coffee granules
2 teaspoons vanilla extract
1 (11-ounce) package piecrust mix
2 cups whipping cream
Chocolate curls

Combine first 4 ingredients in a heavy saucepan; cook over low heat, stirring constantly, until mixture is smooth. Stir in vanilla. Cool mixture to room temperature.

Combine piecrust mix and ¾ cup chocolate mixture in a small bowl; beat at medium speed of an electric mixer until smooth. Divide pastry into 6 equal portions. Press each portion onto bottom of an inverted ungreased

8-inch cakepan to within ½ inch of sides. Bake layers, two at a time, at 425° for 5 minutes. Trim uneven edges of circles; run a knife under pastry to loosen it from cakepans. Invert layers onto wax paper to cool.

Beat whipping cream until thickened but just before soft peaks form; fold in remaining chocolate mixture. Stack pastry on a serving plate, spreading about ⅔ cup whipped cream mixture between each. Spoon remaining whipped cream mixture on top of cake; sprinkle with chocolate curls.

Chill at least 8 hours before serving. Store in refrigerator. Yield: one 8-inch stack cake.   *Pam Garrison*
Leeds, Alabama

FUDGE DESSERT WITH KAHLÚA CREAM

2 cups sugar
½ cup all-purpose flour
¾ cup cocoa
1 cup butter or margarine, melted
5 eggs, slightly beaten
2 teaspoons vanilla extract
1½ cups chopped pecans
Kahlúa Cream

Combine first 6 ingredients; beat 3 to 4 minutes at medium speed of an electric mixer. Stir in pecans. Spoon into 10 lightly greased 6-ounce soufflé dishes or custard cups. Place dishes in a shallow pan; pour warm water to a depth of 1 inch into pan. Bake at 300° for 40 minutes or until tops are crusty. Remove dishes from water, and cool. Dollop or pipe Kahlúa Cream on top. Yield: 10 servings.

Kahlúa Cream

1 cup whipping cream
3 tablespoons Kahlúa
½ cup sifted powdered sugar

Combine all ingredients; beat at medium speed of an electric mixer until soft peaks form. Yield: 2¼ cups.
Paula McCollum
Springtown, Texas

CHOCOLATE-CARAMEL-PECAN CHEESECAKE

1 (14-ounce) package caramels
1 (5-ounce) can evaporated milk
Graham Cracker Crust
1 cup chopped pecans, toasted
2 (8-ounce) packages cream cheese, softened
½ cup sugar
2 eggs
1 teaspoon vanilla extract
¾ cup semisweet chocolate morsels, melted
Pecan halves

Unwrap caramels; combine caramels and milk in a heavy saucepan; cook over low heat until melted, stirring often. Pour over Graham Cracker Crust; sprinkle toasted pecans evenly over caramel layer, and set aside.

Beat cream cheese at high speed of an electric mixer until light and fluffy; gradually add sugar, mixing well. Add eggs, one at a time, beating well after each addition. Stir in vanilla and chocolate; beat until blended. Spoon over pecan layer. Bake at 350° for 30 minutes. Remove from oven, and run knife around edge of pan to release sides. Let cool to room temperature on a wire rack; cover and chill at least 8 hours.

When ready to serve, remove cheesecake from pan; arrange pecan halves around top edge of cheesecake. Yield: one 9-inch cheesecake.

Graham Cracker Crust

1¼ cups graham cracker crumbs
¼ cup butter or margarine, melted

Combine crumbs and butter, stirring well. Press crumb mixture evenly onto bottom and 1 inch up sides of a 9-inch springform pan. Bake at 350° for 6 to 8 minutes. Cool. Yield: one 9-inch crust.   *Jennie L. Callahan*
Louisville, Kentucky

Let Apples Tempt You

It's harvesttime, and apples are appearing everywhere. They make great snacks by themselves, but they can also accent meals.

For recipes that require apple rings, you can core apples before you cut them. If you don't have a corer, cut the rings first and use a small, round cookie cutter to remove the centers.

AMERICAN APPLE PIE

2 cups all-purpose flour
1 cup firmly packed brown sugar
½ cup regular oats, uncooked
½ teaspoon salt
⅓ cup chopped pecans
¾ cup butter or margarine, melted
4 cups peeled and thinly sliced cooking apples (about 3 apples)
¾ cup sugar
1 tablespoon cornstarch
¼ teaspoon salt
½ cup water
½ teaspoon vanilla extract

Combine first 5 ingredients in a large bowl; add butter, and stir until blended. Measure 1 cup firmly packed mixture; set aside for pie topping. Press remaining mixture in bottom and up sides of a 9-inch deep-dish pieplate. Arrange apple slices in pieplate; set aside.

Combine ¾ cup sugar, cornstarch, and ¼ teaspoon salt in a saucepan; stir in water. Cook over medium heat until mixture boils. Stir in vanilla. Pour hot mixture evenly over apples; crumble reserved topping mixture over pie.

Bake at 375° for 40 minutes, covering with aluminum foil the last 15 minutes, if necessary. Serve with ice cream. Yield: one 9-inch pie.
Bess Feagin
Memphis, Tennessee

Pick an Apple

We find them in our lunchboxes, in fresh pies cooling on Grandma's windowsill, or coated in candy and tightly clutched in a child's hand at the fair.

For the meticulous cook, choosing the right apple from more than 7,000 types grown in the United States is an overwhelming decision. But never fear—all apples are not created equal. Some selections are better for baking, while others are mainly good for eating raw and adding to salads.

To help you pick the right apple, here are descriptions of four of the most popular types and some of their characteristics.

Red Delicious: Crunchy, mellow, and sweet, Red Delicious is a favorite snacking apple. Its elongated shape, broad "shoulders," and five knobs found on its blossom end, or base, distinguish these from other apples in the produce section.

The fine-grained flesh and bright-red skin of Red Delicious apples are ideal for an attractive salad, but if cooked, this selection turns mealy.

Golden Delicious: Mildly sweet and oblong, this apple lends itself to any recipe. The flesh of Golden Delicious stays white longer than most apples after it has been cut, which makes it a good choice to add to salads or fruit-and-cheese trays. A Golden also cooks well, and its pale-to-creamy yellow skin does not need to be peeled since it is so tender. Greenish Goldens are tangier than yellow ones.

Granny Smith: Many people enjoy this tart, crisp, bright-green apple as an out-of-hand snack, but it adds zip to salads and stir-fry dishes as well. Be careful not to overcook Granny Smith apples when preparing them whole, or they'll lose their shape.

Rome Beauty: Called the ultimate baking apple, the Rome Beauty has a tough, brilliant-red skin and a large, round shape. Honey and heat bring out the tangy-sweet flavor from its yellowish flesh, and a Rome Beauty can be baked with a mixture of brown sugar, cinnamon, and raisins for a warm and spicy treat.

The apples mentioned above are generally available year-round. The more seasonal types include: **York**—a lopsided, red apple, slightly tart, and good for cooking; **McIntosh**—a two-toned, red-and-green snacking apple; and **Winesap**—a glossy-red, almost purple apple with red-streaked yellow flesh, which makes a spicy cider.

Cold apples stay much fresher, so be sure to place them in a plastic bag in the refrigerator. The plastic keeps the apples moist and prevents food odors from tainting their flavor.

STUFFED APPLE RING SALAD

2 to 3 Red Delicious apples
Pineapple juice or lemon juice
1 (8-ounce) package cream cheese, softened
2 to 3 tablespoons honey
⅓ cup finely chopped dates
¼ cup chopped pecans
Lettuce leaves

Core unpeeled apples, and cut into ¾-inch-thick rings; dip in pineapple juice to prevent browning. Set aside.

Place cream cheese in a small mixing bowl; beat at medium speed of an electric mixer until smooth. Add honey; beat at medium speed until light and fluffy. Stir in dates and pecans. Arrange apple rings on lettuce leaves. Pipe or dollop cream cheese mixture into center of each apple ring. Yield: 6 servings.   *Jan Stallard*
Kingsport, Tennessee

APPLE PORK CHOPS

¼ cup all-purpose flour
½ teaspoon salt
½ teaspoon paprika
⅛ teaspoon white pepper
6 (½-inch-thick) pork chops
¼ cup vegetable oil
2 medium-size cooking apples
2 cups apple juice, divided
3 tablespoons brown sugar
½ teaspoon ground allspice

Combine first 4 ingredients in a shallow bowl; dredge pork chops in mixture. Reserve remaining flour mixture. Brown pork chops in oil in a large skillet. Arrange chops in a 13- x 9- x 2-inch baking dish.

Core unpeeled apples, and cut into rings; place on chops. Pour 1½ cups apple juice over apples. Combine sugar and allspice; sprinkle over apples. Bake, uncovered, at 325° for 1 hour or until chops are tender.

Remove pork chops and apple slices to a serving platter, reserving pan drippings. Dissolve 1½ tablespoons remaining flour mixture in remaining ½ cup apple juice. Combine flour mixture and pan drippings in a saucepan; cook over medium heat until thickened, stirring constantly. Serve sauce over pork chops. Yield: 6 servings.

Mrs. E. W. Hanley
Palm Harbor, Florida

YAM-AND-APPLE SCALLOP

3 medium-size sweet potatoes
2 medium-size cooking apples
1 tablespoon lemon juice
½ cup firmly packed brown sugar
½ teaspoon ground cinnamon
½ teaspoon pumpkin pie spice
½ teaspoon orange extract
½ cup chopped pecans
2 tablespoons butter or margarine

Cook potatoes in boiling water 20 to 25 minutes or until tender. Let cool to touch; peel. Cut potatoes into ¼-inch slices, and arrange in a lightly greased 12- x 8- x 2-inch baking dish. Core unpeeled apples, and slice into ¼-inch rings. Cut apple rings in half; arrange in rows over potatoes. Sprinkle with lemon juice.

Combine brown sugar and next 4 ingredients; sprinkle over casserole. Dot with butter. Bake, uncovered, at 350° for 35 minutes or until apples are tender. Yield: 6 servings.

Sandi Pichon
Slidell, Louisiana

Tip: *When purchasing sweet potatoes, be sure to select well-shaped, firm potatoes with smooth, brightcolored skins. Avoid any potatoes that have cuts and holes.*

QUICK!

Add Dressing To Recipes

Things aren't always what they seem. If you look beyond the obvious, you might find some creative, pleasant surprises. For instance, the next time you pick up a bottle of commercial salad dressing, don't just pour it on a green salad. Instead, think of it as a one-step marinade for meats. Or would you ever guess it could flavor a creamy dip or cheese ball for a fancy appetizer?

Several dressings work well as recipe ingredients and speed the process along in these reader favorites. You'll welcome the convenience of commercial dressing in any spot on the menu—not just the salad course.

CHICKEN-ITALIAN DRESSING BAKE

½ cup Italian-seasoned
   breadcrumbs
¼ cup grated Parmesan cheese
⅛ teaspoon salt
4 chicken breast halves, skinned
   and boned
¼ cup commercial Italian salad
   dressing
Vegetable cooking spray

Combine breadcrumbs, cheese, and salt in a plastic bag; shake to mix. Dip chicken in salad dressing. Place one piece of chicken in bag, and shake to coat. Repeat procedure with remaining chicken. Place in a lightly greased pan. Bake at 400° for 15 minutes. Spray chicken with cooking spray, and bake an additional 5 to 10 minutes or until done. Yield: 4 servings.

Judy McCrary
Thomaston, Georgia

GRILLED MARINATED PORK TENDERLOIN

2 (¾-pound) pork tenderloins
1 (8-ounce) bottle commercial
   Italian salad dressing

Place pork tenderloins in a zip-top heavy-duty plastic bag. Pour dressing over tenderloins; seal and refrigerate 8 hours.

Remove tenderloins from marinade. Insert meat thermometer into tenderloins, being careful not to touch fat. Grill tenderloins, covered, over hot coals 12 to 15 minutes or until thermometer registers 160°, turning them once. Yield: 6 servings.

Lillian Owens
New Castle, Kentucky

OPEN-FACE REUBEN SANDWICHES

1 (12-ounce) can corned beef
1 (16-ounce) jar sauerkraut, well
   drained
½ cup commercial Thousand Island
   salad dressing
½ teaspoon pepper
1 tablespoon bacon bits
8 slices rye bread, toasted
8 (¾-ounce) slices Swiss cheese

Break up corned beef with a fork until crumbly. Add sauerkraut and next 3 ingredients, stirring well. Spread mixture on toast. Bake at 350° for 10 minutes. Cut each slice of Swiss cheese in half. Place 2 strips on top of each sandwich; bake an additional 5 minutes or until cheese melts. Yield: 4 to 6 servings.

Darlene Cates
Forney, Texas

CHEESE-CRAB DIP

1 cup fresh crabmeat, drained and
  flaked (see note)
1¼ cups mayonnaise or salad
  dressing
½ cup (2 ounces) shredded sharp
  Cheddar cheese
¼ cup commercial French salad
  dressing
1 teaspoon prepared horseradish

Combine all ingredients; cover tightly
and refrigerate. Serve with assorted
crackers. Yield: 2½ cups.

Note: You can substitute 1 (6-ounce)
can lump crabmeat for fresh crabmeat, if desired. Yield: 2 cups.
                    Mrs. E. W. Hanley
                    Palm Harbor, Florida

CHEESE BALL

2 (8-ounce) packages cream cheese,
  softened
1 (2.5-ounce) package thinly sliced
  ham, chopped
¼ cup commercial Italian salad
  dressing
¾ cup chopped pecans

Combine first 3 ingredients in a bowl;
refrigerate 30 minutes. Shape mixture
into a ball, and roll in chopped pecans,
coating thoroughly. Serve with crackers. Yield: 2½ cups.
                    Susan Lee Wilson
                    Johnson City, Tennessee

From Our Kitchen To Yours

Get the school year off to a healthy
start by encouraging sensible snacking. Snacks can help meet our daily
nutritional needs no matter what age
we are. These simple suggestions
yield tempting and nutritious treats to
keep on hand for nibbling.

When kids come home from school,
they drop their books and head for a
snack—often junk food with lots of
calories and little nutritional value. Because most commercial snacks are
high in fat, keep ingredients on hand
to make **Pizza Bites.** Separate 1 (11-
ounce) can refrigerated biscuits, and
divide each biscuit in half. Place on a
lightly greased baking sheet, and bake
at 350° for 10 minutes. Spread with ½
cup commercial pizza sauce, and
sprinkle with 4 ounces (1 cup) shredded part-skim mozzarella cheese;
bake an additional 8 minutes, or
freeze, if desired, and bake frozen for
15 minutes.

If you're in a hurry, grab a piece of
fresh fruit, such as a banana, apple, or
pear, instead of a candy bar to satisfy
that mid-afternoon slump. To accompany nature's desserts, make
Orange-Yogurt Dip by combining 1
(8-ounce) carton vanilla yogurt, 1½
teaspoons frozen orange juice concentrate, and 1 tablespoon honey.

Butter-and-Herb Blend perks up
air-popped popcorn, potatoes, and
breadsticks. Combine 2 tablespoons
butter-flavored granules, 1 teaspoon
dried dillweed, ½ teaspoon garlic
powder, and ⅛ teaspoon red pepper;
sprinkle on popped corn and potato
wedges. Separate 1 (11-ounce) can
commercial soft breadsticks, spray
with butter-flavored cooking spray,
and sprinkle with blend; bake according to package directions.

When a balanced meal loses out to a
busy schedule and fast food, try dunk-
ing raw vegetables, such as carrot and
celery sticks and cauliflower and broccoli flowerets, in **Yogurt-Herb Dip** to
supply the missing nutrients. To prepare Yogurt-Herb Dip, stir together ¼

cup plain nonfat yogurt, 1 tablespoon
reduced-calorie mayonnaise, ¼ teaspoon dried dillweed, ¼ teaspoon
dried chives, and a dash of ground
white pepper.

Granola-Peanut Butter Spread
smeared on a graham cracker, bagel,
or popcorn cake answers the call
when a little pick-me-up is needed.
Stir together ⅓ cup 100% natural
oats-and-honey cereal, ¼ cup creamy
peanut butter, 1 teaspoon honey, and
¼ teaspoon ground cinnamon.

If a banana or carrot stick isn't appealing to you, make **Citrus Slush** in
the blender. Process 1 (6-ounce) can
frozen orange juice, lemonade, or
limeade concentrate; ¾ cup water;
and ice cubes added to the 3-cup line.
Serve immediately.

How to Satisfy Snack Attacks—Nutritiously

—Make natural frozen treats by
freezing fruits such as grapes, plums,
or nectarines.

—Make snack mix with bite-size
wheat, rice, corn, and bran ready-to-
eat cereals; coat with butter-flavored
cooking spray, and sprinkle with low-
sodium seasonings, such as garlic, onion, or chili powder. Bake the snack
mix just until it is crisp.

—Combine peanut butter and fruit
spread, and spread the mixture on
whole-grain crackers.

—Blend a fruit cream using 1 cup frozen peach slices or other frozen fruit,
½ cup skim milk, and 2 tablespoons
powdered sugar; freeze.

—Soak apple and pear slices in pineapple juice for added flavor and to
keep fruit from darkening.

—Mix orange juice and ice milk for a
creamy orange slush.

—Team angel food cake with sliced
fruit or fruit-flavored yogurt.

—Add sliced fresh fruit to vanilla yogurt, and sprinkle with granola or
wheat germ.

—Spread peanut butter on vanilla wafers; top with banana slices.

—Cut pita bread rounds into triangles,
spray with butter-flavored vegetable
cooking spray, and sprinkle with
grated Parmesan cheese or a sugar-
cinnamon mixture; bake the chips at
425° for 10 minutes.

—Combine air-popped popcorn, dry-roasted peanuts, and raisins.
—Spread low-fat cheese on whole-grain crackers or plain bagel chips, and eat with an apple or celery.
—Toast a frozen whole grain waffle; top with fruit or yogurt.
—Combine cream cheese, chopped dates, and a dash of honey; spread on crackers or fruit.

Munching Strategies

Plan snacks from three of the basic four food groups—fruits and vegetables, cheese and dairy products, and cereal and grains. Choose a variety of foods that provide dietary fiber and give the most nutrition for the least calories.

To figure the percentage of fat in one serving, first find the number of grams of fat per serving. For example, a serving of pretzels contains 110 calories and 1 gram of fat. Multiply the grams of fat (1) by 9 (the number of calories per gram of fat) to get fat calories per serving. The amount of fat calories is 9. Then divide this number by the total calories (110). You'll find the amount of fat in the pretzels contributes 8% of the calories in one serving ($\frac{9}{110}$ x 100 = 8%).

Plan ahead; if you have a snack available, you won't be tempted. Carry fruit or other healthy snacks with you. To economize, make individual packets from family-size packages. Choose snacks containing safflower, sunflower, soybean, corn, or cottonseed oil instead of coconut, palm, or palm kernel oil. Steer clear of salted peanuts, potato chips, French fries, and onion rings.

Tip: *Fruited and flavored yogurts add a rich texture to shakes and snacks with less fat and cholesterol. Use lemon or vanilla yogurt in fruit dishes and some salad dressings or as toppings for desserts.*

Hush Puppy History

Legend says that at campsites of old, while the catch or kill of the day was cooking over an open fire, man threw his yapping canine best friend bits of fried cornbread and a command to "Hush, puppy!" And so was named a Southern institution.

The recipes here include ingredients such as tomatoes, bacon, and cheese. So you can prepare hush puppies to suit a particular taste.

TOMATO-ONION HUSH PUPPIES

1 (7-ounce) package hush puppy mix
1 egg
⅔ cup buttermilk
½ cup chopped onion
½ cup chopped tomato
Vegetable oil

Combine all ingredients except oil in a medium bowl; stir until smooth. Set aside for 5 minutes.

Pour oil to a depth of 3 inches into a Dutch oven; heat to 375°. Carefully drop batter by rounded tablespoonfuls into hot oil. Fry a few at a time 2 minutes or until golden brown, turning once. Drain on paper towels. Serve immediately. Yield: 2 dozen.

Scotty Dorrough
Birmingham, Alabama

BACON HUSH PUPPIES

6 slices bacon
1½ cups yellow cornmeal
½ cup all-purpose flour
1 tablespoon baking powder
¼ teaspoon salt
½ cup chopped onion
1 egg, slightly beaten
1 cup buttermilk
Vegetable oil

Cook bacon in a heavy skillet 6 to 8 minutes or until crisp. Remove bacon, reserving 2 tablespoons drippings in skillet. Drain bacon, and crumble. Set bacon and drippings aside.

Combine cornmeal and next 3 ingredients; stir in onion and bacon. Make a well in center of mixture. Combine egg, buttermilk, and bacon drippings; add to dry ingredients, stirring just until moistened.

Pour vegetable oil to a depth of 3 inches into a Dutch oven; heat to 375°. Carefully drop batter by tablespoonfuls into hot oil. Fry a few at a time 3 minutes or until hush puppies are golden brown, turning once. Drain on paper towels. Serve immediately. Yield: 20 hush puppies.

CHEESY MEXICAN HUSH PUPPIES

¾ cup yellow cornmeal
½ cup all-purpose flour
1½ teaspoons baking powder
½ teaspoon salt
⅛ teaspoon red pepper
1 cup (4 ounces) shredded Monterey Jack cheese
1 (4-ounce) can chopped green chiles, drained
1 tablespoon minced onion
1 egg
½ cup milk
Vegetable oil

Combine first 8 ingredients in a large bowl; make a well in center of mixture. Combine egg and milk; add to dry ingredients, stirring just until moistened.

Pour oil to a depth of 3 inches into a Dutch oven; heat to 375°. Carefully drop batter by rounded tablespoonfuls into hot oil. Fry a few at a time 3 to 4 minutes or until golden brown, turning once. Drain on paper towels. Serve immediately. Yield: about 2 dozen.

ON THE LIGHT SIDE

Trim Calories Without Sacrificing Sweetness

Each American eats nearly 130 pounds of sugar each year. With this craving for sweets added to our desire for low-calorie meals, a growing interest in sugar substitutes is at an all-time high.

Saccharin, the one most widely used, has been around for more than 90 years. It's very stable and can be heated without breaking down, making it ideal for cooking and baking. At 300 times the sweetening power of sugar, it takes only a pinch to sweeten a recipe. Familiar brands are Sweet 'N Low® and Sugar Twin®.

The safety of saccharin has been the subject of extensive scientific research. The National Cancer Institute conducted one of the largest studies on saccharin and concluded that there was "no evidence of increased risk with long-term use of saccharin in any form, or with the use that began decades ago."

One of the most popular sweeteners on the market today is aspartame, brand named Equal®. It is made from two amino acids found naturally in foods and has about 180 times the sweetness of sugar. Its sugarlike taste sweetens and enhances flavors with very little aftertaste, but it loses its sweetness when heated, making it unsuitable for cooking or baking.

The newest sweetener on the market is acesulfame-K known by the commercial name Sweet One®. Chemically, acesulfame-K is similar to saccharin, and like saccharin, it can be used in cooking and baking. It is about 200 times sweeter than sugar and has less of an aftertaste than saccharin.

Recipes for baked items made with sugar substitutes generally do not have the same texture and volume as those prepared with sugar. For that reason, it's best to stick with recipes that have been tested.

Tip: *Satisfy your craving for sweets by choosing low-fat foods. For example, have a slice of low-fat angel food cake for dessert rather than a slice of cheesecake. Or opt for plain low-fat gingersnaps for a snack instead of a fat-laden doughnut.*

SWEET-AND-SOUR CHICKEN

2 tablespoons cornstarch
2 tablespoons granulated brown sugar substitute sweetened with saccharin
1 tablespoon low-sodium Worcestershire sauce
¾ teaspoon ground ginger
¼ teaspoon garlic powder
1½ cups unsweetened pineapple juice
¼ cup low-sodium soy sauce
¼ cup wine vinegar
¼ cup reduced-calorie catsup
Vegetable cooking spray
3 cups cubed uncooked chicken
½ cup julienne-cut sweet red pepper
½ cup julienne-cut green pepper
3 cups hot cooked rice (cooked without salt or fat)

Combine first 9 ingredients in a medium bowl; stir well.

Coat a nonstick skillet with cooking spray; place over medium-high heat until hot. Add chicken, and sauté 5 minutes. Add sweet red pepper and green pepper; sauté 2 minutes. Gradually stir cornstarch mixture into chicken mixture. Cook over medium heat, stirring until thickened and bubbly. Serve over rice. Yield: 6 servings (299 calories per ⅔ cup mixture and ½ cup rice).

□ *28.6 grams protein, 2.2 grams fat, 38 grams carbohydrate, 66 milligrams cholesterol, 418 milligrams sodium, and 43 milligrams calcium.*

SUPREME BEAN SALAD

1 (16-ounce) can no-salt-added green beans, drained
1 (16-ounce) can yellow wax beans, drained
1 (10-ounce) package frozen English peas, thawed
1 cup chopped green pepper
1 cup thinly sliced purple onion
1 (2-ounce) jar diced pimiento, drained
1 teaspoon minced fresh garlic
¾ cup white vinegar
1 tablespoon vegetable oil
½ teaspoon salt
½ teaspoon pepper
16 packets sugar substitute sweetened with aspartame or 8 packets sweetened with acesulfame-K or saccharin

Combine first 7 ingredients in a large bowl; set aside.

Combine vinegar, oil, salt, and pepper in a small saucepan; bring to a boil. Remove from heat; stir in sugar substitute. Pour over vegetables; toss gently. Cover and chill 3 hours, stirring occasionally. Drain before serving. Yield: 7 servings (106 calories per 1-cup serving).

□ *4.2 grams protein, 2.4 grams fat, 18.4 grams carbohydrate, 0 milligrams cholesterol, 412 milligrams sodium, and 64 milligrams calcium.*

Mrs. Robert Bailey
Knoxville, Tennessee

FRUIT CUP

2 (16-ounce) cans sliced peaches, packed in extra light syrup
1 (8-ounce) can unsweetened pineapple tidbits, undrained
2 cups sliced strawberries
1½ cups sliced bananas
1 teaspoon orange-flavored breakfast beverage crystals sweetened with aspartame
1 (0.9-ounce) package vanilla-flavored instant pudding mix sweetened with aspartame

Drain peaches; cut into bite-size pieces. Combine peaches and remaining ingredients; stir gently until all fruit is coated. Cover and chill thoroughly. Yield: 11 servings (84 calories per ½-cup serving).

□ *1 gram protein, 0.5 gram fat, 20.7 grams carbohydrate, 0 milligrams cholesterol, 9 milligrams sodium, and 18 milligrams calcium.*

Mrs. R. F. Glover
Roanoke, Virginia

BLUEBERRY MUFFINS

⅓ cup reduced-calorie margarine, softened
¼ cup granulated sugar substitute sweetened with saccharin or acesulfame-K
1¼ cups all-purpose flour
1 teaspoon baking powder
¼ teaspoon baking soda
¼ teaspoon salt
1 egg
½ cup skim milk
1 cup frozen blueberries, thawed and drained
Vegetable cooking spray

Beat margarine at medium speed of an electric mixer; gradually add sugar substitute, beating well.

Combine flour, baking powder, soda, and salt. Combine egg and milk; stir well. Add flour and milk mixtures alternately to creamed mixture, beginning and ending with flour mixture. Mix just until blended. Gently stir in blueberries.

Spoon batter into miniature (1¾-inch) muffin pans coated with cooking spray, filling two-thirds full. Bake at 375° for 15 to 20 minutes or until muffins are done. Yield: 2 dozen miniature muffins (50 calories per muffin).

□ *1.2 grams protein, 2 grams fat, 7 grams carbohydrate, 12 milligrams cholesterol, 78 milligrams sodium, and 24 milligrams calcium.*

Shirley Ann Glaab
Hattiesburg, Mississippi

Lunch With An Italian Twist

Italian seasonings mingle with the fresh flavors of vegetables in this luncheon menu. A combination of orzo (a pasta resembling elongated rice) and shrimp fill red, yellow, or green pepper halves to create Peppers Stuffed With Shrimp-and-Orzo Salad.

Long avoided by the health conscious because of its high-cholesterol content, shrimp is being welcomed back to the family of healthful eating. The very low saturated fat content found in shrimp makes it acceptable to cholesterol-conscious eaters because saturated fat has more of an effect on raising blood cholesterol levels than dietary cholesterol.

For this luncheon, welcome guests with a cool glass of Fruit Refresher; then serve Peppers Stuffed With Shrimp-and-Orzo Salad. Place a basket of Garlic Bread on the table. Colorful Spumoni and Berries ends this meal that's less than 15% fat.

Light Luncheon
Fruit Refresher
Peppers Stuffed With Shrimp-and-Orzo Salad
Raw vegetables
Garlic Bread
Spumoni and Berries

FRUIT REFRESHER

⅓ cup sugar
1 cup water
2 cups unsweetened orange juice
¾ cup unsweetened grapefruit juice
¼ cup unsweetened pineapple juice
2 tablespoons lemon juice
1 slice canned unsweetened pineapple, diced
5 maraschino cherries, diced
2 cups cold water

Combine sugar and 1 cup water in a medium saucepan; bring mixture to a boil, reduce heat, and simmer 5 minutes. Cool.

Combine sugar mixture, orange juice, and remaining ingredients. Chill before serving. Yield: 8 servings (80 calories per ¾-cup serving).

□ *0.6 gram protein, 0.1 gram fat, 20 grams carbohydrate, 0 milligrams cholesterol, 1 milligram sodium, and 10 milligrams calcium.*

Mrs. Everett H. Powell
Decatur, Alabama

PEPPERS STUFFED WITH SHRIMP-AND-ORZO SALAD

4 large red, yellow, or green peppers (1½ pounds)
6 cups water
2 pounds unpeeled small fresh shrimp
4 cups cooked orzo or rice (cooked without salt or fat)
1 cup chopped green onions
2½ tablespoons white wine vinegar
1 tablespoon olive oil
¾ teaspoon pepper
⅔ cup (3 ounces) crumbled feta cheese

Cut peppers in half lengthwise, and remove and discard seeds; wash peppers, and set aside.

Bring water to a boil; add shrimp, and cook 3 to 5 minutes. Drain well; rinse with cold water. Chill. Peel and devein shrimp; coarsely chop. Combine shrimp, orzo, and green onions; set aside.

Combine vinegar, olive oil, and pepper. Pour over orzo mixture; toss gently. Add cheese; toss gently. Spoon salad into peppers; cover and chill until ready to serve. Yield: 8 servings (221 calories per serving).

□ *22.8 grams protein, 5.4 grams fat, 18.8 grams carbohydrate, 189 milligrams cholesterol, 328 milligrams sodium, and 100 milligrams calcium.*

Carrie Byrne Bartlett
Gallatin, Tennessee

GARLIC BREAD

½ (1-pound) loaf Italian bread
Butter-flavored vegetable cooking
  spray
⅛ teaspoon garlic powder
2 tablespoons freshly grated
  Parmesan cheese

Slice bread in half horizontally. Spray each half with cooking spray; sprinkle with garlic powder and Parmesan cheese. Wrap in aluminum foil, and bake at 350° for 20 minutes or until thoroughly heated. Yield: 8 servings (92 calories per serving).

☐ *3.1 grams protein, 1.4 grams fat, 15.8 grams carbohydrate, 2 milligrams cholesterol, 188 milligrams sodium, and 29 milligrams calcium.*

SPUMONI AND BERRIES
(pictured on back cover)

2¼ cups lime sherbet, slightly
  softened
2 tablespoons chopped almonds,
  toasted
2¼ cups pineapple sherbet,
  softened
2¼ cups raspberry sherbet,
  softened
16 large fresh strawberries

Line an 8½- x 4½- x 3-inch loafpan with wax paper. Combine lime sherbet and 2 tablespoons almonds; spread in bottom of prepared pan. Cover and freeze 30 minutes.

Spread pineapple sherbet evenly over lime sherbet mixture; cover and freeze 30 minutes. Spread raspberry sherbet evenly over pineapple sherbet; cover and freeze until firm.

Invert onto a platter, and remove wax paper; cut into 1-inch slices. Serve each slice with 2 strawberries. Yield: 8 servings (196 calories per serving).

☐ *2.2 grams protein, 2.6 grams fat, 42.6 grams carbohydrate, 0 milligrams cholesterol, 113 milligrams sodium, and 75 milligrams calcium.*

Slimmed-Down Spinach Quiche

If you've been watching fat and cholesterol in your diet, you probably gave up quiche long ago. Now it's time to rediscover its good taste.

Dr. W. H. Pinkston, of Knoxville, Tennessee, trimmed away calories, fat, and cholesterol in his Spinach Quiche recipe. The pastry shell is made with vegetable oil; low-fat dairy products, such as 1% low-fat cottage cheese and part-skim mozzarella, replace the richer versions in the filling.

SPINACH QUICHE

Vegetable cooking spray
2 cups sliced fresh mushrooms
½ cup diced onion
2 cloves garlic, minced
½ cup egg substitute
1 tablespoon Dijon mustard
¼ teaspoon salt
¼ teaspoon pepper
1 cup 1% low-fat cottage
  cheese
1 (10-ounce) package frozen
  spinach, thawed and drained
Vegetable Oil Pastry
1½ ounces part-skim mozzarella
  cheese slices

Coat a large, nonstick skillet with cooking spray; place over medium-high heat until hot. Add mushrooms, onion, and garlic; sauté until tender.

Combine egg substitute and next 4 ingredients; stir in spinach. Add mushroom mixture, stirring well; spoon into prebaked pastry shell. Bake at 350° for 35 minutes. Arrange cheese slices over quiche; bake 5 minutes or until cheese melts. Let stand 5 minutes before slicing. Yield: 8 servings (220 calories per serving).

☐ *10.4 grams protein, 10.8 grams fat, 20.5 grams carbohydrate, 4 milligrams cholesterol, 398 milligrams sodium, and 106 milligrams calcium.*

Vegetable Oil Pastry

1⅓ cups all-purpose flour
¼ teaspoon salt
1 egg white, slightly beaten
⅓ cup vegetable oil
1 tablespoon cold water

Combine flour and salt; add egg white, oil, and water. Stir with a fork until dry ingredients are moistened. Shape into a ball; place between 2 sheets of wax paper. Roll to a 12-inch circle. Place in a 9-inch pieplate; flute edges. Prick bottom and sides of pastry with a fork. Bake at 450° for 12 minutes. Yield: one 9-inch pastry shell.

COMPARE THE NUTRIENTS		
(per serving)		
	Traditional	Light
Calories	308	220
Fat	22.9g	10.8g
Cholesterol	110mg	4mg

Firing Up The Rib Debate

If you grew up in Georgia, where barbecue sauce runs thick and red, you probably can't imagine dressing your ribs with anything other than a sauce like this one. But folks from North Carolina would have you believe that the best ribs are basted *only* with a thin, vinegar sauce.

Another ribs debate concerns the three cuts most commonly found in the South. Rib enthusiasts partial to gnawing the bone swear by a slab of **spareribs** cut from the brisket area of a pig. Usually the least expensive because they have the lowest ratio of meat to bone, spareribs serve one person per pound.

People who crave more meat opt for **baby loin back ribs** (alias **back ribs, loin back ribs,** or **baby back ribs**). These ribs are cut from the loin of the animal and are meatier than spareribs, although most cooks still buy one pound per person. Baby loin back ribs don't indicate the age of the animal; the ribs are just smaller.

Thick-and-meaty **country-style ribs** offer the best option for a knife-and-fork attack, although most Southerners use the hand-held approach anyway. In contrast to other ribs, which come in slabs, these are cut into individual ribs. And they are so meaty you can count on 1½ to 2 servings per pound.

The debate continues when it comes to cooking the ribs. Only one concept is certain: If you cook them too fast, you'll be in for more gnawing than you bargained for.

Many barbecue enthusiasts maintain that the best flavor comes from ribs grilled directly over low heat for two to three hours. These ribs demand frequent basting and constant supervision to prevent flare-ups.

Another group insists on boiling ribs before grilling them. But without a huge kettle you'll have to cut the ribs into small pieces, and that destroys the "integrity" of the slab.

For our purposes, we cut the slabs in half (one serving for most slabs), placed them in a pan with a vinegar mixture (now *that* made my North Carolina friend happy), and baked them for 30 minutes to an hour, depending on the type rib. They're ready for the grill when only a small amount of pink remains.

It takes at least 30 minutes on the grill to give the ribs that smoky flavor Southerners expect. Either a gas or charcoal grill will do. Generally you'll get more flavor from a charcoal grill, but the temperature is easier to control with a gas grill.

The trick is to grill the ribs just long enough to take on flavor but not burn the sweet sauce on the meat. The sugar in most sauces will blacken if cooked too long or at too high a heat. Our recipe gives exact cooking times.

BARBECUED RIBS

4 pounds pork ribs (spareribs, baby loin back ribs, or country-style ribs)
Vinegar Basting Sauce
Barbecue Sauce

If using slabs, cut each slab in half crosswise. Place ribs in a shallow roasting pan; pour Vinegar Basting Sauce over ribs. Cover with aluminum foil, and bake at 300° for 30 minutes for baby loin back ribs or 1 hour for spareribs or country-style ribs, basting with vinegar mixture halfway through cooking time.

Drain ribs, discarding basting sauce. Grill ribs over low coals (275° to 300°) 15 minutes, turning after 8 minutes. Baste ribs generously with Barbecue Sauce; grill 8 minutes. Turn ribs; baste again with Barbecue Sauce, and grill 7 minutes or until done. Yield: 4 to 8 servings.

Vinegar Basting Sauce

⅔ cup water
⅓ cup red wine vinegar

Combine ingredients in a small bowl. Yield: 1 cup.

Barbecue Sauce

1 cup catsup
1 cup water
½ cup cider vinegar
⅓ cup Worcestershire sauce
¼ cup prepared mustard
¼ cup butter or margarine
½ cup firmly packed brown sugar
1 teaspoon hot sauce
⅛ teaspoon salt

Combine all ingredients in a saucepan, stirring well. Bring to a boil; cover, reduce heat, and simmer 1 hour. Yield: 3 cups.
Millie Givens
Savannah, Georgia

It All Starts With Chicken

What comes first—the chicken or the menu? Often the chicken, and the reasons are obvious. It's economical, usually everyone in the family likes it, and you can create so many dishes with it.

CHICKEN-PECAN QUICHE

1 cup all-purpose flour
1 cup (4 ounces) shredded sharp
   Cheddar cheese
¾ cup chopped pecans
½ teaspoon salt
¼ teaspoon paprika
⅓ cup vegetable oil
3 eggs, beaten
1 (8-ounce) carton sour cream
¼ cup mayonnaise or salad
   dressing
½ cup chicken broth
2 cups chopped cooked chicken
½ cup (2 ounces) shredded sharp
   Cheddar cheese
¼ cup minced onion
¼ teaspoon dried whole dillweed
3 drops of hot sauce
¼ cup pecan halves

Combine first 5 ingredients in a bowl; stir in oil. Set aside one-fourth of mixture. Press remainder of mixture in bottom and up sides of a 9-inch quiche dish. Prick bottom and sides of crust with a fork. Bake at 350° for 10 minutes. Set aside.

Combine eggs, sour cream, mayonnaise, and chicken broth in a medium bowl; stir well. Stir in chicken, Cheddar cheese, minced onion, dillweed, and hot sauce; pour mixture into prepared crust. Sprinkle reserved crumb mixture over filling; top with pecan halves. Bake at 325° for 45 minutes. Yield: 6 to 8 servings.

Mrs. C. B. Williams
Richmond, Virginia

SPECIAL OCCASION CHICKEN

¼ cup butter or margarine
4 chicken breast halves, skinned
   and boned
1 cup sliced fresh mushrooms
2 tablespoons minced shallots
¼ teaspoon salt
¼ teaspoon pepper
1 cup (4 ounces) shredded
   mozzarella cheese

Melt butter in a skillet over medium heat. Add chicken, and cook 10 minutes. Turn chicken; add sliced mushrooms and shallots. Sprinkle evenly with salt and pepper; cook 10 minutes or until tender.

Transfer chicken to a platter. Sprinkle cheese over chicken; top with mushrooms and shallots. Cover and let stand 5 minutes or until cheese melts. Yield: 4 servings.

Susan Cheek
Montgomery, Alabama

ITALIAN CHICKEN

2 pounds chicken breasts, thighs,
   and legs, skinned
1 (14½-ounce) can tomato wedges,
   drained
1 (6-ounce) can whole mushrooms,
   drained
1 (6-ounce) can pitted ripe olives,
   drained
1 (14-ounce) can artichoke hearts,
   drained
1 (8-ounce) bottle Italian salad
   dressing
½ cup dry white wine
1 (1-ounce) envelope onion soup
   mix
1 (8-ounce) package linguine

Place chicken pieces in a lightly greased 12- x 8- x 2-inch baking dish. Arrange tomato wedges, mushrooms, olives, and artichoke hearts on top. Combine salad dressing and wine; pour over vegetables and chicken. Sprinkle with onion soup mix. Cover and bake at 350° for 1 hour or until chicken is done.

Cook linguine according to package directions. Remove chicken from baking dish, and set aside. Combine remaining vegetable mixture, and spoon over linguine on serving platter. Arrange chicken pieces on top, and serve immediately. Yield: 4 servings.

Harriet Heinemann
Roanoke, Virginia

Gumbo From The Gulf

The Bayou State may have invented gumbo many moons ago, but Louisiana's neighbor, Mississippi, can do it up right, too. Take a soup bowl along a good stretch of the Gulf rimming I-10 and, chances are, you'll be served up some authentic renditions—Cajun- and Creole-style.

These two Mississippi readers include tomatoes and okra—key Creole ingredients—in their versions. And you've got a choice of cooking style. You can start with a roux (flour cooked in oil) and simmer the ingredients the old-fashioned way for Spicy Seafood Gumbo, or you can take the shortcuts offered in Okra Gumbo.

OKRA GUMBO

1 large onion, chopped
1 large green pepper, chopped
2 tablespoons vegetable oil or
   bacon drippings
4 cups sliced fresh okra
3 ripe tomatoes, peeled and
   chopped
1 cup corn cut from cob (about 2
   ears)
1 tablespoon white vinegar
½ teaspoon salt
¼ teaspoon black pepper
⅛ teaspoon red pepper

Sauté onion and green pepper in oil in a large skillet until tender. Add okra and remaining ingredients, and cook over medium heat 15 minutes, stirring frequently. Serve immediately. Yield: 8 servings. *Phyllis McCalop*
Cleveland, Mississippi

SPICY SEAFOOD GUMBO

1 cup vegetable oil
1 cup all-purpose flour
4 medium onions, chopped
8 stalks celery, chopped
3 cloves garlic, minced
4 (14½-ounce) cans ready-to-serve chicken broth
2 (28-ounce) cans whole tomatoes, undrained and chopped
2 (10-ounce) packages frozen sliced okra, thawed
1 pound crab claws
¼ cup Worcestershire sauce
1 tablespoon hot sauce
5 bay leaves
½ cup minced fresh parsley
2 teaspoons dried whole thyme
2 teaspoons dried whole basil
2 teaspoons dried whole oregano
2 teaspoons rubbed sage
1 teaspoon pepper
2 pounds unpeeled medium-size fresh shrimp
1 quart Standard oysters, undrained
1 pound fresh crabmeat, drained and flaked
1 pound fish fillets, cut into 1-inch cubes
Hot cooked rice
Gumbo filé (optional)

Combine oil and flour in a cast-iron skillet; cook over medium heat 20 minutes, stirring constantly, until roux is the color of chocolate. Stir in onion, celery, and garlic; cook 10 minutes, stirring often. Transfer mixture to a Dutch oven. Add chicken broth and next 12 ingredients; simmer 2 hours, stirring occasionally.

Peel and devein shrimp. Add shrimp, oysters, crabmeat, and fish to Dutch oven; simmer 10 to 15 minutes.

Remove and discard bay leaves. Serve gumbo over hot cooked rice, and, if desired, sprinkle with filé. Yield: 7 quarts. *Sally Brown*
Pascagoula, Mississippi

A Savory Supper

One night Dyanna Byers of Savannah, Georgia, found herself with 1½ pounds of fresh shrimp and three guests to feed. The result was tasty Shrimp and Pasta, which you can serve with generous amounts of Parmesan cheese and French bread.

SHRIMP AND PASTA

1½ pounds unpeeled medium-size fresh shrimp
1 (12-ounce) package spaghetti
1 tablespoon Old Bay seasoning
1 cup broccoli flowerets
1 clove garlic, minced
3 tablespoons olive oil
1 bunch green onions, chopped
1 (4-ounce) can sliced mushrooms, drained
1 (4-ounce) can sliced water chestnuts, drained
½ cup sour cream
Grated Parmesan cheese

Peel and devein shrimp; set aside.

Cook spaghetti according to package directions, omitting salt and adding Old Bay seasoning. Drain and return to Dutch oven; keep warm.

Sauté broccoli and garlic in olive oil in a large skillet 3 to 4 minutes. Add green onions; sauté 1 minute. Add shrimp, and cook 4 minutes, stirring constantly. Stir in mushrooms and water chestnuts; cook until thoroughly heated. Stir in sour cream; heat thoroughly, but do not boil. Serve over spaghetti; sprinkle with Parmesan cheese. Yield: 6 servings.

A Soup With B.L.T. Flavors

Gary Raymond of Mandeville, Louisiana, blended the flavors of a B.L.T. sandwich in his Bacon, Lettuce, and Tomato Soup. "It's one of the quickest soup recipes I've been able to come up with that can be made relatively inexpensively, and with delicious results," he brags. For a thicker soup, Gary adds more vegetables.

BACON, LETTUCE, AND TOMATO SOUP

3 beef-flavored bouillon cubes
3 cups hot water
8 slices bacon, cut into 1-inch pieces
⅓ cup chopped onion
⅓ cup chopped celery
5 ripe tomatoes, peeled and coarsely chopped
1 tablespoon Worcestershire sauce
½ teaspoon garlic salt
½ teaspoon dried parsley flakes
¼ teaspoon dried whole thyme
¼ teaspoon pepper
Dash of hot sauce
2 cups shredded lettuce
Seasoned croutons

Dissolve bouillon cubes in hot water; set aside.

Cook bacon in a large Dutch oven until crisp; remove bacon, reserving 2 tablespoons drippings in Dutch oven. Drain bacon on paper towels. Add onion and celery to drippings, and sauté until transparent, stirring frequently; drain. Add bouillon, tomato, and next 6 ingredients; bring to a boil. Reduce heat, and simmer, uncovered, 20 to 25 minutes. Add lettuce, and cook 2 minutes or until lettuce wilts. Top with bacon and croutons. Serve immediately. Yield: 5 cups.

Pack A Tailgate Picnic

When you have tickets to a football game, don't miss a great opportunity. Instead of racing to the stadium just in time for kickoff, leave early. This menu fits the needs of busy folks going to a game, even if it takes hours to get there. You can make the recipes a day or two ahead and chill. Ice down the perishable items in a cooler; then spread out food when you're ready.

Tailgate Picnic for 10

Curried Pecans
Cold Pepper Steak   Rolls
Horseradish   Mayonnaise
Lettuce-English Pea Salad
Blue Cheese-Potato Salad

CURRIED PECANS

½ cup butter or margarine
3 tablespoons brown sugar
3 tablespoons commercial plum sauce
2 to 3 tablespoons curry powder
1½ tablespoons ground ginger
¾ teaspoon salt
1½ pounds pecan halves
1 cup raisins

Melt butter in a large skillet. Add brown sugar and next 4 ingredients; stir well. Add pecans, stirring to coat. Spoon mixture into a 15- x 10- x 1-inch jellyroll pan. Bake at 350° for 15 minutes, stirring every 5 minutes. Remove from oven; stir in raisins. Cool. Store in an airtight container. Yield: 7 cups.   *Mrs. E. W. Hanley*
Palm Harbor, Florida

COLD PEPPER STEAK

3 pounds top round steak, about 1¾ inches thick
¼ cup water
¼ cup red wine vinegar
¼ cup vegetable oil
2 tablespoons cracked pepper
2 teaspoons dried whole thyme

Score steak on each side, and place in a shallow dish. Combine remaining ingredients; pour over steak, turning to coat both sides. Cover and refrigerate 8 hours, turning occasionally.

Remove steak from marinade; discard marinade. Place steak on a lightly greased rack of a roasting pan. Broil 4 inches from heat 14 minutes; turn steak, and broil an additional 14 minutes or until meat thermometer registers 140° (rare) or 160° (medium). Place steak on a platter; cover and chill up to 2 days. Slice steak thinly; serve cold. Yield: 10 servings.
Clara B. Givens
Lubbock, Texas

LETTUCE-ENGLISH PEA SALAD

¼ cup vegetable oil
3 tablespoons red wine vinegar
3 tablespoons minced fresh parsley
1½ tablespoons sugar
½ teaspoon salt
½ teaspoon garlic salt
¼ teaspoon dried whole oregano
⅛ teaspoon pepper
½ head romaine lettuce, torn
½ head iceberg lettuce, torn
2 stalks celery, sliced diagonally
2 green onions, sliced
1 cucumber, sliced
1 (10-ounce) package frozen English peas, thawed

Combine first 8 ingredients in a jar. Cover tightly, and shake vigorously. Chill. Combine romaine lettuce and remaining ingredients in a zip-top heavy-duty plastic bag. Cover and chill at least 2 hours.

When ready to serve, combine dressing and salad mixture; toss gently. Yield: 10 servings.
Mrs. Clayton J. Turner
De Funiak Springs, Florida

BLUE CHEESE-POTATO SALAD

10 to 12 new potatoes (about 3 pounds)
¾ teaspoon salt
¼ teaspoon white pepper
2 tablespoons chopped fresh parsley
3 green onions, thinly sliced
3 hard-cooked eggs, chopped
⅓ cup slivered almonds, toasted
1 (8-ounce) carton sour cream
2 tablespoons milk
¼ teaspoon white wine vinegar
1 (4-ounce) package blue cheese, crumbled
Radicchio leaves
4 slices bacon, cooked and crumbled
Garnish: fresh parsley sprigs

Peel potatoes, and cut into ¼-inch cubes. Cook in boiling water to cover 10 minutes or until tender; drain.

Combine potatoes and next 6 ingredients; set aside. Combine sour cream, milk, vinegar, and blue cheese; stir into potato mixture. Cover and chill at least 2 hours.

When ready to serve, spoon salad into a bowl lined with radicchio leaves. Sprinkle bacon over top. Garnish, if desired. Yield: 10 servings.

Tip: *Avoid purchasing green-tinted potatoes. The term used for this condition is "light burn," which causes a bitter flavor. To keep potatoes from turning green once you have bought them, be sure to store in a cool, dark, dry place.*

You'll Cheer For These Beverages

Whether your football crowd gathers at the game or in front of the TV, count on beverages to help kindle the gridiron spirit. The collection we offer here provides a lot of options.

Early in the football season, Spiced Iced Tea makes a good warm-weather refresher, especially at a tailgate picnic. As the temperature drops for subsequent games, consider Mulled Cider; a thermos will keep it warm.

When tuning in the television or radio for a game, you might enjoy one of the spirited recipes that offers a "kick," such as the brandy-based concoction that lives up to its name— Extra-Kick Punch. Or try Whiskey Sour Punch or Cranberry-Vodka Refresher. Each of these makes at least a gallon, so there's plenty to serve guests as they munch on snacks and watch or listen to the game.

MULLED CIDER

8 whole black peppercorns
6 whole allspice
6 whole cloves
2 (3-inch) sticks cinnamon, halved
4 quarts apple cider
2 quarts cranberry juice cocktail

Combine first 4 ingredients in a tea ball or cheesecloth bag.

Combine apple cider and cranberry juice in a large Dutch oven. Add spice bag, and bring to a boil. Cover, reduce heat, and simmer 30 minutes. Remove spice bag; serve beverage hot. Yield: 1½ gallons.   *Peggy H. Amos*
Martinsville, Virginia

ZIPPY RED EYE

1 quart tomato juice
1 cup catsup
1 cup water
2 tablespoons Worcestershire sauce
2 teaspoons hot sauce
1 teaspoon salt

Combine all ingredients; stir gently. Serve beverage over ice. Yield: about 1½ quarts.   *Doris T. Ramsey*
Martinsville, Virginia

SPICED ICED TEA

3 cups boiling water
5 regular-size cinnamon-apple-flavored tea bags
1½ cups sugar
1 (6-ounce) can frozen orange juice concentrate, thawed and undiluted
1 (6-ounce) can frozen lemonade concentrate, thawed and undiluted
2 cups unsweetened pineapple juice
9 cups water
Garnish: lemon slices

Pour boiling water over tea bags; cover and steep 5 minutes. Remove tea bags, squeezing gently. Stir in sugar, orange juice, lemonade, pineapple juice, and 9 cups water. Chill. Serve over ice. Garnish each serving, if desired. Yield: 1 gallon.
Marjorie Pike
Springfield, Tennessee

WHISKEY SOUR PUNCH

3 (6-ounce) cans frozen lemonade concentrate, thawed and undiluted
4 cups bourbon
3 cups orange juice
1 (33.8-ounce) bottle club soda, chilled
4 cups ice cubes (about 28 cubes)
Garnish: orange slices

Combine first 5 ingredients in a punch bowl; stir gently. Garnish, if desired. Yield: 1 gallon.   *Martha Juvelis*
Silver Spring, Maryland

EXTRA-KICK PUNCH

2 quarts water
1 cup firmly packed brown sugar
2 cups rum
1 cup brandy
1 cup lemon juice
1 cup unsweetened pineapple juice
¼ cup peach brandy

Combine water and brown sugar, stirring until sugar dissolves. Add remaining ingredients; chill. Serve over ice. Yield: 3½ quarts.   *Mary Peterson*
Batesville, Mississippi

3 (32-ounce) bottles cranberry-apple
drink
3 to 4 cups vodka
2 cups orange juice
⅔ cup lemon juice
½ cup sugar
1 (28-ounce) bottle mineral water,
chilled

Combine first 5 ingredients, stirring
until sugar dissolves; chill. Stir in mineral water just before serving. Yield:
1¼ gallons.   *Velma Kestner*
Berwind, West Virginia

Toss Spinach Into A Salad

When you think about adding a spinach
salad to the menu, use your imagination, just as our readers did when they
created these recipes.

Spinach-Sesame Salad is simple to
prepare; the entire recipe, homemade
dressing and all, calls for only seven
ingredients.

WILTED SPINACH SALAD

1 pound fresh spinach
4 slices bacon
3 tablespoons finely chopped onion
⅓ cup white wine vinegar
⅓ cup water
1 (2-ounce) jar diced pimiento,
drained
2 tablespoons sugar

Remove stems from spinach; wash
leaves thoroughly, and pat dry. Tear

into bite-size pieces, and place in a
large salad bowl.

Cook bacon in a skillet until crisp;
drain, reserving drippings. Crumble
bacon; set aside. Sauté onion in drippings. Add vinegar and remaining ingredients; bring to a boil. Immediately
pour over spinach; toss gently. Sprinkle with bacon, and serve immediately. Yield: 4 servings.
                      Nancy Whorton
                    New Boston, Texas

ARRANGED SPINACH SALAD

1 pound fresh spinach
1 cup large-curd cottage cheese
2 hard-cooked eggs, cut into
wedges
1 cup (4 ounces) shredded
mozzarella cheese
½ cup walnut pieces, toasted
2 slices bacon, cooked and
crumbled
½ cup sour cream
2 to 4 tablespoons sugar
2 tablespoons white vinegar
2 teaspoons prepared horseradish
½ teaspoon dry mustard
¼ teaspoon salt
¼ teaspoon pepper

Remove stems from spinach; wash
leaves thoroughly, and pat dry. Tear
into bite-size pieces; arrange on individual salad plates. Arrange cottage
cheese and next 3 ingredients on top.
Sprinkle with bacon.

Combine sour cream and remaining
ingredients; stir until sugar dissolves.
Drizzle dressing over salad. Yield: 4
to 6 servings.   *Della Taylor*
                  Jonesboro, Tennessee

SPINACH SALAD WITH POPPY SEED DRESSING

1 pound fresh spinach
1 cup sliced fresh mushrooms
1 small purple onion, sliced and
separated into rings
¼ cup slivered almonds, toasted
2 hard-cooked eggs, sliced
⅓ cup vegetable oil
2 tablespoons white vinegar
1 tablespoon honey
1 tablespoon prepared mustard
2 teaspoons poppy seeds

Remove stems from spinach; wash
leaves thoroughly, and pat dry. Tear
into bite-size pieces. Combine spinach, mushrooms, onion, almonds, and
eggs in a large bowl.

Combine oil and remaining ingredients in a jar. Cover tightly, and shake
vigorously. Pour dressing over spinach mixture just before serving, and
toss. Yield: 6 to 8 servings.
                    Cathy Williams
                  Vale, North Carolina

Spinach Tip

If you've ever purchased fresh
spinach, you're no doubt familiar
with the need to rinse each leaf
very well. Particles of dirt cling
tightly to the curly leaves, and
spinach will be gritty if you don't
wash the leaves carefully. After
washing, pinch the spiny stems
from each leaf.

If this sounds too time-
consuming, many marketers now
wash, trim, and bag fresh produce, including spinach, to help
the harried consumer. Most
stores bag ready-to-use washed
and trimmed spinach in 10-ounce
packages, which are roughly
equivalent to one pound of fresh,
untrimmed spinach.

SPINACH-SESAME SALAD

1 pound fresh spinach
½ head iceberg lettuce, torn
1 green onion, sliced
⅓ cup olive oil
3 tablespoons lemon juice
1 tablespoon honey
1 tablespoon sesame seeds, toasted

Remove stems from spinach; wash leaves thoroughly, and pat dry. Tear into bite-size pieces.

Combine spinach, torn lettuce, and sliced green onion in a large bowl, and set aside.

Combine olive oil, lemon juice, and honey in a jar; cover tightly, and shake vigorously.

Pour dressing over salad just before serving, and toss gently. Sprinkle salad with toasted sesame seeds. Yield: 6 to 8 servings.

Barbara Beacom
Kernersville, North Carolina

EGGPLANT FRITTERS

1 large eggplant (about 1½ pounds)
1½ to 1¾ cups fine, dry breadcrumbs
2 eggs, slightly beaten
½ cup sliced green onions
2 tablespoons minced fresh parsley
1 teaspoon Greek seasoning
¼ teaspoon pepper
⅛ teaspoon garlic powder
Vegetable oil

Peel eggplant, and cut into 1-inch cubes; cook in a small amount of boiling water 10 minutes or until tender. Drain well, and mash. Add 1½ cups breadcrumbs and next 6 ingredients. Add more breadcrumbs if mixture is too soft. Shape mixture into 16 balls.

Pour oil to a depth of 2 to 3 inches into a Dutch oven; heat to 375°. Fry fritters until golden brown; drain on paper towels. Serve fritters with marinara sauce or salsa, if desired. Yield: 16 fritters.

SAUSAGE-STUFFED EGGPLANT

2 medium eggplants (about 1¼ pounds each)
1 pound Italian sausage
1 tablespoon vegetable oil
¾ cup chopped carrots
1 (4-ounce) can sliced mushrooms, drained
½ cup process cheese spread

Cut eggplants in half lengthwise. Remove pulp, leaving a ¼-inch shell; chop pulp. Set both aside.

Remove casings from sausage; brown sausage in a large skillet, stirring to crumble. Drain well, and set sausage aside. Wipe skillet clean with paper towels.

Heat vegetable oil in skillet; add eggplant pulp and carrot, and sauté until tender. Stir in sausage, mushrooms, and cheese. Place eggplant shells in a 12- x 8- x 2-inch baking dish; spoon sausage mixture into shells. Bake at 375° for 15 to 20 minutes. Yield: 4 servings.

Nora Henshaw
Okemah, Oklahoma

Another Look At Eggplant

Maybe eggplant is not for everyone. But aficionados of the usually purple-skinned staple of many Middle Eastern diets can thank Thomas Jefferson for introducing it to our country.

He was a little more successful in selling Americans on familiar European eggplant concoctions, rather than exotic Lebanese and Greek dishes, which also use the vegetable. That explains the ever-popular use of tomato sauce and mozzarella cheese in Eggplant Italiano. You might lure reluctant, first-time eggplant tasters into the experience with Eggplant Fritters. That's as close to Southern cooking as this vegetable gets.

If you're feeling really adventuresome, scour specialty grocery stores or produce stands for white eggplant.

EGGPLANT STACKS

1 small eggplant (about ¾ pound)
1 (2.8-ounce) jar pesto basil sauce or ⅓ cup pesto basil sauce
2 medium tomatoes, peeled and cut into ¼-inch-thick slices
¼ cup freshly grated Parmesan cheese
1 tablespoon chopped fresh parsley (optional)

Peel eggplant, and cut into ½-inch slices. Place in a single layer in a lightly greased 13- x 9- x 2-inch baking dish. Cover and bake at 425° for 10 minutes; remove from oven. Spread half of pesto sauce on eggplant slices; top with tomato slices. Spread remaining pesto on tomato; sprinkle with Parmesan cheese. Cover and bake an additional 10 minutes. Sprinkle with parsley, if desired. Yield: 6 servings.

Nancy Walton
Birmingham, Alabama

Fall Vegetables

■ Prices of fresh vegetables and fruit change with the seasons. It is best to buy seasonal fresh foods when they are most plentiful and at peak quality.

■ When fresh pumpkin is plentiful, substitute 2 cups mashed, cooked pumpkin for one 16-ounce can.

■ Never store uncooked fresh sweet potatoes in the refrigerator as the coolness will cause them to lose their flavor and turn black.

EGGPLANT ITALIANO

1 medium eggplant (about 1¼ pounds)
¾ cup wheat germ
½ cup grated Parmesan cheese
1 teaspoon dried parsley flakes
¾ teaspoon poppy seeds
¾ teaspoon paprika
½ teaspoon pepper
½ cup buttermilk
1 (8-ounce) can no-salt-added tomato sauce
1½ teaspoons fresh or ½ teaspoon dried whole basil
½ teaspoon dried whole oregano
⅛ teaspoon garlic powder
¼ cup (2 ounces) shredded mozzarella cheese
Garnish: fresh basil sprigs

Peel eggplant, and cut into ½-inch slices; set aside.

Combine wheat germ, Parmesan cheese, parsley flakes, poppy seeds, paprika, and pepper in a shallow dish.

Dip eggplant in buttermilk, and dredge in wheat germ mixture. Place eggplant on an aluminum foil-lined baking sheet. Bake at 350° for 25 minutes or until crisp and golden.

Combine tomato sauce, 1½ teaspoons fresh basil, oregano, and garlic powder; spoon on top of eggplant. Sprinkle with mozzarella cheese, and bake an additional 5 minutes or until cheese melts. Place eggplant on a serving dish, and garnish with fresh basil sprigs, if desired. Yield: 6 servings.
Sandy Brauer
St. Louis, Missouri

Tip: *Eggplant flesh darkens rapidly when cut, so don't peel until just before cooking. Remember to rub cut surfaces with lemon or lime juice to prevent darkening.*

Dill—An Herb For All Reasons

Dill, a member of the parsley family, originated in the Mediterranean. The meaning of dill comes from Nordic words, which mean "lull" or "dull." Although its flavor is lively and fresh, the definition refers to dill's early medicinal uses as a means of inducing sleep and soothing indigestion.

Dill comes in three forms. **Fresh dillweed** is the airy foliage of the dill plant and is used in these recipes. The plant also bears **dillseeds,** which boast a pungent, bitter flavor. You can harvest them yourself or buy them at the supermarket. The same is true for **dried dillweed.** One teaspoon of dried dillweed may be substituted for 1 tablespoon of fresh. At some supermarkets you can find bundles of fresh dillweed in the produce section.

■ When Frances B. Davis sent us the recipe for **Turnip-and-Carrot Salad,** she noted that this recipe is a good way to get acquainted with turnips as well as fresh dillweed.

TURNIP-AND-CARROT SALAD

¼ cup olive oil
3 tablespoons lemon juice
2 tablespoons chopped fresh dillweed
1 tablespoon sugar
⅛ teaspoon pepper
1 large turnip, peeled and cut into julienne strips
4 carrots, diagonally sliced
Lettuce leaves
Garnish: fresh dillweed

Combine first 5 ingredients in a bowl; add turnip and carrots, tossing to coat. Chill 30 minutes. Serve on lettuce leaves. Garnish, if desired. Yield: 4 to 6 servings. *Frances B. Davis*
Abilene, Texas

■ **Dilled Chicken Salad,** an excellent luncheon choice, serves eight. Fresh dillweed blended with cream cheese and sour cream lend a rich flavor to this salad favorite.

DILLED CHICKEN SALAD

8 chicken breast halves, skinned
1 teaspoon salt
1 cup chopped celery
3 hard-cooked eggs, chopped
1 (3-ounce) package cream cheese, softened
½ cup mayonnaise or salad dressing
¼ cup sour cream
1½ tablespoons chopped fresh dillweed
1 teaspoon dry mustard
¼ teaspoon salt
⅛ teaspoon pepper
Lettuce leaves
Slices of raw carrot and yellow squash

Combine chicken and 1 teaspoon salt in a Dutch oven; add water to cover. Bring to a boil; cover, reduce heat, and simmer 45 minutes or until chicken is tender.

Drain chicken, reserving broth for other uses. Bone chicken, and cut into bite-size pieces; combine chicken, chopped celery, and eggs in a large bowl, and set aside.

Combine cream cheese and next 6 ingredients in a medium bowl. Add to chicken mixture, and toss well. Cover and chill thoroughly. Serve salad on lettuce leaves with sliced carrot and squash. Yield: 8 servings.
Sharon McClatchey
Muskogee, Oklahoma

■ **Creamy Dill Dressing** calls for white pepper, a mild-flavored member of the ground pepper family. You can find white pepper on the spice rack at the supermarket.

CREAMY DILL DRESSING

1 cup mayonnaise or salad dressing
1 (8-ounce) carton sour cream
¼ cup milk
1½ tablespoons olive oil
1 tablespoon minced fresh dillweed
1 tablespoon dill pickle juice
2 teaspoons paprika (optional)
¼ teaspoon white pepper
⅛ teaspoon garlic powder
⅛ teaspoon salt

Combine mayonnaise and sour cream; gradually stir in milk, mixing well. Stir in remaining ingredients; cover and chill thoroughly. Serve with salad greens. Yield: 2 cups.

Note: Omit milk from recipe to serve as a creamy dip for vegetables.
Daniel Garavelli
Memphis, Tennessee

Jazz Up The Menu With Muffins

Tired of the "same old song" at lunch and supper? Defeat the mealtime blues with these jazzy muffins; their flavor is definitely something to sing about. Pair Caraway-Cheese Muffins with soups, fruit, or chicken salad. Apple-Carrot Muffins glean additional flavor from raisins and coconut. Try them with ham and vegetables at supper, and reheat for breakfast.

Growing Fresh Dillweed

One way to ensure a fresh supply of dillweed is to grow it at home. After flowering, you'll have dillseeds as well.

Dill is an independent sort, not suited to growing in pots. If you buy a transplant and set it out, it will often flower, set seeds, and die very quickly. For the best results, sow seeds directly in the garden. Snip the foliage with scissors rather than a knife to ready it for the kitchen. Just don't trim more than half of the plant's foliage at once. All dill tastes good, but if you're a real connoisseur, try growing Tetra-Dill.

APPLE-CARROT MUFFINS

2 cups all-purpose flour
2 teaspoons baking soda
½ teaspoon salt
2 teaspoons ground cinnamon
1 cup sugar
2 cups grated carrots
1 large tart green apple, peeled, cored, and grated
½ cup raisins
½ cup sliced almonds
½ cup flaked coconut
3 eggs, slightly beaten
⅔ cup vegetable oil
2 teaspoons vanilla extract

Combine first 5 ingredients in a large bowl; stir in carrot, apple, raisins, almonds, and coconut. Make a well in center of mixture. Combine eggs, oil, and vanilla; add to dry ingredients, stirring just until moistened. Spoon into greased muffin pans, filling two-thirds full. Bake at 350° for 20 minutes. Remove muffins from pans. Yield: 2 dozen.
Linda Magers
Clemmons, North Carolina

CARAWAY-CHEESE MUFFINS

1½ cups all-purpose flour
1 tablespoon baking powder
½ teaspoon salt
3 tablespoons sugar
1 cup (4 ounces) shredded Cheddar cheese
1 cup wheat bran cereal
1 to 2 teaspoons caraway seeds
1 egg, beaten
¾ cup milk
2 tablespoons vegetable oil

Combine first 7 ingredients in a large bowl; make a well in center of mixture. Combine egg, milk, and oil; add to dry ingredients, stirring just until moistened. Spoon into greased muffin pans, filling about two-thirds full. Bake at 400° for 20 minutes. Remove from pans immediately. Yield: 1 dozen.
Evelyn Weisman
Corpus Christi, Texas

Win With Snack Cakes

From Little League to the majors, hungry players and fans will snatch squares of these cakes repeatedly, and with good reason. They taste great, offer plenty of sweetness, and travel well in a lunchbox.

KEY LIME CAKE

1 (18.25-ounce) package lemon
  supreme cake mix
1 (3.4-ounce) package lemon
  instant pudding mix
4 eggs
½ cup water
½ cup Key lime juice
½ cup vegetable oil
2 cups sifted powdered
  sugar
¼ cup Key lime juice

Combine first 6 ingredients; beat 2 minutes at medium speed of an electric mixer. Pour batter into a greased and floured 13- x 9- x 2-inch pan. Bake at 350° for 35 minutes or until a wooden pick inserted in center comes out clean. Let cake cool in pan on a wire rack.

Combine powdered sugar and ¼ cup Key lime juice; drizzle over cake. Cut into squares. Yield: 15 to 18 servings.   *Thelma Peedin*
Newport News, Virginia

Tip: *For a successful cake, measure all the ingredients accurately, follow the recipe without making any substitutions, and use the pan sizes recommended in the recipe.*

HONEY BUN CAKE

1 (18.25-ounce) package yellow
  cake mix with pudding
4 eggs
⅔ cup vegetable oil
⅓ cup water
1 (8-ounce) carton sour cream
½ cup firmly packed
  brown sugar
1 teaspoon ground cinnamon
⅔ cup chopped pecans
Glaze (recipe follows)

Combine first 5 ingredients in a mixing bowl; beat at medium speed of an electric mixer until smooth. Set aside.

Combine brown sugar, cinnamon, and pecans; set aside.

Pour half of batter into a greased and floured 13- x 9- x 2-inch baking pan. Sprinkle half of sugar mixture over batter. Repeat procedure. Gently swirl batter with a knife.

Bake at 350° for 30 to 35 minutes or until a wooden pick inserted in center comes out clean. Remove from oven. Drizzle glaze over cake, and cool. Cut into squares. Yield: 15 to 18 servings.

Glaze

1 cup sifted powdered sugar
2 tablespoons milk
½ teaspoon vanilla extract

Combine all ingredients; beat at medium speed of an electric mixer until smooth. Yield: ⅓ cup.   *Marie Davis*
Charlotte, North Carolina

Party-Pretty Dessert

Whether it's a couple or a crowd, Marie Bowers is always ready for the frequent guests in her Joaquin, Texas, home. Her favorite make-ahead dessert for planned parties is Ice Cream Party Squares, and she keeps a batch on hand for drop-in visitors.

ICE CREAM PARTY SQUARES

2½ cups vanilla wafer crumbs,
  divided
4 (1-ounce) squares unsweetened
  chocolate
1⅓ cups butter or margarine
3 cups sifted powdered sugar
1 cup chopped pecans, toasted
¼ cup water
2 teaspoons vanilla extract
½ gallon butter pecan ice cream
  (rectangular carton)
Garnishes: chocolate shavings,
  chocolate-dipped pecan halves

Spread 1 cup vanilla wafer crumbs in bottom of a buttered 13- x 9- x 2-inch dish; set aside.

Combine 4 ounces unsweetened chocolate and butter in a saucepan; cook over low heat until chocolate melts. Remove from heat. Add powdered sugar, chopped pecans, water, and vanilla, stirring until blended. Stir in remaining 1½ cups vanilla wafer crumbs. Spread mixture over crumbs in dish, and freeze at least 3 hours.

Cut ice cream crosswise into ½-inch slices; arrange over chocolate layer, carefully spreading top of ice cream until smooth. Cover and freeze until firm.

Let dessert stand at room temperature 5 minutes before serving. Garnish, if desired. Yield: 12 to 15 servings.

OCTOBER

Pumpkins piled high in roadside stands and supermarkets

signal the coming of fall in the South. Other seasonal

vegetables include carrots, parsnips, rutabagas, turnips, sweet

potatoes—all root vegetables packed with nutrition. As you

turn the pages of this chapter you'll find delicious new ways of

preparing these fall favorites.

Rice Across Our Region

You've probably never given it much thought, but behind every bag of rice you've tossed into your grocery basket is a story of the South, richly textured with heritage and culture. Perhaps those who tell it best are the ones who created the tale, the farmers and cooks of our region's major rice-growing states—Arkansas, Louisiana, Mississippi, and Texas.

Rice farmers across the region may grow virtually the same product, but the dishes made with it are as different as the Southerners who cook them. The mild-tasting grain serves as a canvas for a vivid painting of the flavors of our varied cultures.

You know you're in South Louisiana when you taste spicy jambalayas. Cross the western border into Texas, and you find Tex-Mex cuisine and to the east, you're in Mississippi's catfish country. In Arkansas, rice is a partner for wild game. These foods are a result of the lifestyles, imagination, and ingredients available in different areas. So browse through these recipes, and let them tell you a story.

■ Sybil Arant and her husband, Turner, grow rice and raise catfish in the Mississippi Delta, and she combines the two in her Catfish Gumbo. Okra and tomatoes hint at the Creole influence borrowed from the neighboring state of Louisiana.

CATFISH GUMBO
(pictured on page 226)

1 cup chopped green pepper
1 cup chopped celery
1 cup chopped onion
2 cloves garlic, minced
¼ cup vegetable oil
2 (14½-ounce) cans ready-to-serve beef broth
1 (16-ounce) can tomatoes, undrained and chopped
1 teaspoon salt
½ teaspoon dried whole oregano
½ teaspoon dried whole thyme
½ teaspoon red pepper
1 bay leaf
2 pounds farm-raised catfish fillets
1 (10-ounce) package frozen sliced okra, thawed
Hot cooked rice

Sauté green pepper, celery, onion, and garlic in hot oil in a Dutch oven until tender. Stir in broth and next 6 ingredients; bring to a boil. Cover, reduce heat, and simmer 30 minutes, stirring occasionally.

Cut catfish into 1-inch pieces; add to gumbo, and simmer 10 minutes. Stir in okra; cook an additional 5 minutes. Remove bay leaf. Serve over rice. Yield: about 3½ quarts.

Sybil Arant
Sunflower, Mississippi

■ The translation—"gift with the rice"—is a lot easier to pronounce than the word itself—"jambalaya" (JAM-buh-LIE-yuh). However you say it, Ricky Breaux indeed has a gift with the rice. He won the 1990 World Champion Jambalaya Cook contest at the annual festival in Gonzales, Louisiana. Ricky learned the skill from a master; his father, Charles "Black" Breaux, earned the title in 1984.

CHICKEN-AND-SAUSAGE JAMBALAYA

1 (2½- to 3-pound) broiler-fryer, cut up
¾ pound smoked sausage, cut into ½-inch slices
¼ cup vegetable oil
2½ cups chopped onion (about 1 pound)
½ cup chopped green pepper
2 cloves garlic, minced
2 green onions, chopped
5 cups water
1 pound long-grain rice, uncooked
1 teaspoon salt
¼ to ½ teaspoon black pepper
¼ to ½ teaspoon red pepper

Cook chicken and sausage in oil in a Dutch oven until chicken is golden brown; remove chicken and sausage. Drain, reserving 2 tablespoons drippings in Dutch oven.

Sauté 2½ cups chopped onion and next 3 ingredients in drippings. Add water, rice, salt, peppers, chicken, and sausage; bring to a boil. Cover, reduce heat, and simmer 20 minutes or until rice is tender and water is absorbed. Let stand 5 minutes before serving. Yield: 6 servings.

Ricky J. Breaux
Saint Amant, Louisiana

■ From Louisiana, Craig Shaddock and her husband, Bill, sell family-grown rice to the public nationwide. The rice they grow is an aromatic type, also called "popcorn" rice because of the wonderful way it smells while cooking. You'll love its nutty flavor in Mardi Gras Rice, and the purple, green, and yellow colors of the Bayou State celebration.

MARDI GRAS RICE
(pictured on page 227)

8 cups cooked rice
1 cup frozen English peas, thawed
1 cup frozen corn, cooked and drained
½ head red cabbage, shredded
⅓ cup diced green pepper
3 tablespoons sliced green onions
3 tablespoons chopped fresh parsley
1 cup mayonnaise or salad dressing
1 teaspoon Creole seasoning
1 teaspoon curry powder
Lettuce leaves

Combine first 7 ingredients in a large bowl. Set aside. Combine mayonnaise, Creole seasoning, and curry powder; add to rice mixture, tossing gently. Chill. Serve on lettuce leaves. Yield: 16 servings.   *Craig Shaddock*
Lake Charles, Louisiana

■ More than 30 years ago, **Frankie Meripol** learned to make Mexican Rice with the help of her Mexican neighbor, Felix Cuellar. This trace of Felix's heritage has become a Meripol family tradition as Frankie still enjoys making the favorite in her Dallas kitchen today.

MEXICAN RICE
(pictured on page 226)

1 (10¾-ounce) can condensed chicken broth, undiluted
1 tablespoon vegetable oil
1 cup long-grain rice, uncooked
1 cup chopped cooked chicken
1 medium tomato, peeled, seeded, and chopped
1 clove garlic, minced
2 jalapeño peppers, seeded and minced
½ teaspoon ground cumin
Garnish: jalapeño peppers

Dilute broth according to label directions; set aside. Heat oil in a large skillet. Add rice; cook, stirring constantly, until golden brown.

Stir in broth, chicken, and next 4 ingredients; bring mixture to a boil. Cover, reduce heat, and simmer 25 to 30 minutes or until liquid is absorbed. Garnish with jalapeño peppers, if desired. Yield: 4 to 6 servings.
Frankie Meripol
Dallas, Texas

■ **Steve** and **Ann Mathis** share their love of duck hunting with other Arkansas wild game fans. An invitation to their place in Tollville often includes a hunt guided by Steve. Ann will cook your fresh duck and serve it with her favorite, Rice Dressing.

RICE DRESSING
(pictured on page 227)

1 (6-ounce) package long-grain and wild rice mix
¾ pound bulk pork sausage
1 tablespoon vegetable oil
1 tablespoon all-purpose flour
1 onion, chopped
2 stalks celery, chopped
½ green pepper, chopped
3 green onions, sliced
2 cloves garlic, minced
1 teaspoon Worcestershire sauce
⅛ teaspoon hot sauce
1 chicken-flavored bouillon cube
1 (4-ounce) can sliced mushrooms, undrained
Garnishes: pimiento rose, celery leaves

Cook rice according to package directions. Set aside.

Brown sausage in a Dutch oven, stirring to crumble. Drain; set aside.

Combine oil and flour in Dutch oven; cook over medium heat, stirring constantly, until caramel colored. Stir in chopped onion and next 7 ingredients. Drain mushrooms, reserving liquid. Add water to mushroom liquid to equal 1½ cups. Add mushrooms and

1½ cups liquid to Dutch oven. Bring to a boil; cover, reduce heat, and simmer 1 hour. Stir in rice and sausage; heat thoroughly. Garnish, if desired. Yield: 6 servings.   *Ann Mathis*
Tollville, Arkansas

■ If you know **Fred** and **LaVerne Seidenstricker** in Hazen, Arkansas, then you know that their kitchen is always open. "We're not gonna tell you there's an extra pea in the pot. We'll tell you there's an extra grain of rice in the pot," Fred quips. Try his favorite, LaVerne's Apple Rice Pudding.

APPLE RICE PUDDING

2 eggs
½ cup sugar
½ cup sour cream
1 cup milk
¼ teaspoon salt
2½ cups cooked short-grain rice
1 cooking apple, peeled, cored, and chopped
1 cup (4 ounces) shredded Cheddar cheese
⅓ cup raisins
¼ cup firmly packed brown sugar
1 tablespoon all-purpose flour
½ teaspoon ground cinnamon
1 tablespoon butter or margarine, melted

Combine first 5 ingredients in a bowl; stir in rice, apple, cheese, and raisins. Spoon mixture into a lightly greased 2-quart baking dish. Combine brown sugar and remaining ingredients; sprinkle over rice mixture. Bake, uncovered, at 350° for 45 minutes. Yield: 8 servings.

LaVerne Seidenstricker
Hazen, Arkansas

QUICK!

Entrées For Company

Many readers tell us they'd entertain more if it wasn't such an undertaking. Well, it's not anymore.

Whether you lean toward something casual like Fiery Cajun Shrimp or a fancy spread that features Veal Marsala, each of these entrées can be prepared in 30 minutes or less.

For each recipe, we've given ideas for completing the menu with side dishes that are so simple you probably won't even need a recipe. An easy green salad is almost always appropriate. And don't forget about frozen vegetables like corn on the cob; it's tasty and takes just minutes to prepare in the microwave. As far as dessert goes—no one will know that you picked up a cheesecake from the deli unless you tell them.

■ Add a green salad and corn on the cob to Fiery Cajun Shrimp for a well-rounded menu. Serve with plenty of French bread for dipping in the spicy butter sauce.

FIERY CAJUN SHRIMP

1 cup butter, melted
1 cup margarine, melted
½ cup Worcestershire sauce
¼ cup lemon juice
¼ cup ground pepper
2 teaspoons hot sauce
2 teaspoons salt
4 cloves garlic, minced
5 pounds unpeeled medium-size
   fresh shrimp
2 lemons, thinly sliced
French bread

Combine first 8 ingredients; pour half of mixture into a large ceramic heatproof dish. Layer shrimp and lemon slices in sauce; pour remaining sauce over shrimp and lemon. Bake, uncovered, at 400° for 20 minutes or until shrimp are pink, stirring twice. Drain sauce, and serve with shrimp and French bread. Yield: 6 to 8 servings.
Betty McLendon
Pensacola, Florida

■ Sauté Mahimahi in Grape Sauce for a simple but elegant dinner. Rice, buttered carrots, and a spinach salad will complete the menu nicely.

MAHIMAHI IN GRAPE SAUCE

1 pound mahimahi fillets
⅓ cup all-purpose flour
⅛ teaspoon salt
⅛ teaspoon pepper
¼ cup butter or margarine
½ cup dry vermouth
1 cup seedless grapes
Hot cooked rice

Cut fillets as necessary to make 4 serving pieces. Combine flour, salt, and pepper; dredge pieces of fish in flour mixture.

Melt butter in a large skillet. Add fish; cook about 5 minutes on each side or until fish is almost done. Add vermouth and grapes; cover and simmer 3 minutes. Serve with rice. Yield: 4 servings.
Adele Burkas
Tarpon Springs, Florida

■ With only four ingredients, Italian Sausage Dinner is a snap to put together for a casual meal. Evelyn Mosley serves it with a green salad, creamed potatoes, and French bread.

ITALIAN SAUSAGE DINNER

1 pound Italian link sausage
2 tablespoons water
1 green pepper, cut into strips
2 medium onions, cut into wedges

Combine sausage and water in a skillet; cover and cook over low heat 15 minutes, stirring occasionally. Drain drippings from skillet. Add pepper and onion; cover and cook 4 to 5 minutes or until vegetables are tender, stirring often. Yield: 4 servings.
Evelyn Mosley
Germantown, Tennessee

■ The flavor of Veal Marsala is so sensational that you'll hardly believe it's so easy to prepare. In addition to serving it with vermicelli, offer a broiled tomato and/or your favorite steamed green vegetable.

VEAL MARSALA

¾ cup all-purpose flour
½ teaspoon salt
⅛ teaspoon freshly ground pepper
1¼ pounds thin veal cutlets
½ cup butter or margarine,
   melted
1¼ cups Marsala wine (see note)
Hot cooked vermicelli

Combine first 3 ingredients. Dredge veal in flour mixture; sauté in butter 1 to 2 minutes on each side. Place veal on a serving platter; keep warm. Add wine to skillet, scraping bottom of skillet to loosen browned particles. Cook until bubbly; pour over veal. Serve with vermicelli. Yield: 4 to 6 servings.

Note: 1 cup Chablis or other dry white wine plus ¼ cup brandy may be substituted for Marsala wine, if desired.
Dianna Rudolph
Houston, Texas

Dig Deep For Nutrition

It's high time that root vegetables were raised to their rightful place in healthy eating. Pound for pound, root vegetables have more fiber and nutrients than most green vegetables and are virtually fat and cholesterol free. They are literally buried treasures.

Roots and tubers are nature's storehouses of nutrients and energy for growing stems and leaves. Popular edible roots and tubers include carrots, parsnips, rutabagas, celeriac, turnips, potatoes, sweet potatoes, and jicama. They're sweetest when small or medium size.

If these vegetables haven't been on your menu for a while, now's the time to try some new recipes. Parsnips, one of the lesser known root vegetables, look like big, white carrots and have a sweet, nutty flavor. In Glazed Parsnips, brown sugar, orange juice, and pineapple enhance their natural sweetness. Before cooking, trim both ends and scrape with a vegetable peeler just as you would a carrot.

And knobby, brown celeriac (or celery root) is showing up in supermarkets throughout the South. Its strong celery flavor and dense texture blend well with other vegetables. When combined with carrot strips in Celeriac and Carrots, it makes a colorful and great-tasting side dish.

ROSEMARY CARROTS

2¼ cups thinly sliced carrots
½ cup water
1 tablespoon brown sugar
1 tablespoon chopped chives
1 teaspoon chicken-flavored bouillon granules
½ teaspoon fresh rosemary
⅛ teaspoon pepper

Combine carrots and water in a saucepan; bring to a boil. Cover, reduce heat, and simmer 7 to 8 minutes or until carrots are crisp-tender. Drain, reserving 2 tablespoons liquid.

Combine reserved liquid, brown sugar, and remaining ingredients in a saucepan. Bring mixture to a boil over medium heat, stirring constantly; pour over carrots, and toss. Yield: 4 servings (45 calories per ½-cup serving).

□ *1.1 grams protein, 0.2 gram fat, 10.6 grams carbohydrate, 0 milligrams cholesterol, 260 milligrams sodium, and 24 milligrams calcium.*
Mrs. Edwin J. Mazoch
Corpus Christi, Texas

CELERIAC AND CARROTS

2 cups julienne-sliced celeriac
1 cup julienne-sliced carrots
½ cup ready-to-serve, no-salt-added chicken broth
1 teaspoon reduced-calorie margarine
¼ teaspoon chopped fresh dillweed

Combine all ingredients in a skillet; bring to a boil. Cover, reduce heat; simmer 3 to 5 minutes. Yield: 5 servings (42 calories per ½-cup serving).

□ *1.3 grams protein, 0.7 gram fat, 8.7 grams carbohydrate, 0 milligrams cholesterol, 80 milligrams sodium, and 35 milligrams calcium.*

ORANGE BEETS

1 pound fresh beets
2 teaspoons cornstarch
½ teaspoon ground ginger
½ teaspoon ground nutmeg
¾ cup orange juice
1 (11-ounce) can mandarin oranges, drained

Leave root and 1 inch of stem on beets; scrub with a vegetable brush. Place beets in a saucepan; add water to cover. Bring to a boil; cover, reduce heat, and simmer 30 to 35 minutes or until tender. Drain. Pour cold water over beets, and drain again. Trim off roots and stems, and rub off skins; slice beets, and set aside.

Combine cornstarch and next 3 ingredients in a medium saucepan; bring to a boil, and cook 1 minute, stirring constantly. Add sliced beets and mandarin oranges to sauce; cook until thoroughly heated. Yield: 6 servings (56 calories per ½-cup serving).

□ *1.1 grams protein, 0.4 gram fat, 13.1 grams carbohydrate, 0 milligrams cholesterol, 31 milligrams sodium, 15 milligrams calcium.*   *Barbara Nibling*
San Angelo, Texas

BRAISED TURNIPS

5 cups julienne-cut turnips
1 tablespoon reduced-calorie margarine
1 tablespoon sugar
⅛ teaspoon salt
⅓ cup ready-to-serve, no-salt-added chicken broth
3 tablespoons chopped fresh parsley
1 tablespoon lemon juice

Combine first 4 ingredients in a nonstick skillet; sauté over low heat 8 to 10 minutes, stirring occasionally. Stir in broth, parsley, and lemon juice; cover and cook over low heat 5 to 7 minutes or until tender. Yield: 7 servings (43 calories per ½-cup serving).

□ *0.8 gram protein, 1.1 grams fat, 8 grams carbohydrate, 0 milligrams cholesterol, 121 milligrams sodium, 30 milligrams calcium.*
Frances B. Davis
Abilene, Texas

HONEY RUTABAGA

½ cup dry white wine
1 tablespoon brown sugar
2 tablespoons honey
2 teaspoons reduced-calorie
  margarine
4 cups cubed, uncooked rutabaga

Combine all ingredients in a large saucepan. Bring to a boil; cover, reduce heat, and simmer 40 to 45 minutes. Yield: 5 servings (92 calories per ¾-cup serving).

□ *1.4 grams protein, 1.2 grams fat, 20.6 grams carbohydrate, 0 milligrams cholesterol, 40 milligrams sodium, and 57 milligrams calcium.*

Rublelene Singleton
Scotts Hill, Tennessee

HERBED POTATOES

Vegetable cooking spray
4 medium-size baking potatoes, cut
  into ¼-inch slices (1½ pounds)
2 medium-size white onions, cut
  into ¼-inch slices (12 ounces)
5 plum tomatoes, sliced (1 pound)
½ teaspoon salt
1 teaspoon dried whole thyme
¾ teaspoon dried rosemary,
  crushed
1 tablespoon olive oil
2 tablespoons chopped fresh parsley

Coat a 12- x 8- x 2-inch baking dish with cooking spray. Layer half each of potatoes, onions, and tomatoes in dish; sprinkle with half each of salt, thyme, and rosemary. Repeat layers, and drizzle evenly with olive oil. Cover and bake at 425° for 35 to 40 minutes or until tender. Sprinkle with parsley. Yield: 8 servings (105 calories per ¾-cup serving).

□ *2.9 grams protein, 2.1 grams fat, 19.9 grams carbohydrate, 0 milligrams cholesterol, 158 milligrams sodium, 32 milligrams calcium.* *Virginia Cooper*
Scottsboro, Alabama

GLAZED PARSNIPS

1 pound parsnips
Vegetable cooking spray
1 (8-ounce) can crushed pineapple
  in juice, undrained
½ cup orange juice
2 tablespoons brown sugar
½ teaspoon grated orange rind

Scrape parsnips, and cut into 2-inch pieces; cut each piece into 4 strips. Cook parsnips in boiling water to cover, 10 minutes or until tender; drain. Place in a 10- x 6- x 2-inch baking dish coated with cooking spray.

Combine pineapple and remaining ingredients; pour over parsnips. Bake at 350° for 30 minutes, basting occasionally. Yield: 4 servings (150 calories per ½-cup serving).

□ *1.8 grams protein, 0.4 gram fat, 37.1 grams carbohydrate, 0 milligrams cholesterol, 14 milligrams sodium, 57 milligrams calcium.* *Hilda Marshall*
Front Royal, Virginia

LIGHT MENU

Serve A Healthy Down-Home Menu

Home cooking. Those two words conjure up memories of a favorite menu for everyone. No matter how many gourmet dinners you eat, there's still that occasional longing for a good home-cooked meal.

We've put together a menu that will satisfy a yearning for home cooking and still be healthy. Baked in the oven so it doesn't have all the fat, Chicken Croquettes has a crispy outside similar to deep-fried croquettes. And the low-fat Mushroom Sauce served with the croquettes is almost like gravy.

To top off the meal serve New-Fashioned Apple Cobbler, which has only 169 calories per serving. With apples now at their peak, it's the perfect time to make this dessert.

Family Dinner for 6
Chicken Croquettes and
Mushroom Sauce
Green Beans and Potatoes
Green salad with
oil-free dressing
New-Fashioned Apple Cobbler

CHICKEN CROQUETTES AND MUSHROOM SAUCE

6 (4-ounce) skinned, boned chicken
  breast halves
1 stalk celery, cut into 1-inch
  pieces
1 medium carrot, cut into 1-inch
  pieces
1 small onion, cut into ½-inch
  slices
2 cups water
½ cup diced celery
½ cup diced onion
Vegetable cooking spray
½ cup egg substitute
½ teaspoon salt
½ teaspoon pepper
2 tablespoons cornstarch
½ cup skim milk
½ cup reduced-sodium cracker
  crumbs
¼ teaspoon paprika
Mushroom Sauce

Combine first 5 ingredients in a large saucepan; bring to a boil. Cover, reduce heat, and cook 15 minutes or until chicken is tender. Remove chicken from broth; strain broth, reserving 1½ cups. Set aside.

Position knife blade in food processor bowl. Place chicken in processor bowl; process 45 seconds or until chicken is finely chopped, but not smooth. Set aside.

Sauté ½ cup diced celery and ½ cup diced onion in a large skillet coated with cooking spray. Remove from heat. Stir in chicken, egg substitute, salt, and pepper.

Combine cornstarch, milk, and ½ cup reserved broth in a small saucepan. Cook over medium heat, stirring constantly, until mixture begins to boil; boil 1 minute, stirring constantly. Stir sauce into chicken mixture; shape into 6 croquettes. Combine cracker crumbs and paprika; roll croquettes in crumbs, and place on a baking sheet coated with cooking spray. Bake at 375° for 30 minutes or until croquettes are thoroughly heated. Serve with Mushroom Sauce. Yield: 6 servings (228 calories per croquette with ¼ cup Mushroom Sauce).

□ 30.5 grams protein, 4.8 grams fat, 14 grams carbohydrate, 66 milligrams cholesterol, 445 milligrams sodium, and 66 milligrams calcium.

Mushroom Sauce

2 cups sliced fresh mushrooms
2 tablespoons reduced-calorie margarine, melted
2 tablespoons all-purpose flour
1 cup reserved chicken broth
⅛ teaspoon salt
¼ teaspoon pepper

Sauté mushrooms in margarine in a saucepan over medium heat. Add flour, stirring until smooth. Cook 1 minute, stirring constantly. Gradually stir in chicken broth; cook over medium heat, stirring constantly, until thickened and bubbly. Stir in salt and pepper. Yield: 1½ cups (9 calories per tablespoon).

□ 0.2 gram protein, 0.6 gram fat, 0.7 gram carbohydrate, 0 milligrams cholesterol, 22 milligrams sodium, and 1 milligram calcium.

GREEN BEANS AND POTATOES

4 medium-size red potatoes, cut into eighths
2 (16-ounce) cans no-salt-added green beans, drained
1 medium onion, sliced and separated into rings
2 teaspoons beef-flavored bouillon granules
½ teaspoon garlic powder
¼ teaspoon pepper
1 cup water

Layer all ingredients in a large saucepan in the order given; bring to a boil. Cover, reduce heat, and simmer 20 minutes or until potatoes are fork tender. Yield: 6 servings (143 calories per 1-cup serving).

□ 4.7 grams protein, 0.7 gram fat, 31.3 grams carbohydrate, 0 milligrams cholesterol, 328 milligrams sodium, and 51 milligrams calcium.

Mildred Morgan
Knoxville, Tennessee

NEW-FASHIONED APPLE COBBLER

1 tablespoon cornstarch
½ cup apple juice, divided
5 cups peeled and sliced cooking apples
⅓ cup firmly packed brown sugar
½ teaspoon ground cinnamon
¼ teaspoon ground nutmeg
¼ teaspoon ground cloves
Vegetable cooking spray
½ cup all-purpose flour
2 tablespoons corn oil margarine
1 to 2 tablespoons cold water

Combine cornstarch and ¼ cup apple juice; set aside.

Combine remaining ¼ cup apple juice and next 5 ingredients in a heavy saucepan; bring to a boil. Reduce heat, and simmer 10 minutes, stirring occasionally. Stir in cornstarch mixture; cook over medium heat, stirring constantly, until mixture begins to boil. Boil 1 minute, stirring constantly, until mixture is thickened and bubbly. Remove from heat; pour into an 8-inch square baking dish coated with cooking spray. Set aside.

Place flour in a small bowl; cut in margarine with a pastry blender until mixture resembles coarse meal. Sprinkle water evenly over surface of mixture; stir with a fork until dry ingredients are moistened. Shape into a ball; gently press between 2 sheets of heavy-duty plastic wrap into a 4-inch circle. Chill 15 minutes.

Roll dough to an 8-inch square; freeze 5 minutes. Remove top sheet of plastic wrap; cut dough into strips to fit baking dish. Arrange strips over apples in a lattice design. Bake at 425° for 30 to 35 minutes or until cobbler is bubbly and crust is golden. Yield: 6 servings (169 calories per ½-cup serving).

□ 1.2 grams protein, 4.4 grams fat, 32.6 grams carbohydrate, 0 milligrams cholesterol, 48 milligrams sodium, and 18 milligrams calcium.

Mrs. E. R. Lovell
Jackson, Mississippi

Pastry Tips

■ Roll pie pastry on a lightly floured surface, but remember that too much flour toughens the crust. A stockinette rolling pin cover minimizes the amount of flour needed during rolling.

■ Make a quick job of rolling pastry. Roll lightly; keep in mind that too much handling will result in a tough crust.

■ Slip a cookie sheet or a sheet of foil under a cobbler or fruit pie when baking in the oven in order to catch any bubble-over.

Good-For-You Biscuits

In the South, tender, flaky biscuits are served at breakfast, lunch, and dinner. They're a part of our daily lives that can't be given up—even for healthy eating.

In years past, lard, shortening, or butter were the preferred fats for making biscuits. Nowadays, reduced-calorie margarine, liquid spread, or vegetable oil are used because they're lower in saturated fats—the kind that can raise blood cholesterol levels.

Cut reduced-calorie margarine into the flours for Whole Wheat Biscuits just as you would other solid fats. After stirring in the milk, knead the dough lightly, shape into balls, and bake. Golden-brown Whole Wheat Biscuits prove that good-tasting biscuits can be healthy, too.

WHOLE WHEAT BISCUITS
(pictured on page 228)

1½ cups all-purpose flour
½ cup whole wheat flour
1 tablespoon baking powder
½ teaspoon salt
3 tablespoons reduced-calorie margarine
¾ cup evaporated skimmed milk
Vegetable cooking spray

Combine first 4 ingredients; cut in margarine with a pastry blender until mixture resembles coarse meal. Add milk, stirring until dry ingredients are moistened. Turn dough out onto a lightly floured surface, and knead about 1 minute.

Shape dough into 12 balls; place balls in an 8-inch square baking pan coated with cooking spray. Flatten dough slightly. Bake at 450° for 10 to 12 minutes. Yield: 1 dozen (111 calories per biscuit).

□ *3.7 grams protein, 2.2 grams fat, 19.1 grams carbohydrate, 1 milligram cholesterol, 219 milligrams sodium, and 99 milligrams calcium.*

COMPARE THE NUTRIENTS (per serving)		
	Traditional	Light
Calories	165	111
Fat	9.9g	2.2g
Cholesterol	27mg	1mg

It's All In The Family Cookbook

We were flooded with responses after an article appeared last year in our July issue of *Southern Living* about how to put together a family cookbook. Many folks shared comments about compiling and publishing their own treasured collection of family favorites. We thought these publishing veterans had so much good advice to offer that we wanted to share some of their comments and recipes with you.

■ Patty Cartwright Harvey of Fort Worth, Texas, put together *Cartwright Cuisine* to avoid what she thought would be a more difficult assignment from the reunion committee. She confides that she was wrong about the cookbook being the easier task, but she found it a fun learning experience. One of the many great recipes in the cookbook is Chicken-and-Spinach Enchiladas.

CHICKEN-AND-SPINACH ENCHILADAS

12 chicken breast halves, skinned
1 teaspoon salt
2 (10-ounce) packages frozen chopped spinach
1 cup diced onion
1 tablespoon butter or margarine, melted
1 (10¾-ounce) can cream of chicken soup, undiluted
¾ cup milk
3 (4-ounce) cans diced green chiles, drained
3 (8-ounce) cartons sour cream
3 cups (12 ounces) shredded Monterey Jack cheese, divided
16 flour tortillas

Place chicken in a Dutch oven; add salt and water to cover. Bring to a boil; cover, reduce heat, and simmer 40 minutes or until tender. Remove chicken, and let cool slightly. Bone chicken; dice and set aside.

Cook spinach according to package directions; drain well, and reserve 1 cup spinach broth. Set aside.

Sauté onion in butter in Dutch oven until tender. Stir in spinach and chicken; set aside.

Combine soup, reserved spinach broth, milk, green chiles, sour cream, and half of cheese in a bowl; mix well. Stir half of sauce mixture into chicken mixture. Reserve remaining sauce.

Spoon chicken mixture evenly down center of each tortilla; roll up tortillas, and place, seam side down, in 2 lightly greased 13- x 9- x 2-inch baking dishes. Spoon remaining sauce over tortillas. Bake, uncovered, at 350° for 25 minutes. Sprinkle with remaining cheese; bake an additional 5 minutes. Yield: 4 to 6 servings per casserole.

Note: Casseroles may be frozen prior to baking. To serve, remove from freezer; let thaw in refrigerator. Bake as directed.
Priscilla Lupe
San Antonio, Texas

■ Karen and Bill Hudnall of Paris, Texas, took on the project of compiling *From Hudnall Kitchens* by themselves. Several months prior to their annual July gathering they sent out requests for family recipes. Karen organized everything and drew artwork for the book; then Bill took over and handled the printing. One of the favorite recipes is Scalloped Eggplant.

SCALLOPED EGGPLANT

1 (1-pound) eggplant, peeled and
  cut into ½-inch cubes
1 small onion, grated
3 slices bread, crumbled
½ cup evaporated milk
½ cup chopped green pepper
1 cup (4 ounces) shredded Cheddar
  cheese
3 tablespoons butter or margarine,
  melted
1 egg, beaten
¾ teaspoon salt
¼ teaspoon pepper
¼ cup cracker crumbs
Paprika

Cook eggplant and onion in boiling water to cover 5 minutes or until vegetables are tender; drain well. Add crumbled bread, milk, green pepper, cheese, butter, egg, salt, and pepper, and stir well.

Pour eggplant mixture into a greased 1½-quart baking dish; top with cracker crumbs, and sprinkle with paprika. Bake, uncovered, at 350° for 30 to 35 minutes or until top is lightly browned. Yield: 6 servings.
Irene Shumpert
Gulf Breeze, Florida

■ Letters were sent to 282 descendants of the Pazdera family asking them to submit recipes for the cookbook that bears the family name. Six months from the date of the first letter, the book was in their hands according to Rosia Minden of Fort Smith, Arkansas, who sent a copy of the book to us. The book is full of simple but tasty recipes, such as Maple Heights Baked Beans.

MAPLE HEIGHTS BAKED BEANS

¾ pound ground beef
1 (16-ounce) can baked beans in
  tomato sauce
1 (15-ounce) can Great Northern
  beans, undrained
1 medium onion, chopped
2 tablespoons brown sugar
½ teaspoon salt
½ teaspoon pepper
1 teaspoon dry mustard
1 teaspoon Worcestershire sauce
1 tablespoon molasses
½ cup catsup
4 slices bacon, cooked and drained

Cook ground beef until browned, stirring to crumble; drain. Combine ground beef and next 10 ingredients. Spoon mixture into a lightly greased 2-quart baking dish. Bake, uncovered, at 350° for 55 minutes. Top with bacon strips, and bake an additional 5 minutes. Yield: 8 servings.
Helen Rahon Duda
Maple Heights, Ohio

■ For *Gatlin Family Favorites*, Martha Shelly of Topeka, Kansas, asked every relative to submit five recipes, each from a different food category and each a favorite at their annual reunion in Oklahoma. Honey-Wheat Bread is a favorite in the book.

HONEY-WHEAT BREAD

2 packages dry yeast
½ cup warm water (105° to 115°)
1 egg
¾ cup honey
½ cup nonfat dry milk
1 tablespoon salt
2 tablespoons vegetable oil
1¾ cups warm water (105° to 115°)
3 cups whole wheat flour
4 to 4½ cups all-purpose flour

Dissolve yeast in ½ cup warm water in a large mixing bowl; let stand 5 minutes. Stir in egg and next 5 ingredients. Add whole wheat flour; beat at medium speed of an electric mixer until smooth. Stir in enough all-purpose flour to make a stiff dough.

Turn dough out onto a floured surface, and knead 5 minutes or until smooth and elastic. Cover and let rise in a warm place (85°), free from drafts, 45 minutes or until dough has doubled in bulk.

Punch dough down; divide in half, and shape into two loaves. Place in well-greased 8- x 4- x 3-inch loafpans; cover and let rise 30 minutes or until doubled in bulk. Uncover and bake at 375° for 30 minutes or until loaves sound hollow when tapped, shielding loaves with aluminum foil, if necessary, to prevent overbrowning. Remove bread from pans, and let cool. Yield: 2 loaves.
Debbie Inman
Berryton, Kansas

■ Flora Grantham of Smithfield, North Carolina, says that her family published *The Family Tree* as a fundraiser for their family reunion. The book contains one of her favorite recipes, Peanut Muffins.

PEANUT MUFFINS

1½ cups all-purpose flour
1 tablespoon baking powder
¼ teaspoon salt
¼ cup sugar
2 eggs, beaten
½ cup milk
½ cup butter or margarine, melted
¾ cup dry roasted, unsalted
  peanuts, chopped

Combine first 4 ingredients in a large bowl; make a well in center of mixture. Combine eggs, milk, and butter; add to dry ingredients, stirring just until moistened. Gently stir in peanuts. Spoon into greased muffin pans, filling three-fourths full. Bake at 400° for 15 to 20 minutes. Yield: 1 dozen.
Doris M. Hull
Washington, D.C.

■ Patty Hedge did much of the original typing for *The Anderson Family Cook Book*. She says her family feared they'd be stuck with many of the 200 books the publisher required them to purchase prior to publication, but they sold them easily and had to reorder. Patty's Coconut Pound Cake appears in the book.

COCONUT POUND CAKE

1½ cups shortening
2¼ cups sugar
5 eggs
3 cups sifted cake flour
¼ teaspoon salt
1 cup milk
1 (7-ounce) can flaked coconut

Beat shortening at medium speed of an electric mixer. Gradually add sugar, beating well. Add eggs, one at a time, beating after each addition.

Combine flour and salt; add to creamed mixture alternately with milk, beginning and ending with flour mixture. Mix just until blended after each addition. Stir in coconut.

Pour batter into a greased and floured 10-inch tube pan. Bake at 325° for 1 hour and 25 minutes or until a wooden pick inserted in center comes out clean. Let cool 15 minutes. Remove from pan; cool on wire rack. Yield: one 10-inch cake.   *Patty Hedge*
Hohenwald, Tennessee

Tip: *To measure shortening, use the easy water-displacement method if the water that clings to the shortening will not affect the product. (Keep in mind this important point: Do not use this method for measuring shortening for frying.) To measure ¼ cup shortening using this method, put ¾ cup water in a measuring cup; then add shortening until the water reaches the 1-cup level. Just be sure that the shortening is completely covered with water. Drain off the water before using the shortening.*

■ Proceeds generated from the sale of *The Thomas and Bridges Family Cookbook* help to fund projects of the Thomas-Bridges Association, a nonprofit organization of relatives who incorporated to pass along heritage from one generation to the next. This cookbook contains lots of family favorites, including Cherry-Cola Salad.

CHERRY-COLA SALAD

1 (8-ounce) can crushed pineapple, undrained
1 (10-ounce) bottle maraschino cherries, undrained
1 (3-ounce) package cherry-flavored gelatin
1 (3-ounce) package cream cheese, softened
¾ cup cola-flavored beverage
½ cup chopped pecans

Drain pineapple and cherries, reserving liquids in a medium saucepan. Sprinkle gelatin over liquid mixture, and let stand 1 minute. Cook over medium heat, stirring constantly, until gelatin dissolves; remove from heat. Add cream cheese, stirring until smooth. Stir in fruit, cola-flavored beverage, and pecans. Pour into a lightly oiled 4-cup mold. Cover and chill until firm. Yield: 6 to 8 servings.
Gertrude S. Humphries
Cadiz, Kentucky

Fishing For A Pizza

While on vacation, Sue and Gary Fowler of Middlesboro, Kentucky, sampled an unusual pizza. "It was exceedingly rich, devoid of tomato sauce, and full of bits of shellfish," recalls Sue.

Checking with friends and thumbing through cookbooks didn't turn up a similar recipe, so Sue took to her kitchen to try to re-create the unusual combination. We think you'll agree the results are worth her effort.

SHELLFISH PIZZA

1 (10-ounce) can refrigerated pizza crust
¼ cup butter
2½ tablespoons all-purpose flour
1 cup half-and-half
1 clove garlic, minced
1 tablespoon grated Parmesan cheese
¼ teaspoon dried whole basil
Dash of dried whole thyme
1 cup (4 ounces) shredded Monterey Jack cheese
1 cup (4 ounces) shredded mozzarella cheese
8 large boiled shrimp, peeled and halved
8 ounces crab-flavored seafood mix, coarsely chopped
1 small tomato, seeded and chopped
2 green onions, minced
5 small mushrooms, sliced
¼ cup grated Parmesan cheese

Unroll dough, and press onto bottom and ¼ inch up sides of a lightly greased 15- x 10- x 1-inch jellyroll pan. Prick dough generously with a fork, and bake on lowest rack of oven at 425° for 5 minutes. Cool.

Melt butter in a heavy saucepan over low heat; add flour, stirring until smooth. Cook 1 minute, stirring constantly. Gradually add half-and-half; cook over medium heat, stirring constantly, until mixture is thickened and bubbly. Stir in garlic and next 3 ingredients; spread on pizza crust. Sprinkle with Monterey Jack and mozzarella cheeses. Layer shrimp and remaining ingredients over cheeses. Bake at 425° for 15 to 18 minutes. Let stand 4 to 5 minutes before cutting. Yield: 6 main-dish or 20 appetizer servings.

Right: Satisfy a variety of appetites with South-of-the-Border Chili served over rice, White Chili topped with cheese, or Hot Venison Chili cooled with lettuce and tomato; all are satisfying and heart healthy. (Recipes begin on page 283.)

Catfish Gumbo (page 216) combines the best of Mississippi and Louisiana rice cookery.

Colorful Mexican Rice (page 217) is a classic recipe from our south-of-the-border neighbors.

The South is home to most of our country's major rice-growing states— Arkansas, Louisiana, Mississippi, and Texas.

Celebrate Louisiana's favorite holiday with Mardi Gras Rice (page 217), complete with official colors.

After the hunt, pair Rice Dressing (page 217) with duck—a popular combination in Arkansas.

Whole Wheat Biscuits (page 222) bake up with a tender inside and a crisp golden-brown crust. Best of all, they prove that good-tasting biscuits can be healthy, too. A delicious example of light, healthy cooking, this recipe is offered in the monthly feature, "Light Favorite."

Relax, The Salad's Ready

The scenario may vary, but the problem is common: There's little time to cook dinner. These recipes, along with a little planning, will eliminate one of your worries—the salad.

Our salads offer options from a tangy marinated creation, Zucchini-Artichoke Salad, to a gelatin concoction, Classic Tomato Aspic, to a traditional favorite, Marinated Slaw.

CLASSIC TOMATO ASPIC

2 envelopes unflavored gelatin
⅓ cup cold water
3 cups tomato juice
1 teaspoon sugar
¼ teaspoon pepper
⅛ teaspoon salt
1 teaspoon prepared horseradish
1 teaspoon lemon juice
1 teaspoon Worcestershire sauce
Lettuce leaves

Sprinkle gelatin over cold water in a medium saucepan; let stand 1 minute. Add tomato juice and remaining ingredients except lettuce. Cook over medium heat, stirring until gelatin dissolves. Cool to room temperature. Pour mixture into a lightly oiled 4-cup mold. Cover and chill at least 8 hours. Unmold onto a lettuce-lined plate. Yield: 6 to 8 servings. *Dorsella Utter*
Louisville, Kentucky

MARINATED SLAW

1 medium cabbage, shredded (about 9 cups)
1 large green pepper, chopped
1 medium onion, finely chopped
1 stalk celery, chopped
1½ cups white vinegar
2 cups sugar
¾ teaspoon mustard seeds
½ teaspoon salt
¼ teaspoon ground turmeric

Combine first 4 ingredients in a large bowl, stirring well.

Combine vinegar and remaining ingredients in a saucepan; bring to a boil, stirring occasionally. Boil 1 minute; pour over vegetables. Cover and chill at least 8 hours. Serve with a slotted spoon. Yield: 8 servings.
Hazel Slucher
Taylorsville, Kentucky

ZUCCHINI-ARTICHOKE SALAD

1 (8-ounce) bottle Italian salad dressing
2 (0.4-ounce) envelopes ranch-style dressing mix
4 medium zucchini, sliced
2 (14-ounce) cans artichoke hearts, drained and halved
1 (8-ounce) can whole mushrooms, drained
1 (6-ounce) can pitted ripe olives, drained
1 (8-ounce) can bamboo shoots, drained
1 (2-ounce) jar diced pimiento, drained
Red leaf lettuce

Combine Italian salad dressing and ranch dressing mix; stir in remaining ingredients except lettuce. Cover and chill at least 8 hours. Spoon into a lettuce-lined bowl, using a slotted spoon. Yield: 12 to 14 servings.
Louise Bodziony
Gladstone, Missouri

FRESH VEGETABLE CONGEALED SALAD

1 (3-ounce) package lemon-flavored gelatin
2 teaspoons beef-flavored bouillon granules
1 cup boiling water
1 (8-ounce) carton sour cream
½ cup seeded and chopped cucumber
¼ cup chopped radishes
¼ cup diced green pepper
1 tablespoon sliced green onions
Lettuce leaves

Dissolve lemon gelatin and bouillon granules in boiling water; chill until the consistency of unbeaten egg white. Fold in sour cream until mixture is smooth. Fold in cucumber, radishes, green pepper, and green onions.

Spoon vegetable mixture into lightly greased ½-cup molds. Cover and chill at least 8 hours. Unmold onto lettuce. Yield: 6 servings.
Mrs. James W. Strayer
Hilton Head Island, South Carolina

A Cook With An Eye On Africa

Merriam McLendon may have grown up in Birmingham, but her palate yearns for the flavors of West Africa— fiery, spicy foods that tingle the lips and warm the soul—foods such as Jollof Rice Dinner. Merriam prefers fish and shrimp, but beef and chicken may be substituted. Although yams would be used in Africa, Merriam substitutes sweet potatoes.

The rest of the menu is simple. Merriam tosses a green salad with plump tomatoes and onions. If she's lucky at the wine shop, she serves Tej, a honey-sweet wine from Ethiopia. If that's not available, a sweet white, Vouvray, or a German wine works well. Commercial lemon sherbet for dessert refreshes the tingling taste buds of her guests.

JOLLOF RICE DINNER

3 medium-size sweet potatoes (1¼ pounds), peeled and cut into large cubes
1 (1¾-pound) cabbage, cut into 8 wedges
2 pounds frozen whiting fish fillets, thawed and cut into pieces
½ cup vegetable oil
1 pound medium-size fresh shrimp, peeled and deveined
2 tablespoons vegetable oil
1 large onion, coarsely chopped
1 medium green pepper, coarsely chopped
4 large carrots, scraped and cut into pieces
7 cloves garlic, chopped
1 (6-ounce) can tomato paste
6½ cups hot water, divided
2 teaspoons salt
1 to 2 tablespoons red pepper
1 tablespoon dried whole oregano
2 cups long-grain rice, uncooked

Cook sweet potatoes in boiling water 6 minutes or until tender; drain and set aside. Cook cabbage in boiling water 8 minutes or until crisp-tender; drain and set aside.

Cook one-third of fish fillets in ½ cup oil in skillet until lightly browned, turning once. Remove from skillet, reserving drippings in skillet. Repeat procedure twice with remaining fish. Add shrimp to skillet; sauté 3 minutes or until done. Remove shrimp from skillet, and set aside.

Transfer oil from skillet to Dutch oven; add 2 tablespoons oil to Dutch oven. Add onion and next 3 ingredients; sauté until crisp-tender. Stir in tomato paste, and cook 5 to 7 minutes, stirring often. Add 5 cups water, salt, red pepper, and oregano. Simmer 30 minutes over low heat, stirring occasionally. Remove vegetables, using a slotted spoon, and transfer to a serving platter; keep warm.

Add sweet potatoes to sauce mixture, and heat thoroughly. Remove to serving platter, and keep warm. Repeat procedure with cabbage, fish, and shrimp.

Add remaining 1½ cups water to sauce mixture; bring to a boil. Add rice, and cook 20 minutes or until rice is tender, stirring often. Add additional water, if necessary. Spoon into a serving bowl. Yield: 8 servings.

There's A Party In The Cards

We'll cut a deal with you. You name the game, we provide the menu, and you've got a great card party! Whether it's bridge, canasta, or rook, the event is usually a fun-filled marathon, and good food is a must for sustenance.

Either open the bidding or take a break later to tally the score with a cool beverage and appetizer served right on the game table. Our club sandwich and tangy green salad will be the main course; then you can play your trump with peanut butter-and-chocolate candies shaped into hearts, diamonds, clubs, and spades.

The best part of the strategy is the preparation: the whole meal can be finished a couple of hours beforehand with no frantic, last-minute details. Our menu will suit two tables of four, or you can double the recipes and the fun for a party of 16.

Citrus Spritzers
Apple-Date Spread
Double-Decker Club Sandwiches
Marinated Orange-Onion Salad
Peanut-Fudge Bites

Make the Invitation

You can bet you'll have a full house for your card party with these invitations and RSVP forms, which are both simple and inexpensive. Each invitation requires six cards, so purchase one deck, or more (for more than eight players) of playing cards, glue, red envelopes, smaller white envelopes, and red and black markers.

For each invitation arrange three cards face up and one card face down on top. Glue together, and let dry. Write the pertinent party information in black marker on back of top card.

To make the RSVP form, glue one card face up overlapping one card face down, and let dry. In red or black marker, make two boxes for guests to check their response: "Deal me in" (yes) or "Count me out" (no).

Address the smaller envelope in red to yourself for the RSVP, and enclose the envelope, RSVP, and invitation in a red envelope.

CITRUS SPRITZERS

2 (750-milliliter) bottles white
 wine, chilled
1 (2-liter) bottle lemon-lime
 carbonated beverage, chilled
½ cup lemon juice

Combine all ingredients, stirring well.
Serve immediately. Yield: 4 quarts.

APPLE-DATE SPREAD

1 (8-ounce) package cream cheese,
 softened
¼ cup milk
1½ cups finely chopped pecans
1 cup finely chopped, unpeeled
 apple
¾ cup finely chopped dates
Garnish: apple slices

Combine cream cheese and milk, mixing well. Stir in chopped pecans, apple, and dates. Garnish, if desired,
and serve with assorted crackers.
Yield: 2¾ cups.   *Jennifer Mungo*
Columbia, South Carolina

DOUBLE-DECKER CLUB
SANDWICHES

1 (8-ounce) carton sour cream
2 tablespoons prepared
 horseradish
2 teaspoons honey mustard
¼ teaspoon garlic salt
⅛ teaspoon white pepper
¾ pound thinly sliced ham
12 slices whole wheat bread
4 slices Swiss cheese
8 lettuce leaves
¾ pound thinly sliced turkey
8 slices tomato
4 slices bacon
16 pitted ripe olives
16 pimiento-stuffed olives

Combine sour cream, horseradish,
honey mustard, garlic salt, and white
pepper; stir well. Place 3 ounces of
ham on each of 4 slices of bread. Top
each with 1 teaspoon sauce, 1 slice
cheese, a lettuce leaf, and another
slice of bread. Place 3 ounces of turkey on each slice, and add 1 teaspoon
sauce, lettuce leaf, 2 slices tomato,
and 1 slice bacon. Top with remaining
slices of bread.

Skewer a ripe olive and pimiento-
stuffed olive on each of 16 wooden
picks. Cut each sandwich into 4 triangles, and secure each quarter with a
pick. Yield: 8 servings.

MARINATED ORANGE-ONION
SALAD

2 cups fresh orange sections
1 small purple onion, sliced and
 separated into rings
¼ cup red wine vinegar
¼ cup olive oil
2 tablespoons chopped fresh parsley
8 cups mixed salad greens

Combine orange sections and onion
rings in a medium bowl; set aside.
Combine vinegar and oil; pour over
orange mixture, and sprinkle with
fresh parsley. Cover and chill 3 hours,
tossing occasionally.

Place salad greens in a shallow dish;
arrange orange and onion evenly over
greens, and drizzle dressing over
salad. Serve immediately. Yield: 8
servings.   *Marion Hall*
Knoxville, Tennessee

PEANUT-FUDGE BITES

1 (12-ounce) package peanut
 butter morsels
1 (14-ounce) can sweetened
 condensed milk
3 tablespoons butter or margarine
1 cup semisweet chocolate morsels
1 tablespoon shortening

Combine peanut butter morsels,
sweetened condensed milk, and butter in a 2-quart glass bowl. Microwave
at HIGH 1½ minutes or until morsels
melt; stir well.

Pour mixture onto a cookie sheet
lined with wax paper; spread into a
13- x 11-inch rectangle. Smooth surface with a rolling pin. Chill 45 minutes
or until firm. Turn mixture onto a cutting board; remove wax paper. Cut
into desired shapes with 1-inch and
1½-inch cookie cutters.

Combine chocolate morsels and
shortening in a 2-cup glass measure.
Microwave at HIGH 1 minute; stir until smooth. Spoon chocolate mixture
into a decorating bag, and pipe mixture onto peanut butter shapes. Chill
until piping is set. Store in refrigerator
in an airtight container. Yield: about
11 dozen.   *Mildred Bickley*
Bristol, Virginia

Make It Easy

■ Use sharp kitchen shears to
cut sticky foods such as dates
or marshmallows. For added
ease, dip your kitchen shears in
hot water.

■ Add the dressing to salad
greens just before serving so
that the greens won't wilt.

■ When purchasing meat such
as ham, turkey, or roast beef
for sandwiches, go to the deli
counter in your local grocery
store. The meat can be sliced
as thinly as you desire.

■ Pour carbonated lemon-lime
beverage or ginger ale into ice
cube trays and freeze. Use the
ice cubes to chill and add flavor
to punch.

■ Soften one 8-ounce package of
cream cheese by microwaving at
MEDIUM LOW (30% power)
for 2 to 2½ minutes.

Treat Them To A Festival

These easy recipes and tips are designed to help you plan a neighborhood festival, a salute to the season and the playful spirit it evokes in us and our children. The treats rely on convenience products and have only a few ingredients. Whether you plan an entire event or simply invite neighborhood children to supper, we think these recipes will make fall all the more appetizing.

Plan a Fall Festival

In Jackson, Mississippi, Rev. Barbara A. Oliver of Northminster Baptist Church greets the cooler temperatures armed with a to-do list for her church's fall festival. The event coincides with Halloween and is open to the community. Many families attend the celebration because it's safer than trick-or-treating, and they get a chance to visit with folks from their neighborhood. Here, Barbara shares her successful planning tips. The same ideas may also be applied to school, civic, or neighborhood group functions.

"First, plan activities that can be enjoyed by every age group, from preschool to seniors," she says. Barbara asks each Sunday school class to be responsible for a booth and gives it a list of safe, appropriate games from which to choose. Fifteen booths or activities are enough to occupy 200 folks from 6:30 to 8 p.m.

Festivals work best in a large gym or other open room, allowing revelers to continue to party in case of bad weather. To cover costs and generate mailing lists for other activities, Barbara charges a nominal admission per child and asks each family to fill out a registration card. The card goes into a fish bowl for door-prize drawings. She asks families in the church to donate candy for prizes.

Additional prizes for the games are purchased at discount stores. Once again, Barbara has her eye on safety. "We don't buy anything that can't be used by a child under the age of 3," she says. A committee also solicits piggy banks, pencils, hats, or T-shirts from local banks and businesses. Local pizza restaurants often donate bags to hold the loot.

MICROWAVE CHILI

1 pound ground turkey
1 onion, chopped
1 green pepper, chopped (optional)
1 (15-ounce) can tomato sauce
2 tablespoons chili powder
½ teaspoon dried whole oregano
Dash of garlic powder

Combine turkey, onion, and, if desired, green pepper in a 2-quart casserole. Cover with wax paper, and microwave at HIGH 6 minutes, stirring after 3 minutes; drain. Add tomato sauce and remaining ingredients, stirring well. Microwave at HIGH 10 minutes, stirring after 5 minutes. Serve on hot dogs. Yield: 3½ cups.

Martha Griffey
Sherman, Texas

KRAUT RELISH

1 (16-ounce) jar sauerkraut,
    drained
½ cup finely chopped celery
½ cup finely chopped green pepper
½ cup finely chopped carrot
½ cup finely chopped onion
¼ cup sugar

Combine all ingredients; cover and refrigerate 8 hours. Serve relish with hot dogs, vegetables, or meats. Yield: 1 quart.

Charlotte Pierce
Greensburg, Kentucky

Tricks, Treats, And Carnival Feats

Here's a list of safe, easy-to-make activity booths, including some for young children and adults. You might also include such favorites as apple bobbing and a costume contest.

■ **Ping-Pong Ball Toss**—Place three cans decorated with pumpkin faces on a stepladder. Children get five attempts to toss Ping-Pong balls into all three cans.

■ **Feed the Pumpkin**—Paint a giant pumpkin face on a cardboard box. Cut out the mouth; toss bean bags into the opening.

■ **Pick Up Ducks**—Float rubber ducks or plastic pumpkins in a small swimming pool. Let children pick up three ducks in a turn. If "lucky duck" is written on the duck's belly or bottom of pumpkin, the child wins a prize.

■ **Shoot Out the Candle**—Aim squirt guns at lighted candles. The first one to quench a flame wins a prize.

■ **Treasure Dig**—Fill a small swimming pool with sand; then add candy enclosed in wrappers or unshelled peanuts. Let preschoolers "dig" for their treasure with a sand bucket and shovel.

■ **Balloon Pop**—See who can pop three balloons in six tries with darts. This is a real hit with older children.

■ **Floating Ring**—Throw inflatable or Nerf® balls through a Hula-Hoop® swinging from the ceiling.

■ **Cakewalk**—Reward winners with cupcakes. To encourage reading, have bookwalks.

■ **Concession Stand**—Stock it with hot dogs and the trimmings, brownies, and funnel cakes.

OVEN-MADE CARAMEL CORN

6 quarts freshly popped corn (about
  1 cup unpopped corn)
1 cup dry roasted peanuts
1 cup pecan halves or pieces
1 cup butter or margarine
1 cup firmly packed brown sugar
1 cup sugar
½ cup light corn syrup
1 teaspoon salt
½ teaspoon baking soda

Combine popped corn, peanuts, and pecans in a large roasting pan.

Melt butter in a large saucepan; stir in sugars, corn syrup, and salt. Bring to a boil; boil 5 minutes, stirring often (temperature will be about 244°). Remove from heat; stir in soda.

Pour sugar mixture over popped corn and nuts; stir well. Bake at 250° for 45 minutes, stirring every 15 minutes. Cool. Store in an airtight container. Yield: 6 quarts.

Helen Goggans
Kingsland, Arkansas

OAT 'N' CRUNCH BROWNIES

1 (21.5-ounce) package fudge
  brownie mix
½ cup chopped pecans
⅓ cup quick-cooking oats,
  uncooked
¼ cup firmly packed brown sugar
¼ teaspoon ground cinnamon
  (optional)
2 tablespoons butter or margarine,
  melted
¾ cup candy-coated chocolate
  pieces

Grease bottom of a 13- x 9- x 2-inch pan. Prepare brownie mix according to package directions; spoon into prepared pan.

Combine pecans, oats, brown sugar, and, if desired, cinnamon; stir in butter. Stir in candy; sprinkle over batter. Bake at 350° for 35 minutes. Let cool, and cut into squares. Yield: 3 dozen.

Mrs. E. W. Hanley
Palm Harbor, Florida

NUTTY FUNNEL CAKES

¾ cup sifted powdered sugar
1 teaspoon ground cinnamon
⅔ cup pecan pieces
2½ cups self-rising flour
¼ cup sugar
1⅔ cups milk
2 eggs
½ teaspoon almond or vanilla
  extract
Vegetable oil

Combine powdered sugar and cinnamon; set aside.

Position knife blade in food processor bowl. Add pecans; process until finely chopped. Add flour and next 4 ingredients; process 30 seconds or until mixture is smooth.

Pour oil to a depth of ½ inch in a large skillet. Heat to 375° over medium-high heat. Cover bottom opening of funnel with finger. (Funnel with a ⅜-inch opening works best.) Pour ¼ cup batter into funnel; hold funnel over skillet. Remove finger from funnel end to release batter into hot oil, moving funnel in a slow circle so that batter forms a spiral.

Fry each funnel cake 1 minute or until edges are golden brown; turn and fry until golden. Drain on paper towels. Repeat procedure with remaining batter. Sprinkle powdered sugar mixture over warm funnel cakes, using a sieve. Serve immediately. Yield: about 1 dozen.

Rose Alleman
Saint Amant, Louisiana

It's Pumpkin Time Again

In the fall, pumpkins appear in virtually every supermarket and roadside stand. Large and shapely ones make the most terrifying jack-o'-lanterns. Save the seeds to make Seasoned Pumpkin Seeds, a munchie with flavor and texture similar to popcorn.

When baking with fresh pumpkin, select a smaller pumpkin, one that

weighs about 2½ pounds. Wash the pumpkin, and cut it in half crosswise. Scrape out the seeds, and reserve them for roasting, if desired. Place the halves, cut side down, in a 15- x 10- x 1-inch jellyroll pan. Bake at 325° for 45 minutes or until fork tender; cool 10 minutes. Peel pumpkin, and puree in a food processor, or mash. This size pumpkin yields about 2¼ cups mashed pumpkin.

SPICED PUMPKIN BREAD

¾ cup butter or margarine,
  softened
2 cups sugar
4 eggs
2 tablespoons molasses
⅔ cup orange juice
2 cups canned or cooked mashed
  pumpkin
3⅓ cups all-purpose flour
1 teaspoon baking powder
1 teaspoon baking soda
1¼ teaspoons salt
1 teaspoon ground cinnamon
1 teaspoon ground cloves
1½ teaspoons vanilla extract
1 cup raisins
1 cup chopped pecans

Beat butter at medium speed of an electric mixer. Gradually add sugar, beating well. Add eggs, one at a time, beating after each addition. Add molasses, orange juice, and mashed pumpkin.

Combine flour and next 5 ingredients; add to creamed mixture, mixing just until blended. Stir in vanilla extract, raisins, and chopped pecans.

Spoon batter into four greased and floured 7- x 3½- x 2-inch loafpans. Bake at 350° for 50 to 55 minutes or until a wooden pick inserted in center comes out clean. Cool in pans 10 minutes; remove from pans, and let cool completely on a wire rack. Yield: four 7-inch loaves.

Elizabeth M. Haney
Dublin, Virginia

SEASONED PUMPKIN SEEDS

¾ cup pumpkin seeds
1 tablespoon butter or margarine, melted
½ teaspoon Worcestershire sauce
¼ teaspoon garlic salt
¼ teaspoon seasoned salt

Remove membrane from seeds; rinse and pat seeds dry. Place seeds in an 8-inch square pan; add remaining ingredients, and toss to coat all sides. Bake at 300° for 25 to 30 minutes or until lightly toasted, stirring occasionally. Yield ¾ cup.

Microwave Directions: Remove membrane from seeds; rinse and pat seeds dry. Place seeds in a 9-inch pieplate; add remaining ingredients, and toss to coat all sides. Microwave at HIGH 8 minutes or until lightly toasted, stirring at 2-minute intervals. (Cooking time will vary with size of pumpkin and moistness of seeds. Do not overcook.)   *Sandra Russell*
Gainesville, Florida

FROSTY PUMPKIN-PRALINE PIE

¼ cup firmly packed brown sugar
¼ cup sliced almonds
1 tablespoon butter or margarine
1 teaspoon water
1 cup canned or cooked mashed pumpkin
½ cup firmly packed brown sugar
¼ cup milk
1 teaspoon ground cinnamon
½ teaspoon ground nutmeg
¼ teaspoon ground ginger
¼ teaspoon salt
2 cups vanilla ice cream, softened
Graham Cracker Crust
1 cup whipping cream
1 teaspoon vanilla extract
2 tablespoons sugar

Combine ¼ cup brown sugar, almonds, butter, and water in a 9-inch pieplate. Microwave at HIGH 2 to 3 minutes, stirring every minute.

Spread mixture on wax paper to cool; crumble and set aside.

Combine pumpkin and next 6 ingredients in a 2-quart glass bowl. Microwave at HIGH 3 to 4 minutes, stirring once. Cool. Fold in softened ice cream, and pour mixture into prepared crust. Freeze 1 hour.

Beat whipping cream and vanilla until foamy; gradually add 2 tablespoons sugar, beating until soft peaks form. Spread mixture on top of pie, and sprinkle with almond mixture. Cover and freeze up to 2 weeks. Let stand at room temperature 10 minutes before slicing. Yield: one 9-inch pie.

Graham Cracker Crust

¼ cup butter or margarine
1¼ cups graham cracker crumbs
2 tablespoons sugar

Place butter in a small glass bowl. Microwave at HIGH 1 minute. Add crumbs and sugar; mix well. Press mixture into a 9-inch pieplate. Microwave at HIGH 1 to 2 minutes or until firm. Cool. Yield: one 9-inch crust.
Margaret Cotton
Franklin, Virginia

From Our Kitchen To Yours

Perhaps the spirit of Halloween fills your house as ghosts and goblins play in makeshift haunted houses and you decorate the front door, fill the ceramic pumpkin with treats, and bake cookies for school parties. Try Great Pumpkin Cookies for your special trick-or-treaters. Because a convenience product is used and cleanup is a snap, these cookies aren't time-consuming. The hardest part is to keep from nibbling the candy corn that's leftover.

So help your ghosts and goblins by using our pattern and pictures to produce your own haunting memory.

GREAT PUMPKIN COOKIES

1 (20-ounce) roll refrigerated slice-and-bake sugar cookies
Orange paste food coloring
Green paste food coloring
Candy corn
Licorice strips

Fold a 12-inch square piece of wax paper in half, and place on top of cookie pattern with folded edge aligned with the straight line. Trace around dotted lines; then carefully cut out pattern, and set it aside.

Let cookie dough soften at room temperature approximately 10 minutes. Slice a 1-inch portion of dough, and set aside. Place remaining dough in a large, zip-top heavy-duty plastic bag; add a small amount of orange food coloring, and close top. Knead food coloring into dough, adding extra coloring, if necessary. Place reserved dough in a small, zip-top heavy-duty plastic bag; add a very small amount of green food coloring; close top, and knead food coloring into dough.

Divide orange dough in half. Roll one half out onto a lightly greased cookie sheet to a 10- x 8-inch rectangle. Place pattern on top of dough; using a metal spatula, carefully cut around pumpkin design. Remove pattern, discarding excess dough. Repeat procedure.

Roll green dough out to ¼-inch thickness on wax paper; place stem of pattern on top, and cut around design. Repeat procedure, discarding pattern and excess dough. Remove stems from wax paper, and place on top of pumpkins.

Bake cookies at 350° for 6 minutes; remove from oven, and let stand 5 minutes. Arrange candy corn for eyes and nose; outline mouth and eyes with licorice. Bake at 350° for 2 to 3 minutes; let cookies cool slightly before removing from cookie sheet. Cool on a wire rack. Yield: 2 cookies.

Note: For the best results, cut thick licorice strips in half, using kitchen shears.

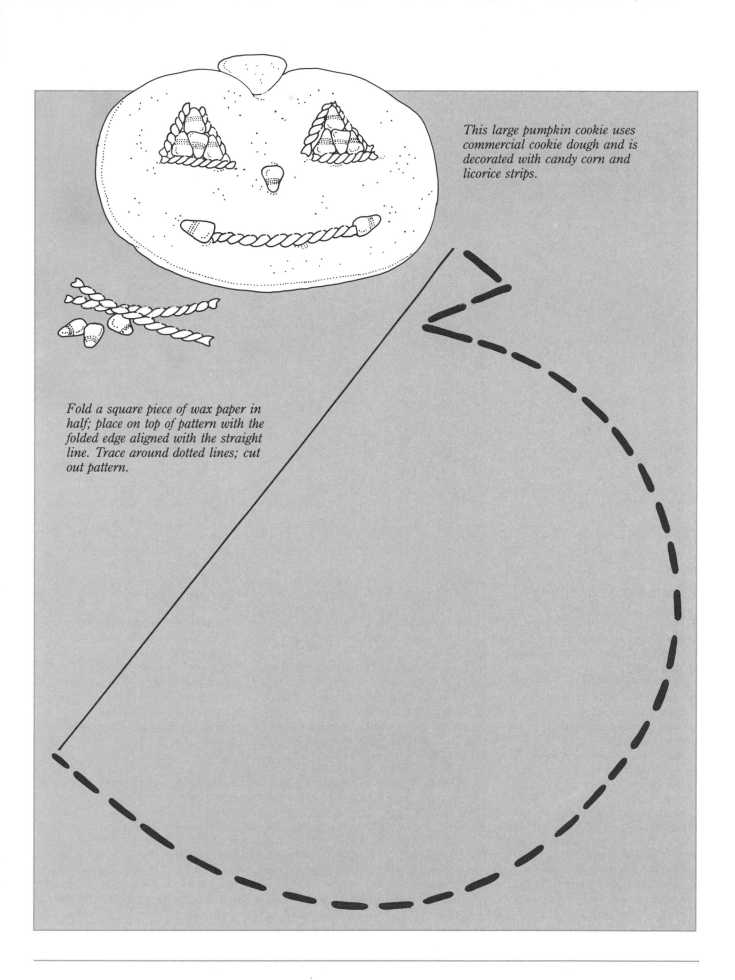

This large pumpkin cookie uses commercial cookie dough and is decorated with candy corn and licorice strips.

Fold a square piece of wax paper in half; place on top of pattern with the folded edge aligned with the straight line. Trace around dotted lines; cut out pattern.

Nuts About Cookies

Let's face it—most of us are absolutely nuts about cookies, especially cookies with nuts. And because you'll pay a pretty penny for those wonderful almonds, walnuts, pecans, and cashews, you want to be sure to make good use of them. We think you'll taste your money's worth in every bite of these sweet treasures. From dainty to robust, there's something here for every nut, and cookie, lover.

BROWN SUGAR-PECAN COOKIES

1 cup butter or margarine, softened
½ cup firmly packed brown sugar
½ cup sugar
1 egg
1 teaspoon vanilla extract
2 cups all-purpose flour
½ teaspoon baking soda
¼ teaspoon salt
½ cup finely chopped pecans
Brown Sugar Frosting
Pecan halves

Cream butter at medium speed of an electric mixer; gradually add sugars, mixing well. Add egg and vanilla; beat well. Combine flour, soda, and salt; gradually add to creamed mixture, mixing after each addition. Stir in chopped pecans. Chill 30 minutes.

Shape dough into 1-inch balls; place on ungreased cookie sheets. Bake at 350° for 10 to 12 minutes. Cool on wire racks, and spread Brown Sugar Frosting over tops. Top each cookie with a pecan half. Yield: 5 dozen.

Brown Sugar Frosting

1 cup firmly packed brown sugar
½ cup half-and-half
1 tablespoon butter or margarine
1½ to 1⅔ cups sifted powdered sugar

Combine brown sugar and half-and-half in a saucepan. Cook over medium heat, stirring constantly, until mixture comes to a boil; boil 4 minutes. Remove from heat. Stir in butter. Add 1½ cups powdered sugar, and beat at medium speed of an electric mixer until smooth. Add remaining powdered sugar to desired spreading consistency. Yield: 1⅓ cups. *Trenda Leigh Richmond, Virginia*

SIMPLY WALNUT COOKIES

½ cup butter or margarine, softened
2 tablespoons sugar
1 cup all-purpose flour
1 teaspoon walnut extract
1 cup walnuts, finely chopped
¾ cup sifted powdered sugar

Beat butter and 2 tablespoons sugar at medium speed of an electric mixer until blended. Stir in flour. Add walnut extract and walnuts, stirring well. Chill 30 minutes.

Shape dough into 1-inch balls; place on ungreased cookie sheets. Bake at 350° for 15 minutes or until done. Roll warm cookies in powdered sugar. Yield: 2½ dozen. *Beverly Garver Anderson, South Carolina*

TEXAN-SIZE ALMOND CRUNCH COOKIES

1 cup sugar
1 cup sifted powdered sugar
1 cup butter or margarine, softened
1 cup vegetable oil
2 eggs
2 teaspoons almond extract
3½ cups all-purpose flour
1 cup whole wheat flour
1 teaspoon baking soda
1 teaspoon salt
1 teaspoon cream of tartar
2 cups chopped almonds
1 (6-ounce) package almond brickle chips
Sugar

Combine 1 cup sugar, powdered sugar, butter, and vegetable oil in a large mixing bowl; beat at medium speed of an electric mixer until blended. Add eggs and almond extract, beating well. Combine flours, soda, salt, and cream of tartar; gradually add to creamed mixture, beating just until blended after each addition. Stir in almonds and brickle chips. Chill dough 3 to 4 hours.

Shape dough into 1½-inch balls, and place at least 3 inches apart on ungreased cookie sheets. Flatten cookies with a fork dipped in sugar, making a crisscross pattern. Bake at 350° for 14 to 15 minutes or until lightly browned. Transfer to wire racks to cool. Yield: about 4 dozen.

Linda Magers
Clemmons, North Carolina

Toss A Fall Fruit Salad

Don't think that the season for fresh fruit salad is over just because strawberries, blueberries, and melons have disappeared from produce stands. The same baskets that once held spring and summer fruit are now brimming with a different selection.

Most of these fruits look pretty in a basket on the counter or dining table while awaiting their use in recipes, but that's not the best way to store them. Unless they're going to be eaten right away, place them in the fruit and vegetable bin in the refrigerator to keep them firm, fresh, and juicy.

PEAR-SWISS CHEESE SALAD

¼ cup sour cream
¼ cup plain yogurt
Dash of ground cardamom
Dash of ground cinnamon
2 pears, cored and sliced
1 cup (4 ounces) shredded Swiss cheese
½ cup chopped roasted cashews
Lettuce leaves (optional)

Combine sour cream, yogurt, cardamom, and cinnamon; add pears, cheese, and cashews, tossing gently. Cover and chill. Serve on lettuce leaves, if desired. Yield: 4 servings.

Sandra Russell
Gainesville, Florida

FROZEN CRANBERRY-PINEAPPLE SALAD

2 cups fresh cranberries, ground
½ cup sugar
1 (8-ounce) can crushed pineapple, drained
1½ cups miniature marshmallows
1 cup whipping cream, whipped

Combine cranberries, sugar, and crushed pineapple; let stand 30 minutes or until sugar dissolves. Stir marshmallows into cranberry mixture; fold in whipped cream. Spoon into an 8½- x 4½- x 2½-inch loafpan lined with plastic wrap. Cover and freeze at least 8 hours. Remove from pan; cut into slices. Yield: 8 servings.

Janice Leake
Richmond, Kentucky

GRAPEFRUIT-BANANA SALAD WITH CELERY SEED DRESSING

½ cup vegetable oil
⅓ cup sugar
1 teaspoon dry mustard
½ teaspoon paprika
3 tablespoons honey
3 tablespoons cider vinegar
1 tablespoon lemon juice
½ teaspoon celery seeds
1 cup thinly sliced celery
1 cup packed celery leaves
1 grapefruit, peeled, sectioned, and seeded
2 bananas, peeled and sliced
¼ cup chopped walnuts

Combine first 7 ingredients in container of an electric blender; process until blended (about 30 seconds). Stir in celery seeds.

Combine celery, celery leaves, grapefruit, banana, and ½ cup dressing, stirring gently. Spoon onto individual salad plates; sprinkle with walnuts. Serve with remaining dressing. Yield: 4 to 6 servings.

Charlotte Moret
St. Louis, Missouri

APPLE-BEET SALAD

2 cups shredded apple
1 (15-ounce) can whole beets, drained and shredded
1 tablespoon lemon juice
1 tablespoon honey
Lettuce leaves
2 tablespoons chopped walnuts, toasted

Combine apple, beets, lemon juice, and honey, tossing gently. Serve on lettuce leaves. Sprinkle with walnuts. Yield: 4 to 6 servings. *Cathy Darling*
Grafton, West Virginia

Using Fresh Fruits

■ Ripe bananas can be refrigerated to keep them an additional 3 to 5 days. Or peel, mash, and freeze in airtight containers for use in baking.

■ When buying fresh citrus, look for fruits that have smooth, blemish-free skins. Indications of high juice content are that fruits feel firm and are heavy for their size.

■ When you use fresh lemons for cooking, remember that one medium lemon will yield 2 to 4 tablespoons juice and 1 tablespoon grated rind.

■ Store lemon, orange, and grapefruit rinds in the freezer; grate as needed for pies, cakes, and cookies. Or use the rinds candied for the holidays.

■ Whenever a recipe calls for both the rind and the juice of citrus fruit, wash and grate before juicing.

Cook Up Some Fun This Weekend

After a hectic week of catch-as-catch-can meals, it's time to slow the pace and actually enjoy your kitchen this weekend. Recreational cooks pull out pots and pans the way shoppers hit the malls and sports fans head to the stadium for fun.

These recipes are involved enough to be interesting, but not so complicated to be frustrating. They serve from 6 to 12 people, so weekend chefs can treat the whole family and even invite a few friends.

While any one of these entrées is baking in the oven, there's plenty of time to brighten the table with a vase of fall blooms or a basket of ivy.

DEVILED CRAB CASSEROLE

1 pound fresh crabmeat, drained and flaked (see note)
2 cups soft breadcrumbs, divided
½ cup chopped celery
2 tablespoons finely chopped green pepper
2 tablespoons chopped fresh parsley
2 tablespoons chopped chives
2 hard-cooked eggs, chopped
½ cup mayonnaise or salad dressing
2½ tablespoons lemon juice
1 tablespoon prepared mustard
½ teaspoon salt
½ teaspoon Worcestershire sauce
½ teaspoon hot sauce
1 egg, beaten
2 tablespoons butter or margarine, melted

Combine crabmeat, 1 cup breadcrumbs, celery, green pepper, parsley, chives, and egg in a lightly greased 2-quart baking dish. Combine mayonnaise and next 6 ingredients, and stir into crabmeat mixture.

Combine butter and remaining 1 cup breadcrumbs; sprinkle on top. Bake at 375° for 35 minutes or until thoroughly heated. Yield: 6 servings.

Note: You can substitute 1 (16-ounce) container pasteurized crabmeat, drained and flaked, for fresh crabmeat. To make casserole ahead, assemble and chill 8 hours before baking. Remove from refrigerator, and let sit at room temperature 30 minutes before baking as instructed.

Marge Killmon
Annandale, Virginia

ITALIAN PORK ROAST

1 (3- to 3½-pound) rolled boneless pork loin roast
4 cloves garlic, halved
1 tablespoon olive oil
1 to 2 tablespoons dried Italian seasoning
1 teaspoon coarsely ground pepper

Place roast in a shallow roasting pan. Cut 8 small slits in roast at 2-inch intervals; insert garlic clove halves deep into slits. Brush olive oil evenly over roast, and sprinkle with Italian seasoning and pepper. Insert meat thermometer, making sure it does not touch fat. Bake at 325° for 1½ hours (30 minutes per pound) or until meat thermometer reaches 155°. Remove from oven, and cover loosely with aluminum foil. Let stand 15 minutes or until meat thermometer reaches 160°. Yield: 10 to 12 servings. *Sara Cairns*
Montevallo, Alabama

SAVORY YOGURT CHICKEN

1 cup fine, dry breadcrumbs
¼ cup grated Parmesan cheese
1 to 2 tablespoons instant minced onion
1 teaspoon garlic powder
1 teaspoon seasoned salt
¼ teaspoon dried whole oregano, crushed
¼ teaspoon dried thyme, crushed
Dash of pepper
1 (8-ounce) carton plain yogurt
8 chicken breast halves, skinned
¼ cup butter or margarine, melted
1 teaspoon sesame seeds
Creamy Yogurt Sauce

Combine first 8 ingredients in a shallow dish; set aside.

Brush yogurt on all sides of chicken breast halves; coat with breadcrumb mixture. Place in a lightly greased 15- x 10- x 1-inch pan. Drizzle with butter, and sprinkle with sesame seeds. Bake, uncovered, at 350° for 50 to 60 minutes or until done. Serve casserole with Creamy Yogurt Sauce. Yield: 8 servings.

Creamy Yogurt Sauce

1 (8-ounce) carton plain yogurt
1 (10¾-ounce) can cream of chicken soup, undiluted
½ teaspoon chicken-flavored bouillon granules
½ teaspoon lemon juice
½ teaspoon Worcestershire sauce
Dash of garlic powder
Dash of seasoned salt

Combine yogurt (at room temperature) and remaining ingredients in a small saucepan; cook over low heat, stirring constantly, until thoroughly heated. Yield: 2 cups.

Mrs. Earl L. Faulkenberry
Lancaster, South Carolina

Tip: *An easy way to cut calories is to substitute yogurt for sour cream in most recipes.*

NOVEMBER

Now is the time to plan for holiday festivities. From appetizers to desserts, "Holiday Dinners" offers a variety of party plans with menus and recipes. Make a meal of appetizers at an informal buffet, or use one or two of the hors d'oeuvres to begin a special dinner party. Colorful side dishes, too, along with interesting entrées, abound in this bonus section. Mouth-watering desserts, both long-time favorites and new versions of old classics, round out the recipe selection.

Sugar & Spice
And Everything Nice . . .

. . . that's what fall baking is made of. Let cinnamon, cloves, ginger, allspice, and nutmeg bring the sweet scents of autumn to your kitchen.

And to your table, bring the sweet and spicy tastes of tea cakes, muffins, cinnamon rolls, or gingerbread that your baking creates.

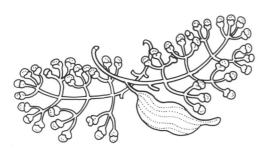

OLD-FASHIONED GINGERBREAD
(pictured on pages 266 and 267)

½ cup butter or margarine,
   softened
1 cup sugar
1 egg
1 cup molasses
2½ cups all-purpose flour
1½ teaspoons baking soda
½ teaspoon salt
1 teaspoon ground cinnamon
1 teaspoon ground ginger
1 cup hot water
Lemon Sauce
Garnish: lemon rind strips

Beat butter at medium speed of an electric mixer. Gradually add sugar, beating well. Add egg and molasses, mixing well.

Combine flour and next 4 ingredients; add to creamed mixture alternately with water, beginning and ending with flour mixture. Mix after each addition.

Pour batter into a lightly greased and floured 13- x 9- x 2-inch pan. Bake at 350° for 35 to 40 minutes or until a wooden pick inserted in center comes out clean. Serve with Lemon Sauce, and garnish, if desired. Yield: 15 to 18 servings.

Lemon Sauce

½ cup butter or margarine
1 cup sugar
¼ cup water
1 egg, beaten
Juice and rind of 1 lemon

Melt butter in a saucepan; add remaining ingredients, stirring constantly. Cook over medium heat until mixture reaches 160°. Yield: 2 cups.

Betsy Rose
Greensboro, North Carolina

RAISIN-CINNAMON ROLLS
(pictured on pages 266 and 267)

1 (16-ounce) loaf frozen bread
   dough, thawed
¼ cup butter or margarine, melted
   and divided
½ cup sugar
2 teaspoons ground cinnamon
⅓ cup raisins
2 tablespoons chopped almonds,
   toasted
2 teaspoons grated lemon rind
½ cup sifted powdered sugar
2½ teaspoons lemon juice

Roll dough on a lightly floured surface to a 14- x 8-inch rectangle. Brush surface of dough with 2 tablespoons melted butter.

Combine ½ cup sugar and next 4 ingredients in a small bowl; sprinkle over dough, leaving a ½-inch border on all sides. Starting with long side, roll up jellyroll fashion. Pinch seam to seal (do not seal ends).

Cut roll into 12 slices; place cut side down in a lightly greased 9-inch square pan. Brush with remaining 2 tablespoons melted butter. Cover and refrigerate 8 hours.

Remove pan from refrigerator, and let rolls rise in a warm place (85°), free from drafts, 50 minutes or until doubled in bulk. Bake rolls at 350° for 20 to 25 minutes.

Combine powdered sugar and lemon juice; drizzle over warm rolls. Yield: 1 dozen.   *Bettye Cortner*
Cerulean, Kentucky

PEAR-GINGER MUFFINS
(pictured on pages 266 and 267)

1 (16-ounce) can pear halves,
   drained
2 cups all-purpose flour
1 teaspoon baking soda
½ teaspoon salt
1 teaspoon ground ginger
1 teaspoon ground cinnamon
⅛ teaspoon ground nutmeg
⅛ teaspoon ground cloves
½ cup firmly packed dark brown
   sugar
1 egg, slightly beaten
1 (8-ounce) carton sour cream
½ cup vegetable oil
3 tablespoons molasses
½ cup chopped pecans
½ cup finely chopped crystallized
   ginger

Dice pear halves; drain on paper towels. Set aside.

Combine flour and next 7 ingredients in a mixing bowl; make a well in center of mixture. Combine egg and next 3 ingredients; add to dry ingredients, stirring just until moistened.

Combine diced pears, pecans, and crystallized ginger; gently stir into batter. Spoon into greased muffin pans, filling two-thirds full. Bake at 350° for 25 minutes. Yield: 16 muffins.

Note: Crystallized ginger can usually be found in the spice section of the grocery store. It is often sold cut up in pieces in a jar.   *Sue-Sue Hartstern*
Louisville, Kentucky

BRANDIED APRICOT
TEA CAKES
(pictured on pages 266 and 267)

1 (6-ounce) package dried apricots, finely chopped
½ cup currants
½ cup boiling water
½ cup butter or margarine, softened
1½ cups firmly packed brown sugar
3 eggs
2 cups all-purpose flour
½ teaspoon baking soda
½ teaspoon salt
1 teaspoon ground allspice
1 teaspoon ground cinnamon
½ teaspoon ground cloves
1 cup apricot brandy
Powdered sugar (optional)

Combine apricots and currants in a bowl; add boiling water. Cover and let stand 8 hours.

Beat butter in a large bowl at medium speed of an electric mixer; gradually add brown sugar, beating well. Add eggs, one at a time, beating well after each addition.

Combine flour and next 5 ingredients; add to creamed mixture alternately with brandy, beginning and ending with flour mixture. Mix after each addition. Stir in fruit mixture.

Spoon batter into paper-lined miniature muffin pans, filling three-fourths full. Bake at 325° for 25 to 30 minutes. Remove muffins from pans, and let cool on wire racks. Sprinkle muffins with powdered sugar, if desired. Yield: 4½ dozen.   *Ellie Wells*
Lakeland, Florida

A Spicy Tradition
In Natchitoches

You probably can't spell it or pronounce it, but you might remember Natchitoches (NACK-uh-tush) from *Steel Magnolias,* the movie that put this small town on the national map.

But Louisianans knew about this spot in the center of their state long before the stars arrived because it's the home of the famous Natchitoches Meat Pie, popular here since before the Civil War. Gone are the street vendors chanting "Hotta meat pies! Get your hotta meat pies right here!" But a Natchitoches native who remembers those cries from childhood has made sure the legend lives on. James Lasyone opened Lasyone's Meat Pie Kitchen & Restaurant almost 25 years ago, and it remains a popular place to enjoy the spicy, meat-filled pastries.

About the same time, Gay Melder was starting another meat pie tradition. Like many other residents, she loves to make the delicacies at home, so she sets aside one day a year to do just that—but not just any day. It is always the first Saturday in December, when about 150,000 visitors descend on the small town to celebrate the Christmas Festival of Lights. Now with us, she shares her recipe.

NATCHITOCHES MEAT PIES

1 pound lean ground beef
1 pound lean ground pork
1 medium onion, chopped
1 medium-size green pepper, chopped
1 bunch green onions, chopped
4 to 5 cloves garlic, minced
1 tablespoon all-purpose flour
1 teaspoon salt
½ teaspoon pepper
¼ to ½ teaspoon red pepper
Pastry
Vegetable oil

Combine meat in a heavy skillet; brown over medium heat, stirring until it crumbles. Remove from skillet; drain, reserving drippings in skillet. Set aside. Sauté onion and next 3 ingredients in skillet until tender. Return meat to skillet; stir in flour and seasonings. Set aside.

Divide pastry into 4 portions. Roll out one portion to ⅛-inch thickness. Cut 5 circles using a 6-inch saucer as a guide and rerolling dough if necessary. Spoon about ¼ cup meat mixture on one half of each dough circle. Moisten edges with water. Fold dough over meat mixture, pressing edges to seal. Crimp edges with a fork. Repeat procedure with remaining dough portions and meat mixture.

Pour oil to a depth of 3 inches into a Dutch oven; heat to 375°. Fry about 4 pies at a time until browned, turning once. Drain on paper towels. Serve immediately. Yield: 20 pies.

Pastry

8 cups all-purpose flour
2 teaspoons baking powder
4 teaspoons salt
1 cup shortening
2 eggs, beaten
2¼ cups milk

Combine flour, baking powder, and salt in a large bowl; cut in shortening with a pastry blender until mixture resembles coarse meal. Combine eggs and milk. Gradually add to flour mixture, stirring with a fork until dry ingredients are moistened. Shape into a ball (pastry will be stiff). Yield: pastry for 20 meat pies.

Note: Pies may be frozen before cooking. Place pies in a single layer on baking sheets; cover and freeze. Transfer from baking sheets to zip-top heavy-duty plastic bags, and return to freezer. To serve, thaw pies overnight in refrigerator, and fry as directed above.

You *Can* Afford A Party

Parties signal the arrival of the holiday season. So do buying gifts, making donations to charities, and booking seasonal travel plans. With so many expenses, you might be tempted to skip entertaining. But go ahead; you can entertain without blowing your budget. Here are some tips to keep costs down—and still have a good time.

Not Every Party Costs a Bundle

■ Hosting a breakfast or brunch is less expensive than a cocktail party and allows guests to plan their own afternoon and evening activities. A dessert buffet, complete with gourmet coffee, cheesecake, pound cake, fruit dessert, or other sweets, is another possibility.

■ Rely on an old favorite, the potluck supper. You supply the entrée; ask each of your guests to bring a side dish or salad and copies of the recipe. For each guest, quickly make a booklet of these recipes to send home as a party favor.

■ Host friends for a game of cards, board games, or holiday scavenger hunt. Offer a hot beverage and cookies or pound cake.

■ Soup and salad buffets lend themselves to easy planning and make controlling costs easier.

A Cocktail Party On a Budget

■ Serve a marinated eye-of-round roast, which is less expensive than beef tenderloin. Thinly slice the meat to go on party rolls. Any meat goes farther if you ask the butcher to professionally slice it after you cook it.

■ Meat is often one of the most expensive items on a menu. Ham or turkey is usually less expensive per pound than beef tenderloin. Offer a chafing dish recipe, such as a beef or sausage stroganoff, or a creamed seafood sauce, and serve it in small pastry shells to get the most from a small amount of meat.

■ Serve a seafood spread and crackers rather than whole marinated shrimp or shrimp cocktail. Substitute less expensive shrimp-, crab-, or seafood-flavored mixes for fresh seafood in casseroles or spreads. The mixes are available at delis or in the frozen foods or seafood section of supermarkets.

■ Instead of serving a dozen appetizers, select three or four that are substantial.

■ It seems that folks always eat the expensive items first; if your supply runs low, be prepared to replenish that tray with an item from the refrigerator or pantry, such as cream cheese topped with chutney or pepper jelly and served on crackers.

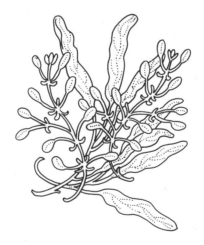

Set a Mood with Things You Have on Hand

Planning the decorations for a party can be as much fun as planning the food. The enthusiasm a party generates isn't always linked to spending a lot of money.

■ Instead of relying on fresh-cut flowers, arrange a grouping of potted poinsettias. Enjoy them the whole season or take them to friends or shut-ins after the party is over.

■ If you have grapevine wreaths and a tablecloth, you have a tablescape. Wind ribbon and greenery through the wreaths, and arrange them on the table. Set the punch bowl in the center of one. Place votive candles (which can be purchased inexpensively at variety stores) on the table for a glittering display of lights.

■ If you enlist the help of a floral designer, ask him or her to do arrangements with natural elements, such as pinecones, greenery, okra pods, and cotton bolls. While the initial cost may be more than many other types, you can enjoy the arrangement throughout the season.

■ Shop after-Christmas sales for next year's party favors and gifts. Tree ornaments, holiday mugs, and tea towels are nice to have on hand. Stock up on bright napkins to line bowls of party snacks, popcorn, or candies.

■ Printed invitations aren't required. Design your own—you can use photographs from last year's party, or unleash your own creativity with a photocopy machine and colored paper. Copy your invitations onto white paper, and let children color them for a personalized family greeting.

Holiday Dinners®

A Dinner In Progress

This holiday party gives new meaning to "places to go and

people to see." That's what this annual progressive dinner is

all about—a chance to meet the neighbors and enjoy a

traveling feast.

John Beckler checks his bow tie one last time in the foyer mirror while his wife, Pat, smooths the skirt of her royal-blue cocktail dress. Anyone would guess that they're headed out for a night on the town.

Actually, the Becklers—and lots of their neighbors—are staying home tonight. Well, not inside their houses, but within the familiar bounds they call home—WildeWood, a neighborhood in Columbia, South Carolina.

Tonight is their long-awaited seventh annual WildeWood Garden Club progressive dinner. After a year of extensive planning, these folks are in for a treat right in their own backyard. They'll spend the evening enjoying a multicourse meal, with each course served in a different location.

Half the fun is moving from place to place and discovering who's there. The whole idea behind this holiday party is that given an organized opportunity to mix and mingle, mere acquaintances will get a start on becoming friends. It is hoped that there will be fewer distant polite waves and more real over-the-fence chats on every block after this annual neighborhood event.

Pat looks over the "assignment sheet" she received two weeks before. She has her dish, Crabmeat Mousse, and they're headed for the Kilmanns' home for hors d'oeuvres, and then on to the Alexanders' for the main course.

Already there's a good bit of scurrying in the neighborhood as others go early for behind-the-scenes duties. Pat pauses briefly in the Kilmanns' large combined living and dining room to admire the touches of Christmas; she then joins a handful of women in the kitchen putting finishing touches on Blue Cheese Soufflé and Caviar-Artichoke Mound. Meanwhile, their husbands enjoy cocktails and each other's company.

The evening is off to a great start even before the rest of the 105 guests arrive for finger-food appetizers. The same scene is taking place a few doors down at the Lewis home. These two neighborhood houses were volunteered because their floor plans can accommodate large crowds.

As it nears 7:30 p.m., a few women search for a telephone. Synchronizing their missions, they call teenagers at home to warm their assigned main

course dishes and have them ready for a quick pickup. Several other couples excuse themselves early to go home and light candles, put on Christmas music, and await their dinner guests. As hosts, they're not asked to prepare any food, only their homes. Wilde-Wood scurries with activity as the 210 participants disperse to 16 homes. A sense of camaraderie prevails as kitchens fill with people carving Beef Tenderloin With Peppercorns and arranging Carrots and Broccoli With Horseradish Sauce.

When each plate is on the table, guests scan place cards for their seats. If hosts have done their job, no one will be next to his or her spouse, but instead near the person he or she knows the least. Throughout the meal, relaxed laughter and animated conversation accompany the quiet clinking of crystal and silver.

But this leisurely pace can't last forever; a final course awaits. With one more round of carefully timed phone calls and quick trips home for a dish, it's off to the evening's grand finale—dessert and coffee—at the WildeWood Country Club. It's large enough that the whole crowd has a chance to be together. And no one's watching the clock now. After sampling four desserts, these neighbors have time for sitting and chatting, or dancing 'til dawn (well, almost) to tunes spun by a disc jockey.

After a final twirl on the dance floor with John, Pat Beckler is ready to call it a night. On the way home, she and John compare notes and deem the event a success. They had a great meal and a good time. And along the way, they had opportunities to meet several new people, as well as to renew old acquaintances. They're already looking forward to next year.

Progressive Dinner In 3 Parts

First stop—A neighbor's home for appetizers

Second stop—Another home for the main course

Third stop—Country club for dessert buffet and dancing

CAVIAR-ARTICHOKE MOUND

4 (14-ounce) cans artichoke hearts, drained
2 (8-ounce) packages cream cheese, softened
¼ cup sour cream
2 tablespoons mayonnaise or salad dressing
½ to 1 cup finely chopped onion
2 (2-ounce) jars black caviar, drained

Chop artichokes; drain well on paper towels. Shape artichokes into a mound in center of dish, and set aside.

Combine cream cheese, sour cream, mayonnaise, and onion; beat at medium speed of an electric mixer 1 minute or until blended. Spread evenly over artichoke mound, flattening top slightly. Spoon caviar on top of mixture.

Refrigerate Caviar-Artichoke Mound until serving time. Serve with crackers. Yield: 15 to 20 servings.

CRABMEAT MOUSSE

1 envelope unflavored gelatin
¼ cup cold water
½ cup boiling water
½ cup mayonnaise or salad dressing
2 tablespoons finely chopped fresh chives or 2 teaspoons freeze-dried chives
2 tablespoons finely chopped fresh dillweed or 2 teaspoons dried whole dillweed
1 tablespoon grated onion
1 tablespoon lemon juice
1 teaspoon salt
¼ teaspoon paprika
Dash of hot sauce
2 cups fresh lump crabmeat, drained and flaked
1 cup whipping cream, whipped

Combine gelatin and ¼ cup cold water in a large bowl. Add ½ cup boiling water, stirring until gelatin dissolves. Cool to room temperature. Add mayonnaise and next 7 ingredients, stirring well. Chill until the consistency of unbeaten egg white.

Fold in crabmeat and whipped cream; spoon into a lightly oiled 6-cup mold. Cover and refrigerate until firm. Unmold and serve with crackers or bread. Yield: about 6 cups.

BLUE CHEESE SOUFFLÉ

1 envelope unflavored gelatin
2 tablespoons cold water
¼ cup butter or margarine, softened
½ (8-ounce) package cream cheese, softened
1 (4-ounce) package blue cheese, softened
1 teaspoon Dijon mustard
¾ cup whipping cream, whipped

Cut a piece of aluminum foil long enough to fit around a 1-cup soufflé dish, allowing a 1-inch overlap; fold foil lengthwise into thirds. Lightly oil one side of foil.

Wrap foil around outside of soufflé dish, with oiled side against dish, allowing it to extend 3 inches above rim to form a collar; secure foil with freezer tape or string.

Sprinkle gelatin over cold water in a small saucepan; let stand 1 minute. Cook over low heat, stirring until gelatin dissolves.

Combine butter, cheeses, and mustard in a mixing bowl; beat at medium speed of an electric mixer until smooth. Add gelatin; mix well. Fold in whipped cream.

Spoon mixture into prepared soufflé dish; cover and chill at least 8 hours. Remove collar, and serve soufflé with crackers or raw vegetables. Yield: about 2 cups.

Putting The Pieces Together

You may be thinking "so many details." WildeWood residents would add "but so much fun." Both their event and planning experience have grown over the years, so learn from these tips and start small in your neighborhood, just as they did. You may choose to adapt their idea to another holiday or theme, or even make your party casual.

■ **Make reservations early.** If you need a nearby clubhouse or public facility, get on the calendar early in the year because these are heavily requested for Christmas parties. Book a band or disc jockey at the same time. Choose hosts several months ahead so they have time to make special decorations or do those home repairs or projects often prompted by company coming.

■ **Plan and practice the menu.** Remember appearance, taste, and practicality when picking the menu. Choose dishes that can be made ahead, transported, and possibly reheated. Nothing is worse than unwelcome surprises the night of the big event, so get a group together and have a "dress rehearsal." Prepare the whole menu, and decide on serving pieces, presentation, and garnishes. Any problems that surface can be smoothed out then.

■ **Communicate and anticipate.** Send interested neighbors a notice with the date of the event a couple of months ahead. Request their commitment no

later than six weeks before the party, and be firm. With so many people involved, each with a dish or other responsibility, any last-minute changes affect everyone. If emergencies arise and someone can't make it, ask that she or a friend still provide the assigned recipe for the evening.

■ **Make a list, and check it twice.** Determine how many people each host can accommodate for the main course, and assign a group of people who don't know each other well to each hosting location. Also assign each person or couple in the group except the hosts one dish of the meal until the whole menu (including appetizers and dessert) is covered. If there are more guests than dishes needed, they can help with decorations, cleanup, or last-minute errands the day of the party.

Two weeks before the event, send each guest an assignment sheet listing the dish to bring and locations and times for each course. Attach a copy of the recipe for the dish, and include any special directions or presentation suggestions.

■ **Footing the bill.** Wilde-Wood's event is sponsored by its garden club, and members pay a

fee to the treasury for the event. This fee covers the cost of the meat or main dish, wine, and bakery rolls, as well as the club rental, the bartender, and the disc jockey. Members pay for the side dishes, appetizers, and desserts up to a certain amount; anything over that is reimbursed. The evening's total cost isn't always covered by the fee; when this occurs, the balance comes from the club's treasury.

If your neighborhood doesn't have an organization, try sending letters to measure interest in a progressive dinner. After determining size and style of the event, carefully estimate the cost of the food and drinks, facility rental, and band, if desired. Divide the total estimate by the number of interested people for a "per person" fee, and gauge interest again.

Appoint a chairman or committee to carry out the details, and see if a bank will arrange a temporary account for the event. If your party involves a very small group and cost, each person can contribute a dish, or one person can buy everything and then be reimbursed.

■ **Finishing touches.** Wilde-Wood volunteers compile cookbooks of the evening's recipes, place cards, and menu cards as keepsakes of the evening. You may also consider inexpensive party favors or printed napkins at the dessert course.

BIBB SALAD WITH RASPBERRY-MAPLE DRESSING

¼ cup raspberry vinegar
2 tablespoons maple syrup
⅔ cup vegetable oil
2 heads Bibb lettuce, torn
1 small purple onion, sliced and
  separated into rings
1 cup (4 ounces) crumbled blue
  cheese
¼ cup pine nuts, toasted

Combine vinegar and syrup; gradually add oil, stirring with a wire whisk. Set dressing aside.

Combine lettuce and sliced onion; arrange on individual salad plates. Sprinkle with blue cheese and pine nuts; drizzle with dressing. Yield: 6 servings.

BEEF TENDERLOIN WITH PEPPERCORNS

1 (5- to 6-pound) beef tenderloin,
  trimmed
3 tablespoons Dijon mustard
1 tablespoon dried whole sage
1½ tablespoons green peppercorns,
  drained
1½ tablespoons whole black
  peppercorns, ground and divided
1½ tablespoons whole white
  peppercorns, ground and divided
2 tablespoons butter, softened

Cut tenderloin lengthwise to within ½ inch of one long edge, leaving edge intact. Open tenderloin out flat. Place heavy-duty plastic wrap on tenderloin; pound meat to flatten slightly. Remove wrap; spread meat with mustard. Sprinkle top of tenderloin evenly with sage, green peppercorns, and ½ tablespoon each of black and white ground peppercorns.

Fold one side of tenderloin back over, and tie securely with heavy string at 3-inch intervals. Spread butter over outside, and sprinkle with remaining ground peppercorns.

Place tenderloin on a rack in a roasting pan; insert meat thermometer into thickest portion of tenderloin.

Bake at 425° for 30 to 45 minutes or until meat thermometer registers 140° (rare) or 160° (medium). Let stand 10 minutes before slicing. Yield: 10 to 12 servings.

SCALLOPED POTATOES WITH SWEET MARJORAM AND PARMESAN CHEESE

½ cup freshly grated Parmesan
  cheese
1 tablespoon dried whole marjoram
1 teaspoon salt
½ teaspoon garlic powder
¼ teaspoon grated nutmeg
¼ teaspoon coarsely ground pepper
4 large baking potatoes, peeled and
  thinly sliced (about 3 pounds)
2 tablespoons freshly grated
  Parmesan cheese
2 cups whipping cream
½ cup water
Garnish: fresh parsley sprigs

Combine first 6 ingredients in a small bowl. Set aside.

Layer potatoes in 12 (8-ounce) lightly greased ramekins, sprinkling each layer with reserved seasoning mixture, and ending with potatoes. Sprinkle top layer with 2 tablespoons Parmesan cheese.

Combine whipping cream and water; pour over potatoes. Put ramekins on baking sheets, and cover with foil. Bake at 350° for 1 hour and 20 minutes; uncover and bake 20 minutes or until lightly browned. Let stand 10

minutes before serving. Garnish, if desired. Yield: 12 (½-cup) servings.

Note: To make casserole, layer one-third of potatoes in a lightly greased 12- x 8- x 2-inch baking dish. Sprinkle half of seasoning mixture over potatoes. Repeat layers with potatoes and seasonings, ending with potatoes. Sprinkle evenly with 2 tablespoons Parmesan cheese.

Combine whipping cream and water; pour over potatoes. Cover with foil, and bake at 350° for 1½ hours. Uncover and bake 30 minutes. Let stand 10 minutes before serving. Casserole may serve only 6 to 8 if guests serve themselves.

CARROTS AND BROCCOLI WITH HORSERADISH SAUCE

½ cup mayonnaise or salad
  dressing
¼ cup milk
2½ tablespoons prepared
  horseradish
2 tablespoons minced onion
⅛ teaspoon salt
Dash of pepper
2 (12-ounce) packages fresh baby
  carrots, steamed
3 cups fresh broccoli flowerets,
  steamed

Combine first 6 ingredients; cook over low heat until hot (do not boil), stirring constantly. To serve, spoon about 2 tablespoons sauce on each plate; arrange warm carrots and broccoli on sauce. Yield: 6 servings.

STRAWBERRY CAROUSEL

2 tablespoons milk
1 tablespoon butter or margarine
¼ cup sugar
1 egg
1 egg yolk
¼ cup sifted cake flour
¼ teaspoon baking powder
½ cup strawberry preserves
2 tablespoons kirsch
White Chocolate Mousse
1 quart fresh strawberries
2 tablespoons minced pistachios

Combine milk and butter in top of a double boiler; bring water to a boil. Reduce heat to low; cook until butter melts. Keep warm over low heat.

Combine sugar, egg, and egg yolk in medium mixing bowl. Place bowl over large saucepan of hot (not simmering) water over low heat. Beat at low speed of an electric mixer 5 minutes or until sugar dissolves and mixture is warm. Remove bowl from hot water; beat at medium speed an additional 5 minutes or until mixture is tripled in volume and the consistency of whipped cream. Combine flour and baking powder; fold flour mixture and warm milk into whipped mixture.

Grease bottom and sides of an 8-inch springform pan. Line bottom with a circle of wax paper. Pour batter into prepared pan. Bake at 375° for 10 minutes or until a wooden pick inserted in center comes out clean. Cool in pan 10 minutes; remove from pan, leaving wax paper on bottom of cake, and cool completely on wire rack.

Remove wax paper from cake, and return cake to springform pan. Cook strawberry preserves in a small saucepan over low heat until melted; strain, and add kirsch. Brush half of mixture over cake, reserving the other half. Spread 1 cup White Chocolate Mousse over cake.

Cut enough strawberries in half lengthwise to line sides of pan. Place berries around edge of cake, points up

and cut sides against pan. Arrange remaining whole berries on top of cake, points up. Spoon or pipe remaining mousse between berries on top of cake. Chill cake at least 3 hours.

To serve, remove sides from pan. Reheat remaining preserves mixture; brush on sides of cake and exposed surface of berries. Press pistachios against sides of cake. Chill at least 30 minutes. Yield: 8 to 10 servings.

White Chocolate Mousse

8 ounces white chocolate, grated
2 tablespoons water
3 tablespoons kirsch
1½ cups whipping cream, whipped

Combine white chocolate and water in a heavy saucepan; cook over low heat, stirring constantly, until chocolate melts. Cool; stir in kirsch.

Fold whipped cream into white chocolate mixture. Yield: 4 cups.

Note: Recipe can be made the day before and refrigerated.

LEMON-RASPBERRY CAKE

1 cup shortening
2 cups sugar
4 eggs
3 cups sifted cake flour
2½ teaspoons baking powder
½ teaspoon salt
1 cup milk
1 teaspoon almond extract
1 teaspoon vanilla extract
1 (10-ounce) jar seedless raspberry preserves
Lemon Buttercream Frosting

Beat shortening at medium speed of an electric mixer; gradually add sugar, beating well. Add eggs, one at a time, beating well after each addition.

Combine flour, baking powder, and salt; add to creamed mixture alternately with milk, beginning and ending with flour mixture. Mix after each addition. Stir in flavorings.

Pour batter into 3 greased and floured 9-inch round cakepans. Bake at 375° for 18 to 20 minutes or until a wooden pick inserted in center comes out clean. Cool in pans 10 minutes; remove from pans, and let cool completely on wire racks.

Split cake layers in half horizontally. Place half of one cake layer, cut side up, on a cake plate; spread with about 2 tablespoons raspberry preserves. Repeat with remaining layers, omitting preserves on top of last layer. Frost top and sides of cake with Lemon Buttercream Frosting, reserving 1 cup frosting to pipe on top and sides of cake. Chill until serving time. Yield: one 6-layer cake.

Lemon Buttercream Frosting

1¼ cups butter or margarine, softened
2 teaspoons grated lemon rind
3 tablespoons lemon juice
3 cups sifted powdered sugar

Combine butter, lemon rind, and lemon juice; beat at medium speed of an electric mixer 30 seconds. Gradually add powdered sugar to mixture until blended. Beat an additional 2 to 3 minutes or until mixture is light and fluffy. Yield: 3 cups.

Tip: *To keep the plate neat while frosting a cake, place three or four strips of wax paper over the edges of the plate. Position the cake on the plate, and fill and frost it; then carefully pull out the wax paper strips.*

HAZELNUT TORTE

6 eggs, separated
¾ cup sugar, divided
⅓ cup dry breadcrumbs
¼ cup all-purpose flour
⅔ cup finely chopped hazelnuts
Creamy Mocha Frosting

Beat egg whites in mixing bowl at high speed of an electric mixer until soft peaks form. Gradually add ¼ cup sugar; beat until soft peaks form. Set mixture aside.

Beat egg yolks at high speed until thick and lemon colored (about 2 minutes). Gradually add remaining ½ cup sugar; beat 1 minute. Add breadcrumbs, flour, and nuts, mixing well (mixture will be very stiff). Stir in about ¾ cup egg whites; fold in remaining egg whites.

Pour batter into a greased and floured 9-inch springform pan. Bake at 325° for 40 to 45 minutes. Let cake cool in pan 10 minutes. Remove carefully from pan, and cool completely on a wire rack.

Slice cake horizontally into thirds. Spread Creamy Mocha Frosting between layers and on sides of layers, and pipe or spread on top of torte. Yield: one 9-inch torte.

Creamy Mocha Frosting

1 teaspoon instant coffee granules
1 tablespoon hot water
1 cup butter, softened
2 (1-ounce) squares semisweet chocolate, melted
2 cups sifted powdered sugar
1 teaspoon vanilla extract

Dissolve coffee granules in hot water; cool. Beat butter at medium speed of an electric mixer. Add coffee and chocolate, mixing well. Add powdered sugar and vanilla; beat 2 minutes or until frosting mixture is light and fluffy. Yield: 2 cups.

CHOCOLATE-ALMOND CAKE

½ cup cocoa
½ cup boiling water
⅔ cup shortening
1¾ cups sugar
2 eggs
2¼ cups all-purpose flour
1½ teaspoons baking soda
¼ teaspoon salt
1½ cups buttermilk
1 teaspoon vanilla extract
Almond Cream Filling
Chocolate Frosting
2 tablespoons sliced almonds, toasted

Combine cocoa and boiling water in a bowl; stir until smooth. Set aside.

Beat shortening. Gradually add sugar, beating well. Add eggs, one at a time; beat well after each addition.

Combine flour, soda, and salt; add to creamed mixture alternately with buttermilk, beginning and ending with flour mixture. Mix just until blended after each addition. Stir in chocolate mixture and vanilla.

Pour batter into 3 greased and floured 8-inch round cakepans; bake at 350° for 20 to 25 minutes or until a wooden pick inserted in center comes out clean. Cool in pans 10 minutes; remove from pans, and let cool completely on wire racks. Spread Almond Cream Filling between layers.

Reserve 1 cup Chocolate Frosting; spread remaining frosting on top and sides of cake. Pipe or dollop reserved frosting on top of cake; sprinkle with almonds. Yield: one 3-layer cake.

Almond Cream Filling

¼ cup all-purpose flour
½ cup milk
¼ cup butter or margarine, softened
½ cup shortening
1 teaspoon almond extract
¼ teaspoon salt
4 cups sifted powdered sugar

Combine flour and milk in a small saucepan; cook over low heat, stirring constantly with a wire whisk, until mixture thickens and just begins to boil. Remove from heat; cool. Cover and chill at least 1 hour.

Beat butter and shortening at medium speed of an electric mixer. Add chilled flour mixture, almond extract, and salt; beat until smooth. Gradually add powdered sugar; beat at high speed 4 to 5 minutes or until light and fluffy. Yield: 2½ cups.

Chocolate Frosting

½ cup butter or margarine, softened
3 (1-ounce) squares unsweetened chocolate, melted
⅓ cup milk
1 teaspoon vanilla extract
1 (16-ounce) package powdered sugar, sifted

Beat butter and chocolate at low speed of an electric mixer until smooth. Blend in milk and vanilla extract. Gradually add powdered sugar; beat at high speed 5 minutes or until fluffy. Yield: enough to frost one 3-layer cake.

Tip: *Sifting flour, with the exception of cake flour, is no longer necessary. Simply stir the flour, gently spoon it into a dry measure, and level the top. Powdered sugar, however, should be sifted to remove the lumps.*

They're Coming For Dinner

"The most stressful part of entertaining is timing. So many things are cooking at once. It's definitely a management situation—and not a day to try out new recipes, at least not for me," says Amy Booker as she flashes a quick, bright smile. A dietetics major with a minor in journalism at Louisiana State University, Amy uses her culinary skills to plan the big meal at her father's house or to host friends during the holidays. After a few attempts at entertaining, she's now a seasoned veteran, and willingly shares her preparation tips. "When I entertain, I carefully schedule what ingredients need to be chilled and what foods need to be baked. Otherwise, something can come out two hours late."

For Amy, selecting the foods she'll serve and creating the setting are crucial parts of hosting a meal. "For a dinner, you need foods with a lot of variety in appearance, color, and texture. Everything looks the same if you're not careful. I like to have dishes of as many sizes and shapes as possible, and *lots* of fresh flowers," she says.

This young cook's thoughts helped us plan the recipes for this menu for the first-time cook—or the experienced cook who's too busy to plan. The recipes came from our readers, and the step-by-step plan was designed by our home economists. They tested this menu with the frantic pace of the "big day" in mind.

Traditional Holiday Spread
Currant-Glazed Ham
Easy Spinach Salad
Sweet Potatoes Royale
Sweet-and-Sour Green Beans
Commercial rolls
Hot Cranberry Bake   Ice cream
Wine or iced tea
Coffee

A Step-by-Step Plan

A Day Ahead: Make Sweet Potatoes Royale; refrigerate. Wash and tear spinach; refrigerate spinach in air-tight container or plastic bag. Wash beans, trim ends, and remove the strings; refrigerate beans. Set table; set up buffet for serving.

Three hours Before Serving: Begin cooking Currant-Glazed Ham. Assemble and bake Hot Cranberry Bake. Begin glazing ham. Remove Sweet Potatoes Royale from refrigerator, and let stand 30 minutes. When dessert comes out of oven, put sweet potato casserole in to bake. When the ham reaches 140°, remove it from the oven. Cover the ham with aluminum foil, and let stand until ready to carve. Assemble Easy Spinach Salad, refrigerating until serving time. Make Sweet-and-Sour Green Beans. Warm commercial rolls in oven immediately before sitting down to eat the dinner.

CURRANT-GLAZED HAM

1 (10-ounce) jar red currant jelly
¼ cup dry sherry
1 (8½-pound) smoked, fully cooked, bone-in ham half

Combine currant jelly and sherry in a small saucepan; cook over low heat, stirring constantly, until jelly melts. Remove from heat; set aside.

Remove skin from ham; if necessary, trim fat to ¼- to ⅛-inch thickness. Place ham, fat side up, on rack in a shallow roasting pan. Cover with aluminum foil; bake at 325° for 1 hour. Remove foil; baste generously with jelly mixture. Bake, uncovered, 30 to 45 minutes or until a meat thermometer registers 140°, basting every 15 minutes. Yield: 16 servings.

Mildred Bickley
Bristol, Virginia

EASY SPINACH SALAD

1½ pounds fresh spinach
2 (11-ounce) cans mandarin oranges, drained
1 (2.25-ounce) package sliced almonds, toasted
Commercial Italian, poppy seed, or spinach salad dressing

Remove stems from spinach; wash leaves thoroughly, and pat dry. Tear into bite-size pieces. Combine spinach, oranges, and almonds in a large bowl. Serve with salad dressing. Yield: 8 servings.

SWEET POTATOES ROYALE

1 (29-ounce) can sweet potato
   pieces, drained and mashed
1 (17-ounce) can sweet potato
   pieces, drained and mashed
½ cup firmly packed dark brown
   sugar
½ cup applesauce
¼ cup butter or margarine, melted
2 teaspoons vanilla extract
¾ cup flaked coconut
20 large marshmallows

Combine first 6 ingredients. Spoon mixture into a lightly greased 12- x 8- x 2-inch baking dish; bake at 325° for 25 minutes.

Remove from oven; sprinkle with coconut. Arrange marshmallows on top; bake 10 to 15 minutes or until marshmallows are golden. Yield: 8 servings.

Note: Casserole may be assembled and refrigerated 8 hours or a day before baking. Remove from refrigerator, and let stand 30 minutes; uncover and bake as directed. *Rose Alleman*
Saint Amant, Louisiana

SWEET-AND-SOUR GREEN BEANS

2 pounds fresh green beans (see
   note)
1 cup water
2 slices bacon
½ cup diced onion
1 tablespoon all-purpose flour
¼ cup white vinegar
2 tablespoons sugar
1 teaspoon salt
¼ teaspoon pepper

Wash beans; trim ends, and remove strings. Bring water to a boil in a Dutch oven; add beans. Cover and cook 10 minutes or until crisp-tender. Drain beans, reserving ¾ cup liquid; set beans and liquid aside.

Cook bacon in a large skillet until crisp; remove bacon, reserving drippings in skillet. Crumble bacon, and set aside. Sauté onion in skillet until tender. Add flour; cook 1 minute, stirring constantly. Stir in reserved liquid, vinegar, sugar, salt, and pepper. Reduce heat, and simmer 8 to 10 minutes or until thickened, stirring constantly. Add green beans to mixture; toss to coat. Cover and heat thoroughly. Spoon into a serving bowl; sprinkle with crumbled bacon. Yield: 8 servings.

Note: If desired, three (9-ounce) packages frozen whole green beans may be substituted for fresh green beans; cook until crisp-tender according to package directions.
Mrs. L. Mayer
Richmond, Virginia

Timely Tips

■ Save time by carefully organizing your shopping list, grouping items according to the layout of the store.

■ While you are out shopping, check your local variety store or kitchen shop for a timer. It will help keep you on track.

■ Plan your table setting ahead to save valuable last-minute time. (Setting the table doesn't have to bankrupt you. For instance, you can buy attractive, inexpensive plates and combine them with other platters and serving pieces.)

HOT CRANBERRY BAKE
(pictured on page 266)

4 cups peeled, chopped cooking
   apples
2 cups fresh cranberries
1½ teaspoons lemon juice
1 cup sugar
1⅓ cups quick-cooking oats,
   uncooked
1 cup chopped walnuts
⅓ cup firmly packed brown sugar
½ cup butter or margarine, melted
Vanilla ice cream

Layer apples and cranberries in a lightly greased 2-quart baking dish. Sprinkle with lemon juice; spoon 1 cup sugar over fruit. Set aside.

Combine oats and next 3 ingredients; stir just until dry ingredients are moistened and mixture is crumbly. Sprinkle over fruit; bake, uncovered, at 325° for 1 hour. Serve dessert warm with vanilla ice cream. Yield: 8 servings.
Sue-Sue Hartstern
Louisville, Kentucky

Appetizers Aplenty

Appetizers typically tease the palate for the dinner menu to come, but just for fun, make a meal of appetizers. These recipes feature meat, cheese, fruit, or vegetables, so they offer enough variety to mix and match like a traditional menu.

Whether your crowd numbers 4 or 40, an appetizer buffet will encourage a casual atmosphere—for guests and party planners alike. Follow these guidelines for personalizing an appetizer menu; then pick and choose your favorites from the categories of recipes that follow.

—Vary the types of food to keep the menu well rounded. One meat and one cheese appetizer will pair well with a fruit or vegetable selection. For variety, make sure only one of the choices features bread or chips.

—Balance the way appetizers are prepared; avoid the common mistake of preparing multiple dips and spreads in one menu.

—Aim for variety in the texture, color, and flavor of the recipes grouped together. It's appealing for one or two of the selections to be hot.

—Select three to five appetizers when the guest list includes up to 25 people, and count on each person sampling 2 to 4 of each item, depending on the number of items offered. Double or triple the number of choices of appetizers accordingly as the number of people multiplies.

—If you'd like to offer dessert, select one or two favorite cookies, candies, or mini-tarts so that guests can easily serve themselves.

—When in doubt as to how much to prepare, err on the side of excess; it's embarrassing to run out of food, but often helpful to have leftovers.

■ **Meaty Appetizers**—Start menu planning with meat appetizers. They're the most expensive and time-consuming to prepare. Beginning with meat helps fit the rest of the menu into your schedule and budget.

APPETIZER SHRIMP KABOBS

2 pounds unpeeled large fresh shrimp
½ cup lemon juice
½ cup vegetable oil
¼ cup soy sauce
3 tablespoons chopped fresh parsley
2 tablespoons finely chopped onion
½ teaspoon salt
½ teaspoon pepper
1 clove garlic, minced

Peel shrimp, and devein, if desired; set aside. Combine lemon juice and remaining ingredients except shrimp in a shallow dish; set aside.

Arrange shrimp on 6-inch bamboo skewers, and place in marinade, turning to coat. Cover and refrigerate 2 to 3 hours.

Remove shrimp from marinade, reserving marinade. Place shrimp on rack of a lightly greased broiler pan. Broil 6 inches from heat 3 to 4 minutes on each side, basting occasionally with remaining marinade. Serve hot or cold. Yield: about 3 dozen.

Myra Williams
Iuka, Mississippi

HONEY-GLAZED CHICKEN WINGS

2 pounds chicken wings
1 cup honey
½ cup soy sauce
2 tablespoons sesame or vegetable oil
2 tablespoons minced fresh gingerroot
2 tablespoons minced scallions
2 tablespoons catsup
1 clove garlic, minced

Cut off and discard wingtips; cut wings in half at joint. Place wing pieces in a 13- x 9- x 2-inch baking dish.

Combine honey, soy sauce, oil, fresh gingerroot, scallions, catsup, and minced garlic in a small bowl; pour mixture over wing pieces, turning to coat. Cover and chill 1 hour.

Transfer wings to a lightly greased 15- x 10- x 1-inch jellyroll pan; bake, uncovered, at 375° for 45 minutes, turning once. Transfer to a serving platter. Yield: 8 to 10 appetizer servings.

DeLea Lanadier
Montgomery, Louisiana

■ **From the Cheese Counter**—Most appetizers with cheese offer make-ahead convenience. Cheese balls and dips can be made a day or two early; Cheesy-Sesame Seed Turnovers can be baked and frozen, then reheated at the last minute. To offer maximum flavor let cheese balls and uncut cheese (such as Honey-Mustard Brie) sit at room temperature for an hour before serving.

FRUIT-AND-NUT CHEESE BALL

4 cups (16 ounces) shredded sharp Cheddar cheese
¾ cup butter or margarine, softened
2 tablespoons Dijon mustard
2 tablespoons milk
2 teaspoons Worcestershire sauce
½ cup mixed dried fruit bits, chopped
½ cup sliced almonds, toasted

Position knife blade in food processor bowl; add first 5 ingredients. Process 1 minute or until smooth. Chill 30 minutes. Shape into a ball. Roll in dried fruit and almonds, pressing gently to make fruit and almonds adhere. Chill up to 2 days. Let sit 1 hour. Serve with crackers. Yield: one 3½-cup cheese ball.

Charlotte Moret
St. Louis, Missouri

Tip: *Refrigerate cheese in its original wrap until opened. After opening, rewrap the cheese tightly in plastic wrap, plastic bags, or aluminum foil, or place in airtight containers and refrigerate.*

CHEESY SESAME SEED TURNOVERS

2 (3-ounce) packages cream cheese, softened
1 cup butter or margarine, softened
2 cups all-purpose flour
3 eggs, beaten
2 cups (8 ounces) shredded Muenster or gouda cheese
2 tablespoons grated onion
½ teaspoon hot sauce
¼ teaspoon salt
2 egg whites, beaten
3 to 4 tablespoons sesame seeds

Combine cream cheese and butter in a large bowl; beat at medium speed with an electric mixer until smooth. Add flour, and beat well. Divide dough in half, and shape into 2 balls; wrap in plastic wrap, and chill at least 1 hour.
Combine eggs and next 4 ingredients, mixing well.
Roll pastry to ⅛-inch thickness on a lightly floured surface. Cut into 2½-inch rounds. Place 1 teaspoon cheese mixture in center. Brush edges of pastry with water, and fold in half; seal edges. Place on ungreased baking sheets, and brush with beaten egg whites; sprinkle with sesame seeds. Bake at 375° for 20 minutes or until golden. Yield: 5 dozen.

Note: To freeze, place baked turnovers on a baking sheet; freeze. Transfer to a plastic bag, and freeze up to 1 month. To serve, bake frozen turnovers at 375° for 5 minutes or until thoroughly heated.

C. M. Grunsten
Yalaha, Florida

Tip: *Do not throw away cheese that has dried out or any small leftover pieces. Grate the cheese; cover and freeze for use in casseroles or to top baked potatoes or toast.*

HONEY-MUSTARD BRIE

1 (15-ounce) round Brie cheese
¼ cup honey mustard
½ cup sliced almonds or chopped pecans, toasted
Apple wedges
1 (6-ounce) can pineapple juice

Remove rind from top of cheese, cutting to within ½ inch of outside edges. Place Brie on a large serving plate, and spread mustard over top; sprinkle with almonds. Cover and let stand at room temperature at least 1 hour.
Toss apple wedges in pineapple juice; drain. Arrange fruit around Brie; serve immediately. Yield: 10 to 14 appetizer servings.

PEPPERONCINI-CREAM CHEESE DIP

1 (10-ounce) jar pepperoncini (salad peppers), drained and stemmed
1 (8-ounce) package cream cheese, softened
¼ cup grated Parmesan cheese
½ cup sour cream

Position knife blade in food processor bowl; add first 3 ingredients. Pulse several times or until smooth. Stir in sour cream. Cover and chill until ready to serve. Serve with pita toast triangles. Yield: 1⅔ cups.

■ Your Pick of Vegetables and Fruits—These hors d'oeuvres offer color, fiber, and flavor to round out the menu, and often can be made ahead of time, too. If you want to serve appetizers from more than one category, this one is a good choice.

TROPICAL DIP FOR FRUIT

1 (8-ounce) carton sour cream
½ cup apricot preserves
½ cup macadamia nuts, chopped and toasted
¼ cup flaked coconut

Combine all ingredients; cover and chill. Serve with assorted fresh fruit. Yield: 1¾ cups.

Ellen Palmer
Atlanta, Georgia

VEGETABLE CANAPÉS

1 (3-ounce) package cream cheese, softened
3 tablespoons sour cream
¼ teaspoon garlic salt
⅛ teaspoon white pepper
½ teaspoon dried whole dillweed
3 tablespoons frozen minced chives, thawed
8 slices very thin white bread
8 slices very thin whole wheat bread
Thinly sliced cucumber, squash, or radishes
Shredded carrot
Sliced cherry tomatoes
Fresh watercress or dillweed sprigs

Beat cream cheese until fluffy. Stir in next 5 ingredients; set aside.
Cut two 1¾-inch rounds from each bread slice. Keep bread covered with damp towels while assembling. Spread each bread round with 1 teaspoon cream cheese mixture. Top with assorted vegetables and watercress as desired. Yield: 32 canapés.

Holiday Turkey Talk

There is more than one way to cook a turkey. Not only do flavoring ingredients vary with these recipes, but the way the turkey is roasted, what part of the turkey is used, and even where the giblets go are also up for debate.

Several years ago, Sunny Tiedemann concocted Madeira Roast Turkey (recipe on next page). The dish was such a hit with family and friends that they haven't allowed her to serve other turkey recipes since.

As for the recipe for Grandmother's Dressing that accompanies this spirited bird, Sunny recalls, "When I was a teenager, my grandmother, Dixie Belle Chesnut McConnell, taught me her turkey dressing recipe by the handful-of-this and pinch-of-that method. I developed specific measurements in 1982 when my daughter wanted to make a traditional Southern Thanksgiving dinner to impress her prospective Yankee in-laws."

HERBED TURKEY-IN-A-BAG
(pictured on page 4)

1 (10-pound) turkey
2 tablespoons dried parsley flakes
1 tablespoon rubbed sage
1 teaspoon dried whole marjoram
1 teaspoon dried whole thyme
1 teaspoon dried whole savory
½ teaspoon dried whole rosemary
1 tablespoon all-purpose flour
Garnish: assorted fresh herbs

Remove giblets and neck from turkey; reserve for other uses. Rinse turkey with cold water; pat dry. Tie ends of turkey legs to tail with cord if legs are not tucked under flap of skin. Lift wingtips up and over back, and tuck under turkey.

Combine parsley flakes and next 5 ingredients in container of an electric blender; process 1 minute. Sprinkle cavity and outside of turkey with herb mixture.

Shake flour in a large oven cooking bag; place in a large roasting dish at least 2 inches deep. Place turkey in bag, readjusting wingtips, if necessary. Close cooking bag, and seal; make 6 (½-inch) slits in top of bag, following package directions. Insert meat thermometer through bag into meaty part of turkey thigh, making sure thermometer does not touch bone. Bake turkey at 325° until meat thermometer reaches 185°.

Remove roasting dish from oven; carefully cut a large slit in top of bag. Remove turkey; let stand 15 minutes before carving. Garnish, if desired. Yield: 10 to 12 servings.

Patsy Bell Hobson
Liberty, Missouri

TURKEY BREAST WITH ORANGE-RASPBERRY GLAZE

1 (5- to 5½-pound) turkey breast, skinned and boned
1 cup orange juice
1 teaspoon grated orange rind
1 teaspoon rubbed sage
½ teaspoon dried whole thyme
½ teaspoon pepper
1 tablespoon cornstarch
¼ cup water
2 cups fresh or frozen raspberries, thawed
⅓ cup sugar

Place turkey breast in a 13- x 9- x 2-inch pan. Pour orange juice over breast, and sprinkle with orange rind, sage, thyme, and pepper. Cover and bake at 325° for 1½ hours or until meat thermometer registers 170°, basting breast frequently with pan drippings.

Transfer turkey to a serving platter. Set aside. Measure 1 cup pan drippings, adding water, if necessary, to make 1 cup; strain and set aside.

Combine cornstarch and ¼ cup water in a small saucepan, stirring well. Add raspberries, sugar, and reserved pan drippings. Cook over medium heat until mixture thickens, stirring frequently. Serve sauce with turkey. Yield: 8 to 10 servings.

Carrie Byrne Bartlett
Gallatin, Tennessee

Tip: *Never add cornstarch to a hot mixture because it will lump. Dilute cornstarch in twice as much cold liquid and stir until smooth. Then gently stir into the hot mixture.*

MADEIRA ROAST TURKEY WITH GRANDMOTHER'S DRESSING

½ cup butter or margarine, melted
1 cup Madeira wine
3 tablespoons soy sauce
3 tablespoons Worcestershire sauce
1 lemon, cut in half
1 (12- to 15-pound) turkey
Vegetable cooking spray
1 to 3 tablespoons cornstarch
¼ cup water
Grandmother's Dressing
Garnishes: purple cabbage, lemon
  slices, fresh parsley sprigs

Combine first 4 ingredients and juice of one lemon half; set aside.

Remove giblets and neck from turkey; reserve for other uses. Rinse turkey with cold water; pat dry. Tie ends of legs to tail with cord if legs are not tucked under flap of skin. Lift wingtips up and over back, and tuck under bird.

Place turkey on rack of a roasting pan, breast side up; rub turkey with other lemon half, squeezing juice over turkey. Spray turkey with cooking spray. Insert meat thermometer into meaty part of thigh, making sure it does not touch bone. Bake at 325° for 3 hours or until meat thermometer reaches 185°, basting every 30 minutes after the first hour with Madeira mixture. If turkey starts to brown too much, cover with aluminum foil.

When turkey is two-thirds done, cut the cord or band of skin holding drumsticks to tail; this will ensure that thighs are cooked internally. Turkey is done when drumsticks are easy to move up and down. Let stand 15 minutes before carving.

Measure remaining basting mixture and pan juices from turkey. Using 1 tablespoon cornstarch to each cup of drippings, combine cornstarch and ¼ cup water, stirring until smooth; stir into pan drippings. Bring to a boil; boil 1 minute, stirring constantly. Serve with turkey. Garnish turkey and Grandmother's Dressing, if desired. Yield: 14 to 16 servings.

Grandmother's Dressing

¼ cup shortening
1 cup cornmeal
½ cup all-purpose flour
1 teaspoon baking powder
½ teaspoon baking soda
½ teaspoon salt
2 eggs, beaten
1 cup buttermilk
8 slices day-old bread, cut into
  ½-inch cubes
¾ cup chopped celery
¾ cup chopped onion
½ cup chopped fresh parsley
2 teaspoons poultry seasoning
2 teaspoons white pepper
2 teaspoons rubbed sage
1 to 2 teaspoons ground thyme
1 teaspoon celery salt
½ cup butter or margarine, melted
3 eggs, beaten
2 (14½-ounce) cans ready-to-serve
  chicken broth

Spoon shortening into an 8-inch cast-iron skillet. Place in a 425° oven for 4 minutes or until hot.

Combine cornmeal, flour, baking powder, soda, and salt in a large bowl; add 2 eggs and buttermilk, stirring well. Spoon into hot skillet, and bake at 425° for 35 minutes or until browned. Cool; crumble cornbread into a large bowl. Add bread cubes and remaining ingredients, stirring well. Spoon into a lightly greased 13- x 9- x 2-inch baking dish, and bake at 325° for 1 hour or until golden brown. Yield: 8 to 10 servings.

Sunny Tiedemann
Bartlesville, Oklahoma

TURKEY WITH GIBLET DRESSING AND TURKEY GRAVY

1 (10- to 12-pound) turkey
1 teaspoon poultry seasoning
½ teaspoon salt
½ teaspoon pepper
Vegetable oil
Giblet Dressing
Turkey Gravy

More Turkey Talk

■ An uncooked or cooked stuffed turkey or chicken should never be refrigerated. The stuffing should be thoroughly removed and refrigerated in a separate container.

■ The giblets and necks should be removed from whole chickens and turkeys, and then washed, and cooked within 12 hours.

■ When you have small portions of meat or poultry leftover, cut it up into bite-size pieces, and freeze it until you have enough to add to a pot pie or casserole.

■ Extend the storage life of your turkey leftovers by freezing them. Slice, chop, or cube the meat, and then package it in meal-size portions.

Remove giblets and neck from turkey; reserve for gravy and dressing. Rinse turkey with cold water; pat dry. Sprinkle cavity with poultry seasoning, salt, and pepper. Tie ends of legs to tail with cord if legs are not tucked under flap of skin. Lift wingtips up and over back, and tuck under turkey.

Place turkey on an oiled roasting rack, breast side up; brush entire bird with oil. Insert meat thermometer into meaty part of thigh, making sure it does not touch bone. Bake at 325° for 2 hours and 45 minutes or until thermometer reaches 185°. If turkey starts to brown too much, cover with aluminum foil.

When turkey is two-thirds done, cut the cord or band of skin holding drumsticks to tail; this procedure will ensure that thighs are cooked internally. Turkey is done when drumsticks are easy to move up and down. Let turkey stand 15 minutes before carving. Reserve 1 cup pan drippings for Turkey Gravy. Serve turkey with Giblet Dressing and Turkey Gravy. Yield: 12 to 14 servings.

Giblet Dressing

Turkey giblets and neck
1 quart water
2 chicken-flavored bouillon cubes
1 teaspoon poultry seasoning
½ teaspoon salt
½ teaspoon pepper
Canned chicken broth
2 cloves garlic, minced
1 stalk celery, chopped
1 medium onion, chopped
1 tablespoon butter or margarine, melted
4 cups French bread cubes, toasted
½ cup mashed potatoes
1 cup self-rising cornmeal
1 teaspoon dried whole parsley
½ teaspoon cream of tartar
½ teaspoon pepper
¼ teaspoon salt
¼ teaspoon ground nutmeg
2 eggs, lightly beaten

Place giblets and neck in a large saucepan; add water, bouillon cubes, poultry seasoning, salt, and pepper. Bring to a boil; cover, reduce heat, and simmer 45 minutes or until giblets and neck are tender. Let cool. Cover and chill at least 8 hours.

Discard layer of fat on top of mixture. Pick meat from neck; set aside for gravy. Chop giblets; set aside for dressing. Add canned chicken broth, if necessary, to make chilled broth measure 4 cups. Set aside.

Sauté garlic, celery, and onion in butter in a Dutch oven until tender; add 2 cups reserved broth (keep remaining 2 cups broth), giblets, bread cubes, mashed potatoes, cornmeal, dried parsley, cream of tartar, pepper, salt, nutmeg, and eggs; stir to blend. Bake at 325° in a lightly greased 9-inch square pan for 45 minutes. Yield: 9 servings.

Turkey Gravy

1 cup pan drippings from turkey
Canned chicken broth
¼ cup cornstarch
2 cups reserved turkey broth, divided
½ teaspoon salt
½ teaspoon pepper
½ to 1 teaspoon poultry seasoning
½ cup chopped turkey
Turkey neck meat

Chill pan drippings; discard layer of fat on top of mixture. If necessary, add canned chicken broth to equal 1 cup drippings.

Combine cornstarch and ½ cup turkey broth in a large saucepan; stir well. Add pan drippings, remaining 1½ cups turkey broth, and seasonings. Bring mixture to a boil, stirring constantly. Add chopped turkey and neck meat; boil 1 minute, stirring constantly. Yield: 3 cups.

Flora Lee B. Powers
Chesapeake, Virginia

Fresh Ideas For Salads

Looking for some variety in your family's annual holiday meal? Your mom's roast turkey and your aunt's pecan pie may be long-standing favorites, but why not try a new salad this year? Raspberry-Wine Salad, a jazzed-up version of a basic cranberry congealed salad, goes especially well with turkey and dressing.

Try Tossed Shell Salad if you're planning a Christmas buffet. It's festive in color and easy for guests to serve themselves.

For a last-minute salad idea, drizzle Honey-Orange Vinaigrette over your own concoction of salad greens, fruit, cheese, and even walnuts. We also recommend this easy salad dressing for gift baskets.

HONEY-ORANGE VINAIGRETTE

¾ cup vegetable oil
¼ cup cider vinegar
¼ teaspoon grated orange rind
3 tablespoons orange juice
2 tablespoons honey
¼ teaspoon onion powder
¼ teaspoon freshly ground pepper
⅛ teaspoon hot sauce

Combine all ingredients in a jar; cover tightly, and shake vigorously. Serve vinaigrette over fruit or green salad. Yield: 1¼ cups.

TOSSED SHELL SALAD

2¾ cups uncooked shell macaroni
1 cup cherry tomato halves
1 cup (4 ounces) shredded Cheddar
 cheese
½ cup sliced green onions
½ cup pitted ripe olives, sliced
1 medium-size green pepper, thinly
 sliced
¼ cup vegetable oil
2 tablespoons lemon juice
2 tablespoons white wine vinegar
1 teaspoon dried whole dillweed
1 teaspoon dried whole oregano
½ teaspoon salt
⅛ teaspoon pepper

Cook macaroni according to package directions; drain. Rinse with cold water; drain. Combine macaroni, tomato, cheese, green onions, olives, and green pepper; set aside.

Combine oil, lemon juice, vinegar, dillweed, oregano, salt, and pepper; pour over macaroni mixture, and toss gently. Cover and chill. Yield: 8 servings.
Jill Rorex
Alexandria, Virginia

RASPBERRY-WINE SALAD

1 (6-ounce) package
 raspberry-flavored gelatin
2 cups boiling water
1 (16-ounce) can whole-berry
 cranberry sauce
½ cup Burgundy or other dry red
 wine
1 (8-ounce) can crushed pineapple,
 undrained
⅓ cup chopped walnuts
Lettuce
Garnishes: grapefruit and orange
 sections
Cheese Fluff Dressing

Dissolve gelatin in boiling water; add cranberry sauce, stirring until sauce melts. Stir in wine. Chill until the consistency of unbeaten egg white. Fold in pineapple and walnuts.

Spoon mixture into a lightly oiled 6-cup ring mold; cover and chill until firm. Unmold onto a lettuce-lined plate; garnish, if desired. Serve with Cheese Fluff Dressing. Yield: 8 to 10 servings.

Cheese Fluff Dressing

1 cup frozen whipped topping,
 thawed
1 (3-ounce) package cream cheese,
 softened
3 tablespoons milk
½ teaspoon grated orange rind

Combine all ingredients; beat with an electric mixer until well blended. Yield: ¾ cup.
Dorothy C. Taylor
Palm City, Florida

ON THE LIGHT SIDE

Heart-Healthy Gifts From Your Kitchen

Gifts from the kitchen are gifts from the heart. And what better way to share the holiday spirit with the special people in your life than with a gift that's not only delicious but heart healthy as well.

Classic Fruitcake will appeal to a friend who enjoys old-fashioned fruitcake. It has all the goodness of traditional fruitcake right down to the hint of bourbon.

Busy cooks will appreciate Herb-Rice Mix. Simply combine the mix with water, and cook in the oven or microwave. It's a flavorful side dish that will complement most entrées.

Look for attractive bags, boxes, and jars to use as containers for food gifts, and decorate the package with holiday labels, ribbons, or ornaments. For a special present, wrap up a kitchen utensil that can be used to prepare or serve the recipe.

Stock a Salad Gift Basket

A fresh green salad can be a refreshing change of pace amid the season's rich, heavy menus. That's why a salad gift basket is a welcome holiday gift. Pack it with salad greens, cheese, fruit, breadsticks, and a homemade salad dressing, such as Honey-Orange Vinaigrette (page 255). Here are other ideas:
■ Baskets come in a variety of shapes and sizes. However, we suggest packing your gift in a wooden produce crate. You may already have one on hand, or

check for one in the produce department at your supermarket.
■ Use shredded office paper to pad the bottom of the wooden crate. It's free and is a great way to recycle.
■ Make the basket simple or elaborate. Consider adding a set of salad tongs, a pepper mill, or a bottle of wine.
■ Add a can of vacuum-packed meat, cheese, croutons, and French bread for a chef salad collection—a great gift for someone who has a busy schedule.

HERB-RICE MIX

4 cups long-grain rice, uncooked
2½ tablespoons beef-flavored bouillon granules
2½ tablespoons parsley flakes
1 tablespoon dried onion flakes
2 teaspoons dried whole basil
1 teaspoon dried whole thyme
½ teaspoon garlic powder

Divide rice and bouillon granules into 4 gift packages; set aside.

Combine parsley flakes and remaining ingredients; stir, and divide among gift packages. Seal. Include recipe with packages. Yield: 4 packages.

Herb Rice

1 package herb-rice mix
2½ cups hot water

Combine ingredients in a 1½-quart casserole. Cover and bake at 350° for 45 minutes or until liquid is absorbed and rice is tender.

Microwave Directions: Combine ingredients in a deep 2-quart casserole. Cover tightly with heavy-duty plastic wrap, and fold back a small corner of wrap to allow steam to escape. Microwave at HIGH 5 minutes. Stir well. Cover and microwave at MEDIUM (50% power) 12 to 14 minutes or until rice is tender and water is absorbed. Let stand 2 to 4 minutes. Fluff rice with a fork. Yield: 4 servings (174 calories per ½-cup serving).

□ *3.7 grams protein, 0.2 gram fat, 38.2 grams carbohydrate, 0 milligrams cholesterol, 473 milligrams sodium, and 17 milligrams calcium.*

PROCESSED PICANTE SAUCE

3 (14½-ounce) cans no-salt-added whole tomatoes, undrained
4 tomatillos, cored and halved
1 small jalapeño pepper, seeded
2 (4-ounce) cans diced green chiles, undrained
1 cup chopped onion
2 cloves garlic, minced
¼ cup white vinegar
1 teaspoon salt
1 teaspoon chili powder
1 teaspoon ground cumin
Light Tortilla Chips

Combine first 3 ingredients in container of a food processor or electric blender; process just until chopped (do not puree). Place chopped vegetables in a Dutch oven, and add remaining ingredients except chips. Bring to a boil, reduce heat, and simmer 30 minutes, stirring occasionally. Spoon hot mixture into hot sterilized jars, leaving 1 inch of headspace.

Cover hot jars at once with metal lids, and screw on bands. Process in boiling-water bath 10 minutes for half-pints. Serve with Light Tortilla Chips. Yield: 7 half-pints (4 calories per tablespoon).

□ *0.1 gram protein, 0 grams fat, 0.8 gram carbohydrate, 0 milligrams cholesterol, 25 milligrams sodium, and 5 milligrams calcium.*

Light Tortilla Chips

12 (6-inch) corn tortillas

Dip each tortilla in water; drain on paper towels. Using a pizza cutter or kitchen shears, cut each tortilla into 8 triangles.

Place triangles in a single layer on an ungreased baking sheet. Bake at 350° for 15 minutes or until chips are crisp and begin to brown. Remove from oven, and let cool. Store in an airtight container. Yield: 12 servings (8 calories per triangle).

□ *0.3 gram protein, 0.1 gram fat, 1.6 grams carbohydrate, 0 milligrams cholesterol, 7 milligrams sodium, and 5 milligrams calcium.*

CRANBERRY RELISH

2 medium-size cooking apples (1¼ pounds), chopped
½ cup raisins
1 (6-ounce) can frozen apple juice concentrate, thawed and undiluted
4 cups fresh or frozen cranberries
¼ cup firmly packed brown sugar

Combine all ingredients in a heavy saucepan; bring to a boil over medium heat, stirring constantly. Cover, reduce heat, and simmer 15 minutes, stirring occasionally. Yield: 4 cups (17 calories per tablespoon).

□ *0.1 gram protein, 0.1 gram fat, 4.5 grams carbohydrate, 0 milligrams cholesterol, 1 milligram sodium, and 3 milligrams calcium.*

Packaging Food Gifts

■ Use brightly colored gift bags as containers for wrapped foods.

■ Be sure to label each food gift, saying what it is and the date when made.

■ Include pertinent information with your food gift, including storing, shelf life, freezing, and instructions for any further cooking that may be needed.

MINESTRONE SOUP MIX

½ cup dried onion flakes
½ cup dried celery flakes
¼ cup dried parsley flakes
2 tablespoons dried whole basil
1 tablespoon dried whole oregano
1 tablespoon dried whole marjoram
1 teaspoon garlic powder
1 teaspoon freshly ground pepper
½ cup beef-flavored bouillon
  granules
1 pound dried navy beans
1 pound dried kidney beans
2 cups elbow macaroni, uncooked

Combine onion flakes, celery flakes, parsley flakes, basil, oregano, marjoram, garlic powder, and pepper; divide into 4 gift packages. Add 2 tablespoons bouillon granules to each package. Label and seal. Combine navy beans and kidney beans; divide into 4 gift packages. Label and seal. Place ½ cup macaroni into 4 gift packages. Label and seal.

Present 1 package herb mix, 1 package bean mix, and 1 package macaroni with recipe for Minestrone Soup. Yield: 4 gift packages.

Minestrone Soup

1 package bean mix
3 quarts water
1 package herb mix
1 carrot, chopped
⅔ cup (4 ounces) chopped lean
  cooked ham
1 (14½-ounce) can no-salt-added
  stewed tomatoes, undrained
1 package macaroni

Sort and wash bean mix; place in a Dutch oven. Cover with water 2 inches above beans; soak 8 hours. Drain beans.

Combine beans, 3 quarts water, herb mix, chopped carrot, and ham. Bring to a boil; reduce heat, and simmer 2 hours, stirring occasionally. Add tomatoes and macaroni; cook 20

minutes or until macaroni is tender. Yield: 8 servings (167 calories per 1-cup serving).

□ *11.7 grams protein, 1.2 grams fat, 28.3 grams carbohydrate, 7 milligrams cholesterol, 976 milligrams sodium, and 78 milligrams calcium.*

CLASSIC FRUITCAKE

Vegetable cooking spray
1½ cups all-purpose flour
2 teaspoons baking powder
½ cup sugar
1½ teaspoons grated orange rind
¾ teaspoon ground cinnamon
½ teaspoon ground nutmeg
½ teaspoon ground allspice
2 cups chopped pecans
1½ cups golden raisins
1 cup red maraschino cherries,
  halved
1 cup green maraschino cherries,
  halved
1 (15¼-ounce) can unsweetened
  pineapple tidbits, drained
1 (8-ounce) package pitted dates,
  diced
1 (8-ounce) package dried apricots,
  diced
1 (8-ounce) package dried peaches,
  diced
1 cup egg substitute
⅓ cup skim milk
1 tablespoon vanilla extract
2 teaspoons lemon extract
½ cup bourbon

Line four 7½- x 3½- x 2-inch loafpans with aluminum foil. Coat foil with cooking spray, and set aside.

Combine flour and next 6 ingredients in a large bowl. Add pecans and next 7 ingredients; stir well. Add egg substitute and next 3 ingredients, stirring until moistened. Divide batter evenly among pans. Bake at 300° for 1

hour and 20 minutes, shielding the last 30 minutes with aluminum foil to prevent overbrowning.

Remove from oven; let cool 10 minutes on a wire rack. Remove cakes from pans; peel foil from cake.

Soak cheesecloth in bourbon; wrap cakes in cheesecloth. Store in an airtight container in refrigerator. Yield: 4 cakes (116 calories per ½-inch slice).

□ *1.8 grams protein, 3.1 grams fat, 21.7 grams carbohydrate, 0 milligrams cholesterol, 20 milligrams sodium, and 21 milligrams calcium.*

SUGAR-FREE SPICED TEA MIX

1 (3.3-ounce) jar sugar-free,
  caffeine-free iced tea mix with
  lemon
2 (1.8-ounce) packages sugar-free,
  orange breakfast drink mix
1 tablespoon plus 1 teaspoon
  ground cinnamon
2 teaspoons ground cloves

Combine all ingredients. Store in an airtight container, or package into three 1-cup gift packages. To serve, stir 1½ teaspoons mix into 1 cup hot water. Yield: 3 cups tea mix (3 calories per 1-cup serving).

□ *0.1 gram protein, 0 grams fat, 0.3 gram carbohydrate, 0 milligrams cholesterol, 1 milligram sodium, and 2 milligrams calcium.*

Susan Hamilton Clark
Greenville, South Carolina

A Wine Guide For The Holidays

The holidays offer the perfect opportunity to sip versatile sparkling wines and other selections that enhance the flavor of this season's foods. Wines also eliminate the pressure of last-minute shopping; they can be bought long before party time and stashed in the basement or another cool room. With the suggestions and tips offered here, making the right choice is easy.

Sparkling Wine— An Instant Celebration

Sparkling wine complements more types of food than any other. The bubbles dance and swirl, inviting us to relax and have a good time. Crisp, dry styles (labeled "brut" or "natural") perk up the flavors of appetizers and party buffets.

Those called "blanc de noirs" (French for white wine made from dark grapes) can be served with many dinner menus, excluding hearty meats such as steaks. Sweeter versions (called "extra dry," "sec," or "Asti spumante") are lively companions for desserts. At the end of your festive holiday season, you may discover that sparkling wines aren't just for holidays; they're perfect choices to serve all year round.

Differentiate "champagne" from "sparkling wine." Any wine with bubbles is a sparkling wine, but only sparkling wine made by a specific process in the Champagne region of France should be called champagne. While some wine producers in other countries borrow the word for their labels, savvy wine drinkers always make the distinction by noting from where the wine comes.

The following sparkling wine selections are generally available throughout the South, with prices varying from place to place because of local and state taxes. Wine merchants can sometimes special order and give case discounts. Unfortunately, many champagnes are fairly expensive because of the exchange rate of the dollar and global demand.

Light styles for cocktails, aperitifs, or light hors d'oeuvres: Taittinger Brut la Française (France), Schramsberg Blanc (California), and Freixenet Cordon Negro (Spain).

Medium-body for hors d'oeuvres and light courses: Veuve Clicquot Brut Yellow Label (France), Domaine Mumm Cuvée Napa Brut Prestige (California), Hanns Kornell Brut (California), and Codorniu Anna de Codorniu (Spain).

Full-body styles for buffets, dinners: Bollinger Special Cuvée Brut (France), Iron Horse Blanc de Noirs 1987 (California), Domaine Chandon Blanc de Noirs (California), and Gratien-Meyer Brut Blanc de Noirs (France).

Lightly sweet to sweet for desserts, after dinner, or aperitifs for "people who say they don't like sparkling wines": Henkell Extra Dry (Germany), Cinzano Asti Spumante (Italy), Korbel and Balatore Spumante (California).

Reach for New Choices, Too

Sparkling wines are just one option for the holidays. In addition to mainstays such as Chardonnays, Cabernet Sauvignons, and White Zinfandels, favorites throughout the year, reach for zesty, sweet-tart Rieslings, crisp Chenin Blancs, food-friendly Semillons, berry-like Pinot Noirs, mellow Merlots, and the highest quality Beaujolais Crus.

Among the white varieties, Riesling and Chenin Blanc can be dry (the opposite of sweet). They are often made in lightly sweet styles, which make them successful choices for holiday meals with sweet side dishes, such as sweet potatoes and spiced fruit.

Germany is the world specialist in Riesling, a grape with excellent fruit acidity that pairs perfectly with fish, chicken, or light pork dishes. Chenin Blanc grapes flourish in the Vouvray region along the Loire River in France, where they are paired with fish and ham. Semillon is seldom seen on American wine labels, but it and Sauvignon Blanc are the two mainstays of white Bordeaux wines; both are popular in Australia.

White Selections: Wiltinger Scharzberg 1985 Kabinett Schmitt Sohne (Germany), Trefethen 1989 White Riesling (dry) (California), Vouvray Marc Bredif (France), Simi 1989 Chenin Blanc Mendocino (California), Tyrrell's 1986 Semillon (Australia), and Wente 1989 Semillon Estate (California) are available.

Few red wines are better food mates than Pinot Noirs. This is the grape variety responsible for the alluring taste of red Burgundy. While the California and Oregon versions of this wine are quite different from Burgundy, they are rich with flavor. These wines are also skimpy on tannins that can make other red wines harder to pair with food.

Merlot is another great choice for a solid red wine with youthful flavors. It is grown in France's Bordeaux region, especially in the Pomerol district, and has found success in America's vineyards. Beaujolais wines are always good choices with foods, but the holidays are the right time to move up from the ordinary Beaujolais categories to the top echelons, the Beaujolais Crus called Fleurie, Morgon, Juliénas, Brouilly, Côtes de Brouilly, Moulin-à-Vent, St. Amour, Chiroubles, Regnie, and Chenas.

Red Selections: Rodney Strong 1985 Pinot Noir (California), Louis Jadot 1988 Pinot Noir (France), Hogue Cellars 1987 Merlot (Washington), M. G. Vallejo 1989 Merlot (California), and Georges Duboeuf 1989 Fleurie or Chiroubles (France).

Toasty Beverages

Welcoming guests with a warm drink is a wonderful touch, but don't forget to treat yourself to a quiet moment while sipping these toasty beverages.

During the hurried holiday season, these simple recipes combined with a few minutes of relaxation will renew your holiday spirit.

HOT BUTTERED PINEAPPLE DRINK

1 (48-ounce) can pineapple juice
⅔ cup orange juice
2 tablespoons butter or margarine
2 teaspoons brown sugar
4 (3-inch) sticks cinnamon

Combine all ingredients in a large saucepan; bring to a boil. Reduce heat, and simmer 20 minutes. Remove cinnamon sticks, and serve hot. Yield: 5 cups. *Mildred Clute Marquez, Texas*

CHRISTMAS DREAMS IN WINE

2 (12-ounce) cans frozen apple juice concentrate, thawed and undiluted
1 (12-ounce) can frozen cranberry juice concentrate, thawed and undiluted
4 cups dry red wine
4 cups water
⅓ cup sugar
10 whole cloves
5 (3-inch) sticks cinnamon
Orange slices (optional)

Combine juice concentrates, wine, water, and sugar in a Dutch oven. Tie whole cloves and cinnamon sticks in a cheesecloth bag; add spice bag to juice mixture. Cover and chill at least 6 hours, stirring occasionally.

Remove and discard spice bag. Serve hot or cold with an orange slice, if desired. Yield: 12¾ cups.
Clairiece Gilbert Humphrey Charlottesville, Virginia

SPIRITED HOT MOCHA
(pictured on page 266)

2 cups milk
1 (1-ounce) square semisweet chocolate, grated and divided
1 to 2 tablespoons sugar
1 tablespoon instant coffee granules
¼ cup brandy (optional)
Sweetened whipped cream

Pour milk into a 4-cup glass measure; microwave at HIGH 5 to 6 minutes or until thoroughly heated. Stir in 4½ tablespoons grated chocolate, sugar, and coffee granules. Add brandy, if desired, and pour beverage into mugs. Top with whipped cream, and sprinkle with remaining grated chocolate. Yield: 2 cups. *Linda Tompkins Birmingham, Alabama*

DECEMBER CIDER

1 (12-ounce) can frozen apple juice concentrate, thawed and undiluted
1 (12-ounce) can frozen cranberry juice concentrate, thawed and undiluted
1 (6-ounce) can frozen lemonade concentrate, thawed and undiluted
9 cups water
7 whole cloves
1 teaspoon ground nutmeg
5 (3-inch) sticks cinnamon
½ cup rum (optional)

Combine first 7 ingredients in a large Dutch oven. Bring mixture to a boil; reduce heat, and simmer 15 minutes. Remove cloves and cinnamon sticks, and discard. Stir in rum, if desired. Yield: 3 quarts. *Elizabeth M. Haney Dublin, Virginia*

HOLIDAY WASSAIL

6 cups apple cider
2½ cups apricot nectar
2 cups unsweetened pineapple juice
1 cup orange juice
1 teaspoon whole cloves
4 whole allspice
3 (3-inch) sticks cinnamon

Combine all ingredients in a Dutch oven; bring to a boil. Reduce heat, and simmer 15 minutes. Strain and discard spices. Serve hot. Yield: about 3 quarts. *Cynda A. Spoon Broken Arrow, Oklahoma*

Right: *This elegant dinner begins with Acorn Squash Soup (page 294), served in squash shells.*

This simple menu sparkles with holiday spirit. Chicken Alouette, Vegetables Tossed in Olive Butter, and Cranberry Congealed Salad are served from the buffet. (Recipes and serving tips begin on page 294.)

Above: *Cranberry Congealed Salad (page 296) adds vibrant color to the holiday buffet.*

Above left: *Chicken Alouette (page 295), elegant but easy to prepare, will dazzle your guests.*

Vegetables Tossed in Olive Butter (page 295), a festive side dish for the holidays, makes a colorful presentation at any meal.

Offer guests Strawberry Divinity, Caramel Fudge, and Pecan Brittle. These homemade treats will satisfy even the most serious candy craving. (Recipes, pages 272 and 273.)

Add this healthy and colorful side dish, Fruit Salad With Oriental Dressing (page 277), to your holiday menu.

Make your holiday open house memorable. For an impressive party presentation, float a heart-shaped mold of frozen ginger ale and strawberries in slushy Party Punch (page 278).

Fill your home with the spicy aroma of baked goods; choose from (clockwise from top) Brandied Apricot Tea Cakes, Pear-Ginger Muffins, Raisin-Cinnamon Rolls, and Old-Fashioned Gingerbread. (Recipes begin on page 240.)

Above: *During the busy holiday season, set aside time to relax with a mug of Spirited Hot Mocha (page 260). Once you taste it, you'll want to serve the warm drink to guests.*

Top: *Hot Cranberry Bake (page 250) is much easier to make than a fancy pie or cake. Served in a compote, it's an elegant and appetizing dessert.*

The holiday season wouldn't be the same without a luscious dessert like Coconut Cream Cake (page 269).

Holiday Dinners.

The Sweetest Tradition Of All

During the holiday season more people take to their kitchens—mixing bowls in hand—than at any other time of year. It's part of that long-standing tradition of holiday baking and candy-making. With our readers' help, we present sweets for each of the 12 days of Christmas.

Christmas for Cathy Wallace of Oak Ridge, Tennessee, means it's time to make Danish Pudding Cake. The recipe came from her great-grandmother whom she never met, but she remembers both her grandmother and mother preparing and serving the dessert during the holidays.

COCONUT CREAM CAKE
(pictured on page 268)

1 cup butter or margarine, softened
2 cups sugar
3 eggs
3 cups all-purpose flour
2 teaspoons baking powder
1 cup milk
1 teaspoon vanilla extract
1 teaspoon lemon extract
½ teaspoon butter flavoring
½ cup water
1 tablespoon sugar
Coconut Frosting
1 (1¼-pound) fresh coconut, grated, or 3 cups canned or frozen coconut

Beat butter in a large bowl at medium speed of an electric mixer. Gradually add 2 cups sugar, beating well. Add eggs, one at a time, beating after each addition.

Combine flour and baking powder; add to creamed mixture alternately with milk, beginning and ending with flour mixture. Stir in flavorings.

Pour batter into 3 greased and floured 9-inch round cakepans. Bake at 350° for 25 to 30 minutes or until a wooden pick inserted in center comes out clean. Cool cake in pans on wire racks 10 minutes; remove from pans, and let cake layers cool completely on wire racks.

Combine water and 1 tablespoon sugar in a small saucepan; bring to a boil. Reduce heat, and simmer 3 minutes. Drizzle sugar mixture over cake layers. Stack layers, spreading about 1 cup Coconut Frosting between layers, and sprinkling ½ cup grated coconut on frosting between layers. Spread top and sides with remaining Coconut Frosting, and sprinkle with remaining coconut. Store in refrigerator. Yield: one 3-layer cake.

Coconut Frosting

2 cups whipping cream
½ cup sugar
1 teaspoon vanilla extract
1 teaspoon lemon extract
2 drops of butter flavoring

Combine all ingredients in a medium bowl; beat at medium speed of an electric mixer until soft peaks form. Yield: 4 cups.   *Mae Harkey*
Mount Pleasant, North Carolina

DANISH PUDDING CAKE

1 cup butter or margarine, softened
1¾ cups sugar
3 eggs
3 cups all-purpose flour
1½ teaspoons baking soda
1 teaspoon salt
1 cup buttermilk
1 cup chopped pecans
1 cup pitted dates, chopped
1 tablespoon grated orange rind
1 tablespoon orange juice
1½ teaspoons grated orange rind
½ cup orange juice
½ cup sugar

Beat butter in a large bowl at medium speed of an electric mixer; gradually add 1¾ cups sugar, beating well. Add eggs, one at a time, beating well after each addition.

Combine flour, soda, and salt; add to creamed mixture alternately with buttermilk, beginning and ending with flour mixture. Stir in pecans and next 3 ingredients.

Pour batter into a greased and floured 10-inch tube pan. Bake at 350° for 55 minutes to 1 hour or until a wooden pick inserted in center of cake comes out clean. (Do not remove cake from pan.)

Combine 1½ teaspoons orange rind, ½ cup orange juice, and ½ cup sugar in a small bowl, stirring until sugar dissolves. Spoon over hot cake, and cool in pan on a wire rack. Yield: one 10-inch cake.   *Cathy Wallace*
Oak Ridge, Tennessee

BOURBON-PECAN POUND CAKE

1 cup shortening
2½ cups sugar
6 eggs
3 cups all-purpose flour
2 teaspoons baking powder
½ teaspoon salt
½ teaspoon ground nutmeg
1 (8-ounce) carton sour cream
½ cup bourbon
1 cup finely chopped pecans
Glaze (optional)

Beat shortening in a large bowl at medium speed of an electric mixer; gradually add sugar, beating well. Add eggs, one at a time, beating well after each addition.

Combine flour and next 3 ingredients. Combine sour cream and bourbon; add to creamed mixture alternately with flour mixture, beginning and ending with flour mixture. Mix just until blended after each addition. Stir in pecans.

Pour batter into a greased and floured 10-inch tube pan. Bake at 325° for 1 hour and 10 to 15 minutes or until a wooden pick inserted near center comes out clean. Cool in pan on wire rack 10 to 15 minutes; remove from pan, and let cool completely on wire rack. Drizzle glaze over cake, if desired. Yield: one 10-inch cake.

Glaze

2¼ cups sifted powdered sugar
2 tablespoons bourbon
2 tablespoons water

Combine all ingredients; stir well. Yield: ½ cup.   *Eleanor K. Brandt*
Arlington, Texas

CHOCOLATE-RASPBERRY TRUFFLE CHEESECAKE

2½ cups chocolate wafer crumbs
⅓ cup butter or margarine, melted
½ cup sugar
1 (8-ounce) package semisweet chocolate squares, cut into ½-inch cubes
¼ cup hot strong coffee
3 (8-ounce) packages cream cheese, cut into 1-inch cubes
1 (8-ounce) carton sour cream
1 cup sugar
2 eggs
2 tablespoons whipping cream
1 teaspoon vanilla extract
¼ cup Chambord or other raspberry-flavored liqueur
Raspberry Sauce
Garnish: whipped cream, fresh mint sprigs

Combine wafer crumbs, butter, and ½ cup sugar; blend well. Press on bottom and 1½ inches up sides of a 9-inch springform pan. Set aside.

Position knife blade in food processor bowl; add chocolate cubes, and process until finely ground. With food processor running, pour hot coffee through food chute. Process until chocolate is melted and smooth. Add cream cheese cubes and next 6 ingredients, and process until mixture is smooth, stopping once to scrape down sides of processor bowl.

Pour mixture into prepared crust, and bake at 350° for 55 minutes. (Center will still be soft.) Let cheesecake cool to room temperature on a wire rack. Cover and chill at least 8 hours. Carefully remove sides of pan. Place each serving on a pool of Raspberry Sauce. Garnish, if desired. Yield: 10 to 12 servings.

Raspberry Sauce

1 (10-ounce) package frozen raspberries, thawed
2 teaspoons cornstarch

Drain raspberries, reserving juice. Put raspberries through a food mill, and discard seeds. Combine raspberry juice, puree, and cornstarch, stirring until smooth. Cook over medium heat, stirring until smooth and thickened. Let cool. Yield: ¾ cup.
Carol Y. Chastain
San Antonio, Texas

BUTTERSCOTCH CAKE

⅔ cup butterscotch morsels
¼ cup water
½ cup shortening
1¼ cups sugar
3 eggs
2¼ cups all-purpose flour
1 teaspoon baking soda
½ teaspoon baking powder
½ teaspoon salt
1 cup buttermilk
Butterscotch Filling
Sea Foam Frosting

Combine butterscotch morsels and water in a small saucepan; place over low heat, and stir until melted. Set aside to cool.

Beat shortening in a mixing bowl at medium speed of an electric mixer; gradually add sugar, beating well. Add eggs, one at a time, beating well after each addition. Add butterscotch mixture to creamed mixture.

Combine flour and next 3 ingredients; add to creamed mixture alternately with buttermilk, beginning and ending with flour mixture.

Pour batter into two greased and floured 9-inch cakepans. Bake at 375° for 25 to 30 minutes or until a wooden pick inserted in center comes out clean. Cool in pans 10 minutes. Remove layers from pans, and cool completely on wire racks.

Place one cake layer on cake platter; spread with 1 cup Butterscotch

Filling. Repeat with second cake layer, spreading filling to within ½ inch of edge. Frost sides and top edge of cake with Sea Foam Frosting. Yield: one 2-layer cake.

Butterscotch Filling

½ cup sugar
1 tablespoon cornstarch
½ cup evaporated milk
⅓ cup water
⅓ cup butterscotch morsels
1 egg yolk, slightly beaten
2 tablespoons butter or margarine
1 cup chopped pecans
1 cup flaked coconut, chopped

Combine sugar and cornstarch in a heavy 2-quart saucepan. Stir in milk and water. Add butterscotch morsels and egg yolk; stir well. Cook over medium heat, stirring constantly, until mixture is smooth and thickened. Remove from heat; stir in butter and remaining ingredients. Let cool. Yield: enough for one 2-layer cake.

Sea Foam Frosting

⅓ cup sugar
⅓ cup firmly packed brown sugar
⅓ cup water
1 tablespoon corn syrup
1 egg white
¼ teaspoon cream of tartar

Combine sugars, water, and corn syrup in a medium-size heavy saucepan; cook over medium heat, stirring constantly, until mixture is clear. Cook without stirring until mixture reaches soft ball stage (240°).

Combine egg white and cream of tartar in a small mixing bowl; beat at high speed of an electric mixer until soft peaks form. Continue to beat, slowly adding hot syrup in a steady stream. Beat constantly until mixture reaches spreading consistency. Yield: about 2½ cups.   *Sandra Russell*
Gainesville, Florida

RASPBERRY TEA CAKE

¼ cup butter or margarine, softened
¾ cup sugar
1 egg
2 cups all-purpose flour
2 teaspoons baking powder
½ teaspoon salt
½ cup milk
2 cups fresh or frozen raspberries, thawed
½ cup sugar
¼ cup all-purpose flour
½ teaspoon ground cinnamon
¼ cup butter or margarine

Beat ¼ cup butter in a mixing bowl at medium speed of an electric mixer; gradually add ¾ cup sugar, beating well. Add egg, beating well.

Combine 2 cups flour, baking powder, and salt; add to creamed mixture alternately with milk, beginning and ending with flour mixture. Gently stir in raspberries.

Spoon batter into a greased and floured 9-inch round cakepan.

Combine ½ cup sugar, ¼ cup flour, and cinnamon in a small bowl. Cut in ¼ cup butter with a pastry blender until mixture resembles coarse meal. Sprinkle over cake batter. Bake at 375° for 35 to 40 minutes or until a wooden pick inserted in center comes out clean. Cool in pan 10 minutes; remove from pan, and cool completely on a wire rack. Yield: one 9-inch coffee cake.   *Rozanne Weidemann*
Fayetteville, Arkansas

PRALINE COOKIES

1 egg, beaten
¼ cup plus 2 tablespoons butter or margarine, melted
1¼ cups firmly packed brown sugar
1 teaspoon vanilla extract
1 cup plus 2 tablespoons all-purpose flour
¼ teaspoon salt
1¼ cups pecan halves

Combine first 4 ingredients, stirring well. Add flour and salt, stirring well. Stir in pecans. Drop by tablespoonfuls onto ungreased cookie sheets. Bake at 350° for 10 minutes (do not overbake). Yield: 3 dozen.   *Ann Howell*
East Prairie, Missouri

BLONDE BROWNIES WITH CHOCOLATE CHUNKS

1 (6-ounce) vanilla-flavored baking bar
⅓ cup butter or margarine
2 eggs, beaten
½ cup sugar
¼ teaspoon vanilla extract
1½ cups all-purpose flour
½ teaspoon baking powder
¼ teaspoon salt
⅔ cup chopped pecans
⅔ cup semisweet chocolate chunks

Combine baking bar and butter in a heavy saucepan; cook over low heat until melted. Set aside to cool slightly.

Combine eggs, sugar, and vanilla in a large bowl, stirring until blended. Add butter mixture, mixing well.

Combine flour, baking powder, and salt; stir into butter mixture. Fold in pecans and chocolate. Spoon into a greased 9-inch square pan. Bake at 350° for 25 minutes. Cool and cut into 1½-inch squares. Yield: 3 dozen.

ORANGE SHORTBREAD

1 cup butter, softened
¾ cup sifted powdered sugar
1 teaspoon grated orange rind
2 teaspoons frozen orange juice
  concentrate, thawed and
  undiluted
1¾ cups all-purpose flour
Sliced almonds

Beat butter in a mixing bowl at medium speed of an electric mixer; gradually add powdered sugar, beating well. Add orange rind and concentrate; stir in flour.

Press dough into a lightly greased 15- x 10- x 1-inch jellyroll pan; prick all over with a fork. Cut into 1½-inch diamonds. Place a sliced almond in center of each diamond. Bake at 300° for 30 minutes or until done. Recut diamonds while warm. Let cool in pan on a wire rack. Yield: about 4 dozen.

CHOCOLATE-PECAN PIE

½ cup butter or margarine, melted
1 cup light corn syrup
1 cup sugar
¼ cup cocoa
4 eggs
1 teaspoon vanilla extract
¼ teaspoon salt
1 cup chopped pecans, divided
½ cup flaked coconut
1 unbaked 9-inch pastry shell

Combine first 4 ingredients in a heavy saucepan; cook over low heat, stirring constantly, until sugar dissolves. Let cool slightly. Add eggs, vanilla, and salt, stirring well. Stir in ½ cup pecans and coconut; pour filling into unbaked pastry shell, and top with remaining ½ cup pecans. Bake at 325° for 55 minutes. Yield: one 9-inch pie.
Catherine Morris
Dibble, Oklahoma

LEMON-BUTTERMILK PIE

¾ cup sugar
¼ cup cornstarch
⅛ teaspoon salt
2½ cups buttermilk
½ teaspoon grated lemon rind
¼ cup lemon juice
3 eggs, separated
1 baked 9-inch pastry shell
1 tablespoon cornstarch
⅓ cup sugar

Combine first 3 ingredients in a heavy saucepan. Combine buttermilk, lemon rind, and lemon juice; gradually stir into sugar mixture. Cook over medium heat, stirring constantly, until mixture thickens and boils. Boil 1 minute, stirring constantly. Remove from heat.

Beat egg yolks at medium speed of an electric mixer until thick and lemon colored. Gradually stir about one-fourth of hot mixture into yolks; add to remaining hot mixture, stirring constantly. Cook over medium heat, stirring constantly, until mixture thickens and boils. Boil 1 minute, stirring constantly. Pour into pastry shell.

Beat egg whites and 1 tablespoon cornstarch at high speed of an electric mixer just until foamy. Gradually add ⅓ cup sugar, 1 tablespoon at a time, beating until stiff peaks form and sugar dissolves (2 to 4 minutes). Spread meringue over hot filling, sealing to edge of pastry. Bake at 325° for 25 to 28 minutes or until golden brown. Cool. Yield: one 9-inch pie. *Willa Govoro*
Bossier City, Louisiana

STRAWBERRY DIVINITY
(pictured on page 264)

3 cups sugar
¾ cup water
¾ cup light corn syrup
¼ teaspoon salt
2 egg whites
1 (3-ounce) package strawberry-
  flavored gelatin
1 cup chopped pecans

Combine first 4 ingredients in a heavy 3-quart saucepan; cook over low heat, stirring gently, until sugar dissolves. Cover and cook over medium heat 2 to 3 minutes to wash down sugar crystals from sides of pan. Uncover and cook over medium heat, without stirring, to hard ball stage (258°). Remove from heat.

Beat egg whites in a large bowl at high speed of an electric mixer until foamy. Add gelatin, and beat until stiff peaks form. Pour hot syrup mixture in a thin stream over egg whites while beating constantly at high speed until mixture holds its shape (3 to 4 minutes). Quickly stir in pecans, and drop mixture by rounded teaspoonfuls onto wax paper. Let cool. Yield: 4½ dozen.
Sandra Russell
Gainesville, Florida

PECAN BRITTLE
(pictured on page 264)

1 cup pecan pieces
1 cup sugar
½ cup light corn syrup
⅛ teaspoon salt
1 tablespoon butter or margarine
1 teaspoon vanilla extract
1 teaspoon baking soda

Line a 15- x 10- x 1-inch jellyroll pan with aluminum foil. Butter foil, and set pan aside.

Combine pecan pieces, sugar, corn syrup, and salt in a heavy 2-quart saucepan, and cook over low heat, stirring gently, until sugar dissolves. Cover and cook over medium heat 2 to 3 minutes to wash down sugar crystals from sides of pan.

Uncover and cook to hard crack stage (300°). Stir in butter, vanilla, and soda. Pour mixture into prepared pan, spreading thinly. Let cool. Break into pieces. Yield: ¾ pound.

Microwave Directions: Combine first 4 ingredients in a 2-quart glass bowl. Microwave at HIGH 4 minutes; stir and microwave at HIGH 3 to 4 minutes. Stir in butter and vanilla, and microwave at HIGH 1 minute. Stir in soda. Pour mixture into prepared pan, spreading thinly. Let cool. Break candy into pieces.   *Doris Campbell*
Spartanburg, South Carolina

CARAMEL FUDGE
(pictured on page 264)

5 cups sugar, divided
2 cups half-and-half
¼ cup butter
½ cup milk
2 cups miniature marshmallows
1 teaspoon vanilla extract
1 cup chopped pecans

Combine 4 cups sugar, half-and-half, and butter in a heavy Dutch oven. Cook over low heat, stirring gently, until sugar dissolves. Cover and cook over medium heat 2 to 3 minutes to wash down sugar crystals from sides of pan.

Sprinkle remaining 1 cup sugar in a large heavy skillet; cook over medium heat, stirring constantly, until sugar melts and turns light golden brown.

Pour caramelized sugar and milk into fudge mixture. (Mixture will lump but will become smooth with further cooking.) Cook over low heat, stirring constantly, until caramelized sugar dissolves. Continue cooking, without stirring, until mixture reaches soft ball stage (240°). Cool to 160°. Add marshmallows and vanilla. Beat with a spoon until marshmallows melt and mixture begins to thicken. Stir in pecans. Pour into a buttered 9-inch square pan, spreading with a spatula. Cool candy, and cut into squares. Yield: 2½ pounds.   *Judy Luker*
Talladega, Alabama

Reindeer Cookies Steal The Show

Baking Christmas cookies can be time-consuming. Mixing dough, rolling it out, cutting it with seasonal cookie cutters, sprinkling it with red or green sugar crystals, and finally baking until lightly browned require patience. One smart grandmother has a better, and easier, idea.

"My five grandchildren really enjoyed making these reindeer cookies last Christmas," Flo Burtnett of Gage, Oklahoma, wrote about this recipe. Instead of all the mixing and baking, Flo simply stirred together three ingredients for the frosting, then set out graham crackers, red cinnamon candies, pretzels, and mini-morsels, and let the children have at it.

Whether an adult or a child makes these cookies, it's a good idea to have a few extra graham crackers on hand because they break easily. The kids will enjoy eating the "mistakes" while new crackers are prepared. When slicing the graham crackers, be sure to use a serrated knife, gently sawing across the top of each. If you try to cut the crackers in one firm motion, they will probably break.

JOLLY REINDEER COOKIES

1 cup sifted powdered sugar
2 tablespoons whipping cream
1 teaspoon vanilla extract
12 (2½-inch-square) graham crackers
24 semisweet chocolate mini-morsels
12 red cinnamon candies
12 mini-pretzels, broken in half

Combine first 3 ingredients; mix well, and set frosting aside.

Cut a graham cracker diagonally in half with a serrated knife, using a gentle sawing motion. Spread a small amount of frosting over top side of cracker half. Top with remaining cracker half, placing cut sides opposite each other so that 2 narrow ends meet to form reindeer nose (see illustration below). Spread a small amount of frosting to cover top cracker. Press chocolate morsels on reindeer for eyes and cinnamon candy for nose. Add pretzel halves for antlers. Repeat procedure with remaining ingredients. Let dry on a wire rack. Yield: 1 dozen.

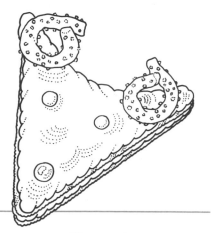

Special Gift Wrap

Decorating gift wrap personalizes packages, making them as memorable as the gifts you carefully choose. Each of these wraps is easy to make and requires only a few supplies. Have fun experimenting with your own variations.

Stenciled Gift Wrap
Materials:
Large brown mailing paper
Stencils—A variety of designs are available at most craft shops; prices vary, depending on quality and design.
Florist paint—Available at craft shops and some florists.
Yarn or Rope

Spread a large sheet of brown mailing paper in a well-ventilated area, and anchor corners. Place stencil on paper, and spray with florist paint. Repeat, placing stencil over paper to fill out the design. When paper is dry, wrap your packages with the paper and tie with yarn or rope.

Holiday Stamp Gift Wrap
Materials:
Holiday stamps (10 to 20)
Photocopy machine—Check the Yellow Pages for print shops located near you.

When holiday cards start coming through the mail, tear the stamps off the envelopes. Place the stamps in a random pattern, face down on a photocopy machine. Place a piece of white or brightly colored paper over them to make a background for the stamps. Enlarge the stamps for a dramatic look. Each copy becomes a sheet of gift paper.

QUICK!

An After-Shopping Feast

The menu presented here is your ticket to sanity during the holiday season. You can spend an hour in preparation before shopping, then return home, and in 20 minutes offer your friends or family a wholesome, satisfying meal that puts the crowded parking lots, busy store clerks, and endless lines behind you.

Kielbasa-Vegetable Dinner is a one-dish meal that casts off the chill and warms the spirit. Christine Orth of Signal Mountain, Tennessee, says even her teenage daughter, Holly, has prepared Kielbasa-Vegetable Dinner for supper. This easy menu, complete with homemade rolls and a refreshing pie for dessert, serves six.

An Hour Before Shopping: Make Tart Lemon Pie. While pie bakes in the oven, mix up batter for Spoon Rolls, and refrigerate. Make Creamy Clam Spread. Wash and cut up vegetables and slice sausage for Kielbasa-Vegetable Dinner.

Upon Arriving Home: Offer Creamy Clam Spread and assorted crackers for an appetizer. While friends relax, bake Spoon Rolls and finish Kielbasa-Vegetable Dinner.

After-Shopping Menu
Creamy Clam Spread
Kielbasa-Vegetable Dinner
Spoon Rolls
Tart Lemon Pie

CREAMY CLAM SPREAD

2 (3-ounce) packages cream cheese, softened
1 (6½-ounce) can minced clams, drained
2 green onions, chopped
1 tablespoon honey mustard

Combine all ingredients; stir well. Spoon into a serving bowl; cover and chill at least 2 hours. Serve with assorted crackers. Yield: 1 cup.
Nancy Seamon
Hilton Head, South Carolina

KIELBASA-VEGETABLE DINNER

3 slices bacon
1½ pounds small red potatoes, thinly sliced
1 cup chopped onion
3 large carrots, thinly sliced
½ teaspoon dried whole marjoram
1½ pounds kielbasa sausage, diagonally sliced
1½ pounds fresh broccoli, cut into flowerets
1 cup water

Cook bacon in a large Dutch oven until crisp; remove bacon, reserving drippings in Dutch oven. Crumble bacon, and set aside. Add potato, onion, carrot, and marjoram to drippings in Dutch oven; cook over medium heat 7 minutes, stirring often.

Add kielbasa, broccoli, and water to vegetables in Dutch oven; bring mixture to a boil. Cover, reduce heat, and simmer 10 minutes or until vegetables are crisp-tender, stirring occasionally. Serve dinner in soup bowls; sprinkle with crumbled bacon. Yield: 6 servings.   *Christine Orth*
Signal Mountain, Tennessee

SPOON ROLLS

1 package dry yeast
2 tablespoons warm water (105° to 115°)
½ cup vegetable oil
¼ cup sugar
1 egg, beaten
4 cups self-rising flour
2 cups warm water (105° to 115°)

Dissolve yeast in 2 tablespoons warm water in a large bowl; let stand 5 minutes. Add vegetable oil and remaining ingredients to yeast mixture, and stir until mixture is smooth.

Cover tightly, and refrigerate at least 4 hours. Stir again, and spoon into well-greased muffin pans, filling three-fourths full. Bake at 400° for 20 minutes or until rolls are golden. Yield: 20 rolls.   *Janet Williams*
Franklin, Tennessee

TART LEMON PIE

3 eggs
1 medium lemon, unpeeled, quartered, and seeded
1¼ cups sugar
2 tablespoons lemon juice
¼ cup butter or margarine, melted
1 unbaked 9-inch pastry shell
Vanilla ice cream or frozen yogurt

Combine first 4 ingredients in container of an electric blender; process 3 minutes or until smooth. Add melted butter; process 30 seconds. Pour mixture into pastry shell. Bake at 350° for 30 to 35 minutes. Serve pie with vanilla ice cream or frozen yogurt. Yield: one 9-inch pie.   *Eunice Killcrease*
Albertville, Alabama

Here Comes Santa!

It's a big decision—what to leave for Santa and his reindeer. For many children, it's simply cookies and milk, with a carrot or raisins for Rudolph, of course. In some homes, Santa has been known to eat a sandwich and chips or even a full-size meal. But whatever the choice, let your children help with the cooking.

PEANUT BUTTER ELF BITES

½ cup sugar
½ cup light corn syrup
1 cup peanut butter
2 cups crisp rice cereal

Combine sugar and syrup in a medium saucepan; cook over medium heat until mixture comes to a boil, stirring constantly. Remove from heat; add peanut butter, stirring until mixture is smooth. Stir in cereal. Drop mixture by tablespoonfuls onto wax paper; let cool completely. Yield: 3 dozen.
Joyce M. Swisdak
Birmingham, Alabama

SANTA'S PINWHEELS

1 (3-ounce) package cream cheese, softened
5 slices bacon, cooked and crumbled
2 teaspoons finely chopped onion
1 teaspoon milk
1 (8-ounce) can refrigerated crescent dinner rolls
2 teaspoons grated Parmesan cheese

Combine first 4 ingredients; stir well, and set aside.

Separate dough into 4 rectangles; press perforations to seal. Spread one-fourth of cream cheese mixture over each dough rectangle, leaving a ¼-inch margin on one long side and no margin on other sides. Roll dough, jellyroll fashion, starting at long side with filling spread to edge; pinch seams to seal. Cut each roll into 8 slices; place cut side down on a greased baking sheet. Sprinkle with Parmesan cheese. Bake at 375° for 10 to 12 minutes or until lightly browned. Yield: 32 appetizers.

Note: To make ahead, prepare pinwheels, and bake at 375° for 8 minutes. Cool. Freeze on baking sheet. When frozen, place in heavy-duty zip-top plastic bags. To serve, place frozen pinwheels on baking sheet; bake at 375° for 5 minutes or until thoroughly heated.   *Linda Griffeth*
Richmond, Texas

REINDEER MUNCHIES

1 cup chopped walnuts
1 cup raisins
1 cup pitted dates, chopped
2 tablespoons honey
Colored sprinkles, ground walnuts,
   or graham cracker crumbs
   (optional)

Position knife blade in food processor
bowl; add 1 cup walnuts. Process 1
minute or until nuts are ground. Remove from processor bowl; set aside.

Place raisins, dates, and honey in
food processor bowl; cover and pulse
2 or 3 times or until combined. Stir
into ground walnuts.

Shape mixture into 1-inch balls; if
desired, roll in sprinkles, ground walnuts, or graham cracker crumbs.
Yield: about 2½ dozen.

Mrs. Chris Bryant
Johnson City, Tennessee

CHRISTMAS EVE PECANS

1 egg white
4 cups pecan halves
½ cup sugar
1½ tablespoons ground cinnamon
¼ teaspoon salt

Beat egg white until foamy. Add pecan
halves, and stir gently until coated.
Set aside.

Combine sugar, cinnamon, and salt;
sprinkle over pecans, and stir gently
until coated. Spread pecans in a lightly
greased 15- x 10- x 1-inch jellyroll
pan. Bake at 300° for 30 minutes, stirring every 10 minutes. Cool completely, and store in an airtight
container. Yield: 4 cups.

Charlotte Moret
St. Louis, Missouri

Celebrate With Citrus

Baskets of sweet-tasting oranges and
tangy grapefruit are always welcome
gifts. Citrus fruits, bursting with fresh
flavor and nutrients, can be enjoyed
anytime and help you meet the recommended five servings of fruits and
vegetables each day. A bonus is that
the entire fruit is usable. Here are
suggestions for getting the most from
your citrus.
—Alice Little Hobbs of Marion, North
Carolina, uses citrus to sweeten the
Christmas air. To make the potpourri,
combine the rind of 1 grapefruit, 2 oranges, and 2 lemons with 1 teaspoon
whole cloves, 1 teaspoon whole allspice, and 3 (2-inch) sticks cinnamon
in a Dutch oven. Cover with 6 cups
water; simmer. Add water as needed.
—When using only the juice or pulp of
an orange, grate the colored rind
(avoiding the bitter white membrane)
before cutting the orange, and freeze.
—Dry citrus rind for use in spiced tea
mix or potpourri; spread grated rind

or ¼-inch strips on a baking sheet,
and bake at 200° for 1 hour. Cool and
store in a tightly covered container.
—Freshly squeezed orange juice
freezes up to four months; however,
the juice from navel oranges may become bitter.
—Citrus shells freeze well and make
convenient serving containers for
sauces and desserts. (Freezing whole
citrus fruits is not recommended.)
—Store oranges and grapefruit in a
cool, dry place up to 10 days or in the
refrigerator's covered crisper up to 3
weeks. (Keeping citrus in sealed plastic bags or plastic-wrapped trays may
promote mold growth.)
—You'll enjoy making these easy salad
recipes and serving Orange Fruit Cup
or Fantastic Ambrosia as a refreshing
ending to dinner. If you have extra
fruit, section it, being sure to collect
the juice, and pack the pieces along
with the juice in jars to share with
your friends.

GRAPEFRUIT-ORANGE SALAD

1 large grapefruit, peeled and
   sectioned
1 orange, peeled and sectioned
¾ to 1 cup orange juice
1 (3-ounce) package lemon-flavored
   gelatin
1 cup boiling water
½ cup coarsely chopped
   pecans

Drain grapefruit and orange sections;
reserve juice. Add enough orange
juice to make 1 cup. Dissolve gelatin
in boiling water; add juice mixture.
Chill until mixture is the consistency
of unbeaten egg white. Fold fruit sections and pecans into gelatin mixture.
Pour into a 9-inch square dish. Cover
and chill until firm. Cut into squares to
serve. Yield: 9 servings.

Mary Robinson
Montevallo, Alabama

FRUIT SALAD
WITH ORIENTAL DRESSING
(pictured on page 265)

3 cups torn Bibb lettuce
3 cups torn iceberg lettuce
1 pint strawberries
3 oranges, peeled and sectioned
3 grapefruit, peeled and sectioned
1 banana, sliced
1 tablespoon sesame seeds, toasted
Oriental Dressing

Place lettuce on a platter; arrange fruit over lettuce. Sprinkle with sesame seeds; serve immediately with Oriental Dressing. Yield: 6 servings.

Oriental Dressing

1 teaspoon cornstarch
⅛ teaspoon garlic powder
⅛ teaspoon ground ginger
⅔ cup apricot nectar
¼ cup red wine vinegar
3 to 4 tablespoons honey
1 teaspoon sesame or vegetable oil

Combine cornstarch, garlic powder, and ginger in a saucepan. Stir in apricot nectar and remaining ingredients; cook over medium heat, stirring constantly, until mixture is thickened and bubbly. Cool; cover and chill 2 hours. Yield: 1 cup.   *Marion Anderson*
Kingsport, Tennessee

FANTASTIC AMBROSIA

4 bananas, sliced
¼ cup orange juice
2 cups orange sections
1 cup fresh strawberries, halved
¼ cup salad dressing or
   mayonnaise
1 tablespoon sugar
½ cup whipping cream, whipped
2 tablespoons flaked coconut,
   toasted

Toss banana slices in orange juice; drain and reserve juice. Layer orange sections, bananas, and strawberries in a serving bowl; cover and chill.

Combine salad dressing, sugar, and reserved orange juice; fold in whipped cream. Spoon mixture over fruit, and sprinkle with coconut. Yield: 6 to 8 servings.   *Marie A. Davis*
Charlotte, North Carolina

ORANGE FRUIT CUP

¾ cup water
¼ cup sugar
1 (3-inch) stick cinnamon
1 (4-inch) lemon rind strip
1 (4-inch) orange rind strip
4 oranges, peeled and sliced
1 apple, unpeeled and cut into thin
   wedges
1 pear, unpeeled and cubed
1 tablespoon lemon juice
2 bananas, sliced

Combine first 5 ingredients in a saucepan. Bring to a boil; cover, reduce heat, and simmer 8 minutes. Cool. Remove and discard cinnamon stick and citrus rind.

Combine sugar mixture, oranges, apple, pear, and lemon juice in a shallow dish. Cover and chill at least 3 hours. Add banana slices, and serve immediately. Yield: 6 to 8 servings.
Louise Osborne
Lexington, Kentucky

Tip: *To section citrus fruit, peel in a spiral motion to remove rind. Cut off remaining white membrane, slicing from top to bottom. Slip knife, cutting edge up, between membrane and section. Slide the blade from the center up the other side of membrane.*

Get A Head Start
With Punches

Ready to fill your punch bowl or favorite pitcher for drop-in guests, an open house, or a spontaneous neighborhood gathering? You can plan ahead for the season with the frozen fruity beverages we offer here. Each punch can be divided into several batches and stored in heavy-duty zip-top plastic bags in the freezer up to four months. So whether the group is large or small, you can serve the amount you need. Be sure to save one batch to sip while trimming the tree, waiting for Santa, or watching bowl games.

AMARETTO PUNCH

2 cups sugar
1 quart boiling water
1 (46-ounce) can unsweetened
   pineapple juice
1 (12-ounce) can frozen orange
   juice concentrate, thawed and
   undiluted
1 (6-ounce) can frozen lemonade
   concentrate, thawed and
   undiluted
2 quarts water
2 cups amaretto or other almond-
   flavored liqueur
2 tablespoons vanilla extract
1 tablespoon almond extract

Dissolve sugar in boiling water; stir in remaining ingredients. Divide mixture evenly into 6 quart-size, zip-top, heavy-duty plastic bags; freeze. Remove each bag from freezer as needed; let stand at room temperature until mixture is slushy. Yield: about 6 quarts.   *Linda Griffeth*
Richmond, Texas

PARTY PUNCH
(pictured on page 265)

2 quarts boiling water
4 to 5 cups sugar
¼ cup citric acid
1 (46-ounce) can unsweetened
  pineapple juice
1 (12-ounce) can frozen pink
  lemonade concentrate, thawed
  and undiluted
1 (10-ounce) can frozen strawberry
  daiquiri mix, thawed and
  undiluted
4 quarts water
8 (10-ounce) bottles ginger ale

Combine 2 quarts boiling water, sugar, and citric acid in a ceramic heatproof container, stirring until citric acid dissolves.

Combine pineapple juice, next 3 ingredients, and citric acid mixture in a large plastic container. Divide mixture evenly into 4 gallon-size, zip-top, heavy-duty plastic bags; freeze.

Remove each bag from freezer 30 minutes before serving. Place mixture in a punch bowl, and break into chunks; add 2 bottles ginger ale to each bag of mixture. Stir until slushy. Yield: 2½ gallons or 2½ quarts per bag of mixture.

Note: Citric acid may be found in the canning section of your grocery store.
Patsy Black
Edgemoor, South Carolina

FRUIT SLUSH PUNCH

2½ quarts water
3 (6-ounce) cans frozen lemonade
  concentrate, thawed and
  undiluted
2 (46-ounce) cans unsweetened
  pineapple juice
2 (0.14-ounce) envelopes cherry or
  lemon-lime flavored unsweetened
  drink mix
8 (10-ounce) bottles ginger ale

Combine all ingredients except ginger ale; stir until drink mix dissolves. Divide mixture evenly into 4 gallon-size, zip-top, heavy-duty plastic bags; freeze. Remove each bag from freezer 1 hour before serving. Place in a punch bowl, and break into chunks; add 2 bottles ginger ale to each bag of mixture. Stir until slushy. Yield: 2½ gallons or 2½ quarts per bag of mixture.
Frances Christopher
Iron Station, North Carolina

Make an Ice Mold

To prepare the strawberry ice mold pictured on page 265, pour 2 cups ginger ale into a 7-inch heart-shaped cakepan; freeze at least 4 hours. Arrange about 1 cup sliced strawberries in heart shape on top of frozen ginger ale; freeze ice mold 30 minutes. Slowly add ½ cup ginger ale; freeze up to 2 months.

To unmold, let pan sit at room temperature 5 minutes or until mold is loosened. Carefully place the mold in punch.

APRICOT BRANDY SLUSH

9 cups boiling water, divided
4 regular-size tea bags
2 cups sugar
1 (12-ounce) can frozen orange
  juice concentrate, thawed and
  undiluted
1 (12-ounce) can frozen lemonade
  concentrate, thawed and
  undiluted
2 cups apricot brandy
4 (10-ounce) bottles ginger ale

Pour 2 cups boiling water over tea bags; cover and steep 5 minutes. Remove tea bags, squeezing gently.

Combine remaining 7 cups boiling water and sugar, stirring until sugar dissolves; stir in orange juice concentrate, lemonade concentrate, and brandy. Divide mixture evenly into 2 gallon-size, zip-top, heavy-duty plastic bags; freeze.

Remove each bag from freezer 30 minutes before serving. Place in serving container, and break into chunks; add 2 bottles ginger ale to each bag of mixture. Stir until slushy. Yield: 19 cups or 9½ cups per bag of mixture.
Ruth A. Smith
White Hall, Maryland

Welcome The Carolers!

Caroling is a holiday tradition across the whole United States. And here in the South we can enjoy our milder weather as we greet the Christmas season in song.

To get the carolers going on time, we suggest a make-ahead menu,

starting with the Easy Club Sandwich Bar. Make and refrigerate Peppered Cheese Kabobs and Roasted Corn-and-Avocado Dip a day in advance. Picadillo Tarts, filled with Mexican hash, may be assembled ahead of time, then baked and served in only eight minutes.

Carolers' Menu
Roasted Corn-and-Avocado Dip
Peppered Cheese Kabobs
Easy Club Sandwich Bar
Picadillo Tarts
Assorted commercial cookies

ROASTED CORN-AND-AVOCADO DIP

1 cup frozen whole kernel corn, thawed
2 teaspoons vegetable oil
2 large avocados, peeled
1 medium tomato, finely chopped
3 tablespoons lime juice
2 tablespoons minced onion
2 cloves garlic, minced
1 small canned jalapeño, chopped
½ teaspoon salt
¼ teaspoon ground cumin
Garnish: tomato wedges

Combine corn and oil in a shallow pan. Bake at 400° for 8 minutes or until lightly browned, stirring twice. Cool and set aside.

Mash 1 avocado, and coarsely chop remaining avocado. Combine roasted corn, mashed avocado, chopped avocado, and next 7 ingredients, stirring until blended. Cover and chill up to 24 hours. Garnish, if desired, and serve with yellow and blue cornmeal chips. Yield: 3 cups.
Belinda Carmichael
Nashville, Tennessee

PEPPERED CHEESE KABOBS

¼ cup diced onion
1 teaspoon dried red pepper flakes
1 bay leaf
¼ cup olive oil
1 tablespoon lemon juice
1 (8-ounce) package Monterey Jack cheese, cut into ½-inch cubes
1 (6-ounce) can pitted large ripe olives, drained
1 large sweet red pepper, cut into 24 pieces
Purple cabbage (optional)

Sauté first 3 ingredients in olive oil until onion is tender. Remove from heat, and cool slightly. Stir in lemon juice.

Combine olive oil mixture, cheese, olives, and sweet red pepper; toss gently. Cover and marinate in refrigerator up to 24 hours, stirring mixture occasionally.

Alternate cheese cubes, olives, and red pepper on 6-inch skewers. Trim core end of cabbage to form a flat base; insert kabobs in cabbage to serve, if desired. Yield: 2 dozen.
Nora Henshaw
Okemah, Oklahoma

EASY CLUB SANDWICH BAR

1 dozen sourdough rolls
¾ cup mayonnaise or salad dressing
¾ cup commercial Russian salad dressing
¾ pound thinly sliced deli roast turkey
¾ pound thinly sliced deli roast beef
½ pound bacon slices, cooked and halved
12 slices Swiss cheese
1 small head leaf lettuce, separated into leaves
2 medium tomatoes, thinly sliced

Slice rolls in half horizontally. Arrange rolls and remaining ingredients buffet style, and allow guests to build their own sandwiches. Yield: 12 servings.

PICADILLO TARTS

½ pound ground chuck
1 medium onion, chopped
⅓ cup slivered almonds, toasted and chopped
⅓ cup currants
¼ cup tomato sauce
1 teaspoon brown sugar
¼ teaspoon salt
¼ teaspoon ground allspice
¼ teaspoon pepper
10 sheets commercial frozen phyllo pastry, thawed
½ cup butter, melted
Garnish: fresh parsley sprigs

Cook ground chuck and onion in a skillet until meat is browned; drain well. Stir in almonds and next 6 ingredients.

Place 1 sheet of phyllo on a damp towel (keep remaining phyllo covered with a damp towel). Lightly brush phyllo with melted butter. Top with another sheet, and brush with melted butter. Fold in half, placing long edges together to make a 17- x 6¾-inch rectangle. Cut into 10 equal portions, using kitchen shears or a sharp knife. Repeat procedure with remaining phyllo and butter.

Press each portion of phyllo into a lightly greased miniature (1¾-inch) muffin cup to form a shell. Spoon about 1 teaspoonful beef and onion mixture into each tart shell. Cover tarts with plastic wrap, and refrigerate until ready to bake.

Bake at 400° for 8 minutes or until golden brown. Gently remove from pan. Serve warm or at room temperature. Garnish, if desired. Yield: 50 appetizers.
Susan Williams
Texarkana, Texas

Build Our Christmas Cottage

So you waited until the busy season has arrived to make the family a gingerbread house. And now all the mixing and rolling and cutting and baking, not to mention the decorating, seem overwhelming. You know what to do about it?

Forget the gingerbread! You can build this sturdy little cottage with a base of graham crackers, side it with graham bites, and roof it with colorful corn puffs cereal. Candies and crackers provide the trim and landscaping, so all you have to make is the icing. We assembled the house in less than six hours, not including drying time. Just work a little each day, and let that day's work dry overnight.

The ingredients won't cost much, and there'll be extra pretzels, gumdrops, and other goodies to nibble on as you work. If you don't have scrap wood, you'll need to purchase a 25-inch round piece of ¼-inch plywood from a hardware store to use as the base of the house. If you have a jigsaw, trim the edges of the plywood so that the yard will be more natural looking.

While the actual construction needs to be done by an adult, some tasks, such as adding cereal to the roof and landscaping the yard, can easily be done by a child.

Royal Icing has long been the favored icing for "gluing" this type project together because it dries to a firm, durable finish. But because of the USDA's current recommendation against eating uncooked eggs, this type icing is no longer considered edible. It remains our icing of choice for projects of this kind, though, because most people don't eat decorative houses anyway.

For an edible icing, you can make Royal Icing using meringue powder,

which can be purchased at cake decorating supply stores. Follow package directions carefully.

After the holidays, carefully wrap the cottage in large pieces of plastic, such as dry-cleaning bags, and store it in a cool, dry place. Properly stored, it can last several years.

QUICK-FIX CHRISTMAS COTTAGE
(pictured on page 304)

1 (16-ounce) package graham crackers
5 to 6 recipes Royal Icing
3 (5-stick) packages red cinnamon-flavored chewing gum
1 (3.5-ounce) package white chocolate sticks
1 (8-ounce) package fruity frosted corn puffs cereal
1 (10-ounce) package graham bites
5- to 7-pointed ice cream cones
Green paste food coloring
1 (4.5-ounce) package red twist licorice
1 (10-ounce) package sun-toasted wheat crackers
About 25 large green gumdrops
About 50 small green gumdrops
1 (18.3-ounce) package all-bran cereal
1 (10-ounce) package tiny twist pretzels

Step 1: Lay 3 large pieces of wax paper on a flat surface. On one piece of wax paper, lay out front of house in this fashion: Lay 2 unbroken graham crackers side-by-side, right side down. Lay another cracker crosswise at top of the 2 crackers, right side down. Using gentle pressure with a serrated knife, carefully saw top cracker from each bottom corner (touching the other crackers) to the top center to make extension for roof

to rest on. Repeat to make back of house. (See Diagram A.)

On second sheet of wax paper, lay 2 sets of 3 unbroken crackers side-by-side, right side down, to make sides of house. (See Diagram B.)

On third sheet of wax paper, lay 2 sets of 4 unbroken crackers, side-by-side, right side down, to make roof. (See Diagram C.)

Step 2: "Glue" crackers together as they are positioned using Royal Icing and tip No. 6 (mix Royal Icing as needed, one batch at a time unless otherwise specified). To do so, pick up crackers, one at a time, and pipe a thin line of icing where edges of crackers meet. Lay piped cracker back in position, pressing crackers to help them stick. Leaving crackers on surface, right side down, gently spread a thin layer of icing using a metal spatula across backs of all crackers to add stability and help prevent breakage.

Step 3: Trim about ¾ inch from 8 sticks of gum. Lay 2 sets of 4 sticks of gum lengthwise, side-by-side, on wax paper to arrange bases for windows on sides of house. Cut white chocolate sticks to appropriate lengths to frame windows. Pipe a small amount of icing on back of each white chocolate stick, and "glue" sticks to gum base. Trim 1 inch from 3 sticks of gum; assemble these with additional white chocolate sticks to make smaller window for front of house. Assemble a door using 3 untrimmed sticks of gum, gluing gum to a thin piece of cardboard because door will need reinforcement. Let everything you've assembled so far dry at least 5 hours. (Cover and chill any leftover Royal Icing to use in remaining steps.)

Step 4: Invert each section of roof; spread a thin layer of icing to cover front of each section. Sprinkle icing with corn puffs cereal, rolling cereal as necessary to cover icing with cereal.

Step 5: Assemble the 4 sides of the house, attaching each side with icing and stabilizing sides by propping them with appropriate size cans of food until icing dries. Let the parts assembled in Steps 4 and 5 dry for at least 5 hours. (See Diagram D.)

Step 6: "Brick" all 4 sides of house with graham bites and Royal Icing, gently sawing them in half with a serrated knife as necessary to fit crackers at sides of house.

Step 7: Pipe a strip of icing along top edges of roof extensions and house. Lay the 2 sides of roof together on top of house, and prop bottom of each roof with an appropriate size can for support until dry. Pipe a strip of icing along top seam of roof, and sprinkle additional corn puff cereal to hide seam. (See Diagram E.) Attach windows and door to house with icing. Let icing dry at least 5 hours.

Step 8: Prepare 5 to 7 ice cream-cone trees in varying heights. (Vary the height of trees by sawing off part of wide end of cones using a serrated knife.) To make trees, color about 2 cups frosting with green food coloring. Spread green icing (or pipe with metal tip No. 233 or 65) to cover outside of cones; let dry at least 5 hours.

Step 9: Position house on plywood base. Attach house to base with icing. Pipe icing along outer edges of roof, and attach red licorice trim as desired. Trim around door with additional white chocolate sticks. Add yellow corn puff for door knob.

Step 10: Prepare 2 recipes fresh Royal Icing. Spread a small amount of icing in position for walkway. Brick walkway with wheat crackers. Spread additional icing to cover half of board, smoothing it to cover edges. Arrange large and small gumdrops around house, and small gumdrops around walkway. Crush small amount of all-bran cereal, and sprinkle around gumdrops as pine bark. Invert pretzels in icing around edges of board to make a fence. Repeat procedure to finish the other half of board. Scatter trees in snow as desired.

Royal Icing

3 egg whites
½ teaspoon cream of tartar
1 (16-ounce) package powdered sugar

Combine egg whites and cream of tartar in a large mixing bowl. Beat at medium speed of an electric mixer until egg whites are frothy. Gradually add powdered sugar to beaten egg whites, mixing well. Continue to beat mixture at high speed 5 to 7 minutes. Yield: about 2 cups.

Note: Royal Icing dries very quickly, so be sure to keep icing covered at all times with plastic wrap. Because of the uncooked egg whites, this icing is not edible.

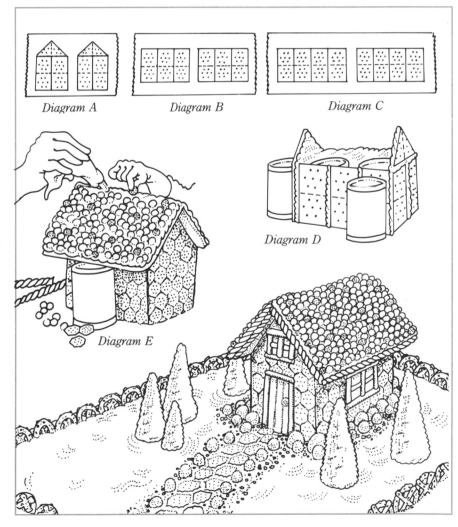

Diagram A   *Diagram B*   *Diagram C*

Diagram D

Diagram E

Sweet Rites Of Passage

We treasure holidays by passing traditions on to our children, making sure their future includes a little of our past. Two of our readers share annual baking rituals that have become special memories for their families.

■ Carolyn Johnson remembers learning to make Moravian Christmas Cookies at her mother's side in Winston-Salem, North Carolina.

MORAVIAN CHRISTMAS COOKIES

2 cups molasses
1 cup shortening
1 cup firmly packed brown sugar
6 to 6½ cups all-purpose flour, divided
2 tablespoons baking soda
Pinch of salt
1½ tablespoons ground cinnamon
1½ tablespoons ground cloves
1½ tablespoons ground ginger

Combine first 3 ingredients in a saucepan; cook over medium heat until shortening melts; cool. Combine 1 cup flour, soda, salt, and spices; stir into molasses mixture. Stir in 2½ cups flour. Cover and keep cool (not refrigerated) 8 hours.

Spoon mixture onto a heavily floured surface; knead in remaining 2½ to 3 cups flour. (Dough will become shiny.) Roll dough to ¹⁄₁₆-inch thickness on a floured surface. Cut with a 2-inch round cookie cutter, and place on a lightly greased cookie sheet. Bake at 275° for 8 minutes or until firm. Cool on cookie sheets. Yield: about 22 dozen.

Carolyn Johnson
Birmingham, Alabama

■ Years ago Blanche Michel picked up a set of Hannukah cookie cutters at her temple's gift shop and started making Symbol Sugar Cookies annually with her children.

SYMBOL SUGAR COOKIES

⅔ cup shortening
¾ cup sugar
1 egg
1½ tablespoons milk
½ teaspoon grated orange rind
½ teaspoon vanilla extract
2 cups all-purpose flour
1½ teaspoons baking powder
¼ teaspoon salt
Decorator Frosting

Beat shortening at medium speed of an electric mixer; gradually add sugar, beating well. Add egg and next 3 ingredients, stirring until blended. Combine flour, baking powder, and salt; gradually add to creamed mixture, mixing well. Cover and chill 1 hour.

Divide dough in half. Roll each half to ¼-inch thickness on a lightly floured surface. Cut with desired cookie cutters; place on ungreased cookie sheets. Bake at 375° for 6 to 8 minutes; cool on wire racks. Spoon Decorator Frosting into a decorating bag, and pipe an outline onto cookies. Yield: about 4 dozen.

Decorator Frosting

1½ tablespoons butter or margarine, softened
1 cup sifted powdered sugar
1 tablespoon milk
¼ teaspoon vanilla extract
Blue paste food coloring

Beat butter at medium speed of an electric mixer. Add sugar and milk, beating until blended. Stir in vanilla. Divide mixture in half. Stir food coloring into one half, leaving other half white. Yield: ½ cup. *Blanche Michel*
Lake Charles, Louisiana

Cookie Tips

■ Let cookies cool completely before storing. To keep cookies fresh, store soft and chewy ones in an airtight container and crisp cookies in a jar with a loose-fitting lid.

■ Use shiny cookie sheets and cakepans for baking. Dark pans absorb more heat and cause baked products to overbrown.

■ To loosen cookies or cake layers that have been left in the pan too long, return the pan to a 350° oven for 2 minutes; then remove the food from the pan immediately.

■ Quick-cooking oats, browned in a small amount of butter or margarine, make an economical substitute for chopped nuts in many kinds of cookie recipes.

■ For perfectly shaped round cookies, pack homemade refrigerator cookie dough into clean 6-ounce juice cans (don't remove bottoms) and freeze dough. Thaw cookie dough about 15 minutes; then open bottom of can and push up, using the top edge as a cutting guide.

■ To shape cookies without rolling and cutting, roll dough into 1-inch balls and place on cookie sheet 2 inches apart; flatten each ball with bottom of glass dipped in sugar.

ON THE LIGHT SIDE

Ladle Up A Bowl Of Healthy Chili

It's virtually impossible to get two people to agree on what makes good chili: chopped meat versus ground meat; red pepper, hot sauce, or fresh green chiles; beans or no beans; vegetables or no vegetables. Plus every chili cook has a secret ingredient.

With all this controversy over ingredients, a few adjustments for health-conscious eating seem minor. The kind and amount of fat used is important. Monounsaturated fat (canola, olive, or peanut oils) or polyunsaturated fat (safflower, sunflower, or corn oils) are the best choices. Sauté vegetables in a small amount of one of these oils or in a Dutch oven or skillet coated with vegetable cooking spray to keep saturated fat low.

Ground chuck, top round, and game (venison, buffalo, or elk) are good lean choices for chili. Ground or chopped chicken or turkey may replace red meat in many recipes.

Traditionally, chili is high in sodium. Cutting down or omitting salt and using no-salt-added canned products will decrease the sodium content significantly. Rinse beans canned with salt under cold water to lessen the sodium, or use dried beans that have soaked overnight and been cooked until soft. Beans add complex carbohydrates, nutrients, and fiber to chili.

SOUTH-OF-THE-BORDER CHILI
(pictured on page 225)

1 pound lean boneless top
   round steak, trimmed
Vegetable cooking spray
½ cup chopped onion
1 clove garlic, minced
2 tablespoons chili
   powder
1 tablespoon cocoa
1 teaspoon dried whole
   oregano
½ teaspoon salt
½ teaspoon ground cumin
1 (8-ounce) can no-salt-added
   tomato sauce
2 cups water
2 cups hot cooked rice (cooked
   without salt or fat)

Partially freeze top round steak; cut into ½-inch cubes, and set aside.

Coat a Dutch oven with cooking spray; place over medium-high heat until hot. Add onion and garlic; sauté until tender. Add meat, and cook until meat browns, stirring often. Stir in chili powder and next 6 ingredients; bring to a boil. Cover, reduce heat, and simmer 1 hour, stirring often. Serve over rice. Yield: 4 servings (370 calories per ¾ cup chili and ½ cup rice).

□ *31.2 grams protein, 5.9 grams fat, 46.2 grams carbohydrate, 65 milligrams cholesterol, 407 milligrams sodium, and 46 milligrams calcium.*

Ruth A. Colosimo
Copperas Cove, Texas

HOT VENISON CHILI
(pictured on page 225)

2 pounds lean venison stew meat,
   diced
1 tablespoon olive oil
1¾ cups chopped onion
1 cup diced celery
3 cloves garlic, crushed
3 cups water
3 (14½-ounce) cans no-salt-added
   tomatoes, undrained and chopped
2 (10-ounce) cans diced tomatoes
   with green chiles, undrained
2 tablespoons chili powder
1½ tablespoons reduced-sodium
   Worcestershire sauce
¼ teaspoon dried whole thyme
¼ teaspoon dried whole oregano
¼ teaspoon ground cumin
¼ teaspoon salt
1 (16-ounce) can no-salt-added
   kidney beans, undrained
3 cups finely shredded iceberg
   lettuce
¾ cup (3 ounces) shredded reduced-
   fat sharp Cheddar cheese
¾ cup diced tomato

Brown venison in hot oil in a Dutch oven, stirring until it crumbles. Stir in onion, celery, and garlic; cook until tender. Add water and next 8 ingredients; bring to a boil. Reduce heat, and simmer, uncovered, 2 hours, stirring occasionally. Add beans, and cook 30 minutes. Ladle chili into individual bowls. Top each serving with ¼ cup lettuce, 1 tablespoon cheese, and 1 tablespoon tomato. Yield: 3 quarts (286 calories per 1½-cup serving).

□ *31.5 grams protein, 5.7 grams fat, 25.2 grams carbohydrate, 59 milligrams cholesterol, 529 milligrams sodium, and 111 milligrams calcium.*

VEGETARIAN CHILI

1 pound dried pinto beans
5 quarts water
1 teaspoon garlic powder
½ teaspoon salt
5 cups chopped tomatoes
2 cups diced onion
1 cup diced celery
2 (16-ounce) cans no-salt-added
  kidney beans, undrained
1 (6-ounce) can tomato paste
1 tablespoon chili powder
1 teaspoon ground cumin
½ teaspoon pepper
7 cups hot cooked brown
  rice (cooked without salt
  or fat)

Sort and wash beans; place in a large
Dutch oven. Cover with water
2 inches above beans; let soak 8
hours. Drain.
  Combine beans, 5 quarts water,
garlic powder, and salt; bring to a boil.
Reduce heat, and simmer, uncovered,
1 hour or until beans are tender, stirring occasionally. Add tomato and
next 7 ingredients; bring mixture to a
boil. Reduce heat, and simmer, uncovered, 2½ hours, stirring often.
Serve chili over rice. Yield: 14 servings (369 calories per 1½ cups chili
with ½ cup rice).

□ *15.1 grams protein, 1.4 grams fat,
75 grams carbohydrate, 0 milligrams
cholesterol, 120 milligrams sodium,
and 91 milligrams calcium.*
                    Bonnie Dockery
                    Cedar Hill, Texas

WHITE CHILI
(pictured on page 225)

1 cup dried navy beans
3 (10½-ounce) cans ready-to-serve,
  no-salt-added chicken broth
1 cup water
1¼ cups chopped onion
1 clove garlic, minced
¼ teaspoon salt
2 cups chopped cooked chicken
  breasts (skinned before cooking
  and cooked without salt)
1 (4-ounce) can chopped green
  chiles
1 teaspoon ground cumin
¾ teaspoon dried whole oregano
¼ teaspoon ground red pepper
⅛ teaspoon ground cloves
¾ cup (3 ounces) shredded
  40%-less-fat Monterey Jack
  cheese

Sort and wash beans; place in a Dutch
oven. Cover with water 2 inches
above beans; let soak 8 hours. Drain
beans, and return to Dutch oven. Add
broth and next 4 ingredients. Bring to
a boil; cover, reduce heat, and simmer
2 hours, stirring occasionally.
  Add chicken, chiles, cumin, oregano, red pepper, and cloves to bean
mixture; cover and cook 30 minutes.
Spoon into serving bowls; top each
with cheese. Yield: 6 servings (273
calories per 1-cup serving).

□ *30.5 grams protein, 4.1 grams fat,
26.9 grams carbohydrate, 51 milligrams cholesterol, 199 milligrams sodium, and 229 milligrams calcium.*

SOUTHWESTERN CHILI

Vegetable cooking spray
1½ pounds raw skinless turkey
  breast, cut into 1-inch cubes
1½ cups chopped onion
1½ cups chopped green pepper
4 cloves garlic, crushed
4 (14½-ounce) cans no-salt-added
  stewed tomatoes
2 (15-ounce) cans pinto beans,
  drained and rinsed
2 (4-ounce) cans chopped green
  chiles, undrained
1 (6-ounce) can no-salt-added
  tomato paste
1 (1¾-ounce) package chili
  seasoning mix
⅔ cup water
½ cup chopped fresh parsley or
  cilantro
1 tablespoon seeded and diced
  jalapeño pepper
1 tablespoon lemon juice
1 teaspoon ground cumin
¼ teaspoon ground cloves

Coat a Dutch oven with cooking
spray; place over medium-high heat
until hot. Add turkey and next 3 ingredients; sauté until turkey is cooked.
Stir in stewed tomatoes and remaining
ingredients. Simmer over low heat 1
hour, stirring occasionally. Yield: 10
servings (267 calories per 1½-cup
serving).

□ *28.1 grams protein, 2.3 grams fat,
35.8 grams carbohydrate, 56 milligrams cholesterol, 164 milligrams sodium, and 121 milligrams calcium.*

Vegetable Savvy

■ Be sure to save your celery
leaves. The outer leaves can
serve as seasonings in soups,
stuffings, and other cooked
dishes. The inner leaves of the
celery add a nice flavor to
tossed salads.

■ Keep celery fresh and crisp
by wrapping in paper towels;
place in a plastic bag in the refrigerator. The towels absorb
any excess moisture.

■ When you are out of canned
tomatoes for a recipe try substituting 1 (6-ounce) can tomato
paste plus 1 cup water. It will
make very little difference in
most kinds of recipes.

■ Leftover vegetables may be
folded into a cream sauce to
serve over a plain omelet, added
to fritter batter, or marinated
with French dressing for a delicious salad.

■ Always store onions in a cool,
dark place with air circulation to
prevent sprouting.

A Healthful Breakfast Casserole

Weekends and holidays often find cooks looking for something easy to fix for breakfast. For years a breakfast casserole was a favorite because it could be made ahead and baked first thing in the morning. Concerns over fat and cholesterol caused many folks to cross this recipe off their lists, but with revisions it can be added back.

Skim milk, low-fat cheese, and egg substitute keep fat and cholesterol to a minimum without sacrificing the creamy texture. And lean ham or Italian turkey sausage plus several seasonings give this healthful version the flavors of the original recipe.

BREAKFAST CASSEROLE

3 cups cubed French bread
Vegetable cooking spray
¾ cup diced lean cooked ham
2 tablespoons diced sweet red
  pepper
1 cup (4 ounces) shredded, reduced-
  fat sharp Cheddar cheese
1⅓ cups skim milk
¾ cup egg substitute
¼ teaspoon dry mustard
¼ teaspoon onion powder
¼ teaspoon white pepper
Paprika

Place bread in an 8-inch square baking dish coated with cooking spray. Layer ham, red pepper, and cheese over bread; set aside.

Combine milk and next 4 ingredients; pour over cheese. Cover and refrigerate 8 hours. Remove from refrigerator; let stand 30 minutes. Bake, uncovered, at 350° for 30 minutes; sprinkle with paprika. Serve immediately. Yield: 6 servings (196 calories per ¾-cup serving).

☐ *16.4 grams protein, 5 grams fat, 18.2 grams carbohydrate, 25 milligrams cholesterol, 579 milligrams sodium, and 218 milligrams calcium.*

Note: One-half pound Italian turkey sausage may be substituted for ham. Coat a nonstick skillet with cooking spray; place over medium heat. Cook turkey sausage until browned, stirring until it crumbles. Drain and pat dry with paper towels. Yield: 6 servings (269 calories per ¾-cup serving).

☐ *17.2 grams protein, 13 grams fat, 17.9 grams carbohydrate, 36.1 milligrams cholesterol, 627 milligrams sodium, and 257 milligrams calcium.*

COMPARE THE NUTRIENTS		
(per serving)		
	Traditional	Light
Calories	645	196
Fat	48.9g	5g
Cholesterol	312mg	25mg

Standby Vegetable Casseroles

When you run out of creativity, when you just can't make another involved recipe, when one more dinner party is more than you can take, turn to an old standby—casseroles.

All these recipes—except Greek-Style Squash—can be made ahead. (The phyllo pastry gets soggy if you let it sit.) Simply prepare the casseroles, and refrigerate 8 hours. Let them stand 30 minutes to come to room temperature before cooking for the amount of time directed.

GREEK-STYLE SQUASH

2½ pounds yellow squash, sliced or
  3 (10-ounce) packages frozen
  sliced yellow squash, thawed
1 large onion, chopped
1 teaspoon salt
1 cup water
1 (16-ounce) container ricotta
  cheese
1 cup cottage cheese
½ cup grated Parmesan cheese
¼ teaspoon salt
¼ teaspoon white pepper
1 (16-ounce) package frozen phyllo
  pastry, thawed
Butter-flavored vegetable cooking
  spray

Combine squash, onion, 1 teaspoon salt, and water in a Dutch oven. Bring to a boil over medium heat. Reduce heat, and simmer 5 to 7 minutes or until squash is tender; drain. Set mixture aside.

Combine ricotta cheese and next 4 ingredients. Set aside.

Keep phyllo covered with a slightly damp towel until ready for use. Place 1 phyllo sheet horizontally on a flat surface. Coat phyllo with cooking spray. Layer 5 more phyllo sheets on first sheet, spraying each with cooking spray; place phyllo in a lightly greased 13- x 9- x 2-inch baking dish, letting excess phyllo pastry extend over sides of dish.

Spoon half each of squash mixture and cheese mixture over phyllo in dish. Repeat procedure with 6 more sheets of phyllo and remaining squash mixture and cheese mixture. Coat remaining phyllo with cooking spray, and place on top of casserole. Using scissors, trim overhanging edges of phyllo around dish. Bake at 350° for 40 minutes or until golden brown. Yield: 10 to 12 servings.
*Carol Yarbro
Birmingham, Alabama*

LAYERED VEGETABLE CASEROLE

1 (10¾-ounce) can cream of
   mushroom soup, undiluted
1 (6-ounce) roll garlic cheese, sliced
1 (5-ounce) can evaporated milk
1 (16-ounce) can whole green
   beans, drained
2 (14-ounce) cans artichoke hearts,
   drained and quartered
1 (8-ounce) can sliced water
   chestnuts, drained
2 (4-ounce) cans sliced mushrooms,
   drained
1 (16-ounce) package frozen
   broccoli cuts
¾ cup sliced green onions
½ cup soft breadcrumbs
¼ cup butter or margarine, melted

Combine soup, cheese, and milk in a
medium saucepan. Cook over medium
heat until mixture is smooth, stirring
often. Remove from heat.

Combine green beans and next 5 ingredients. Spoon half of vegetable
mixture into a lightly greased 12- x 8-
x 2-inch casserole; pour half of sauce
over vegetables. Repeat procedure
with remaining vegetables and sauce.

Combine breadcrumbs and butter;
sprinkle over casserole. Bake at 350°
for 40 minutes or until bubbly and
lightly browned. Yield: 8 to 10
servings.
                          Carol Barclay
                          Portland, Texas

VEGETABLE-CURRY CASSEROLE

1 (16-ounce) package frozen
   broccoli, green beans, celery,
   red pepper, and mushrooms
1 (10¾-ounce) can cream of
   chicken soup, undiluted
1 cup (4 ounces) shredded sharp
   Cheddar cheese
¼ to ⅓ cup mayonnaise or salad
   dressing
½ teaspoon curry powder
¼ cup fine, dry breadcrumbs
2 tablespoons butter or margarine,
   melted

Cook vegetables according to package
directions; drain. Combine vegetables
and next 4 ingredients; spoon into a
lightly greased 1-quart casserole.
Combine breadcrumbs and butter;
sprinkle over casserole. Bake at 350°
for 30 minutes or until bubbly. Yield: 4
servings.
                          Lois M. Peele
                  Greensboro, North Carolina

Fresh Vegetables, Simple Sauces

The old saying that the simple things
in life are best certainly holds true for
vegetables. When you really want to
taste the fresh flavor of a vegetable,
you don't need a cookbook full of complicated recipes—you just need to
know how to cook it. And when it's
done to perfection, drizzle one of
these simple sauces over the top.

The secret to cooking vegetables
actually begins at the grocery store.
Select only the best produce; if what
is on display looks wilted or blem-
ished, ask if there's anything fresher
in the stockroom. Steaming and microwaving provide the freshest flavors
because these methods use the least
amount of water to dilute flavor and
nutrients, but boiling is a good
alternative.

SOUR CREAM-LIME SAUCE

1 (8-ounce) carton sour cream
2 tablespoons chopped fresh parsley
1 tablespoon prepared mustard
1 tablespoon lime juice
¼ teaspoon onion salt
⅛ teaspoon white pepper

Combine all ingredients, stirring well.
Cover and chill 2 hours. Serve over
hot or chilled cooked vegetables.
Yield: 1 cup.   *Sue-Sue Hartstern*
                  Louisville, Kentucky

CHEDDAR CHEESE SAUCE

3 tablespoons butter or margarine
3 tablespoons all-purpose flour
1½ cups milk
½ teaspoon salt
¼ teaspoon dry mustard
1 cup (4 ounces) shredded Cheddar
   cheese

Melt butter in a heavy saucepan over
low heat; add flour, stirring until
smooth. Cook 1 minute, stirring constantly. Gradually add milk; cook over
medium heat, stirring constantly, until
mixture is thickened and bubbly. Stir
in salt, dry mustard, and cheese.
Yield: 2 cups.   *Letha Burdette*
                  Greenville, South Carolina

HOT LEMON-HERB SAUCE

¼ cup butter or margarine
2 tablespoons all-purpose flour
1 teaspoon chicken-flavored
   bouillon granules
1 cup chicken broth
2 tablespoons lemon juice
½ teaspoon dried whole dillweed or
   dried whole tarragon

Melt butter in a heavy saucepan over
low heat; add flour and bouillon granules. Cook 1 minute, stirring constantly. Gradually add chicken broth;
cook over medium heat, stirring constantly, until mixture is thickened and
bubbly. Stir in lemon juice and dillweed. Yield: 1¼ cups.
                          Mary F. Jackson
                          Wedowee, Alabama

Cooking 1 Pound of Vegetables

Vegetable	Preparation	Boiling	Steaming	Microwaving
Asparagus	Wash; Snap off tough ends. Remove scales with vegetable peeler, if desired.	Cook, covered, in ½ cup boiling water 6 to 8 minutes.	Cook, covered, on a rack above boiling water 8 to 12 minutes.	Arrange in dish with stem ends out; add ¼ cup water. Cover and microwave at HIGH 6 minutes.
Broccoli	Remove outer leaves and enough ends of lower stalks. Wash; cut into spears.	Cook, covered, in ½ cup boiling water 10 to 15 minutes.	Cook, covered, on a rack above boiling water 15 to 20 minutes.	Arrange in dish with stem ends out; add ¼ cup water. Cover and microwave at HIGH 6 to 8 minutes.
Carrots	Scrape; remove ends, and rinse. Leave tiny carrots whole; slice large carrots, or cut into strips.	Cook, covered, in ½ cup boiling water 6 minutes (slices) or 7 minutes (strips).	Cook, covered, on a rack above boiling water 6 to 8 minutes (slices) or 8 to 10 minutes (strips).	Place carrots in dish; add ¼ cup water. Cover and microwave at HIGH 6 minutes (slices) or 7 minutes (strips).
Cauliflower	Remove outer leaves and stalk. Wash; break into flowerets.	Cook, covered, in ½ cup boiling water 8 minutes.	Cook, covered, on a rack above boiling water 8 to 10 minutes.	Place cauliflower in dish; add ¼ cup water. Cover and microwave at HIGH 4 to 5 minutes, giving dish a half-turn after 2 minutes. Let stand 2 minutes.
Green Beans	Wash; trim ends, and remove strings. Cut into 1½-inch pieces.	Cook, covered, in ½ cup boiling water 10 to 12 minutes.	Cook, covered, on a rack above boiling water 12 minutes.	Place in dish; add ¼ cup water. Cover and microwave at HIGH 10 to 12 minutes, stirring twice.

A Splash Of Cranberry Vinegar

Vinegar is a common ingredient in salad dressings, but Trudy Dunn's approach to salad is anything but common. Purchased wine vinegar becomes spectacular in her Dallas, Texas, kitchen once she adds herbs, spices, or fruits to make her own flavored vinegars.

VEGETABLE-CHICKEN SALAD

1 cup julienne-sliced carrots
½ cup julienne-sliced jicama
1 cup julienne-sliced zucchini
1 cup julienne-sliced yellow squash
1 cup julienne-sliced celery
½ cup julienne-sliced sweet red pepper
4 cups julienne-sliced cooked chicken
6 cups torn romaine lettuce
Cranberry-Orange Dressing
Garnish: fresh parsley sprigs

Place carrot and jicama in boiling water to cover for 30 seconds; drain. Immediately place in ice water; drain. Combine carrot, jicama, and next 4 ingredients, tossing gently. Arrange vegetables and chicken on top of lettuce. Serve with Cranberry-Orange Dressing. Garnish, if desired. Yield: 6 servings.

Cranberry-Orange Dressing

¼ cup fresh orange juice
¼ cup Cranberry Vinegar (see recipe, next page)
1½ teaspoons grated orange rind
½ teaspoon salt
½ cup vegetable oil

Position knife blade in food processor bowl. Add first 4 ingredients, and pulse 2 or 3 times or until mixture is blended. With processor running, pour oil through food chute in a slow, steady stream; process until blended. Yield: 1 cup.

CRANBERRY VINEGAR

1 quart white wine vinegar
2 cups fresh cranberries, divided
4 (3-inch) sticks cinnamon
½ cup honey
1 orange
10 (6-inch) wooden skewers

Combine vinegar, 1 cup cranberries, and cinnamon in a saucepan; bring to a boil. Remove from heat; let stand 2 minutes. Stir in honey.

Using a citrus zester or paring knife, cut a 12- x ¼-inch strip of rind from orange, reserving orange for other uses. Thread remaining 1 cup cranberries and orange rind on skewers; place in decorative bottles or jars. Cut rind into pieces if necessary to divide evenly among bottles.

Strain vinegar mixture, discarding cranberries. Pour liquid over skewers in bottles. Store at room temperature 2 weeks before using to let flavor develop. Remove skewers from vinegar to prevent spoilage of cranberries as vinegar level drops from use. Yield: 4½ cups.

Roasts: Easy, Practical, And Oh-So-Good

Let's face it. A good beef roast is hard to beat. With strong family values emerging as a part of the nineties lifestyle, it's no wonder that this old favorite is making a comeback. Although many cooks never stopped serving roast, newcomers to the kitchen are discovering how easy and economical it is to cook.

Here's a quick overview of the difference in tender and less-tender beef cuts, appropriate cooking methods, and tips on smart shopping. Most important, these recipes promise juicy roasts—in time for dinner.

Two Choices

When you stop at the meat counter, you have two options—tender and less-tender cuts of beef. Moist-heat cooking methods, which involve steaming or cooking in liquid, tenderize less-tender cuts of beef. Tender cuts can stand up to dry-heat cooking methods, such as roasting or broiling and they also work well with moist-heat methods.

Cooking Less-Tender Cuts

The following cooking methods transform less-tender cuts into juicy, succulent entrées:
—*Braising:* Meat is browned to develop color and flavor. Then it's slowly cooked in a small amount of liquid in a pan with a tight-fitting lid. Example: Fruited Chuck Roast.
—*Pressure Cooking:* Roasts of 3 to 4 pounds are cooked in less than an hour in liquid under pressure. Pressure cookers, available at hardware stores or discount stores, are completely safe. Just follow the manufacturer's instructions. Example: Pressure-Cooker Roast.
—*Using Oven-Cooking Bags and Tents:* Add 1 tablespoon flour and liquids—often beer, wine, or other flavored beverages—to less-tender or tender cuts of meat inside an oven-cooking bag; bake to desired degree of doneness. Example: Herbed Roast. Cooking roasts tented or wrapped in foil is a similar method—steam from soup or other liquids added to the roast cooks the meat.

You Can Roast Tender Cuts

Tender cuts of roast are suited to both moist- and dry-heat methods of cookery. *Roasting* is the easiest way to cook tender meat. Place thawed or fresh roast (straight from refrigerator) fat side up on a rack in a shallow pan. Insert a meat thermometer; don't let tip rest on bone or fat. Do not add water or cover; cook to desired degree of doneness. Example: Dijon Wine-Marinated Roast.

Savvy Use of Leftovers

Unless you serve a large group, roasts yield great leftovers. To make quick barbecue sandwiches, chop roast, and add barbecue sauce; reheat and serve on buns. Add chopped meat to casseroles or soup. For a Southwestern twist, mix meat with mayonnaise and salsa; roll up in a tortilla, and serve with shredded lettuce and chopped tomatoes.

HERBED ROAST

2 to 3 cloves garlic
1 (3-inch) piece of carrot
1 (3-inch) piece of celery
1 (3- to 4-pound) boneless
   eye-of-round roast
1 tablespoon all-purpose flour
1 tablespoon dried whole rosemary
1 tablespoon dried whole basil
1 tablespoon beef-flavored bouillon
   granules
1 teaspoon rubbed sage
½ teaspoon garlic powder
¼ teaspoon salt
½ teaspoon pepper
1 cup dry red wine
¼ cup olive oil

Cut garlic, carrot, and celery into 8 to 10 small strips; make 8 to 10 (3-inch) slits in roast with a sharp knife. Insert strip of garlic, carrot, and celery into each slit.

Shake flour in an oven cooking bag. Place bag in a 13- x 9- x 2-inch baking dish. Combine rosemary and next 6 ingredients; rub on outside of roast. Place in bag. Combine wine and olive oil; pour over roast in bag. Close bag with nylon tie. Marinate roast 8 hours in refrigerator.

Remove from refrigerator. Make six ½-inch slits in top of bag. Bake roast at 325° for 50 to 60 minutes or until a meat thermometer registers 140° to 150°.

Cut top of bag open carefully; remove roast. Yield: 10 to 12 servings.
Laura Hunter
Saint Charles, Missouri

DIJON WINE-MARINATED ROAST

1 (3- to 4-pound) boneless rib-eye
  roast or rump roast
½ cup red wine
2 tablespoons freshly ground black
  pepper
2 tablespoons olive oil
1 tablespoon Dijon mustard
½ teaspoon salt
⅛ teaspoon dried whole tarragon
1 clove garlic, crushed

Place roast in a zip-top heavy-duty plastic bag; set aside.

Combine wine and remaining ingredients; pour into plastic bag. Seal bag, and refrigerate 8 hours. Remove roast, and place on rack in a shallow roasting pan; insert meat thermometer, making sure thermometer does not touch fat. Bake roast at 350° for 18 to 20 minutes per pound for rare or until thermometer registers 140°. Yield: 10 to 12 servings.

Note: Rib-eye roasts are also packaged as "rib roasts."
Georgie O'Neill-Massa
Welaka, Florida

PRESSURE-COOKER ROAST

1 tablespoon vegetable oil
1 (3- to 3½-pound) boneless chuck
  roast or sirloin tip roast
1½ cups water
1 onion, cut into eighths
1 carrot, cut into 1-inch pieces
1 stalk celery with leaves, cut into
  1-inch pieces
1 clove garlic, minced
2 bay leaves
1 teaspoon dried whole oregano or
  rosemary
1 teaspoon salt
¼ teaspoon pepper
⅛ teaspoon hot sauce
2 tablespoons cornstarch
2 teaspoons water

Heat oil in a 4-quart pressure cooker. Add roast; brown on both sides. Add 1½ cups water and next 9 ingredients; close cover securely. Place pressure regulator on vent pipe, and cook 55 minutes with pressure regulator rocking slowly. Remove from heat.

Run cold water over pressure cooker to reduce pressure instantly. Remove lid so that steam escapes away from you.

Remove roast to serving platter; keep warm. Pour drippings over crushed ice in a colander to remove excess fat. Reserve 2 cups strained drippings in a saucepan. Combine cornstarch and 2 teaspoons water, stirring until smooth; add to drippings. Cook over medium heat, stirring constantly, until gravy is thickened and bubbly. Serve with roast. Yield: 8 to 10 servings.

FRUITED CHUCK ROAST

12 pitted prunes
18 dried apricot halves
1 cup ginger ale
2 tablespoons vegetable oil
1 (3½- to 4-pound) boneless
  chuck roast
1 large onion, sliced
¼ cup firmly packed brown sugar
2 teaspoons salt
½ teaspoon pepper
½ teaspoon ground cinnamon
¼ teaspoon ground ginger
½ cup water
6 medium potatoes, sliced
1 tablespoon cornstarch
2 tablespoons water

Soak prunes and apricot halves in ginger ale; set aside.

Heat oil in a Dutch oven. Add roast, and brown on both sides; remove roast. Add onion to Dutch oven, and cook until golden. Sprinkle roast with brown sugar, salt, pepper, cinnamon, and ginger. Return roast to Dutch oven; add ½ cup water. Cover and simmer 2½ hours; add potatoes. Simmer 20 minutes. Drain fruit; add the fruit to roast. Cook 10 minutes or until the potatoes are tender. Arrange roast, potatoes, and fruit on a platter.

Combine cornstarch and 2 tablespoons water. Add enough water to reserved drippings to make 1½ cups; stir in cornstarch mixture, and cook over medium heat, stirring constantly, until smooth and slightly thickened. Serve gravy with roast. Yield: 6 to 8 servings.
Trenda Leigh
Richmond, Virginia

Serve Up A Roast

■ At the grocery store, look for meat cuts that have the most lean meat for the money. When you buy less expensive cuts make sure you are not paying for large amounts of gristle, fat, and bone.

■ Buy meat such as ham or pot roast in bulk; cut and freeze it in serving-size portions.

■ Packaged meat from the market should be rewrapped before freezing. Tape the store label on the freezer wrapper to retain a description as to cut, weight, cost, and date.

■ Baste a roast with wine or wine vinegar for a wonderfully distinctive flavor.

■ Always use a meat thermometer when roasting to prevent overcooking. It's also best to get in the habit of using a minute timer for precise cooking.

■ After removing a roast from the oven, allow it to cool 15 minutes for easier carving.

Wild Game Is On The Menu

Bob Neill is seldom at a loss for words. A storyteller, writer, and banquet speaker, Bob can spin a yarn with the best of them. Even his own life makes a pretty good story.

He started out farming, and hard times hit. Then a knee injury forced him into a 33-pound cast that covered him from his hip to his foot. During his recuperation, he armed himself "with a handful of sharp pencils and an armload of legal pads." A writer was born, and now Bob's company is one of the largest publishers of outdoor books in the South.

At their home in Leland, Mississippi, Bob and Betsy Neill host an annual plantation dove hunt for about 150 folks, most of them high school and college buddies and neighbors.

Whether the hunting party is large or small, the Neills are prepared to dress and cook the wild game. Here they share some tips:
—Try to field dress game as soon as possible to avoid a gamey taste.
—Before freezing, soak any feathered game, squirrel, or rabbit in salted water. (Bob recommends soaking before cooking fresh game, too.) Rinse well in cold water, and place in a zip-top heavy-duty plastic bag. Remember to label and date the bags. Game can stay frozen without a loss of quality for 6 to 8 months.
—Because many types of game, particularly venison and dove, are leaner than domestic cuts of meat, add fat or liquid during cooking to be sure that the meat is moist and tender.

■ When Betsy makes gumbo, she usually ends up clearing the wild game out of her freezer. "It takes every pot in the house and all day to cook," she says. We think it's worth the effort.

WILD GAME GUMBO

2 quarts water
1 (2½- to 3-pound) broiler-fryer
1½ teaspoons salt
8 dove breasts (about 1 pound)
1 pound venison roast, cut into 1-inch cubes
1 squirrel, dressed and cut into pieces (optional)
1 rabbit, dressed and quartered (about 2 pounds)
2 quail, dressed
1 small onion
1 stalk celery
1 bay leaf
1 tablespoon salt
¼ teaspoon red pepper
1½ pounds smoked link sausage, cut into ½-inch slices
¼ cup bacon drippings
½ cup all-purpose flour
1 cup chopped onion
1 cup chopped celery
2 to 3 teaspoons pepper
1 teaspoon hot sauce
½ teaspoon red pepper
1 teaspoon Worcestershire sauce
Hot cooked rice

Combine 2 quarts water, chicken, and 1½ teaspoons salt in a large Dutch oven. Bring to a boil; cover, reduce heat, and simmer 1 hour or until tender. Remove chicken from broth. Chill broth; remove fat from broth. Remove chicken from bones, and chop into bite-size pieces. Set aside.

Combine dove breasts and next 8 ingredients (or 9, if you add squirrel) in a large Dutch oven; add water to cover. Bring to a boil; cover, reduce heat, and simmer 2 hours. Remove meat from broth; strain broth. Set aside. Remove meat from bones, and chop into bite-size pieces. Set aside.

Brown sausage in a large heavy skillet over medium heat. Remove to paper towels, leaving drippings in skillet. Add bacon drippings to skillet. Heat over medium heat until hot. Add flour, and cook, stirring constantly,

■ Betsy cooks this dove recipe in a cast-iron skillet. She seasons a new skillet by rubbing vegetable oil in it and placing the skillet in a hot oven until it smokes.

SHERRIED DOVES

10 to 12 dove breasts
¼ teaspoon salt
¼ teaspoon pepper
¼ cup butter or margarine
2 cups sherry
2 tablespoons cornstarch
¼ cup water
Hot cooked rice

Sprinkle doves with salt and pepper. Melt butter in a 10-inch cast-iron skillet; add doves and sherry. Cover and bake at 400° for 35 to 40 minutes. Remove doves, and keep warm; reserve 2 cups pan drippings. (Add water to measure 2 cups, if necessary.) Combine cornstarch and ¼ cup water, stirring well; stir into pan drippings. Bring mixture to a boil over medium heat; boil 1 minute. Serve gravy and doves over rice. Yield: 5 to 6 servings.

until roux is the color of caramel (15 to 20 minutes). Add chopped onion, celery, and pepper; cook 10 minutes.

Combine roux and reserved chicken broth in a large Dutch oven; cover and simmer 30 minutes. Add game, sausage, chicken, hot sauce, red pepper, and Worcestershire sauce. Add reserved stock from game if additional liquid is desired; simmer, uncovered, 2 hours, stirring occasionally. Remove bay leaf. Serve gumbo over hot cooked rice. Yield: 4½ quarts.

■ Bob warns against overcooking the kabobs for this recipe. While he makes the kabobs, which are his specialty, Betsy makes the rice.

GRILLED DUCK KABOBS WITH ALMOND RICE

4 duck breast halves, skinned and boned
1 (15¼-ounce) can pineapple chunks, undrained
1 (8-ounce) bottle Italian salad dressing
12 cherry tomatoes
1 green pepper, cut into 12 (1¼-inch) squares
12 small fresh mushrooms
1 (6-ounce) can frozen orange juice concentrate, thawed
⅔ cup Worcestershire sauce
Almond Rice

Cut each duck breast half into 3 lengthwise strips; set aside.

Drain pineapple, reserving juice; set pineapple aside. Combine juice and Italian salad dressing. Alternately thread duck breast strips onto six 6-inch wooden skewers with pineapple chunks, cherry tomatoes, green pepper squares, and mushrooms. Place kabobs in a 13- x 9- x 2-inch baking dish; pour pineapple-dressing mixture over top. Chill at least 8 hours, turning kabobs occasionally.

Drain kabobs, reserving pineapple-dressing marinade. Grill kabobs, uncovered, over medium coals (300° to

400°) about 15 minutes or until meat is done, turning occasionally.

Combine marinade, orange juice concentrate, and Worcestershire sauce in a small saucepan. Bring mixture to a boil; reduce heat, and simmer 5 minutes. Serve kabobs over Almond Rice with marinade sauce. Yield: 6 servings.

Almond Rice

1½ cups long-grain rice, uncooked
1 (10¾-ounce) can cream of mushroom soup, undiluted
1 (4-ounce) can mushroom stems and pieces, undrained
1 (2¼-ounce) package slivered almonds, toasted
½ cup butter or margarine, melted
¼ to ½ teaspoon ground nutmeg

Cook rice according to package directions, omitting salt; stir in mushroom soup and remaining ingredients. Spoon into a lightly greased 12- x 8- x 2-inch baking dish; bake, uncovered, at 350° for 30 minutes or until thoroughly heated. Yield: 6 servings.

Serving Wild Game

■ Remember that small game such as rabbit or squirrel may be substituted in most recipes calling for chicken.

■ Be sure to offer tangy relishes or chutneys with game.

■ Choose an appropriate bread to accompany platters of game, including hot buttered biscuits, French bread and garlic bread, cornbread and corn muffins, cornpone, and homemade rolls.

■ Consider other classic game accompaniments that include cabbage, turnips, chestnuts, mushrooms, and onions, as well as hot buttered grits or rice.

Vegetables In A Flash

One little, two little, three little . . . ingredients. The song applies well to these vegetable recipes, but you'll have to stop singing at six instead of ten—the recipes are that simple. And the best part about them is you probably have all the ingredients on hand.

MUSHROOM-BACON GREEN BEANS

4 slices bacon
½ pound fresh mushrooms, sliced
1 medium onion, chopped
2 (16-ounce) cans green beans, drained
⅛ teaspoon pepper

Cook bacon in a large skillet until crisp; remove bacon, reserving 2 tablespoons drippings in skillet. Crumble bacon, and set aside.

Add mushrooms and onion to drippings in skillet; sauté until onions are tender. Add beans and pepper; cook until thoroughly heated. Spoon into a serving dish; sprinkle with bacon. Yield: 6 servings.
Karen Wood
Crescent, Oklahoma

GLAZED BABY CARROTS

1 (16-ounce) package baby carrots, scraped
2 tablespoons butter or margarine
3 tablespoons brown sugar
2 to 3 tablespoons pineapple juice
½ teaspoon ground ginger
Garnish: chopped fresh parsley

Cook carrots in a small amount of boiling water 5 minutes or until crisp-tender; drain.

Melt butter in a small saucepan; add brown sugar, pineapple juice, and ginger. Pour mixture over carrots, and toss gently; garnish, if desired. Yield: 4 servings.
Linda Wright
Tulsa, Oklahoma

BROCCOLI
WITH LEMON SAUCE

1½ pounds fresh broccoli
½ clove garlic, minced
2 tablespoons olive oil
2 tablespoons lemon juice

Remove large leaves from broccoli, and cut off tough ends of lower stalks; discard. Wash broccoli thoroughly, and cut into spears. Cook in a small amount of boiling water 6 to 8 minutes or just until tender; drain.

Sauté garlic in hot olive oil until tender. Add lemon juice; pour over broccoli, tossing gently. Yield: 6 servings.
Caroline W. Kennedy
Newborn, Georgia

APPLESAUCE
SWEET POTATOES

4 medium-size sweet potatoes
  (about 2 pounds)
1 cup unsweetened applesauce
⅔ cup firmly packed brown sugar
2½ tablespoons butter or
  margarine, melted
¼ teaspoon salt

Cook sweet potatoes in boiling water to cover 30 minutes or until they are tender. Let cool to touch; peel potatoes, and slice ½-inch thick. Arrange slices in a lightly greased, 1½-quart baking dish.

Combine applesauce and remaining ingredients; pour over potatoes.

Bake, uncovered, at 350° for 20 minutes or until thoroughly heated. Yield: 6 to 8 servings.

Microwave Directions: Peel sweet potatoes, and slice ½-inch thick. Arrange in a shallow 2-quart baking dish; add ¼ cup water. Cover tightly with heavy-duty plastic wrap; fold back a small corner of wrap to allow steam to escape. Microwave at HIGH 15 minutes, stirring after 10 minutes. Drain. Arrange slices in a lightly greased 1½-quart baking dish.

Combine applesauce and remaining ingredients; pour over potatoes. Microwave, uncovered, at HIGH 4 minutes.
Mrs. Marvin Jackson
Silas, Alabama

ZUCCHINI TOSS

1 pound fresh zucchini, cut into
  ¼-inch slices
1 tablespoon olive oil
1 tablespoon freshly grated
  Parmesan cheese
⅛ to ¼ teaspoon grated lemon rind
¼ teaspoon salt
¼ teaspoon pepper

Sauté zucchini in hot oil 5 minutes or until crisp-tender. Remove from heat; cover and let stand 5 minutes. Spoon into a serving dish.

Combine cheese and remaining ingredients. Sprinkle over squash; toss gently. Serve immediately. Yield: 3 servings.
Shirley McGehee
Spring Branch, Texas

Vegetable Know-How

■ Use liquid that is leftover from canned or cooked vegetables and fruit in congealed salads, stews, savory sauces, or casseroles.

■ Immediately before using fresh mushrooms, wipe them clean or quickly rinse them in a colander; never immerse mushrooms in water.

■ For a small amount of grated onion, place in a garlic press.

■ For best results, sauté fresh mushrooms before freezing them. Thaw mushrooms and add to recipe.

■ Freshen wilted vegetables by letting them stand 10 minutes in cold water to which a few drops of lemon juice have been added; drain, and store the vegetables in a plastic bag in refrigerator.

■ A special topping for cooked vegetables or casseroles can be made by crushing ½ cup herb-seasoned stuffing mix and combining it with 2 tablespoons melted butter or margarine; top the dish with this mixture, and then sprinkle with 1 cup shredded cheese.

■ Marinate leftover vegetables (beets, carrots, beans, broccoli, cauliflower, corn, and brussels sprouts) in pourable salad dressing for relishes and salads.

■ To retain white color of fresh mushrooms, slice just before using or dip in lemon juice.

■ Remember that overcooking destroys nutrients in vegetables. Warm leftovers carefully in a double boiler or a microwave. Even better, just mix them cold in a salad.

DECEMBER

Christmas is the favorite time of the year for entertaining

family and friends. With recipes and menus from Southern

Living, *it's easy to set the mood for holiday parties. An*

elegant dinner, for instance, can be planned and carried out

with ease and flair, thanks to the plans and ideas featured in

"Elegance Comes Easy." And for desserts, the selections in

this chapter are spectacular, with recipes that appeal to

children and adults alike.

Elegance Comes Easy

Easy-to-make, scented with spice, and ripe with the flavor of winter-kissed vegetables, Acorn Squash Soup beckons folks to the table. To the delight of guests, this colorful appetizer soup is served in squash shells and then garnished with white kale. And it is nestled in the midst of a wonderful holiday setting.

Inspiration for the table setting (see page 261) comes from the deep greens of winter squash and the rosy reds and pinks of blooming gloxinia. Antique green majolica dishes were mixed with china and silver to provide a warm background for this meal. Containers of fresh flowers and ivy were placed in terra-cotta pots for quick, simple floral arrangements.

Silver candlesticks set off the table, which is accented with small wrapped packages. Cheerful reminders of the holiday season, the packages are perfect hiding places for small tree ornaments or other party favors that your guests can take home.

The tablescape is oversized, so it limits talk across the table, but guests can chat with friends seated on either side. If it's too big, simply reduce the size of the arrangement to improve the flow of conversation.

With the main meal on the buffet, guests serve themselves, cutting down on last-minute work in the kitchen. Stacked cake stands provide a tall, proud piece from which to serve the Cranberry Congealed Salad. Silver lends elegance and sophistication, but many combinations of glass and other serving pieces might be mixed and matched. The recipes require little garnishing, a nice plus for the cook who leaves the party for a few minutes to set up the buffet.

A Menu for 6

Acorn Squash Soup
Chicken Alouette
Vegetables Tossed in Olive Butter
Cranberry Congealed Salad
Chocolate Mousse au Grand Marnier
Wine   Coffee or tea

Make-Ahead Plan

To host the party with ease, follow this preparation guide. Most of the cooking is done the day before. Final baking, arranging, and serving is reserved for party day.

The Day Before: Bake acorn squash for soup; reserve pulp and shells. Make Cranberry Congealed Salad and Chocolate Mousse au Grand Marnier. Wash lettuce for salad, and refrigerate. Cut up vegetables, and make butter sauce for Vegetables Tossed in Olive Butter; refrigerate. Set up buffet and table.

Starting Four Hours Before the Party: Make Chicken Alouette, and refrigerate. Reheat squash soup bowls in the oven, or bring them to room temperature. Make Acorn Squash Soup, and simmer one hour. Steam the vegetables, and reheat the butter sauce. Combine the steamed vegetables with the butter sauce, and toss gently; keep warm. Unmold the congealed salad onto lettuce leaves; keep salad refrigerated until ready to serve. When it's time for dinner, add half-and-half to soup, heat thoroughly, and serve. While guests enjoy the soup, bake the chicken bundles.

ACORN SQUASH SOUP
(pictured on page 261)

4 acorn squash
3 carrots, sliced
1 onion, sliced
⅓ cup water
2 tablespoons butter or margarine
1 tablespoon all-purpose flour
1 teaspoon salt
½ to 1 teaspoon pepper
2 (14½-ounce) cans ready-to-serve chicken broth
½ cup sherry
½ teaspoon ground nutmeg
⅛ teaspoon paprika
Dash of ground allspice
Dash of red pepper
1 cup half-and-half
1½ tablespoons sherry (optional)
Kale leaves
Paprika

Cut squash in half lengthwise, and remove seeds. Place squash, cut side down, in a broiler pan. Add hot water to pan to a depth of 1 inch. Bake at 350° for 30 minutes. Spoon pulp from squash halves to create eight bowls, reserving pulp.

Place carrot and onion in a saucepan; cover with water. Bring to a boil; cover, reduce heat, and simmer 15 minutes or until vegetables are tender. Drain; combine vegetables with reserved pulp and ⅓ cup water in container of an electric blender or food processor. Process 30 seconds or until mixture is smooth. Set aside.

Melt butter in a large Dutch oven over low heat; add flour, salt, and pepper, stirring until smooth. Cook 1 minute, stirring constantly. Gradually add pureed vegetable mixture, chicken broth, and next 5 ingredients; bring to a boil. Cover, reduce heat, and simmer 1 hour, stirring occasionally. Stir in half-and-half and, if desired, 1½ tablespoons sherry. Cook until heated. If desired, serve in squash shells on a bed of kale. Sprinkle with paprika. Yield: 8 servings.
Kaki Hockersmith
Little Rock, Arkansas

CHICKEN ALOUETTE
(pictured on pages 262 and 263)

1 (17¼-ounce) package frozen puff pastry sheets, thawed
1 (4-ounce) container garlic-and-spice-flavored Alouette cheese (see note)
6 skinned and boned chicken breast halves
½ teaspoon salt
⅛ teaspoon pepper
1 egg, beaten
1 tablespoon water
Garnish: kale leaves

Unfold pastry sheets, and roll each sheet into a 14- x 12-inch rectangle on a lightly floured surface. Cut one sheet into four 7- x 6-inch rectangles;

cut second sheet into two 7- x 6-inch rectangles and one 12- x 6-inch rectangle. Set large rectangle aside. Shape each small rectangle into an oval by trimming off corners. Spread pastry ovals evenly with cheese.

Sprinkle chicken breast halves with salt and pepper, and place one in center of each pastry oval. Lightly moisten pastry edges with water. Fold ends over chicken; fold sides over, and press to seal. Place each bundle, seam side down, on a lightly greased baking sheet.

Cut remaining large pastry rectangle into 12- x ¼-inch strips. Braid 2 strips together, and place crosswise over chicken bundles, trimming and reserving excess braid; braid two additional strips, and place lengthwise over bundle, trimming and tucking ends under. Repeat procedure with remaining strips. Cover and refrigerate up to 2 hours, if desired.

Combine egg and 1 tablespoon water; brush over pastry bundles. Bake at 400° on lower oven rack 25 minutes or until bundles are golden brown. Garnish, if desired. Yield: 6 servings.
Nancy Clark
Columbia, South Carolina

Note: One-half cup chives-and-onion-flavored cream cheese may be substituted for Alouette cheese, if desired.

VEGETABLES TOSSED IN OLIVE BUTTER
(pictured on pages 262 and 263)

4 small red potatoes, unpeeled and sliced
1 pound fresh asparagus, cut into 2-inch pieces (see note)
1 small sweet red pepper, cut into 2-inch julienne strips
1 zucchini, sliced
½ pound fresh mushrooms, sliced
1 (7-ounce) jar baby corn ears
Olive Butter

Place potatoes in a steaming rack in a large Dutch oven; add water to a

depth of 1 inch. Bring to a boil; cover and steam 5 minutes. Add asparagus and red pepper; cover and steam 5 minutes. Add zucchini and mushrooms; cover and steam 5 minutes. Add corn; cover and steam 1 minute. Transfer vegetables to a bowl; toss with Olive Butter. Yield: 6 servings.

Note: One (10-ounce) package frozen asparagus can be substituted for 1 pound fresh asparagus. To cook, add thawed asparagus with red pepper, zucchini, and mushrooms.

Olive Butter

⅓ cup butter, melted
3 tablespoons lemon juice
⅓ cup sliced ripe olives
1 tablespoon lemon zest

Combine ingredients. Yield: ¾ cup.
Roberta Boyack
Miami, Florida

Fresh Mushroom Tips

■ After purchasing fresh mushrooms, refrigerate immediately in their original container. If mushrooms are in a plastic bag, make a few holes in the bag for ventilation.

■ For fluted mushrooms, cut 4 pairs of slits at even intervals around mushroom cap, cutting from center of cap to edge and allowing 1/16 inch between slits. Remove and discard thin strips of mushroom between the slits.

■ Depending on the condition when purchased, fresh mushrooms can be refrigerated for 7 to 10 days.

■ To slice mushrooms quickly and uniformly, use an egg slicer.

CRANBERRY CONGEALED SALAD
(pictured on pages 262 and 263)

1 (3-ounce) package cherry-flavored gelatin
¾ cup boiling water
1 (16-ounce) can whole-berry cranberry sauce
1 orange, peeled, sectioned, chopped, and drained
½ cup diced apple
½ cup chopped pecans
Lettuce leaves
2 tablespoons sour cream
2 tablespoons mayonnaise or salad dressing

Combine gelatin and boiling water; stir until gelatin dissolves. Add cranberry sauce, stirring until blended. Chill until the consistency of unbeaten egg white. Fold in orange, apple, and pecans. Spoon mixture into 6 lightly oiled ⅔-cup molds or custard cups; cover and refrigerate molds until firm.

Unmold onto lettuce leaves. Combine sour cream and mayonnaise; serve alongside salad, or top each with a dollop. Yield: 6 servings.
Eva Billings
Sparta, North Carolina

Note: Salad may be prepared in one large 5-cup mold.

CHOCOLATE MOUSSE AU GRAND MARNIER

1 (4-ounce) package sweet baking chocolate
4 (1-ounce) squares semisweet chocolate
¼ cup Grand Marnier or other orange-flavored liqueur
2 cups whipping cream
½ cup sifted powdered sugar
Garnish: chocolate curls

Combine 8 ounces of chocolate and Grand Marnier in a heavy saucepan; cook over low heat until chocolate melts, stirring constantly. Remove from heat, and cool to lukewarm.

Beat whipping cream until foamy; gradually add powdered sugar, beating until soft peaks form. Gently fold about one-fourth of whipped cream into chocolate; fold in remaining whipped cream. Spoon into individual serving dishes. Chill until ready to serve. Garnish, if desired. Yield: 6 servings.
Susan Hamilton Clark
Greenville, South Carolina

Sweet Decadence

Stacks of recipes collected all year long tell the same tale in kitchens across the South. Promises to try that spectacular dessert "sometime" are finally met in December when the holiday baking fever strikes.

So what are some of this year's temptations? There are Chocolate Kahlúa Cake, the perfect fulfillment of any chocoholic's wish, and Apricot Mousse, a showstopper fit for a posh party. Need an elegant finale for a seated dinner? Try Holiday Pears With Crème Chantilly. And don't forget the kids. For them, Chocolate Pizza is simple, and best of all, fun.

PISTACHIO-CREAM ÉCLAIRS
(pictured on page 301)

1 cup water
½ cup butter or margarine
1 cup all-purpose flour
¼ teaspoon salt
4 eggs
1 (3.4-ounce) package pistachio-flavored instant pudding mix
1 cup milk
1⅓ cups whipping cream, whipped
Chocolate Glaze

Combine water and butter in a medium saucepan; bring to a boil. Add flour and salt all at once, stirring vigorously with a wooden spoon over medium-high heat until mixture leaves sides of pan and forms a smooth ball. Remove from heat, and cool 4 to 5 minutes.

Add eggs, one at a time, beating thoroughly, with a wooden spoon after each addition; continue beating until dough is smooth.

Drop dough by level one-fourth cupfuls 2 inches apart on greased baking sheets. Shape each éclair into a 5- x 1-inch rectangle. (Or spoon dough into a pastry bag, and pipe into rectangles on sheets.)

Bake at 375° for 35 minutes or until browned. Cut a 2-inch slit in the side of each éclair, and bake an additional 10 minutes. Cool on wire racks.

Combine pudding mix and milk in a bowl. Beat at low speed of an electric mixer until smooth and thickened (about 2 minutes). Fold in whipped cream; refrigerate.

Cut off top of each éclair; pull out and discard soft dough inside. Spoon about ½ cup filling into bottom halves, and cover with top halves. Drizzle or pipe Chocolate Glaze on top of each éclair. Yield: 10 servings.

Chocolate Glaze

½ cup semisweet chocolate morsels
1 tablespoon butter or margarine
1½ teaspoons light corn syrup
1½ teaspoons milk

Combine all ingredients in a 1-cup glass measure. Microwave at MEDIUM (50% power) 1 to 2 minutes or until morsels and butter melt, stirring after 1 minute. Yield: ⅓ cup.
Clara B. Givens
Lubbock, Texas

Tip: *When melted, semisweet chocolate morsels and semisweet chocolate squares can be used interchangeably.*

PUMPKIN ROLL
(pictured on pages 302 and 303)

3 eggs
1 cup sugar
⅔ cup mashed, cooked pumpkin
1 teaspoon lemon juice
¾ cup all-purpose flour
1 teaspoon baking powder
¼ teaspoon salt
1 teaspoon ground cinnamon
1 teaspoon pumpkin pie spice
¼ teaspoon ground nutmeg
1 cup chopped pecans
1 to 2 tablespoons powdered sugar
1 (8-ounce) package cream cheese, softened
⅓ cup butter or margarine, softened
1 cup sifted powdered sugar
1 teaspoon vanilla extract
Garnishes: sweetened whipped cream, chopped pecans

Grease and flour a 15- x 10- x 1-inch jellyroll pan; set aside.

Beat eggs in a large bowl at high speed of an electric mixer until thick; gradually add 1 cup sugar, and beat 5 additional minutes. Stir in pumpkin and lemon juice.

Combine flour and next 5 ingredients; gradually stir into pumpkin mixture. Spread batter evenly in pan; sprinkle with 1 cup pecans, gently pressing into batter. Bake at 375° for 12 to 15 minutes.

Sift 1 to 2 tablespoons powdered sugar in a 15- x 10-inch rectangle on a cloth towel. When cake is done, immediately loosen from sides of pan, and turn out onto sugared towel. Starting at narrow end, roll up cake and towel together; cool completely on a wire rack, seam side down.

Beat cream cheese and butter in a large bowl at high speed of an electric mixer; gradually add 1 cup powdered sugar and vanilla, beating mixture until blended.

Unroll cake; spread with cream cheese mixture, and carefully reroll. Place cake on plate, seam side down. Garnish with whipped cream or pecans, if desired. Yield: 10 servings.
Marie W. Harris
Sevierville, Tennessee

APRICOT MOUSSE
(pictured on cover and pages 302 and 303)

20 ladyfingers
3 (16-ounce) cans apricot halves, undrained
2 envelopes unflavored gelatin
5 egg yolks
1¼ cups sugar, divided
⅛ teaspoon salt
1 cup milk
2 tablespoons apricot brandy or light rum
1 (2-ounce) package slivered almonds
1½ cups whipping cream
¾ cup whipping cream
2 tablespoons powdered sugar
⅛ teaspoon almond extract
Garnishes: apricots, fresh mint, sliced toasted almonds

Cut a 30- x 3-inch strip of wax paper; line sides of a 9-inch springform pan with strip. Split ladyfingers in half lengthwise; line sides and bottom of pan with ladyfingers. Set aside.

Drain apricots, reserving ½ cup juice. Set aside 4 apricots for garnish. Place knife blade in bowl of food processor; add remaining apricots, and process 1 minute or until mixture is smooth. Set aside.

Sprinkle gelatin over reserved ½ cup apricot juice. Set aside. Combine egg yolks, ¾ cup sugar, and salt in a heavy saucepan. Gradually add milk; cook over medium heat, stirring constantly, 4 minutes or until mixture thickens and thermometer reaches 160°. Add softened gelatin, stirring until gelatin dissolves. Stir in pureed apricots, brandy, and slivered almonds. Chill mixture until the consistency of unbeaten egg whites (about 30 minutes).

Beat 1½ cups whipping cream until foamy; gradually add remaining ½ cup sugar, beating until soft peaks form. Fold whipped cream into apricot mixture; spoon into prepared pan. Chill mixture 8 hours.

Remove ring from springform pan; remove wax paper. Beat ¾ cup whipping cream until foamy; gradually add powdered sugar and almond extract,

beating until soft peaks form. Pipe or dollop on top of mousse. Slice reserved apricots, and arrange on whipped cream. Garnish, if desired. Yield: 8 to 10 servings.
Ann Kolb Garner
Ozark, Alabama

HOLIDAY PEARS WITH CRÈME CHANTILLY

¼ cup water
¼ cup sugar
2 tablespoons lemon juice
¼ teaspoon ground mace
6 to 8 medium pears
1 (10-ounce) package frozen raspberries, thawed
Crème Chantilly

Combine water, sugar, lemon juice, and ground mace in a shallow 2-quart casserole, stirring until sugar dissolves; set aside.

Peel pears, leaving stems intact. Place pears in sugar mixture; spoon over pears. Cover and bake at 350° for 50 minutes or until pears are tender but still hold their shape. Carefully remove pears from sugar mixture. Discard sugar mixture; return pears to casserole.

Place raspberries in a strainer over a bowl; mash berries with the back of a spoon. Discard seeds. Pour raspberry juice over pears; cover and refrigerate 8 hours, spooning juice over pears occasionally.

To serve, spoon about 3 tablespoons Crème Chantilly on individual plates, and place pear upright on crème. Yield: 6 to 8 servings.

Crème Chantilly

1 cup whipping cream
1 to 2 tablespoons powdered sugar
½ teaspoon vanilla extract

Beat all ingredients at medium speed of an electric mixer until thickened, but not stiff. Yield: 1½ cups.
Mildred Bickley
Bristol, Virginia

CHOCOLATE KAHLÚA CAKE

¾ cup butter or margarine,
  softened
2¼ cups sugar
4 eggs
2 (1-ounce) envelopes premelted
  unsweetened chocolate
⅓ cup Kahlúa
2¼ cups sifted cake flour
1 teaspoon cream of tartar
½ teaspoon baking soda
¼ teaspoon salt
¾ cup milk
¾ cup chopped hazelnuts or
  pecans, toasted and divided
Chocolate Kahlúa Frosting

Beat butter at medium speed of an
electric mixer; gradually add sugar,
beating well. Add eggs, one at a time,
beating well after each addition. Add
chocolate and Kahlúa; beat until well
blended.

Combine flour and next 3 ingredients; add to creamed mixture alternately with milk, beginning and ending
with flour mixture. Mix well after each
addition.

Pour batter into 3 greased and
floured 9-inch round cakepans. Bake
at 350° for 18 to 23 minutes or until a
wooden pick inserted in center comes
out clean. Cool in pans 10 minutes; remove from pans, and cool completely
on wire racks.

Stir ½ cup hazelnuts into 1 cup
Chocolate Kahlúa Frosting; spread between layers. Spread remaining frosting on top and sides of cake. Sprinkle
remaining ¼ cup hazelnuts on top.
Yield: one 3-layer cake.

Chocolate Kahlúa Frosting

¼ cup butter, softened
1 (8-ounce) package cream cheese,
  softened
1 (16-ounce) package powdered
  sugar, sifted and divided
3 (1-ounce) envelopes premelted
  unsweetened chocolate
¼ cup Kahlúa

Beat butter and cream cheese at medium speed of an electric mixer. Add 1
cup powdered sugar and chocolate;
beat until smooth. Gradually add
remaining powdered sugar and
Kahlúa, beating at low speed until
spreading consistency. Yield: enough
for one 3-layer cake.   *H. W. Asbell*
Leesburg, Florida

CHOCOLATE COOKIE CHEESECAKE

1½ cups cream-filled chocolate
  sandwich cookie crumbs
2 tablespoons butter or margarine,
  melted
¼ cup firmly packed brown sugar
1 teaspoon ground cinnamon
4 (8-ounce) packages cream cheese,
  softened
1¼ cups sugar
⅓ cup whipping cream
2 tablespoons all-purpose flour
1 teaspoon vanilla extract
4 eggs
1½ cups coarsely chopped cream-
  filled chocolate sandwich cookies
2 (8-ounce) cartons sour cream
¼ cup sugar
1 teaspoon vanilla extract
1 cup whipping cream
1¼ cups semisweet chocolate
  morsels
1 teaspoon vanilla extract

Combine first 4 ingredients in a medium bowl; firmly press mixture
evenly onto bottom and 1 inch up
sides of a 10-inch springform pan.
Bake at 350° for 5 minutes; set aside.

Beat cream cheese at medium
speed of an electric mixer until
smooth. Gradually add 1¼ cups sugar,
beating well. Add ⅓ cup whipping
cream, flour, and 1 teaspoon vanilla;
beat well. Add eggs, one at a time,
beating after each addition. Pour one-
third of batter into prepared pan. Top
with cookie pieces; pour in remaining
batter. Bake at 350° for 45 minutes.

Combine sour cream, ¼ cup sugar,
and 1 teaspoon vanilla; spread evenly
on cheesecake. Bake at 350° for 7
minutes. Turn oven off, and leave in
oven 30 minutes. Remove cheesecake
from oven, and let cool completely on
a wire rack.

Combine 1 cup whipping cream and
semisweet chocolate morsels in a
saucepan; stir over low heat until
chocolate melts. Stir in 1 teaspoon vanilla. Pour mixture over cheesecake
while still warm. Refrigerate until
serving time. Yield: 12 to 14 servings.
Linda Keith
Carrollton, Texas

CHOCOLATE PIZZA
(pictured on page 304)

1 pound chocolate-flavored candy
  coating
1 (12-ounce) package semisweet
  chocolate morsels
2 cups miniature marshmallows
1 cup chocolate-flavored corn puff
  cereal
1 cup peanuts
⅓ cup red candy-coated chocolate
  pieces
⅓ cup green candy-coated
  chocolate pieces
⅓ cup flaked coconut (optional)
1 (2-ounce) square vanilla-flavored
  candy coating
1 teaspoon vegetable oil

Melt chocolate candy coating and
chocolate morsels in a heavy saucepan
over low heat, stirring often. Remove
from heat. Add marshmallows, cereal,
and peanuts; stir until coated. Pour
mixture into a well-greased 12-inch
pizza pan; sprinkle with candies and, if
desired, coconut.

Melt vanilla candy coating with oil in
a heavy saucepan over low heat, stirring often. Drizzle over pizza. Let cool
at room temperature or chill until firm.
Cover and store at room temperature.
Cut into squares or wedges. Yield: 20
servings.

Add Chocolate To The Cheese

Melanie Smith of Monroe, North Carolina, loves chocolate. Her family and friends were never surprised when she whipped up wonderful desserts made with this rich confection—until the day she laced a cheese spread with chocolate nuggets.

It sounds unusual, but the combination works. Melanie stirs cinnamon and powdered sugar into a mixture of cream cheese and chocolate mini-morsels, and serves the clever concoction with gingersnaps. She prefers to make her own cookies, following the recipe her mother used when Melanie was a little girl. But you can purchase gingersnaps when you are pressed for time.

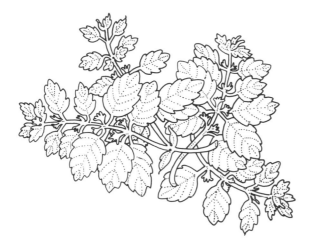

CHOCOLATE CHIP CHEESE LOAVES

3 (8-ounce) packages cream cheese, softened
1½ cups semisweet chocolate mini-morsels
1 cup sifted powdered sugar
1 tablespoon ground cinnamon
1 (7-ounce) milk chocolate candy bar
1¼ cups chopped pecans
Gingersnaps

Combine first 4 ingredients, stirring until blended; divide mixture in half, and spoon each half into a plastic wrap-lined 7½- x 3- x 2-inch loafpan. Cover and chill 5 hours or until ready to serve.

Pull a vegetable peeler down long edge of candy bar, letting chocolate curl up on vegetable peeler.

To serve, invert each cheese loaf onto a serving plate; remove plastic wrap. Press pecans around sides of loaves. Sprinkle chocolate curls on top. Serve with Gingersnaps. Yield: two 2-cup cheese loaves.

Gingersnaps

¾ cup shortening
1 cup sugar
1 egg
¼ cup molasses
2 cups all-purpose flour
2 teaspoons baking soda
¼ teaspoon salt
1 tablespoon ground ginger
1 teaspoon ground cinnamon
Sugar

Beat shortening in a large bowl at medium speed of an electric mixer; gradually add 1 cup sugar, beating well.

Add egg and molasses and mix until thoroughly blended.

Combine flour and next 4 ingredients; add one-fourth of mixture at a time to creamed mixture, mixing after each addition.

Shape dough into ¾-inch balls, and roll in sugar. Place on ungreased cookie sheets, and bake at 350° for 8 minutes. (Tops will crack.) Remove to wire racks to cool. Yield: 8 dozen.

Note: To make larger gingersnaps, shape dough into 1-inch balls, and bake 10 minutes. Dough will yield 4 dozen large ginger snaps.

Chocolate Tips

■ Three tablespoons of unsweetened cocoa powder plus 1 tablespoon shortening may be substituted for each 1-ounce square of unsweetened chocolate called for in a recipe.

■ Chocolate must be treated delicately. It should always be stored at a temperature under 78°F. Sometimes a gray color develops on the chocolate. This is called "bloom," and it is a sign that the cocoa butter has risen to the surface. The flavor and quality will not be lessened, and the gray color, or bloom, will disappear when the chocolate is melted.

■ Temperature, time, and stirring are important when melting chocolate. Chocolate will scorch at too high a temperature; heating too long and stirring too much will cause chocolate to separate into particles that will not melt and blend together.

From Our Kitchen To Yours

We are happy to have had the opportunity to answer so many of your questions about preparing, serving, and preserving food. Here is a sampling of those most frequently asked.

How do you safely serve food during a party?

There are basically three food safety guidelines to remember: Keep food clean, keep cold food cold, and keep hot food hot. Food should not sit at room temperature for more than two hours. An exception is egg dishes, which should not sit for more than one hour.

All cold foods should be kept cooler than 40°, and hot foods should be kept warmer than 140°.

To accomplish this, serve chilled food such as shrimp in a dish placed on a bed of crushed ice, and serve a hot dip from a chafing dish. (Caution: Chafing dishes don't always keep food at a high enough temperature, and some warmers hold at only 110°.)

If your party is longer than two hours, keep extra trays refrigerated and hot food in the oven prior to serving. After two hours, replace containers with fresh, full ones.

If a partially empty container has been sitting at room temperature more than two hours, do not replenish it with fresh food.

If the food has been prepared carefully and held at safe temperatures throughout the party, you can enjoy the leftovers. Divide the remaining food into smaller portions for quick freezing.

Use anything you refrigerate within one to two days, and thoroughly reheat food that is served hot. If there is any question about the safety of leftovers, discard them.

Why didn't the salad congeal properly?

When working with gelatin, always make sure the gelatin granules dissolve before proceeding to the next step. Gelatin is completely dissolved when all the granules vanish.

Don't confuse "softening" with "dissolving"; softening gelatin in a cold liquid helps the granules swell. Then they are dissolved in a boiling liquid or as the softened mixture is beaten, stirring constantly for 2 minutes.

Avoid using fresh pineapple, figs, kiwifruit, papaya, or prickly pears in gelatin; these fruits contain enzymes that destroy protein, preventing the gelatin from setting. Also keep in mind that lemon juice, vinegar, wine, and other acids also make a mold softer and more fragile; use no more than 2 tablespoons per 1 cup of liquid. A general guideline we follow is that one envelope of flavored or unflavored gelatin will gel 2 cups of liquid.

If you're adding chopped fruit, vegetables, or meat to gelatin, reduce the amount of liquid by ¼ cup. If you're using flavored gelatin, follow the instructions on the package for adding solids. Be sure you don't try to congeal the salad in the same container you used for mixing.

What keeps a piecrust from becoming soggy?

To prevent pastry from absorbing any liquid, bake the pie immediately after assembling. If the crust isn't flaky, next time try glazing the pastry for fruit pies with currant jelly or a slightly beaten egg white or brushing the pastry for vegetable and meat pies with a beaten egg white or Dijon mustard before baking.

For single-crust pies, prick the bottom and sides of the brushed pastry with a fork; bake at 400° for 3 minutes. Remove from oven, and gently prick with a fork. Bake the crust an additional 5 minutes, and add the uncooked filling.

Are jams and jellies with a paraffin seal safe?

Paraffin does not form an airtight seal, needed to prevent mold growth. For long-term storage, all kinds of jams, jellies, and preserves should be processed in a boiling water bath for five minutes. If they are not processed, be sure to store them in the refrigerator up to six months.

What can be substituted for raw egg whites?

There isn't a simple solution. To replace beaten egg whites in some recipes, such as a chilled soufflé or mousse, you can fold in whipped cream, but you'll be adding calories, too. However, there are alternatives. For Ice Cream Party Squares, featured in our September chapter on page 214, we increased the vanilla wafer crumbs in the original recipe to replace 8 egg whites; this change reduces the cost without adding another ingredient or too many calories.

What causes a cheesecake to crack?

A small crack or two is characteristic of some cheesecakes. However, a deep crack can be the result of baking too long or at too high a temperature. To help prevent cracks, avoid overbeating the batter after adding the eggs, and avoid opening the oven door during the first 30 minutes of baking. When you remove the cheesecake from the oven, carefully loosen the cake from the sides of the springform pan to let it contract freely as it cools. Let it cool away from drafts.

What is meat-cure mix?

Some recipes for homemade sausage sticks and beef sticks call for meat-cure mix, a national brand product that contains a fine-quality salt and a combination of meat-curing ingredients. This product can be found at most grocery stores in the food preservation section or on the baking aisle labeled Tender Quick®, "a cure for fresh and frozen meats."

Right: *In Pistachio-Cream Éclairs (page 296), homemade cream puffs hold a fluffy filling that starts with pistachio pudding mix.*

A slice of Pumpkin Roll (page 297), a treat for the senses, will delight any holiday guest.

Save the best for last; both Apricot Mousse and Pumpkin Roll are memorable endings for holiday meals. (Dessert recipes begin on page 296.)

Kids will love the novelty of Chocolate Pizza (page 298), a rich dessert of chocolate candy made on a pizza pan and served in squares.

Stroll through the aisles of a grocery store and you'll find candy, crackers, and cereal just right for constructing Quick-Fix Christmas Cottage—you won't need to bake a thing. (Recipe and instructions begin on page 280.)

Update Your Eggnog Recipe

The holidays are here, and that means it's time to search your recipe file for those old family favorites that you prepare year after year.

The eggnog recipe that may have been in your family for generations is probably no longer considered safe. We now know that uncooked eggs can be contaminated with salmonella bacteria. If your recipe contains raw eggs, throw it away, and try one of these recipes when you're craving eggnog.

EASY EGGNOG

2 pints vanilla ice cream, softened
1 quart commercial dairy eggnog
½ to ¾ cup bourbon

Just before serving, spoon heaping tablespoons of ice cream into punch bowl. Pour eggnog over ice cream; add bourbon to taste, and stir gently. Yield: 2 quarts.
Janet Marett
Chesterfield, Missouri

COOKED CUSTARD EGGNOG

1 quart milk
6 eggs
Dash of salt
½ cup sugar
¼ teaspoon ground nutmeg
1 teaspoon vanilla extract
1 cup whipping cream, whipped
Ground nutmeg

Heat milk in a large saucepan (do not boil). Beat eggs and salt in a large bowl; gradually add sugar, mixing well. Gradually stir about ¼ of hot milk into egg mixture; add to remaining hot milk, stirring constantly. Cook over medium-low heat, stirring constantly, until mixture thickens and reaches 160°. Stir in ¼ teaspoon nutmeg and vanilla. Set saucepan in larger pan of ice for 10 minutes to rapidly cool mixture. Cover and refrigerate up to 48 hours. When ready to serve, fold in whipped cream, and sprinkle eggnog with ground nutmeg. Yield: 7 cups.

QUICK!

Plan For A Group

When it's your turn to plan refreshments, try this menu. Most of the recipes can be made ahead of time or within 30 minutes of the party. Offer them at your holiday office party or a meeting of your civic group, bridge or garden club, or Sunday school class. Or prepare a favorite recipe for a potluck party.

An Easy Party for 15
Tuna Spread
Pita chips
Assorted vegetables
Marinated Mushrooms
Fruited Cream Cheese Spread
Commercial gingersnaps and crackers
Chocolate-Peanut Butter Chip Brownies
Percolator Punch

When You Volunteered: Tips and Ideas

—Be realistic about the time you can invest; ask friends to help you plan a party that will be fun. If your group has a budget, don't hesitate to work with a caterer.
—Keep the party environmentally sensitive. If you have to buy disposable tableware, choose paper (preferably recycled paper) instead of foam or plastic. The best choice is unlaminated paper; it's biodegradable and recyclable, especially by composting.
—Candles add plenty of atmosphere with little cost; tie them with raffia or bows. Serve food in baskets, and decorate with seasonal greenery. During the holidays a departure from traditional red and green often inspires interest. Try combinations of teal, brown, cranberry, gold, and blue.

TUNA SPREAD

1⅓ cups commercial chowchow
2 (6⅛-ounce) cans solid white tuna in water, drained
⅔ cup mayonnaise or salad dressing
1 large leafy cabbage

Place chowchow in a sieve to drain. Combine chowchow, tuna, and mayonnaise; stir well. Cover and chill thoroughly to blend flavors.

Cut out the center of cabbage to form a bowl. Fill the cabbage with tuna mixture. Serve mixture with cherry tomatoes, carrot sticks, and pita chips. Yield: 3 cups.

Note: To make pita chips from 6-inch pita bread rounds, separate each pita bread into 2 rounds; cut each into 8 wedges. Spray with vegetable cooking spray; sprinkle lightly with garlic salt. Bake at 350° for 15 minutes or until crisp and lightly browned.
E. G. Golding
Winston-Salem, North Carolina

Tip: *When you intend to use tuna for salads, sandwich fillings, creamed dishes, or even casserole dishes, you can save money by buying the less expensive "light meat" packs of tuna.*

MARINATED MUSHROOMS

2 (12-ounce) packages fresh
    mushrooms
1 (8-ounce) bottle Italian salad
    dressing
1 (4-ounce) jar pimiento, drained
¼ cup chopped fresh parsley

Clean mushrooms with damp paper towels; trim ends from stems.

Combine salad dressing, pimiento, and parsley in a large zip-top heavy-duty plastic bag. Add mushrooms, tossing gently to coat with salad dressing. Chill 20 minutes. Yield: 16 appetizer servings.

Note: To make ahead, chill 8 hours, stirring occasionally.

FRUITED CREAM CHEESE SPREAD

¼ cup chopped almonds
2 (8-ounce) packages cream cheese,
    softened
Lettuce leaves
½ cup mango chutney or other
    fruit-flavored chutney

Spread almonds in a shallow pan, and bake at 350° for 4 to 5 minutes; set toasted almonds aside.

Place cream cheese on lettuce leaves on a serving tray. Coat the top with chutney, allowing some of the chutney to run off the sides. Sprinkle with toasted almonds. Serve with gingersnaps or wheat crackers. Yield: 32 appetizer servings.

Note: Spread can be made ahead and refrigerated.

CHOCOLATE-PEANUT BUTTER CHIP BROWNIES

1 (21½-ounce) package brownie
    mix
1 cup peanut butter morsels

Prepare brownie mix according to package directions, stirring in peanut butter morsels. Spoon mixture into a greased 13- x 9- x 2-inch pan. Bake at 350° for 33 to 35 minutes. Cool and cut into squares. Yield: 2 dozen.

PERCOLATOR PUNCH

5 cups unsweetened pineapple juice
4 cups cranapple juice cocktail
4 cups water
¾ cup firmly packed brown
    sugar
2 tablespoons whole allspice
4 (2-inch) sticks cinnamon

Pour first 3 ingredients into a large percolator. Place brown sugar, allspice, and cinnamon in percolator basket. Perk through complete cycle of electric percolator. Yield: 13 cups.

Bunny Campbell
Gainesville, Florida

ON THE LIGHT SIDE

Dairy Products: Read Between The Labels

If you're concerned about the amount of fat in your diet, chances are you've switched from whole milk to 2% milk. After all, it's only 2% fat so that makes it a low-fat food, right? Wrong.

Two percent milk actually contains 35% fat—that's enough to keep it from meeting the American Heart Association's standards of a low-fat food, which is 30% or less calories from fat.

The labeling terms used by the manufacturer had you thinking that 2% milk was low in fat. Actually 2% milk is 2% fat by *weight*. If you take a closer look at the nutrition label of 2% milk, you'll find that an 8-ounce glass has about 121 calories and 4.7 grams of fat.

To figure the percentage of fat, multiply the grams of fat (4.7) by 9 (which is the number of calories per gram of fat) to get fat calories per serving. The amount of fat calories is 42.3. Then divide this number by the total calories (121). You'll find the fat in 2% milk contributes 35% of the calories in one serving ($42.3 \div 121 = 35\%$).

Percent of Calories from Fat
2% Low-Fat Milk
Nutrition Information Per Serving
Serving Size........................1 cup
Calories................................121
Protein ....8.1 grams
Carbohydrates...............11.7 grams
Fat ....4.7 grams

Milk and milk products are important in health-conscious eating because they are a major source of calcium. Low-fat and nonfat dairy products are as rich in calcium, protein, riboflavin, and vitamins A, B_6, and B_{12} as their higher fat counterparts, and in some cases they are actually higher in calcium and protein because of the nonfat dry milk solids added to give color and body. Cottage cheese, yogurt, ricotta cheese, evaporated milk, cream cheese, and even Cheddar cheese now have low-fat or nonfat versions available.

Armed with the knowledge that the key to measuring the true fat content of food is the percentage of calories from fat and *not* the percent of fat by weight, you'll be able to choose products that are lowest in fat. And if you're still drinking 2% milk, now's the time to ease down to 1%, ½%, or skim milk. The taste isn't much different, but the differences in fat content are considerable.

CREAMY BROCCOLI SOUP

1 (10-ounce) package frozen
    chopped broccoli, thawed
2¼ cups skim milk
1 tablespoon reduced-calorie
    margarine
1 (2-ounce) envelope instant
    mashed potato flakes
2 teaspoons instant minced onion
1 (10½-ounce) can ready-to-serve,
    no-salt-added chicken broth
¼ teaspoon salt
¼ teaspoon pepper

Cook broccoli according to package directions, omitting salt; set aside.

Combine milk and margarine in a medium saucepan; cook over medium heat, stirring constantly, until thoroughly heated (do not boil). Stir in potato flakes and onion. Place in container of an electric blender; add broccoli, and process 30 seconds. Scrape down sides; process an additional 30 seconds or until almost smooth. Return to saucepan.

Stir in broth, salt, and pepper; simmer 10 minutes, stirring often. Yield: 4 servings (142 calories per 1-cup serving).

□ *8.1 grams protein, 2.3 grams fat, 22.5 grams carbohydrate, 3 milligrams cholesterol, 278 milligrams sodium, and 220 milligrams calcium.*

Elizabeth M. Haney
Dublin, Virginia

CREAMY BLUE CHEESE DRESSING

1 cup 1% low-fat cottage cheese
⅓ cup skim milk
2½ tablespoons lemon juice
¼ teaspoon prepared horseradish
¼ teaspoon coarsely ground
    pepper
2 tablespoons crumbled blue cheese

Combine first 4 ingredients in container of an electric blender or food processor; process until smooth. Stir

in pepper and cheese. Pour into an air-tight container; chill. Yield: about 1½ cups (11 calories per tablespoon).

□ *1.5 grams protein, 0.3 gram fat, 0.6 gram carbohydrate, 1 milligram cholesterol, 52 milligrams sodium, and 15 milligrams calcium.*

Judith Jones Canterbury
Gray, Georgia

POTATO-CHEESE DREAM

4 cups thinly sliced, peeled
    potatoes
1 cup 1% low-fat cottage cheese
¼ cup egg substitute
Dash of red pepper
Vegetable cooking spray
½ cup (2 ounces) shredded 40%
    less-fat sharp Cheddar cheese
¼ cup sliced green onions
¼ cup chopped fresh parsley

Cook potatoes in boiling water to cover 8 to 10 minutes or just until tender. Drain. Place cottage cheese, egg substitute, and red pepper in container of an electric blender or food processor; process 1 minute or until smooth. Set mixture aside.

Place half of potatoes in an 8-inch square baking dish coated with cooking spray. Layer with half each of cheese, green onions, parsley, and

cottage cheese mixture. Repeat layers with remaining ingredients, reserving parsley. Bake, uncovered, at 375° for 25 to 30 minutes or until lightly browned. Sprinkle remaining parsley over top. Yield: 7 servings (133 calories per ¾-cup serving).

□ *8.9 grams protein, 1.9 grams fat, 19.4 grams carbohydrate, 7 milligrams cholesterol, 206 milligrams sodium, and 118 milligrams calcium.*

Sheree McIntosh
Flag Pond, Tennessee

CRANBERRY SMOOTHIE

1 cup cranberry juice cocktail
1 (8-ounce) carton plain nonfat
    yogurt
2 tablespoons honey
Ice cubes

Combine first 3 ingredients in container of an electric blender. Add enough ice to measure 3 cups; blend. Serve immediately. Yield: 3 cups (136 calories per 1-cup serving).

□ *4.5 grams protein, 0.2 gram fat, 30.1 grams carbohydrate, 2 milligrams cholesterol, 59 milligrams sodium, and 157 milligrams calcium.*

Brenda Berger
Austin, Texas

Do Your Heart a Favor . . .

. . . and make a move toward drinking skim milk or milk with only ½% or 1% fat. Compare the amount of fat in the different milks listed below.

	Calories per cup	Fat grams	Percent Fat	Calcium milligrams
Skim milk	86	0.4	4%	302
½% milk	91	1.3	13%	300
1% milk	102	2.6	23%	300
2% milk	121	4.7	35%	297
Whole milk	150	8.2	49%	291
Buttermilk*	99	2.2	20%	285

*Commercial buttermilk is made from skim or 1% milk.

BANANA COOLERS

1 ripe medium-size banana
¼ cup unsweetened orange juice
1 cup skim milk
1 tablespoon honey
¼ teaspoon almond extract
Ice cubes

Combine all ingredients except ice cubes in container of an electric blender. Add enough ice cubes to measure 3 cups; blend until smooth. Serve immediately. Yield: 3 cups (96 calories per 1-cup serving).

□ *3.3 grams protein, 0.3 gram fat, 21.2 grams carbohydrate, 2 milligrams cholesterol, 43 milligrams sodium, 105 milligrams calcium.* Louise Ellis
Talbott, Tennessee

Discover Yogurt Cheese

Versatile yogurt cheese is showing up in a variety of light-and-healthy recipes. Its thick, smooth texture and tangy flavor are similar to cream cheese and sour cream—but without all the fat.

To make yogurt cheese, place plain nonfat yogurt in a colander lined with 2 layers of cheesecloth or a coffee filter. Cover with plastic wrap; place over bowl and drain in the refrigerator 12 to 24 hours. After liquid has drained from yogurt, the yogurt cheese will remain. For the best results, choose nonfat or low-fat yogurt without added gelatin. It takes 16 ounces of yogurt to make 1 cup of yogurt cheese.

Yogurt cheese made from vanilla low-fat yogurt or fruit-flavored low-fat yogurt yields a slightly sweeter yogurt cheese that's great for spreading on bagels or bread.

LEMON CHEESECAKE

3 cups nonfat yogurt
1 envelope unflavored gelatin
⅓ cup lemon juice
¾ cup sugar
1½ cups 1% fat cottage cheese
½ cup light process cream cheese product
2 teaspoons grated lemon rind
Graham Cracker Crust
Garnish: lemon rind curls, fresh mint sprigs

Place colander in a large bowl. Line colander with 2 layers of cheesecloth or a coffee filter. Spoon yogurt into colander. Cover loosely with plastic wrap; chill 24 hours. Discard liquid. Cover and refrigerate yogurt cheese.

Sprinkle gelatin over lemon juice in a small saucepan; let stand 1 minute. Add sugar, and cook over low heat, stirring until gelatin dissolves. Remove from heat, and place in container of a food processor or electric blender. Add cottage cheese; cover and process until smooth. Add cream cheese and grated lemon rind; process until smooth. Add yogurt cheese, and process until smooth; pour mixture into Graham Cracker Crust. Cover and refrigerate 8 hours. Garnish, if desired. Yield: 10 servings (218 calories per slice).

Graham Cracker Crust

¾ cup graham cracker crumbs
3 tablespoons reduced-calorie margarine, melted
¼ cup sugar

Combine all ingredients; mix well, and press mixture firmly into a 9-inch springform pan. Bake cheesecake at 350° for 8 to 10 minutes. Cool. Yield: one 9-inch crust.

□ *10.4 grams protein, 5.3 grams fat, 33.1 grams carbohydrate, 9 milligrams cholesterol, 334 milligrams sodium, and 175 milligrams calcium.*

Company Dinner With An Oriental Flair

Flavors of the Orient season this healthy, low-fat menu that's great for entertaining. Wait until guests arrive to cook Chinese Roast Pork, so it will be warm and juicy. Red Cabbage-and-Apple Slaw and Lemon Sherbet can be prepared ahead of time, and Vegetable-Rice Toss can be started just before guests arrive.

Chinese Dinner for 8
**Chinese Roast Pork
Vegetable-Rice Toss
Steamed broccoli
Red Cabbage-and-Apple Slaw
Lemon Sherbet**

CHINESE ROAST PORK

4 (8-ounce) pork tenderloins
¼ cup low-sodium soy sauce
¼ cup bourbon
1 clove garlic, minced
1½ tablespoons peeled, minced gingerroot
1 tablespoon sugar
Vegetable cooking spray

Trim fat from tenderloins; place in a shallow dish. Combine soy sauce and next 4 ingredients; pour marinade over tenderloins, turning to coat all sides. Cover and chill 2 to 3 hours, turning tenderloins occasionally.

Remove tenderloins from marinade, reserving marinade. Place tenderloins on a rack coated with cooking spray. Place rack in broiler pan; add water to pan. Broil 6 inches from heat

15 to 18 minutes, turning often, and basting with reserved marinade. Meat is done when meat thermometer inserted in thickest portion of tenderloin registers 160°. Yield: 8 servings (176 calories per 3-ounce serving).

□ *25.8 grams protein, 4.3 grams fat, 1.9 grams carbohydrate, 83 milligrams cholesterol, 255 milligrams sodium, and 9 milligrams calcium.*

Lula Bell Hawks
Newport, Arkansas

VEGETABLE-RICE TOSS

1 teaspoon sesame oil
¾ cup diced onion
½ cup diced carrot
2 cloves garlic, minced
2 (10½-ounce) cans ready-to-serve, low-sodium chicken broth
¼ teaspoon Chinese Five Spice powder
¼ teaspoon pepper
¼ teaspoon salt
1¼ cups long-grain rice, uncooked
½ cup frozen English peas, thawed
½ cup diagonally sliced green onions

Heat oil in a wok or skillet until hot. Add onion, carrot, and garlic; sauté until tender. Add chicken broth and next 3 ingredients; bring to a boil. Stir in rice; return to a boil. Cover, reduce heat, and cook 20 minutes. Add peas and green onions; toss gently. Yield: 8 servings (139 calories per ⅔-cup serving).

□ *3.4 grams protein, 1.5 grams fat, 27.1 grams carbohydrate, 0 milligrams cholesterol, 89 milligrams sodium, and 22 milligrams calcium.*

RED CABBAGE-AND-APPLE SLAW

7 cups finely shredded red cabbage
1½ cups diced Golden Delicious apple
⅓ cup cider vinegar
2 teaspoons olive oil
1 teaspoon sugar
1 teaspoon Dijon mustard
¼ teaspoon salt
¼ teaspoon pepper
½ teaspoon caraway seeds (optional)
8 red cabbage leaves (optional)

Combine cabbage and apple; set mixture aside.

Combine vinegar, olive oil, sugar, Dijon mustard, salt, and pepper in a jar; add caraway seeds, if desired. Cover tightly, and shake vigorously. Drizzle over cabbage; toss gently. Cover and chill thoroughly.

Serve slaw on red cabbage leaves, if desired. Yield: 8 servings (43 calories per ¾-cup serving).

□ *0.9 gram protein, 1.4 grams fat, 8 grams carbohydrate, 0 milligrams cholesterol, 99 milligrams sodium, 34 milligrams calcium.*

Delana W. Pearce
Lakeland, Florida

LEMON SHERBET

1 envelope unflavored gelatin
½ cup skim milk
¼ cup sugar
2½ cups skim milk
1 (6-ounce) can frozen lemonade concentrate, thawed and undiluted
½ teaspoon grated lemon rind

Sprinkle gelatin over ½ cup skim milk in a medium saucepan; let stand 1 minute. Add sugar, and cook over low heat until gelatin dissolves, stirring constantly. Remove from heat. Stir in 2½ cups milk and remaining ingredients (mixture will curdle). Pour into an 8-inch square pan; freeze 3 hours or until mixture is firm but not frozen.

Position knife blade in food processor bowl; chop sherbet mixture into chunks, and place in processor bowl. Process until smooth. Return mixture to pan; freeze 4 hours or until frozen. Let stand 10 minutes before serving. Yield: 8 servings (98 calories per ½-cup serving).

□ *4 grams protein, 0.2 gram fat, 20.7 grams carbohydrate, 2 milligrams cholesterol, 50 milligrams sodium, and 115 milligrams calcium.*

Calorie Savers

■ Choose dairy products that are made from skim or low-fat milk as a way to keep fat and calories lower.

■ Instead of serving sauces or creams over vegetables, use seasonings such as bouillon, lemon juice, herbs, spices, or butter substitutes.

■ Save calories at mealtime by eating your meal from a small luncheon plate rather than a large dinner plate. Smaller portions of food will look larger.

■ Try a little calorie-free club soda in grape or apple juice to add a bubbly sparkle and to make the fruit juice calories go further.

■ Reduce calories in meat dishes by trimming away visible fat before cooking the meat.

Italian Fare For Two

Welcome winter with this light Italian dinner that makes it easy to set a romantic mood at home. The menu spotlights Veal Marsala served over fettuccine. Rich Marsala wine mingles with other flavors for an entrée that's not soon forgotten.

For an authentic Italian ending to the meal, serve Light Biscotti with coffee. The crunchiness of the Light Biscotti is mellowed by dipping it into the beverage.

Italian-Style Dinner
**Veal Marsala
Hearts of Romaine
With Caper Vinaigrette
Commercial Italian bread
Light Biscotti
Coffee**

VEAL MARSALA
(pictured on page 189)

6 ounces veal cutlets
2 tablespoons all-purpose flour
Olive oil-flavored vegetable cooking
 spray
⅓ cup Marsala wine
1 cup sliced fresh mushrooms
½ cup sweet red pepper strips
½ cup sliced onion, separated into
 rings
⅔ cup no-salt-added chicken broth
1 teaspoon lemon juice
¼ teaspoon salt
¼ teaspoon pepper
1 cup hot cooked fettuccine (cooked
 without salt or fat)

Place veal between 2 sheets of heavy-duty plastic wrap, and flatten to ¼-inch thickness, using a meat mallet or rolling pin. Cut veal into 1-inch squares. Place flour in a shallow container, and dredge veal in flour. Coat a nonstick skillet with olive oil-flavored cooking spray, and place skillet over medium-high heat until hot. Add veal to skillet, and cook veal on both sides until browned. Transfer veal to a lightly greased 1-quart casserole. Deglaze pan by pouring wine into skillet; pour pan drippings over veal in casserole, and set aside.

Combine mushrooms, red pepper strips, onion, chicken broth, lemon juice, salt, and pepper in skillet; cook until vegetables are tender. Spoon vegetables and pan drippings over veal in casserole. Bake at 400° for 15 to 20 minutes or until mixture is bubbly. Serve veal mixture over ½ cup hot cooked fettuccine. Yield: 2 servings (262 calories per serving).

□ *24 grams protein, 3.8 grams fat, 31.6 grams carbohydrate, 71 milligrams cholesterol, 375 milligrams sodium, and 37 milligrams calcium.*

HEARTS OF ROMAINE WITH CAPER VINAIGRETTE
(pictured on page 189)

3 cups inner leaves of romaine
 lettuce
¼ cup sliced cucumber
1 slice red onion, separated
 into rings
Caper Vinaigrette

Combine first 3 ingredients; toss. Divide on 2 serving plates. Drizzle 1½ tablespoons Caper Vinaigrette over greens. Yield: 2 servings (31 calories per 1½-cup serving).

□ *1.7 grams protein, 0.8 gram fat, 4.6 grams carbohydrate, 0 milligrams cholesterol, 247 milligrams sodium, and 35 milligrams calcium.*

Caper Vinaigrette

1 teaspoon cornstarch
½ cup water
3 tablespoons rice vinegar
1 tablespoon reduced-sodium soy
 sauce
1 tablespoon sherry
¼ teaspoon minced fresh
 garlic
1 teaspoon olive oil
1 teaspoon sugar
2 tablespoons capers

Combine first 8 ingredients in a small saucepan; stir well. Place over medium heat; bring to a boil, stirring constantly. Cook 1 minute, stirring constantly. Remove from heat; stir in capers. Cover and refrigerate. Yield: ¾ cup (9 calories per tablespoon).

□ *0.1 gram protein, 0.4 gram fat, 1 gram carbohydrate, 0 milligrams cholesterol, 159 milligrams sodium, and 1 milligram calcium.*

LIGHT BISCOTTI

½ cup firmly packed brown
 sugar
½ cup egg substitute
3 tablespoons vegetable oil
1 teaspoon grated lemon rind
1 teaspoon almond extract
⅓ cup ground almonds
1¾ cups all-purpose flour
1 teaspoon baking powder
¼ teaspoon salt
Vegetable cooking spray

Combine first 5 ingredients in a large mixing bowl; beat at medium speed of an electric mixer until smooth. Add almonds; beat until well blended. Combine flour, baking powder, and salt; gradually add to batter, beating mixture until well blended. Cover and refrigerate at least 3 hours.

Coat 2 sheets of heavy-duty plastic wrap with cooking spray. Divide dough in half; shape each half into a 12-inch log on plastic wrap. Transfer to a baking sheet coated with cooking spray. Using lightly floured hands, flatten logs to ½-inch thickness. Bake at 325° for 25 minutes.

Transfer logs to a wire rack; let cool. Slice each log diagonally into ½-inch slices. Place slices, cut side down, on cookie sheets. Bake at 300° for 15 minutes or until slices are dry. Cool on wire racks (biscotti will be crisp when cool). Store in tins. Yield: 40 slices (50 calories per slice).

□ *1.3 grams protein, 2.1 grams fat, 6.8 grams carbohydrate, 0 milligrams cholesterol, 28 milligrams sodium, and 14 milligrams calcium.*

Potatoes: Plain To Fancy

A little name-calling may be in order for one of our favorite vegetables. Some say just plain "potatoes," while others opt for the spunkier "spuds."

BAKED POTATO SOUP

4 large baking potatoes
⅔ cup butter or margarine
⅔ cup all-purpose flour
6 cups milk
¾ teaspoon salt
½ teaspoon pepper
4 green onions, chopped and divided
12 slices bacon, cooked, crumbled, and divided
1¼ cups (5 ounces) shredded Cheddar cheese, divided
1 (8-ounce) carton sour cream

Wash potatoes and prick several times with a fork; bake at 400° for 1 hour or until done. Let cool. Cut potatoes in half lengthwise; then scoop out pulp.

Melt butter in a heavy saucepan over low heat; add all-purpose flour,

stirring until smooth. Cook 1 minute, stirring constantly. Gradually add 6 cups milk; cook over medium heat, stirring constantly, until mixture is thickened and bubbly.

Add potato pulp, salt, pepper, 2 tablespoons green onions, ½ cup bacon, and 1 cup cheese. Cook until thoroughly heated; stir in sour cream. Add extra milk, if necessary, for desired thickness. Serve with remaining onion, bacon, and cheese. Yield: 10 cups.
La Juan Coward
Jasper, Texas

CRAB-STUFFED POTATOES

6 large baking potatoes
Vegetable oil
½ cup butter or margarine
½ cup sour cream
1 cup (4 ounces) shredded Cheddar cheese
½ teaspoon salt
½ teaspoon Old Bay seasoning
¼ teaspoon pepper
½ pound fresh lump crabmeat (see note)
¼ cup finely sliced green onions
2 tablespoons fine, dry breadcrumbs
¼ teaspoon paprika
¼ teaspoon Old Bay seasoning

Wash potatoes, and rub skins with vegetable oil. Prick each potato several times with a fork. Bake at 400° for 1 hour or until done. Let cool. Cut a 1-inch lengthwise strip from top of each potato. Carefully scoop out pulp, leaving a ¼-inch shell intact; mash pulp.

Combine potato pulp, butter, and next 5 ingredients; gently stir in lump crabmeat and green onions. Stuff shells with potato mixture. Sprinkle with breadcrumbs, paprika, and ¼ teaspoon Old Bay seasoning. Bake stuffed potatoes at 425° for 15 minutes. Yield: 6 servings.

Note: One 6-ounce can lump crabmeat, drained, may be substituted for ½ pound fresh lump crabmeat.
Sandra Rhodes Potter
Cambridge, Maryland

POTATOES WITH EGGS AND MEAT

¼ pound bulk pork sausage
1 tablespoon vegetable oil
2 medium potatoes, peeled and diced
4 eggs, slightly beaten
8 (6-inch) flour tortillas
Picante sauce

Brown sausage in a large nonstick skillet, stirring until it crumbles. Drain and set aside.

Heat oil in skillet; add potatoes, and cook until tender, stirring often. Return sausage to skillet; pour eggs over potatoes and sausage. Draw a spatula across bottom of skillet until egg forms large curds; then remove skillet from heat.

Heat tortillas according to package directions. Spoon potato mixture evenly down center of each tortilla; top with picante sauce. Roll up tortillas, and serve immediately. Yield: 4 servings.
Sharon Franklin
Lewisville, Texas

BARBECUED POTATOES

1 tablespoon butter or margarine, melted
1 tablespoon honey
2 teaspoons chili powder
⅛ to ¼ teaspoon garlic powder
⅛ teaspoon pepper
3 medium-size baking potatoes, cut into ½-inch slices

Combine first 5 ingredients; add potatoes, tossing to coat. Spread potatoes evenly on a lightly greased 15- x 10- x 1-inch jellyroll pan. Bake at 425° for 20 minutes or until potatoes are tender. Yield: 4 servings.
Dee Gilbert
Knightdale, North Carolina

After The Turkey, Make Soup

We've all heard the promise of a chicken in every pot, but during the holiday season you're more likely to find a turkey left from the holiday family feast. The turkey carcass and leftover meat are just right for simmering in a soup or chowder for a warming winter's meal.

If you like to make recipes more healthful, try this tip to reduce fat and calories in recipes that start with a turkey carcass. Once the broth is made from the carcass, chill it several hours until the fat congeals and rises to the surface. Then just scoop and discard, and continue with the recipe.

TURKEY CHOWDER

Vegetable cooking spray
1 small onion, chopped
1 cup turkey or chicken broth
1 (8¾-ounce) can cream-style corn
1 medium potato, peeled and cubed
½ cup chopped celery
1 cup cubed cooked turkey
¼ teaspoon salt
Dash of pepper
⅛ teaspoon paprika
⅛ teaspoon ground ginger
½ cup milk
1 cup half-and-half
2 teaspoons chopped fresh parsley

Coat a large, nonstick skillet with cooking spray; place over medium-high heat until hot. Add onion, and sauté until tender. Add broth and next 4 ingredients; bring to a boil. Cover, reduce heat, and simmer 20 minutes or until potato is tender. Add seasonings; gradually stir milk and half-and-half into soup. Cook over low heat until soup is thoroughly heated, stirring occasionally. Ladle soup into bowls, and sprinkle evenly with parsley. Yield: 1 quart.   *Hazel Sellers*
Albany, Georgia

TURKEY-BARLEY SOUP

1 turkey carcass
6 quarts water
12 peppercorns
3 to 4 stalks celery, cut into fourths
2 bay leaves
1 large onion, cut into eighths
Pinch of garlic powder
1 cup barley, uncooked
2 (16-ounce) cans tomatoes, drained and chopped
1 cup chopped onion
1 cup chopped celery
1 cup chopped carrot
2 teaspoons salt
¼ teaspoon pepper

Combine first 7 ingredients in a large Dutch oven; bring to a boil. Cover, reduce heat, and simmer 1 hour. Remove carcass from broth, and pick meat from bones; set aside.

Measure 4 quarts broth, and return broth to Dutch oven; refrigerate remaining broth for other uses. Bring broth to a boil. Add barley; reduce heat to medium, and cook 45 minutes. Add turkey, tomatoes, and remaining ingredients; simmer 30 minutes. Remove and discard bay leaves. Yield: about 5 quarts.   *Richard A. Goff*
Birmingham, Alabama

TURKEY-VEGETABLE SOUP

1 turkey carcass
4 quarts water
1 small onion, chopped
2 tablespoons butter or margarine, melted
2 medium potatoes, peeled and diced
2 carrots, scraped and diced
½ cup chopped celery
1 teaspoon salt
⅛ teaspoon pepper
2 tablespoons all-purpose flour
2½ cups milk, divided

Place turkey carcass and water in a large Dutch oven; bring to a boil. Cover, reduce heat, and simmer 1 hour. Remove carcass from broth, and pick meat from bones. Set meat aside. Measure 2 cups broth; refrigerate remaining broth for other uses.

Sauté onion in butter in Dutch oven until tender. Add 2 cups broth, turkey, potato, and next 4 ingredients. Bring to a boil; cover, reduce heat, and simmer 10 minutes or until vegetables are tender.

Combine flour and ½ cup milk, stirring until smooth; add remaining milk, and stir into turkey mixture. Cook over medium heat until soup is slightly thickened, stirring occasionally. Yield: 1¾ quarts.   *Adelyne Smith*
Dunnville, Kentucky

TURKEY-NOODLE SOUP

1 turkey carcass
4 quarts water
½ cup finely chopped onion
½ cup finely chopped celery
1 teaspoon salt
¼ teaspoon pepper
4 ounces medium egg noodles, uncooked

Place turkey carcass and water in a large Dutch oven; bring to a boil. Cover, reduce heat, and simmer 1 hour. Remove carcass from broth, and pick meat from bones. Set meat aside. Measure 8 cups broth, and return it to Dutch oven; refrigerate remaining broth for other uses.

Add onion and next 3 ingredients to broth in Dutch oven. Bring to a boil; cover, reduce heat, and simmer 1 hour. Stir in turkey and noodles; simmer, uncovered, 8 minutes or until noodles are tender. Yield: 2 quarts.
Gloria Pedersen
Brandon, Mississippi

Put Salad On The Menu

If salad is on the menu, include one of these. Our readers take a simple green salad to new heights, adding seasoned meats, beans, noodles, and vegetables. In the variety offered here, you'll find salads such as Spinach Pesto-Pasta that are best served alongside an entrée. Others make a one-dish meal.

ORIENTAL SHRIMP SALAD

4½ cups water
1½ pounds unpeeled medium-size fresh shrimp
1 cup bean sprouts
1 (8-ounce) can sliced water chestnuts, drained
¼ cup chopped green onions
¼ cup chopped celery
¾ cup mayonnaise or salad dressing
1 tablespoon soy sauce
1 tablespoon lemon juice
¼ teaspoon ground ginger
1 cup chow mein noodles, divided
Lettuce leaves

Bring water to a boil; add shrimp, and cook 3 to 5 minutes. Drain well; rinse with cold water. Chill. Peel, devein, and chop shrimp.

Combine shrimp, bean sprouts, chestnuts, green onions, and celery in

a bowl. Combine mayonnaise and next 3 ingredients, and add to shrimp mixture; toss well. Cover and chill. Just before serving, stir in ¾ cup noodles. Spoon onto lettuce-lined plates, and sprinkle with remaining noodles. Yield: 4 servings.
Connie Burgess
Knoxville, Tennessee

SOUTHWESTERN TURKEY SALAD

1 egg
1 tablespoon water
½ cup yellow cornmeal
1 teaspoon chili powder
¼ to ½ teaspoon salt
1 pound turkey cutlets or 6 skinned and boned chicken breast halves, pounded
Vegetable cooking spray
¼ cup vegetable oil
2 tablespoons lime juice
2 tablespoons rice vinegar
1 tablespoon chopped fresh cilantro or parsley
¼ teaspoon sugar
⅛ to ¼ teaspoon crushed red pepper
⅛ teaspoon salt
4 cups red leaf lettuce, torn
3 cups romaine lettuce, torn
1 avocado, sliced
12 cherry tomatoes, halved
Garnish: fresh cilantro sprigs

Combine egg and water; set aside. Combine cornmeal, chili powder, and ¼ to ½ teaspoon salt. Dip turkey in egg mixture, and dredge in cornmeal mixture. Cook 2½ minutes on each side over medium heat in a nonstick skillet coated with cooking spray. Cut into strips and set aside.

Combine oil and next 6 ingredients in a jar. Cover tightly, and shake vigorously. Pour dressing over lettuce, tossing to coat. Place lettuce on individual plates; arrange turkey strips, avocado slices, and tomatoes on top. Garnish, if desired. Yield: 6 servings.
Edith Askins
Greenville, Texas

BEAN-AND-SAUSAGE SALAD

1 pound kielbasa sausage, sliced
1 large onion, chopped
2 cloves garlic, minced
2 tablespoons olive oil
2 (16-ounce) cans white beans, rinsed and drained
1 cup sliced, pitted ripe olives
1 (7.95-ounce) jar roasted red peppers, drained and chopped
⅓ cup red wine vinegar
1 teaspoon hot sauce
½ teaspoon dried whole oregano
1 pound fresh spinach

Cook sausage, onion, and garlic in olive oil in a Dutch oven over medium-high heat 5 minutes; drain, if needed. Stir in white beans and remaining ingredients except spinach; cook until thoroughly heated.

Remove stems from spinach; wash leaves thoroughly and pat dry. Tear into bite-size pieces. Arrange spinach on individual plates, and top with hot sausage mixture. Yield: 6 servings.
Mrs. Earl Maurer
Christmas, Florida

GAZPACHO SALAD

½ cup commercial French salad dressing
1 teaspoon lime juice
½ teaspoon dried whole oregano
⅛ teaspoon pepper
1 cup chopped tomato
½ cup chopped cucumber
¼ cup chopped green pepper
2 tablespoons sliced green onions
4 cups shredded lettuce
2 avocados, peeled and halved

Combine first 4 ingredients; set aside. Combine tomato, cucumber, green pepper, and green onions; stir in dressing mixture, and set aside.

Arrange lettuce on individual plates; top with avocado halves, cut side up. Spoon tomato mixture into avocado; serve immediately. Yield: 4 servings.
Debbie Cornett
Murchison, Texas

HOT GERMAN-STYLE BEAN SALAD

1 pound fresh green beans
½ cup water
¼ teaspoon salt
5 slices bacon
1 small onion, chopped
¼ cup chopped celery
1 tablespoon all-purpose flour
3 tablespoons sugar
¾ cup water
¼ cup white vinegar
⅛ teaspoon pepper

Wash beans; trim ends, and remove strings. Cut beans into 1½-inch pieces. Combine ½ cup water and salt in a saucepan; bring to a boil. Add beans; reduce heat and simmer 10 to 15 minutes or until tender. Drain.

Cook bacon in a large skillet until crisp; remove bacon, reserving 2 tablespoons drippings in skillet. Crumble bacon, and set aside. Sauté onion and celery in bacon drippings until tender. Stir in flour and sugar; cook over low heat 1 minute, stirring constantly. Gradually add ¾ cup water and vinegar; cook until smooth and thickened, stirring constantly. Add beans and pepper; heat thoroughly. Sprinkle with bacon. Yield: 4 servings.

Barbara E. Bach
Clearwater, Florida

SPINACH PESTO-PASTA

1 (10-ounce) package frozen
 chopped spinach, thawed
½ cup grated Parmesan cheese
⅓ cup fresh basil leaves
¼ cup pine nuts, toasted
1 teaspoon crushed garlic
½ teaspoon coarsely ground pepper
¼ teaspoon anise seed, ground
¼ teaspoon salt
2 tablespoons butter or margarine,
 softened
½ cup olive oil
1 (12-ounce) package egg noodles

Drain spinach on paper towels. Combine spinach and next 9 ingredients in food processor bowl fitted with knife blade. Process 30 seconds, scraping the sides of processor bowl once.

Cook noodles according to package directions; drain well. Add pesto to hot noodles, tossing gently. Serve immediately. Yield: 8 to 10 servings.

Gwen Louer
Roswell, Georgia

Warm Up With Curry

The first culinary reaction to winter's chill is often a steaming pot of soup, but there are some delightful options that do the job just as well. Have you thought about curry? Its heat is subtle, spreading warmth slowly, gently.

Curry powder is a blend that usually includes turmeric, ginger, cumin, red and black peppers, coriander, cinnamon, and cloves. Although the traditional East Indian cuisine combines curry with meat in a sauce over rice, Americans use curry powder in a variety of dishes. Warm up with some reader favorites.

CURRIED TEA SANDWICHES

1 (8-ounce) package cream cheese,
 softened
¼ cup orange marmalade
2 teaspoons curry powder
16 slices very thin white bread
Garnishes: sliced green onions,
 chopped walnuts, chutney,
 toasted and flaked coconut

Beat cream cheese at medium speed of an electric mixer until fluffy. Stir in marmalade and curry powder. Cut two 2-inch rounds out of each bread slice with a cookie cutter. Spread 1½ teaspoons cream cheese mixture on each bread round. Garnish, if desired. Yield: 32 sandwiches. *Mary Pappas*
Richmond, Virginia

TURKEY APPETIZERS

1 cup all-purpose flour
1½ teaspoons baking powder
1 teaspoon onion salt
½ teaspoon curry powder
¼ cup butter or margarine,
 softened
½ cup milk
1 cup finely chopped cooked turkey
1 cup (4 ounces) shredded Cheddar
 cheese
1 tablespoon finely chopped green
 pepper

Combine first 4 ingredients; cut in butter with a pastry blender until mixture resembles coarse meal. Sprinkle milk (1 tablespoon at a time) evenly over surface; stir with a fork until dry ingredients are moistened. Stir in turkey, cheese, and green pepper.

Drop mixture by rounded teaspoonfuls onto greased baking sheets; bake at 400° for about 15 minutes or until browned. Serve appetizers warm. Yield: 4 dozen. *Cornelia Thomson*
Monticello, Georgia

CHICKEN-BROWN RICE BAKE

½ cup chopped onion
2 tablespoons vegetable oil
2 teaspoons curry powder
3 cups chicken broth
1 cup brown rice, uncooked
1 (16-ounce) package frozen mixed
 vegetables
2 cups chopped cooked chicken

Sauté onion in oil until crisp-tender. Add curry powder, and cook 1 minute, stirring constantly. Add chicken broth; bring mixture to a boil. Cover, reduce heat, and simmer 15 minutes. Stir in rice; cover and cook over low heat 50 minutes or until liquid is absorbed. Stir in vegetables and chicken. Spoon into a lightly greased 12- x 8- x 2-inch baking dish. Cover and bake at 350° for 30 to 35 minutes. Yield: 6 servings.

Marion Szydlik
Bremond, Texas

CHICKEN-BROCCOLI CASSEROLE

1¼ pounds fresh broccoli
2 cups diced cooked chicken
1 (10¾-ounce) can cream of mushroom soup, undiluted
1 (10¾-ounce) can cream of chicken soup, undiluted
2 cups (8 ounces) shredded Cheddar cheese
½ cup chicken broth
½ cup chopped fresh mushrooms
½ to 1 teaspoon curry powder
3 tablespoons fine, dry breadcrumbs
Paprika

Trim off large leaves of broccoli, and remove tough ends of lower stalks. Wash thoroughly, and cut into spears. Cook broccoli, covered, in a small amount of boiling water 8 minutes or until crisp-tender. Drain well. Arrange in a lightly greased 12- x 8- x 2-inch baking dish; top with chicken.

Combine soups and next 4 ingredients; pour over chicken. Sprinkle with breadcrumbs and paprika. Bake at 350° for 30 minutes or until bubbly. Yield: 6 servings.

Ann C. McConnell
Kensington, Maryland

CURRIED CAULIFLOWER

1 cauliflower (about 2¾ pounds), cut into flowerets
½ teaspoon salt
3 cups water
1 (10¾-ounce) can cream of chicken soup, undiluted
1 cup (4 ounces) shredded Cheddar cheese
⅓ cup mayonnaise or salad dressing
½ teaspoon curry powder
½ cup fine, dry breadcrumbs
3 tablespoons butter or margarine, melted

Combine cauliflower, salt, and water in a large saucepan; bring to a boil. Cook 8 minutes or until tender; drain. Place cauliflower in a lightly greased shallow 2-quart casserole; set aside.

Combine soup and next 3 ingredients; spoon over cauliflower. Combine breadcrumbs and butter; sprinkle over soup mixture. Bake at 350° for 30 minutes. Yield: 6 to 8 servings.

Sharon McClatchey
Muskogee, Oklahoma

CURRIED APRICOTS

1 (17-ounce) can apricot halves, drained
2 tablespoons butter or margarine, melted
¼ cup firmly packed brown sugar
1 to 1½ teaspoons curry powder

Place drained apricots, cut side up, in a pieplate. Combine butter, sugar, and curry powder; spoon over apricots. Bake at 350° for 30 minutes. Serve warm with pork. Yield: 5 to 6 servings.

Lynn Aigner
Woodsboro, Texas

Give Breakfast A New Tune

If you're one who rushes around on weekday mornings—lucky to get breakfast at all—you probably like to sit back and *enjoy* the morning meal on weekends. If so, these breakfast recipes are for you.

BRAN PANCAKES WITH CINNAMON SYRUP

1 (7-ounce) package bran muffin mix
1 egg, beaten
⅔ cup milk
1 tablespoon vegetable oil
Cinnamon Syrup

Place muffin mix in a bowl; make a well in center. Combine egg, milk, and oil; add to muffin mix, stirring just until dry ingredients are moistened.

For each pancake, pour about ¼ cup batter onto a moderately hot, lightly greased griddle. Turn pancakes when tops are covered with bubbles and edges look cooked (watch carefully for quick browning). Serve with Cinnamon Syrup. Yield: 8 pancakes.

Cinnamon Syrup

1 cup sugar
½ cup light corn syrup
¼ cup water
½ teaspoon ground cinnamon
½ cup evaporated milk

Combine first 4 ingredients in a small saucepan; stir well. Bring to a boil over medium heat, stirring constantly; boil 2 minutes. Remove from heat; stir in evaporated milk. Serve warm over pancakes or ice cream. Yield: about 1⅔ cups.

Linda Hanson
Deltona, Florida

HOMESTYLE MUESLI

2 cups regular oats, uncooked
1 (8-ounce) carton vanilla low-fat yogurt
1 cup milk
2 tablespoons brown sugar
1 (11-ounce) can mandarin oranges, drained
1 banana, sliced
1 apple, chopped
½ cup chopped pecans or almonds, toasted

Place oats in a 15- x 10- x 1-inch pan. Bake at 375° for 10 minutes, stirring occasionally. Cool. Combine oats and next 3 ingredients, stirring well. Cover and refrigerate 8 hours.

Stir oranges, banana, and apple into oat mixture. Spoon into serving bowls; sprinkle with pecans. Yield: 4 servings.

Linda Keith
Carrollton, Texas

BREAKFAST TACOS

1 large potato, peeled and cubed
8 slices bacon
4 green onions, sliced
6 (7-inch) flour tortillas
3 eggs, slightly beaten
¼ teaspoon salt
¼ teaspoon pepper
½ teaspoon Worcestershire sauce
¼ cup half-and-half
Sour cream
Picante sauce

Cook potato in boiling salted water 10 minutes or until tender; drain well. Set potato aside.

Cook bacon in a large skillet until crisp; remove bacon, reserving 2 tablespoons drippings in skillet. Crumble bacon, and set aside. Cook potato and green onions over medium heat in reserved bacon drippings until the potato is browned. Drain off excess drippings.

Wrap tortillas securely in aluminum foil; bake at 350° for 10 minutes or until thoroughly heated.

Combine eggs and next 4 ingredients; pour over potatoes, and cook over medium heat, stirring gently, until eggs are set. Stir in bacon.

Spoon about one-sixth of egg mixture lengthwise down center of a tortilla. Fold bottom third of tortilla over filling. Fold sides of tortilla in toward center, leaving top open. Repeat with remaining tortillas and filling. Serve with sour cream and picante sauce. Yield: 6 tacos. *Claudia Kinkel*
New Braunfels, Texas

Gifts Kids Can Make

As soon as kids are old enough to have friends, they want to remember them with presents at Christmastime. Gifts of food often head the list of options because they offer the chance to be creative. These recipe choices offer varying degrees of difficulty to accommodate cooks of all ages.

Minted Hot Cocoa Mix is a good choice for a gift because it's easy to make and a favorite with all ages. When the gift is for a teacher or other adult, adding instant coffee granules turns the mix into a mocha-flavored drink (directions immediately follow the original recipe).

With cocoa mix or any food gift, be sure to attach a gift card telling the name of the recipe and, if appropriate, how to prepare it.

SPICED NUTS

2 tablespoons butter or margarine
1 tablespoon sugar
1 teaspoon garlic salt
½ teaspoon ground cinnamon
2 cups pecan halves
2 cups unsalted dry roasted peanuts

Place butter in a 12- x 8- x 2-inch baking dish; microwave at HIGH 45 seconds or until melted. Stir in sugar, garlic salt, and cinnamon. Add nuts; toss gently to coat well. Microwave at HIGH 7 to 8 minutes, stirring after 4 minutes. Let stand until cooled, stirring often. Yield: 4 cups.
Diane Logan
Bowie, Texas

CHOCOLATE CRUNCH COOKIES

1 (18.25-ounce) package German chocolate cake mix with pudding
1 egg, slightly beaten
½ cup butter or margarine, melted
1 cup crisp rice cereal

Combine cake mix, egg, and butter. Add cereal; stir until blended. Shape dough into 1-inch balls. Place on lightly greased cookie sheets. Dip a fork in flour, and flatten cookies in a crisscross pattern. Bake at 350° for 10 to 12 minutes. Cool slightly; remove to wire racks to cool. Yield: 4 dozen.
Carrie Treichel
Johnson City, Tennessee

CHOCOLATE-SESAME STICKS

4 (1-ounce) squares chocolate-flavored candy coating
2 tablespoons peanut butter
3½ dozen sesame mini-breadsticks

Combine candy coating and peanut butter in a saucepan; place over low heat until coating melts, stirring frequently. Pour mixture into a 10-ounce custard cup. Dip one end of each breadstick into coating mixture, and place on wax paper until firm. Yield: 3½ dozen.

Delana Smith
Birmingham, Alabama

MINTED HOT COCOA MIX

3 (4½-inch) sticks hard peppermint candy
1 cup powdered non-dairy coffee creamer
1 cup sifted powdered sugar
¼ cup cocoa

Place candy in a heavy-duty zip-top plastic bag; crush candy with a mallet. Combine crushed candy and remaining ingredients. Store in an airtight container. To serve, combine ¼ cup cocoa mix and ¾ cup boiling water; stir well. Yield: 2¼ cups mix.

Note: To make **Mocha-Flavored Hot Cocoa Mix,** add ½ cup instant coffee granules. *Patsy Black*
Edgemoor, South Carolina

Appendices

MICROWAVE COOKING CHART

Food Item	Amounts	Time	Procedure
Beverages			
Boiling Water (for tea)	½ cup 1 cup 2 cups	1½ to 2½ minutes 2 to 3½ minutes 4 to 5½ minutes	Place in a glass measure and microwave, uncovered, at HIGH until boiling.
Hot Milk (for cocoa)	½ cup 1 cup 2 cups	1 to 2 minutes 2 to 3½ minutes 4 to 5 minutes	Place in a glass measure and microwave, uncovered, at HIGH until thoroughly heated (do not boil).
Cereal			
Quick Cooking Oats	⅓ cup	2 to 3 minutes	Place in a serving bowl; add ¾ cup water. Microwave, uncovered, at HIGH until boiling.
Conveniences			
Toasting Almonds, Peanuts, Pecans, Walnuts	¼ cup ½ cup 1 cup	2 to 4 minutes 3 to 4 minutes 4 to 5 minutes	Spread in a pieplate and microwave, uncovered, at HIGH until lightly toasted.
Toasting Coconut	½ cup	2 to 3 minutes	Spread in a pieplate and microwave, uncovered, at HIGH until lightly toasted (will darken upon standing).
Melting Chocolate Morsels	1 cup	3 to 3½ minutes	Place in a glass measure and microwave, uncovered, at MEDIUM (50% power) until softened. Stir well.
Cheese and Butter			
Melting Butter or Margarine	¼ cup ½ cup 1 cup	55 seconds 1 minute 1½ to 2 minutes	Place in a glass measure and microwave, uncovered, at HIGH until melted.
Softening Cream Cheese	3-ounce package 8-ounce package	30 to 40 seconds 45 seconds to 1 minute	Place in a glass measure and microwave, uncovered, at HIGH until softened.
Fish and Shellfish			
Fish Fillets	4 (4-ounce)	5 to 8 minutes	Place in a baking dish. Cover and microwave at HIGH until fish flakes easily when tested with a fork.
Shrimp, peeled	1 pound	3 to 5 minutes	Place in a baking dish. Cover and microwave at HIGH until tender and pink.
Meat			
Ground Beef	1 pound	5 to 8 minutes	Place in a baking dish. Cover and microwave at HIGH until no longer pink.
Bacon	2 slices 4 slices 6 slices	2 to 3 minutes 3½ to 4½ minutes 5 to 7 minutes	Place on a bacon rack. Cover with paper towels and microwave at HIGH until crisp.
Frankfurters	1 link 2 links	25 to 30 seconds 30 seconds to 1 minute	Pierce each link with a fork. Place in a baking dish. Cover and microwave at HIGH until thoroughly heated.
Poultry			
Whole Broiler-Fryer	1 (3-pound)	40 to 50 minutes	Place on a rack in a baking dish. Cover and microwave at MEDIUM (50% power) until drumsticks are easy to move.
Cut-up Broiler-Fryer	3 pounds	18 to 20 minutes	Place in a baking dish. Cover and microwave at HIGH until tender.

EQUIVALENT WEIGHTS AND MEASURES

Food	Weight or Count	Measure or Yield
Apples	1 pound (3 medium)	3 cups sliced
Bacon	8 slices cooked	½ cup crumbled
Bananas	1 pound (3 medium)	2½ cups sliced, or about 2 cups mashed
Bread	1 pound	12 to 16 slices
	About 1½ slices	1 cup soft crumbs
Butter or margarine	1 pound	2 cups
	¼-pound stick	½ cup
Cabbage	1 pound head	4½ cups shredded
Candied fruit or peels	½ pound	1¼ cups chopped
Carrots	1 pound	3 cups shredded
Cheese, American or Cheddar	1 pound	About 4 cups shredded
cottage	1 pound	2 cups
cream	3-ounce package	6 tablespoons
Chocolate morsels	6-ounce package	1 cup
Cocoa	1 pound	4 cups
Coconut, flaked or shredded	1 pound	5 cups
Coffee	1 pound	80 tablespoons (40 cups perked)
Corn	2 medium ears	1 cup kernels
Cornmeal	1 pound	3 cups
Crab, in shell	1 pound	¾ to 1 cup flaked
Crackers, chocolate wafers	19 wafers	1 cup crumbs
graham crackers	14 squares	1 cup fine crumbs
saltine crackers	28 crackers	1 cup finely crushed
vanilla wafers	22 wafers	1 cup finely crushed
Cream, whipping	1 cup (½ pint)	2 cups whipped
Dates, pitted	1 pound	3 cups chopped
	8-ounce package	1½ cups chopped
Eggs	5 large	1 cup
whites	8 to 11	1 cup
yolks	12 to 14	1 cup
Flour, all-purpose	1 pound	3½ cups
cake	1 pound	4¾ to 5 cups sifted
whole wheat	1 pound	3½ cups unsifted
Green pepper	1 large	1 cup diced
Lemon	1 medium	2 to 3 tablespoons juice; 2 teaspoons grated rind
Lettuce	1 pound head	6¼ cups torn
Lime	1 medium	1½ to 2 tablespoons juice; 1½ teaspoons grated rind
Macaroni	4 ounces (1 cup)	2¼ cups cooked
Marshmallows	11 large	1 cup
	10 miniature	1 large marshmallow
Marshmallows, miniature	½ pound	4½ cups
Milk, evaporated	5.33-ounce can	⅔ cup
evaporated	13-ounce can	1⅝ cups
sweetened condensed	14-ounce can	1¼ cups
Mushrooms	3 cups raw (8 ounces)	1 cup sliced cooked
Nuts, almonds	1 pound	1 to 1¾ cups nutmeats
	1 pound shelled	3½ cups nutmeats
peanuts	1 pound	2¼ cups nutmeats
	1 pound shelled	3 cups
pecans	1 pound	2¼ cups nutmeats
	1 pound shelled	4 cups
walnuts	1 pound	1⅔ cups nutmeats
	1 pound shelled	4 cups
Oats, quick-cooking	1 cup	1¾ cups cooked
Onion	1 medium	½ cup chopped
Orange	1 medium	⅓ cup juice; 2 tablespoons grated rind
Peaches	2 medium	1 cup sliced

EQUIVALENT WEIGHTS AND MEASURES *(continued)*

Food	Weight or Count	Measure or Yield
Pears	2 medium	1 cup sliced
Potatoes, white	3 medium	2 cups cubed cooked or 1¾ cups mashed
sweet	3 medium	3 cups sliced
Raisins, seedless	1 pound	3 cups
Rice, long-grain	1 cup	3 to 4 cups cooked
pre-cooked	1 cup	2 cups cooked
Shrimp, raw in shell	1½ pounds	2 cups (¾ pound) cleaned, cooked
Spaghetti	7 ounces	About 4 cups cooked
Strawberries	1 quart	4 cups sliced
Sugar, brown	1 pound	2⅓ cups firmly packed
powdered	1 pound	3½ cups unsifted
granulated	1 pound	2 cups

HANDY SUBSTITUTIONS

Ingredient Called For	Substitution
1 cup self-rising flour	1 cup all-purpose flour plus 1 teaspoon baking powder and ½ teaspoon salt
1 cup cake flour	1 cup sifted all-purpose flour minus 2 tablespoons
1 cup all-purpose flour	1 cup cake flour plus 2 tablespoons
1 teaspoon baking powder	½ teaspoon cream of tartar plus ¼ teaspoon soda
1 tablespoon cornstarch or arrowroot	2 tablespoons all-purpose flour
1 tablespoon tapioca	1½ tablespoons all-purpose flour
2 large eggs	3 small eggs
1 egg	2 egg yolks (for custard)
1 egg	2 egg yolks plus 1 tablespoon water (for cookies)
1 (8-ounce) carton commercial sour cream	1 tablespoon lemon juice plus evaporated milk to equal 1 cup; or 3 tablespoons butter plus ⅞ cup sour milk
1 cup yogurt	1 cup buttermilk or sour milk
1 cup sour milk or buttermilk	1 tablespoon vinegar or lemon juice plus sweet milk to equal 1 cup
1 cup fresh milk	½ cup evaporated milk plus ½ cup water
1 cup fresh milk	3 to 5 tablespoons nonfat dry milk solids in 1 cup water
1 cup honey	1¼ cups sugar plus ¼ cup water
1 (1-ounce) square unsweetened chocolate	3 tablespoons cocoa plus 1 tablespoon butter or margarine
1 tablespoon fresh herbs	1 teaspoon dried herbs or ¼ teaspoon powdered herbs
¼ cup chopped fresh parsley	1 tablespoon dried parsley flakes
1 teaspoon dry mustard	1 tablespoon prepared mustard
1 pound fresh mushrooms	6 ounces canned mushrooms

EQUIVALENT MEASUREMENTS

3 teaspoons	1 tablespoon	2 cups	1 pint (16 fluid ounces)
4 tablespoons	¼ cup	4 cups	1 quart
5⅓ tablespoons	⅓ cup	4 quarts	1 gallon
8 tablespoons	½ cup	⅛ cup	2 tablespoons
16 tablespoons	1 cup	⅓ cup	5 tablespoons plus 1 teaspoon
2 tablespoons (liquid)	1 ounce	⅔ cup	10 tablespoons plus 2 teaspoons
1 cup	8 fluid ounces	¾ cup	12 tablespoons

CHEESE SELECTION GUIDE

Cheese	Flavor, Texture, and Color	Used For	Goes With
American	Very mild; creamy yellow	Sandwiches, snacks	Crackers, bread
Bel Paese (Italy)	Mild; spongy; creamy yellow interior	Dessert, snacks	Fresh fruit, crusty French bread
Brie (France)	Sharper than Camembert; soft, creamy, with edible crust	Dessert, snacks	Fresh fruit
Blue (France)	Piquant, spicy; marbled, blue veined, semisoft; creamy white	Dessert, dips, salads, appetizers, cheese trays	Fresh fruit, bland crackers
Brick (United States)	Mild; semisoft; cream-colored to orange	Sandwiches, appetizers, cheese trays	Crackers, bread
Camembert (France)	Mild to pungent; edible crust; creamy yellow	Dessert, snacks	Especially good with tart apple slices
Cheddar (England) (United States)	Mild to sharp; cream-colored to orange	Dessert, sandwiches, salads, appetizers, cheese trays; use as an ingredient in cooking	Especially good with apples or pears
Chèvre (French)	Goat cheese; very pungent; creamy	Relishes, appetizers, sauces	Crackers, fruit
Cottage Cheese (United States)	Mild; soft, moist, large or small curd; white	Appetizers, fruit salads, snacks; use as an ingredient in cooking	Canned or fresh fruit
Cream Cheese (United States)	Mild; buttery, soft, smooth; white	Dessert, sandwiches, salads; use as an ingredient in cooking	Jelly and crackers
Edam (Holland)	Mild; firm with red wax coating	Dessert, appetizers, cheese tray	Fresh fruit
Feta (Greece)	Salty; crumbly, but sliceable; snow white	Appetizers; use as an ingredient in cooking	Greek salad
Fontina (Italy)	Nutty; semisoft to hard	Dessert, appetizers, sandwiches	Fresh fruit, crackers, bread
Gjetost (Norway)	Sweetish; firm, smooth; caramel-colored	Appetizers	Crackers
Gouda (Holland)	Mild, nutty; softer than Edam, with or without red wax coating	Dessert, appetizers	Fresh fruit, crackers
Gruyère (Switzerland)	Nutty; similar to swiss; firm with tiny holes	Dessert, appetizers	Fresh fruit
Jarlsberg (Norway)	Mild, nutty; firm	Sandwiches, snacks	Fresh fruit, bread
Havarti (Denmark)	Mild; rich and creamy	Snacks, sandwiches	Crackers, bread, fresh fruit
Liederkranz (United States)	Robust; texture of heavy honey, edible light-orange crust	Dessert, snacks	Fresh fruit, matzo, pumpernickel, sour rye, thinly sliced onion
Limburger (Belgium)	Robust, aromatic; soft, smooth; creamy white	Dessert	Fresh fruit, dark bread, bland crackers
Monterey Jack (United States)	Mild; semisoft; creamy white	Snacks, sandwiches, sauces, casseroles	Bread, crackers
Mozzarella (Italy)	Delicate, mild; semisoft; creamy white	Pizza; use as an ingredient in cooking	Italian foods
Muenster (Germany)	Mild to mellow; semisoft	Sandwiches, cheese trays	Crackers, bread
Parmesan (Italy)	Sharp, piquant; hard, brittle body; light yellow	Use grated as an ingredient in cooking; table use: young cheese, not aged	Italian foods; combine with Swiss for sauces
Pineapple Cheese (United States)	Sharp; firm, pineapple-shaped	Dessert, appetizers, salads, snacks	Fresh fruit
Port Salut (France)	Mellow to robust, fresh buttery flavor; semisoft	Dessert, appetizers, cheese trays	Fresh fruit, crackers

CHEESE SELECTION GUIDE *(continued)*

Cheese	Flavor, Texture, and Color	Used For	Goes With
Provolone (Italy)	Mild to sharp, usually smoked, salty; hard; yellowish-white	Dessert, appetizers; use as an ingredient in cooking	Italian foods
Ricotta (Italy)	Bland but semisweet; soft; creamy white	An ingredient in main dishes, filling, or pastries	Fresh fruit
Romano (Italy)	Sharp; hard, brittle body; light yellow	Use grated as an ingredient in cooking; table use: young cheese, not aged	Italian foods, salads, sauces
Roquefort (France)	Sharp; semisoft, sometimes crumbly; blue veined	Desserts, dips, salads, appetizers	Bland crackers, fresh fruit, demitasse
Stilton (England)	Semisoft; slightly more crumbly than blue; blue veined	Dessert, cheese trays, dips, salads	Fresh fruit, bland crackers
Swiss (Switzerland)	Sweetish; nutty with large holes; pale yellow	Dessert, cheese trays, salads, sandwiches, appetizers, use as an ingredient in cooking	Fresh fruit, squares of crusty French bread

WINE SELECTION GUIDE

Type of Wine	Specific Wine	Serve With	Temperature	When to Serve
Appetizer	Sherry (dry), Port Vermouth (dry)	Appetizers, nuts, cheese	Chilled, room temperature, over ice	Before dinner
Table Wines (white)	Rhine, Chablis, Sauterne, Light Muscat, Riesling, White Chianti	Fish, seafood, poultry, cheese, lamb, veal, eggs, lighter foods, pork (except ham)	Chilled	With dinner; any time, with or without food
Table Wines (red)	Rosé	Curry, patio parties, Chinese food, any food	Slightly chilled	With dinner; any time, with or without food
	Claret	Game, Italian food, beef, Hawaiian food	Slightly chilled	With dinner
	Chianti	Red meat, cheese, roasts, game, Italian food	Slightly chilled	With dinner
	Burgundy	Cheese, Italian food, game, ham, heartier foods, roasts, steaks	Slightly chilled	With dinner; any time, with or without food
Sparkling Wines	Champagne, dry	Appetizers, fish, seafood, poultry, main courses, desserts, cheese, any festive meal	Chilled	Any time, with or without food
Dessert Wines	Port, Muscatel, Tokay, Champagne (sweet), Sherry (cream), Madeira (sweet), Sauterne, Marsala, Malaga	Desserts, fruit, nuts, cheeses, cakes, pastries	Cool or room temperature	After dinner with dessert

GLOSSARY

à la King—Food prepared in a creamy white sauce containing mushrooms and red and/or green peppers

à la Mode—Food that is served with ice cream

al Dente—The point in the cooking of pasta at which it is still fairly firm to the tooth; that is, very slightly undercooked

Aspic—A jellied meat juice or a liquid held together with gelatin

au Gratin—Food served crusted with breadcrumbs and/or shredded cheese

au Jus—Meat served in its own juice

Bake—To cook any food in an oven by dry heat

Barbecue—To roast meat slowly over coals on a spit or framework, or to roast in an oven, basting intermittently with a special kind of sauce

Batter—A mixture of flour and liquid that is thin enough to pour

Baste—To spoon pan liquid and/or a sauce over meats while they are roasting to prevent surface from drying

Beat—To mix vigorously with a brisk motion with spoon, fork, egg beater, or electric mixer

Béchamel—A white sauce of butter, flour, cream (not milk), and seasonings

Bisque—A thick, creamy soup usually of shellfish, but sometimes made of pureed vegetables

Blanch—To dip food briefly into boiling water

Blend—To stir 2 or more ingredients together until well mixed

Blintz—A cooked crêpe stuffed with cheese or other filling

Boil—To cook food in boiling water or liquid that is mostly water (at 212°F. at sea level) in which bubbles constantly rise to the surface and burst

Boiling-water-bath canning method—Used for processing acid foods, such as fruit, tomatoes, pickled vegetables, and sauerkraut. These acid foods are canned safely at boiling temperatures in a water-bath canner

Borscht—Soup containing beets and other vegetables; it is usually made with a meat stock base

Bouillabaisse—A highly seasoned fish soup or chowder containing two or more kinds of fish

Bouillon—Clear soup made by boiling meat in water

Bouquet Garni—Herbs tied in cheese-cloth which are cooked in a mixture and removed before serving

Bourguignon—Name applied to dishes containing Burgundy and often braised onions and mushrooms

Braise—To cook slowly with a small amount of liquid in a covered utensil (less tender cuts of meat may be browned slowly first on all sides in a small amount of shortening; then the meat is seasoned, and water is added)

Bread, to—To coat with crumbs, usually in combination with egg or other binder

Broil—To cook by direct heat, either under the heat of a broiler, over hot coals, or between two hot surfaces

Broth—A thin soup, or a liquid in which meat, fish, or vegetables have been cooked

Brown—To cook in a skillet or oven or under a broiler until brown

Bruise—To partially crush an ingredient, such as herbs, to release flavor for seasoning food

Capers—Buds from a Mediterranean plant, usually packed in brine and used as a condiment in dressings or sauces

Caramelize—To cook white sugar in a skillet over medium heat, stirring constantly, until the sugar forms a golden-brown syrup

Casserole—An ovenproof baking dish, usually with a cover; also the food cooked inside it

Charlotte—A molded dessert containing gelatin, usually formed in a glass dish or a pan that is lined with ladyfingers or pieces of cake

Clarified butter—Butter that has been melted and chilled. The solid is then lifted away from the liquid and discarded. Clarification heightens the smoke point of butter. Clarified butter will stay fresh in the refrigerator for at least 2 months

Coat—To cover completely, as in "coat with flour"

Cocktail—An appetizer; either a beverage or a light, highly seasoned food served before a meal

Coddle—To gently poach in barely simmering water

Compote—Mixed fruit, raw or cooked, usually served in "compote" dishes

Condiments—Seasonings that enhance the flavor of foods with which they are served

Consommé—Clear broth that is made from meat

Cool—To let food stand at room temperature until not warm to the touch

Court Bouillon—A highly seasoned broth made with water and meat, fish or vegetables, and seasonings

Cream, to—To blend together, as sugar and butter, until mixture takes on a smooth, creamy texture

Cream, whipped—Cream that has been whipped until it is stiff

Crème de Cacao—A chocolate-flavored liqueur

Crème de Café—A coffee-flavored liqueur, sometimes used in cooking

Crêpes—Very thin pancakes

Crimp—To seal pastry edges together by pinching

Croquette—Minced food, shaped like a ball, patty, cone, or log, bound with a heavy sauce, breaded, and fried

Croutons—Cubes of bread, toasted or fried, served with soups or salads

Cruller—A doughnut of twisted shape, very light in texture

Cube, to—To cut food into cube-shaped pieces

Curaçao—An orange-flavored liqueur

Cut in, to—To incorporate by cutting or chopping motions, as in cutting shortening into flour for pastry

Demitasse—A small cup of coffee served after dinner

Devil, to—To prepare with spicy seasoning or sauce

Dice—To cut into small cubes

Dissolve—To mix a dry substance with liquid until the dry substance becomes a part of the solution

Dot—To scatter small bits of butter over top of a food

Dust—To lightly sprinkle with a dry ingredient, such as flour

Dredge—To coat with something, usually flour or sugar

Filé—Powder made of sassafras leaves used to season and thicken foods

Fillet—Boneless piece of meat or fish

Flambé—To flame, using alcohol as the burning agent; flame causes caramelization, enhancing flavor

Flan—In France, a filled pastry; in Spain, a custard

Florentine—A food containing or placed upon spinach

Flour—To coat with flour

Flute—To make a decorative edge on pastry

Fold—To add a whipped ingredient, such as cream or egg white, to another ingredient by very gentle over-and-under movement

Frappé—A drink whipped with ice to make a thick, frosty consistency

Fricassee—A stew, usually of poultry or veal

Fritter—Vegetable or fruit dipped into, or combined with, batter and fried

Fry—To cook in hot shortening

Garnish—A decoration for a food or a drink

Glaze (To make a shiny surface)—In meat preparation, a jelled broth applied to meat surface; in breads and pastries, a wash of egg or syrup; for doughnuts and cakes, a sugar preparation for coating

Grate—To obtain small particles of food by rubbing on a grater or shredder

Grill—To broil under or over a source of direct heat

Grits—Coarsely ground dried corn, served boiled, or boiled and then fried

Gumbo—Soup or stew made with okra

Herb—Aromatic plant used for seasoning and garnishing foods

Hollandaise—A sauce made of butter, egg, and lemon juice or vinegar

Jardinière—Vegetables in a savory sauce or soup

Julienne—Vegetables cut into strips or a soup containing such vegetables

Kahlúa—A coffee-flavored liqueur

Kirsch—A cherry-flavored brandy

Knead—To work a food (usually dough) by hand, using a folding-back and pressing-forward motion

Marinade—A seasoned liquid in which food is soaked

Marinate, to—To soak food in a seasoned liquid

Meringue—A whole family of egg white-sugar preparations including pie topping, poached meringue used to top custard, crisp meringue dessert shells, and divinity candy

Mince—To chop into very fine pieces

Mornay—White sauce with egg, cream, and cheese added

Mousse—A molded dish based on meat or sweet whipped cream stiffened with egg white and/or gelatin (if mousse contains ice cream, it is called bombe)

Panbroil—To cook over direct heat in an uncovered skillet containing little or no shortening

Panfry—To cook in an uncovered skillet in small amount of shortening

Parboil—To partially cook in boiling water before final cooking

Pare—To shave away the skins of fruits or vegetables

Pasta—A large family of flour paste products, such as spaghetti, macaroni, and noodles

Pâté (French for paste)—A paste made of liver or meat

Petit Four—A small cake, which has been frosted and decorated

Pilau or pilaf—A dish of the Middle East consisting of rice and meat or vegetables in a seasoned stock

Pipe—To squeeze a smooth, shapeable mixture through a decorating bag to make decorative shapes

Poach—To cook in liquid held below the boiling point

Preheat—To turn on oven so that desired temperature will be reached before food is inserted for baking

Puree—A thick sauce or paste made by forcing cooked food through a sieve

Reduce—To boil down, evaporating liquid from a cooked dish

Rémoulade—A rich mayonnaise-based sauce containing anchovy paste, capers, herbs, and mustard

Render—To melt fat away from surrounding meat

Rind—Outer shell or peel of fruit

Roast, to—To cook in oven by dry heat (usually refers to meats)

Roux—A mixture of butter and flour used to thicken gravies and sauces; it may be white or brown, if mixture is browned before liquid is added

Sauté—To fry food lightly over fairly high heat in a small amount of fat in a shallow, open pan

Scald—To heat milk just below the boiling point; to dip certain foods into boiling water before freezing them (procedure is also called blanching)

Scallop—A bivalve mollusk of which only the muscle hinge is eaten; to bake food in a sauce topped with crumbs

Score—To cut shallow gashes on surface of food, as in scoring fat on ham before glazing

Sear—To brown surface of meat over high heat to seal in juices

Set—Term used to describe the consistency of gelatin when it has jelled enough to unmold

Shred—Break into thread-like or stringy pieces, usually by rubbing over the surface of a vegetable shredder

Simmer—To cook gently at a temperature below boiling point

Soufflé—A spongy hot dish, made from a sweet or savory mixture (often milk or cheese), lightened by stiffly beaten egg whites or whipped cream

Steam—To cook food with steam either in a pressure cooker, on a platform in a covered pan, or in a special steamer

Steam-pressure canning method—Used for processing low-acid foods, such as meats, fish, poultry, and most vegetables. A temperature higher than a boiling temperature is required to can these foods safely. The food is processed in a steam-pressure canner at 10 pounds' pressure (240°) to ensure that all of the spoilage micro-organisms are destroyed

Steep—To let food, such as tea, stand in not quite boiling water until the flavor is extracted

Stew—A mixture of meat or fish and vegetables cooked by simmering in its own juices along with other liquid, such as water and/or wine

Stir-fry—To cook quickly in oil over high heat, using light tossing and stirring motions to preserve shape of food

Stock—The broth in which meat, poultry, fish, or vegetables has been cooked

Syrupy—Thickened to about the consistency of egg white

Toast, to—To brown by direct heat, as in a toaster or under broiler

Torte—A round cake, sometimes made with breadcrumbs instead of flour

Tortilla—A Mexican flat bread made of corn or wheat flour

Toss—To mix together with light tossing motions, in order not to bruise delicate food, such as salad greens

Triple Sec—An orange-flavored liqueur

Truss, to—To tie or secure with string or skewers the legs and wings of poultry or game in order to make the bird easier to manage during cooking

Veal—Flesh of milk-fed calf up to 14 weeks of age

Velouté—White sauce made of flour, butter, and a chicken or veal stock, instead of milk

Vinaigrette—A cold sauce of oil and vinegar flavored with parsley, finely chopped onions, and other seasonings; served with cold meats or vegetables or as a dressing with salad greens

Whip—To beat rapidly to increase air and increase volume

Wok—A round bowl-shaped metal cooking utensil of Chinese origin used for stir-frying and steaming (with rack inserted) of various foods

Zest—Gratings of the colored portion of citrus skin

HERBS AND SPICES

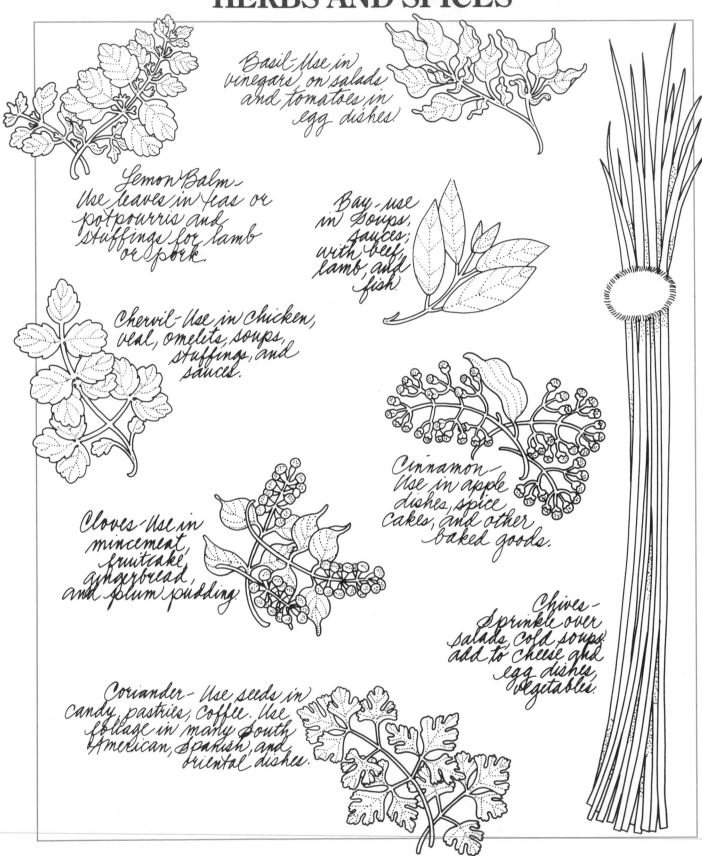

Basil-Use in vinegars, on salads and tomatoes, in egg dishes.

Lemon Balm- Use leaves in teas or potpourris and stuffings for lamb or pork.

Bay- use in soups, sauces; with beef, lamb, and fish.

Chervil-Use in chicken, veal, omelets, soups, stuffings, and sauces.

Cinnamon- Use in apple dishes, spice cakes, and other baked goods.

Cloves-Use in mincemeat, fruitcake, gingerbread, and plum pudding.

Chives- Sprinkle over salads, cold soups, add to cheese and egg dishes, vegetables.

Coriander- Use seeds in candy, pastries, coffee. Use foliage in many South American, Spanish, and oriental dishes.

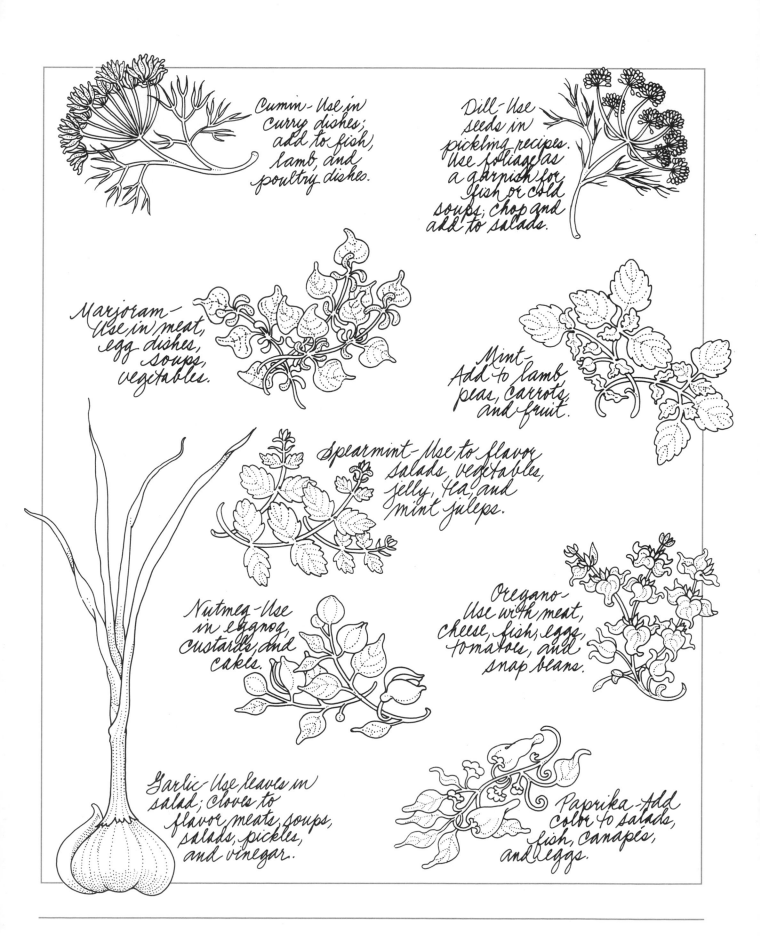

Cumin - Use in curry dishes; add to fish, lamb, and poultry dishes.

Dill - Use seeds in pickling recipes. Use foliage as a garnish for fish or cold soups; chop and add to salads.

Marjoram - Use in meat, egg dishes, soups, vegetables.

Mint - Add to lamb peas, carrots, and fruit.

Spearmint - Use to flavor salads, vegetables, jelly, tea, and mint juleps.

Nutmeg - Use in eggnog, custards, and cakes.

Oregano - Use with meat, cheese, fish, eggs, tomatoes, and snap beans.

Garlic - Use leaves in salad; cloves to flavor meats, soups, salads, pickles, and vinegar.

Paprika - Add color to salads, fish, canapés, and eggs.

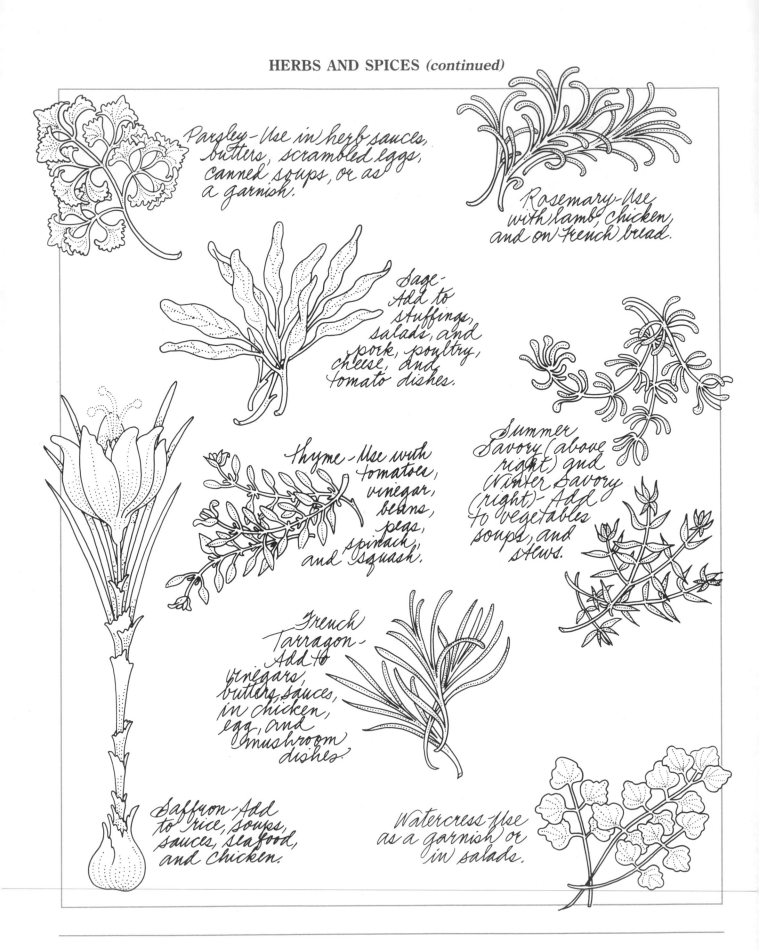

Parsley—Use in herb sauces, butters, scrambled eggs, canned soups, or as a garnish.

Rosemary—Use with lamb, chicken and on French bread.

Sage—Add to stuffings, salads, and pork, poultry, cheese, and tomato dishes.

Thyme—Use with tomatoes, vinegar, beans, peas, spinach, and squash.

Summer Savory (above right) and Winter Savory (right)—Add to vegetables soups, and stews.

French Tarragon—Add to vinegars, butters, sauces, in chicken, egg, and mushroom dishes.

Saffron—Add to rice, soups, sauces, seafood, and chicken.

Watercress—Use as a garnish or in salads.

Recipe Title Index

An alphabetical listing of every recipe by exact title
All microwave recipe page numbers are preceded by an "M"

Month-by-Month Index

An alphabetical listing within the month of every food article and accompanying recipes
All microwave recipe page numbers are preceded by an "M"

General Recipe Index

A listing of every recipe by food category and/or major ingredient
All microwave recipe page numbers are preceded by an "M"

Ham. *See also* Pork.
Biscuits, Southern Ham and, 12
Casserole, Breakfast, 285
Casserole, Ham Roll, M127
Glazed Ham, Currant-, 249
Glazed Ham, Strawberry-, 84
Prosciutto-Wrapped Asparagus, 98
Rolls, Asparagus Ham, 117
Sandwiches, Double-Decker Club, 231
Sandwich Loaf, Pineapple-Ham, 167
Spread, Horseradish-Ham, 167
Steak, Glazed Ham, 13
Hominy
Mexican Hominy, 133, 162
Honey
Bread, Honey-Banana, 68
Bread, Honey-Wheat, 223
Brie, Honey-Mustard, 252
Chicken Wings, Honey-Glazed, 251
Pancakes, Honey, 139
Pork Chops, Honey-Lime, 33
Rutabaga, Honey, 220
Vinaigrette, Honey-Orange, 255
Yogurt, Orange Slices with
Honey, 68
Honeydew. *See* Melons.
Hors d'Oeuvres. *See* Appetizers.
Hot Dogs. *See* Frankfurters.

Ice Creams and Sherbets
Banana-Graham Ice Cream, 56
Chocolate Ice Cream, Mexican, 162
Dessert, Decadent Ice Cream, 56
Galore and More, Ice Cream, 144
Grapefruit Ice, 122
Lemon Ice Cream, 65
Lemon Sherbet, 309
Pie, Chocolate Ice Cream, 56
Pie, Nutty Ice Cream, 180
Piña Colada Ice Cream, 181
Squares, Ice Cream Party, 214
Vanilla Ice Cream, 174
Watermelon Ice, 173

Kabobs
Beef-and-Vegetable Kabobs, 148
Cheese Kabobs, Peppered, 279
Duck Kabobs with Almond Rice,
Grilled, 291
Fruity Mermaid Kabobs, 177
Shrimp Kabobs, Appetizer, 251

Lamb
Chops, Grilled Lamb, 163
Lasagna
Crawfish Lasagna, 89
Florentine, Creamy Lasagna, 94
Noodles Lasagna, Lots of, M127
Turkey Lasagna, 130
Lemon
Asparagus, Lemon-Sesame, 31
Carrot Bundles, Lemon-, 80
Chicken Sauté, Lemon-Dill, 186
Chips, Lemon-and-Herb Bagel, 139
Chips, Lemon-and-Herb Wonton, 138

Desserts
Cake, Lemon-Raspberry, 247
Cheesecake, Lemon, 308
Cream, Lemon, 119
Frosting, Lemon Buttercream, 247
Ice Cream, Lemon, 65
Mousse with Raspberry Sauce,
Lemon, 96
Pie, Lemonade, 42
Pie, Lemon-Buttermilk, 272
Pie, Tart Lemon, 275
Sauce, Lemon, 240
Sherbet, Lemon, 309
Tarts, Berry Good Lemon, 119
Marinade, Lemon-Soy, 194
Punch, Strawberry-Lemonade, 175
Sauce, Broccoli with Lemon, 292
Sauce, Hot Lemon-Herb, 286
Sauce, Lemon-Cheese, 24
Turkey Picatta, 137
Lentils
Soup, Lentil, 28
Lime
Cake, Key Lime, 214
Chicken, Grilled Lime-Jalapeño, 87
Pie, Key Lime, 42
Pork Chops, Honey-Lime, 33
Sauce, Sour Cream-Lime, 286
Linguine
Spinach, Linguine with, 30

Mangoes
Salsa, Mango, 182
Marinades. *See* Sauces.
Marshmallows
Sauce, Marshmallow, 91
Melons
Balls and Cherries in Kirsch, Melon, 91
Cantaloupe Green Salad, 126
Cantaloupe Surprise, Sherbet-, 105
Honeydew Melon with Grapes, 91
Watermelon Ice, 173
Watermelon Mousse, Frozen, 96
Microwave
Appetizers
Nuts, Spiced, M316
Beverages
Mocha, Spirited Hot, M260
Desserts
Crust, Graham Cracker, M234
Fudge, Microwave, M92
Glaze, Chocolate, M296
Peanut-Fudge Bites, M231
Pecan Brittle, M272
Pie, Frosty Pumpkin-Praline, M234
Main Dishes
Beans and Franks, Jiffy, M172
Chicken Mexicana, M127
Chili, Microwave, M232
Fish-and-Vegetable Dinner, M196
Fish with Greek Sauce,
Poached, M183
Ham Roll Casserole, M127
Ham Steak, Glazed, M13
Lasagna, Lots of Noodles, M127
Peppers, Beef-Stuffed, M127
Snapper Provençal, M170
Pumpkin Seeds, Seasoned, M234
Rice, Herb, M257

Salad, Green Beans-and-
Cheese, M159
Vegetables
Artichokes, Stuffed, M117 .
Asparagus-Carrot-Squash Toss, M45
Asparagus, Lemon-Sesame, M31
Asparagus with Almond Sauce, M117
Green Beans, Baked, M159
Green Beans, Garlic, M159
Green Beans Oriental, M158
Green Beans with Marjoram,
Fresh, M159
Medley, Garden Vegetable, M45
Peas, Company Green, M31
Potatoes, Twice-Baked, M185
Spinach Casserole, M31
Sweet Potatoes, Applesauce, M292
Tomatoes with Walnut-Rice
Stuffing, M102
Mousses
Apricot Mousse, 297
Chocolate Mousse au Grand
Marnier, 296
Crabmeat Mousse, 244
Lemon Mousse with Raspberry Sauce, 96
Pumpkin Mousse, 96
Watermelon Mousse, Frozen, 96
White Chocolate Mousse, 247
Muffins
All-Bran Oat Bran Muffins, 134
Apple-Carrot Muffins, 213
Applesauce Muffins, 141
Blueberry Muffins, 140, 203
Bran Muffins, Freezer, 141
Caraway-Cheese Muffins, 213
Cheddar-Raisin Muffins, 51
Chive Muffins, 34
Cornmeal Muffins, 19
Oat Bran-Banana Muffins, 18
Oatmeal-Bran Muffins, 83
Peanut Muffins, 223
Pear-Ginger Muffins, 240
Poppy Seed Muffins, 34
Southwestern Muffins, 34
Squash Muffins, 69
Mushrooms
Green Beans, Mushroom-Bacon, 291
Marinated Mushrooms, 306
Sauce, Mushroom, 221
Sautéed Peppers and Mushrooms,
Herb-Stuffed Chicken with, 26 .
Stuffed Mushrooms, Sausage-, 164
Mustard
Brie, Honey-Mustard, 252
Spread, Chive-Mustard, 12

Noodles
Casserole, Vegetable Noodle, 30
Lasagna, Lots of Noodles, M127
Soup, Turkey-Noodle, 312

Oatmeal
Bread, Dill-Oat, 95
Brownies, Oat 'n' Crunch, 233
Muesli, Homestyle, 315
Muffins, Oat Bran-Banana, 18
Muffins, Oatmeal-Bran, 83

Strawberries
Butter, Strawberry, 71
Carousel, Strawberry, 247
Daiquiris, Creamy Strawberry, 66
Divinity, Strawberry, 272
French Toast Sandwiches,
 Strawberry-, 160
Frozen Strawberry Cups, 173
Ham, Strawberry-Glazed, 84
Ice Mold, Strawberry, 278
Punch, Strawberry-Lemonade, 175
Romanoff, Strawberries, 126
Salad, Strawberry-Spinach, 169
Soup, Sherry-Berry Dessert, 180
Spumoni and Berries, 204
Tartlets, Fresh Berry, 98
Tarts, Berry Good Lemon, 119
Torte, Spring, 57
Stuffings and Dressings
Giblet Dressing, 255
Grandmother's Dressing, 254
Rice Dressing, 217
Walnut-Rice Stuffing, Tomatoes with, 102
Sweet-and-Sour
Beans, Sweet-and-Sour Green, 250
Chicken, Sweet-and-Sour, 202
Dressing, Sweet-and-Sour, 126
Syrups
Cinnamon Syrup, 315

Tacos
Beef Tacos, Soft, 88
Biscuit Bites, Taco, 89
Breakfast Tacos, 316
Deep-Dish Taco Squares, 88
Joes, Taco, 167
Tea
Mint Tea, Easy, 187
Mint Tea, Fruited, 81
Mix, Sugar-Free Spiced Tea, 258
Spiced Iced Tea, 209
Tomatoes
Aspic, Classic Tomato, 229
Caviar Tomatoes, 12
Gazpacho, 94
Green Tomatoes, Oven-Fried, 122
Hush Puppies, Tomato-Onion, 201
Salad, Gazpacho, 313
Salad, Tomato-Feta, 168
Salsa, Fresh Tomato, 182
Sauce, Tomato Basil, 85
Sauce, Turkey Cutlets with
 Tomato-Caper, 61
Soup, Bacon, Lettuce, and Tomato, 207
Spaghetti with Tomatoes and Garlic, 47
Stuffed Tomatoes, Cheese-, 69
Walnut-Rice Stuffing, Tomatoes
 with, 102
Tortillas. *See also* Burritos, Enchiladas.
Chips, Corn Tortilla, 17
Chips, Light Tortilla, 257
Chips, Tortilla, 137
Huevos Rancheros, 77
Tuna
Grilled Tuna with Poblano Salsa, 135
Salad, Tuna-Pasta, 43
Sandwich Boats, Tuna, 166
Spread, Tuna, 305

Turkey
Appetizers, Turkey, 314
Breast with Orange-Raspberry Glaze,
 Turkey, 253
Burgers, Grilled Turkey, 61
Chili, Southwestern, 284
Chowder, Turkey, 312
Curried Cream Sauce, Turkey Slices
 with, 60
Cutlets with Tomato-Caper Sauce,
 Turkey, 61
Giblet Dressing and Turkey Gravy,
 Turkey with, 254
Gravy, Turkey, 255
Herbed Turkey-in-a-Bag, 253
Italiano, Turkey, 62
Lasagna, Turkey, 130
Oven-Fried Turkey Cutlets, 121
Picatta, Turkey, 137
Roast Turkey with Grandmother's
 Dressing, Madeira, 254
Salad, Southwestern Turkey, 313
Sandwiches, Double-Decker Club, 231
Skillet Turkey Dinner, 61
Sloppy Toms, 51
Soup, Turkey-Barley, 312
Soup, Turkey-Noodle, 312
Soup, Turkey-Vegetable, 312
Stir-Fry, Turkey-Broccoli, 62
Stroganoff, Turkey, 61
Tarragon Cream, Turkey with, 60
Turnips
Braised Turnips, 219
Dip, Turnip Green, 13
Salad, Turnip-and-Carrot, 212

Vanilla
Ice Cream, Vanilla, 174
Veal
Marsala, Veal, 218, 310
Vegetables. *See also* specific types.
Barley and Vegetables, 81
Bites, Veggie, 171
Cabbage Rolls, Vegetarian, 86
Canapés, Vegetable, 252
Casserole, Layered Vegetable, 286
Casserole, Vegetable-Curry, 286
Casserole, Vegetable Noodle, 30
Cheesecake, Layered Vegetable, 62
Chicken and Vegetables, Creamed, 90
Chicken and Vegetables with Ginger-Soy
 Sauce, 32
Chili, Vegetable, 28
Chili, Vegetarian, 284
Fish-and-Vegetable Dinner, 196
Kabobs, Beef-and-Vegetable, 148
Kielbasa-Vegetable Dinner, 274
Marinated Veggies, 46
Meatballs and Vegetables with Horseradish
 Dressing, 32
Medley, Garden Vegetable, 45
Nachos, Vegetable, 17
Nests, Scallops in Vegetable, 70
Olive Butter, Vegetables Tossed in, 295
Pilaf, Barley-Vegetable, 33
Primavera, Chicken-Pasta, 72
Primavera, Garden Spiral, 30
Rice Toss, Vegetable-, 309

Salads
Chicken Salad, Vegetable-, 287
Congealed Salad, Fresh
 Vegetable, 229
Marinated Salad, 186
Pasta Salad, Vegetable, 143
Pebble Salad, 27
Tortellini Salad, Garden, 44
Salsa, Garden, 182
Soup, Quick Veggie, 31
Soup, Turkey-Vegetable, 312
Spaghetti, Shrimp-and-Vegetable, 170
Steamed Fish and Vegetables, 32
Stir-Fry, Orange
 Roughy-and-Vegetable, 50
Summer Vegetables, 136
Vinaigrette, Grilled Chicken with
 Vegetables, 26
Venison
Chili, Hot Venison, 283
Gumbo, Wild Game, 290
Vinegars
Cranberry Vinegar, 288

Waffles
Cornbread Waffles, 90
Gingerbread Waffles, 68
Light Waffles, 139
Walnuts
Cookies, Simply Walnut, 236
Stuffing, Tomatoes with Walnut-Rice, 102
Watermelon. *See* Melons.
Wild Rice. *See* Rice/Wild Rice.
Wok Cooking
Beef and Asparagus, Stir-Fry, 124
Beef and Broccoli, Quick, 123
Beef-and-Broccoli Stir-Fry, 46
Chicken Stir-Fry, Easy, 124
Chicken Stir-Fry, Hurry-Up, 124
Orange Roughy-and-Vegetable Stir-Fry, 50
Turkey-Broccoli Stir-Fry, 62
Wontons
Chips, Baked Wonton, 138
Chips, Cinnamon-and-Sugar Wonton, 138
Chips, Garlic Wonton, 138
Chips, Lemon-and-Herb Wonton, 138
Chips, Parmesan Cheese Wonton, 138

Yogurt
Chicken, Savory Yogurt, 238
Fruit Medley, Yogurt-Granola, 58
Honey Yogurt, Orange Slices with, 68
Pineapple-Yogurt Whirl, 132
Pops, Pineapple-Yogurt, 173
Rolls, Yogurt Crescent, 123
Sauce, Creamy Yogurt, 238

Zucchini
Coleslaw, Fiesta Zucchini, 168
Fans, Zucchini, 33
Oven-Fried Zucchini Spears, 121
Salad, Zucchini-Artichoke, 229
Scalloped Zucchini Bites, 165
Soup, Watercress-Zucchini, 72
Toss, Zucchini, 292

Favorite Recipes

Record your favorite recipes below for quick and handy reference.

Appetizers	Source/Page	Remarks

Beverages	Source/Page	Remarks

Breads	Source/Page	Remarks

Desserts	Source/Page	Remarks

Main Dishes	Source/Page	Remarks
Honey-Glazed Wings 351		great!

Salads	Source/Page	Remarks

Soups and Stews	Source/Page	Remarks

Vegetables and Side Dishes	Source/Page	Remarks